Advertising Pro

STUDIES IN INDUSTRY AND SOCIETY
Philip B. Scranton, *Series Editor*
*Published with the assistance of the Hagley Museum and Library*

Related titles in the series:

David A. Hounshell   *From the American System to Mass Production, 1800–1932: The Development of Manufacturing Technology in the United States*

JoAnne Yates   *Control through Communication: The Rise of System in American Management*

James P. Kraft   *Stage to Studio: Musicians and the Sound Revolution, 1890–1950*

Lindy Biggs   *The Rational Factory: Architecture, Technology, and Work in America's Age of Mass Production*

# ADVERTISING PROGRESS

*American Business*
*and the*
*Rise of Consumer Marketing*

Pamela Walker Laird

THE JOHNS HOPKINS UNIVERSITY PRESS
*Baltimore & London*

*This book has been brought to publication with the generous assistance of the Hagley Museum and Library, the History Department of the University of Colorado at Denver, Jay Last, and an anonymous donor.*

Johns Hopkins Paperbacks edition, 2001
2 4 6 8 9 7 5 3 1

The Johns Hopkins University Press
2715 North Charles Street
Baltimore, Maryland 21218-4363
www.press.jhu.edu

Library of Congress Cataloging-in-Publication Data will be found at the end of this book.
A catalog record for this book is available from the British Library.

ISBN 0-8018-6645-6 (pbk.)

*To my parents,*
*Lillie J. Walker and Joseph G. Walker,*
*with love*

# Contents

## Part Three
### Consumption as Progress

# Illustrations

## Plates

*Color illustrations appear after page 256*

## Figures

# Preface and Acknowledgments

More than twenty years ago I began to learn about remarkable treasures in nineteenth-century art—advertisements that still shine with color and exquisite printing. Pretty women and children and cuddly animals populated many of the scenes, all splendid and bountiful. Although I enjoyed looking at these lovely images, the pictures that lured me onto this long adventure featured industrial images, motifs that clashed with my experience of advertising content. Factories and locomotives filled large posters and small trade cards; at other times they appeared in corner vignettes adorning complex prints or, in some advertisements, even as industrial scenes seen through the windows of fashionable homes. The mustachioed faces of business owners looked over their domains, and their names blazed across these vintage advertisements in large, opulent letters. Cornucopia and other symbols of plenty abounded, including images of the advertising manufacturers' mansions.

Clearly, the businesspeople who commissioned these complex visual messages had a different notion of what they wanted to show the public than the people who create today's advertisements. Yet when I searched publications on the history of advertising, I found no explanation for the riddle. Even more surprising, business and cultural historians had largely ignored these artifacts, focusing instead on the dark and densely worded newspaper and magazine advertisements of the period. Only occasional, unflattering comments about posters for circuses and patent medicines broke the rule. Art historians, on the other hand, had recognized these materials as the important output of commercial printers, the only large-scale communications producers who could offer printed color to the nation. Collectors and other antiquarians who wrote about vintage advertisements appreciated them for their beauty and nostalgic interest. However, no one described the motivations behind those motifs of a century ago, except by a passing intuition or two. And nowhere could I find why, if those messages were so important to nineteenth-century manufacturers, did they all but vanish by the 1910s. Why are industrial images so rare now?

These questions sparked my adventure. I began by unraveling why the smokestacks and other motifs that seemed strange to me posed no riddle when they were created. I found that smokestacks and progress, mansions and success, new consumer technologies and social progress, industrialists' portraits and their ambitions for cultural authority, all fit together as symbols and goals in the culture of mainstream business that I explored. When this culture changed, when advertisements proclaimed brand names rather than owners' names, and advertising specialists rather than owners created commercial messages, the messages changed. The new advertisements promoted a different vision of progress—one driven by consumers' purchase decisions as guided by the new marketing professionals, who also sought cultural authority for themselves and their work. My odyssey resulted in this book when I had accounted for the transition by which those earlier symbols of progress had lost their standing as commonplace. Solving that puzzle, in turn, explained something about how nineteenth-century U.S. business culture and commercial messages gave way to those of the twentieth.

As I look back on this adventure, I am filled with gratitude for the friends and strangers who have helped me on my way. The intellectual path led me to strangers; some of those strangers became friends who have shared and enriched my personal path beyond measure.

After several years of working alone, I discovered the benefits, both intellectual and personal, of other scholars' fellowship. Bayla Singer encouraged me to enter a doctoral program to develop as a historian. Under the tutelage of Lori Breslow, David D. Hall, and my dissertation committee at Boston University—Joseph Boskin, Robert V. Bruce, Saul Engelbourg, Richard Wightman Fox, and Thomas Glick—I learned both the challenges and the gratifications of the academic life. Robert V. Bruce, in particular, opened up the world of business history to me. I especially value Joe Boskin's guidance and support, then and still.

Bayla's advice also led me to John M. Staudenmaier, S.J., who encouraged my thinking about advertising's past as well as its present. His encouragement and help began at a critical time and have continued. John is often the invisible audience for whom I write. At his suggestion, I began participating in the Society for the History of Technology (SHOT), another turning point for me. The people of this organization welcomed me as they have so many other interdisciplinary scholars, providing fellowship and intellectual stimulation with their productive eclecticism. My friendships and activities within SHOT have given me strength and ideas.

My friends have brought their affections and wisdom to me from many directions. Jeanne Johnson, Carole Levin, and Dolores Leal Owens have been with me for three decades, guiding and supporting me through personal and professional developments. Friends and colleagues who have shared my life in important ways in the last dozen years as the adventure expanded my world include Lindy Biggs, Lori Breslow, Amira Salinas Cranor, Colleen Dunlavy, Moya Hansen, Susan Lanman, Iola McMurray, and Terry R. Reynolds. Each of these people brings special blessings into my life.

Among the people whose insights and knowledge have enlightened many a discussion on historical advertisements, I thank first Don J. Lurito. Long ago, he and I developed an appreciation for the beauty of nineteenth-century chromolithographed advertisements and their importance as cultural icons—an appreciation we share to this day. Jack Golden's apparently infinite knowledge of historical printing has inspired and taught me beyond measure. In the academic world, I have learned from discussions on marketing history with many people, especially Regina Lee Blaszczyk, the late Roland Marchand, Daniel Pope, and Timothy B. Spears.

Although academic researchers increasingly appreciate material culture as a resource, they often underappreciate private collectors' commitments to both the preservation and the study of historical artifacts. There are many ways in which I could not have conducted my research without access to private collections of vintage advertisements. (Unless otherwise noted, all illustrations come from private collections.) In particular, I would like to mention David and Bettie Briggs, Jack Golden, and Don J. Lurito, who provided knowledge, insights, and photographs to this project. David Cheadle shared some of his extensive research on trade-card history with me. The generosity of Jay Last and another, anonymous, donor has helped bring this book to publication. I deeply appreciate all of the ways in which the collecting community has encouraged and enlightened me.

This manuscript has benefited from readings of earlier versions, in part or whole, by Joseph Corn, David Morton, Daniel Pope, Gail Reitenbach, and Regina Lee Blaszczyk and her Boston University students Jennifer R. Green and Kathleen McDonald. I wish I could write a second book to satisfy all their questions; I hope the present volume will answer most of them.

The History Department of the University of Colorado at Denver has provided me with support, collegial and professional, and I have appreciated the opportunity to teach in this community of students who reward my every effort.

I am grateful for financial assistance for research from the Englebourg Travel Fellowship, the Hagley Museum and Library's Business History Scholar's Grant, and the Smithsonian Institution's Short-Term Visitor Grant. I also thank the Hagley Museum and Library and the History Department of the University of Colorado at Denver, who generously contributed toward publication of this book.

In the course of pursuing evidence, I received capable and enthusiastic assistance from many archivists and librarians, especially those at the Archives Center of the National Museum of American History (NMAH), the Hagley Museum and Library, the N. W. Ayer Archives (when they were still at Ayer Corporate Communications), and the J. Walter Thompson Company Archives in the Manuscript Department, William R. Perkins Library, Duke University. In particular, Vanessa Broussard-Simmons and Lorene Mayo at the Archives Center, NMAH, and Ellen Gartrell at Duke University greatly assisted my research; their respect and appreciation for the treasures under their care inspires them to see those materials used and their research value recognized. Eugene L. Schwaab Jr., of Western Hemisphere, Inc., Stoughton, Massachusetts, and Robert Topp, of Hermitage Antiquarian Bookshop, Denver, Colorado, have helped me complete this project while at a distance from major research centers. I appreciate their enthusiasm for scholarly pursuits.

The relationships and education I have gained pursuing answers to my questions will continue to bless my life, and I am grateful. Most especially, I treasure the home and life Frank N. Laird and I have built. We met by the good grace of strangers who had become friends along my path toward this book. Frank has taken valuable time from his own work to help me with the words, the ideas, and the production of this project. He is my partner in every aspect of our lives. There is no measure of the joy and comfort such a true partner can bring into one's life.

# Advertising Progress

# Introduction

*While much history has in it nothing in common with our surroundings or purposes, and cannot, therefore, yield us anything of direct value, the history of advertising, being a record of the adaptation of business methods to modern business conditions, is peculiarly rich in helpful information, and a careful study of it in the manner Emerson suggests should greatly benefit the modern business man.*

—Francis Wayland Ayer, "Advertising in America," 1895

In 1977, the DeCordova Museum in Lincoln, Massachusetts, exhibited a remarkable array of nineteenth-century advertisements with striking images that challenged the limited notions about "old-fashioned" ads most familiar to denizens of late-twentieth-century consumer culture. Amid this bounty, bewhiskered men like the Smith Brothers, who still stare at each other across their cough-drop boxes, and corseted, lace-bedecked women seemed less like clichés than when pasted on today's gift cards and the walls of "country stores." The colorfully lithographed show cards, containers, trade cards, and novelty items featured as elements of "An American Dream: The Art of Free Enterprise" did evoke apparent amusement and nostalgia from many viewers. Yet their sheer abundance and variety made these vintage artifacts seem less like quaint and curious anomalies and more like materials that must have some historical import. How could this legacy of marketing tools not hold some historical and cultural significance? Here were factories topped with profligate clouds of smoke; there, cruel caricatures of (non-Anglo-Protestant) ethnic groups. Everywhere flourished images of women: ethereal nudes averted angelic eyes in some advertisements, while in others clothed prostitutes stared at their audiences audaciously. Other feminine images represented Victorian standards of propriety and prosperity as they portrayed good wives and daughters. Symbols of technological achievement proliferated—electricity, clocks, trains, steamships, mercantile buildings, and a plenitude of factories. The names, and often the faces, of the men (and, rarely, women) who founded and/or operated the firms presided over nearly every advertisement on display.

Westerners of the late twentieth century have mixed feelings about industrialization. Although we attribute to it the benefits of our standards of living, we also have become sensitive to the injustices and hardships of industrialization and urbanization and their consequent social and environmental problems. The advertisements at the DeCordova therefore struck a perplexing chord as emissaries from the more optimistic heyday of industrialization. The images of factories and machines in advertisements directed to consumers especially challenged current notions of how advertisements should look. Why had advertising styles changed since then? Had they simply modernized in some deterministic manner or perhaps because people had tired of these fashions? Did their origins in the enthusiasm of the modern era's adolescence explain them? Did the decline of industrial imagery from manufacturers' advertisements reflect other, larger, trends in U.S. cultural and business history? Furthermore, might this transformation shed some light on the evolution of the consumer culture from the production ethos of the nineteenth century? Seeking out and assembling the pieces of this puzzle promised to help explain the relationships between all advertisements, their creators, and their cultural contexts.

Since the decade before the DeCordova exhibition, skepticism about progress and its nature has begun to darken many Americans' views of their horizons. Some people have come to challenge the faith that unrestricted economic growth through industrial expansion is possible, fair, or even safe. Others have girded themselves for political and martial battles with self-righteous rhetoric, trying to defend claims to what they see as their "share" of a zero-sum world economy. This loss of optimism, however apt, throws into sharp relief the people who created advertisements in earlier styles, because as a whole they knew no such despair. Instead, they and many of their contemporaries debated—then as now—whose values and activities best served the general progress and thereby earned legitimacy.

Because they realize, or at least sense, that advertisements serve not only as tools for business success but also as factors in competitions for cultural authority, businesspeople often express their notions of progress in their advertisements. Hence, I have labeled advertising, past and present, as *the business of progress*. The theme of progress runs through advertising history, tying it to the broader contexts of U.S. business and cultural history, always offering paths to a better world, illuminated by disparate notions of what "better" entails.

Notions of progress contributed to many Americans' frames of reference between the Civil War and World War I. Definitions of progress came to them from poets, politicians, scientists, and philosophers. In the context of the vast changes of the nineteenth and early twentieth centuries and the demands that these changes made on citizens' conduct and values, endorsing a material standard for progress became a dominant, albeit not universal, practice. It helped its advocates to define the rewards of change and to justify its costs. Through remarkable innovations and transformations in both content and media, advertising messages during this period took on an important role in articulating and shaping the available definitions of progress. Since the decisions and values of U.S. industrialists drew attention that exacerbated both their self-consciousness as a new class and their perceived needs for cultural legitimation, their advertisements allowed them to present themselves as the entrepreneurial heroes of progress. Their advertisements provided owner-managers with a communication strategy in competitions for both cultural authority and for business success. When manufacturers, in particular, created their own advertisements, they boasted of their roles in progress through advertising messages that glorified industry and technology as the means to new abundance and cultural advancement.

Changes in business practices, distribution methods, and cultural values had a symbiotic, reciprocal relationship with changes in advertising between 1870 and 1920—the period of its so-called modernization. For example, when the nation's first transcontinental railroad traffic began in 1869, businesspeople still wrote and designed their own advertising messages, commissioning printers and publishers to produce them. But by the 1910s, when the United States had developed a powerful economy, leading advertisers—that is, businesspeople who advertised—commissioned advertising professionals—practitioners who included agents, copywriters, and artists—to create and distribute their messages, sometimes using techniques developed for wartime propaganda. Advertisements prior to the Civil War generally heralded the increased availability of traditional goods like spices, shoes, and textiles. By midcentury, however, both merchants and manufacturers began to promote altogether new types of goods like sewing machines and reapers for which no ready demand existed. New printing technologies helped advertisers to spread information and promotions for their products.

What causal links between all these changes made most twentieth-century advertisements differ so much from their nineteenth-century precursors? Modernization in general has not proceeded deterministically or along a single course; what modernity entailed at any point in time and space was not always clear or desirable to its participants. Innumerable actors made their decisions within a maze of variables, such as those that people considered when making their decisions about marketing strategies. How did they decide about messages, media, and audiences at different points in time? Did their decisions vary by industry or type of business or cultural context? What options did they have? We know that the volume of advertising expanded dramatically after 1870 and that much of it consisted of forms relegated to the status of ephemera and novelties—those show cards and containers that now reside abundantly in museums, private collections, and archives but appear as minor components in the armamentarium of today's advertising. What functions did these serve? What is the significance of their disappearance and this century's domination by advertising through periodicals and, later, broadcasting?

What accounts for the shifts in advertising practices, and how do they relate to the larger changes in American business and culture during this period? How did the move away from owner-managed firms in major industries to bureaucratized corporations affect advertising? What impact did developments in communication technologies and networks have as printed advertisements assumed increasingly important marketing functions as the main components in a consumer-oriented "pull" strategy that reinforced, and sometimes replaced, the middlemen's "push" of goods toward consumers? How did the growing dominance of periodicals as mass media affect the process and the content of advertising? Did Progressivism have any effect?

I have sought to answer these and other questions by examining the marketing problems that motivated businesspeople to advertise, by studying advertising practitioners' activities, expectations, and how they responded to changes in the business environment and communication networks, and by studying the advertising messages in that rich context. In doing so, I have sought to explain the evolving processes for creating, producing, and distributing advertisements in terms of business practices and personnel as well as the technologies available to advertisers. My goal has been to construct a dynamic analytic framework that explains the evolution of advertising content and styles along with the professionalization of advertising practices. My research has ranged over a variety of historical materials, including advertising and printing-trade literature, agency archives, and pertinent secondary literature on business and cultural history. I also returned to the advertisements themselves —to newspapers and magazines, and most especially to the lithographed images that first piqued my interest, although this study does not exhaustively analyze images or written messages except for what they say about their creators.

As with any other form of communication, advertisements' meanings differ for their creators and their audiences. Because advertisements supply useful historiographical resources for studying the values and perceptions of the people who created them, it is important to know who selected advertising messages between 1870 and 1920 and how they made their decisions. As I seek to explain why as well as how advertisements took on their twentieth-century form, I have focused on their creators' perspectives and goals, leaving others to answer the question of whether or not the advertisements of this or any period also reflect their audiences' interests and concerns. This study does not interpret advertising messages as much as it explains how and why they took the forms and contents they did.

My arguments revolve around the well-documented change in the personnel who performed advertising functions for U.S. firms in this period. Prior to the 1890s, the vast majority of advertisements were created by merchants and manufacturers, aided by printers but not by specialized advertising professionals. This is still the case for the legions of small advertisers in all media. Furthermore, until managerial operations became widely specialized, owners or their close associates managed most companies, taking a personal interest in the advertisements that represented their firms to the public. Once managerial specialists dominated any given firm's operations, a different sort of professional with different ambitions and interests designed and wrote and placed its advertisements. Owner-managers and advertising specialists held different positions vis-à-vis the firms they advertised as well as different attitudes toward the functions of advertising. Under both types of managements, advertisements served as components of the discourse of cultural politics, as products of their creators' interests that necessarily changed as their creators changed. Reconstructing these two groups' frames of reference and interests regarding advertising practices and content makes it possible to explicate their different modes of advertising.

Two related themes explain why consumer advertising shifted from producer-oriented styles, emphasizing a production ethos and notions of progress that were tied to production and producers, to consumer-oriented styles, which gave greater importance to consumption as the driving force of progress. One theme comprises an institutional, business history that focuses on the changing marketing problems to which actors in the advertising process both contributed and responded. The companion theme forms a cultural history concerning marketers' perceptions of their roles in progress.

During the decades when industrialists used their advertisements to promote both their products and their contributions to material progress, advertising agents played but minor roles in publicity efforts. Agents placed advertisements in newspapers and magazines, for manufacturers as well as for other pre-1890 clientele, like retailers, patent-medicine vendors, and entertainers; they rarely created copy. Despite the proliferation of progress discourse in the nineteenth century, advocates and advisers for the advertising profession in these years made no claim that their field contributed to progress. Before 1900, practitioners seldom saw their functions in any context broader than the business successes of their clientele. Their claims to professional esteem they limited to how efficiently and effectively they placed messages that their clients had already created. Yet by the 1910s, advertising professionals had for a decade acted and written as purposeful innovators and agents of modernity. Their remarkable shift from narrow to broad statements of professional purpose and self-promotion by advertising practitioners between 1895 and 1905 coincided with changing conditions both external and internal to the field. The accelerating concentration of businesses during this period and the decline of the owner-manager in favor of specialized, professional management working on behalf of stockholders, for example, affected many industries producing nationally distributed consumer goods. During the same years, large-circulation magazines expanded into national markets with the help of nationwide rail networks, and reformers challenged the credibility and desirability of unregulated advertising. Pressures within the advertising field also encouraged professionalization, growing competition among agencies, and changes in the nature of clientele. This study examines how these and other developments combined to inspire the expanded functions and revised statements of professional purpose that first appeared in the middle 1890s.

Beginning at the very end of the old century, advocates of the advertising profession frequently and ardently adopted the prevailing progress discourse on behalf of themselves and their work. Manufacturers and advertising professionals increasingly differed about whose contributions to progress deserved priority. Advertising's advocates asserted its legitimacy by itemizing its contributions to national progress, both material and cultural. As marketing professionals transformed their field, they appropriated progress rhetoric and purposefully denied it to producers, thereby refashioning the visions of progress and its sources presented to the public through advertisements. Fewer and fewer ads featured manufacturers as the heroes of progress; indeed, advertising professionals frequently argued with their clients against using industrial imagery in their promotions. Newly empowered professionals designed messages that separated material and cultural progress from the processes of production. They emphasized neither the heroics of producing abundance nor even the celebration of abundance but, instead, the challenges of selecting between and using properly an assumed abundance. Advertisements portrayed individual, cultural, and national progress as the end results of consumers' decisions—decisions informed and guided by the new prophets of modernity, the specialists who created the advertisements. In doing so, advertising practitioners helped both to fuel and to direct the maturing consumer culture. Advertising's advocates still proclaim that it "builds growth," that it is a "Unifying Force for the 21st Century," and that, above all else, "it pays to advertise." A special issue of *Advertising Age* in 1988, "The Power of Advertising," once again promoted its field as "a remarkably accessible universal service" that builds markets and reduces prices, paving the way for progress through consumption.[1]

Earlier practices and beliefs never disappeared, but the proportions changed. Many factors sped the rate of change, among them World War I, the increasing amounts of consumer goods manufactured by corporations using continuous process machinery, and the increasing costs of national advertising with broadcasting as a new option. But, as with many processes, a century has not been enough to drive all firms away from owner-manager control over advertising. And there is no reason to think that another century will bring much change in the current ratios: small-business owners retain their intimate links with their operations; founders of innovative businesses often want a hand in presenting their products or services to the public. What was rare in the nineteenth century is now common, but not universal; what was common in the nineteenth century still occurs in the late twentieth, especially when owners operate their own firms.

The pre-nineteenth-century sense of an advertisement as an announcement that might or might not be commercial has almost entirely passed into obscurity in the English language. Today most people in the United States think of manufacturers' commercial messages for trademarked products when they think of advertising. In recent decades, any other use of "advertising" has to be qualified by a modifying adjective, such as "classified" or "retail," to avoid confusion. While I have analyzed transformations within the advertising field overall, I have focused on "brand name" advertising because manufacturers have dominated national marketing innovations and public awareness since the 1890s. Although retail advertising has always exceeded the expenditures of all other categories of advertisements, it fell behind others in innovations after the 1880s. Therefore, unless specified otherwise, this study focuses on manufacturers' advertising practices and products. Although I have tried to avoid teleological statements and perspectives—other choices could certainly have driven this past to a different present—the dominance of national (rather than retail) brand-name advertising in our century's commercial and popular culture is a reality that calls for explanation, especially when compared with very different nineteenth-century conditions and styles.

This analysis attributes much of the development of business and advertising procedures to business and advertising peoples' responses to competition because that is what falls out of the evidence. Whether or not this dynamic proceeded in an ideal or humane fashion or yielded an ideal or humane system, competition did prevail during these primordial stages, although opportunities to compete were almost always restricted to male members of the hegemonic classes. By recognizing that successful competitors directed advertising's course, I do not intend to lend legitimacy to the system that resulted.

In preparing this study, I have tried to avoid gendered language as much as possible. However, using *businesspeople* in place of *businessmen* does not change the reality that the vast majority of individuals operating businesses other than retail and artisan shops—and writing about them—were men. Nonetheless, by the end of the century, women such as Kate Griswold, publisher of *Profitable Advertising*, did figure in the advertising field as well, and there were enough women in business who advertised that comparing advertisements according to the advertisers' gender would be well worth the effort.[2] Given this book's focus on the mainstream, I have only scratched the surface of many questions about gender and ethnicity and the advertising processes during these decades. This study also leaves unexplored possible influences on U.S. advertising from abroad, with the exceptions of a few advertisers who operated extensively in the United States. As a study primarily of how actors in this field presented themselves to the public and of the internal dynamics between the actors, issues of international influence rarely appeared in the evidence before the 1890s, and then largely concerned the impact of European design. Pertinent questions remain regarding international sharing and mutual influences.

---

Advertisements are the most public, and in many ways the most evocative, components of today's Western marketing process. They are important elements of our material culture as well as messages commissioned for marketing purposes. Because advertising has been a major conduit between businesses and the general population, its history can help us look at the interrelations between business and the larger culture. In order to use advertisements as material history, we must appreciate how complex and convoluted the relationships between advertising messages, their creators, and their audiences have been and remain. And although advertisements do not provide totally reliable materials for reconstructing their creators' business and cultural attitudes and intentions, they are richly resonant products of those attitudes, beliefs, and intentions. My goal has been to examine advertisements as elements of material history in the context of the business and cultural dynamics in which they were produced. That method has provided an explanation for—rather than simply the traditional observations about—the modernization of advertising.

Part One

---

# PRODUCTION
## AS
# PROGRESS

# 1

# Marketing Problems and Advertising Methods as America Industrialized

*When competition increased after the war the manufacturer did not wait for trade to turn up, but sent out salesmen, catalogues, circulars and what has now come to be a mass of trade literature, much of it elaborately designed to gain the attention of busy men.*

—"Methods of Selling Goods," *Iron Age* editorial, 1896

The roots of the tremendous growth in American advertising that took place after the Civil War were laid down over centuries of evolution in Western marketplaces.[1] Conspicuous traces of the earliest history remained in the 1870s. As people walked through commercial districts, they still saw and heard advertisements in two media that harkened back to ancient towns: trade signs with emblems but no lettering still hung from buildings and stood on the streets to announce the locations of merchant, banking, and artisan businesses, and in the larger towns, street criers and peddlers still shouted their chants very much as they had for centuries. The latter was clearly the liveliest medium of the period. In earlier times, many street sellers had represented merchants, publishers, or medicine dealers who hired them to sing their wares. Street criers had provided advertisers with their best opportunities for emotional advertising appeals, applying humor, rhyming, and exaggerated descriptions. Prior to the 1820s, news, official announcements, and commercial announcements all fell under the rubric of advertisements, so the street criers' occupation held a measure of prestige.

The bourgeois pedestrian of the 1870s, in contrast, had little respect for either the business or the practitioners of street selling.[2] In the commercial capitals of New York City and Philadelphia, a few retailers still attracted attention with flamboyant additions to the street crier's repertoire, such as ostriches and elephants laden with sandwich boards. These extravagances were the street sellers' swan song, however, and did not revive the ancient advertising medium. With rare exceptions, such as department-store parades, only peddlers offering goods for sale on the spot have survived the nineteenth century, and they occupy the lowest rung on the entrepreneurial and social ladders.

The conditions that destroyed the viability of street crying as an advertising medium of any consequence were those that dominated the transformation of the entire nation through the course of the nineteenth century. The impacts of industrialization and urbanization appeared so vast and profound that both contemporary and later observers were inclined to declare them inevitable, even deterministic, processes. Like other historical processes, however, they resulted from countless decisions by countless individuals driven by their personal needs, ambitions, and expectations; together, they determined the transformations of nations.

Whether these changes improved or worsened people's lives, whether participants harkened back with nostalgia or looked forward with anticipation, nineteenth-century Americans usually attributed the changes in their material and cultural lives to *progress*. Even those who romanticized the preindustrial past with its street criers and picturesque towns generally forged ahead. Sometimes, innovators in advertising such as the retailer John Wanamaker and the editors of the *Inland Printer* (a leading printers' trade journal) idealized visions of the rural past even while they promoted cosmopolitanism and steam-powered presses, helping to generate and define the modern age. Countless individuals played out another dualism, as both observers and participants in a progress that proceeded by competition. So merchants switched their advertising patronage from street criers to print in order to compete with others who had already made this "progressive" shift. As the ancient medium lost credibility, its attractiveness and prestige spiraled further downward; youths inclined to performance occupations turned instead to the growing audiences for traveling troupes and repertory shows. Printers used their increasing revenues to invest in ever more sophisticated ways of pleasing their advertising patrons, and merchants, in their turn, advertised and sold more and greater varieties of goods, helping thereby to develop markets. Both winners and losers had a word for this reciprocal, competitive dynamic: *progress*. Moreover, whatever else they thought of the changes, Americans' goals increasingly, if not universally, absorbed materialist criteria for progress. So, instead of the appearance of spiritual or political worthiness determining the value of a person's contributions to the commonweal, at least in principle, as in the Puritan communities and the early Republic, material successes became major criteria for leadership and social prominence. This was notoriously so in the Gilded Age metropolis.

The dramatic expansions in population, wealth, income, and territory that characterized the United States in the nineteenth century paralleled equally dramatic expansions in the size and character of markets for both consumer and industrial goods. Then, as now, businesspeople defined their marketing problems in terms of what they wanted to accomplish in selling their goods or services and the circumstances that they encountered in doing so. Advertising is only one component of addressing a marketing problem, namely, paid communications with one's market.[3] To canvas their potential markets, whether urban, suburban, regional, or national, as markets changed, businesspeople came to define their marketing problems as entailing communication goals that required advertising media with far greater reach than street criers. An 1890 authority on advertising summarized why these changes increased the use of printed promotions:

> The manufacturer once made everything in one shop, and sold to everybody near him. Now he only makes one or a few things, and must supply more customers, who are widely scattered. The consumers . . . must now use the products of numerous and remote manufacturers. Thus there is an ever-widening distance between the producer and the consumer.
>
> But the producer and consumer should know each other. . . . The railroad only allows producer and consumer to drift farther and farther from an acquaintance with each other. Only the printer's ink can bridge the distance, and bring the producer and consumer into relations of intimacy. The locomotive and printing press must go hand in hand.[4]

As early as the 1820s, even the concentrated domains of urban merchants became larger, busier, and noisier than street criers could manage. By midcentury, the available varieties of products and services exceeded the carrying capacity of an unaugmented aural medium. Advertisers experimented with other on-the-scene media, such as wagons covered with signs, decorated clocks, and mechanical trade stimulators, devices highly ornamented with brand names that drew people into a store by performing tasks, from cutting the tips off cigars to providing therapeutic electric shocks. Advertisers even tried sending their messages out on coins.[5] All these methods, however, suffered from limited reach or exposure to the market, so over the decades, advertisers increasingly chose printed media to disseminate information and appeals, exchanging liveliness for reach. Only later could the technical capacities of print replace some of the street criers' color.

Printed media expanded the reach of advertisers' communications, but until midcentury, in newspapers and broadsides they rarely permitted anything other than short announcements decorated with simple woodcuts. Steel or copper engravings were costly and relatively rare in American advertising before mid-nineteenth century, and almost never appeared in newspapers; only the more affluent merchants and tradespeople in the larger cities adopted the English custom of commissioning finely engraved bill heads and shop cards. Dating back in England to the seventeenth century and flourishing in the United States in the eighteenth, these advertising sheets ranged from quite small to twelve inches across and were used to wrap small purchases, to record transactions, and as papers for public posting.[6] Then by the 1850s, woodcuts and other print forms began to proliferate in newspapers and elsewhere. As limited as the earlier options for print advertisements were by our standards, there was little else for people to read that was new each week; hence, the merchants' unadorned lists of goods received ample attention.

## Advertising Methods in Pre–Civil War Markets

Prior to the 1820s, most printed advertisements in America were primitive in both their styles and their communication techniques. With few exceptions, advertisements were little more than announcements of whatever goods a merchant had to sell or whatever services someone desired or offered. Only as commercial advertising activities expanded did the term *advertisement* gradually narrow to encompass primarily commercial announcements, excluding other announcements such as legal notices, which had once been considered advertisements. (Reminders of the roots of the word *advertisement* in *to advert* or *to turn the attention*, remain in older newspapers' names such as the *Daily Advertiser* and also the Spanish use of *advertencia* as a notice or warning and of *anuncio* for *advertisement*.) Frequently, merchants began their announcements by craving "the public's indulgence," "beg[ging] to offer," or "respectfully inform[ing] friends and the public" of their offerings. These deferential, almost servile, prose styles derived from the social customs of service and self-conscious pretensions of gentility shared by politicians and merchants alike that preceded the Jacksonian era's revolution in rhetorical styles. Moreover, the simple announcement, with or without such deferential stylistic conventions, sufficed for sellers and consumers alike at this stage of marketing because most items offered before 1820 were traditional, generic services and goods such as foodstuffs, cloth, or ribbons. There was no need to educate the public about their uses or desirability except in the few circumstances where fashion had begun to generate discretionary demand, such as in ceramics, textiles, and apparel accessories. The attractions of fashion had begun to build a consumerist culture in Britain and Europe during the eighteenth century. Before the War of 1812, fashion lured Americans into consumerism primarily by example and travel to Europe rather than advertising.[7] And the public did not have to be taught to distinguish between goods within most categories: consumers judged products by inspection and by merchants' reputations, not by brand names. Common understanding in America—more than in Britain or Europe—assumed that demand typically exceeded supply, obviating expenditures to generate interest in goods. Merchants in the United States deemed it necessary only to announce the availability, quality, and affordability of their offerings to market them, unlike in eighteenth-century London, where Dr. Samuel Johnson represented many observers when he noted in 1759 that "[a]dvertisements are now so numerous that they are very negligently perused, and it is therefore become necessary to gain attention by magnificence of promises, and by eloquence sometimes sublime and sometimes pathetic."[8] Both purveyors and consumers in the United States, in contrast, presumed that people already knew what they wanted and that they bought what they could. Retailers, including artisans selling their own products, sometimes claimed that their goods met the standards for fashion, but enticing and instructional illustrations of just what fashion entailed did not yet accompany such declarations.

The U.S. distribution system, or marketing channels, until the 1810s centered around unspecialized merchants acting as the primary intermediary between producers and retailers and other middlemen. Whether in towns or rural areas, retailers ran comparatively small operations, and no individual retailer came close to wielding the marketplace impact of the general merchants until the middle of the century. With their roots in the colonial period, such merchants dominated the economy of the Federal and Jacksonian periods; they were the "business class." They imported and distributed to retailers goods from abroad, distributed raw materials to many trades, distributed the few domestically manufactured goods that were available to retailers, and also exported. General merchants also had important functions as a major source of credit for both businesses and governments.[9] Advertisements before the 1820s reflected the importance of the general merchants as their announcements of arriving ship cargos and other sources of inventory were major features in port city newspapers. They directed announcements primarily to retailers, both in the port city itself and those from the hinterlands who came into the cities to purchase their stocks several times a year. Most commercial advertisements not placed by these wholesaling merchants were placed by retailers who had acquired much of their inventories from them. At either level of merchandising, wholesale or retail, lists with occasional, brief descriptions characterized the prevailing style of advertisements. Auctioneers, agents for ships, entertainers, schools, medical practitioners and medicine sellers, lawyers, lottery companies, and financial services such as insurance companies and bankers placed most of the remainder of the commercial announcements in the typical newspaper up through the 1860s.

Merchants and patent-medicine purveyors dominated the early newspaper pages. The differences in their promotions demonstrate the connections between marketing problems and advertising forms, the latter supplying the exceptions that proved the rule of the announcement format. Preparers and purveyors of medicinal products and services faced different marketing problems than did most contemporary advertisers. Unlike most goods that were identified and sold generically, that is by type, and that required no explanation to sell, proprietary, or branded, medicines all claimed to offer unique solutions to consumers' difficulties that had to be explained. (Medicinal products that sold at retail in England and the United States were considered proprietary or patent goods because the preparers and/or sellers declared ownership and filed legal claims to their unique names, or brands, and secret compositions.)[10] Also, unlike the merchants selling most other goods in that era's marketplace, medicinal promoters operated in "an economy of abundance," according to historians David M. Potter and James Harvey Young; that is, even though people's ailments and lack of effective medical care combined to create high levels of demand for remedies, the proliferation of entrepreneurial medicine preparers sufficed to motivate intense competition for market share and to expand markets geographically when conditions created apparent opportunities.[11] This set of circumstances set up three basic marketing problems for the medicine sellers: how to phrase and present their claims; how to communicate their claims; and how to connect those claims in people's minds with specific nostrums. The advertising forms that nostrum sellers practiced, therefore, argued their products' merits and associated those merits with a specific identity through a name or an emblem, which we have since come to call a trademark or brand name. The trademark often served a second purpose, linking nostrums with symbols for reassurance, such as saints, angels, herbs, doctors, or grandmothers, or symbols of power such as electricity or swords, or symbols for exotic resources, such as non-European peoples or exotic places and plants.

Another, related, marketing device that set nostrum promoters apart within the American marketplace before mid-nineteenth century was their extensive use of consumer-sized packaging. Only a few other products, such as cosmetics, alcohol, and tobacco, had both the marketing needs and the profit margins to justify the tremendous expense that packaging entailed before the availability of industrialized packaging. The traditional, generic goods that filled people's basic needs, in contrast, were sold unlabeled and in bulk. Patented, processed, and packaged as pills, lozenges, or solutions in alcohol, medicines, however, were sold in small units. Unlike most other goods, they were therefore easy to store and ship for distribution outside of their immediate production areas. Competition between producers encouraged expanding the geographical boundaries of their markets, with the result that nostrums were the first branded products promoted widely as early as the eighteenth century, and more widely as the transportation networks of the nineteenth century developed. With each incremental increase in the networks, medicine sellers expanded the size of their campaigns until, in the transcontinental, national markets that existed by the 1870s, they became the largest group of advertisers.[12] Medicine bottles, boxes, and wrappings carried products' identifying shapes or marks as well as their claims. Identifiable packaging with a strong symbol, whether name or image, also served as a cognitive link between the product itself and advertising for it in other media. Indeed, before medicine promoters routinely patented their products, many of them patented the shapes of their containers or copyrighted their labels in order to protect their unique appearances, as the Coca-Cola Company did for its bottle adopted in 1916.

One other characteristic distinguished the nostrum sellers from all other early-nineteenth-century American businessmen other than entertainers, namely, a tradition of showmanship that went at least as far back as ancient Greece. Perhaps this tradition followed simply from their special need to compete for attention, or perhaps a flair for theatrics and exaggeration inclined an entrepreneur to selling nostrums. Whatever the explanation for the high correlation, selling snake oil and the like has been rivalled in hyperbole and dramatics only by such famed showmen as P. T. Barnum. Such lessons were not lost when, later, other promoters had to solve similar marketing problems. As James Harvey Young, historian of medical promotion, has concluded: "While other advertising in the press was drab, his [the medicine seller's] was vivid; while other appeals were straightforward, his were devilishly clever. The patent medicine promoter was a pioneer, marching at the head of a long procession of other men with ships and shoes and sealing wax to sell."[13]

In all the alternatives tried during the primordial stages of American advertising, promoters of successful nostrums and entertainments led the fields because their plentiful, lively, colorful, optimistic, and enticing messages successfully resonated with enough of their audiences to have powerful impacts.

**Fig. 1.1.** Densely packed pages that often did not distinguish between commercial and other announcements typified newspapers until printing technologies in the 1870s permitted increased illustrations. The customized banner for Anderson's Cough Drops on this front page of the *Massachusetts Spy* (Worcester; 10 October 1821) illustrates how patent-medicine promoters stood out from others in their advertising techniques; most other woodcuts in early newspaper ads were of stock images, such as ships, set in at the advertiser's request.

*Production as Progress*

Despite the dismay of elitist naysayers, most Americans eagerly experimented with the new medicinal and experiential options offered to aid both ancient ills and modern ambitions. Nostrum sellers and sideshow operators also offered Americans a freedom from authority that appealed to many still reveling in the decline of deference that characterized the century between 1750 and 1850.[14] The growing confidence that citizens could simultaneously purchase independence from pain and elitist authorities, such as doctors, also resonated with the spirit of the times. Many considered this a form of progress, albeit one that would wane with the waxing of professionalism at the end of the century. Patent medicines and their narcotic content also offered consumers opportunities to violate the temperance strictures of the times, another aspect of the nostrums' appeal. Nostrum sellers—like circus people—flourished in this environment, leading the way for other entrepreneurs whose ambitions and promises later laid claim to growing abundance as the century moved along.

The attributes of the thirty advertisements on the front page of the *Massachusetts Spy* of 10 October 1821 (fig. 1.1) illustrate the contrasts between medicinal and other announcements of the period. Nine announce legal matters, hearings, or meetings; ten list goods "respectfully" submitted by merchants, both wholesale and retail; two seek workers and two offer services; one combines a legal announcement and a mercantile listing; at the top of the page, Harvard University offers "Medical Lectures," and at the bottom the publisher announces a medicine just arrived at his bookstore; a notice informs readers of the availability of real estate; another tells of a "Premium Bull, Columbus"; and the *Spy*'s publisher announces his almanac for 1822. Only black lines and variation of font differentiate these messages, but a thirtieth, an advertisement for Anderson's Cough Drops, displays a woodcut of an elaborate banner encasing the lone brand name on the page. Immediately under this banner lies the claim, "*The most valuable Medicine in use for* COUGHS AND CONSUMPTIONS." The intensely argumentative copy that follows exemplifies the genre of nostrum advertising:

> This new and healing Balsam bids fair to rival every Medicine heretofore discovered, for Coughs and complaints of the lungs, leading to Consumption, and even in seated Consumptions it has lately been used by many, with the most surprizing success. If Certificates [testimonials] from persons of the highest respectability, or the great and increasing demand for it, may be called proof of its good effects, it is proved. Scarcely a case of Colds, Coughs, pain in the side, difficulty of breathing, want of sleep, arising from debility, or even Consumptions, but may be relieved by the timely use of this Medicine.———Many certificates of its efficacy accompany each bottle.

*Caution.*— Be particular that every genuine bottle has "*Anderson's Cough Drops*" stamped on the bottle, and the directions are all signed by JAMES MELLEN.[15]

(In the above quotation, as in all quotations throughout the book, unless otherwise noted, the emphases are as in the originals.) Two lengthy testimonials follow the declarations quoted above, and the message concludes with information about retailers and the wholesaler who carried the medication around New England. The illustration, the many claims, the use of testimonials, the relatively wide geographic distribution, and the caution about competing substitutes came to typify techniques in marketing all varieties of goods after the Civil War.

The language of excitement, promise, and innovation exhibited in medical advertisements continued for decades. Samples from the *New York Tribune* of 26 May 1865, include the following:

MRS. M. G. BROWN, METAPHYSICAL PHYSICIAN, from Philadelphia, discoverer and proprietor of the celebrated "METAPHYSICAL DISCOVERY" for DEAFNESS and every disease which flesh is heir to, is now at her office, No. 51 Bond-st., and would be glad to see all who are using her Metaphysical Discovery; also those afflicted in any way. She positively assures the world that there is no other ANTIDOTE that will reach the CAUSE of DISEASE. Her discovery treats the CAUSE, and not the EFFECT.

Sharing twenty-one inches with twenty-nine other advertisements, Mrs. S. A. Allen offered her World's Hair Restorer in six different two- and three-line notices. But, while Mrs. Brown tried a long entry to reach her audience and Mrs. Allen tried many short entries, Weeks and Potter tried a startling headline to sell WHEATON'S OINTMENT [which] WILL CURE THE ITCH IN 48 HOURS.

ITCH! ITCH! ITCH!
SCRATCH! SCRATCH! SCRATCH![16]

Whatever healing powers the ointment had were probably those of suggestion, much as the headline held the power to stir an itch in readers.

From the 1870s through the end of the century, medicine producers and entertainers such as theaters, circuses, and exhibitions dominated advertising to such an extent that many people associated the entire field of advertising, other than local retail and noncommercial announcements, with these dubious but lucrative trades. By far the largest category of businesses through the end of the century that advertised beyond local limits, patent-medicine companies accounted for more than one-half of the 104 firms listed as spending more than $50,000 on national advertising as late as 1893.[17] Much of the public opposition that the whole advertising field faced when the Progressive movement attacked the enterprise resulted from the strength of this association. Notwithstanding the many criticisms that have been directed at entertainers and patent-medicine advertisers, it was the patronage of these clients that subsidized the era's printed media—as, today, advertisers of all sorts continue to subsidize most media. Entertainers and medicine sellers also set the standards for color and liveliness in visual style and for drama and hyperbole in copy of the period. Conversely, by the end of the century, they set standards against which all advertisers were judged, both by modernizing advertisers and by the mainstream public.[18] Although the mainstream public—that vocal portion of the population dominating the press and other political institutions—may have represented larger portions of the population even less than it does now, its impact was profound.

## The Evolution of Retail Advertising

This first stage of U.S. industrialization, between the 1820s and the 1870s, provided the market conditions for the heyday of retail advertising, when retailers contributed many innovations in advertising content, style, and placement that determined the direction of the whole field. Ever-growing quantities of both industrial and agricultural goods, together with concomitant developments in urbanization and in transportation and communication technologies, made increasing numbers of traditional, generic products available to consumers, who were increasingly concentrated in cities. Consequently, the new market conditions of midcentury were characterized by a gradual shift to a buyers' market. Responding and contributing to these developments, producers, wholesalers, and merchants expanded and changed their marketing activities. As they did, they altered the distribution channels through which goods passed from the producers of raw materials to processors and industrialists and then to consumers.

This early stage of industrialization began the slow shift away from the announcement-style of retailers' and manufacturers' print advertisements that prevailed at midcentury—fueled, perhaps, by the plentiful exceptions in medical and entertainment advertising. Most of the consumer-directed products of industry and commerce from the 1820s into the post–Civil War period remained traditional, generic goods (domestic foodstuffs, textiles, shoes, and iron products). Developments in manufacturing techniques and technologies (manufacturing generally included the processing of raw materials, such as foodstuffs, into usable forms, as well as the assembly of products) increased the volume of these traditional goods but rarely resulted in different types of goods for the general marketplace. Consumers already knew the nature of most goods for sale and businesspeople did not recognize any need to educate consumers at the expense of advertising costs. Furthermore, most advertisements still promoted merchants, not brand-name products, so the basic marketing needs during this period changed primarily by a quantum increase in the intensity of competition between known entities; that is, between merchants selling generic products.

Yet increasing competition does not alone explain retailers' marketing innovations in this period. With the exception of the printing and advertising trade presses that specifically targeted advertisers in all fields, the extensive but conservative trade and industrial advertising directed to wholesalers, processors, and industrialists had virtually no impact on the overall development of advertising methods in the nineteenth century (or in the twentieth, for that matter). Transportation enterprises advertised extensively as well, but until the late 1800s their consumer-directed messages usually listed space available for people and cargo, schedules, and claims for speed; they gave essential information but the formats changed little. Therefore the following analysis examines changes affecting the distribution channels for bringing goods from importers, processors, and industrialists to consumers.

In 1820, the wholesale and general merchants dominated not only commerce but the entire U.S. economy. As marketing conditions changed after 1850, wholesaling changed. The general merchants' prominence faded as commodity dealers and full-service wholesalers came to divide the intermediary functions of the distribution channels. Even though these more specialized wholesalers dominated the distribution channels as a group, their decisions to advertise decreased relative to the vastly expanding marketplace. Moreover, like other forms of trade advertising, as a rule the wholesalers' messages remained stylistically conservative. Thus, although wholesalers, like most businesspeople, increased their absolute amounts of spending on promotion, their share of and innovations in advertising expenditures declined relative to the dramatic expansion in advertising bought by retailers and manufacturers after the Civil War. Instead, wholesalers increasingly relied on traveling salesmen and catalogs to promote their stocks, both to processors and to retailers.[19]

In contrast to the wholesalers' marketing mix, consumer-directed advertisements have always been the primary means by which retailers of all sizes have regularly communicated to their potential markets. Until the 1930s, most store operators continued to maintain small inventories and to sell to neighborhood residents. Most of these neighborhood stores confined vertising to trade signs outside their stores, to small spaces in local ne and to leaflets announcing promotions or pictures and calendars from printers with their names overprinted on them.[20] Specialized the other hand, provided the earliest retailing innovations in respon first stage of industrialization and urban population concentrations. Specialized retailers, as distinct from artisans' shops, operated as early as the 1830s selling particular types of clothing or hats, usually men's, or dry goods. Such specialized storekeepers had to solve a new marketing problem through advertisements, namely, to draw customers from outside their immediate neighborhoods. As a result, the successful among them bought space in citywide newspapers and had flyers printed for distribution on outdoor walls, by mail, and for handouts. They also wrote more aggressive copy to tout their wares than had previously been typical for retailers, competing with neighborhood shops by convincing customers to travel extra distances to shops previously unknown to them. While American cities did not yet possess "economies of abundance" according to Potter's designation, competition between retailers did indeed accelerate after 1820, and retail advertisements began to take on greater intensity as a result. Even so, until the 1870s, price and occasionally the quality of goods remained the primary inducements normally touted in these advertisements.

Unlike the unadorned lists placed by merchants in the 1821 *Massachusetts Spy*, merchants' advertisements by 1865 showed that they had learned that their primary advertising goal was to create a sense of urgency with which to attract customers into their stores without fail, and immediately—which is still the rule in retail advertising. Sampling advertisements from the *New York Tribune* of 26 May 1865 demonstrates this trend with large, bold, uppercase lettering, extravagant punctuation, and rising levels of hyperbole. Using a woodcut illustration of a man in an elaborately tailored shirt—one of only two woodcuts in the entire, eight-page paper—Ira Perego & Sons offered "*PEREGO'S* PATENT BOSOM *SHIRT*. IN ADDITION to our usual stock of MEN'S FURNISHINGS, we have opened a full assortment of FASHIONABLE *CLOTHING*, AT POPULAR PRICES." L. Binns, Millinery offered "BONNETS at HALF PRICE this week. STRAW BONNETS at $1, $2, and $3 each, worth $2, $4, and $6. CRAPE BONNETS and SILK BONNETS at $10, worth $16." An unusually coaxing entry promised that, "Heads win a new charm from the superb Summer HATS just brought out by GENIN for the special adornment of the beau sex. Have you seen them, Ladies? If not a new delight is in store for you; and mark this! the prices will not alarm you." Of course, the patent-medicine and entertainment advertisements in that same paper far outshine Genin's one-half column inch in their claims and hyperbole. For Barnum's American Museum, the master showman listed sixteen different attractions that day, *plus* "a million curiosities."[21] Still, the promise to add to ladies' charms and the use of a question within the copy to engage readers placed Genin in the vanguard of copywriting enthusiasm.

Merchants who recognized the growing potential for profits in selling industrially produced, processed, and transported goods to urban consumers built a new type of institution—the mass retail store. American cities of the mid- and late nineteenth century increasingly concentrated population and wealth, first in port cities, then in hubs of the railroad networks. Because the people in these burgeoning population centers made their livelihoods in specialized occupations, they had to buy, rather than make, more and more of what they needed and desired. Adequate output of both domestic and foreign industries and some means by which to inform people that these goods could be had in desirable selections and at favorable terms fostered centralized retail outlets. The earliest mass retailers carried large stocks of many varieties of dry goods, augmented often by jewelry and domestic wares organized by category or department.[22]

In meeting their marketing problems, owners of large stores entered the ranks of the most prolific and innovative individual advertisers, especially during the decades following the Civil War.[23] Like specialty stores, large stores could not exist by drawing only on neighborhood-sized markets that had traditionally attracted urban spending.[24] In centralizing consumer activities, they joined and often led the trends to pass up the announcement-style of advertisement, and they vastly expanded the volume and pace of retail advertising. Price became, as it remains, a focus of department-store advertising to foster high-volume, high-turnover selling at low margins. Part of "price advertising" featured the policy of selling goods at one, nonnegotiable price at any given time. All department stores eventually adopted this policy because of their interests in maximizing efficiencies and turnover and because they grew to employ more sales clerks in larger numbers of transactions than any businesses had previously required. All this activity ruled out traditional negotiations.[25] Since brand names did not yet guide consumer purchase decisions, major retailers also increasingly featured merchandise guarantees.[26] Stores trying to attract consumers away from neighborhood and small-town stores found such confidence-raising policies invaluable competitive tools.

Two main paths led to the early department store, the first developing when wholesalers opened up retail showrooms to the public. An advertisement in the 1865 issue of the *New York Tribune* cited above promoted the goods of

Clark, Traphagen, and Hunter, who offered clothing for men, boys, and children at reduced prices from their "entire wholesale stock at retail."[27] By this route, Alexander T. Stewart built a prototype department store, the Marble Palace, in New York City as early as 1846, and then, in 1862, the first fully departmentalized store in the United States, the Cast Iron Palace. Still, of his total annual sales that reportedly reached $50 million by 1870, all but $8 million came from his wholesale operations. By 1841, Stewart already advertised "regular and uniform" prices, and he usually receives credit for originating both the one-price policy and the storewide guarantee, although Lord & Taylor in fact preceded him by three years in advertisements for their dry goods, claiming "no deviation from first price."[28]

Augmenting a specialized clothing store or dry-goods store with other types of goods marked the second path by which retailers developed department-store operations. As late as 1889, Marshall Field resisted adding items other than dry goods to his enormous store in Chicago, but competition and younger managers prevailed. By virtue of this diversification, Field's retail trade gradually overtook his wholesale operations, although those had still made 95 percent of the firm's total profits through the 1870s.[29]

John Wanamaker began business—and began to change retail advertising—in 1861 in partnership with Nathan Brown, his brother-in-law, selling men's clothing in Philadelphia. Unlike Stewart's sedate newspaper announcements intended to inspire confidence, Wanamaker's promotions proclaimed his store's goods and prices loudly and frequently. He often ran one advertisement several times in the same newspaper edition. Wanamaker competed for attention, and he succeeded notoriously. For example, a couple of days before the store opened, he spread countless small handbills through Philadelphia with only the initials "W. & B." Just before the store opened, a second set of handbills announced the opening. After taking in $20.67 his first day, he spent all but the sixty-seven cents on newspaper advertisements offering men's suits at bargain prices. He opened his department store in 1869 and continued with flamboyant promotions throughout his long career, including advertising in newspapers to an extent considered profligate by many. According to an advertising agent, by 1870 he had already "caused the universal 'Wanamaker & Brown' to be chiseled on the street crossings, painted on rocks, and mounted on house-tops," thereby gaining the praise of a major figure in the advertising field at the time. His most famous aphorism about advertising responded to critics who accused him of wasting half of his advertising expenditures: Yes, he agreed, but since he was not sure which half that was, he intended to continue on. As extravagantly as he advertised, Wanamaker did not intentionally waste money. For instance, when he recognized that advertising the wholesale enterprises he later opened did not carry the same advantages as retail advertising, he minimized it.[30]

Highly personalized organization and operations so characterized all mid- and most late-nineteenth-century businesses that the impact of owner-managers on the practices and styles of advertising cannot be overemphasized. Stewart's and Field's reserved styles as well as Wanamaker's spiritedness derived directly from their personalities and attitudes toward business. Likewise, Rowland H. Macy's copy was unique, not only winning great success for his retail business but also setting new standards for the literary quality of department-store advertisements. Macy opened a dry goods store in 1858 outside of the busiest shopping districts in New York City. He had little capital and could not buy newspaper space for his first month in business. Once he began, he used aggressive advertising techniques to compensate for his poor location and lack of financial resources, drawing customers from well-established stores with low, one-priced, guaranteed goods offered for cash only. His advertisements read more interestingly than his competitors', and he used white space creatively by distributing words with a bit of distance between them, or by repeating words to give a designed appearance, practices he might have learned from the display advertisements (those laid out for attention-getting, unlike classified advertisements) of some innovative publishers, such as S. N. Dickinson of Boston, or patent-medicine sellers. His copy also read pleasantly, with few of the conventional, stilted clichés. For instance, he asked readers about their preferences regarding purchases and then told them that their answer could be found at his store. He also announced his wares and then told readers, "You want them, of course." After about 1863, Macy's marketing problems dwindled compared with the administrative problems brought on by his successes. Macy chose to take less interest in writing copy, and his advertisements lost their freshness.[31] Even so, he had made his mark on the advertising field.

Mail-order retailing, and the newspaper and magazine advertising to support it, grew steadily through the nineteenth century, picking up pace just before 1870. Even so, until 1872, the nation lacked a retailer concentrating on marketing a wide variety of goods solely through catalogs. At that time, Aaron Montgomery Ward and his brother-in-law George A. Thorne took advantage of the transportation and communications developments that fostered the mail-order magazines. Ward's varied background of selling to rural consumers in several capacities had prepared him to communicate and appeal to them. He was particularly aware of their concerns both about the costs that middlemen's profits added to most of their purchases and also about getting fair value for their money. The National Grange of the Patrons of Husbandry, an agrarian social, educational, and political movement founded in 1867, endorsed Ward and Thorne in 1873 as a means by which rural folks could bypass middlemen, including wholesalers, drummers (traveling salesmen), and creditors. Accordingly, they promoted their operations as The Original Grange Supply House and promised to save purchasers 40 to 100 percent of the "profits of the middle men." To do so, they aimed at purchasing goods directly from manufacturers for cash; they also sold for cash. By 1874, in addition they guaranteed their goods, reassuring distant purchasers of recourse that was sometimes more reliable than that available from their local general storekeepers. Because Ward recognized that gaining the rural consumers' confidence was his most important promotional goal, his copy focused attention less on specific items for sale and more on his institution, encouraging people to send for the catalog. Ward wrote his company's extensive advertising himself. He placed it in the general presses as well as specialized mail-order magazines and, following the lead of the patent-medicine advertisers, he also mailed almanacs to farmers. In the 1890s, he even sent out promotional railroad cars loaded with both merchandise and entertainers. Ward continued to write most of his advertisements through the 1880s, self-consciously maintaining a friendly tone and repeatedly inviting readers to his establishment.[32] Although many other firms exploited the nation's burgeoning railroad networks, postal system, and presses by selling specialized lines through the mails, Ward did not face major competition until Sears and Roebuck began their general line of catalog sales in 1893—also out of Chicago, the Midwest's hub.

By the time that Montgomery Ward and Company started up, large, urban retailers had been advertising dry goods and other wares to the urban public for decades. But because consumers visited their stores, these retailers perceived less need for illustrations. Marshall Field, for instance, built the largest store in the Midwest using few illustrations in his newspaper advertisements right up to the last years of the century, despite protests from his top managers.[33] By the early 1880s, in contrast, Ward offered such abundance in watches, notions, gloves, toilet goods, cutlery, jewelry, fans, albums, trunks, harnesses, ready-made clothing, boots, hats, and so on, that he deemed woodcuts, and, later, electroplated or photoengraved images, necessary to illustrate the variations and entice consumers.[34] Ward and Field made their different decisions according their perceptions of their different marketing problems. Other urban-market retailers, such as Wanamaker, showed more enthusiasm than did Field for illustrations, but in general large retailers' marketing problems tended to diverge from those of other types of advertisers after the 1870s. As a result, with a few notable exceptions, such as Wanamaker's 1880 decision to hire a specialized copywriter, John Powers, their later innovations rarely addressed the marketing problems of the brand-name advertisers, whose activities were to determine the next major thrust of advertising evolution. Although retailers as a whole still buy more advertising space and time than national, brand-name advertisers, their techniques and strategies developed in a different direction from that of branded-product advertising, at least until the 1970s when fast-food chains and other retailers began to blur the distinctions between advertising products and advertising retail outlets.

As nineteenth-century businesspeople learned by competition and comparison to appreciate the value of eliciting emotional responses from the audiences for their advertisements, retailers and manufacturers found that different appeals satisfied their different personal and business interests. Whereas manufacturers tended to make their claims on excitement in terms of technological progress and their sense of its ramifications, retailers featured services and their handling of burgeoning varieties and volume of goods as their contributions to progress. The excitement of buying and selling, of competing on price and quality and sometimes integrity, has proven consistently compelling for retailers. As prominent advertising agent George Rowell argued in 1870, competing with aggressive advertising marked the "progressive spirit" of the era:

> Much less than a hundred years ago, in the days of slow-coaches and very slow people, when business men were content with few sales and small profits, it made little difference whether a tradesman advertised his goods or not. But the whole course of trade and traffic has undergone as much change as other things, and now it is indispensible [sic] that he should keep up with the progressive spirit of the times, and he is certain to succeed best who in business tact, and the liberal expenditure of money, leads rather than follows in the race. It is doubtful if any retailer clothier in the United States scatters as much money among newspaper people as John Wanamaker.[35]

Despite all the activity and dynamism Wanamaker and others poured into their advertising, until the 1890s, when retailers moved from seeing service as deference and fashion as nonessential to new views of service and fashion as progress and boons to society, even their most elaborate advertising images in the 1870s lacked the dramatic iconography they showed by the end of the century.

The divergence between urban retailers and manufacturers in their marketing problems and advertising styles came to the fore just as the latter started to assert themselves as advertisers to consumers, with considerable consequence for their messages. Indeed, just as marketplace leadership had gradually moved from wholesalers to retailers by 1870, it then moved to manufacturers.

Impersonal market forces did not determine this movement: manufacturers aggressively and deliberately developed advertising techniques to wrest control of the marketplace away from retailers and wholesalers. Because of manufacturers' highly visible successes at developing branded products, most people today identify "modern" advertising with branded-product advertising. As a 1909 article in the *Yale Review* explained, "the older [newspaper] advertisements were almost exclusively of localities and persons," informing the reader at what retailers various goods could be purchased. "To-day," on the other hand, the majority of the advertisements one sees "are issued by the manufacturers of a particular article or special kind of articles . . . [that] may be obtained 'anywhere,' and the only request made is that the name of the brand be not forgotten. It is one more striking illustration of the shrinkage in distances and the unification of demand that are almost world-wide."[36]

## Early Developments in Manufacturers' Advertising

The second stage of industrialization, approximately 1870–1900, with its surge of invention and increased productivity, coincided with a dramatic expansion of world trade and provided the context for new developments in the marketplace. These factors combined to add immeasurably to the types and quantities of material goods available to consumers—sewing machines, spool thread, musical instruments, clocks, polishes, packaged foods and drinks, and countless varieties of tools and devices for everyone in every type of work, including housework. The shift from a sellers' market to a buyers' market begun by the first stage of industrialization became even more apparent with all these new varieties of goods competing for the consumers' spending. The postwar expansion of new types of goods into the marketplace propelled the emergence of modern product marketing, with brand-name advertising as its primary tool. Manufacturers experimented with introducing their branded products to the public and with generating both general demand for their type of product and specific demand for their brands. As remarkable as the manifestations of material progress were, people could not very well want to buy what they did not know existed, did not understand, or did not perceive as a need. Advertisements served as a major means by which the public became aware of the fruits of invention, industry, and world trade. In this way, advertising truly became the business of material progress: it helped create desire for the new and improved, even as it made the very existence of the "new" financially possible. Moreover, advertisements provided a public forum for presenting progress, in word and image, according to the visions and interests of their creators.

With promises and threats, often with novel imagery and vitality, advertising messages helped to define both progress and the expectations and rewards of the Victorian lifestyle in terms of materialistic criteria for personal and material success.

Accelerating population concentrations, growing income levels that allowed increasing levels of discretionary spending, the growth of transportation systems (particularly the railroad networks), and the rapid growth of communication systems (telegraph, the postal system, and the press), all continued prewar trends. Although these preconditions facilitated the development of brand-name marketing by manufacturers, modern advertising did not develop as a simple, direct result. Nor did aggressive advertising by manufacturers just appear because of a ready and accessible audience, for example, or simply because industrialists' new productivity left them with unforeseen supplies to sell. Instead, the complex economic conditions on both the demand and the supply sides created opportunities and marketing problems that entrepreneurs recognized and responded to variously. The most successful exploited their opportunities and resolved their marketing problems through methods that often included advertisements. Indeed, marketing decisions often determined a business's success as much as, and in some cases more than, did technological innovations.[37]

For instance, to step back another century, advertising did not simply appear from nowhere in the consumer and industrial revolutions of eighteenth-century England, where what I have referred to as the first and second stages of American industrialization occurred as a single, more graduated, process. Merchants and manufacturers first used advertisements extensively as a deliberate means of exploiting novel economic opportunities. Historian Neil McKendrick writes that attitudinal changes overcame traditions in a "consumer revolution [that] was the necessary analogue to the industrial revolution." McKendrick specifies that the key to the novel opportunity that successful entrepreneurs recognized in eighteenth-century England was fashion; that is, they saw the potential to exploit popular desires to emulate the rich and powerful, and the new capability for doing so. Furthermore, "all of these small items of household consumption [particularly clothing and beer] offered the lure of profit for those who flocked to make and sell them." McKendrick contends that this era's substantial economic development required the pursuit of luxury by "an ever-widening proportion of the population," which "became an engine for growth, a motive power for mass production." A case in point, Josiah Wedgwood very deliberately promoted his potteries with such success that he created an "'epidemical' sickness to possess his wares amongst the upper and middling ranks." He did so by first winning the patronage of the nobility for a style of pottery, then gradually cheapening the pottery to attract what he called "the middling People" through advertisements and showrooms. Wedgwood's implementation of promotional innovation responded to his perceptions of marketing problems that stood in the way of selling large quantities of his goods to various markets.[38]

In the United States, the specific marketing problems of selling manufactured goods, such as textiles and ceramics, were quite different than in cosmopolitan and affluent areas of England. During the first stage of American industrialization, merchants, not manufacturers, promoted the consumer goods subject to fashion. Because the engineers of fashion by and large remained British and, to a much smaller extent, continental, comparisons with fashionable persons and households of England and France, or with those who had contacts or experience there, sufficed to lure scant discretionary income from Americans quite self-conscious of their cultural distance from cosmopolitan centers.[39] American merchants and manufacturers generally merely copied European fashions for which demand already existed. Only later, when American manufacturers began to produce goods that were unknown or as yet undesired by their markets, did they need to generate demand by developing innovative marketing techniques. Until after the Civil War, American manufacturers apparently left the determination of fashion to the Europeans, since the first innovative goods they produced for the consumer markets and promoted directly to consumers were what they themselves called the mechanical wonders of their day.

Through the century, producers developed a sense of their participation in technological changes that they believed was worthy of widespread notice because of its presumed value to the progress of both society as a whole and their potential customers. That spirit increasingly pervaded their commercial messages. While retailers emphasized the prices, the "latest fashions," and the variety in their stores, artisans and larger-scale manufacturers described their contributions to prosperity in terms of "improvements"; at best, merchants could claim only to carry the manufacturers' improvements to consumers. These different claims on progress symbolized an increasingly antagonistic relationship between manufacturers and merchants that played out in their marketing strategies into the next century.

In this context of a rapidly changing economy, the first American manufacturers to develop nontraditional distribution channels did so to meet their specific, nontraditional marketing problems. In the mid-nineteenth century, the usual distribution channels positioned the wholesaler between manufacturers and retailers and normally saved manufacturers considerable money and effort in product distribution. The wholesalers or jobbers who purchased goods, then stored, marketed, and distributed them to retailers, bore the burden of these costs and activities, as well as the attendant risks. The wholesalers' traveling salesmen—"drummers," or commercial travelers—also provided easy and quick ways of introducing new products to the retail trade (as, today, for many types of products, they still do, although their control of most markets has substantially diminished). For manufacturers to give up those benefits and to try new alternatives, they had to have expected substantial countervailing benefits.[40] For instance, the Fairbanks Scale Company of St. Johnsbury, Vermont, founded in 1830 and producer of the earliest business machines (reliable scales for weighing goods for sale and shipping) spent $3,000 on advertisements at one time in the *New York Tribune*—the largest single pre–Civil War expenditure by any advertiser—and paid out more than $30,000 annually on various media through the 1860s.[41] Fairbanks also sent out catalogs with woodcuts at least as early as 1847,[42] and by the 1850s he hired "itinerant agents" around the country to supervise sales through regional offices.

Advertisements in the *New York Tribune* of 26 May 1865, referred to earlier, hint at why some mid-nineteenth-century manufacturers, like Fairbanks, chose to bypass wholesalers and retailers, devising new distribution channels despite the costs and risks involved. Other than publishers and medicinal promoters, most of the producers seeking to reach consumers directly in this issue manufactured complex machines and sold out of their own showrooms. Musical instruments, especially pianofortes and organs, predominated, followed by another expensive and novel machine, the sewing machine. Unlike the myriad generic goods, such as notions, ribbons, hats, foodstuffs, and so on, advertised by wholesalers and retailers and certified by their reputations, the public's estimation of assembled devices relied solely on their manufacturers' reputations. For example:

> STEINWAY & SONS' GOLD MEDAL GRAND AND SQUARE PIANOS are now considered the best in Europe as well as this country, having received the first Prize Medal at the World's Exhibition in London, 1862. The principal reason why the Steinway Pianos are superior to all others, is, that the firm is composed of five practical piano-forte makers (father and four sons), who invent all their own improvements, and under whose personal supervision every part of the instrument is manufactured.[43]

No marketer of that era knew a complex product as well as its manufacturer. Therefore, no one could argue such a product's benefits better or explain its use. To that end, Steinway spent more than $50,000 on advertising in 1868.[44]

When a product possessed a unique and attractive differential, its "own improvements" in Steinway's case, its manufacturer often considered that feature at least as important if not more important than its price. Whereas retailers and wholesalers generally competed by offering generic goods at competitive prices, manufacturers of complex, expensive, consumer goods discovered that instead they fared best by promoting their differentials as arguments for fixed and profitable prices. In this situation, retailers and manufacturers had conflicting interests that inclined the latter to market their own goods so they could better compete on nonprice variables. They could also balance saving middlemen's markups against the expenses of their own showrooms, advertisements, and itinerant agents. Furthermore, effectively promoting a product's differential through advertisements or salespersons required forming an association between the product and the differential through some symbolic representation that functioned as a trademark. Before the 1890s, that symbol was usually the name of the producer or inventor; for their part, wholesalers and retailers generally saw little merit in promoting another's name, unless they had exclusive rights to that product. The marketing advantages of establishing a wide reputation associated with a brand name cannot be overestimated; after 1870, they drove many of the most important innovations in the advertising field.

For the same reasons that Steinway and Sons sold from their own showrooms and spent more than $50,000 in 1868 on advertising, the manufacturers of sewing machines, another complex product, recognized the need to control their own sales and distribution.[45] Manufacturers of other complex machineries, such as agricultural equipment and printing presses, followed similar practices. Accordingly, Elias Howe Jr., placed an unimposing advertisement in the 1865 *New York Tribune* for "THE ORIGINAL HOWE SEWING MACHINES." Like Steinway, Howe invited customers to view his machines at his own showroom in New York City. Unlike Steinway, Howe also sought agents with this advertisement.[46] In selling from his own showroom and seeking agents, Howe followed the patterns originated by his antagonist both in courtroom and marketplace, Isaac Singer.[47] In 1851, Singer and his partners began selling the sewing machine that incorporated Singer's first improvements through specialized showrooms, a practice that had evolved out of the artisan's shop tradition. Singer initiated its unique successes by inviting women, through advertisements, into the showrooms to learn how to use the new technology from other, trained, women. This merchandising by instruction was an important, albeit intangible, differential and one well worth associating with the company's name and machine through advertising. Accordingly, most Singer advertisements in the 1850s and 1860s showed a woman working at a machine.[48] Because of the mechanical inadequacies of these machines, the advertisements soon thereafter offered guarantees, at the same time touting "the best" sewing machine available.

In 1855, Singer's lawyer and partner, Edward Clark, wrote that "a large part of our own success we attribute to our numerous advertisements and publications. To insure success only two things are required: 1st to have the best machines and 2nd to let the public know it." Since we know that Singer did not produce the most reliable machines, we might well doubt Clark's judgment about the second requirement, too, except for the many other times that advertising has successfully compensated for inadequate products. By the end of the 1850s, the Singer Manufacturing Company and its major competition also began to put agents around the country on salary and to open up branches rather than franchises, thereby eliminating the independent agent as well as the wholesaler and independent retailer.[49] Singer's early centralized control over marketing and distribution resulted in commercial success that derived more from his marketing prowess and innovation than from technological innovation, despite advertisements proclaiming technological progress. Indeed, the company managed to dominate competing firms that had superior production methods and machines. Reversing the expected causality, the Singer Manufacturing Company seems to have been forced into improving its production methods in order to meet the demand achieved by its sales techniques.[50] Thus, the nature of the product—a novel, complex, and expensive device for consumer use—and not surplus inventory, drove Singer's marketing innovations.

Cyrus Hall McCormick developed solutions along similar lines in turning to advantage the special marketing problems faced in promoting new and complex agricultural technologies. He recognized that his harvesting machine required demonstration and explanation, in part because it was novel and in part because of intensive competition from other harvester manufacturers, most notably Obed Hussey in the early years. Hussey and McCormick patented their machines within a year of each other, 1833 and 1834, respectively. In the early years, both men sold their machines by traveling personally in the countryside near their origins. While they continued to invent and "borrow" mechanical improvements to improve their imperfect machines, McCormick forged ahead of Hussey and the other manufacturers by promoting his machines beyond his personal contacts: his first advertisements appeared the year before he filed for his patent. Then, during the 1840s, McCormick developed a network of agents and advertised widely in agricultural publications, while Hussey continued to rely heavily on his own personal salesmanship and free publicity from contests and exhibitions.[51]

McCormick advertised aggressively early on, unusually so by comparison with other manufacturers or retailers of the pre–Civil War era. Indeed, in Mc-Cormick's enthusiasm for the hard sell, his advertisements strongly resembled those of the medicine sellers. Like them, McCormick heavily employed testimonials that he not only solicited from well-known figures but that he sometimes wrote as well. His advertisements attacked his competitors by implication and even by name, which also paralleled patent-medicine purveyors' assaults on medical doctors' snobbery, faulty treatments, and expenses. In addition, McCormick engaged in unabashed puffery; that is, he paid or coerced editors of publications in which he advertised to write favorably of his machinery or to print his copy as editorial comment. McCormick also used job printing (printing done to order, such as cards, tickets, and brochures) early and heavily. He had pamphlets printed during the 1840s for distribution at fairs and exhibitions, and his first advertising pamphlet for distribution by mail and agents appeared before the harvest of 1859. McCormick used chromolithography, too, commissioning his first multicolored posters in 1867. The handbills and newspaper advertisements that McCormick began using at least as early as 1851 demonstrated his recognition of the importance of both touting and explaining his products to his potential customers. His advertisements continued for decades to combine claims for his machines' prowess with instructions for their assembly, operation, and repair.[52]

By 1870, the marketing problems that retailers and producers faced were changing in many ways as they participated in and contributed to the developing national marketplace. Those who adapted their advertising methods to their specific circumstances best succeeded in extending their reputations and expanding their sales. In turn, they altered their own marketplace and influenced future marketing conditions. While not all nineteenth-century manufacturers built their own marketing organizations, those producing goods for the widely dispersed American consumer increasingly began to find merit—that is, profit—in exerting increasing control over the distribution channels through which their goods passed to the consumer. Increasingly aggressive and extensive advertising methods often led manufacturers' marketing strategies in achieving this control.

# 2

# Owner-Manager Control of Advertising

*The Humphryes Manufacturing Company is the creature of [John Humphryes Jr.'s] brain, his excellent business ability and his untiring energy. He organized it, fostered it and, as its secretary and general manager, made it the prosperous plant it is—in fact, to his intense application in furthering its business may be traced the impairment of his health.*

—Obituary for John Humphryes Jr., *Iron Age*, 1893

## Whose Ads Were They?

All too often, people think of historical advertisements as easily accessible windows onto past attitudes and practices. In part, this questionable assumption follows from the belief that popular culture at any time can be discovered in the plentiful messages advertisers pay to project onto it. However, the relationships between advertising messages, their creators, and their audiences are much too complex and convoluted for any such facile conclusions.[1] Societies do not produce advertisements—specific people within societies produce advertisements. Advertisements present us with messages prepared by advertisers—that is, the businesspeople who advertise and their collaborators, such as printers, publishers, and advertising agents, according to their combined notions about their audiences, how best to communicate to them, and to what purpose. Commercial messages therefore better represent their creators than their audiences, much less the population at large. Advertising messages at most reflect the perceptions that the advertisers and their co-creators have of their audiences' values and lifestyles. More likely, they reflect what marketers expect will appeal to their audiences as well as the values and lifestyles marketers hope to promote to their audiences. Advertisements share this characteristic with any form of message created to influence people at a distance, such as religious missives and political posters. To the extent that the creators of advertisements share their audiences' perceptions, their messages may communicate common attitudes. To the extent that audiences adopt marketers' messages, the ads influence popular culture. So when we interpret advertisements, do we seek their meanings for their creators or their meanings for intended or unintended audiences—or perhaps their meanings for ourselves? Or, more unsoundly, do we seek their meanings for some abstractly defined, ambient society, as if it were a single entity? Each of these approaches has merit as a distinct direction of analysis requiring contextualization and identification; each is problematic and not to be taken lightly. As in translating any symbols and discourse of any period and culture, each direction should be taken deliberately and explicitly.

Advertisements, both historical and contemporary, do reflect something of their social and cultural environments, but they do so unclearly and with varying degrees of representation, because no single group of people or messages can represent an entire population with all its diversity. Advertisements reflect what their creators thought audiences wanted to see, or what they thought their audiences should see, according to the creators' ideological, social, and business biases. Since the advent of formalized market research and motivation research after World War II, we can surmise that the fit between commercial messages and their audiences has become tighter in some ways, but the pipers still play their patrons' tunes and not the tunes of their audiences.

How, then, and by whom, have advertisements been created? The advertising process, in the nineteenth century as now, comprised five basic steps: deciding to advertise, conceiving the message, producing it, distributing it, and paying for it. Advertisers must always perform the first and last steps, initiating the process and paying for it. What, if any, of the middle three steps they perform has varied over time and according to custom and other factors, especially the size and organization of their firms and the passage of time since their founding.

In the century before 1920, specialists gradually took over the three steps between marketers' deciding to advertise and their paying for it. Conception, production, and distribution of the message devolved to specialists at different rates over the years, according to advertisers' desires for assistance and many other factors. By 1870, most advertisers who were not printers themselves routinely delegated the production of their advertisements to others. Whether or not advertisers delegated distribution depended on the medium used. Distributing advertisements through advertising agents to the periodical media, newspapers and magazines, increased rapidly between 1870 and 1890 as the complexities and size of the marketplace grew, especially when advertisers tried to reach national or large metropolitan markets. When, on the other hand, advertisers used nonperiodical media, such as posters and trade cards, they or their sales agents or wholesalers retained for decades, sometimes even to the present, the responsibility for distributing their messages to their publics. The critical and highly individualistic matter of conceiving the advertising messages shifted only gradually, and after 1890, to specialized communication professionals. Nevertheless, advertisers still retain ultimate control of the content of their commercial messages.

Important though small and owner-operated firms are to today's economy and society, they no longer dominate the direction or the popular image of U.S. business or its political economy. In contrast, entrepreneurial capitalism prevailed in American business before the 1890s. In part because the owners, or their extended families, often founded and always managed most nineteenth-century enterprises, they were intimately involved in their functions. Furthermore, these firms operated without corporate stockholders for financing, relying on retained earnings, silent partners, or the growing domestic and foreign banking and institutional investment resources.[2] Then, as now, owner-managers answered to themselves and to their partners and families.

Prior to the merger movement of the 1890s, an owner or small group of partners could oversee the entire operations of most firms, assisted by a single layer of supervisors between themselves and the majority of their employees, and managerial specialization had only begun to set standards for operating the largest U.S. businesses. Although a few leaders in managerial practices, such as some railroads, had passed through the owner-manager, entrepreneurial style by the 1870s, small enterprises remained in the majority and important to operation and innovation in the U.S. business system into the present.[3] Manufacturers' trade journals continually praised and idealized "Men Who Succeed"—to quote the *Manufacturers' Gazette* of 1890. Such men gain both "reputation and wealth" by having "grown up in the business, becoming familiar with every detail and every branch. They do not have to rely upon any one for the successful operation of their plant."[4] In 1869, James A. Garfield admonished young men aspiring to business success that "whatever you win in life you must conquer by your own efforts, and then it is yours—*a part of yourself*" (emphasis added). Along with the extended passage from Garfield's speech, Seymour Eaton reiterated the substance of this message in other forms throughout his *One Hundred Lessons in Business*. For instance, the first lesson consisted of a page of advice from "a Brooklyn man of long experience in business life" that instructed young men to learn all aspects of their business, to be "master of [their] own business" in every way.[5] This was, after all, the highly proclaimed managerial style of two of America's most famous businessmen, Andrew Carnegie and John D. Rockefeller, notwithstanding the sizes of their operations.

Many of the major figures and firms of nineteenth-century American business, like Carnegie and Rockefeller, had little impact on consumer-directed advertising practices. For instance, the infrequent but powerful exceptions to the small-business rule that had already, by the 1870s, developed corporate structures and middle managerial practices, such as the large Massachusetts textile mills, railroads, telegraph companies, and insurance companies, mostly sold to other businesses, or their goods were generic products sold through traditional wholesale distribution channels. Railroads, which advertised extensively to the public and to businesses, did so to raise capital, but they advertised comparatively little to nontrade consumers before 1890, except to publicize rates and timetables. Although they purchased substantial newspaper space and ordered multitudes of posters and timetable brochures, their advertising policies rarely deviated from conventions developed by other advertisers, particularly retailers. Rarely did they lead in advertising as they did in the evolution of managerial or financing practices. An early example of a railroad's experimenting with novel forms came in 1892 with the Santa Fe Railroad's beginning successful campaigns to attract tourists to the Southwest, using artists' romantic renditions of the area and its people, under the direction of an advertising specialist. An editorial in Printers' Ink stated that it was "not poverty that keeps the railways out of the enormous benefits they might reap by a suitable advertising scheme." The reason was their "conservative tradition," as it was for the insurance companies, too.[6] Similarly, despite Carnegie Steel Company's size, and Andrew Carnegie's early adaptation to production of the managerial innovations that he had learned in the telegraph and railroad industries, neither he nor other large manufacturers of capital goods advertised to the consumer sufficiently to have any interest in developing that field. Indeed, in The Empire of Business, Carnegie's 345-page collection of advice on business written in 1902, he included not a word on advertising as a pertinent tool of business success.[7]

The nineteenth-century businesses that determined the course of the century's advertising practices began as small enterprises and were marketed initially by their founders. Individuals started owner-managed businesses, such as that begun by Dr. C. E. Welch, a Methodist dentist, who in 1869 invented a nonalcoholic grape drink as a substitute for wine in communion. Favorable responses encouraged him to market it, so he began by typesetting, printing, and distributing advertisements, mostly "circulars and booklets to churches and members of the medical profession."[8] G. G. Mennen also provided his own early, and rather more flamboyant, promotions. Around 1880, this pharmacist concocted a pleasing talcum powder that he first marketed by distributing samples to local mothers. He then nailed signs on fences and trees in the area, still selling from his drugstore. After Mennen gave up his store, he sold from the back of a wagon that carried, in addition to quantities of talcum powder, a troupe of entertainers. Later he advertised with painted boards, signs on barns and rocks, painted theater curtains, and circus programs, then distributed novelty giveaways through retailers and the mails and bought magazine and newspaper space. Not until after 1910 did Mennen seek an ad agent's assistance in creating his messages.[9]

Firms operating under this nonbureaucratic style have continued these practices, regardless of the date or the size of business. In 1910, Otto Leisy, a partner and the "Sole Manager" of a moderate-sized brewery, reminded his employees of his monopoly on decision making within the company; he did this in a document entitled, "Rules to be strictly adhered to in 1910 by every employee in the I. Leisy Brewing Company."[10] On a much larger scale, according to Ida Tarbell, John D. Rockefeller continued to control his business even after it reached massive proportions. "To know every detail of the oil trade, to be able to reach at any moment its remotest point, to control even its weakest factor, this was [his] ideal of doing business." As Tarbell explained, there "must be nothing—*nothing* in his great machine he did not know to be working right."[11] And in the 1920s, Henry Ford still managed the firm he founded as closely as possible, considering its great size. For fifty years beginning in 1937, Edwin H. Land, inventor and promoter of the self-developing camera, and the Polaroid Company operated as "a man and a company who occupied the same space, and often, but not always, spoke with the same voice."[12]

Before the advent of the advertising/newspaper agent in the 1840s, advertisers always worked directly with the newspaper or magazine publishers or job printers who produced their messages. Between the 1840s and 1890s, advertising agents increasingly distributed advertisements to the presses for their clients, but they provided only minimal, if any, creative services. Thus, almost always before 1890, but decreasingly thereafter, advertisers initiated the process, decided upon the message, and then, with or without an agent as a liaison, communicated it and a set of expectations for it to a printer or publisher. The letters between advertising businesses and printers or agents before 1890 were always written by or addressed to officers of the advertising firm or their secretaries. Even during the 1890s, on most occasions when *Printers' Ink* or any other advertising trade journal praised advertising successes, they credited the founder or highest officers of the advertising firms for the relevant decisions or innovations.[13] Although printers and publishers often exerted considerable influence on an advertisement's content and style, the final determination on an advertisement always belonged to someone keenly interested in the public image of the firm and its products.

J. Estey & Company exemplified owner-managers' identification with their firms. In 1849, Jacob Estey became a silent partner in a firm, founded in Brattleboro, Vermont, three years before, that manufactured reed organs. In 1857, he and a Mr. Greene took over the firm and named it after themselves. After Greene retired a few years later, Estey controlled the company and continued to so do for several decades, as partners and relatives came and went. The firm grew, and by 1870 Estey employed at least two hundred people, producing more than three hundred organs each month. Estey's own reputation and that of the firm's were the same to him, even when he had partners, as evinced by the diatribe he wrote into the company's catalog in response to his competitors' price-cutting during the hard times of the 1870s:

> The age of humbug is not past, and this is one of the most arrant humbugs of all. Such a policy carried to the end can only result in ruin and disgrace. "My reputation, Iago, my reputation!" cried the repentant Cassio. . . . Messers. ESTEY & Co. value the reputation of the ESTEY ORGAN as they do their own. They have earned an honorable name, and their great success has been achieved by honest, plain, straightforward dealings with patrons, agents, and all concerned.[14]

Such a defense for a business, invoking personal reputation, reflected, as it still does, owner-managers' identity with their firms.

There is a certain irony in Estey's declaration that the "age of humbug" had not passed. *Humbug*, as the indignant Estey used the term, referred originally to promotional deception, but it came to be associated also with the bright and extravagant advertisements made possible by advances in printing technologies after the Civil War. In this latter sense, Estey sponsored numerous advertising forms common to nineteenth-century entrepreneurs later called "Barnum & Baileys of the industrial scene."[15] For example, one Estey multicolored poster, circa 1890, features an expansive factory complex as the dominant image (plate 1). Vignettes fill the lower corners: on the left, an idealized bourgeois parlor scene features an Estey organ as the focus of genteel attention, all under Jacob Estey's gaze, and on the right, Jacob Estey's portrait appears again, flanked by his two current partners. This print demonstrates the showmanship of the period's colorful advertising outside of periodicals. The factory complex, the founder's portrait, all topped by the oversized and elaborate lettering shouting the company's name, were standard fare for these signs, frequently accompanied by scenes of products in use. Such flourishes had more in common with circus promotions than they did with the dark and staid announcements typical before the Civil War, and that were still prevalent in newspapers and magazines.

## "Bill It Like a Circus" and Other Innovations

To "bill it like a circus" became a common expression among aggressive advertisers.[16] And many manufacturing advertisers would not have objected to a label that likened them to the master of humbug, Phineas Taylor Barnum. Indeed, one of the largest shoe industrialists of the period, William L. Douglas, readily acknowledged having been inspired by posters with Barnum's portrait to use his own face for his trademark, and he did so very successfully. Some in the advertising business took the impact of Barnum's humbug, if not its content, so seriously that *Printers' Ink,* the period's main advertising trade journal, mourned his death. According to the eulogy, Barnum had served, after all, as "one of the shining examples of success attained through judicious advertising."[17] In his *Autobiography,* Barnum stated with his characteristic bombast that "I thoroughly understand the art of advertising, not merely by means of printer's ink, which I have always used freely, and to which I confess myself much indebted for my success, but by turning every possible circumstance to my account." For fifty-six years, beginning in 1835, Barnum entertained and challenged Americans and Europeans, drawing them into his sideshows, museums, concerts, lectures, and, of course, circuses with flamboyant and extensive promotions. Far from disclaiming humbug, he titled one of his popular lectures, "The Science of Money-Making and the Philosophy of Humbug." With his humbug, he "bought Americans with brass, for gold and silver I had none."[18] Certainly, the tales of Barnum's promotions have astonished generations with his extravagant imagination. He employed the press to his advantage with both paid advertisements and with his skills at obtaining free publicity for his entertainments, and he generated advance publicity with trainloads of brightly colored posters, favoring them over newspapers for the towns along his itinerary.[19]

Neil Harris's analysis of Barnum's talents and accomplishments provides useful insights for understanding other successful advertisers of the nineteenth century. Harris contends that Barnum, like the patent-medicine purveyors, appealed to Americans' "egalitarian self-confidence." They relished the chance to challenge experts and sought to make their own decisions about the verac-

*Production as Progress*

ity of claims and propositions. Consequently, when they paid their nickels to see the "Fejee mermaid" that Barnum promoted as the subject of learned doctors' debates, they were pleased to be able to see clearly for themselves that it was only a monkey's head and torso joined to the tail of a large fish. "Who is to decide," his advertisements asked, "when *doctors* disagree?" The more controversy Barnum could whip up, the greater his profits, especially if he could engage experts with impressive credentials to challenge him publicly. In explaining Barnum's successes, Harris "reconstruct[s] the language of showmanship that meant so much to nineteenth-century Americans." He argues that, despite the popular conceptions of Barnum, he was not simply a "brash huckster." Barnum was "neither a good-natured deceiver nor an evil-minded philistine, but an intelligent, complex, and well-organized entrepreneur whose business involved the myths and values of a self-proclaimed democracy." Likewise, much of the popular attraction to patent medicines derived from the independence that, users believed, the medicines gained them from doctors.[20]

Barnum did not train in any formal sense as an advertiser, promoter, or showman. Beginning in rural New England and then moving to New York City, he tried shopkeeping, newspaper editing, boarding-house managing, and lottery selling. The only one of these ventures that fared well was Barnum's lottery enterprise, but most states outlawed that activity before he could make his fortune. Barnum found his calling at last when the opportunity to promote a provocative entertainment piqued his fancy. Despite accusations that he fabricated a hoax in 1835 by purchasing and exhibiting a very old slave as George Washington's nurse, Barnum's genius lay not, in Harris's words, so much "in the invention or manufacture of curiosities as in their discovery, purchase, and advertisement." Barnum succeeded because of what he called "my monomania to make the Museum [and other projects] the town wonder and town talk. . . . I often seized upon an opportunity by instinct, even before I had a very definite conception as to how it should be used, and it seemed, somehow, to mature itself and serve my purpose." This statement made good on Barnum's claim of "thoroughly" understanding the advertising of his time, for it contains the key to other nineteenth-century advertisers' successes in appealing to consumers. None were trained to promote; they all grew up without the communication technologies they employed as adults. Those who had a flair for promotion, those who shared Barnum's intuition and passion for it, succeeded at that portion of their business efforts. As Barnum put it, "I fell in with the world's way, and . . . my 'puffing' was more persistent, my posters more glaring, my pictures more brilliant."[21] Instance after instance, Barnum, like Singer and McCormick, turned marketing problems, including obscurity at some times and controversy at others, into profitable opportunities. Advertisers other than Barnum faced different marketing problems, of course, and generally had more in the way of tangible, functional products for their customers to judge. But their promotional efforts achieved marketing advantages for them if, by their intuition and personal inclinations, they too "fell in with the world's way."

During the Civil War, the Union government experienced a unique marketing problem—that of selling massive numbers of war bonds to a cautious population not accustomed to such matters. The promotional campaign that Jay Cooke devised, the likes of which the country had never seen and would see again only rarely until after 1890, resulted in a hybrid of standard contemporary techniques and a harbinger of future ones. The unique marketing problem combined with the size of the sponsoring institution, the required geographical and social reach of the campaign, and the impact of the single entrepreneur in charge and resulted in a remarkable campaign. Although Cooke operated as an agent of the federal government, his independence, personal investments, and payment by commission from the bonds he sold gave his activities the character of an innovative, owner-managed enterprise.

Jay Cooke was a self-made man in the best of the nineteenth-century tradition. By 1860, he headed a Philadelphia banking firm. He had had experience with advertising throughout his business career: as a teenager, his duties for the Washington Packet & Transportation Company included writing its advertisements. One of his biographers, Henrietta M. Larson, claims that his messages distinguished themselves from the competition's by acting as "sales talks" rather than "merely trite announcements." Cooke's enterprise in that position drew the attention of financier E. W. Clark, who gave the young man his start in banking in 1839. With E. W. Clark & Company, Cooke learned to sell railroad securities, municipal and state bonds, and real estate, and his experience included generating advertisements for the firm's offerings. At the beginning of the Civil War, Cooke established his reputation as a promoter of bonds by a precedent-setting campaign to sell bonds for the State of Pennsylvania. Even conservative institutional investors were persuaded to purchase these bonds by Cooke's appeals to their "patriotism and State pride of Pennsylvania in this hour of trial," as well as to their financial "self-interest." Furthermore, Cooke successfully advertised to ordinary citizens to buy bonds in denominations as low as $50. By reaching many levels of wealth, Cooke succeeded in oversubscribing the bond sales.[22]

On the basis of Jay Cooke's Pennsylvania bond campaign, Secretary of the Treasury Salmon P. Chase appointed him to sell Union bonds with the intention that Cooke would direct his efforts not only to the banking and finance community but, more importantly, to the general public. Cooke combined both traditional and innovative practices for the campaign. He created a massive organization with 2,500 selling agents traveling around the country, but he controlled it out of his own home in true entrepreneurial fashion, calling in assistance only as he needed it. For instance, Cooke's ambitions for the universal reach of newspaper, poster, handbill, and mailer advertisements required working through advertising agencies. His purpose was less to use the agents in the manner of most contemporary businesses—namely, to achieve the most favorable rates—than to ensure complete coverage with the greatest efficiency. Using the agents' placement capacities, Cooke distributed not only advertisements—for which he made a point of paying generously—but also "reading notices"; that is, prepared "editorials" and information that he expected the newspapers to run without additional compensation.

Besides the remarkable size of this operation, Cooke innovated in copywriting, combining rational with emotional, patriotic, appeals to draw out citizens' savings. Cooke credited his inspiration in part to the impressions made on him by the evocative advertisements of Dr. Jayne, an early and extraordinarily successful patent-medicine promoter, and John Wanamaker, already the consummate retailer. Cooke also used professional writers to help him get his ideas into print. Journalists Samuel Wilkerson and John Russell Young worked under Cooke's direction, supplementing his own writing, to turn out the massive volume of copy that the campaign required. Working as an entrepreneur, essentially as an agent for the Union government, Cooke paid for all the advertising expenses out of his own commissions on the bond sales.[23] In a sense, therefore, Cooke operated in this campaign very much as does an account executive in advertising today, defining the campaign's character and writing and directing copywriting and media placement with other, more specialized professionals, except that he was paid by a commission on sales.

---

Without any formal, studied set of conventions to follow, and without professional guidance, except from printers, advertisers experimented with the many fast-developing alternatives available to them for communication and transportation in a changing environment. Conventional practices grew out of these experiments.

The major marketing problems besetting most advertisers are competition for consumers' attention and competition for consumers' expenditures. The lack of easy access to homes and businesses through attractive, national mass media compounded these challenges in most of the nineteenth century. Different marketing problems fostered and rewarded different advertising policies, and not all restrained businesspeople deserved George P. Rowell's stern admonition, "The man who refuses to patronize the newspaper is the man of morbid disposition, of small ideas and no business talent."[24] Needless to say, advertisers' resemblance to P. T. Barnum in their practices ranged from the near likenesses of the patent-medicine sellers to the contrasts of stolid industrialists who advertised quietly and sold only through their trade presses and forums.[25] For patent-medicine purveyors and entertainers, extravagant advertising and other methods of self-promotion became so much a part of their business that any reticence in style doomed their sales. Macy and Wanamaker dominated the retail markets in their respective cities through personally devised, distinctive, and extensively distributed advertisements; Singer, McCormick, and Fairbanks likewise set precedents for manufacturers nationally. Despite exceptions to the stereotypes within each category, businesspeople made their marks when they matched their promotional efforts to their fields' marketing needs; those matches, collectively, created the conventions.

## Patent-Medicine Purveyors and the Power of Printers' Ink

The promotional styles of patent-medicine seller Dr. David Jayne inspired many other campaigns, including Jay Cooke's bond-selling strategies. Jayne had begun his career practicing medicine in New Jersey in the 1840s, which made him one of the few nineteenth-century patent-medicine sellers with a certified medical education. He moved to Philadelphia to sell his nostrums, and once there, according to George P. Rowell, a major figure in advertising for fifty years after the Civil War, "he had the good sense to see that no matter how much merit his medicines possessed it was necessary to make them known. In the matter of advertising, Dr. Jayne led all competitors in the race for fame and fortune." Rowell admiringly recounted that Jayne's "fortune was counted by millions, and his income itself was so large that he had to conjure up ways and means to dispose of it."[26] In addition to extensive newspaper advertising, by 1850 Jayne expanded on the custom of taking out advertisements in someone else's almanac by designing and commissioning an entire almanac as his own medium, setting an example that patent-medicine sellers followed for almost a century. His intuitive notion of how best to attract attention to his *Medical Almanac and Guide to Health* and to win sales for his vermifuge and other potions resulted in picturing a large, bug-eyed worm on the cover. Jayne and his successor seemed satisfied with this imagery, keeping it on their almanacs' covers in one form or another until 1911.[27]

James C. Ayer followed Jayne's lead in distributing almanacs and other nonperiodical printed advertisements to become one of the world's most prominent patent-medicine men. No immediate kin to advertising agent F. Wayland Ayer, James Ayer began in the medicine business around 1855 as a pharmacist who claimed the title of "Dr.," as did many of his contemporary peers. After a decade of heavy promotion, his sales supported a large industrial complex in Lowell, Massachusetts. By 1871, this complex included his own lithograph and letterpress printing departments, from which he oversaw the production of eight million almanacs annually. In 1889, Ayer's facilities produced one hundred thousand almanacs daily, published, over the course of the year, in twenty different languages.[28] In addition to the almanacs that Ayer produced out of his own shops, he also ordered advertisements in other formats from job printers, sending posters, trade cards, paper fans, and countless other novelties into the marketplace. For instance, a single country store in Mattawaumkeag, Maine, had on hand at least twenty-five Ayer posters, some of them never unwrapped, when it closed sometime after 1890.[29] In addition to directing these multitudes of lithographed advertisements, Ayer enhanced his reputation as a competent businessman with his close control over newspaper advertisements. He required that newspapers place his messages exactly according to specifications and trained his staff to watch for "shortcomings," for which he would personally demand compensation. He also trained what Rowell called "the best corps of advertising men that ever traveled in the interest of a patent medicine." Rowell's earliest memory of an advertisement was the label on his family's ever-handy bottle of Ayer's Cherry Pectoral, one of many tributes by which Rowell and others acknowledged Ayer's successes. In 1900, the journal *Advertising Success* declared that the "evolution of the science of American advertising can be traced by a review of Ayer announcements."[30]

Any number of others made their fortunes at selling patent medicines in the nineteenth century. As late as 1894, the *New York Times* declared, in a full-page article subtitled, "Vast Fortunes Made by the Patent-Medicine Kings," that "In Printer's Ink [is] the Secret" (printer's ink was a popular expression for periodical advertising). Reporting on a dinner at Delmonico's sponsored by the Association of Manufacturers and Wholesale Dealers in Proprietary Articles of the United States, the *Times* told the stories of some of those men "who had advertised themselves into fame and fortune," who were "better known than Cabinet members," and "whose business ventures extend to all quarters of the world." The article concluded hyperbolically that these successes demonstrated that "a pot of printer's ink is better than the greatest gold mine."[31] Not surprisingly, this tribute neglected to mention the regular criticisms made in that very paper and other public forums against many of the medicine sellers' practices, such as covering rocks, trees, and barns along public thoroughfares and railroads with painted reminders of their brands.[32] Furthermore, by 1894, many critics had begun to assail these same "patent-medicine kings" for the alcohol and narcotic contents of their nostrums and for their problematic copy techniques, which included unverified testimonials and frightening descriptions of illnesses and the horrible consequences of doing without their medications. Because of the dubious, often times harmful, nature of their products, few of the early patent medicines survived as household remedies past the 1920s.[33] A few of the more benign products, such as Lydia Pinkham's Female Remedy, did survive well into the twentieth century, but with a much diminished popularity; corporate rather than individual names have come to control the trade. To this day, old-time patent-medicine sellers remain more noted for their advertising strategies and techniques than for their nostrums. Leaders among them set the pace for lavish spending, and, like Barnum, they exploited their idiosyncratic flairs for self-promotion. Their successes demonstrated the value of competitive exposure, and gaining audiences through volume advertising and attention-getting devices became the standards for aggressive advertising.

## Selling Nationally

Manufacturers and retailers offering consumers products with more objective and tangible qualities than the nostrums often chose to pursue some of the same promotional tactics. Even before Richard W. Sears began to compete with Montgomery Ward's general-lines mail-order business, he advertised aggressively, primarily in newspapers. He began in 1886 selling watches through catalogs, writing his first newspaper copy at the end of that year. After moving from Minneapolis to Chicago in 1887 to have better access to the nation's transportation and communication networks, Sears advertised his watches heavily, putting copywriting high on the list of activities to which he personally attended. He brought watchmaker and tinker Alvah Curtis Roebuck into the firm to supervise the more mechanical aspects of the business so that he could devote his time to marketing. Despite heavy competition, Sears's promotions, which included complete guarantees, garnered more than enough business to foster rapid growth. Sears added other products to his offerings, and by 1894 his catalog had 322 pages with a wide variety of items, by then competing directly with Ward's catalog. Sears's sales eventually overtook his competitors because, according to Boris Emmet and John E. Jeuck, his "spellbinding advertisements exerted a telling effect on farm readers. His compelling messages pulled the reader into his copy and kept that reader's attention to the end."[34] Historian of marketing Richard Tedlow has agreed with this assessment, concluding that Sears's "panache" was the determining factor. He quotes Louis E. Asher, a turn-of-the-century Sears executive who declared: "The 'Send No Money' advertisements violated every rule of good advertising except one—the advertisements pulled! As Sears once said, 'They almost pulled the ink off the paper.' They were unattractive to the eye, set in crowded five-point type that was hard to read. There was no white space. But every ad carried the magic three-word message in heavy black type: 'Send No Money,' followed by the simple direction: 'Cut out and return this ad.'"[35] The cluttered copy and those "magic" words were all part of Sears's personal style of advertising; they were more like the traditional merchants' style than circus posters, to be sure, but quite in step with the standards of voluminous advertising set by the patent-medicine purveyors and entertainers. Although Sears's firm went through several forms during those years, none of those changes affected his control over advertising output.

After the Civil War, Cyrus Hall McCormick, manufacturer of harvester equipment, continued expanding his marketing nationally, although his brothers still did not allow their agents to place large newspaper advertisements in local newspapers; they encouraged, instead, small newspaper advertisements, personal selling, "puffery" (i.e., paid-for editorial statements), and limited use of other media. By 1870, however, Cyrus developed more extensive advertising practices, having overcome his brothers' fears that production could not keep up with orders. After first using lithographed posters, or show cards, in 1867, he increased expenditures, using more color and flourish as the years went on. In spring 1871, he distributed eighteen thousand copies of a chromolithographed show card to agents whose names and towns were overprinted by letterpress in red in spaces left blank for that purpose. In 1871, McCormick imitated a competitor's methods by publishing a trade newspaper full of praise for his machines alongside nonpromotional information and advice. His agents freely distributed this paper, which quickly replaced the McCormick pamphlet as a major, long-term selling tool. In the early years, McCormick had no agents to assist him in selling and he wrote his own advertising pamphlets of necessity, but even though the firm grew substantially during his lifetime, he always maintained personalized control over marketing. According to his grandson, the elder McCormick believed that "the heads and frequently the originators of their businesses, knew more than other men" about their machines, and therefore there was no need for a "specialized science" of advertising. So McCormick spent his last thirty years (he died in 1884) attending entirely to marketing and patent legalities. His grandson credited McCormick's successes in great measure to—in addition to his "undying service to humanity" in inventing modern agriculture as well as modern industry—his advertising virtuosity.[36]

After 1880, Cyrus H. McCormick Jr. gradually took over his father's promotional work, writing most of the advertisements as well as the puffery pieces sent to newspapers and journals. In the 1880s, the son came to supervise the annual production of 350,000 copies of the house advertising organ, the *Farmers' Advance*, 800,000 pamphlets, and 7,000 to 8,000 chromolithographed show cards. As a nonspecialist working within the fast-changing field of advertising, McCormick Jr. continued his father's extensive advertising practices, continuing also the family's debate upon the merits of those practices. In 1886, McCormick Jr. wrote a revealing commentary on the "fashions in methods of advertising," calling them "capricious." He argued, "Trying to do business without advertising is like winking at a pretty girl through a pair of green goggles. You may know what you are doing, but no one else does. Quitting advertising in dull times is like tearing out a dam because the water is low. Either plan will prevent good times from coming. . . . People who advertise only once in three months forget that most folks can not remember anything longer than about seven days." McCormick Jr.'s defense of his own advertising policies showed his determination to pursue his deceased father's high-profile policies despite continuing family opposition.[37]

## Publishers as Advertisers

George P. Rowell's listing of major advertisers of the 1870s pointed out the importance of publishers as advertisers.[38] Years later, Cyrus K. Curtis set new standards for publishers as advertisers and also came to wield enormous power within the advertising business overall, building what became, before broadcasting, two of the most important national advertising media, the *Ladies' Home Journal* and the *Saturday Evening Post*. Curtis had early developed a belief in the importance of advertising by first working in a store and then selling newspaper space to Boston merchants. He started up his first magazine in the burgeoning national marketplace of the 1870s and 1880s, a context that inspired hundreds of people to start up magazines. After that first try failed, Curtis started again in 1879, this time in Philadelphia. For this new farmers' weekly, *Tribune and Farmer*, his wife, Louisa Knapp Curtis, wrote a column addressed to women. Her feature became so popular that she expanded it first to a full section then, in December 1883, to a monthly supplement entitled the *Ladies' Journal*. The immediate success of this publication, which came to be known as the *Ladies' Home Journal* by a common misreading of its masthead by which readers mistakenly incorporated the *Home* under a cottage scene as part of the title, convinced the Curtises to focus all of their energies on building it.[39]

Curtis fully appreciated publishing's money-making potential that lay in attracting advertising revenues rather than subscription revenues or partisan patronage. He spent unprecedented amounts of money developing the *Ladies' Home Journal* as an attractive, well-written publication, successfully targeted to the prosperous classes. He raised circulations by advertising these merits extensively in other publications, both magazines and newspapers. The *Journal's* circulations, in turn, lured more advertising revenues than any previous publication. As part of this process, in 1885 Curtis sought out the agency of N. W. Ayer & Son in order to place the messages he had written more efficiently. Then, after several years of building the *Journal* slowly, Curtis decided to accelerate the process; in 1888 he went to Francis Wayland Ayer with a request for $400 in advertising credit. Curtis reported years later, in eulogizing Ayer, that he received the credit with the single stipulation that the agency could "spend it where we think it will do you the most good." The advertisements achieved such remarkable results that Curtis continued expanding his advertising until he challenged Ayer with a second request a year later, this time for $200,000 in advertising credit. Ayer granted this request as well, collecting payment for the loan by placing advertisements from his other clients into the *Journal* without paying Curtis for the space. With these campaigns behind him, Curtis continued aggressive advertising through the Ayer agency, building his circulations to the largest of the century. Also in 1889, Curtis hired Edward Bok to edit the *Journal* so that he and his wife could devote their efforts to what they considered more appropriate activities—she to her home and he entirely to advertising and promotion.[40]

## Advertising Soaps

Competition for consumers' expenditures increased during the nineteenth century as markets grew, productivity rose, local markets became regional, and some regional markets became national. Not only did similar products and services compete with each other, but new products competed with older alternatives and different types of products and services competed with each other. At the same time, the competition for consumers' attention increased as the intensity of promotional efforts grew in a self-fueling spiral, each advertiser attempting to wrest attention from other promoters. Entrepreneurs devised new advertising practices and exploited existing ones, building up a range of con-

ventional practices and attitudes that valued broad, frequent, and often intense exposure. The cumulative consequences of this spiral, of course, added
to each advertiser's perceived need for ever-increasing promotion. As the
decades after the Civil War passed, businesspeople who were determined to
compete through innovative advertising began to divide according to whether
they became more expert by specializing in marketing themselves, secured the
services of advertising specialists, or combined both approaches. As yet, a pattern had not crystallized; in this period of flux, when advertisers experimented
with form and content and media, advertisements reflected their notions of
what served their interests best, whatever their effectiveness as selling tools.

Selling soap during this period, for example, presented acute marketing
problems; it was a field that especially rewarded innovative advertising. The
market was extremely competitive because of rapid increases in manufacturing
productivity and the relative ease of transporting the finished goods; indeed,
the geographic range of competition was so large that several British soaps
competed effectively in the American market during this period. An additional factor that exacerbated competition between soap makers resulted from
their decisions to market their products in small, consumer-sized units packaged with identifying wrappers. The soap manufacturers then faced several
marketing challenges that involved generating both generic demand all
around as well as specific demand for their own brands. First, they had to convince buyers to consume more soap to absorb their collective productivity.
Second, they had to convince buyers to cast off long-standing traditions of either making their own soap or buying it in blocks from their storekeepers'
generic cakes. Third, they sought to foster brand loyalty—that is, specific
demand—for products with only minor differentials. As early as 1851, B. T.
Babbitt began a promotional program offering premiums in exchange for
quantities of soap wrappers, and all of the major soap companies developed
variations on this practice at one time or another.

In 1865, Thomas A. Barratt, a Briton who became one of the best-known
late-nineteenth-century advertising innovators, bought a partnership in a
prosperous London soap company founded seventy-five years earlier by An-
thony Pears and operated until then entirely by the Pears family. Barratt had
been admitted into this firm earlier to be joint proprietor, bookkeeper, salesman, and traveling salesman. Prior to his partnership, the firm had advertised
very little, and the Pears family became quite distressed when Barratt expanded advertising expenditures not only beyond limits acceptable to them
but beyond those of any previous nonmedicinal manufacturer in England. His
lavish use of posters and newspaper advertisements containing testimonials
from doctors, chemists, and even British-born Lillie Langtry, the renowned ac-

tress and beauty, drove the Pears family out of the business in dismay at how their family name appeared so ubiquitously and indiscreetly—although not before they had become quite wealthy. In 1883, Barratt began promoting his soaps in the United States, following the same extravagant practices and achieving the same successes; for example, in 1888 he made a $35,000 appropriation for advertising in the United States alone.

Barratt's innovations in advertising strategies had great impact in America as well as in England. One of his many famous contributions to advertising practice came in 1886, when he purchased a painting by Sir John Millais to be published on both sides of the Atlantic as an advertisement for his soap. The great success of this novel tactic in gaining widespread attention and publicity, not to mention sales, began a fashion of using fine art in advertisements that many, including Millais's son, credited for "rais[ing] the character of our illustrated advertisements."[41]

In the late 1880s, Barratt worked at developing questions as popular slogans in order to identify cleanliness with the use of Pears' Soap. Slogans had been used before, but most of them were dull and prosaic and did not pique the fancy the way that Barratt's questions did. For example, he asked "How do you spell soap?" to which his advertisements responded, "Why, P-E-A-R-S', of course." His most famous question became a fad: "Good Morning! Have you used Pears' Soap?" Children, adults, even political cartoonists and writers of the caliber of Mark Twain, reportedly teased their acquaintances and foes with the question for years.[42]

Although Barratt owned and directed his firm, he cared nothing for its history or manufacturing operations; he had no personal connection with either of these. He presaged twentieth-century marketers' attitudes toward manufacturing and selling with the remark that "Any fool can make soap. It takes a clever man to sell it."[43] Barratt, like George P. Rowell, an advertising agent who started up a patent-medicine manufactory in order to devise its advertising, at that time had to own a company to control its advertising campaign. He operated, therefore, as a transitional innovator, less like a traditional owner-manager and more like a twentieth-century advertising specialist. His talents and interests lay more with advertising than with any other aspect of managing his firm.

Elbert Hubbard, another innovative contributor to advertising history, held several other claims to fame, including authorship of "A Message to Garcia" in 1899 and the founding of an American center for the Arts and Crafts movement, the Roycroft Shop. Before literary and artistic accomplishments of this stature occupied him, however, Hubbard had pursued several trades, most notably a partnership in the Larkin Soap Company of Buffalo, New York. Beginning as a salesman, Hubbard soon became a partner and directed advertising and promotions for Larkin from 1882 until 1893. In this position, he took the strategy of offering premiums for soap wrappers well past its modest origins. In 1889, for instance, he offered unusually substantial attractions, such as lamps and furniture for wrappers plus a small amount of cash, a combination that today is called a self-liquidating premium. When Hubbard decided that he had achieved fortune enough, at the age of thirty-five, he sold his interests in the company to his partner, John D. Larkin, for $75,000.[44]

According to all reports, Elbert Hubbard truly enjoyed selling; he eagerly began each day as a salesman and advertising director for Larkin Soap. In his career after leaving Larkin, he epitomized the transitional advertising entrepreneur, but differently from Barratt. Although he claimed to leave the soap business in order to free himself from commercial activities, he continued, as a freelance, to write copy with a rather unusual flourish—one of the few copywriters who ever signed his works; and he did so with pride. He so relished copywriting that he wrote many essays promoting and guiding the profession, including "The Adman's Philosophy," "The Science of Advertising," and "A Message to Ad-Men."[45] Hubbard lived later than Thomas Barratt, surviving until a time when an advertising specialist could pursue the trade without owning a company. In that sense, Hubbard not only was a transitional figure, but he lived the transition himself.

In the 1880s, beginning gradually, more and more advertisers consulted with advertising specialists about conceiving, producing, and distributing their commercial messages. By the 1920s, only a few major advertisers did not use specialists, either as in-house employees or outside agencies. Despite this historical correlation, however, we cannot equate specialization in advertising with modernity. Since World War I, several of the United States' most notable technological and marketing innovators have had strong and even controlling influences on their firms' public images. Prominent examples have included Henry Ford; Tim Gill of Quark, Inc.; and Steve Jobs, when he was first with Apple, Inc. Less prominent, but well known in every locale, are the retailers whose broadcast voices and gesticulations promote their wares—cars, jewelry, electronics—with a vigor only the dedicated can generate. The strongest predictor of owner-manager control of advertising is neither date nor size of firm, but whether or not an enterprise is operated by its founder.

# 3

# Printers, Advertisers, and Their Products

*I felt the pride that every thoughtful person connected with journalism must feel when he looks back at what the press has done for the world and the evident greatness of its function in the future. We can trace all that we have of practical science, of industrial art, of political freedom and social advancement to the comparatively short period of less than 500 years since the invention of printing. Before that the world presented a more or less dreary waste of ignorance, superstition and tyranny. The efficiency of the press [is] an element of progress.*

—David Williams, publisher of the *Iron Age*, address to the
New England Iron and Hardware Association, 1896

Printed materials held a special significance in nineteenth-century United States. Books, periodicals, and printed art represented both progress and the potential for future progress, as well as functioning as arenas in which to contest various notions of progress. For advertisers and printers, printed art and promotional copy provided key tools for expressing their worldviews, as well as for advancing their ambitions. Printed advertising also placed printers and advertisers in a mutually dependent relationship; together, they developed and experimented with a wide range of advertising media. Newspapers and magazines constituted the category most like our present commercial mass media. Another category of printed advertising media comprised matter sent through the mails, mostly "circulars" but also mail-order materials. Freestanding, specialty formats offered countless options for illustrated messages, making up a third category that ranged from broadsides still in the style of eighteenth-century woodcuts to colorfully lithographed calendars, almanacs, posters, trade cards, playing cards, and even metal household and office implements, such as shoehorns, rulers, and ink blotters.

As did many tradespeople, printers began the nineteenth century performing most tasks in all-purpose shops; then as they diversified their skills and technologies and demand for specialized work increased, printers and their shops specialized. During the eighteenth and early nineteenth centuries, most printing offices in the United States produced newspapers, simple magazines, and small books. Additional revenues came from speculation work, such as art prints or sheet music for sale by subscription, wholesale, or retail, plus job printing, that is, printing to order anything from dance tickets to advertising posters to stationery to government publications. By midcentury, the demand for special orders encouraged many shops to specialize in job printing; book and periodical publishers and job printers gradually diverged, providing advertisers with increasingly diverse formats. In addition to examining the printing business, this chapter surveys the printers' products, nonadvertisements as well as advertisements, because they formed the iconographic and verbal contexts within which advertisers generated their messages and with which industrialists, including printers, defined progress.

## Print in Nineteenth-Century American Culture

In many ways, printers operated at the center of U.S culture until film and broadcasting undermined their preeminence and their own automated technologies reduced individual printers' sense of contribution. Writing copy, composing type, and generating images by hand within relatively small print shops gave many nineteenth-century printers a sense of pride in their craft as a key component of the modernizing, progressive culture. Early in the next century, a veteran of more than fifty years described printing as "one of the greatest of world industries, the thing that makes civilization possible, the art that permits coöperation among mankind." He explained that "no education worthy of the name, no industrial progress, no general dissemination of knowledge, no development of the mechanic arts, nor of chemistry and science, would be possible without the art of printing as a basis." Because printing "is the mouthpiece of all American industry, . . . we are the advance agents of liberty and prosperity."[1] Given the near monopoly that print had on educational materials and mass communications prior to film and broadcasting, and the presses' central role in political activities, printers had a strong case in making the most of their impact. As the nexus of political and business activity, printers credited their craft with much of the world's progress to date, and they accepted responsibility for its continuance. In "the interest of all humanity, discovery, enlightenment and civilization . . . ," printers' "requirement, to keep pace with the demands of the age, calls for incessant vigilance and continued improvement in workmanship, material, machinery, and labor-saving inventions."[2]

The presses' centrality to politics not only justified printers' claims to importance but also formed a link between political and commercial discourses. Long before the flourishing of print advertising and its revenues after the Civil War, printers produced argumentative copy as a matter of both principle and enterprise. Newspapers had often functioned as party organs in the first half of the century, relying on political patronage, and printers also produced broadsides for political factions, again out of both principle and enterprise. As a result, printers filled their products with polemics and insults directed at rival politicians and publishers, and in later years many factors reinforced this tradition of the presses' political activism.[3] Moreover, only after the 1850s did Americans regularly distinguish between commercial and noncommercial announcements by reserving the term *advertisements* for the former. The newspapers' traditions of political patronage also helps explain many publishers' notorious willingness to accept puff advertising, that is, paid or pressured endorsements that appeared as editorial copy. After the Civil War, many newspapers perpetuated maudlin and sensational styles to continue the level of excitement that prevailed during the conflict,[4] drawing on and fostering the polemical styles of patent-medicine and other commercial messages. For instance, although journalism only began to exploit the public's interest in stories of ordinary folks by midcentury,[5] patent-medicine purveyors had employed such techniques in their testimonials much earlier, such as the Anderson's Cough Drops copy reproduced in chapter 1.

The imagery and rhetoric of the nineteenth-century's political and commercial persuasions frequently intersected in lively pictures in both the periodical and nonperiodical presses. These intersections reflected political cartooning's long tradition as a polemical force and the fact that the same printers often produced both political and commercial images. For instance, a political cartoon of the Civil War period entitled "The Great Remedy" (fig. 3.1) mimicked the polemics of patent-medicine advertising to make its political claims for Lincoln's protecting the Union against contraband to the Confederacy. About thirty years later, a trade card for "Empire" Wringer participated— somewhat obliquely—in widespread fiscal debates by showing a playful Uncle Sam blithely wringing gold coins into a basket while exclaiming, "Just look at

THE GREAT REMEDY.

**Fig. 3.1.** Patent medicines and politics were central to printers whose products sometimes linked the imagery and polemics of the two. This 1862 print supported the Union cause by promoting Lincoln as "The Great Remedy." The kittens' names (barely visible in this reproduction), Abe (curled up in the liberty cap) and Jeff (being pulled away by a noose) for the white pair, and Contraband for the black kitten, carry both political and racial meanings. Courtesy of the Dearborn (Michigan) Historical Commission.

that! And too much surplus in the treasury already? My 'Empire' beats the world." The copy on the back of the card concludes, "Use the Empire Wringer—Will Pay for Itself" (fig. 3.2).

The roots of political cartooning run deeply into the history of print, and, until photography became the primary reproductive mechanism for advertising, the styles and symbols of one resembled those of the other, including eagles, Brother Jonathan, Uncle Sam, and Columbia, plus other goddess-like figures, to represent the values of the nation.[6] The same racial, ethnic, class, and gender stereotypes can be found in each; for instance, Thomas Nast's images of minorities continued for decades as visual clichés for mainstream prejudices in advertisements and cartoons. Occasionally, artists even advertised their own services as both lithographer and caricaturist.[7] In the post–Civil War era,

*Fig. 3.2.* A somewhat mischievous Uncle Sam cranks the Empire Wringer to mint gold coins during the early years of the 1890s, when a federal surplus and related fiscal issues dominated political discussions. The back of this trade card claims that by reducing "the Labor One-Half," the wringer will save enough "strength every week" to make it worth "much more than the small additional cost." Producers often portrayed their innovations in household technologies as the means of transforming domestic tasks from drudgery to pleasure. By this they felt they contributed to progress on social as well as industrial fronts.

art styles for both political and commercial art evolved together, sometimes engaging the same artists. Lithographer Joseph Keppler was publisher, printer, and artist, drawing in a style quite similar to many chromo advertisements by his contemporaries. His cartoon creations in the 1880s and 1890s, with their political and social commentaries, made the American magazine *Puck* a success in both English and German. Keppler's cupidlike figure for the Puck in the trademark derived from the convention that used cherubs frequently, in both advertisements and almost every other lithographed medium. His Uncle Sam figure likewise resembled that found in countless advertisements, such as that for the "Empire" Wringer. Keppler occasionally illustrated advertisements in his journals as well.[8] Although Thomas Nast, the century's most influential political cartoonist, did not illustrate advertisements, his drawings for Christmas established the nation's vision of Santa Claus and seasonal trappings that marketers have used ever since.[9] Palmer Cox began his career as a political cartoonist, but found advertising and book illustration more attractive venues for his cartoons of elves named Brownies. The popular character the Yellow Kid likewise began in political commentary but moved back and forth between it and advertising.[10] There is no need here to determine if either field—politics or commerce—led the other in polemical styles, but it is essential to recognize that the same people printed and sometimes drafted both types of messages at a time when personal contact characterized almost all transactions.

Printers' centrality to U.S. culture between the Civil War and the end of the century also rested on the rise of lithography as a nonperiodical mass-communication medium.[11] Lithography was invented in 1796 in Germany as the first printing method that did not require the preparation of either engraved or embossed surfaces. Lithographers, who were almost always job printers, operated as "agencies of mass impression," as did publishers. Once chromolithographs (color lithography, first used in the United States in 1840) were produced and marketed in vast quantities by the 1870s, both as artworks and as advertisements, their impact on the cultural environment was incalculable. Many of the most popular printed images harkened back to nonindustrial settings, such as rural scenes, biblical stories, and romantic or patriotic scenes, while others pictured various aspects of modernity, such as visions of prosperity and architectural development, fashion, national expansion, new forms of transportation, and world explorations. In a sense, the accessibility of all lithographs, including the pretty and nostalgic images, evinced material progress. In a culture not yet saturated with manufactured images, this accessibility evoked widespread excitement and acquisitiveness, and particularly when pictures were free because they carried advertisements. Although the free advertising pictures were banished from the "better sort" of parlors, they were almost universally welcomed into kitchens, laundry rooms, children's rooms, college dormitory rooms, work and public places, and barns, as well as ladies' scrapbooks. As photographs of the period frequently indicate, giveaway chromo advertisements also brightened shops, offices, hotels, restaurants, railroad stations, and taverns.

The penetration of prints into almost every environment and storms of protest against that ubiquity contributed to printers' sense of their importance to the emerging culture. The advent of large numbers of affordable prints in the mid-nineteenth century fostered a widespread enthusiasm for art that many patriots and entrepreneurs nurtured. Excitement about the new communication technologies resembled today's reactions to the Internet—a mix of fascination and trepidation. Art education became a national cause, in part to further civilization itself, in part to advance industrial prowess. Louis Prang opened an educational department in his lithography firm in 1874, established the Prang Educational Company in 1882, and devoted the last decades of his life to art education. Many articles in the general press on the subject of lithography evinced interest in the printing technologies themselves, even though publishers and lithographers used competing technologies.[12] At the great expositions—the Centennial Exposition in Philadelphia, 1876, and the Columbian Exposition in Chicago, 1893—printers, their machines, and their products drew massive crowds. Even unveiling the first sixteen-sheet billboard in Cincinnati in 1878 attracted crowds that it required extra police to control.[13] As has happened since with other imitative innovations, chromolithography served as an arena for cultural politics: traditional elites often drew the line that divided them from the rest of society through attitudes toward printed reproductions. Fearing that broad diffusion of cultural materials, in this case reproductions of paintings and other images, would cheapen them in some way, critics attacked the "chromo-civilization," as later critics would attack the cultural effects of plastic. So, even while the general public welcomed chromolithographs into their lives, if not all their parlors, many elitists believed that democratized art was debased art. The very realism that the technology made possible was "the ultimate in deception." A strong denunciation in 1897 asked, "Do we prefer infinite productivity . . . chromos, universal competency of a certain sort, universal cheapness—cheap goods and inexpensive men, or can we afford to deny ourselves the luxury of infinite cheap things . . . and live according to human ideas?" The chromo was one of many industrial goods that some feared were "homogenizing taste and destroying individuality."[14] The chromolithographed advertisements that promoted myriad other industrial goods were doubly dangerous as accessible and colorfully enticing emissaries of a burgeoning and turbulent industrial culture.

Supporters' defenses of chromolithography aligned its achievements with progress, both material and cultural. Louis Prang's work drew strong and early criticisms because of his techniques for copying paintings realistically. Although Prang's current reputation rests primarily on his introduction in 1873 and development thereafter of the greeting card, followed by his extensive productions of advertisements and his later involvement in art education as well as chromo reproductions of paintings, he first gained celebrity for his "artistic prints." He marketed these reproductions widely, won national and international prizes with them, and his success led him into a series of heated exchanges with leading authorities on cultural standards, including E. L Godkin of the *Nation* and Clarence Cook. The public controversy began in 1866 with Cook's attack in the *New York Tribune* calling Prang an ambitious perpetrator of "clever imitation." Prang defended his work, asserting that lithography "helps progress in art" in the same way that books aid other aspects of culture. He also published testimonials in his promotions from supportive cultural leaders, including Harriet Beecher Stowe, John G. Whittier, Henry W. Longfellow, and Wendell Phillips.[15] A letter from James Parton, the renowned historian, appeared in the first issue of the house organ *Prang's Chromo: A Journal of Popular Art*. Parton referred to Prang's prints as "exquisite specimens" and wrote that they satisfied "a favorite dream" of reproducing paintings so that "a great picture can adorn a hundred thousand homes, instead of nourishing the pride of one," while better supporting artists.[16]

Indeed, most commentary on the impact of "republicanized and naturalized" art was positive, although the vast quantities of "street lithography"—that is, the commercial art that appeared for entertainments and other advertisers—eventually reduced support for it.[17] As George Ward Nichols explained in an influential book of 1877, some critics claimed "that the general reproduction of works of art makes them commonplace, and their influence injurious rather than beneficial." Certainly, "one gets very tired of chromo-lithographs and poorly executed prints of the works of great masters; but it is well to consider if it is not better to try to have these copies made in the best way, rather than reject them altogether."[18] Of course, many in the printing trade believed that "commercial art," too, had kept "pace with modern progress" and had had a positive impact on business and society in general; posters in the streets raised the common appreciation for art.[19] Whatever their merit, advertisers' colorful and free chromos came to adorn interior and exterior walls everywhere, public and private, from the lowly abodes of Jacob Riis's subjects to the business places, kitchens, scrapbooks, and carriage houses of the prosperous.[20]

Parton's 1868 letter of praise for chromolithography interpreted the bur-

**Fig. 3.3.** This exquisitely printed advertisement of 1845 for S. N. Dickinson's job-printing services epitomizes both the craftsmanship and the cultural claims of important printers. Symbols of technologies, both abstract and specific, surround Dickinson's offerings and a vignette representing printing's cultural contributions. Courtesy of Jack Golden, Designers 3, Inc.

geoning technology in terms of industrialization and material progress in a way that coincided with the printers' own portrayals of their trade. Parton appreciated Prang's "enthusiasm" for his "beautiful vocation" because the "business of this age is to make every honest person an equal sharer in the substantial blessings of civilization; and one of the many means by which this is to be effected is to make the products of civilization cheap."[21] From the early decades of their technological breakthroughs in the 1830s and 1840s, printers expressed their goals for producing inexpensive pictures and text with their machines. Advocates of the printing trade often pointed to its contributions to modern enlightenment through the high volume and low costs of books and newspapers.[22] An influential Boston printer and typefounder, S. N. Dickinson, advertised in 1845 with an image that glorified his press and its products accordingly (fig. 3.3). Light radiated from a press onto books that nestled into the border flourishes, thence to a woman reading with her child, surrounded by symbols of progress: a single large gear, a globe, a train, a steamboat, and a building with neoclassical design. Almost one-half of an 1841 Dickinson advertisement showed a printer at a small rotary press, turning out cards. An eagle with flags topped an 1847 Dickinson advertisement that also featured the Muses of art, literature, and music on a pedestal. In 1849, the *Saturday Evening Post* promoted itself as "a mammoth paper" and used one-third of its display to show men working a press almost twice their height. In 1869, Hatch & Company, New York, advertised itself with a chromolithographed calendar featuring two Muses, abstract industrial scenes, the Hatch building, busy traffic, itemizations of the firm's services entwined in greenery, and all topped by an eagle.[23]

Printing was one of the largest industries in the nation, and some believed that the printer's "reward of right rated higher than the ordinary manufacturer, because his productions demand greater energy, skill, and brain." Printers' constant emphasis on production, on manufacturing, and on their skills and technologies evinces a technological enthusiasm strongly associated with the nineteenth century generally (and with technologically oriented trades still), and a value system that rated productivity above all other measures of merit. In 1874, the first year of Prang's educational department, he published a series of educational lithographs of *Trades and Occupations*. All twelve prints, including that for "The Kitchen," showed people at work using their tools. Prang gave his own trade disproportionate representation with one scene for typesetters and another for lithographers.[24] The *Inland Printer: A Technical Journal Devoted to the Art of Printing*, the period's leading trade journal for printers and their patrons, rarely commented on advertisements for other industries, but it praised as "artistic" an image that exhibited the value manufacturers placed on

**Fig. 3.4.** The *Inland Printer*'s editors praised this trade advertisement that compared "Two Magicians" and their products. Aladdin, portrayed as Far Eastern rather than Persian, merely smiled and rubbed his lamp as he sat, in contrast to the heroic "modern mechanic" who plied new and complex technologies to build monuments that were not restricted to aristocratic luxuries. The Chicago Pneumatic Tool Co., *Inland Printer* 26 (January 1901): 677.

production (fig. 3.4). "Two Magicians" portrays Aladdin as languorous, simply rubbing his lamp to create a "most beautiful palace," whereas the "modern mechanic" takes a heroic stance, wielding the pneumatic power tool with which he built the Eiffel Tower, a skyscraper, a railroad bridge, and an ocean liner.[25] A press manufacturer expressed this emphasis on production, and printing as production, in 1891: "As much as a producer is above a non-producer—as much as success itself is above all mere appearances of success—so much is the *press that you run* more important than the looks of your building, your counting room, your stationery or your furniture."[26]

As large-scale machinery became increasingly essential to printers, many artisan shops developed into factories; the Boston print shops of Forbes Lithograph Manufacturing Company, with 400 workers by 1875, and Louis Prang, with 281 employees in 1881, were among the earliest large shops in the country. Their advertisements and trade literature increasingly featured entire establishments and their facilities.[27] In 1885, an unusually long article in the *Inland Printer* on the history of inks since ancient times studied a prominent firm, founded in 1816 and operated continuously by the same family, as exemplary of modern progress. The apology that engravings of the factory's interior and exterior yielded "only a faint idea of its capacity and magnitude" indicates the purpose of such illustrations. In 1890 and 1891, the same journal ran three articles on typefoundries and five on paper mills, each describing and usually illustrating the firms' buildings, technologies, products, and sales practices. One typical article described the subject's large, new building in detail, and extended the owners' invitation to customers and the public to "inspect" because "they are justly proud, being satisfied that when their inspection is over they will be convinced that the ability of the 'Central' to furnish the best of everything wanted in a printing office is unsurpassed."[28] In keeping with this conviction that buildings and the machines in them warranted both owners' pride and customers' confidence, advertisements in the *Inland Printer* before the mid-1890s frequently pictured and commended such evidence of technological progress, especially as it might apply to the practical needs of potential customers.


## Printers' Images

Printers' enthusiasm for the graphic potentials of their century's technological innovations and their competitive desires to demonstrate their individual prowess motivated the ornate displays in both typesetting and lithography for which Victorian printing is notorious. Beyond this stylistic tendency, which reigned, despite challenges, until the mid-1890s, printers drew pictorial content from two different inspirations. Romantic, evocative images ignored, more often than not, the impact of industrialization, while other images glorified industrial innovation and the constructed environment, including views of town and factory and scenes of locomotives and steamboats conquering frontiers.

Printers' success with selling images both to consumers and to their advertising customers depended on their being able to match popular notions about what was pretty, humorous, or pleasantly evocative, and that therefore would please their patrons, their patrons' families, and their patrons' customers.[29] As Thomas Sinclair & Son declared on their catalog cover, their work was "in the highest style of the art," to which they credited their firm's longevity.[30] Sales differentials gave printers feedback, so the successful among them did work with some sense of popular taste, doing experimental work on speculation, including ideas for stock advertisements, and dropping from their repertoires what they could not sell. For example, after an initially difficult period, Louis Prang did exceptionally well during and immediately after the Civil War once he started lithographing and hand tinting military subjects—maps, diagrams of land and sea battles, and generals' portraits; he also did images of Lincoln. When he turned his hand to chromolithography in 1866, however, Prang sold poorly until he reproduced a series of barnyard scenes and Eastman Johnson's nostalgic *Barefoot Boy*.[31] Prang and other lithographers learned from such feedback to draw on the same types of images for stock advertisements (including increasingly, by the 1890s, their own advertisements), greeting cards, sheet music, and other prints marketed directly to consumers. The resulting genres featured lovely ladies; pretty children; adorable animals; flowers; patriotic, religious, or sentimental scenes; beautiful scenery; and motifs considered humorous. The latter included various series of racial and ethnic caricatures that many mainstream Americans considered amusing at the time, such as the popular series of trade cards produced by Currier and Ives in the 1880s. In the 1870s, this major printing firm also produced a very popular series of stock trade cards with horse-racing scenes, usually serious but sometimes humorous. The persistence of these styles in advertising and speculative prints attests to the printers' successes with them.[32]

Evocative prints of industrial images, such as Currier & Ives's lithographs of trains, were rarely as popular as the countless nonindustrial images sold to consumers. Yet their occasional successes evinced strong interest in the applications of technologies that were quite dramatically changing everyone's world. Advertisers, in their turn, purchased stock images from the printers' inventories of nonindustrial images, combining the printers' advice with their own tastes and notions about what was appealing, knowing that the stock advertisements told the public nothing more about their business or accomplishments than that they had selected them. However, when advertisers ordered specialized prints for their messages, the distribution of images balanced quite differently.

## Printers and Advertisers

Under the noncorporate systems of operation common to most nineteenth-century businesses, custom held that since no one could know a business as well as its owner-manager, no one else could write appropriate advertising copy for it. Yet whatever notions advertisers had about their abilities to write copy and design layouts, only printers could *produce* their own advertisements. Amateur printers could operate the many small presses sold between the Civil War and the 1920s, but without training and expensive equipment, they could not go beyond simple typeset messages.[33] Novel or large illustrations required sophisticated equipment and skills for making woodcuts, engravings, or lithographs; hence, even advertisers who felt sufficiently confident of their artistic skills to draw out a design could rarely reproduce it themselves.

Printers' assistance ranged from simply the mechanical processing of a fully designed display to joint collaboration with the advertisers. The majority of transactions fell in midrange during the decades after the Civil War, although specialists mediated between increasing numbers of advertisers and printers by the end of the century. As a rule, personal contact between advertisers and printers or their salespeople produced most advertisements, so much so that advertisers sometimes made it difficult to maintain an orderly and efficient print shop. According to the *Inland Printer,* clients' tendency to distract the compositors typesetting their advertisements called for occasional warnings that they "will be paying for [their] garrulity and the compositor be absolved from all errors."[34] A veteran of more than fifty years in the trade explained that "up to about 1875 most printing was sold over the counter like dry goods and wearing apparel."[35]

This same veteran explained that after 1875 "the drumming salesman came into existence. These earlier salesmen went out with great scrap books under their arms, containing samples of crack jobs."[36] As the print shops grew larger and sought clients over wider areas, sales forces took the printers' options to clients, maintaining personal contacts, because "those who want printing done desire, in nearly every case, to interview the printer and personally explain their wants."[37] Some large advertisers even owned their own, large, professional print shops, as did James C. Ayer, patent-medicine producer of

*Production as Progress*

Lowell, Massachusetts, and the Sherwin-Williams [paint] Company, which operated seven presses for its labels and promotions in one of Cleveland's largest printing houses in the 1890s.[38] Regardless of the setting, printers contended often that "the printer, as a rule, is one of the main springs in the arrangement of judicious advertising. Much of the success of the advertiser is due to him."[39] Yet a 1900 book of business advice to printers quoted an 1872 statement by "a leading printer of New York" that advised printers to "persuade your customer to furnish his own copy, written in ink. Avoid writing it for him. If it must be done by you, notify him distinctly that he is responsible for its supposed accuracy as to names, places, and figures."[40] Even though printing advertisements for other businesses was an important part of their occupation, printers did not generally accept responsibility for the content of advertisements before 1890, any more than did advertising agents. In the end, advertisers held responsibility for the content of their messages. As late as 1900, some printers still believed that "if other men had written their ads as well [as they], that there would have been fewer bankruptcies during the last few years."[41]

Advertisers' dependence on printers to produce their messages mirrored the printers' dependence on them, as the two groups participated in the symbiotic relationships typical between advertisers and popular communications firms in the United States, although it was not logically necessary. Printers readily acknowledged the importance of advertising revenues, and they aggressively competed for them. Writing on the business aspects of printing in that era, Paul Nathan advised that "the intelligent job printer will never permit himself to forget that printing is allied to advertising, and that almost all of the printing that he does depends in some way upon its success as an advertisement or as an advertising medium." Nathan warned that job printers who did not please their well-paying advertising patrons would have difficulty affording to update their presses.[42] To acquire such accounts, printers advertised in manufacturers' and merchants' trade journals and even *Printers' Ink*, despite its strongly expressed editorial preference for periodical advertising, especially local newspapers and national magazines.

Job printers and publishing printers frequently challenged each other's claims to be the superior advertising medium. The former believed that an "advertisement in a circular or blotter form is seen by the person whose business is sought while he is seated at his desk, rather than at the breakfast-table or in the [street] cars." Job printers at the turn of the century also charged that publishers participated in "campaigns" in their columns against nonperiodical forms of advertising, creating "a prejudice in [the advertiser's] mind against profitable forms of advertising which would be grist to the commercial printer's mill." It was "useless for newspapers to decry" such forms of publicity as streetcar signs, because they were "a rival that has come to stay."[43] On their side, publishers attacked the "pretty and novel devices for hanging advertisements" and other such "schemes" as inadequate and unprofessional as compared with newspapers and magazines, which were "essential for the successful conduct of all lines of business." "Specialties," another critic asserted, "partake too much of the claim-all patent medicine character."[44]

Rapidly increasing revenues going to printers for advertising throughout the nineteenth century subsidized developments in their technologies and contents. Advertisers drove the printers' competition as they sought state-of-the-art media to carry their messages, operating on two principles: one, that status accrues to a message according to the attractiveness and modernity of its medium; and two, that a message's audience and impact increase with the attractiveness of its medium.[45] Through the century, and accelerating in the last three decades, both newspapers and magazines increasingly competed to attract advertisers' accounts by the quality of their presses, the accuracy of their typesetting, their rates, and, above all, their circulations. Advertising revenues also facilitated many newspapers' metamorphosis from political to commercial organs in the mid-1800s.[46] Magazines remained small and meagerly illustrated through the early 1880s, paying contributors poorly and requiring little advertising income, until they, too, began to engage in a competitive spiral that made them the leading medium for advertisers seeking national exposure. Praising this advertiser/media symbiosis, the *Ladies' Home Journal*'s editor, Edward Bok, paid tribute to his magazine's advertisers in an 1898 editorial, for "it is the growth of advertising in this country which . . . has brought the American magazine to its present enviable position in points of literary, illustrative, and mechanical excellence. The American advertiser has made the superior American magazine of today possible."[47] In effect, Bok identified advertising as the business of progress in the limited senses of the mutual advancement of advertised products and of publishing.

The dynamic Bok celebrated was even more salient for other printers than for publishers. Newspapers and magazines, after all, have their editorial content and, more important, their circulations by which to attract advertising revenues; job printers have nothing but their craft and their presses to attract clients. The essay on printing in *The Great Industries of the United States* attested to a positive effect by 1873 of competition between printers: "Now great and small job establishments in all the cities vie with each other in turning out work which displays not only admirable mechanical skill, but frequently the highest artistic taste."[48] From the printers' view, this "wild scramble for advertising patronage" did not seem so benign as it too often resulted in their having to "obtain custom . . . at a sacrifice."[49]

# Advertising in Periodical Media

Newspapers and magazines have always offered advertisers very different environments for their messages. Newspapers, since their inception, have relied on advertising revenues for major portions of their incomes, although during the Jacksonian era partisan papers began a period of dependency on party subsidies; this diminished after the Civil War.[50] Through the eighteenth century and into the first decades of the nineteenth century, newspaper publishers routinely placed announcements, both commercial and noncommercial, on the preferred first page (see, for example, fig. 1.1). Some publishers sought clientele so avidly that they bartered space for advertisers' goods, which they then sold to local wholesalers and retailers. This practice highlighted the symbiosis between publishers and advertisers, because in such cases the former essentially operated as sales agents for the manufacturers.[51] By the end of the century, all types of businesspersons tried to reach consumers through newspapers, including brand-name manufacturers seeking national markets. Advertising filled three-fourths of some papers.

The format of newspaper advertisements was quite simple after the Civil War—basically what it had been for a century, namely, columns of type. The most significant breakthroughs in newspaper technologies to date had come in the 1830s, when the availability of cheap newsprint and the early cylinder and power presses made possible the large-format penny papers.[52] Yet while developments throughout the century made possible larger papers and faster printing, advertising pages did not significantly change until the 1860s, when the use of web presses made placing line illustrations from woodcuts easier. Until then, the most radical developments in display followed the lead of Robert Bonner, who promoted his *New York Ledger* in the 1850s by repeating regulation-sized type, down and/or across columns, to form striking visual effects.[53] Pages of advertisements in 1870 newspapers therefore still looked very much like the classified sections of today's newspapers, differing only in that the individual messages were often larger than today's classifieds, and their fonts varied more. Rarely, however, did individual messages cover more than a single column on a page or run for more than four or five inches. In fact, in the 1860s, George P. Rowell, one of America's earliest and most influential advertising agents, began placing many of his clients' advertisements at the rate of one insertion of one column inch in one hundred papers for $100.[54]

So many advertisers thought this "card" style offered adequate space that the practice became a great success for Rowell and the many who soon imitated him. For instance, Jay Cooke & Co. and other financial houses advertised with such cards in the *Commercial and Financial Chronicle* after the Civil

War. The Rising Sun Stove Polish Company, one of the period's most prolific promoters in all available media, placed small "card" advertisements in four thousand newspapers in 1896. James Pyle, founder of the Pearline Soap Company, a prolific advertiser and an industry leader for decades, started such simple newspaper advertising before the Civil War, despite his initial reluctance to make the expenditure. Horace Greeley convinced Pyle that he could not afford not to advertise and offered a year's free insertions of a fourteen-line, one-inch card in the *Tribune* if the ads did not pay.[55] Advertisers in the 1870s issues of *Puck* were sufficiently satisfied with cards, and unimpressed by the opportunity to include Joseph Keppler's drawings, gratis, in their messages, that most chose not to pay for enough space to do so, even though Keppler was already acknowledged as one of the nation's leading illustrators.[56] Instead of illustrations, printers usually employed headlines, in heavy, often elaborate, typefaces, to draw attention to the individual advertisements. Some purveyors did pay for small generic woodcuts, as they had for a century, or provided their own, when presses began using more and larger woodcuts for editorial material, such as cuts made from Mathew Brady's Civil War photographs.

The combination of many small advertisements on a page with few illustrations resulted in a cluttered appearance. The large retailers—Macy, Wanamaker, Lord & Taylor, and A. T. Stewart—led the field in running large display advertisements in the 1860s and 1870s, setting their images apart. More dramatic changes came in the last two decades of the century, when many city papers featured photoengraved line, half-tone, and, occasionally, colored illustrations, and advertisers could send in their own "electros" for insertion as fully prepared displays.[57] ("Electro" was the commonly used term for a photoengraved, mounted plate, easy to reproduce and ready to be inserted in newspapers and magazines. Some electros included only illustrations, around which compositors set type, whereas others were fully prepared displays that needed only to be set into purchased space.) Publishers often placed advertisements in the order received, except for those whose patronage warranted "preferred" placement, such as important local merchants. Sometimes "foreign" advertisers (that is, nonlocal) received preferred placement if they could convince the publishers to do so, or bribe the compositors who made up the paper.[58]

While most newspapers of the nineteenth century generally tried to raise at least half of their revenues from advertisers, magazines presented a mixed welcome for advertisers. Some of the most important literary and political periodicals of the 1870s and earlier refused to accept commercial announcements except those deemed proper, such as for books, lectures, and stitching patterns. *Harper's Monthly* allowed advertising privileges only to other publications of the Harper publishing house—unlike *Harper's Weekly*, which typically ran three pages of advertising by the end of the Civil War. Bonner advertised his pathbreaking literary publication the *New York Ledger* at the rate of $27,000 a week at that time, meanwhile refusing to accept advertisements himself.[59] And not until the 1880s did respectable magazines mix advertisements with editorial material. Nonetheless, many periodicals were more than happy to sell their back pages, if not other pages, to advertisers. After the Civil War, a flood of magazines began publication, raising the number of journals in the United States from seven hundred in 1865 to twelve hundred in 1870. That number doubled again by 1880, on its way to yet higher figures by the turn of the century. New publications averaged fewer than four years of life, and success hinged greatly on the ability to attract advertising revenues.[60] Poetry, literature, fashion, advice to women, and essays that collectively preached or expounded on a wide range of topics made up the journals' stock in trade, attracting the readers most likely to have discretionary income enough to spread beyond the local grocery store. Yet to a great extent, magazine advertisements after the Civil War resembled those in newspapers: individual advertisements were relatively small, often packed a dozen per page, each filled with dark, heavy type. Because the pages were quite small, however, rarely more than ten inches high by seven inches wide, the clutter of printing appeared less oppressive than it did in newspapers. Also, magazine publishers often employed new printing technologies for illustrations faster than did newspapers, facilitating illustrated messages and adding considerably to the attractiveness of both individual advertisements and whole pages of them.

By the mid-1880s, magazines began to compete effectively with newspapers as more convenient and effective means by which advertisers could reach the burgeoning national markets; a single magazine insertion could reach into many communities. The larger a magazine's geographical spread across the growing railroad networks, the more it attracted manufacturers of branded products, and the less appropriate it was for urban merchants, who generally continued to rely on newspapers to offer daily specials and to project the requisite sense of newsiness and urgency into their advertising.

Americans had ordered products through the mails at an accelerating pace all through the 1800s, but a type of mail-order advertising just emerging by the 1870s demonstrated the attractiveness of magazines as an advertising medium that crossed regional boundaries. In 1869, E. C. Allen of Augusta, Maine, started up the *People's Literary Companion* primarily as an advertising medium for a line of inexpensive products such as recipes and art prints he wished to sell through the mails. Within a few years, Allen's mail-order magazine so successfully attracted the advertising of other promoters that at least a dozen similar mail-order magazines started up during the 1870s.[61] Postal rates for periodicals had declined steadily after 1825, and all magazines, including the new advertising magazines, received a timely boost in 1879 when Congress established the bulk rate system for second-class mail, thereby reducing rates for magazines substantially.[62]

## Advertising in Nonperiodical Media

Job printers competed fiercely with each other and with publishers for advertisers' expenditures. As they sought innovative ways to attract accounts, they generated a wide variety of forms to carry messages into the marketplace, employing typesetting, engraving, or lithography, or all three on occasion. Advertisers wanted the printed carriers to be attractive to businesspeople, workers both male and female, homemakers, and even children. They intended some forms to be sent for and others to be taken by consumers from local retailers or other distributors to their homes or work places. By the 1870s, these media included trade cards, posters, boxes and bottles with beautifully printed labels, calendars, bookmarks, and almanacs; in the next three decades, the options grew to include tin containers, metal rulers, paper dolls, trays, and even metal potscrapers. Even though these forms were and are labeled as ephemera, they often outlasted periodicals in ordinary circumstances. Calendars, puzzles, office implements, and so forth typically stayed in use longer than the daily newspaper. Untold millions of such advertising specialties, poured forth over the years, were used and displayed everywhere except fine parlors.[63] Despite the huge numbers, their historical presence suffers from their ephemeral nature; when they were bound and preserved, it was informal and personal, not systematic and institutional, in contrast to periodicals.

Despite the complexities of selecting from and using the many options job printers offered for nonperiodical advertising, many businesspeople did not want to be limited to magazine or newspaper advertisements before the 1890s. The uncertainties of appearing in those dark, cluttered pages, with their dubious circulations, did not always warrant their costs and inconveniences. Some advertisers sought a means of exposure that directly pinpointed their potential markets; distributing job-printed forms through retailers, local agents, and the mails could accomplish this on a national scale. Moreover, the nonperiodical media, particularly lithographs, allowed for the prolific reproduction of images, which few periodicals could offer before the development of photoengraving in the 1880s.[64] Pictures were still prizes, often literally so, during the nineteenth century. The graphic flexibility of lithography offered advertisers an infinite range of colorful images that could use humor, sentimentality, lust, and other appeals that were more evocative than the wordy claims typical of contemporary newspaper and magazine advertisements.

Two formats dominated the public presence of the commercial ephemera printed between the Civil War and the end of the century. One category of commercial forms, "circulars"—typically typeset mailers and flyers—likely outnumbered all other forms. Although mail-order and junk mail in the 1870s made but a whisper of their future roar, their importance grew through the century as sellers tried to reach consumers directly. Circulars generally but not always went out on the flimsiest paper, with minimal illustrations, and despite their collective numbers, relatively few have survived to represent the abundance of ancient junk mail. An irritated citizen wrote a letter in 1875 to the editors of the *New York Times* that the newspaper titled "The Nuisance of Circulars." Accusing "those industrious gentlemen who take contracts to address and deliver business circulars" of "making life a burden to me," he wrote:

> When the old-fashioned, unmistakable, and matter-of-fact circular of tradespeople was in vogue the evil was not so great. Bridget could sweep up the day's deposit and make it useful in the kitchen-range. But the circular-senders have headed us off in that direction. Their documents are deceptive and seductive. They come in nice envelopes, and with monograms and postage stamps regularly affixed. One cannot weed them out of his morning's mail. He must go through the lot with circumspection. . . . It is a great nuisance. I am pursued by circulars every hour in the day.

Of course, printers promoted their abilities to accomplish this very deception, even boasting of the "blurred appearance" that mimicked the effects of putting typed and handwritten letters in a copy book.[65]

The second broad category of media that printers created to compete for advertisers' expenditures encompassed items illustrated by either lithography or engraving (woodcut or photoengraving, rarely steel engraving), such as trade cards (usually postcard-sized and somewhat stiff, with printing on both sides), and posters, catalogs, paper dolls, and any number of other illustrated novelty items. Until the mid-1870s, most trade cards and posters were in black and white, whether lithographed, typeset, or woodcut.[66] During the Centennial Exhibition at Philadelphia in 1876, chromolithographed trade cards became all the rage. Thereafter, children and women collected them, often by the hundreds, into scrapbooks, or they decorated walls, screens, and trunks with the cards. As leading lithographer Louis Prang wrote, "Millions upon millions . . . of the most varied designs were thrown on the market. . . . Hardly a business man in the country has not at one time or another made use of such cards to advertize his wares."[67] For instance, in 1881 I. L. Cragin & Company informed retailers that it had already distributed more than one million cards in a single ongoing promotion for Dobbins' Electric Soap.[68] Posters varied more widely in size, some being quite large. Because all but typeset broadsides were much more expensive than trade cards, they were not printed in such large quantities. Posters included illustrated advertisements intended for display in stores, on walls and in windows, in other public places such as hotels, stations, and restaurants, and in homes, offices, and workshops. "Show cards," as they were then called, often were mounted on plaster composition boards or stretchers (internal frames) and then varnished to give them luster and greater longevity.

Advertisers had many decisions to make in the process of arranging for lithographic advertisements, and their first decision—whether or not to order a customized design or a stock design—determined their messages' degree of originality and cost. The McCormick Company could afford substantial customized lithographed advertising to supplement newspaper advertisements and its own publications. In 1881, for example, McCormick ordered about eight thousand newly designed show cards printed and framed at a cost of approximately 75¢ each. The company's regional salespeople received these during the winter so that they could place them by spring. McCormick's agents also distributed about 175,000 circulars, plus trade cards, at state and county fairs each year through the 1870s and 1880s.[69] Many advertisers, including all but the very largest of retailers, however, had much smaller budgets than this industrial colossus; they therefore had to rely on stock images upon which their names and locations could be overprinted. The *Iron Age* reported on the calendars that manufacturers sent in during 1893, and approximately one-third were stock designs; among retailers, stock images were almost universal. The very low costs of these stock prints indicate the economies of scale that lithographers could achieve on large runs requiring no original artwork. For instance, Thomas Sinclair & Son, Philadelphia lithographers whose 1885 catalog offered "Advertising Specialties for the Trade," could sell stock "cabinet show cards" of a standard size, nineteen by twenty-four inches, at $50 for one thousand prints; that is, 5¢ each.[70] Advertisers often had more tailored, word-only messages printed on the reverse sides; these could be typeset locally and inexpensively in black and white. Some manufacturers took advantage of all these options, as the New Home Sewing Machine Company did in the 1880s when it distributed at least eighty customized images on lithographed trade cards, plus dozens of stock images with overprinted messages, flyers, and booklets with agents' information overprinted on the back covers,[71] as well as show cards and hangers (long, narrow posters that hung from a metal strip).

Frequently a brand-name producer or distributor and willing retailers

shared the costs and efforts of getting the advertising messages to the consumers. In this subcategory of the specially ordered advertisement (today
called a "cooperative") a distributor or manufacturer made up an advertisement for a brand-name product and local dealers inserted their names and addresses next to the preprinted (or today, prerecorded) area. The retailers then
distributed the advertisement to their customers, often merely placing the
items on their counters or walls. Retailers could thereby receive goods that
ranged from paper bags to cookbooks or almanacs, all printed with advertising
and "for gratuitous distribution." If they purchased sufficient quantities of the
products being promoted, retailers could have their "own card" printed on the
booklets' covers "free of all expense."[72]

Some printers worked at expanding their markets by making it convenient
for advertisers to purchase stock prints through the mails, leaving us with some
notion of their dealings. In the 1880s, the Jno. [Jonathan] B. Jeffery Printing
Company of Chicago distributed form letters soliciting business informing potential customers, "We are continually getting up new designs. . . . We are now
completing several fine pictures of Running Horses, in colors, which we would
be pleased to send you on application."[73] Thomas Sinclair & Sons offered to
supply "all our regular customers with samples of new goods as soon as they are
issued." Furthermore, "To large advertisers and jobbers, who desire to examine
goods with a view to purchase, we will send our full line on receipt of two dollars, which amount will be deducted from the first bill of fifty dollars or over."
However, this "purely lithographic" firm discouraged customers from requesting typeset advertising from them, as they had no facilities for printing individual messages on the stock cards. Sinclair's chromo trade cards averaged
about $1.75 per set of one thousand stock images, and they would contract out
typesetting on one side of the cards for an additional 50¢ per thousand on orders of five thousand or more. By dealing directly with their local typesetter,
the Sinclairs' catalog suggested, "our customers can get this printing done as
cheaply as we can, and presumably more to their taste."[74] In terms of absolute
numbers, such images, nonadvertiser specific, accounted for the largest single
portion of all nonperiodical advertisements, some 30,000 basic stock images in
trade cards alone, each typically varied with each reprinting, resulting in many
multiples of that number.[75]

After 1870, the makers of more and more proprietary—that is, branded—
consumer and trade products ordered uniquely designed lithographed advertisements. Arranging for these generally required more contact between advertisers and printers than did the purchasing of stock prints. Because of
having to conduct complex negotiations about format and content, the printing industry had to be relatively decentralized, and all but the smallest of

towns possessed typesetting shops, many of which also published local newspapers. Lithographers were more rare, but many excellent and well-known lithographers prospered outside of the major metropolises because of the need for accessibility. For example, Strobridge and Company of Cincinnati began in 1849 and became one of the largest lithographic firms in the country by the 1880s, serving the alcohol and tobacco industries in the region, plus Cincinnati's Procter & Gamble, a prolific advertiser from early in its history, and the Barnum and Bailey Circus.[76] Sometimes independent solicitors intermediated between advertisers and the "practical lithographers" to whom they would contract the printing. Even when printers obtained business from outside their areas, they facilitated direct contact whenever they could, usually by traveling themselves or sending employees or agents to clients.[77] As one printer explained, "personal acquaintance" was important because "it is entirely necessary that we know what your wants are in detail, before proceeding on a speculative basis."[78]

As difficult as it was to work out the details of unique, individualized designs through the mails, some advertisers attempted it. Fortunately, a few examples of such correspondence survive, indicating something of the nature of the interactions between job printers and advertisers, and showing at the same time how difficult the procedure could be. Sometimes printers received only the broadest instructions from advertisers, such as, "I wish you to take pains in the printing to have them get up in *good* style . . . —with the name of the company printed in plain and pretty capitals—I will leave it for your taste to arrange the form of the printing. . . . P. s. I wish you to put on some pretty vignette."[79] More often the instructions and resulting correspondence entailed more complex negotiations. For instance, many printers responded to potential customers' requests for estimates by sending samples from which customers could select, or which they could use to develop their own designs. One printer suggested, "If you will make us a small pencil layout we can tell better what you want and if you will explain what kind of a lithograph you want, it might be possible that we shall have something in stock that by relettering would be useful for your purpose."[80] Sometimes the materials that the customer sent to the printer were inadequate for an attractive design, and the printer returned it, as one did, explaining, "We enclose herewith copy, which was made up from the matter you sent us, but we do not think in this form that it will be satisfactory to you."[81] At other times the information sent to initiate work was unclear, such as the following request for a price estimate and a speculative design (one done without guarantee of compensation): "Please quote us price on about 100,000 folders similar to the one enclosed, except that we want an original design, and, of course, the matter will be different. Kindly return a sample [design] with your reply."[82] On occasion, a customer rejected a printers' work if the lack of direct contact had led to misunderstandings.[83]

Even though the printers' advertising customers generally wrote and designed their messages, and then decided whether or not to purchase and distribute any given print, the printers influenced the final product. Printers were therefore warned not "to parade [their] notions about taste . . . [as advertisers wanted their] own notions carried out," yet they often had to guess their patrons' taste; that is, how they would like their designs and copy actually set up. Proofs went back and forth between printers and advertisers as the printers sought to please their customers, even when they came "up with new ideas to be incorporated."[84] As a result, the relationships between printers and their patrons included continuous negotiations about the content of the advertisements. Sometimes the customers' input continued even as printers worked, disrupting the print shop.[85] Nevertheless, it was unavoidable that printers and their artists and compositors impose something of their own styles, techniques, and technologies upon the finished pieces. For instance, the European origins of lithographers often left their traces on their styles in preparing images for American audiences,[86] as with an entire series of posters and metal trays produced for Barbee Whiskey: the illustrations showed Bavarian peasant girls outside an American log cabin that had on its wall a coonskin cap and Kentucky rifle. Occasionally, a printers' impact was less subtle, such as repeating very similar layouts in advertisements for different advertisers. For example, Louis Prang's artists virtually repeated a design for two different breweries, two years apart. Donaldson Brothers, of Five Points, New York, was another important lithography firm, despite an occasional impropriety; they, too, produced similar images for two breweries around 1890. These repetitions may well have resulted from the difficulties printers faced in trying to work conventional motifs into their works too frequently. The motifs in the two Donaldson sets of posters included oversized beer bottles, crates with the brewers' trademarks on them, mythical Germanic kings and fertility goddesses, and goats' faces, although the brewery, in each case, was that of the advertiser, and the crates had the right trademark.[87] All of these motifs were quite popular with brewers throughout the nineteenth century and remained important parts of their advertising until the brewers' advertising styles caught up with the twentieth century after Prohibition.

## Marketing Advantages of Nonperiodical Advertisements

The nonperiodical media helped advertisers to achieve national distribution of large illustrations before magazines and newspapers did so effectively. Locomotive builders numbered among the earliest industrialists to use lithographed images in meeting their nonlocal marketing problems. In their attempts to sell a product that did not lend itself to salesmen's samples, these manufacturers began to order the highest quality lithographed show cards of the 1830s. Because lithographs were still quite expensive at this time, as were the chromolithographs that often replaced black-and-white prints by the 1850s, they served as appropriately prestigious emissaries for such costly machinery to railroad officials, financiers, railroad contractors, engineers, and other potential purchasers, or advisers to purchasers of engines, such as mining operators and industrialists. An 1856 article in the *Railroad Advocate* reported on the importance of these prints:

> They are the appropriate adornments for the offices of every variety of business connected with railroads; they are consulted by master mechanics and locomotive buyers; they are the master-pieces in the parlors of many engineers of good taste. . . . Two prominent locomotive builders have informed us that they owed orders simply to handsome lithographs of their engines, having had no other communication whatsoever with the parties who gave the orders. The lithographs told the whole story just as well as a long conference would have told it. One locomotive sold by a picture, ought to pay for all the pictures a builder would issue in three years. And the builder circulating the best picture, of course, stands the *best* chance of introducing his work. Again, lithographs are now so common, that they are *expected* by all locomotive users. The builder who does not issue them is considered behind the times.[88]

Railroads also commissioned paintings and chromolithographs for self-promotion. The most famous of these included *The Lackawanna Valley* and the *Delaware Water Gap* painted then printed for the Delaware & Lackawanna Company in the 1850s by George Inness.[89] The Santa Fe Railroad mounted an influential promotional campaign in 1892 to attract tourists to the Southwest by using lithographs of artists' romantic renditions of the area and its people.[90]

The national advertising campaigns of McCormick, Fairbanks, and Singer discussed in chapter 1, like the locomotive promotions, were exceptionally grand *before* the Civil War. These advertisers built innovative marketing systems early because of their special needs in selling highly technical, specialized equipment. However, they were no longer exceptions between the Civil War and the 1890s. Indeed, the "post–Civil War revolution in the structure of American marketing" motivated rather than resulted from the federal legal environment for free trade within the United States. Industrialists marketing their products nationally fought extensive judicial battles to establish the "idea of a [national] free-trade unit" on the grounds that progress through "the changing structure of business enterprise" required it.[91] This national character of the industrialists' marketing activities before the mergers of the 1890s is only partially represented by evidence in periodicals, including the advertising trade press, because published media had not before then resolved most problems related to extensive national advertising. Advertisers therefore explored other options. For instance, in 1881, Johnson, Clark and Company of Union Square, New York City, commissioned a chromolithographed poster, or show card, to promote its sewing machine. It portrays a family on their homestead with snow-capped mountains in the background, and the headline reads, "The 'New Home' in the Far West," indicating that the most likely setting is either the Rocky Mountain region or California (fig. 3.5). The firm also distributed show cards and trade cards showing "The 'New Home' in the Sunny South." The Far West poster listed Chicago as one of the firm's two main regional offices for distributing the New Home sewing machine; the other was in Massachusetts. Chicago had grown rapidly as the second hub of national trade, in part because of the extensive marketing of industrial goods from there into the hinterlands and back to the East as well. Cyrus Hall McCormick had moved to Chicago as early as 1847 and for decades sent his advertisements and agents from there into the heartland in ever-increasing volume. In the spring of 1871 alone, McCormick's agents distributed eighteen thousand chromolithographed show cards, and through the 1870s and 1880s they took hundreds of thousands of printed pieces to fairs throughout the country.[92]

In the days when even small communities were likely to have multiple newspapers, when no general (nontrade) magazines had extensive national reach, and when circulation figures were unreliable, newspaper advertising required a complex and inefficient set of operations that often left the advertisers unsure of just what they were getting for their expenditures. This uncertainty remained even if the advertisers worked through advertising agents. At the same time, many industrialists, following the leads of McCormick, Singer, and Fairbanks, were developing marketing networks that included agents on commission or traveling salesmen, then called drummers, on salary. An 1871 writer estimated that fifty thousand drummers traveled American roads.[93] Through these representatives, manufacturers distributed their show cards, trade cards, calendars, or other promotional items, and took orders for their products. A good drummer could effectively distribute the advertisements, be

**Fig. 3.5.** "The 'New Home' in the Far West," 1881, was one of a series of trade cards and chromolithographed show cards (posters) distributed nationally to sell a popular sewing machine. The setting, with its linen tablecloth and flowering vines coupled with the woman's clothing and the entire family's demeanor, all belie the difficulties of homesteading.

sure that retailers or other recipients put the advertisements on display, and gain considerable feedback information as well.[94] In industries that did not employ traveling agents, wholesalers operated as intermediaries between manufacturers and retailers and distributed their own and manufacturers' advertisements with their own drummers or with deliveries of orders. Around 1885, for instance, a six-foot-tall chromolithograph poster for Sapolio household cleaner hung as a sample of smaller posters available to retailers in the window of a wholesaler in the Boston-Providence area.[95] Advertisers or their sales agents frequently hired boys to paste or hand out broadsides and handbills and even chromo posters, all over cities, often covering each other's postings by way of competition. Advertising show cards or other items often went out to merchants through the mails as well, usually not mounted but rolled into mailing tubes; to facilitate this practice, long, narrow posters were designed that

**Fig. 3.6.** Inside stores, arrays of advertising materials greeted the shopper. Fashion, their own ambitions, and traveling salesmen encouraged shopkeepers to use advertisements, distributed to them without charge, to create visual extravagance. Unidentified store interior, 1906. Courtesy of Frame Central, Boston, Mass.

came to be called roll-downs and hangers. This distribution method, while costing very little, gave the advertiser no assurance that retailers displayed the advertisements.

Photographs of stores taken in the decades between 1870 and 1910 show a plethora of chromolithographed advertisements in place. Retailers used them profusely to increase the sales of products on their shelves and to decorate every inch of space not occupied by products for sale. Retailers' storefronts typically deployed advertisements on sidewalks, on outside corners and walls, and in windows, and advertisements filled interior walls and any shelf spaces that happened not to be covered with products for sale. Posters and promotional gadgets even hung from ceilings (fig. 3.6). These colorful point-of-purchase sales devices appealed to manufacturers because they encouraged retailers to carry products that offered such vivid promotional support. Such items also presented consumers with promotional messages at the last possible moment before their purchase decisions. Accordingly, a distributor for Ivory and Lenox Soaps offered retailers the "Services of an Efficient Saleswoman for

Nothing" in the form of a "beautifully colored lithograph of a handsome young woman, life-size, mounted on heavy pulp board." Retailers would benefit because of "the attention she attracts and how much Soap she will sell. This is by far the most costly advertisement they [Procter & Gamble] have ever given away, but they feel justified in the expense, because of the large increase in the sales of their Soaps she is sure to make."[96] Similarly, Humphreys' Medicine Co. offered retailers a "new upright counter show case" of cherry wood with a "front lithographed in ten rich colors" if only they stocked up $25 worth of "preparations." Retailers ordering goods worth $50 would receive "Case, signs, printed matter, etc., gratis."[97] Although the resulting retail ambience was, by today's tastes, more than a bit cluttered, it was lively and colorful. Both retailers and manufacturers expected this abundance of stimulation to increase sales, just as their counterparts today expect point-of-purchase marketing programs to do.

With advertisers seeking out state-of-the-art mass communication technologies to gain a competitive advantage in getting their messages to their markets in the brightest, most vivid manner then available, lithographers, in their turn, competed with each other by continually developing their technologies. They also competed openly with typesetters, who could not offer lithography's inexpensive visual texture before the entry of photoengraving in the late 1880s, nor its freedom from straight-line copy before the introduction of the twisted rule, a device for laying out type in curves, in the 1880s, nor its color before 1900. The contrast of these colorful and popular prints, with their many format options, to the dark, cluttered, and monotonous pages of advertisements in contemporary newspapers and magazines explains something of the attraction businesspeople showed for this alternative. The arguments that advertising agents and publishers repeatedly voiced in trying to dissuade advertisers from using chromolithographed advertisements and other nonperiodical media seemed to have had little effect until the 1890s. By 1900, publishers had succeeded in dominating the advertising arena,[98] but the contest had been intense and often vituperative. Whether the advertising practitioners argued that expenditures on lithography were "money thrown away" out of a genuine concern for advertisers' success or because they regretted losing commissions on those expenditures, the amounts of job printing done for advertising sufficed to attract considerable attention. O. Kling wrote an article with those very words as title, for the *Denver Road*—an article *Printers' Ink* reprinted as part of its campaign against lithography's hold on advertisers' expenditures. Kling cited having received "not less than thirteen calendars for the year 1891" as evidence for his case. "These calendars are so elegant in design that many may be classed as works of art, but owing to their being so numerous the effect that advertisers intended is wholly lost." He also criticized the "flaming lithographs of women and children whose beauty is chiefly imaginary and whose costumes are, what little there is of them, made attractive by conspicuous draping and plenty of red in the brush."[99]

The proportions Enoch Morgan's Sons spent on Sapolio advertising reinforce the impression that the amounts many advertisers spent on job printing were "extensive" relative to publication space, to use Kling's assessment of "money thrown away." In 1885, this leading and innovative marketer of cleanser reportedly bought $15,100 worth of space in publications, meanwhile spending $29,200 in various printed, nonperiodical media.[100] Moreover, chromo advertisements survive from an assortment of companies that includes virtually all manufacturing companies that marketed products to the American consumer during the decades before 1900. There certainly were many hundreds of thousands, perhaps more, uniquely designed and printed lithographed advertisements—the medium of prestige as well as the most cost-effective way available then to get a high-quality, multicolored advertising message into peoples' lives and businesses. The lithography industry grew rapidly during this period, indicating the demand for its services. In 1860, approximately 60 American companies employed about 800 workers. By 1880, the conservative figures of the census listed 167 companies with 4,332 employees. By 1890, there were 700 lithographic companies employing approximately 8,000 people, and having an annual production of more than $20 million—a figure that of course includes both job printing and speculative printing for sales to consumers.[101]

Why did so many manufacturers and other advertisers employ a category of advertising media for which advertising agents had so little regard? No particular trade had yet established itself as the presumed adviser to advertisers. Not only were agents' opinions not yet authoritative, in some cases agents' poor advice drove clients away from periodical advertising altogether, and toward relying entirely on job printers' media. In 1889, for instance, the Lydia Pinkham patent-medicine firm spent its entire advertising budget on trade cards bearing pictures of granddaughters of the deceased Mrs. Pinkham. Charles Pinkham's concerns about the reliability of his agent's services had led to his decision to curtail all newspaper advertising.[102] Moreover, advertisers' extensive promotions outside of the periodical press met many needs that the newspaper and magazine advertisements could not, as advertisers and printers worked together to generate a multitude of ways to solve the problem of getting advertising messages into the ken of customers everywhere. Examples abound. For a century, starting with the 1820s, almanacs served as an especially important advertising medium for the patent-medicine firms as well as many farm-equipment manufacturers. Prior to the general availability of frequently produced, illustrated sources of information such as magazines, almanacs provided much useful and entertaining information, frequently carrying evocative family scenes or work-related illustrations on their covers and in advertisements throughout. In many cases, the front or back covers also had a local retailer's identification overprinted. Catalogs distributed information about manufacturers' various products to jobbers, retailers, and consumers—as they still do.

Many industrialists' trade journals, such as *Iron Age* and *American Industries*, carried regular columns on advertising that devoted much of their space to describing and commenting on catalogs. From the 1870s, novelty advertising forms carried commercial messages disguised as useful or decorative objects, such as calendars (sometimes embossed and die-cut), rulers, potscrapers, paper and cloth dolls, match holders, puzzles, pocket mirrors, thermometers, cookbooks, paperweights, hangers, corkscrews, games, ashtrays, cigar cutters, mugs, hand-held fans, and shoehorns (fig. 3.7).[103] Although *Business: A Practical Journal of the Office* often carried an advertisement for N. W. Ayer & Son, Newspaper Advertising Agents, on its title page in the early 1890s, its regular "Art and Practice of Advertising" featured point-of-purchase items, novelties, and catalogs more than newspaper copy. A novelty was just as likely as a periodical ad to be described as "a clever bit of advertising" in a regular column in the *Tobacco Leaf*.[104] Another column explained that manufacturers used novelties "to gain the interest of both merchants and consumers." For "catching of the consumer, many houses devote a large share of time and attention and considerable sums of money. For his personal use and delectation are provided pictures and photographs in endless variety; pocket-books, diaries and calendars; writing pads and blotters; pens, pencils and rubbers; cigar and cigarette cases and holders; match boxes, and even hats and caps for summer wear, etc., etc."[105] When manufacturers made such novelties available, they competed for dealers as well as consumers because the latter preferred carrying products supported by so much promotional activity. The price to the consumer was these items' advertising messages—the same price carried now by most periodicals and the commercial broadcast media.

Most Americans eagerly embraced the "chromo-civilization," ignoring the elites who decried it and instead taking the giveaway advertising chromos into their homes and workplaces. The fashion reached its peak in the 1880s, when the *New York Times* ran several lengthy articles about it, such as "High Art on Card-Board." Most of these articles noticed favorably "the rage for picturesque advertising." One article included an interview with a lithographer who declared that "there is a steadily increasing demand for the most expensive kind"

**Fig. 3.7.** The Standard Art Calendar Co., Inc., advertised a wide assortment of printed and embossed items used as advertising in the *Advertising Specialty Manufacturers' Directory*. The firm's "Standard Directory of American and Foreign Manufacturers, Jobbers and Dealers in the Advertising Specialty Trade" listed manufacturers of thermometers, thimbles, tin cups, tobacco tags, and items beginning with every other letter of the alphabet onto which advertisements could be placed. (Chicago: Schulman Bros., 1917), p. 176.

of lithographed novelty. He also noted that "[t]his kind of advertising must pay, for some of the largest New York firms have steadily increased their expenses in this direction during the last three years." The *Times* reporter noted that the "more beautiful and artistic a card or plaque is, it is argued, the longer it will be kept in sight and talked about." Indeed, "ladies mak[e] little purchases in [the] stores for no other reason than as an excuse to ask for one of the firm's elaborate spring announcements."[106] Magazine publishers acknowledged and exploited the popularity of the chromo prints from the 1860s through the 1890s by offering them as premiums for people who solicited sufficient numbers of subscribers.[107]

Some industrial advertisers took this notion even farther in order to meet their unique marketing problems. When soap manufacturers, including the four major companies, Babbitt, Larkin, Pears, and Procter & Gamble, started putting their goods into small, consumer-sized packages, they had difficulty in convincing buyers to switch from the centuries-old practices of either making their own soap or buying it in unpackaged, irregular chunks chopped off of storekeepers' large cakes. By making the wrappers themselves valuable commodities, the companies broke through this bottleneck; they encouraged consumers to save their wrappers to exchange them for desirable goods, first offering chromolithographed prints as premiums, then later everything from more soap, to lamps, to furniture. Procter & Gamble offered many attractive chromos in exchange for Star Soap wrappers, for instance, including one with a picture titled *Ethel*. Retailers were to display this picture of a pretty child as an inducement for customers to buy to Star Soap and thereby acquire their own copy of the print without promotional lettering on the front, but with extensive advertising on the reverse.[108] Thurber, Whyland & Co., a large New York food and tobacco distributor, often offered "free advertising novelties" for many of its goods, "to reach the customer direct." In 1890, they invited retailers to take advantage of the "sort of mania, on the part of the small boy, for the collection of the largest quantity of tobacco tags, postage stamps, buttons, etc." by offering cigars and cash as incentives to boys who collected enough cigar bands.[109]

Advertisers and printers even devised ways to encourage popular demand for the advertisements themselves, making them collectible items; observers referred to them as "souvenirs" in a "craze" that was "absolute" in its intensity. Some coffee and tea processors and many tobacco companies induced trade-card collecting by ordering sets with themes, such as flowers, exotic peoples, actresses, game birds, tropical birds, city newspaper editors, military heroes, Native Americans, and sports champions. In many cases, manufacturers distributed a chromo poster to local retailers to show all of the cards in any given set. Instead of trade cards, the Arbuckle Brothers Coffee Company, a foodstuffs processor, often put recipe cards into their packages. Together, these poster and card sets illustrate how advertisers, in getting their advertising messages into the consumers' lives, encouraged brand loyalty and high frequency of use.[110] Cream of Wheat explained this marketing principle to retailers in 1900: "The Object of Advertising Is to Bring People Into Your Store." The company offered its assistance to this end in the form of eighteen "elegant gravures of Northwestern scenery" packed in each case of cereal to be given to purchasers, plus "a large colored placard" for the window to announce the terms of the promotion to the public. This "scheme" would "bring crowds of new customers into your store without one cent of expense to you"; the pictures, said Cream of Wheat, were "not 'cheap truck,' but are real works of art."[111] Large numbers of scrapbooks survive demonstrating the success of the collectible strategy, with trade cards and small chromos often preserved next to gift cards and other nonadvertising items.

## Advertisers' Images

Business historian Edward C. Kirkland explains the "general silence by businessmen regarding issues of interest to historians": precious few, he writes, were as "garrulous" as Andrew Carnegie; the industrialists' and merchants' trade presses recorded their views on many matters extensively, but these were internal literature, not intended for general communication. Kirkland attributes this to their preoccupation with "business affairs and activities [that] were dirty, dusty, and personal," and not considered "literary material."[112] Similarly, in *The Progress of Economics*, Warren Catlin observes that nineteenth-century economists and most writers on business emphasized production, international trade, and banking rather than entrepreneurship itself. H. G. Wells noted that Victorian business "was carried about in people's heads" and therefore "perhaps the great part of Victorian management went undocumented." Memos and other forms of documentary internal communication evolved only at the end of the nineteenth century as the size of firms grew.[113] In lieu of written resources, therefore, nineteenth-century advertisements serve as valuable historiographical resources for studying the business people who created them.

When owner-managers dominated U.S. businesses, founders, partners, officers, and their kin performed most managerial functions, including advertising decisions, through direct contact with printers and publishers. Many large corporations still communicated with their printers via "daily visits" as late as the 1890s.[114] Moreover, contemporary accounts almost always gave company

THE PERILS OF LEAP YEAR.
USE CORTICELLI THE BEST SILK.

**Fig. 3.8.** Late-nineteenth-century advertisers often scoffed at cherished notions of romantic love and companionate marriage, as in this trade card for Corticelli Best Twist silk thread, circa 1885. They did so even when their products' purchasers were those most likely to want to believe in romance, however unrealistic those dreams might have been. Advertisers' frequent insensitivity to consumers' interests and attitudes, often in the name of humor, fueled the arguments of copywriters and artists, who by the turn of the century sought advertisers' patronage.

*Production as Progress*

heads, officers, or kin credit for their advertising campaigns and successes.[115] As a result, advertising messages of the nineteenth century, especially in the nonperiodical media such as chromolithography, represent entrepreneurs' perceived interests and concerns more than do advertisements created by advertising professionals for their clients.

Advertisements served as businesspeople's primary channel of direct, albeit one-way, communication with the public. As such, they fulfilled several functions, only the most obvious of which was to promote and sell the advertisers' products and services. Whether or not advertisements sold their wares effectively in the past is even less knowable than the effectiveness of most advertisements today, but this study's concern with the advertisers and their messages rather than with the audiences' reactions to the messages eliminates having to calculate effectiveness. Nevertheless, considering a few apparent incongruities in advertisers' messages vis-à-vis their audiences yields some insight toward interpreting those messages and their significance for the advertisers.

Humor occurs in these older images frequently. Except for the instances in which anthropomorphized animals played out the jokes, demographic groups other than that to which most advertisers belonged—white, Protestant, bourgeois males—were the objects of ridicule or indignity. Such stereotypes were common in the period's iconography in general, including in manufactured children's books and games, plus countless political cartoons and advertisements that demonstrated their creators' racial, ethnic, gender, and class prejudices. Derogatory portrayals occur in both specially commissioned advertisements and stock prints because their creators considered them amusing.[116] Yet, despite their prejudices and their unabashed publication of them, most manufacturers eagerly sold to anyone, including the objects of their derision. Accordingly, at the end of the last century, advertisements flourished in nearly one thousand foreign-language newspapers in this country, and many industrial and retail firms printed their brochures and packages in several languages. Some advertisers clearly targeted their products to women—pins, thread, and other notions that early on did not require male purchase decisions—through media such as trade cards that were explicitly intended for woman and children. Yet they jested about marital relations frequently, such as picturing women relying on physical restraints such as thread and glue to win and hold their spouses (fig. 3.8). That many advertisers did not hesitate to demean large segments of the population, some of whom counted as potential customers, displayed levels of demographic and cultural centrism impervious to self-consciousness or empathy.[117]

Advertisers also expressed their insensitivity to their audiences by frequently violating today's "one-step-up-rule" in portraying socioeconomic status. Instead of considering their market's most likely status and then portraying their products in use by people in the next higher bracket, nineteenth-century advertisers almost always portrayed their consumers as prosperous members of the upper-middle and upper classes or their servants. For example, the Rising Sun Stove Polish Company often showed women in finery expressing their great satisfaction with a product that women of their position might never even touch. Similarly, a trade card for Scourene portrayed a woman in a lacy dress happily scrubbing pans, while lawn-mower advertisements frequently showed elegantly dressed children mowing lawns. Twentieth-century advertising textbooks routinely warn against offending or intimidating potential customers by presenting too great a gap between consumers' lifestyles and the ones the advertisements present as lures; today, associations of mustard and such with limousines are spoofs. Yet, rather than offering their products as the means to or symbol of a realistic increment in status, nineteenth-century advertisers more often associated their products with the level of status to which they, the advertisers, and their peers were likely to aspire.

In an era noted for its intense emphasis on decorum and propriety among the hegemonic classes, and those aspiring thereto, countless advertisements featured women's forms, and occasionally men's, not at all clothed according to public fashion. Women clothed as actresses or prostitutes staring confidently at their audiences violated norms of female decorum (plate 2). Full female nudity generally appeared only in pictures directed to the male market; these included trade journals as well as advertisements for alcohol and tobacco products, and presumably the only women who would see them there were "crude" or already "fallen." Less frequently, nude and near nude women frolicked on patent medicine, soap, and cosmetic advertisements, the ethereal innocence of their expressions belying their erotic bodies (fig. 3.9). In contrast, not only in advertisements but in every printed medium not primarily intended for children, atavistic variations on classical drapery revealingly clung to countless figures, as it did in the theater of the time. In many cases, the drapery protected modesty (at least that of the viewer) only by adhering strategically if implausibly to breasts and thighs. Debates on the artistic and cultural merits of nudity during the century, such as that inspired by Hiram Power's "The Greek Slave" in 1858 and the abundance of nudity in fine art of the era, may have justified and encouraged the use of such commercial art. Scholars in several fields have analyzed the significance of nude female figures in fine art, theater, and other visual media, reaching various conclusions about its symbolism.[118] Regardless of and in addition to nudity's use as artistic symbol, this

**Fig. 3.9.** Nymphs offer Dr. Hall's Balsam to male representatives from many nations on this chromolithographed sign on metal, circa 1885. Despite their nudity, these otherworldly creatures smile angelically as they serve the world this potion, in contrast to the very worldly stare on the Lorillard image (see plate 2). Cases of the healing balsam await shipment, apparently produced without benefit of industry. Courtesy of the Don Lurito collection.

practice certainly manifested an insensitivity to propriety and audiences as well as artistic pretension. Significantly, nudity declined in the advertisements of later decades, when artistic expression was less challenged by Victorian prudery and when attitudes toward the clothing actually worn by women were more relaxed. By then, formally educated specialists, more aware of their audience, determined advertising styles.

Another example of advertiser insensitivity to consumer perspectives in nineteenth-century advertisements was the frequent portrayal of factories in settings that seem incongruous now. For example, the Sterling Piano Company issued a chromolithographed show card and matching trade cards in the 1880s that featured a young girl at a piano and a boy with a violin (plate 3). Not only were the children dressed in the highest of fashion, but their parlor setting displayed as many of the trappings of domestic ostentation as would fit the frame, and of all the furnishings, the piano was by far the least ornate. Associating a product, especially an expensive one, with luxuries and cultural enrichment is a time-honored promotional strategy, although the extravagance portrayed here strikes the late-twentieth-century viewer as out of the ordinary. Yet today, two other components do seem quite anomalous for an advertisement directed to consumers: Charles A. Sterling's portrait over the piano and the firm's factory outside the window. If such a luxurious residence actually bordered an industrial site (we might think today), why not draw those heavy drapes? And do not Mr. Sterling's stern countenance and dark attire contrast starkly with the Venus-like statue and the bright children? At it turns out, the home was Sterling's own, situated in a prestigious neighborhood on a ridge that really did overlook his and other factories.[119]

Factories appeared in a wide range of formats directed to women and children. The Mason and Hamlin Piano and Organ Company, the Estey Organ Company, the Chris. Lipps Soap Company, and the Boston Rubber Shoe Company number among the very many that published trade cards with factory scenes, even though that medium was intended primarily for women and children. The Rising Sun Stove Polish Company's factory provided the only illustration that the firm placed in its quarter-page ad on the inside front cover of a children's book in 1888.[120] A Dixon Pencil Company hanger (a long, narrow poster) juxtaposes—with no sense of irony—a finely dressed woman drawing her child as she sat in front of a framed factory portrait on her parlor wall.[121] Beyond questions of relevance and interest, the repeated use of this important motif disregarded, even affronted, the many people who found factories distasteful or harmful. In addition to the workers whose limited discretionary incomes often prevented them from being major marketing targets for many products anyway, many prosperous people associated negative connotations with the sight of a factory. This included reformers concerned about urban blight or workers' conditions, artisans angry over the deskilling of production, nativists concerned about the immigrants who filled the factories, as well as many of the old elites, especially the merchant classes, who saw their neighborhoods and statures decline as the industrialists' rose.[122]

B. T. Babbitt's Best Soap often used an image in countless trade and show cards in the 1880s and 1890s that demonstrates how a particular advertiser's intuition could combine with his failure to consider others' perspectives. The sooty factory complex in the central scene contrasts sharply with five vignettes of non-Western peoples eagerly receiving crates of soap. The slogans "Soap for all nations" and "Cleanliness is the scale of civilization" boosted Babbitt's contributions to progress as a provider of soap's civilizing touch. Of course, the nineteenth-century ethnocentric implication that exotic peoples could not be civilized until they received the stuff of Western production, in this case Babbitt's soap, was not limited to industrialists.[123] Today it is hard to understand how anyone could miss the incongruity and irony of associating the cleanliness that defined "civilization" with what even then some saw as industrial-urban blight, while judging as uncivilized and needful of soap peoples who still lived under blue skies.

While it is in the nature of prejudices that people tend to be oblivious of their own and sensitive to others', why did nineteenth-century industrialists often affront some of the very audiences whose trade they sought? Even though mainstream Americans have only in recent decades become widely aware of the need for sensitivity regarding other peoples and lifestyles, communications and advertising professionals began to learn that lesson earlier in this century, at least regarding people they sought as markets; even their tones and messages were more condescending and officious than empathetic. In contrast, communication has never been the primary occupation of most advertisers, with the frequent exception of patent-medicine sellers and entertainers. Until advertising professionals, replacing advertisers as advertisement designers, began to make effective communication the focus of their vocations, questions of feedback and market analysis rarely arose. In the meantime, advertisers projected their messages according to their intuitive senses of what was important or attractive or funny. For the most part, they judged according to their own tastes and those of people like themselves; so all of the above themes filled their trade journals as well as their advertisements, making no distinction between their peers and others as audiences.

Nineteenth-century businesspeople cared so little for empathetic communication with their audiences because, to use David Riesman's terms, they were "inner-directed" people, rather than the "other-directed" people who have since had to function within bureaucratic organizations. The earlier, innovative owner-managers worked in a society "characterized by increased personal mobility, by a rapid accumulation of capital (teamed with devastating technological shifts), and by an almost constant *expansion*: intensive expansion in the production of goods and people, and extensive expansion in exploration, colonization, and imperialism." Inner-directed businesspeople focused their attention "on products . . . and less on the human element." When marketing their products, these people "did not need to look at [themselves] through the customer's eyes,"[124] or at least they did not recognize such a need. Neither their business conditions nor their culture inclined these owner-managers to consider how their behavior might offend or distress others. Owner-managers at any time are more likely than employees or corporate managers to be "inner-directed"; hence, the inability of many entrepreneurs to retain control of firms they found but that grow large enough to require bureaucratic management more than innovation.

Given this frame of reference, we can see that the advertising patterns described above are anomalies only judged by our twentieth-century concepts of what advertisements are supposed to do; that is, to communicate effectively with audiences according to the *audiences'* needs and interests. Precisely because the early advertisers did not attempt to second-guess their audiences, we can usefully evaluate their messages more as projections of the owner-managers' interests and perceptions than as audience-sensitive communications. Doing so, of course, requires that we contextualize the messages, to try to reconstruct the authors' social realities and explicate their implicit as well as explicit meanings to themselves.[125] So, while advertisers initiated and justified their messages and expenditures as marketing tools, the contents sprang from the advertisers' intuitive senses of what to tell their audiences based on their own interests and esteem, with little regard for the interests and esteem of the audiences. The clearest shared trait that all the messages indicate is their creators' claim of predominance over the people and institutions they pictured. Whether this claim followed from arrogance, defensiveness, or wishfulness is another question; it was probably a mix of motives according to the advertisers' sense of their status relative to their messages' subjects. So we might surmise it was arrogance toward racial and ethnic minorities, defensiveness against the excessively wealthy portrayed using their products, and a combination of wishfulness and arrogance toward the unclothed, inviting, and vulnerable females pictured emerging from flowers or floating in a businessman's reveries with the caption, "It's Tempting."[126] When specialists later created advertisements, operating as self-conscious communication professionals, they still carried the prejudices of their hegemonic cohort, but they softened their

*Fig. 3.10.* Walter A. Wood called up explicit visual and verbal symbols to convey important qualities of the firm's agricultural equipment on this trade card, circa 1880. Such attention to focusing on communicating clearly product attributes with both words and pictures indicates this advertiser's concern for his audiences' perceptions.

expression: both the changing strategies and the changing mores required greater awareness of other groups through the next century.

All this is not to say that nineteenth-century advertisements contained no pro-sales arguments about their products. Of the countless commercial messages sent into the public arena, many carried comparisons, explanations, demonstrations, exaggerations, and other means of making claims. Thread manufacturers pictured their products pulling Jumbo, Barnum's prize elephant, towing ships, or replacing cables on bridges. Patent-medicine and cosmetic promoters frequently showed or described consumers before and after using their products; this practice included the frequent use of testimonials. Other producers, too, often used testimonials, although they only rarely claimed the before-and-after changes in the fashion that became common for many products after 1910. Instead, the comparisons were often between wise and progressive people who used the advertised product and the foolish, old-fashioned people who did not. The Blair Manufacturing Company, for one, commissioned a series of trade cards that showed little girls effortlessly pushing lawn mowers ("child's play" was a common strategy); another set illustrated a mowing contest in which a neatly-dressed, handsome young man always easily defeated a variety of bumpkins struggling with other makes. Manufacturers of agricultural equipment often portrayed prize racehorses or carriage horses drawing their machinery—the equivalent in both impracticality and visual appeal of showing an expensive sports car plowing a road. Of thousands of images to sell such equipment, however, rarely did a manufacturer try to incorporate a complex selling argument by visualizing its products' qualities. Walter A. Wood Machines commissioned an exceptional trade card that translated the qualities of "strength, lightness, and simplicity" into visual symbols: a strong man, a ballerina, and an infant (fig. 3.10). Such apparently deliberate attempts to communicate with, rather than address, an audience were rare, as was the large, simple type running diagonally on the back of the card to explain the machines' benefits to users. Wood's trade card shows that advertisers' intuitive messages did not have to convey more about their creators than about their products and what those products offered consumers. Advertisements that did focus on their creators' concerns and ambitions, however, preserved those messages as part of their legacy.

# 4

# Advertising Progress as a
# Measure of Worth

*The nineteenth century is a century of industrial triumphs. Steam and electricity, and the thousands of useful inventions to which they have been applied, have made a complete revolution in society and changed the whole face of the world. Agriculture, the foundation of all civilization, has shared in this revolution. The United States of America is to-day the greatest agricultural nation in the world. The agricultural greatness of America is due to its perfect, labor-saving farm machinery. We lead the world because we use good tools.*

Thus began *One of the Triumphs of the 19th Century*, an advertising booklet prepared for distribution at the 1893 Columbian Exposition in Chicago as a paean to progress in general and to "the mammoth manufactory of Wm. Deering & Co. in Chicago and the machines made there" in particular.[1] This booklet of thirty-two pages, plus covers, belongs to a genre of commercial messages that expressed the advertisers' worldviews and interests in two competitive arenas, business and cultural legitimacy and authority. As the advertising capacities of printing technologies developed in the nineteenth century, businesspeople learned not only to exploit them for selling goods and services, but at the same time to communicate their own views of the world and their places in it. Not empathetic to their audiences' concerns and attitudes, advertisers projected their own concerns and attitudes into the public arena through their commercial messages. Seeking to legitimize and fortify their cultural and political positions, they used the media ostensibly to promote their products and services but also as means for nonbusiness forms of aggrandizement. In 1710, Joseph Addison had already ridiculed the eagerness with which businesspeople purchased their publicity when he observed that "advertisements are of great use to the vulgar: first of all, as they are instruments of ambition. A man that is by no means big enough for the *Gazette*, may creep into the advertisements."[2] Of course, businesspeople had other ways of promoting their interests through the press, either directly, as did Andrew Carnegie with great success, or indirectly, through sympathetic editors and essayists. And, as highly motivated, practical people, they all too often achieved their ends, both proximate and long term, without concern for public opinion at all, as William Vanderbilt so pithily declared in his 1882 retort, "The public be damned." Advertisements were but one possible route to political and popular influence for businesspeople. C. W. Post, an insatiable advertiser, not only spent most of his energies on his firm's advertisements but also purchased a newspaper as an avenue for expressing his views generally.[3] For the vast majority, however, advertisements alone provided a ready conduit to the public, one that they already had to patronize for their marketing.

While nineteenth-century advertisements themselves pique our interest on their own merits as popular art and literature, their value as expressions of businesspeople's concerns vastly increases their historiographical significance. Given owner-managers' identification with their firms, the advertisements they shaped so directly can serve as valuable interpretive tools for understanding how advertisers saw their role in both business and public spheres. These messages can also help us examine those owner-managers' ideological responses to their competitions for success—both cultural as well as in business. In order to understand the messages, independent of their impact, we must locate the confluence of the advertisers' business, social, and spiritual concerns from which the messages flowed. Within that context of the prevailing production ethos and progress ideologies, businesspeople, especially industrialists, projected themselves as agents of change—as the engines of material and, therefore, cultural progress.

## Criteria for Worth and the Victorian Compromise

The fiercest battles in the West's perpetual war between spiritual and material values may well have been fought in nineteenth-century America, and they very much colored the popular culture, including the advertisements, of that period. Never before had such material opportunities presented themselves to so many, and never since has outspoken religious morality had such a hold on those same people. The tensions between these two powerful attractions pulled at everyone. The decisions about how to balance the opposing attractions dominated some people's public lives, pushing them to take strong positions—a few ascetics at one extreme and the most ostentatious of the robber barons and their families at the other. Most people who had the option found a more even balance comfortable, and their compromise contributed to the formation of the Victorian-era American middle class and its bourgeois cultural style.[4] Even missionaries and advocates of the Social Gospel concerned themselves more with justice than with fears of declension toward materialism like those of the Puritans or the New Lights. To be sure, diversity was a salient characteristic of nineteenth-century U.S. society. Not all Americans during Queen Victoria's reign (1837–1901) were Victorians. Generally, white American Protestants of the bourgeois classes, and those who aspired to the American bourgeois gentry, made up mainstream Victorian America. They identified with the era's hegemonic cultural style and its ambivalence regarding the mix of abundance and poverty around them.[5]

Businesspeople often operate in the center of the battle between materialism and moralism, the targets of proselytizing from all sides, receiving both praise and criticism. Nineteenth-century entrepreneurs experienced the lures of materialism in part because money measured their business success, yet they also carried the still-strong traces of a deeply rooted tradition of wrestling with materialism. As social historian Alan Dawley concludes in his *Class and Community: The Industrial Revolution in Lynn*, the "fusion of worldly ambition and religious duty is the essence of the Protestant ethic."[6] In this context, those who took on the task of advising people with ambitions in business always addressed the problem of balancing the tensions between materialism and moralism. For instance, in Haines's *Worth and Wealth: Or the Art of Getting, Saving and Using Money*, the chapter on "Money-Getting" began with the assertion that "Money-getting is the aim, the paramount end, of business." The 1884 tome described in tantalizing detail the merits of money and "its secret charm" for meeting practical and social needs, despite the "intonation of contempt [with which] the word is sometimes uttered." But then the author joined ranks with thousands of others in print and pulpit who warned the ambitious of the difficulties of seeking both money and salvation, for "Money is king; and here lies the danger. . . . For money is hardening to the heart. . . . [Every] true business man . . . [must] feel . . . that while he is laboring for the increase and distribution of wealth, he is working for the elevation and civilization of the masses." If men followed the commandments "to be diligent in business, to be active, to contrive, to invent, to waken up intellect, to render to material world tributary and subservient, and to accumulate the products of art and nature," then they would be able "to accumulate money to enhance their own and others' happiness." In *The Rise of Silas Lapham*, William Dean Howells dramatized the poignancy and multifaceted nature of the battle between materialism and morality for a businessman and his family.[7]

Most nineteenth-century writers offering this kind of advice identified their own balances as "success." Thousands of missives, including trade journals, proclaimed the Victorian compromise that exalted character as the sure road to success. *One Hundred Lessons in Business*, 1887, preached typically, "Let a young man *fear God, be industrious, know his business, spend a little less than he earns*, and success is sure."[8] The popularity of the Victorian compromise did not reside only in print. In 1867, Horace Greeley spoke to thousands of young men on at least two occasions at the behest of S. S. Packard, the president of Bryant & Stratton Business College in New York. Indeed, people were turned away for lack of space when Greeley gave his "Address on Success in Business." Inspired by the opportunities for success in an America that was destined "to bound forward on a career of prosperous activity such as the world has not known," Greeley extolled his audiences to "believe that success in life is within the reach of every one who will truly and nobly seek it." Reciting the usual list of characteristics that ensured success, Greeley emphasized "that thrift, within reasonable limits, is the moral obligation of every man; that he should endeavor and aspire to be a little better off at the close of each year."[9]

Yet wealth alone could not serve as the measurement of success for Victorian businesspeople in the United States. An 1891 trade journal article with advice to young men began: "Being an American, you are ambitious. If that ambition is of the right kind, you are striving for two things: first of all, reputation, and second, money. Success in these two things will make you an example of what is every American young man's ideal—'The successful business man.'"[10] Moral character, in turn, determined the success or failure of a person's business career. Thus, young people were extolled to piety, industry, honesty, frugality, punctuality, and like virtues—the standards of middle-class respectability—plus the virtues of masculine, middle-class heroics, such as initiative and competitiveness, all entirely within the range of any young man's potential. By this logic, success implied that a person must have followed the path of rectitude. The success ethos therefore vindicated those already doing well in business according to the popular success biographies and biographies and obituaries in the trade press.[11] So the "great task of the character ethic had been to spiritualize commerce without commercializing the spirit," according to cultural historian Richard M. Huber in *The American Idea of Success*.[12]

Young people and the general public may actually have been ill-served if they believed that their material success or failure was irrefutable evidence of character. The principle allowed anyone with a claim to material success also to claim virtue, despite prominent examples to the contrary, such as Jay Gould. As explained in *The Imperial Highway to Fortune, Happiness, and Heaven,* 1881, "I can truly say, that nearly all those who began life with me have succeeded or failed as they deserved."[13] In this revision of the Protestant ethic, worldly success provided once again the tangible signs of other-worldly salvation, especially if the wealth so acquired was dispensed with taste and an element of philanthropy.[14] Furthermore, success evinced the desirability of one's business activities, for the "wants of society raise thousands to distinction who are not possessed of uncommon endowments. The *utility* of actions to mankind is the standard by which they are measured."[15] An often quoted biblical legitimation of this ethos proclaimed, "Seest thou a man diligent in his business? He shall stand before kings."[16]

## Linking Business and Personal Industry

The intimate association between owner-managers and their businesses linked the industrialists' sense of personal worth with that of their firms. The owner-manager represented more than the typical mode of operating the American firm before 1890: the owner-manager also exemplified the ideal of the businessperson for the century. Owning and managing well one's own business was everywhere cited as how one could elevate oneself above anonymity without artistic or literary genius, but with the steadfast application of good character. Within this context that so prized self-employment, one's business and its reputation became an extension of one's self and personal reputation. Sociologist David Riesman contrasted the inner-directed businessperson with the modern type by observing that when the former "founded a firm, this was his lengthened shadow," whereas "today the man is the shadow of the firm, the institution."[17] How well or poorly firms did, therefore, measured their owners and their owners' character, as credit reports by the Bradstreet Agency and R. G. Dun concluded explicitly. Andrew Carnegie declared that for business men, "Your firm is your monument." Similarly, Cyrus Hall McCormick frequently made it known that he was, according to his biographer William Hutchinson, "proud of his industry, and to have his name synonymous with harvesting machinery the world over was the chief ambition of his life." McCormick's grandson accorded the inventor the accolade that "the reaper was his life."[18] In 1883 and 1884, just before McCormick Sr. died, his family set aside its differences about advertising expenditures to put out chromo posters honoring him and commemorating the fiftieth anniversary of the harvester's invention by featuring the machine's history.[19]

The ethos of work pervaded popular literature of that century, and the businesspeople of whom we have direct reports seem to have gloried in their never-ending labors. Particularly the materially successful employers of others, or those who sought their patronage, praised the virtues of discipline and work in a marketplace allegedly teeming with opportunities for the diligent. The multitudinous nineteenth-century declarations on the virtues of work include *Triumphant Democracy*, throughout which Carnegie proclaims that work is the mark of the Republic.[20] Of all the character traits that the advice literature of the period expounded upon to guide ambitious young people, willingness to work was the most central. The messages typically followed this pattern: "Accordingly, labor has ever been the indispensable condition of success in any and all departments of life. We are now pointing out to you, reader, an imperial highway to fortune, but we do most earnestly assure you that this highway can never be built without the most unremitting and indefatigable exertion on your part. . . . Industry is the price of excellence in everything."[21] A firm's success, therefore, indicated the hard-working, good character of its owner-manager.

Embedded within this ethos of work was the importance of productiveness, as both an extension of the Protestant ethos of calling and as a major component of the traditional middle-class critique of nonproductive elements in society, both upper- and lower-class. The impulse to measure success in some way that transcended wealth derived in part from industrialists' desire to distinguish themselves from the traditional elites, the mercantile, financial, or idle rich. As Kirkland points out, after the Civil War "the title of 'producer' had taken on the lustre formerly inherent in the word 'merchant.'" Increasing employment and the stocks of available goods, in addition to lowering costs, were grand accomplishments for innovative producers.[22] Under the title of "The Greatest Wealth Producers," the lead editorial in an 1893 issue of the *Iron Age* praised those whose work created more wealth than they consumed.[23] Printers claimed this measure of worth, consistently referring to themselves as manufacturers, and all types of manufacturers extolled their own and others' achievements in this regard. The double meanings of *industry*—more widely applied then than now—as a production activity and as diligence in personal character, also indicates these linkages.

Dramatic increases in productivity in nineteenth-century America, as elsewhere, accompanied the enterprising application of new technologies and the increasing application of research, albeit most of the latter still informal. In Carnegie's encomium to the "republican success" of the United States, he rejoiced that "man is ever getting Nature to work more and more for him."[24] Michael Adas has recently argued that "scientific and technological measures of human capacity" rose to great importance in Western thinking during the eighteenth and nineteenth centuries. Furthermore, "few disputed that machines were the most reliable measure of humankind." Although Adas developed his thesis to explain one way by which Americans and Europeans have justified their "global hegemony," his analysis of "machines as the measure of men" applies equally well to attempts at more local hegemonies. Hence, people using or controlling new, impressive capital equipment might well consider that power a reflection of their own importance, especially in the last decades of the nineteenth century, which historian of technology Thomas Hughes characterizes as "an era of technological enthusiasm."[25] In light of the degree to which industrialists identified with their firms, then, their strong sense of personal identification with the technological aspects of their enterprises and accomplishments makes complete sense.

The social history of the early automobile industry, which was characterized by owner-manager operation into the early twentieth century, provides a useful illustration of the intimate relationship between entrepreneurs, their firms, their products, and their public statements. Automotive manufacturing used and produced many of the most exciting new technologies of the decades before and after the turn of the century. It attracted entrepreneurs eager to pioneer in developing and producing the single most important manufactured status symbol available to consumers in the past one hundred years.

In *Conspicuous Production: Automobiles and Elites in Detroit, 1899–1933*, Donald Davis shows that each manufacturer produced and then advertised his automobiles according to his own self image and social ambitions. With an insightful twist on Thorstein Veblen's concept of conspicuous consumption, Davis argues that the manufacturers believed that status accrued to them according to the status of their products. In other words, Detroit's turn-of-the-century elites produced cars designed and priced to impress their peers, whereas others, most notably Henry Ford, identified with and built their cars for the middling classes.[26]

Automobile manufacturers also manipulated their public images according to their social interests. Naming their companies and their automobiles after themselves, the presidents of automobile companies commonly wrote or signed their advertising copy personally as late as the 1910s. According to Davis, the manufacturers, especially Ford, attached their personal prestige to their products through their advertisements. At the same time, they deliberately sought to promote their social ambitions through their advertisements and the status associated with their automobiles. For example, the owner-managers' advertising copy often featured as assurances about quality their personal applications of the latest technologies or statements about their own purposes and ambitions. Briscoe Automobile, for one, placed advertisements from 1917 to 1919 that began with the claim that the "name of Benjamin Briscoe is indelibly written in the annals of motor car history. He has won fame both as a designer and a manufacturer of high-grade, quality automobiles." Furthermore, "truly the automobile business and the motoring public at large have been the gainers from the efforts of this master designer and manufacturer."[27] Like the entrepreneurs who pioneered the earlier stages of industrialization, the owner-managers of the automobile industry's initial period saw their firms and their products as extensions of their own character and identity,[28] as, more recently, have owner-managers of the early, most innovative stages of new technologies such as photographic equipment, computers, and software.

## Progress as the Measure of Legitimacy

The productivity on which the nineteenth-century industrialists prided themselves required not only their own diligent labors but also their employment of the period's newest technologies of production, transportation, and communication. The larger cultural context within which manufacturers operated was a century of phenomenally dramatic changes in people's material and cultural experiences. As David Landes generalizes the earlier British reaction to their industrialization and urbanization, they "knew they had passed through a revolution." This phenomenon was,

> moreover, a revolution like nothing ever experienced. Previous transformations, political or economic, had always finished by stabilizing at a new position of equilibrium. This one was clearly continuing and bid fair to go on indefinitely. . . . [The] pessimists, vociferous though they were, were a small minority of that part of British society that expressed an opinion on the subject. The middle and upper classes were convinced by the marvelous inventions of science and technology, the increasing mass and variety of material goods, the growing speed of movement and convenience of everyday activities, that they were living in the best of all possible worlds, and what is more, a world getting better all the time. For these Britons, science was the new revelation; and the Industrial Revolution was the proof and justification of the religion of progress.[29]

The British experienced their material revolution early, and it drew the fortunate among them toward a progressive view of worldly history. J. H. Plumb writes of "how quite humble men and women, innocent of philosophical theory," were in eighteenth-century Britain already drawn into "the modernity of their world, and to relish change and novelty and to look with more expectancy towards the future." With the increasing availability of new communications opportunities, new technologies, and more goods of all kinds, "improvement" came to be "the most over-used word" of the time. "Advertisements use the word to the point of boredom: after 'improvement,' the phrase in which salesmen put their faith was 'new method,' after that 'latest fashion.'"[30]

By the 1870s, the eighteenth-century's Enlightenment had long since combined with the material evidence of progress to give intellectual respectability to the idea of a cumulative, noncyclic human history. Industrialization and concomitant developments in science, technology, marketing, and communications seemed to confirm that Western civilization was changing inexorably and irreversibly. As Leo Marx has observed, "with rapid industrialization, the notion of progress became palpable; 'improvements' were visible to everyone. . . . To look at a steamboat, in other words, is to *see* the sublime progress of the race."[31] Notions of the significance and the inevitability of progress thus became general, operating at many different levels of understanding. Although most histories of progress address philosophers' debates on the idea, a popular notion of progress developed quite independently of intellectuals as people saw their world change and as they acted within the changes to further, or occasionally to slow, them. In the Victorian compromise, the popular ideas of progress blended religious and traditional attitudes with the new materialism to allow enterprising people to share in prosperity without violating their adjusted spiritual values.[32] This was the progress that the majority of successful U.S. business owners experienced and the progress in which they believed.

Once American industrialization was under way, debates abounded about what sort of changes might best move society closer to perfection, but only the hopeless and rare skeptics did not adopt some version of progress. Even working-class people generally hoped that their children would someday share in the abundance that their exploited labor produced.[33] The artisans whose shops were outmoded by mechanization tended to displace their distress, blaming immigrants or other minorities, including women factory workers; Luddism was rare. Peter Bowler, in *The Invention of Progress: The Victorians and the Past*, concludes that a "naive progressionism [was] represented by the assumption that industrialization is the goal towards which all social developments must tend." Although some scientists and philosophers held more sophisticated interpretations of progress, many shared the popular views that "the growth of free-enterprise commercialism as the driving force of progress paved the way for a social evolutionism in which the attainment of middle-class values was the last step in the ascent of a linear hierarchy of developmental stages." At the core of this process was "the individual's effort to conquer his environment through the exploitation of better technology." Debates on the primacy of technological innovation for progress aside, by the mid-1800s the two seemed inextricably linked in most Western minds.[34]

Praise, icons, and monuments to material progress flourished in many forms from the last half of the American nineteenth century to the present.[35] A lawyer speaking at a trade meeting in 1896 declared that

> the very foundations of the earth are shaken by the pulsations of the mighty mechanisms that do our bidding and render us essential service. What were luxuries a little time ago are now necessities. A thousand devices minister to our comfort and convenience. Space is annihilated, and the whole world is joined in one mad race against time. . . . The miracles of yesterday have become the commonplaces of to-day. . . . This is no time for skepticism, for all things seem possible. The world owes more to American inventors than to those of any other nation, and our amazing progress has in large measure been due to their tireless efforts and clear brains. The producer is a benefactor.[36]

The Photography Association of America erected a monument to Louis Daguerre in 1890 with the inscription, "Photography, the electric telegraph, and the steam engine are the three great discoveries of the age. No five centuries in human progress can show such strides as these."[37] The cover of "Dawn of the Century," a 1900 march by the popular music publisher E. T. Paull, portrayed a goddesslike figure surrounded by various state-of-the-art technological accomplishments (fig. 4.1). The list of similar paeans to material progress is endless, including the glorification of industrial and commercial abundance that trade publications often vividly portrayed. The cover of *Trade Magazine: Helpful Hints to Merchants and Business Men* for at least several months in 1894 featured a bountiful goddess figure holding a cornucopia as she gazed approvingly over an industrial scene. Elements of this vision of abundant productivity included three forms of transport, factories, telegraph and telephone lines, an electric light, and men moving amid stockpiles of products (fig. 4.2).[38] An 1878 Currier & Ives print, *The Progress of the Century,* crowded similar icons into a scene that also showed printers at work and a telegrapher sending and receiving grand and patriotic messages. These and similar motifs had become conventions in American artistic and literary representations of the technological sublime.[39] They also appeared regularly in the advertisements that nineteenth-century industrialists commissioned for their firms.

Virtually every writer in the late nineteenth century who addressed con-

**Fig. 4.1.** Icons of technological developments swirled around goddesses of progress in media besides advertisements, as on the cover of sheet music for "Dawn of the Century" by E. T. Paull (New York: E. T. Paull Music Company, 1900). Gift of Melissa Faulkner Motschall.

**Fig. 4.2.** Figures of white women as bearers, approvers, and beneficiaries of plenty, but not the producers of it, abound in the business imagery of the nineteenth century, as on this front cover of *Trade Magazine: Helpful Hints to Merchants and Business Men* 2 (May 1894).

temporary issues included references to achieved progress, hopes for more, programs to ensure it, or concerns for its inequities. In fact, the concept was so ubiquitous that it is almost meaningless to refer to a separate literature of progress. Rather, the themes of improvement on personal, national, and world levels pervaded the century's writing and iconography. In particular, the vast majority of writers favorably associated technological developments with positive change and, hence, progress. Horace Greeley wrote in 1872 that industrial growth "is in the line of progress, in the direction of securing to each individual the largest liberty for his personal endeavors, and for society at large the greatest amount of material for its collective comfort and well-being." Even those who criticized the destructive and exploitative aspects of American development generally believed that industrialization itself was not the source of problems. Both Henry George in *Poverty and Progress* and Edward Bellamy in *Looking Backward* firmly believed that a positive progress through the advances of technology and industry could be had, although it required significant redirection of the nation's patterns of power and distribution. Most writers did not debate the merits of contemporary progress as generally defined, but simply accepted the changes as natural and appropriate. For example, a reference manual of "facts and figures" on American development was entitled *The National Hand-Book of American Progress*, expressing the connection between quantitative development and the author's notions of progress.[40]

The industrialist class was prominent among the many Americans "convinced," as Landes put it, of both the reality and the merits of progress, as they experienced it. Indeed, as important actors in the material developments of their era, industrialists, including printers, helped to define progress by their enterprise both in production and in marketing.[41] Their industries made available new and increasingly abundant material goods; their messages to the public about the desirability of those goods helped to set the direction and pace of America's sense of progress. Yet they also experienced great anxieties about their status as a new class as well as tensions when their materialism challenged their traditional values. They were, therefore, of all Americans, particularly likely to find attractive the notions of industrialization as progress. For them, participation in the developments of the era became an important indication of success because it combined control over technological power and acquiring wealth from it with a transcendent value, namely, the betterment of humankind. Such notions of progress resolved their internal tensions between spiritual and worldly ambitions; they gave industrialists a measure of their successes and thereby legitimated their agency in the century's transformations. Of the various transcendent values that industrialists could have adapted to project their successful enterprises, such as piety, charity, family devotion, and so on, progress offered the most powerful explanation and legitimation for the revolution in which they participated.

Yet material progress was not an unmixed blessing, then any more than now. The transformations entailed enormous costs, and some of those costs have been accounted extensively. From our vantage point, we are recently sensitive to the environmental costs. Other costs included the greatest mass dislocation—still ongoing—in history, as wave after wave of rural and village peoples subjected themselves to industry's regimentation of time and behavior. City living eliminated cheap, fresh food from most people's diets, even during harvest season, as it also did away with traditional communities and quiet. The exploitation and degradation of the laboring classes have been well documented, as have myriad other tragic consequences.

Such lists of the costs of the industrial, urban transformation typically focus on the people who suffered most obviously and who had the least control over the conditions under which they struggled. Other Americans seemed to have gained more than they had lost in the transformation. The Victorian bourgeois, for example, and those close enough to aspire to join that dominant stratum, were generally reckoned the successes of the era. Certainly in terms of material goods, they had opportunities to partake of the new profusion of goods from industry and world trade that marked material progress. Yet there were costs for these successful people, too. Indeed, the dislocations and stresses of "modern" living generated new ailments for Victorian women and men, such as neurasthenia and varieties of depression and anxiety.[42] Furthermore, explosive urbanization and industrialization threatened and often destroyed the spaces people had known and trusted. Confrontations with the new technological systems, living conditions, and multicultural melange that were intrinsic parts of the changes at every level created tensions even as they fascinated and challenged people, individually and collectively. According to Earl Hess, many felt that "self-interest had to be infused with a healthy moral sense to prevent harm both to the individual's character and to the commonwealth." Particularly those Americans born before 1870, who included the generation of post–Civil War businesspeople, feared that "the dynamic progress of the economy would destroy the traditional values of the simple culture in which they were raised."[43]

Why, then, did Victorian Americans subject themselves to such stresses and dislocations? Unlike the laboring classes, who mainly sought modest improvements in their meager standards of living through their decisions, the middle and upper classes had to have been driven by ambitions beyond subsistence. To a great extent, a desire to keep up with the processes of industrial, urban transformation propelled many people; they did not want to be left behind by either their peers or the abstract standards of success that signified participation in the progress of the time. Their cultural inheritance also attributed spiritual as well as worldly value to work as the means to success and progress. In 1883, *The Golden Gems of Life* typified how the Victorian compromise tied together the work ethos with success and progress. "Labor may be a burden and a chastisement, but it is also an honor and a glory. Without it nothing can be accomplished. All that to man is great and precious is acquired only through labor. . . . It is by labor that mankind have risen from a state of barbarism to the light of the present. It is only by labor that progression can continue. Labor [is] the grand measure of progress."[44] In a complex and powerfully motivating spiral, the very people whose access to the means of production made them the prime actors in the era's transformations, themselves felt a compelling need to keep step with the processes that they and their peers drove forward. In a serious verse on the politics of abolition that became a broadly applied cliché, James Russell Lowell wrote in 1844,

New occasions teach new duties, time makes ancient good uncouth;
They must upward still and onward, who would keep abreast of truth.[45]

This ideology of progress linked material and social improvements. Its power to justify and to motivate enterprise helps explain why industrialization and urbanization dominated the American nineteenth century despite their disruptions and costs. Although these processes have appeared so vast and profound that both contemporary and later observers have been inclined to declare them inevitable, even deterministic processes, they were not. Like any other historical process, they resulted from countless decisions by countless individuals driven by their personal needs, ambitions, and expectations. There were, of course, different orders of self-determination in people's decision making; investors generally had more freedom of choice than did unskilled laborers, for example. Whatever their circumstances, people generally tried—as they do now—to weigh as well as possible the consequences of alternative decisions. The sum total of infinite numbers of individual decisions determined the nature of the industrial and urban transformations the nation experienced. In this context, Victorian beliefs about progress dominated a worldview that could explain what people experienced, while motivating them and providing some direction for their efforts. Attributing changes to progress, with its positive connotations, legitimized, even glorified, both the changes and their consequences, however unfortunate or disruptive they appeared in the short run.

As Lewis Mumford has written of the American nineteenth century, "Life was judged by the extent to which it ministered to progress, progress was not judged by the extent to which it ministered to life."[46] Successful participation in the new order could also validate an individual's activities and values by placing them into the perspective of this grand historical sweep. Since the products of material progress themselves defined the rewards of participating in modern times, producing as well as acquiring and using modern manufactured and marketed goods became a primary measure of one's successes, and hence one's worth in the new order.

## Competition and Progress

Besides self-justification, why might nineteenth-century industrialists try to project a public image of themselves as progressive producers? Without question, a fiercely competitive experience dominated businesspeople's activities and thoughts. In a collection of biographies, *Men of Business*, written for Scribner's Men of Achievement series in 1893, William O. Stoddard compared business with the "ancient idea that war is the normal condition of the human race." In the "warlike rivalry" of business, "there is perpetual conflict. Business men of all occupations still speak of the season before them as 'the campaign.' In it they expect to meet with competition, and . . . enemies in the field."[47] Accounts and trade were, and are still, *won* in the business world. Some commentators even attributed the intensification of competition to the very technological developments also responsible for material progress. "With the introduction of such forces as steam, machinery and electricity, the laws which prevailed fifty years ago no longer avail. This is aptly shown in the remark of the French economist, who said: 'In ancient days, when fortunes were made by war, war was a business; in these later days, when fortunes are made by business, business is war.'"[48] Exacerbating this sense of competition were business owners' very realistic fears for the survival of their firms and the personal finances and commitments tied up in them. Kirkland indicates that "contemporary observers were prone to assert that ninety-five per cent of all capitalists, 'men carrying on business,' failed." As a result, fears and anxieties about "hazardous" and "perilous" businesses and times filled their letters and conversations, including those of highly successful figures such as Andrew Carnegie and John D. Rockefeller.[49] Furthermore, entrepreneurs ever "tend to seek novel ventures in the context of an environment of uncertainty" and to operate during rapidly changing times, and these conditions also add to their sense of insecurity.[50] In light of the industrialists' perceptions of the world as dominated by risky competition, imperiling business survival, Social Darwinism gained adherents much more as a reflection than a cause of their worldviews, including racism. It provided a discourse to explain and communicate their experiences in terms of "the survival of the fittest" and a "struggle for success."[51] It also allowed the successful to discount the suffering of others whose failures allegedly evinced their inferiority. Participation in progress could validate their efforts and investments, and demonstrating that participation to others argued for the merits of their activities as well as their wares.

Industrialists of this period also experienced competition outside of the marketplace. Louis Galambos characterizes the United States' nineteenth-century "national culture" in terms of "the individualistic orientation of an atomistic competitive society."[52] An intense competition for cultural authority determined whose ideas and whose values would direct the nation's course in the throes of unprecedented change. Writers and speakers of innumerable persuasions proselytized avidly and prolifically, competing to influence the populace or portions thereof. The American industrialists figured as important actors in the dominant changes that some people praised, some questioned, and yet others decried. As a prospering and highly visible new class, the industrialists often felt uneasy about their status and identity relative to the ambient value systems. Even the Boston patricians who founded and profited from the Merrimack River's industrialization experienced this source of concern in the first half of the nineteenth century, when factories were a new and alien phenomenon in the United States.[53] As a study of later American business attitudes theorized, "the content of the business ideology can best be explained in terms of the *strains* to which men in the business role are almost inevitably subject." They respond to "the emotional conflicts, the anxieties, and the doubts engendered by [their] actions" and the "conflicting demands of other social roles which they must play in family and community." Within the constraints of their cultural contexts, businesspeople shape their ideology "to resolve these conflicts, alleviate these anxieties, overcome these doubts."[54] In the nineteenth-century competition for cultural hegemony, the industrialists had investments of time and financial resources, family security and status, and personal reputation to enhance as well as to protect. The ideologies of the American Victorian compromise and progress through increased productivity served these functions in their time. The industrialists' advertisements sent these messages into the commercial and cultural arenas.

# Symbols of Progress

## *Abundance*

Many of the nineteenth-century industrialists' advertisements make sense only by reconstructing the significance of abundance—a phenomenon newly present if hardly universal. Although countless entries in literature and journalism, including most prominently Charles Dickens and Jacob Riis, indicate the salience of poverty to the bourgeoisie, adults had witnessed the rapidly growing availability of material goods, from food products, textiles, domestic decorations, and furniture to agricultural and domestic tools and devices. Most observers interpreted this positively and desired to participate in it one way or another. Industrialists seeking to impress upon their audiences their own contributions to this abundance repeatedly commissioned chromolithographed advertisements with exaggerated images of plenty, sometimes crossing over into fantasy. Plump babies and children appeared frequently, sometimes saved from "dyspepsia" or other digestive ills by a packaged, processed food.[55] The New England Mince Meat Company often showed a dozen children, some dressed like Dickensian waifs, perched on a huge tabletop eagerly watching a gigantic pie being cut. In other advertisements, children playfully romped amid bounty, innocent of the deprivations they might have had to endure without a manufacturer's "high-class preserves" that could only result from "doing business on a large scale." The back of a Thurbers' Fruit Preserves and Jellies trade card, circa 1880, includes an excerpt from the *American Grocer* praising the economies and improvements that resulted from industrially preserving foods.

Industrialists not only produced more goods for consumers, but they also made available goods that were in turn more productive. The "Empire" Wringer portrayed Uncle Sam effortlessly producing a huge basket of gold coins as he turned its crank (see fig. 3.2). Yeast producers showed dough that rose so effectively it threatened the integrity of ovens; likewise, soap manufacturers showed soapsuds that rose to the ceiling. While such effectiveness in reality would not have appealed much to frugal or fastidious homemakers, the advertisers' enthusiasm for their products combined well with the era's conventions for evoking anomalies of scale to humorous ends. H. J. Heinz Co. commissioned hundreds of different die-cut trade cards with children or food preparers, such as chefs, emerging from giant pickles. Confectioners like N. S. Dickey & Co. of Boston showed children playing on huge pieces of candy (fig. 4.3). Huge tomatoes dwarfed the men carrying them on the trademark for Anderson and Campbell, precursor to Campbell Soups.

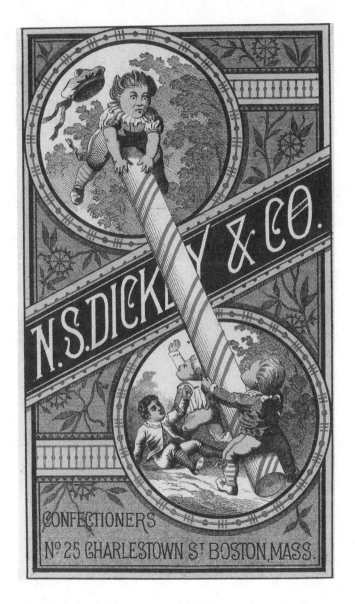

**Fig. 4.3.** Oversized objects often conveyed the nineteenth-century fascination with proportions and abundance, such as on this trade card for Boston confectioner N. S. Dickey & Co., circa 1885. Children playing on a candy cane as large as a teeter-totter fit in with the growing attitudes of mainstream, bourgeois families that childhood should be a time of pleasure and indulgence. Although industrial progress made this possible for some children, it subjected others to greater burdens than ever before.

Advertisers who specially commissioned messages did not celebrate the new abundance in the abstract. In copy for their own publications—booklets, almanacs, flyers, and so on—they credited themselves with fine qualities such as heroism and altruism. Steele & Price published a booklet titled *The Hand and Cornucopia*, "full of good things for everybody." In a story that supplemented the recipes and testimonials, the young heroine asked, "Why do men like Dr. Price spend the greater part of their lives in searching after things that make our food so much more palatable and healthy, and lighten our labor?" Through the heroine's voice, Steele & Price answered that such men "are aiming after something good for humankind."[56] In the industrialists' imagery, and even when scenes of opulence had no direct link to using a product line—as with lavishly exotic scenes shown to associate cosmetics, food items, or medicines with their presumed origins—advertisers' priorities clearly included linking their names with the pictured abundance. The lush colors and ample design possibilities that lithographers made available to advertisers lent themselves to communicating this link. Even retailers or small manufacturers who could not afford to commission unique messages could take advantage of the newly available media to purchase colorful stock images and imprint their names on them. There was no room for modesty as the advertisers competed in taking credit for the industrial cornucopia that flowed into the marketplace.

### Success and Industrial Imagery

Businesspeople projected their business success and, by implication, their own good character, in these accessible media through a discourse of verbal and visual motifs that represented success to the industrialists. Such a discourse need not have appealed to another audience for it to have been attractive to the industrialists themselves. They might have simply displayed their wealth instead, yet because of the strong cultural needs to "identify the secular pursuit of material goods with some more transcendent end," portraying wealth alone as the measure of success and self-worth would not have sufficed in the nineteenth century.[57] Progress, on the other hand, measured success in a way that carried the transcendent values essential to the Victorian compromise. Technologies and other manifestations of material progress lent themselves to visual representations that industrialists incorporated into their advertising messages. Many of these associations offered no explicit indication of how the progress portrayed or symbolized therein benefited the consumer; the implicit benefits of progress sufficed for the advertisers. Sometimes advertisers even neglected the use and nature of the product in favor of self-aggrandizement through displaying ownership and control of those technologies. Henry

Adams remarked at the beginning of the twentieth century about how many "new" Americans seemed to be the products of "so much mechanical power, and bearing no distinctive marks but that of its pressure." Rather than numbering themselves among the ranks of those who were "servant[s] of the powerhouse," in Adams's term, these advertisers proclaimed through their advertisements that they were the masters.[58]

The frequency with which owners named their businesses after themselves and used their portraits as trademarks and advertising motifs indicates their interests in raising themselves above the crowded anonymity of modern life. Given the intimate associations between owner-managers and their businesses, publicizing the ties between a firm and its owner-managers was, of course, a reasonable marketing strategy when personal reputation was a major criterion for judging a firm, from retail to high-level finance. During this period, both R. G. Dun & Co. and the Bradstreet Agency reported on company creditworthiness in part according to the personal character of a firm's principals. At a time of no business regulation or product regulation of any kind, the portrait of a firm's founder or a product's inventor presumed to offer customers a reassurance of a product's reliability; this convention therefore flourished in the field that most needed to inspire confidence—the selling of patent medicines. Even so, virtually all firms, whether in retail, finance, or production, used a surname in their titles, and examples of founders' or owners' portraits abound in all fields. (CEOs again appeared as spokespersons and promotional figures in the 1970s, when American industry felt the press of international competition and needed to inspire confidence anew in American goods.) Even when advertisers did not link their own portraits with those of their factories, they always prominently displayed their names.

Portraits of business places featured prominently in all nature of promotions as printing technologies developed sufficiently during the century to make them feasible. By midcentury, merchants as well as manufacturers and owners of other edifices, such as hotels and depots, increasingly displayed their establishments in their advertisements and periodicals as well as more ephemeral media. All manner of business owners sought recognition for their contributions to community growth in lithographed city views, paying extra to have their establishments featured in vignettes around the main view or to have their trade signs or buildings emphasized disproportionately. Boosters encouraged the printing of these views to advertise their towns as a whole. Associations and towns also published expensive volumes published to illustrate "the great manufacturing industries by which, in large measure, our present commercial importance has been attained."[59]

The factory portrait as an instrument of image making reaches as far back as the building and promotion of the Waltham and Lowell mills in the early 1820s. Factory owners and other major investors commissioned paintings of their properties to hang in their homes, reception halls, and offices. They also commissioned black-and-white prints, at first without advertising messages, for free distribution to municipal authorities, to creditors, to visitors, and, for a price, to the general public. In the 1830s, these factory portraits became frequent images on labels on bolts of cloth and on advertisements. With these lithographed factory and city portraits, the investors in early U.S. textile industries explicitly promoted their land, wares, and stocks, as well as their manufacturing system, at a time when Americans were not all convinced that industry was the way to foster the growth of the new Republic. Whether as advertisements or in other formats, factory owners used their plants' portraits purposefully to help transform public attitudes as well as to attract investors. They sought to legitimate industrial production, sometimes, as already mentioned, by placing cornucopia or other symbols of prosperity in the factory portraits, at other times by featuring bucolic surroundings to minimize the impression that industry disturbed nature, and always by presenting the factories as grand and solid structures.[60]

By the late 1880s, industry was widely, albeit not completely or permanently, accepted as a means to prosperity and progress. Yet tensions about the merits of wealth from industry remained; individual industrialists still had to make their own cases for inclusion in the halls of heroic and meritorious enterprise. Looking at a poster for Dr. Kilmer's Standard Herbal Remedies in the light of cultural politics reveals that the good doctor's countenance and its setting serve as more than a warranty of his honesty and uprightness; they form a political campaign poster of sorts (plate 4). His factory, offices, and the activity around them proclaim together that Kilmer's products came from modern facilities, that the new industrial technologies were something to be proud of, and that Kilmer himself successfully participated in the progress of modern times; he labeled himself "The Invalid's Benefactor" and "A Successful Physician." Even General Electric, in a brochure prepared for the 1893 Columbian Exposition, promoted its massive factories, and their evolution from smaller ones, as evidence of that fledgling corporation's prowess.

Industrialists and company officers often took active parts in creating their advertisements and other publicity formats that featured their factories, enhancing both the buildings and their surroundings. In a lengthy correspondence in 1898 between Robert Bell, secretary of the Alexandria Chemical Company, in Alexandria, Virginia, and Leonhardt Lithography of Philadelphia, Bell began by requesting that the printer use accompanying photographs of the company's buildings to design a letterhead. A second letter from Bell expressed dissatisfaction with the sample sketch because "the buildings do not show up as <u>bold</u> as they should." Furthermore, the "ships are too small." After a series of other complaints, the letter closed with the suggestion that "the wharf could be made more natural if a RR track could be added with several cars shown. . . . The arrangement of buildings is all o.k. though we must admit that the affect [sic] is not as pleasing as it might be." A third letter accepted the final, more impressive, image as "all # o.k."[61] A large poster for the Estey Organ Company of Brattleboro, Vermont (see plate 1), shows considerable embellishment compared with the actual site, as happened frequently.

Architectural imagery appeared in every medium available to nineteenth-century owner-managers attempting to promote themselves and their wares. Letterheads and billheads almost always showed a firm's buildings. Advertisements in manufacturers' trade journals, directed to peers, almost always featured factory portraits or pictures of the items offered, with little or no nonindustrial imagery like that found in the Inland Printer and other printers' journals, at least before the 1890s. Almanacs, tin containers, boxes of all sorts, and entries in city directories also carried industrial and mercantile buildings. Some factory portraits dominated their layouts; others occupied vignettes off to the side. A show card for George E. Mitchell of the Novelty Plaster Company (fig. 4.4) displayed an exterior view of the factory as its centerpiece and featured the interior rooms of his factory as well as his own visage. Only the pictured diversity of the forms of Novelty Plasters, around the main image, indicated any merits of the product line other than its means of production. Many firms, among them breweries and tobacco companies, targeted their advertisements directly to consumers, often using nothing more to promote their product than factory portraits, with or without auxiliary vignettes. Another Mitchell, of Mitchell, Lewis & Company, illustrated his success with vignettes comparing his 1834 factory with his massive manufactory in 1883 (fig. 4.5). He did, however, also promote his product—his wagons, featuring a fierce battle in which male pioneers fought American Indians, their women and children remaining safely ensconced within circled wagons that look as solid as concrete barricades. Not only did Mitchell, Lewis, & Co. thereby participate in industrial progress, they also contributed to others' capacity to participate in progress of a different sort, fulfilling what Euro-Americans then considered their Manifest Destiny.

The styles of factory portraits varied imaginatively to convey the impressiveness of their operations. The enormous coconut framing the "immense" Huyler's Cocoanut and Candy factory in an 1909 postcard typifies the preoccupation with scale that people often expressed in those expansive times (fig. 4.6).[62] For a different effect, a large August Wolf show card contrasted state-

**Fig. 4.4.** Mr. George E. Mitchell surveyed his domain—the interior and exterior views of the Mitchell Novelty Plaster Company—and its products on this chromolithographed show card, circa 1880. The scenes, lists, and pictures of products are the only sales arguments that Mitchell presented.

of-the-art factory lighting, and arc lights outside, with the dark of night (plate 5). In these cases, as in many others, the images carry an important selling argument as well; namely, that the activity that centered on their factories—the endless parade of wagons leading into the Huyler factory and August Wolf's nighttime operations—attests to the success of these firms. Accordingly, the Huyler copy reads, in part, "If the amount of Cocoanuts used annually by Huyler's could be condensed into one single nut it would be large enough to enclose Huyler's immense factory. It would take 222 double trucks to carry the Cocoanuts, Pecans, Filberts and Peanuts used by Huyler's every year." Even the smoke that billowed from the factories, and from the trains and steamships that transported goods to and from them, represented progress to industrialists and many others. Countless advertisements glorified smoke as a symbol of success.

**Fig. 4.5.** Progress, according to this industrialist (pictured on the elaborate first letter of his name) included the Anglo-American drive West and the growth of his firm's capacity to manufacture covered wagons as bulwarks against the frontier's defenders. This vision of social progress also idealized masculine protection that made it unnecessary for women and children to contribute to their own safety. Chromolithographed poster (known as a show card) for Mitchell, Lewis, & Co., 1883.

Although we can surmise a sales pitch that customers should select goods according to the size and modernity of a facility and the activity around it, this genre of advertisement only rarely spelled out that argument; the declarations about and images of factories seem, in an overt sense, to have fulfilled other competitive needs. George E. Mitchell joined the contest of factory sizes in the 1870s with no explicit statement of how factory size benefited consumers: the top of a box of his U.S. Standard Porous Plasters for store display has a line drawing of the same scenes of his Novelty Plasters Works as on the sign already discussed; the inside of the lid contains another set of five line drawings, this time of the factory complex from four directions, plus a bird's-eye view, and in copy wrapped around the five vignettes Mitchell informed his customers, "This is no fancy sketch got up to please the eye, like mythical pictures

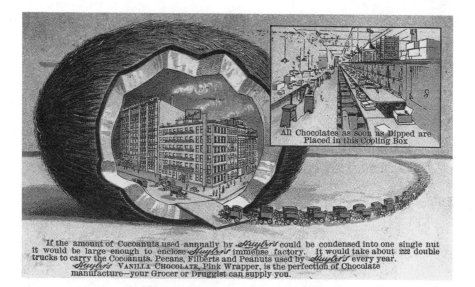

If the amount of Cocoanuts used annually by *Huyler's* could be condensed into one single nut it would be large enough to enclose *Huyler's* immense factory. It would take about 222 double trucks to carry the Cocoanuts. Pecans, Filberts and Peanuts used by *Huyler's* every year. *Huyler's* VANILLA CHOCOLATE, Pink Wrapper, is the perfection of Chocolate manufacture—your Grocer or Druggist can supply you.

**Fig. 4.6.** The Huyler's Coconut and Candy factory, "immense" though it was in the manufacturer's estimation, could be encased in one huge coconut as large as all the coconuts it processed in one year. On this 1909 postcard, the other raw materials the firm processed stretched to the horizon. Such levels of production proclaimed a worthy product and a worthy producer.

of 'immense works,' published by some of my competitors. Come and see me, and see for yourselves." The print glued to the bottom of the box gave instructions for using the plasters; nowhere on the box did Mitchell indicate anything about the quality of the plasters themselves or how they promised to benefit consumers. Even Huyler's copy only implied the connection between size of factory and modernity and the benefits to consumers: he called one of their products "the perfection of Chocolate manufacture" and put a slogan, "Her first choice, her last choice and her choice at all times," atop the scene. In a similar implication, if August Wolf's products were not good, would the factory have had to run at night producing them? The argument remains implicit here and in almost all instances of consumer advertisements.

In contrast, industrialists and their advocates made the argument explicitly in the trade presses, using size, activity, and machinery to argue for quality of product. These visual conventions represent, therefore, a shared discourse among business classes that, when applied to consumer advertisements, measures, once again, the nonattention nineteenth-century owner-managers paid to their consumer audiences. Consumers, especially women, did not read trade

*Production as Progress*

journals or share their internal discourse, and yet advertisers apparently assumed that everyone's reactions would parallel their own. For instance, a factory portrait complete with clouds of smoke provided the frontispiece for an advertising booklet put out by The Knickerbocker Press in 1896. The firm had recently moved to this new building, and the author of the booklet "thought that a brief description of its new quarters may not prove uninteresting to those who have had work done for them bearing the imprint of TKP." The copy merely implied that the quality of the product had made the move necessary because "for several years the demands made upon the Press have so steadily increased as to make it important that its facilities should be materially enlarged." The remainder of the twenty pages describes the building, its design, its equipment, and the technological processes by which printing is accomplished.[63] None of this descriptive material gives any direct evidence, other than its own pages, of the quality of the product that the booklet promotes. The advertisement's contents likely interested the writer and his peers more than his customers, even if they, too, shared the discourse of business success and its links with technological advances.

In rare cases, copy directed to consumers made the argument from production facility and activity to quality of product explicitly. A lithographed store dispenser for Family Matches, circa 1888, pictured the Barber Match Company factory works across the front of the tin container and a large amount of copy on the sides and back. The copy included a statement by C. C. Barber, treasurer of the Diamond Match Company, that tied together the progress of his company with the overall progress of technology and business. Pointing out the parallels between such historical events as the development of the telegraph and the invention of matches, Barber cited the progress by which the firm "now has a daily capacity of sixty million matches, one match for each man, woman and child in the United States." He explained this prodigious success by the company's "strict attention to business, improvements in machinery and methods of manufacture, and by creating a demand for goods that are always good and as cheap as the cheapest. This factory makes about one-third of all the matches consumed in this country."[64] Although the Diamond Match Company was one of the earliest of the nation's industrial corporations, Barber, as a member of the founding family of the largest of the four firms that merged in 1881, still adhered to the entrepreneurial ethos prevalent in the business community of the era. Barber's point-of-purchase advertising projected this interpretation of his firm's diligent and successful participation in progress.

G. G. Green of Woodbury, New Jersey, founded and operated one of the leading patent-medicine companies in America between 1867 and 1910. A prolific advertiser, he, too, made explicit the argument that his production facility and activity proved his products' desirability. Many of his posters and the covers and interior pages of his widely distributed almanacs showed his laboratory, his factory, or his mansion. Sometimes (for example, in an 1890 booklet) the portrait of Green's mansion carried the caption, "Result of True Merit." In the 1880 almanac, Green retold the story of his business under the title of "Wonderful Success." After eleven years of manufacturing and selling his medications, he declared that "it has the largest sale of any medicine in the world . . . and during the last four months our factory has been running until midnight to fill its orders. This wonderful success we attribute to the great virtues of the medicine alone. . . . It seems to have no equal. Try it." On page 29 of this almanac, Green placed a full-page engraving of his "New Laboratory Building. Correct View, not Enlarged." The image included a train steaming past, a smokestack billowing, and well-dressed people walking by.[65]

In his 1889 almanac, Green addressed the question of his own promotional use of industrial imagery by responding to comments from people "who had seen the drawings of our grounds and place of business, but could not be convinced that they were genuine reproductions of the same." He assured readers that the engravings and lithographs had been created "from no spirit of vanity, then, but a sincere desire to gratify our world-wide friends . . . that the house . . . knows how to do successful business."[66] The inquiries that prompted Green's denials indicate that the strategy was rather transparent. Other people knew, and some mistrusted, what the industrialists were trying to do. Green's 1889 almanac announced that he had made a photograph album available to assure customers of the veracity of his advertisements. On the first page of text in this hardbound book, a long, uncredited poem includes the following lines:

There is no luck, whether of good or bad;
For luck is what a man will make of life,
Of time, endowment, present circumstance.
Luck is the man, the man the luck. And so,
These things came not by chance, but were possessed
By foresight, thrift, skill, honest wares and dealing,
Sending the world what it did mostly need,
And for good money giving money's worth.

The thirty-one photographs that follow show Green's possessions, including interior views of his mansion and private railcar.[67] The poem, together with the photographs, indicates that Green very deliberately pictured his laboratory and his personal wealth both as proud evidence of his character and as an argument that he was "for good money giving money's worth."

# Advertising the Technological Sublime

Leo Marx has analyzed the "exhilarating" experiences that many British and Americans shared during industrialization, remarking on an "unusual aspect of the progressive world view"— namely, "the extent to which it was disseminated, without benefit of words or ideas, by the mere appearance of the new instruments of power. Their physical presence alone enabled the new machines, in John Stuart Mill's words, to inculcate 'a feeling of admiration for modern, and disrespect for ancient times' in the entire population, 'down to the wholly uneducated classes.'" Certainly, many of the advertising images disseminated through chromolithographed advertisements during the throes of industrialization communicate the technological sublime that Marx describes as "the sensuous presence of the new power [that] encouraged each successive generation to think of its situation, as well as that of its own successor, as superior to the situation of all previous generations."[68]

## *Images of Technological Progress*

In 1872, a professional publicist and publisher very much caught up in the era's mainstream notions of progress designed a promotional image that equates technological and cultural progress in just this manner. George Crofutt commissioned John Gast to paint and then lithograph *American Progress* as a premium for subscribers to *Crofutt's Western World*, a monthly newspaper dedicated to Western tourism and development. He gave Gast precise instructions for this image of a coast-to-coast panorama that placed it into a popular genre romanticizing the West. Although Crofutt intended to promote interest in the American West, rather than industry per se, he did so by attributing intellectual and racial superiority to abstractions of the same technological and cultural developments to which the industrialists appealed; Gast's work is an allegory of the march of civilization across the American continent, with education and the telegraph leading the way for armies and railroads. Crofutt credited the ensuing expansion of his subscription list to the print's appeal and he commissioned a steel engraving for black-and-white copies he used in his other publications.[69] Crofutt's interpretation of the print's positive impact on his targeted public may not in fact tell us much about the public's reactions; after all, only a small percentage of the public at large had to seek copies of *American Progress* to boost his subscription list significantly. Still, his reactions provide us with a strong indicator of his beliefs, just as the countless illustrations of technological progress created for public dissemination evince their appeal for their creators, not necessarily for their audiences.

The industrialists' own sense of their "new power" added a compelling reason to promote themselves as well as their firms and products through industrial imagery. The Masury Paint Company combined these two messages in an advertisement that expressed both the near-supernatural power of industry and the advantages of mechanical standardization. In allegory style, a well-attired young man confidently points to a packaged product bathed in a celestial glow. This ideal pigment and the machine that cleanly, accurately produced it according to "the acknowledged standard," contrast sharply to the messiness, and hence the unreliability, of an old artisan's work. Through this visual allegory, the Masury firm explicitly distanced itself from the handcrafted tradition, identifying itself with modern technological progress.

August Wolf's night scene also represents heroic industrialism, with clouds of smoke billowing against the moonlight while bright lights emanate from buildings and arc lamps atop towers. This chromolithograph's glorification of the power under Wolf's control—human labor as well as electricity and steam power—testify to his forceful participation in the progress of the times. Although the daytime factory portraits lack some of the epic quality of the Wolf print, they, too, communicated the industrialists' amplified sense of the technological sublime. For example, G. E. Mitchell's countenance floated over the image of his Novelty Plaster Works to remind the viewer that he presided over both machinery and labor in his factory. The B. T. Babbitt's Best Soap image discussed earlier placed the facilities and products of Babbitt's industry at the core of civilization.

For hundreds of years, storekeepers and other advertisers had used symbols in their trade signs, trademarks, promotions, and packages that gave little or no information about the product but attempted to evoke emotional responses. As discussed in chapter 1, these symbols drew on popular motifs, such as patriotic icons or meaningful creatures. Nineteenth-century advertisers often used popular technological motifs, whether they held a logical connection to their businesses or not—such as industrial smoke. The smokestacks and smoke-filled skies depicted on a Milltown Stogies tin place this Pittsburgh advertiser among the many to whom the smoke motif appealed as a positive symbol, despite the hardships felt by people living and working under such skies.[70] Dr. King's 1903 "Guide to Health" showed a boxed bottle of his New Discovery for Consumption surrounded by the "Greatest Discoveries of the 20th Century"—a locomotive, an automobile, a phonograph, and other machines—by which its creator intended to lend credibility to "the greatest [discovery] of all for saving human life" (fig. 4.7)[71]

Locomotives and steamships, the most popular expressions of the technological sublime and mechanical progress, sometimes represented a firm's move-

**Fig. 4.7.** Although Dr. King's New Discovery for Consumption was actually "discovered" in the 1880s, this frontispiece for a 1903 "Guide to Health" booklet surrounded its old-fashioned box with the "greatest discoveries of the 20th century," many of which similarly had nineteenth-century origins. Could Dr. King's nostrums cure all he claimed for them, they would truly rank high among these forms of technological progress. This common promotional strategy sought to enhance products by association with the excitement and esteem of technological advance.

ment of raw materials and finished goods. As the population's experience with locomotives grew, many advertisers exploited the engines' power to evoke the technological sublime even when it bore no connection to their product's quality, manufacture, or distribution. As Leo Marx explained, the "image of the railroad in the landscape was one of the more vivid embodiments of the American ideal of material progress that emerged in the nineteenth century." The Bagley Tobacco Company of Detroit, Michigan, named The Fast Mail tobacco brand for William Vanderbilt's 1874 highly touted improvement in transporting mail. Extensively promoted, the tobacco brand's advertisements and packages always showed a racing, smoking locomotive carrying the mail across the prairie. The image derived from an 1876 painting by John McPhee commissioned by Vanderbilt and first lithographed to advertise his "Lake Shore and Michigan Southern, RY." Another tobacco company, Century Fine Cut, explicitly associated itself with "Centuries of Progress in Boats and Tobacco" by illustrating diverse generations of transportation technologies in its advertisements at the turn of the century.[72]

In some images, however, such as that for the Alexandria Chemical Company cited earlier in this chapter, locomotives and steamships were added or enlarged for the sake of the impressiveness of the scene. These puffing symbols appeared even in advertisements by nonindustrialists, such as retailers, wholesalers, and financial services, who often featured their buildings, showrooms, and warehouses in their advertisements and their packages. Since all merchants and distributors relied on transportation for their trade, their use of these icons said more about their competitive style than their conditions of business. Similarly, the United Brotherhood Mutual Aid Society of Pennsylvania commissioned a chromolithographed show card on tin featuring its "municipal office," a stylish, imposing structure. Enumerations of the society's assets and activities surround the scene, reinforcing the impression of prosperity and strength that the building itself imparts; the locomotive passing immediately in front of the building might have risked the desired impression of stature but for the generally positive contemporary associations of such proximity.

### Electricity and Symbols of Progress

Electrical motifs were also used frequently to associate nineteenth-century firms and products with progressive technologies.[73] Throughout the century, practical electrical applications had gradually developed to whet the appetite for electrical progress—the telegraph, telephone, and public uses in transportation, lighting, and industry. As the realities grew, the general public became ever more aware—through wild claims, spectacles, news and publicity reports, and public utilizations—that this was a force that had unparalleled promise.[74] Still, until the twentieth century, ordinary people had little or no opportunity to use or apply electricity in any practical fashion in their domestic lives. In this market setting, enough enterprising people associated themselves with this most modern of technologies through their trademarks and advertisements to create a genre of promotional materials with electricity as a theme. Whether firms promoted food, tobacco, medical treatments, soaps, or polishes, they could associate their products with electricity through a set of visual motifs that became popular conventions by the 1880s. A sample of these motifs filled a poster for the 1884 International Electrical Exhibition at the Franklin Institute in Philadelphia. The images ranged from functioning technologies to fanciful, ethereal figures, representing electricity as a combination of wonderful applications and limitless prospects. Juxtaposing the figures of goddesses with the products of technological progress attributed to electricity near mystical connotations similar to those evoked by the goddess of abundance (see fig. 4.2 for the association made with industry and commerce on the cover of *Trade Magazine*).[75]

Some entertainers and other entrepreneurs developed a rather controversial area in which electrical motifs were used, a practice now known as electroquackery—the making of medical claims based on real or alleged application of electrical energy.[76] Such advertisements indicate their creators' interests in associating themselves and their products with progressive technologies, whatever the truth about the effectiveness and safety of the treatments, or the artifice of their promoters. Electricity was a prime candidate for both orthodox and fringe medical experimentation in the nineteenth century. Because neither scientists nor lay people knew then what electricity *could* do, they also did not know what it could *not* do, resulting in unrealistic expectations for the health benefits of electricity. Entrepreneurs readily offered more than they could possibly deliver in exploiting the gap between what people wanted and what they could get from electricity. Electroquacks sold two very different types of products, one using electricity directly, the other not, but both with similar appeals to electrical enthusiasm: some claimed that their devices produced medicinal electrical effects through generators, batteries, or magnets; others medicated with pills or bitters. All evoked the technological sublime through a common set of electrical phrases and visual motifs—telegraph and telephone lines and equipment, generators, ticker-tape machines, light bulbs, arc lamps, and so on. With these motifs, promoters associated themselves with a major feature of scientific and technological progress. Dr. H. N. Brown of New Haven, Connecticut, advertised his services in 1875 by promising to give "special attention to the remedial effects of Electricity,

**Fig. 4.8.** Of all the technological advances of the nineteenth century, those related to electricity promised to deliver the most benefits. Electricity's mysteries and the rapid progress in exploring and applying them left much to imagination and hope in an age when routine medicine offered so little to most people. The German Electric Belt Agency was one of many firms ready to claim electrical cures in its booklet, circa 1890, *The Electric Era.*

Magnetism, Dietics, Hygenics and Sanative Science." To highlight the point of this list, Brown inserted "progress" as the central word of the layout, using the largest type on the page other than that for his name.

Dr. George A. Scott's electroquackery advertisements of the 1880s and 1890s included long lists of medicinal claims for his magnet-laden products, such as hairbrushes and toothbrushes, ladies' corsets, and "gents'" devices. Scott embossed many of these items with designs that included an armored fist holding lightning bolts and the slogan "The Germ of All Life is Electricity," touting them all as "remarkable" inventions in his advertisements. In his advertising booklet titled 90 *Years of Pleasure! A Treatise on Electricity and Electro Magnetism,* Scott proclaimed both the continuing mystery of "the nature of the electro-magnetic power" and the progress of its practical applications. Scott aligned his products with progress in telephony and electric lighting, crediting "science" and not medical practice for the success of his products.[77] Similarly, the German Electric Belt Agency promoted its batteried products with endless claims for their medicinal potency. The cover of the advertising booklet "The Electric Era" carries an image suggestive of the Franklin Institute's poster, picturing a goddess cavorting with cherubs, all surrounded by a generator, a ticker-tape machine, and a light bulb (fig. 4.8). According to a flyer for another product, a Dr. Thomas named his product Eclectric Bitters to make a word play on "selected and electrized," by which he invoked a "union of the words Eclectic, to choose, and Electric, containing electricity." However, in the same publication he mentions nothing other than the chemistry of combining special ingredients to explain his "astonishing results."[78]

Just as *atomic* became part of the faddish appellations of various products after World War II—from sandwiches and bubble gum to fashions and colors—nineteenth-century marketers incorporated electricity and electrical motifs into the names and promotions of products. Even when promoters made no pretense about their product's direct application of electricity to a consumer's needs, they might still exploit the contemporary buzz-word value of progress in electrical technologies. For instance, H. E. Bucklen's Electric Bitters purported to be "The Great Electric Remedy"; yet its label and advertisements linked it to electricity only by showing the bottle on a platform between electrodes. Only the electrical motifs, including lightning bolts emanating from the bottle, distinguished this bitters and its claims from countless other brands. Similar motifs adorned packages and advertisements for George E. Sawyer's Electric Cough Drops, although he made no claim to electrical potency. By virtue of connotation only, many advertisers sought to associate themselves and their otherwise unremarkable products with contemporary progress. Such products included a line of canned vegetables packaged as the Electric Brand, featuring a goddess of electricity holding an electric light and a miniature battery, standing in front of two cherubs chatting over telephones. Electric Lustre Starch, Electric Soap, and the Electric Razor also used the name and the conventional visual motifs, despite having no other connection with electricity.[79] The Electric Razor, for example, was a standard straight razor that was embossed with lightning bolts. Tobacco products included the Flor de Franklin Cigar and the Flor D'Edison Cigars, both advertised with scenes of electrical progress. Pace's Electric Mixture Tobacco tin showed the genre's requisite light bulbs, street lamps, telegraph lines, and lightning bolts on the lid and around the sides, plus four dancers from an 1891 German ballet, "Pandora," that celebrated the triumph of electrical progress. The dancers—representing telephony, photography, phonography, and telegraphy—were pictured on the tin identically to their images in the program. In the ballet, all four "technologies" served the prima ballerina, who represented electricity and who was the story's heroine.[80] Neither this tobacco nor any of the other products in this category were promoted with any hint of why one should purchase them other than through their association with electrical progress.

Another technique for promoting products by linking them to electrical progress during this era tied electricity back into industrial imagery. Some advertisers used their industrial applications of electrical power and technologies to promote their products, as the August Wolf Milling Company did with its large show card. Food companies promoted the cleanliness of manufactories run by electrical power rather than by coal-generated steam. The H. J. Heinz Company occupied "a clean spot in Pittsburgh . . . operated throughout by electricity."[81] Interestingly, despite these claims about clean production, the trade card shows smoke billowing from a towering smokestack, locomotives, and steamboats. The Natural Food Company, an early name for the Shredded Wheat Company, took up electricity and industrial imagery enthusiastically in 1901, naming its new electrically powered factory at Niagara Falls a "Palace of Light." Henry Drushel Perky, an adventurous entrepreneur who had started the firm in Denver in 1891, advertised public tours of the plant as an inviting part of Niagara tourist activities. Perky proudly proclaimed that his was "a temple of cleanliness to house the purest and cleanest of foods." Fulfilling his vision of a "show factory," Perky manufactured both Shredded Wheat Cereal and Triscuits in a climate-controlled, sealed plant with superlative facilities for employees as well as products. Between 1901 and 1905, when he retired, Perky advertised this connection between Triscuits and progress extensively, featuring the Falls and usually picturing the "electric baked biscuits" surrounded by lightning bolts.[82]

The numbers of nonelectrical products advertised and packaged with electrical motifs declined rapidly after 1900, having peaked in the 1880s and 1890s; increased access to household electrical appliances diminished the mysticism. Triscuit and Shredded Wheat were among the last major products that were not themselves electrical devices, actual or pseudo, to be promoted with the evocative imagery of the new power. Moreover, they differed from most of the nineteenth-century products promoted by claims about or associations with electrical progress in that they were in fact manufactured through the new technologies. They differed from most twentieth-century products in that they and their early advertisements resulted from the innovations of an entrepreneur in the owner-manager cast, only too eager to proclaim his own and his products' successes by associating them with the progressive technologies of his time.

## Advertising Personal Prosperity

The technologies of industrialization provided advertisers with a set of visual motifs by which they could publicly project their successes while drawing on the transcendent virtues of industrial and material progress. Some advertisers also displayed their personal wealth, publishing visual representations of their consumption, as well as, or instead of, their production. Advertisers' mansions, usually portrayed on the grounds of their businesses, epitomized conspicuous consumption. Perhaps advertisers justified this practice believing that personal wealth, like productive facilities, attested to their wares' merits directly, and indirectly to the producers' good character, in keeping with the aforementioned Victorian moral compromise. In many cases, the picturing of an industrialist's home in an advertisement may not have been a deliberate decision; some entrepreneurs simply may not have distinguished between their homes and their factories as complementary components of their domains. For instance, August Wolf, Dr. Kilmer, and many others built their homes at or near their factories, the better to supervise their facilities. Excluding them from their advertised landscapes would, therefore, have required an overt decision to separate their homes from their work for their publicity, and to deny possible promotional gains from having the public see that these owner-managers personally attended to their businesses. If they did not make such a distinction in their lifestyles, they were unlikely to have made it for their advertisements.

While most advertisements portrayed the mansions as secondary to the manufacturing facilities, some owner-managers featured the evidence of personal wealth more prominently. G. G. Green, for example—he of the poem quoted earlier in this chapter—frequently included both his production facilities and living accommodations in his advertisements because it attested to his success at "for good money giving money's worth." Expanding the strategy, Green often, by virtue of the angle of view, showed his mansion as larger than his production facilities; on occasion he even publicized interior rooms. In his 1883–1884 almanac, Green included another variation with a scene with his family relaxing on the mansion's porch, watching an elegant carriage pull away. In a more unusual but not unique ploy, Green illustrated his private railcar in various media, ostensibly because he used it to travel to health resorts on "investigations." A large chromolithographed show card for Green's August Flower Boshee's German Syrup depicts the interior of Green's elaborate private car with a young girl looking out the window at a rural scene complete with a farmer in his field. Only a barn roof painted with the name of the tonic connects the product to the image. On the back, Green directed "In Explanation" to retailers:

> This is a picture of a daughter of Dr. G. G. Green, Manufacturer of Boshee's German Syrup and Green's August Flower. It represents the young lady seated in a parlor car, enjoying the magnificent scenery of an overland trip to California. The peculiar charm of this picture is that it is real. The artist, one of our best portrait painters, had for his guidance a photograph, and strove above all things for a faithful likeness. The excellent reproduction of the familiar appearance of a parlor car will be at once appreciated by everyone, while the view through the windows is typical of those one is constantly passing all across the continent. The artistic merits of this exquisite souvenir need no comment to engage the attention or enlist the admiration of the public. They will speak for themselves and win so readily a popularity as to render it unnecessary for us to ask that you give this beautiful banner the prominent position in your store that it unquestionably deserves.[83]

Green's certainty that his "beautiful banner" would strike a responsive chord in its viewers evinces a typical insensitivity to his audiences, both retailers and consumers. Few people would find the interiors of private parlor cars "familiar." Moreover, it is not clear how many people would have been enticed to buy a tonic just because its manufacturer indulged his little girl in luxurious travel and then portrayed it to "enlist the admiration of the public." Clearly, some entrepreneurs found the Victorian compromise a difficult balance, Green's frequent reminders that all of this prosperity was the "Result of True Merit" notwithstanding.

The manifestations of entrepreneurial success that extended beyond industrial imagery to personal possessions and activities reinforce the importance of competitiveness in nineteenth-century advertisements. Businesspeople built extravagant houses in part as "a sort of visible bank balance," according to Kirkland, even though they generally absorbed relatively small proportions of their owners' wealth. Riesman points out that "the sphere of pleasure and consumption is only a side show" for inner-directed businesspeople; indeed, some of these people "turn consumption into work," which functions as "an externalized kind of rivalry."[84] Thorstein Veblen's contemporary observations reinforce the connection between entrepreneurship and competition through conspicuous consumption.

Elijah Morse, founder and owner-manager of the Rising Sun Stove Polish Company, commissioned and widely distributed many proofs of his success as one of the nineteenth-century's most prolific nonmedicinal advertisers. As a story in Morse's hometown paper put it in 1904, he, "like P. T. Barnum, believed if you have a dollar's worth of goods for sale, take another dollar and advertise them." Furthermore, "energy, perseverance, and a liberal amount of originality on the Founder's part have been the real cause of success."[85]

Elijah Morse was in many ways the exemplary nineteenth-century business success, with a national reputation as "one of New England's, if not the country's, most successful and energetic business men." According to an interview in 1898, he had started with "no money, and nothing but a hand-mold, a carpet bag, an old white horse and a factory 12 × 15," ultimately building a factory that was at the time of the interview "the largest . . . of its kind in the world, having a capacity of over ten tons a day, and covering over four acres, and buildings containing over four millions of bricks." Morse attributed his success to "good goods, push, and persistent advertising."[86] Many of Morse's illustrated advertisements followed the conventional patterns of industrial imagery, showing his manufactory either as their central image or embedding the factory portrait as a framed picture displayed on a user's wall, or a scene through a window. In one case, the factory portrait decorated an elaborate screen within a prosperous woman's drawing room. In his early factory portraits, Morse's first modest house was shown in front of the production facilities. In the 1880s, after Morse built his mansion across the street from the old house, facing the rising sun, his factory portraits switched direction, looking over the grounds, past the old house to the new one. Although at the far side of the scene, the mansion remained prominent, even disproportionately large relative to the factory buildings. The industrial imagery and mansion in his advertisements indicated that he prized his worldly success.

Elijah Morse's advertisements illustrate how community and political involvement also have often provided successful businesspeople with an important arena in which to compete for cultural authority as well as for more obvious forms of power. His father had been a Congregational minister, and Elijah was a deacon in the church and very active in his hometown of Canton, Massachusetts. According to the *Canton Journal* and local reminiscences, the townspeople considered Morse a generous and fair employer; he continued to pay his employees half of their wages whenever the company shut down during hard times. Morse also supported the YMCA and campaigned actively against smoking and drinking; he was frequently referred to in town as "the Good Elijah." Once he had solidly established his business, Morse entered local politics, representing Canton in the Massachusetts House of Representatives, then the state senate, and finally, until two years before he died, as a congressman.[87] An advertising message very different from his earlier industrial imagery communicated his satisfaction with his prestige and electoral office: a set of cartooned trade cards that Morse distributed for at least a decade carried a story line that hinged prosperity on a decision to purchase stove polish (see fig. 8.3). As the story goes, the professional lives of two men rise or fall as results of their wives' timely cleaning of their cast-iron stoves. Because the first man bought his wife an inferior product, she could not have his dinner ready on time. This "foolish man," therefore, could not spend enough time at his business and was reduced to begging. The "wise man," on the other hand, bought Rising Sun Stove Polish, and because he could conduct his business, he became "enormously wealthy and highly respected," rising to the pinnacle of success: being "elected to Congress." While no man could become as successful by buying Rising Sun Stove Polish as by producing it, this morality tale expresses both Elijah Morse's pride in his own accomplishments and his satisfaction that these successes identified him as a valued member of his community.

## The Demands of Progress

In *The Theory of the Leisure Class*, one of Veblen's most useful insights derived from his analysis of prosperous people who did not obviously fit into his category of the "leisure class." He rejected the Victorian compromise by which the bourgeoisie protested that they worked and sought material success at least in part as a transcendent quest. Veblen lacked sympathy for the "head of the middle-class household" who must "turn his hand to gaining a livelihood by occupations which often partake largely of the character of industry, as in the case of the ordinary business man of to-day." To include this class of working persons in the leisure class, Veblen argued, perceptively, that middle- and upper-class women and children take up the appearance, and in some cases the reality, of "vicarious leisure and vicarious consumption." If we look past Veblen's disdain for these people, we can merge his explanation with the concept of the Victorian compromise and its attempt to balance spiritual and material success to good effect. Thus, in a community that valued industry and required men to work, yet measured success in part by wealth and leisure, some of the competition for cultural authority engaged men's dependents. In other words, "the good name of the household and its master" could depend on the apparent consumption and leisure in the lives of his family.[88]

We cannot know how often the models for advertisements were owner-managers' family members, although sometimes advertisers' children were so identified, as in the cases of Green's daughter and Lydia Pinkham's grandchildren. In many cases, as with the Sterling Piano scene, the portrayal of an advertiser or his family can be deduced to demonstrate the compatibility of Veblen's concepts of vicarious leisure and consumption with the Victorian compromise. Such representation recalls the practice by which Renaissance patrons and their families modeled for paintings of religious themes, the legitimating medium of their times. In a chromolithographed poster for the Diamond Wine Company, for instance, the proprietor promoted his champagne as the refreshment for a small, proper, daytime party (plate 6). (The period's brewery and wine industries attempted through many means to convince the U.S. public that moderate consumption of fermented, not distilled, alcohol products contributed to health and gracious living, a prominent theme in the *American Brewers' Review*). The portrayal of leisure, the champagne, the women's fashionable clothing, and the expensive setting for the gathering all presumably indicate the advertiser's level of prosperity: two of the young women are hatless and therefore at home, entertaining a third woman, and the factory scene outside their embellished window implies that this is the advertiser's home. Although the women are oblivious to the factory, train, and workers in the background, the advertiser chose to remind his audience that industry provided the young women's luxury. More specifically, it was his successful industry that permitted, perhaps required, these young women, maybe his daughters, to indulge in vicarious consumption and leisure.

Youth and wealth combined to allow the young women represented on the Diamond Wine poster to enjoy their daytime champagne party. Victorian adults, however, were subject to ever-increasing demands if they hoped to keep pace with progress. Not only did nineteenth-century businesspeople feel pressures to succeed in terms of progress, their advertisements also convey that their notions of progress included higher expectations for domestic accomplishments and, most especially, for the efficient use of time by both sexes in whatever they did. The industrialists believed that the new technologies they had made available to housewives and other domestic workers required of those workers, especially housewives, increased cleanliness, fashionableness, serenity, and the other virtues of the nineteenth-century's feminine gentility.[89] Married women's growing responsibilities precluded frivolity and often even leisure, except for the very wealthy. At the same time, adult women of the Victorian classes were still expected to display family success through conspicuous consumption and leisure. Their role expectations, therefore, were complex and more than a little paradoxical. On the one hand, wives and mothers shared the younger women's obligation to behave as status symbols; on the other, they also shared the Victorian man's obligation to work. Veblen analyzed the result of these apparently contradictory obligations to conclude that "the leisure rendered by the wife in such cases is, of course, not a simple manifestation of idleness or indolence." Furthermore, it "almost invariably occurs disguised under some form of work or household duties or social amenities, which prove on analysis to serve little or no ulterior end beyond showing that she does not and need not occupy herself with anything that is gainful or that is of substantial use."[90]

The importance of vicarious consumption and leisure to nineteenth-century bourgeois gender expectations, and therefore to how industrialists projected their understandings of men's and women's roles onto their advertisements, followed from one of the fundamental dislocations entailed by industrialization and urbanization. As men left their traditional occupations in or near their homes to enter a separate business/industrial world of wage labor or entrepreneurship, gender roles diverged, changing the ways both men and women contributed to their families' homes, well-being, and status. The work ethic gave social value to men's labors as they contributed to commodity production, whether as farmers, artisans, engineers, or capitalists; so idealized images of men in advertisements and other popular media invariably identified them by their trades or class. Idealized women, on the other hand, most frequently appear idle, or working in ways not obviously essential to their families' subsistence. This, according to the mainstream ideals of the times, constituted progress. An advertising puzzle for the White Sewing Machine contrasts images of an artisan and an engineer or inventor with an ethereal goddess (fig. 4.9). While the men are identified by their work and are surrounded by the symbols of their proud participation in progress, the woman is an abstract figure who stands next to a closed sewing machine. Her participation in progress, like the timeless goddesses elsewhere in the era's promotional art, is portrayed by her serenity. She is best seen not working, even as she stands by her own tool, because of the leisure made possible because of men's labor.

Whether on the farm or in industry, as the century continued, men's status and self-esteem began to depend more exclusively than before on their in-

**Fig. 4.9.** Advertisers have always sought ways to get their messages into people's homes. The W. J. Morgan Lithography Company of Cleveland offered wood puzzles, gluing clients' ads to one side and maps of the United States to the other, thereby creating educational toys suitable for the home. This 1886 chromolithographed image for the White Sewing Machine Company shows a goddess on a pedestal, holding out a laurel wreath as a reward for the inventiveness and labor of men. This evident pride in masculine labor contrasts with denial of the women's labor for which this domestic tool was built: goddesses do not labor at machines.

*Advertising Progress as a Measure of Worth* 143

come-producing abilities. As the family's liaison with the progress—and its products—of the economic world, all men came to be judged as successful according to their abilities to buy, rather than on their abilities to make a standard of living for their families. Their character as hardworking, diligent men could no longer be witnessed by their families and neighbors; only their incomes could attest to this, and this reality strongly reinforced the Victorian compromise that equated character with material success, most obviously indicated by the condition and appearances of their homes and their families. Style, status, and loving indulgence could absorb almost any income, and since income production fell into men's sphere, they have since then felt the pressure of this relentless demand—in recent decades, increasingly shared with women. One of the countless advertisements that have exploited and exacerbated such pressures showed a well-dressed father and young daughter on a trade card, circa 1880. As they stroll by a store window, the girl asks, "Papa, please buy me a pair of Sollers & Company's Shoes; all the stylish girls wear them." Ever since the Victorian era, advertisers have invited men to compare themselves to models whose success allows them to indulge their families' every wish.

In projecting their own concerns about status, the industrialists of this period often promoted their goods as—in Veblen's terms—"items of conspicuous consumption," offering household goods in terms of separate spheres for the sexes: "apparatus for putting in evidence the vicarious leisure rendered by the housewife."[91] Their doing so substantiated Veblen's critique of their affluence, to be sure, but they also evinced a more genuine anxiety about achieving a balance between material and spiritual goals than Veblen is willing to credit them with. Advertisements for household goods projected industrialists' notions of women's practical, spiritual, and social duties within this Victorian compromise. Additionally, they instructed women on how they might participate in progress and thereby become better partners for their spouses, better mothers, and better symbols of their families' well-being. Dixon Pencil Company promoted this ethos with a chromolithed illustration of a mother drawing her child in an affluent room that included the Dixon Company's factory portrait on the wall.

Many advertisements illustrate the industrialists' expectations that women would use advertised technologies to improve the lot of their families according to progressive bourgeois values. In a lithograph for the New Home Sewing Machine Company, an elegantly dressed woman stands next to her sewing machine as she paints an allegory for progress (plate 7). In her painting, she instructs an eighteenth-century woman on the merits of industrial technologies by pointing out to her predecessor a new sewing machine in front of a window looking out on the manufactory. This message gives credit to the sewing machine for enabling the progressive woman to sew elaborate clothes for herself and her daughter while leaving her with time for artistic pursuits. It also credits the industrial system in general for broad improvements in the quality of life since colonial times. This model woman was busy and productive, as a proper Victorian should be, according to the industrialists, but not at gainful work. Although many of her most valued activities were not at all essential to her family's physical survival, obligations—including status-seeking through art and fashion—absorbed her every moment.

A large genre of late nineteenth-century advertisements encouraged both men and women to judge themselves according to the rising expectations of their age of progress; fashion, the appearance of leisure, education, and a new level of attention to children, for instance, all now marked the successful Victorian home. The increasingly complex standards for comparisons with peers extended far beyond subsistence. A period journalist, for example, praised dress-pattern manufacturers for their contributions to "the development of the useful and the beautiful"; for "in its magnitude as a commercial enterprise, [the industry] best illustrates the progress of the age and the civilization of the nineteenth century."[92] As leaders in this field, Mme. Demorest and her husband not only printed and marketed huge quantities of paper patterns that simplified sewing and fitting very complicated clothes, they also edited and published *Demorest's Monthly and Mme. Demorest's Mirror of Fashion*, among other magazines. This highly respected magazine, along with Mme. Demorest's innumerable trade cards and other advertising media, encouraged elaborate fashion standards that more than absorbed the time women saved by using the patterns and sewing machines. All this flourished despite the slogan that called for fashion's "Utility and Beauty rather than its Frivolity and Extravagance."[93] With the benefits of sewing machines, inexpensive spool thread, pins, patterns, and new fabrics, Victorians measured sartorial beauty by complexity, in part because it was newly possible and in part because, if she could not afford a seamstress, it measured the time a woman could spend sewing for herself and her children, rather than attending to subsistence. From every direction, advertisements and other popular media proclaimed new standards for sewing, washing, and ironing that required the new devices.[94] As an advertisement for the Empire Wringer of the 1890s cheerily declared on its reverse side, "You can do twice the work! And no more labor required!" (fig. 3.2).

Even before industrialization, Americans were no strangers to the idea of guarding their time, as the eighteenth-century popularity of Benjamin Franklin's writings and the prevalence of town clocks and criers and other marks of public time testify.[95] Industrialization and urbanization intensified the requirements that individuals regiment their time with increasing energy and focus. In order for an industrial system to function tightly and efficiently, its ambient cultural system must prepare participants to value the hours and minutes of their lives. This acceleration of life's pace and each individual's perceived need to exploit every minute in order to be a valued person has been one of the harshest costs of material progress.[96] Industrialists of necessity were early sensitized to the importance of time and efficiency. They projected onto their advertisements their preoccupation with regimenting time in both their private and public lives, for themselves as well as their families and their workers. In an industrial system with large numbers of interdependent workers and massive investments in capital equipment, inefficiency and breakdowns that lead to underutilization of either labor or machines are always costly, then as now. Advertisers constantly offered to factory operators remedies for inefficiency. A brochure for Smith's Patent Belt Fasteners did so more colorfully than usual: in a series of cartooned panels, a factory manager, Mr. Energy, struggled for efficiency in his factory despite the continual breaking of the belts that transmitted power to his machinery. During downtime, a clock on the wall counted the minutes while workers stood idly with their hands in their pockets or stared out the window. On one such occasion, a paternalistic Uncle John came to the rescue, offering his belt fasteners to the beleaguered industrialist. Mr. Energy later told Uncle John that the new belt fasteners "are worth their weight in gold to us" if they could keep the machinery and workers producing. To reinforce this message, the brochure's copy explained, "You cannot afford to use anything else . . . [to avoid] loss of time." After all, time is money. An 1891 McCormick advertising booklet symbolized the link between time and production with a full-page illustration of a pocket watch on which tiny schematics of McCormick machines marked the minutes; beside the watch, a picture of the McCormick factory accompanied the message, "A complete machine is built every minute."[97]

Clocks in Victorian advertisements generally measured the efficiency of the promoted technological innovation, for home as well as industry. The American Chopper Company advertised by comparing the time-consuming and wasteful preindustrial ways of chopping food with their invention's new, easy, and efficient way that left time for nurturing children. In one scene on a double trade card, the ineffectiveness of an old technology kept a tired, eighteenth-century woman working into the dark of the night. With the American Chopper in the second scene, a modern mother fulfilled more idealized familial duties: she reads to her daughter, who operates the new chopper easily, her attention on her mother's social and spiritual instructions. Advertisements for many laundry products, both chemical and mechanical, also compared the success of two women, as measured by how early their laundry hung on the line. The first woman always demonstrated the harmful consequences of her trying to meet the Victorians' new standards of cleanliness with old-fashioned or inferior products, and her family was distressed because she had to neglect them—like the woman whose husband failed to buy proper stove polish. The progressive woman, on the other hand, could attend to her family's practical, emotional, and social needs because she used the advertised product. In one comparison, an unkempt Mrs. Fogy still washed at noon with "common soap," glaring at her crying child, whereas a calm and attractive Mrs. Enterprise could comfort her child at nine o'clock in the morning because she used Dobbins' Electric Soap. The standards distinguishing the old-fashioned, and therefore unacceptable, with the progressive were often exceedingly harsh. For instance, the 9:00 A.M. standard for finishing the washing in the Dobbins' Electric Soap story line pervaded late-nineteenth-century advertisements for laundry products. One manufacturer even named a laundry soap Nine O'Clock Washing Tea, and its trademark, a tall case clock, dominated its advertisements and packages. The hands on the clock pointed to nine o'clock, and a woman (simply but well-dressed) happily saluted the clock because her wash was already on the line. In reality, however, laundry still took at least half a day until well after the turn of the century, when electrically powered machines became available. This genre of advertisements set stringent standards for women to accomplish the nearly impossible.

The importance of clocks in the Victorian advertisements for domestic technologies heralded the arrival of regimentation in the lives of homemakers and other domestic workers that came along with modernization. The industrialists who commissioned these advertisements patterned them after that discipline of the clock long since known to them and their workers. Probably not intended as deliberately unkind attempts to regiment homes, these messages reflected the experiences and presumptions of the advertising manufacturers and the mode of operation in their own sphere. It only made sense that homes, like factories, would operate more efficiently if on a strict schedule. Women numbered among the strongest advocates of efficiency in the home during the second half of the nineteenth century and much of the twentieth. Home economics in 1899 became the title for the movement to measure women's housework by the same time-and-motion criteria as industrial work, and to improve its efficiency, if not its satisfaction. Home economics advocates were often subsidized by industry;[98] that way, as through advertisements, businesses could advance progress, as they saw it, in the American home.

In the last decades of the century, the Ansonia Clock Company offered its products as a way of relieving the tensions and anxieties that plagued the pro-

**Fig. 4.10.** Many chromo-lithographed advertisements featured pictures created by printers that were unrelated to the product being advertised. Most of these were stock images on which retailers and wholesalers overprinted their names and locations. In the 1890s, manufacturers increasingly purchased large quantities of stock images in thematic sets, especially on trade cards like this one called "Morning of Life" for John Reardon & Sons. This was one in an 1887 series of twenty-five portraits that they distributed across the country seeking to maximize their reach, if not the specificity of their message. Even the backs of the cards in this series made no mention of product features, not even that the soaps might foster such loveliness as the cards portrayed.

gressive individual who recognized the importance of punctuality but who lacked the technology to ensure success. One of their mechanical trade cards (one that folds to form two different scenes) begins by picturing an insomniac—a man distraught with worry about how to keep his appointments. Anxiety about waking up in a timely fashion each morning had kept him awake too many nights, and his health was failing. A patent-medicine bottle on the table indicates the sad state to which he has been brought by his concerns. When opened, the card shows that the modern hero has solved his problems with an alarm clock that gives him the confidence to get adequate rest and be "fat and happy." The efficient use of time characterized successful Victorians, men and women, because their access to novel technologies facilitated their achieving all their other goals for personal worth according to progressive standards. Clocks measured the enhanced efficiency with which people were expected to fit more and more tasks into their days. As historian David Landes has stated, in our modern world "time is the most inexorable of disciplinarians."[99]

*Production as Progress*

# Nonindustrial Images: Abundance and Stock Pictures

Compared with the spareness of twentieth-century design, Victorian advertisements—like most of the period's decorative arts—exude a striking opulence. The era's stylistic proclivities can be attributed, in part, to the combined effects of more people having more wealth to display, to the competition between manufacturers for market share with increased mechanical capacities to produce objects for display, and to the allure of novelty. Certainly, printers' fascination with all of their typographic options compounded their competitiveness in the production of printed extravagances. Not all of their excesses can be credited to other sources of fashion. To judge by their advertisements, many manufacturers seem to have exulted in the abundance they produced. They showed yeast and soap products making mammoth mounds of bread and suds. They showed giant candy canes, corncobs, and coconuts, or copious quantities of jellies, pies, soup, and other foods delighting children and adults. In this genre of bounty far removed from any hint of industry—as either factory production or personal diligence—they pictured exotic lands, fanciful dreams, cherubs, and fairies as their products' origins. Children were plump and never had to miss play because their shoes fell apart; packaged foods saved castaways who always fed babies first. These nonindustrial messages of abundance, like the frequent cornucopia within industrial images, associated manufacturers with the provision of great abundance. Whether motivated by pride, self-congratulation, or even a nascent concern with consumer-oriented messages, this genre of advertisements portrayed, if with some considerable exaggeration, what the industrialists' cornucopia could provide.[100] Whether it actually might benefit consumers—be it yeast that expanded to overfill an oven or a candy cane large enough to serve as a seesaw—mattered less than the industrialists' claims as producers.

Advertisers paid printers to create unique images for all of the advertisements discussed in this chapter thus far. Yet many chromo advertisements, especially trade cards, were overprints; that is, printers' stock images on which advertisers had printed or stamped their business identity and location. Retailers could rarely afford to have a special image designed and printed for themselves and therefore used stock overprints almost exclusively. Some manufacturers also used overprints as a cost expedient; others sometimes commissioned prints with basic, generic images that can only be discriminated from stock prints by the way in which their names were printed onto the images. The New Home Sewing Machine Company distributed many series of trade cards on themes that pertained little or not at all to their product, such as scenes from foreign lands. John Reardon & Sons commissioned a set of trade

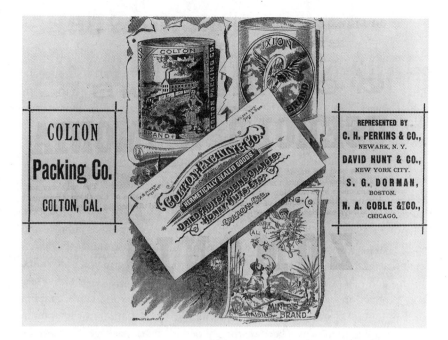

*Fig. 4.11.* The Colton Packing Company advertised the variety of its labels in the *American Grocer* 43, no. 2 (1890): 4. The firm offered food processors a range of images, from generic pictures of pretty scenes to cultural symbols that were irrelevant to specific firms but overlaid with a trademark. Portraits of factories could also be commissioned. Courtesy of Library of Congress.

cards as premiums in 1887 featuring lovely women—with no claims on either front or back of the cards regarding their soaps' contributions to such loveliness; there was only the implied association. In many cases, the pretty pictures in these generic advertising images gave consumers no information about the advertisers or their products other than that they existed and that they supported the printing and distribution of the prints (fig. 4.10). As a group, these generic images designed by printers provide an important contrast to specifically commissioned advertisements; they were created by different people for different purposes. The contrasts between these two categories of images therefore corroborate the thesis that the specifically commissioned creations reflected advertisers' own interests and preoccupations. A contemporary advertisement for a packing company showed the range of images it made available to clients, from pretty or allegorical stock images to grand, customized factory scenes (fig. 4.11).[101] In the light of the printers' feedback about what people bought and enjoyed as consumers of images—feedback that printers likely made available to their custom-work clients—the advertisers must have indeed been strongly motivated to project the images they did.

As a genre, stock images evince several important aspects of nineteenth-century advertising practices precisely because of their images' irrelevance to the firms they advertised and the businesspeople who purchased them. Showing nothing about the services or products being offered, advertisers simply intended the stock prints to act as a conduit by which to place their names before their markets as frequently as possible—a colorful analogue to the contemporary strategy of repeated small "cards" in the press media; often, not even the reverse side of a print carried more than a firm's name, location, and the nature of its business. Such images aimed for their audiences' tender emotions or humor—pretty women, adorable children, cunning animals, beautiful flowers or scenery, and religious or humorous scenes. Stock images rarely included images designed to evoke the grander emotions of national pride or industrial progress, such as eagles, steam engines, or abstract factories. Nor did they instruct consumers on the rising standards for bourgeois achievements— the Victorian compromise—or the value of work and time, as did the industrialists when they created their individualized messages. Consumer-oriented content, such as that which already flourished in the printers' stock images, only gradually became a standard advertising practice after professional communication and marketing experts began to assume the creative functions of advertising, in some cases wresting those functions from the advertisers.

Part Two

# SPECIALIZATION AS PROGRESS

# 5

# Early Advertising Specialists

*It is no longer practicable to have such an accurate or general knowledge of the value of advertising mediums as was possible before they became so very numerous, unless the whole time of several persons is devoted to it, and most advertisers, therefore, are content to leave this matter with an acute and well-informed advertising agent, of whom one or more are to be found in the larger cities.*

—George P. Rowell, Men Who Advertise, 1870

## The Original Niche

People calling themselves advertising agents operated in the United States by the 1840s, but they did not perform many of the functions we now associate with the advertising profession. Even in 1870, when George Rowell asserted that "most advertisers" turned to agents for assistance, those specialists performed a much narrower set of functions than they came to perform in the 1890s.

The economic developments of the first half of the nineteenth century changed the mechanisms as well as the volume of advertising practices. As long as merchants, both wholesale and retail, conducted their businesses on a local basis, they placed their advertisements directly with the people who operated the media where they wanted their messages seen or heard. Proprietors of merchant houses negotiated with a handful of newspaper publishers, job printers, sign makers, or even street criers, who then produced their advertisements. The messages themselves were generally straightforward, except for whatever flourishes street criers or sign painters took the liberty of adding as means of getting attention. This simple, localized system needed no intermediaries. By the 1840s, however, the first stage of U.S. industrialization was in full swing, with growing cities, developing transportation and communication networks, and increasing numbers of newspapers expanding their reach and size. Advertising, too, grew, facilitating the merchants' distribution of products from industry and world trade, and as it grew it became more complicated. As merchants all along the distribution channels competed more aggressively, their advertising alternatives increased. Job printers offered more options for handbills, almanacs, and posters, and an abundance of local newspapers and trade journals spread across the increased distances over which merchants and producers now competed. All of this increased the numbers and difficulties of transactions for the businesspeople who advertised, and those growing complexities very clearly coincided with the origins in the 1840s of the advertising agent as an intermediary.

Printers relied heavily on advertisers' expenditures during this period of business expansion, as they have ever since, whether they produced job printing to order, sold stock pictures to businesses in large volume, published periodicals, or took part in all of these. Periodical publishers always recognized the need for advertising revenues if they were to be competitive and expand their facilities; the American colonies' first successful newspaper, the *Boston News-Letter*, solicited advertisements in its first issue in 1704. By the 1840s, the increasing costs of their new printing presses and the rapidly expanding competition exacerbated publishers' long-standing needs for advertising revenues. The first advertising agents recognized the publishers' plight as an opportunity, and they exploited that opportunity by soliciting accounts on behalf of the publishers. By agreement, the agents drew most of their compensation in the form of commissions from the publishers based on the value of the space purchased by advertisers, setting precedents that have yet to be entirely overridden. So, even though Volney B. Palmer, the first such agent known to have operated in the United States, acquired accounts by convincing merchants that they would benefit from advertising and by offering to facilitate the transactions, he had to assure his prospects that they would not have to pay additionally for his services. They had only to pay for their advertisements at rates from the publishers that he assured were the best available. Through the nineteenth century, agents who could afford it sometimes also purchased space at reduced, high-volume rates, then sold that space in smaller units to advertisers at a profit, but still allegedly lower than the advertisers could have purchased on their own.

Operating essentially as independent agents for publishers but claiming to benefit advertisers, agents did not begin to question dividing their allegiances between publishers and advertisers until the 1870s. When this became an issue, the field split into two groups. One group consisted of advertising agents who served the advertisers, recognizing them rather than the publishers as their primary clients. The second group became newspaper and magazine agents who represented the interests of publishers explicitly. Still, the ambiguities of the agents' loyalties remained at issue for decades. Advertising agents thus carved a niche within the expanding marketplace at the point where the needs of advertisers and publishers intersected, and both sets of clients gradually, grudgingly accepted the agents' brokerage functions.[1] By 1869, a New York City business directory listed only forty-two advertising agents; in 1892, another listed 288.[2]

Many of the early advertising agents entered the field from publishing, having observed the publishers' needs first hand. Palmer, for example, solicited merchants' advertisements for his father's newspaper in New Jersey. Francis Wayland Ayer, whose agency, N. W. Ayer & Son, remains one of the world's largest, discovered the field by chance after a family friend hired him in 1868 for a job that included soliciting advertisements in Philadelphia for a weekly religious newspaper. Claude C. Hopkins, who became a leading copywriter in a later generation of advertising professionals, also had his interest first piqued in advertising while working for his father's small-town newspaper, soliciting advertisements from and distributing handbills for local merchants. The merchants' determination to get their messages in the paper, whether by cash payment or barter, made a strong impression on the young Hopkins.[3] George P. Rowell, who became one of the most influential advertising practitioners of the nineteenth century, got his first city job in 1858 collecting bills and accounts for the Boston *Post*. The newspaper had no advertising solicitor then, so in quiet periods his employer sent Rowell out to inquire of merchants advertising in other papers whether their messages "should not also appear in the *Post*." Throughout Rowell's memoirs, *Forty Years an Advertising Agent*, he writes of advertising agents as "advertising solicitors" and "canvassers" whose most reliable alliances in the business world were with "newspaper men." Advertisers, on the other hand, remained uncertain components of the advertising trade, according to Rowell, even in the first decade of the twentieth century, when he produced his memoirs. Some advertisers promoted products that made fortunes for themselves and their agents, he wrote; mostly, however, they did not. Other times they produced trouble, and it was all rather unpredictable: "Sometimes unpromising customers will develop into good ones and again an apparently honest enterprise will turn out to be a trick or a fraud."

Rowell believed that only the newspapers and the agents themselves had clearly defined functions in the business world and could be relied upon to act predictably. Still, he regularly reminded the publishers of their debts to advertisers, including his 1867 parody of the testimonials of proprietary medicine advertisements: "Brandreth's Pills saved the life of the New York *Herald* in its infancy. It advertised them, and the sum paid for the work paid the printers."[4]

Because buying and selling space in newspapers and magazines and obtaining commissions from the publishers worked so readily, they, of all the media, fit best with the agents' operations. (Advertisements are commissionable if the medium wherein they are placed, usually a mass distribution medium such as a newspaper, magazine, or broadcast, makes available a commission to encourage middlemen to recruit advertisements.) In contrast, advertising agents generally discouraged advertisers from using noncommissionable media—such as posters and trade cards—which they attacked as "misuse" of expenditures. In this way, advertising agents tried to block the use of certain types of advertising forms that had, in some cases at least, proved to advance the progress of business. Rowell and other agents frequently argued that, "if the sign and show-card are successful in attracting patrons, so much the more so would be an attractive notice in the columns of the newspaper. It is then," he asserted, "not only the passers-by who read, but thousands beside, who never would think of gazing into a shop window for what they desire. The paper reaches a class that can be reached in no other way, and produces results to be arrived at by no other medium."[5] That said, Rowell was pained to admit in his memoirs that he successfully advertised his own business on one occasion with posters.[6] N. W. Ayer & Son flatly refused to assist clients with poster advertisements until the late 1890s. Prior to then, the Ayer agency "regarded [posters] as an unsightly and undignified method of sales promotions." Ayer deemed posters inappropriate for any firm other than a patent-medicine company because of their content and also because they were put up in public and private places indiscriminately, often without the permission of the owners of those places. Furthermore, it was difficult to ensure that posters for which the agency had paid were displayed according to contract. Billboards therefore did not receive favorable evaluations from Ayer and other major advertising agents until the late 1890s, after bill posters and distributors began to consolidate and formalize their organizations, improving their reliability and making it possible for advertising agents to collect their fees. (In the early twentieth century, advertising organizations and publications likewise widely opposed advertising on radio broadcasts. They even lobbied Congress to block it, until they found ways to earn commissions from that medium, too.)[7] Finally, in 1900, the Ayer agency proclaimed that "thirty years' experience in advertising has given us our own ideas about Posters and Posting." Neglecting to remind potential advertisers that those ideas had been quite negative until a few years before, the notice continued, "If you have an idea your posting can be bettered, we would like to give you our idea as to the 'how' of doing it."[8]

By the 1840s the administrative efforts to place advertisements in newspapers throughout expanding markets had become a burden on many businesses. As early as 1842, Palmer offered his services to "the enterprising business portion of the community" to assist them in the increasingly complex business of advertising outside of their own purview. His agency "afford[ed] an excellent opportunity" to "publish extensively abroad their respective pursuits—to learn the terms of subscription and advertising, and accomplish their object here without the trouble of perplexing and fruitless inquiries, the expense and labour of letter writing, the risk of making enclosures of money &c, &c."[9] In 1874, Rowell divided "the patrons of advertising agencies" into two groups based on their needs for the services Palmer had outlined thirty-two years earlier. The first group comprised "advertisers in the largest cities" who needed assistance in advertising locally. However, "the principal patrons of the Advertising Agent are those who wish to reach distant points." The majority of these were patent-medicine sellers and entertainers drumming in advance of their shows, but they also included manufacturers seeking sales agents around the country or who were selling their products directly to consumers through the mails. In 1874, Rowell claimed that "the Advertising Agency is a convenience; it is nothing more."[10]

Although some business owners, such as Wanamaker and Macy, appreciated early on the value of advertising broadly, others were more reluctant, and some flatly refused to incur the expenses of such an uncertain undertaking. Enough of the intermediate group—those who were simply reticent—responded to the advertising agents' solicitations to feed the agents' ambitions. Beginning with Palmer, agents visited and wrote businesses to argue both for the potential of advertising to increase revenues and for their own abilities to facilitate placing the advertisements most effectively and efficiently. By the 1870s, some agents had begun to publish periodicals and brochures, such as Rowell's *Advertising Gazette: A Magazine of Information for Advertisers*, to tout the benefits of advertising in general and their authors' agencies in particular. Advertising agencies also applied their skills on behalf of their own businesses by placing their own advertisements in business publications, in general publications, and even on city walls.

## Advertising Agents' Secondary Functions

Because the first generations of advertising practitioners did not, as a rule, write copy or lay out advertisements, their contributions have been generally demeaned by their successors and others. The epithet *space broker* has usually been preceded by *only* or *just*, then accompanied by the assessment that these were unproductive middlemen who merely kept accounts and ran errands between advertisers and publishers. Yet however we value their efforts, some pre-1890s agents provided four functions secondary to placing advertisements that affected the market's evolution. They all built up the volume of advertisements in periodicals; some worked to regularize the rates and procedures for placing advertisements in the press; many sought to prevent substitution of unadvertised for advertised products; and most offered free guidance to advertisers about the practice of advertising. Whether or not drawing businesspeople into the advertising process was a social or a business good, these activities certainly did accelerate the growth of the advertising field and those businesses, such as periodical publishing and large-scale consumer product manufacturing, that came to depend on it.

Space brokering's rewards were directly proportional to the space sold, and the records of the early advertising agents are full of prideful tales of successful forays into the business world to solicit and encourage clients. (In the late twentieth century, other means of compensation have been developed to lessen the correlation between buying time and space in media and agency revenues.) Indeed, early agency work centered on solicitation. Francis Wayland Ayer, who named the Ayer agency after his father, N. W. Ayer, "devoted most of the ordinary working hours to canvassing prospective customers," then executing the orders in his "spare time." Once the agency grew large enough to specialize internally, Ayer's Business-Getting Department remained the core of the agency until the 1920s, promoting "the use of advertising and to urge advertisers to employ the Ayer agency." Self-proclaimed advertising experts offered plenty of advice about the best ways to solicit. Rowell's advice to young admen in 1905, for instance, included keeping "your health good, your conscience clean." Increasing their billings (the dollar volume of advertising placements) was so essential to them that agents felt compelled to deny frequently that they succumbed to the "temptation to urge upon the client a greater expenditure for advertising than his business situation really justifies." Their own long-term interests were best served, they assured the world, by successful, not extravagant, clients. Rowell told young canvassers that their most important tool was believing that their successes would result from soliciting orders "that you think the advertiser would do well to give you."[11]

Practitioners increased their arguments' reach by soliciting potential clients through their own publications and by advertising their services in the press. In 1850, Volney B. Palmer quoted a strongly worded essay by Horace Greeley, himself a newspaperman, who linked advertising with business progress, although less as a cause of change in itself than as a tool for aggressive competitors who cause change. "Extensive advertising of itself," Greeley assessed, "is morally certain to work a revolution in trade, by driving thousands of the easygoing out of it, and concentrating business in the hands of the few who know how to obtain and keep it."[12]

Greeley's concept became a key notion in the field; in 1886, N. W. Ayer & Son began publicizing its motto, "Keeping Everlastingly At It Brings Success." This phrase summarized the attitudes of many other advertising agents in promoting their field to advertisers. Accordingly, other agency mottos in the 1880s and 1890s included Harlan P. Hubbard's "Judicious Advertising is the Keystone of Success" and T. C. Evans's "Systematic and Persistent Advertising The Sure Road to Success in Business."[13] In 1867, Rowell asserted the case even more strongly. "The man who refuses to patronize the newspaper," he declaimed, "is the man of morbid disposition, of small ideas and no business talent. His light, if *he has any*, is so completely concealed beneath the bushel of self that it will never burn to any practical purpose." Two decades later, he borrowed an editorial from *Table Talk* that declared, "Any individual or firm who is unwilling to keep pace with modern progress and adjust his methods to the wants of his age, does not merit success; neither can he reasonably expect to secure it to any large degree." An illustrated advertisement for Rowell's agency in 1889 again exhorted businesses to display their individual lights by advertising. It showed that the light emanating from "America" was blocked by a bushel, perhaps the same bushel that had plagued unprogressive businessmen in 1867.[14] In the same vein, Rowell later advised that although "as a general thing the advertiser cannot tell whether a particular advertisement pays him or does not, . . . the most he knows, as a rule, is that when he advertises most he does most business, and makes most money."[15]

As space brokers, early advertising agents faced conflicts of interest with no established procedures or standards. Many practitioners did their best to exploit the situation, playing publisher off against advertiser, and vice versa. Still, the advertising professionals whose names have survived for a century worked zealously to establish standards and procedures for their field. F. Wayland Ayer and J. Walter Thompson tried to improve conditions largely through the practices of their own agencies. Their influence as models resulted, in large part, because in the process of reevaluating and reforming their profession, they built two of the most successful agencies in the country.

George Rowell tried to change public and business opinions on a broad scale through his publications. According to him, one of the great sources of corruption and inefficiency in the business world was irregularity in advertising procedures; therefore, through the *Advertiser's Gazette* and later through *Printers' Ink,* he urged publishers to state their circulation figures honestly. In 1869 he founded the first newspaper directory in America—the first anywhere that included circulations. Of course, the rates for advertising space that publications could ask of their advertisers depended primarily on their circulations, then as now, so publishers were highly motivated to exaggerate their reports. For decades, Rowell tried to convince publishers that businesses would be more likely to advertise overall, benefiting all publishers, not to mention agents, if they could trust the commodity they were buying; namely, quantities of audience per dollar. Despite his indignation at the dishonest figures of "circulation-swindlers," Rowell was accused by publishers of padding the figures in the *Directory* on behalf of papers that advertised in it. Whatever the truth of those accusations, many other advertising agencies recognized the advantage of circulation information to their clients and started up their own directories; like Rowell's, these doubled as promotions for themselves.[16] When advertising practitioners began to form professional organizations in the last years of the century, these set high priorities on regularizing placement rates and procedures.

It also concerned agents when retailers and wholesalers substituted unadvertised products for heavily advertised products, thereby profiting while reducing advertisers' incentives and threatening agents' livelihoods. Many agents attacked such practices and promoted action against substitution on behalf of producers. Artemas Ward for instance, a leading member of the third generation of advertising specialists, argued that some manufacturers, including nostrum sellers, could and should claim limited protections from the courts because their products, labels, and often even container shapes were patented, and those who had international sales could claim protection through the existing trademark statutes. So despite the poverty of laws protecting domestic trademarks, he criticized manufacturers for their legal inaction, writing in 1891 that they were "much to blame for this condition of affairs. Very few of them have the courage of their convictions." Ward also reminded manufacturers that their expenditures on newspaper advertisements were enough to expect editorial support of their interests. "The gross [dollar value of] advertising of most proprietary articles is larger than the [manufacturers'] net profits, and therefore the newspapers are the largest stockholders in these enterprises. In defending manufacturers against the evils of substitution, publishers will be really defending themselves and their own interests."[17] If manufacturers lost their profits and their ability to advertise nationally, newspapers would thereby lose their primary source of revenues.

Advertising agents served their interests as space brokers and developed the field in yet another indirect way by offering free guidance to clients about the practice of advertising on an informal, ad hoc basis; agents published some advice to advertisers about preparing messages both in agents' own advertisements and in trade journals. In 1886, for instance, N. W. Ayer & Son placed an advertisement in *Farm Implement News*, a "monthly illustrated newspaper devoted to the manufacture, sale and use of agricultural implements and their kindred interests." Ayer admonished manufacturers to remember the consumer and to "talk to the man who USES your line of goods. . . . The consumer READS, & in *his* newspaper you can talk to him THOUGHTFULLY— CONVINCINGLY— PERSISTENTLY— PROFITABLY." But then, manufacturers should not "expect to master the science of advertising in a few days or even months." That was what years of experience had taught the Ayer agency.[18]

In the matter of educating the advertising businessman, George Rowell took a leading position because he broadcast more than isolated tips by which to attract clients. His directory of newspapers made public in 1869 what had been the private domain of advertising agencies—information collected at great expense. By 1874, he also set up the first reading room that made available to advertisers "all newspapers published in the United States or Dominion of Canada." His house publications spread his reputation and expertise through the business community, beginning with the *Advertiser's Gazette* in 1866. In its first year, Rowell's "Writing Advertisements" assured advertisers that there was "no reason, except lack of industry and wit, why advertisements are not intrinsically attractive. Advertising is not simply to tell people who want hats where to find them, but to make them want hats, or think they do."[19] Rowell sought to educate advertisers through *Printers' Ink* starting in 1888, fondly dubbing it "The Little Schoolmaster in the Art of Advertising." *Printers' Ink* remained the leading trade journal of the advertising business through the 1930s, continuing publication through the 1950s. Like his directory, Rowell's journal was quickly imitated, and advertisers had no end of advice available to them for the cost of a subscription. For example, "Do Your Advertisements Pay?" advised advertisers in 1888 to evaluate feedback by comparing the results of advertisements placed in different periodicals. The article also addressed issues of content, asking advertisers if they were "sure that the advertising itself is properly worded and displayed" and advising against using multiple typefaces in a single advertisement.[20]

## Owner-Manager Agency Operations

Like other owner-managed businesses, early advertising agencies operated entirely idiosyncratically, and they varied widely in degrees of honesty, inventiveness, and ambition, as well as in the services they offered to the advertisers. Founders' and proprietors' insights, characters, and abilities determined the directions that their individual businesses took. Their origins, experiences, and predilections shaped their agencies and their solutions to the problems of fitting into and generating a profit from the niche between advertisers and publishers. The names of the early agencies, N. W. Ayer & Son, George P. Rowell & Company, and J. Walter Thompson Company, for instance, indicate their entrepreneurial nature. Each founder saw fit to give his business his own name, except for F. Wayland Ayer (who, as noted earlier, named his agency after his father; he did so in part out of filial loyalty and in part to give it the appearance of longevity). The agencies themselves were small, usually consisting of the proprietor, an "estimator" who calculated rates, a checking clerk who certified that advertisements had, in fact, been placed by the newspapers, a bookkeeper, and an office boy. Generally the proprietor solicited new clients, negotiated with publications, and serviced any needs that clients had beyond figuring their advertising rates and keeping their accounts. Rowell's agency was the largest U.S. agency in the 1870s and 1880s, and its staff had about seven persons until late in that period, two more than most agencies, one to correspond and negotiate with the newspapers and another to collect payments.[21]

Small firms with entrepreneurial owner-managers have great flexibility in responding to both opportunities and problems.[22] The unsettled, rapidly expanding business environment that prevailed during the first half-century of the advertising agency combined with the absence of established patterns within the advertising field to foster diverse practices. People experimented within this primordial niche, but although hundreds of agents searched for profitable directions and practices for their firms, only a small number hit upon the combinations of policies that prospered in the early decades, thereby setting the precedents for their profession's course. It would be easy to credit them with genius and exemplary enterprise in accomplishing this, but their often fortuitous adaptations of specialization were largely responsible for their success.

During the formative periods of nineteenth-century entrepreneurial capitalism, as now, specialization spelled progress because it could reduce a business's transaction and information costs. As a result, a firm could handle, and profit from, more transactions by operating in a systematized, routinized manner than it could if it worked in more traditional, generalized, decision-by-decision fashion.[23] Accordingly, as the first generations of advertising men experimented within their volatile environment, seeking ways to exploit their new niche, successful agents each pioneered some specialized aspect of the interactions between advertisers and publishers. Significantly, while the specialties of each of the leaders undoubtedly overlapped with other, now largely unknown, competitors, they overlapped relatively little with each other in the first two generations of agents. When overlaps occurred, these owner-managers specialized further to gain differential competitive edges. In a sense, therefore, between them, a few leaders covered the major successful options as they existed before 1890. This complementary relationship was not planned; there was a market opportunity for each of their sets of functions and policies, and admen who, often by chance, took on the various opportunities first and most competitively became the leaders, as did Rowell, Ayer, and Thompson on the East Coast and Lord & Thomas in Chicago. The latter had dominated the Chicago market since 1873 and became prominent nationally by the end of the century. When early advertising agents tried other combinations of functions, including writing copy on a regular basis, no matter how much intelligence and enterprise they exhibited, the market did not reward their inventiveness.

## Agency Management and Specialization—The Leaders

George P. Rowell made an important mark on advertising history with his campaigns for honest circulation figures, his efforts to systematize the field, and his publications to educate both advertisers and other advertising practitioners. Still, it was his "system" to broker newspaper space that made him prosper. Started in 1874 and reported in 1875 by the *New York Times,* this new system had "succeeded in working down a complex business into so thoroughly a systematic method that no change in the newspaper system of America [such as, changing rates or circulations] can escape notice, while the widest information upon all topics interesting to advertisers is placed readily at the disposal of the public." Rowell's new system included specializing in newspaper advertising "to make ourselves master of it," and taking responsibility for full payment to publishers for advertisements printed; the system attracted clients by guaranteeing them the lowest rates. In turn, Rowell was able to use the size of his clientele to negotiate favorable rates with newspaper publishers.[24] His thinking about the nature of the agents' services led him to assert, when announcing this new system, that while his business represented both the publisher and the advertisers, "advertising agencies succeeded best when studying the interests of advertisers not newspapers." According to this new system, advertisers who wished Rowell's services would have to accept his statements that his rates were in fact the best available to them and not demand that he bid against other agencies for their business. Nonetheless, despite his insistence that "we will not hereafter be a party to any competition for advertising contracts," Rowell in fact often underbid Ayer for accounts.[25] His system was, therefore, a goal, not an immediately established reality.

The most important aspect of Rowell's system for the long-term development of the advertising field was its nascent orientation toward the advertisers as the agency's clients. Rowell continued to feel more comfortable with the newspaper publishers as business associates, but as early as the 1870s he recognized that the direction of specialization that held the most potential for advertising agents was toward becoming independent advertisers' agents and away from the limitations of newspapers' agents. The ambiguities of the agents' position vis-à-vis the advertisers and the publishers took decades to resolve.[26] In declaring his new system, Rowell began the client-centered perspective in the hectic, volatile, highly competitive business environment between 1870 and 1890. Even so, it was F. Wayland Ayer, not Rowell, who would truly make service to the client his keynote. Ayer took Rowell's statement immediately to heart because he saw Rowell's declaration as a challenge as well as a solution for a personal dilemma. Nonetheless, neither man actually turned their field around yet, and bidding continued.[27] Other business and operating conditions had to change first.

Of all of the early agents, we have the most information about Ayer, and his story perfectly exemplifies the success to be gained from a chance matching of personal characteristics with a potentially lucrative niche. Of those early figures who had any renown at all, Ayer's reputation for a high moral character and religious fervor was unsurpassed. His closest competitor, Rowell, described Ayer as "an indomitable worker; thinks of work all the time, eats little, drinks nothing but water; has no vices, small or large, unless overwork is a vice; is the picture of health; and I sometimes think a good deal such a man as Oliver Cromwell would have been had Oliver been permitted to become an advertising agent."[28] Like many other agents, Ayer had started out his advertising agency as a means to a livelihood that required little capital. Unlike most of the others, however, Ayer considered his career a calling, and he always operated honestly. Like the other leaders, Ayer avoided the short-term gains taken by those who pressured publishers for low rates to supplement commissions while charging advertisers high rates and using the veil of trade secrecy to cover the deception.

Given these inclinations, Ayer experienced a personal crisis in 1874 when a respected friend of his deceased father accused him of being "nothing but a drummer." This man offered Ayer a position in another business of greater repute so that the young man might redeem himself. This assault on his self-esteem came just about the same time that Ayer learned of Rowell's rethinking of the nature of the advertising business, and the combination of challenges prompted Ayer to revamp his agency's practices and policies. In a sense, he later wrote, that was "really for me the beginning of this business. I said to myself, 'I will not be an order taker any longer. I will . . . not be satisfied just to make money. I will have a business, I will mean something to somebody every time I take any business, and I will have clients rather than people who just give me orders.'"[29] Whether or not his epiphany occurred just as Ayer reported it is not as important as the fact that this principle did come to govern his business behavior. And because of the responsiveness of small firms to their proprietors' inclinations, Ayer was able to move his agency in the direction he wished. It was his good fortune that taking this direction at that time made Ayer wealthy and made N. W. Ayer & Son "the greatest institution of the sort that has thus far come into being in any part of the world," in Rowell's admiring words.[30]

Ayer restructured his agency's practices in such a way as to set the standards for service in the field for decades. As he reiterated the firm's purpose at its fiftieth anniversary celebration, it was "to make advertising pay the advertiser, and at the same time to develop, magnify and dignify advertising as a business." From the time of Ayer's new insights, "we asked our customers to recognize that what they needed was service; that we were in position to supply that service; . . . that we were entitled to payment with a profit, and that a commission added to the net amounts credited to publishers was the fairest basis for our payment and profit." Ayer claimed that his new approach, the "open contract," was ridiculed by other agents—until it began to reduce failures and to gain business.[31] In 1925, when Albert Lasker wrote his reminiscences, he recalled that he "never knew a time when they [N. W. Ayer & Son] didn't have the very finest of business practice. . . . He [F. W. Ayer] gave service."[32]

Among the early consequences of Ayer's determination to realign agency functions was the first known concerted market survey, in 1879, taken on in order to lure a valuable client from Rowell. In this case, Henry Nelson McKinney, Ayer's partner since January 1878, took seriously the prospective client's challenge to come up with a more efficient list of newspapers in which to place his advertisements for threshing machines. All agency personnel, including Ayer and McKinney, searched governmental and published sources to build lists of counties producing threshable grains and the rates and circulations of the newspapers most likely to be read by the farmers in those areas.

Such unprecedented information gathering won a lucrative contract from the surprised manufacturer.[33] This was only one of countless instances when doing what Ayer wanted to do—namely, making his agency a respectable, responsible, service business—enhanced his agency's material success at the same time.

Although Ayer liked to claim years later that the new, open-contract system was soon instituted, in fact it took years of patient adjustment on the part of both agent and clientele. It required a level of trust between both parties that was not standard practice in the advertising niche of the 1870s. Indeed, it was almost a year before Ayer signed his first client under the new regime. In order to keep his profits up, Ayer still purchased and sold space through the 1890s, and he still negotiated with publishers in order to obtain profitable rates.[34] Nonetheless, Ayer promoted his agency from the middle 1870s forward as the firm from which advertisers could receive the best and most honest service. By 1880, he encouraged his staff to reject accounts that "were not of a character to do credit to the agency or because the results would be disappointing to the advertiser," according to a newspaper article of 1887.[35] In 1886, he began to advertise his agency as a professional counselor. He went so far in 1887 as to distribute a circular entitled "Our Creed" to communicate his principles of service first and foremost in the clients' interests.[36] In his *Directory* for 1888, Ayer wrote, "Having large experience, unequaled facilities, and abundant capital, we believe we can be of real service to such advertisers as desire intelligent, thoughtful, honest service." That same year, a *Manual for Advertisers*, which actually contained promotions for N. W. Ayer & Son rather than instructions for advertisers, included the proposal that advertisers should "Ask N. W. Ayer & Son what they can do for you."[37]

J. Walter Thompson, the third major advertising agent of this period, specialized in magazine advertising. He prospered in part because he claimed this branch of advertising first and in part because he recognized what advertisers have known ever since: that magazines optimize the targeting of many profitable markets. As with the other successful agents, Thompson succeeded in his specialty by a combination of chance and personal inclinations. His first job in advertising came in 1868 as a clerk for W. J. Carlton's agency in New York City, having been earlier rejected by George Rowell, who misjudged that the young applicant "would be too easily discouraged for an advertising man." Carlton and his early partner, a Mr. Smith, had chosen to specialize by placing advertisements for clients into religious weeklies and then later branched out into general magazines. In 1864, the religious weeklies were an open field, and Carlton & Smith solicited heavily as special agents for their "list" of these publications. After Smith retired, Carlton's personal bent inclined him toward literary magazines. He preferred reading them to soliciting for them, however,

*Specialization as Progress*

and left the advertising field to open a bookstore in 1878. Thompson then purchased the agency, renamed it, and discovered that the firm was at risk unless he could quickly increase its income. He decided that developing further the firm's existing specialization held the most promise and focused his energies on developing the general magazine as an advertising medium.[38]

Thompson quickly surpassed Carlton's level of business by soliciting additional accounts for the magazines he already handled. He then began to build up his reputation and income by acquiring the exclusive rights to place advertisements in many of the best, and previously aloof, literary magazines, most notably *Harper's Monthly*. He operated, therefore, as a special agent; that is, essentially as a representative for the magazine publishers on his list. This alone would have assured him a good income. His great success, however, came when he learned to convince advertisers to place advertisements through his listings by arguing for the differential identities of the magazines' audiences, both between each other and as a group that was distinct from newspapers. According to his successor, Stanley Resor, Thompson's major contribution to advertising practice was his "realization that the high grade magazines had a commercial value as a vehicle for reaching a desirable market under desirable auspices." As late as 1889, when he began to handle newspaper accounts as well, Thompson handled 80 percent of national magazine advertising as special agent for almost all American magazines. Through his contracts with magazines, he controlled general magazine advertising so tightly that other advertising agents had to share publishers' commissions with him in order to place their clients' advertisements.[39] Furthermore, his influence on the magazines he handled was sufficient to persuade them to carry products they otherwise had opposed, including some patent medicines. For example, he bragged in 1883 that he had compelled *Century* to carry Lydia Pinkham advertisements even though "they may not like it."[40]

By carving his own specialization out of the niche between advertisers and magazine publishers, Thompson competed directly with no established agencies; he seems, therefore, to have earned the respect of the field without incurring resentment. Nonetheless, given how much the magazine industry had grown prior to Thompson's studied exploitation of it as an advertising medium, it seems unreasonable to credit him, as many observers did, with its continued expansion after 1878. The growth of urban and rural markets, the continued development of railroad networks, improved printing technologies, and the favorable postal rates offer more adequate explanations. And then there were the newly aggressive publishers, foremost among them, Cyrus K. Curtis, founder with Louisa Knapp Curtis of the *Ladies' Home Journal*. While not questioning the value of Thompson's labors in bringing advertisers and magazines together, it seems that there could scarcely have been a more propitious microniche for an ambitious and capable young man to have come across at the time. What was remarkable was his capacity to stake a monopoly claim on this opportunity, leaving us to wonder how the magazine field might have developed had he not controlled it so closely. In any case, there is no question that the field of general magazines expanded with, if not because of, his encouragement.

Between 1880 and 1890, the number of magazines increased 93 percent, average circulation increased 50 percent, and advertising revenues grew twofold or threefold. The growth was so great that Thompson's success worked against him by the turn of the century. Once publishers began to appreciate the competitive edge that income from advertising could bring them, they no longer needed persuasion to open their pages to it. Similarly, once advertisers came to appreciate the benefits of sending their messages to the magazines' select circulations, they no longer needed Thompson's persuasion, and they in turn encouraged the magazines to let their exclusive contracts with Thompson lapse. N. W. Ayer & Son began to place magazine advertisements in 1896, shortly after Thompson's announcement that he would begin newspaper placements. N. W. Ayer & Son shared their commissions with Thompson when they had to, but encouraged magazines to work independently of Thompson's exclusive listing, underbidding Thompson when necessary. The result was that by the time Resor took over J. Walter Thompson Company in 1916, the firm had temporarily lost its preeminence, even though Thompson had moved into newspapers.[41]

Thompson's reputation as an advertising pioneer also derived from another aspect of his work with magazines. Because magazine audiences are generally defined by interest and social class rather than geography and ethnicity, as are newspaper audiences, Thompson came to a rudimentary appreciation for what is now called target marketing, that is, reaching and appealing to specific market segments. This notion formed when he began to argue the advantages of magazines over newspapers because of their more select audiences. In 1889, the agency's first house advertisement argued that magazines "reach the homes of well-to-do people who have the means to purchase and intelligence to appreciate the desirability of an article brought to their notice." Thompson also realized that magazines were the primary means to reach women in these "well-to-do" homes.[42] When he combined that observation with his intuitive conclusion that women made or controlled many types of family purchasing decisions, he both enhanced the value of advertising in "better" magazines and made an important, albeit coarse, step toward segmenting the population into markets defined by characteristics other than geography, ethnicity, or occupation.

In both the limited sense of the word *specialist* as used by the advertising business and the broader business sense, Thompson as well as the other leading advertising men were all quite notable. In true owner-manager fashion, J. Walter Thompson was still the "Man at the Helm" in 1898, according to a headline in *Profitable Advertising*, a trade publication out of Boston. He would remain so until he retired in 1916. The article below the headline ended with the assessment that "Mr. Thompson is one of the most notable examples of the development of the specialist in commercial life this country has ever produced."[43] Of course, if one were to consider avenues of specialization outside the advertising field, this evaluation was more than a little hyperbolic. Within the field, however, it was an accurate assessment. Specialization maximized transactions by minimizing costs per transaction. It also provided a way to differentiate one's business, as did each of these leading early advertising agents. As Rowell put it, a "new advertising agency must specially represent something; must be headquarters for something, and depend upon that special representation to gain a hearing. These are days of specialization even more than in the past." Because advertisers were "not looking for people who can do everything, they are more interested in those who can do some one thing well that nobody else can do at all."[44] Each of these agencies—N. W. Ayer & Son, George P. Rowell Advertising Agency, and J. Walter Thompson Company— pioneered in different opportunities available within the niche between advertisers and publishers. Each of them took on different combinations of the possible alternatives as their specialized functions, defining the advertising agency business according to their own experiences and inclinations. Others worked in the niche, but these three happened upon the combinations first that proved most profitable and reasonable to the advertisers, defining the field for those early decades within an increasingly complex business environment.

## Responsibilities for Copywriting

When advertising agents wrote advertisements to publicize their own brokerage services, that was the only regular occasion on which they wrote copy before the changes in business practices of the early 1890s. Exceptions existed, such as Harlan Page Hubbard, who offered to write his clients' copy and often found himself at odds with them about the results.[45] In 1874, Rowell stated the typical policy, writing, "Advertisers desiring to avail themselves of the facilities possessed by our agency, are requested to send a concise statement of what they wish to do, accompanied *always* with a copy of the advertisement." Two years earlier he even declared that "the man who cannot do this is not fit to advertise." In his 1906 memoirs, Rowell continued to warn other practitioners that "if an advertiser develops a tendency to trust his advertising plans entirely to you, you should go slow; . . . for if he fails to succeed he will blame you."[46] Many of the most successful agents of the first two generations opposed absorbing copywriting as a regular function, even when it became necessary to compete with others. After all, the advertising agents considered themselves businesspeople, not "literary men," as early copywriters were called. S. M. Pettengill and many other early agents willingly offered "valuable suggestions as to the size, style and position which will make the most effective advertisement for the object to be attained," but they generally expected the advertisers or printers to write the words.[47] As it suited his fancy, Pettengill might write an advertisement, but more for the pleasure of writing than with any sense that he might write more effective copy because of his experience. I. N. Soper saw little need or opportunity for creativity in advertisements in 1874. His *Advertisers' Manual* did not claim "many *original* features, for the whole subject of advertising has been so frequently and thoroughly canvassed, that it has become singularly barren of freshness and novelty." It offered simply "many facts and figures, which advertisers, with the exercise of ordinary tact and intelligence, can utilize [in creating their own advertisements] with profit and advantage."[48]

Even in 1892, when N. W. Ayer & Son hired its first full-time copywriter, John J. Geisinger, founder F. Wayland Ayer told the new man that advertisers were still the persons best qualified to write their own messages. (Jarvis A. Wood had started writing copy for Ayer part time in 1888, but he had not been specifically hired for that purpose.) Daniel M. Lord, founder of Lord & Thomas, the major Chicago agency, felt likewise after an early client rebuked his advice about how an advertisement might be improved, "Young man, you may know a lot about advertising, but you know very little about the furniture business." By the 1880s, Lord reportedly was "aghast, and rather resented the idea that he should be asked to do the advertiser's work for him," according to contemporary Charles Raymond. Lord & Thomas hired a part-time copywriter in the 1890s.[49] As late as 1916, J. Walter Thompson, another of the field's founding fathers, continued to oppose routinely offering additional creative services to clients, especially those advertising to consumers. In 1931, his successor Stanley Resor explained that "Mr. Thompson had been so successful he found it hard to meet changing conditions. He resented the idea of time devoted to plans, copy and other preparation work, with the result that the business was slipping, and it was not showing a profit." Despite his personal attitudes, Thompson had offered to assist advertisers with preparing advertisements for trade journals as early as 1889; he charged extra only if clients required assistance preparing illustrations.[50]

Consequently, if advertising agents wanted to experiment with copywriting and advertising content on a regular basis before the 1890s, they generally did so for their own companies, either their advertising agency or some proprietary (that is, brand-name) product—almost always a patent medicine. For many reasons, ad agencies often came to own patent-medicine firms, and for them they engaged in copywriting. In 1891, George Rowell decided that his twenty-five-year wish "to own a trademark, a proprietary article that might be advertised" could be best satisfied with a medicine. Determining that such a medicine "should be something so clean that no one could object to it on the score of impropriety" and that it should be useful for many ailments, Rowell and a medical friend spent a long time coming up with the formula for Ripans Tabules. They chose the name as a meaningless acronym of the medicine's components with which the public could associate the attributes Rowell claimed for the compound. He recorded his astonishment at "the great amount of work and thought involved in the preparation of the printed matter that must go with a proprietary article." After decades as a leading "adman," placing other people's advertisements, he found himself needing the advice of a man who had made a career of promoting patent medicines: "Write your advertisements to catch damned fools—not college professors . . . and you'll catch just as many college professors as you will of any other sort." After an initial period of massive advertising with no success, the public finally responded and bought Ripans Tabules in large quantities.[51] George Rowell might not have known how to write copy, but he knew how to get his messages placed to advantage.

Freelance writers often set the copywriting pace in the 1880s and 1890s; some could even make reasonable incomes from copywriting, indicating advertisers' growing willingness to pay for such assistance. John E. Powers was already an innovative and successful freelance when John Wanamaker set a precedent by hiring him in 1880, setting him up as the first American recorded to have worked full time on salary as a copywriting specialist. After writing copy that generated astounding sales and making an excellent income with Wanamaker—who refused to abdicate enough authority over his copy to suit Powers—the copywriter left to make a notoriously good income freelancing again after 1886. Even so, Powers saw the copywriter's role as a surrogate for the advertiser, performing only those functions that advertisers themselves could not: "Whatever a manufacturer can do better than anyone else, and has time to do, let him do it himself, or let it be done immediately under his supervision. Whatever parts of his process he cannot do himself, let him get it done by the person or concern that can do it honestly, capably and thoroughly." As publisher of the *Nation* for several years, he tried to educate advertisers in his publication about how they might make their advertisements more "distinctive" and, therefore, more effective. Powers led contemporaries toward his motto to "Say the right thing to the right people in an acceptable way," and to give audiences "reasons why" they should make their purchases.[52] "Pithy" and honest to a fault have been the usual epithets for Powers's style. He deliberately wrote without the formal, flowery, and effusive language that was standard for the time. He advocated short headlines and large type rather than maximizing the number of words in any given space, as did most advertisers. Powers's "common-place" and honest style came to be a standard for many retailers and other advertisers. In 1890, Wanamaker's management estimated that more than fifty retailers nationwide were imitating the Powers style.[53]

Despite Powers's success, in 1885 most freelances could do little more than "eke out a slender livelihood by writing advertisements for business houses whose proprietors lack the ability to attract attention by their own printed announcements," according to the *New York Times*.[54] Part of the freelances' difficulties resulted from the advertising agencies' gradual adaptation to advertisers' increasing concerns about copywriting. The major advertising agencies had begun to write copy and to assist with design before 1890, but only when their clients asked for help, and then often reluctantly. As the competition and intensity of advertising in periodicals increased after the mid-1880s, more and more advertisers felt the need for more effective copywriting and design. In their turn, whatever the agents' initial reluctance, they risked losing clients to competition if they ignored the growing requests from clients who did not want to incur the expense of freelance writers. As a rule, early assistance amounted to "polish[ing] up an occasional phrase or rewrit[ing] the message to fill a smaller space," according to N. W. Ayer & Son's historian Ralph Hower. Even so, in 1880 that agency announced to the business world that the "Composition, Illustration and Display of Newspaper Advertisements has so long been a study with us that we have become admittedly expert in preparing the best possible effects. Having at our command the services of an Artist, a Wood Engraver, and a number of Printers who have been for years engaged almost exclusively in this work under our direction, we possess entirely unequaled facilities for serving those who desire to entrust their business to our care." Yet, even with this announcement, Ayer and his partner John McKinney did not, according to Hower, truly consider the "actual writing of advertisements as the proper work or responsibility of the agent."[55]

Ayer and McKinney had accepted the responsibility of assisting their clients only when competition between clients and between agencies had reinforced their dawning realization that ineffective advertisements discouraged advertisers from buying space altogether. Therefore, despite their reluctance, in 1888 a new employee began spending much of his time at writing, and a house advertisement in 1889 showed increasing interest in encouraging clients to advertise effectively:

> Advertising *will not* make a permanent sale for a fraudulent thing, nor will it sell a thing that nobody wants. On the other hand, it *always* pays to wisely advertise a good thing if it meets a popular want, but in order to be profitable the advertisement must *attract* the attention of those who will become buyers, *convince* them of its merit and *interest* them in its purchase.
>
> *Therefore*, the wording and display of the advertisement, and the proper selection of newspapers are of *vital* importance. To secure these, experience and good judgment are necessary. We will be glad to assist you in the matter.

In 1884, Ayer's agency had produced its first complete campaign for a client, as a solitary experiment, but it hired its first full-time copywriter only in 1892. Rowell brought copywriting and graphics specialists aboard his agency in 1891.[56]

An article in the first issue of *Profitable Advertising: A Monthly Journal Devoted Exclusively to Advertisers* in 1891 analyzed the state of the practice. It praised those established "general advertisers who have attained that degree of financial success, through newspaper and magazine advertising, . . . [and who] are a species of authority and objects of veneration." With them, the advertising agent will "act only as a middle man . . . [who] simply follows definite instructions. He does not originate schemes, does not write advertisements, but simply does as he is told." In these cases, "the agent does not, even morally, become responsible for the success of the advertising." He is not an "architect but a mechanic." On the other hand, for the "weaker advertiser, the advertiser that is new to the business," the responsible agent is obligated to explain the business, including the necessity for "an experienced and high-priced brain to write the advertisements" and, "probably, a first-class artist to furnish the illustrations."[57] In a postscript to a long article on the importance of professional assistance in *placing* advertisements that appeared in J. Walter Thompson's 1887 catalog, he noted that, "special attention [is] given to the preparation of business announcements for new enterprises." Two years later, Thompson did not distinguish between experienced and new advertisers when he offered to prepare advertisements at no extra charge for advertisers who desired this service.[58]

# Early Specialization in Copywriting

If owner-managers in either manufacturing or retail felt inadequate to write and design their own advertisements in the increasingly competitive markets of the 1880s, they could, and some did, acquire the services of a copywriter or artist by putting a specialist on salary, contracting a freelance, or soliciting assistance from an advertising agency. To judge by the reputations of the campaigns produced, only the first of these three options, hiring a specialist, offered advertisers substantial benefits toward improving their campaigns' impacts in the 1880s. All of the major innovations in advertising styles and content before the 1890s came either from owner-managers themselves, officers, or from their employees. This reinforced the widely held belief that advertisers knew their products best and were therefore the best-equipped to write their own copy. Advertising agencies increasingly made their assistance available, but no one could, or was, expected to try to do more than improve on expressing the clients' own ideas. Neither freelance writers nor advertising agents yet recognized the importance of understanding their clients' products and markets sufficiently to know how products might specifically benefit consumers or how those benefits might best be communicated to consumers. Powers wrote his best and most effective advertisements while working exclusively for a client or employer and taking the responsibility and time to know the firm and its products or services. Therefore, before the 1890s, as a rule, only persons directly involved with a firm became sufficiently interested in its products and activities to develop consumer-oriented advertising messages unique to that firm.

On a strictly practical level, advertising agencies were also limited in the creative services they could offer their customers because of their own lack of personnel and internal specialization. Among the few advertising agents who did accept copywriting as a routine responsibility through the 1880s, Harlan P. Hubbard of New Haven was one of the most successful; he was the only agent whom Rowell named in his memoirs as a success despite working outside of a major metropolitan hub.[59] Even so, his agency was no more specialized internally than the others of the 1880s; Hubbard simply took on copywriting as part of his own overall activities. Although Hubbard never became one of the nation's major agents, his billings were substantial during the years the Lydia Pinkham family, from neighboring Massachusetts, favored him with their patronage.

The evolution of advertising practices for Lydia Pinkham's Vegetable Compound and the Pinkham family's interactions with Harlan P. Hubbard and his successor illustrate how a patent-medicine firm could prosper for decades by fitting its copywriting practices to the market environment. In 1875, Lydia

Pinkham and her four children began selling her already-popular herbal remedy for "female ailments." She had generally given bottles of it away before, but times were hard, and Isaac Pinkham, husband and father, had not only lost the family's financial reserves, once again, in the Panic of 1873, but had become enfeebled as well. Together, the family developed the nostrum's name, production, and promotions. The two older sons acted as drummers, while their mother kept the books, directed the other children in producing the tonic, answered letters, and wrote the advertising copy for pamphlets and, later, newspapers. After a couple of years of struggling to sell by using only the pamphlets to supplement personal salesmanship, one of the sons spent most of a large profit on a single newspaper advertisement, much to the dismay of the rest of the family. However, his notion of reaching a broad circulation with a single large insertion paid off with substantial orders. Convinced then of the benefits of newspaper advertising, the family contracted first with a Boston agent, soon turned to Hubbard for more aggressive placements, and then mortgaged their home to buy newspaper space. The family also wrestled with their product's need for a visual trademark. They decided, in 1879, to use Mrs. Pinkham's image as its trademark, and the product's sales "boomed," to use Hubbard's term. The image itself became a popular icon, the subject of songs and jokes—all of which contributed to brand recognition and sales. By 1881, the Vegetable Compound was selling at the rate of two hundred thousand bottles annually. The copy that had achieved this success was largely the product of Mrs. Pinkham's pen, with advice from her family. Her technical phrases came from her home copy of John King's *American Dispensary* and other popular reading material, including other patent-medicine labels. Mrs. Pinkham's genuine sense of her role as a female reformer, as the "Savior of Her Sex," gave her a unique appeal. She blamed overwork, worry, and the bearing of unnatural burdens and lifestyles for women's physical ailments, offering them her tonic as their only source of relief in a difficult world.[60]

In 1881, Lydia Pinkham's two eldest sons died and her own health broke. To continue the business, her last son, Charles, took over management. Harlan Hubbard's influence on newspaper copy increased gradually from offering an occasional suggestion and rewrite to regularly revising the existing sales pitches, although keeping their basic messages consistent with those Mrs. Pinkham had developed. Nonetheless, because of Hubbard's practices of exploiting the account to his benefit, leaving the Pinkhams with small profits despite large sales, he fell out of favor with the family. Charles decided to do without newspaper advertising altogether in 1889 in order to solidify the firm's finances, advertising only through trade cards that pictured his young daughters, who were identified simply as "Lydia E. Pinkham's Grandchildren."[61]

Hubbard had apparently only served the Pinkhams' needs for copywriting assistance in order to induce greater space buying on their part, not because of a sense of client-centered service. In 1889, Charles Pinkham ceased all business connection with Hubbard, and the agent went into bankruptcy, a casualty of the era's typically short-sighted notions about the nature of advertising service. Later that year, a young Bostonian, James J. Wetherald, offered Charles Pinkham a range of services that promised the shape of trends to come. The Pinkhams' past successes and their rejection of Hubbard's limited range of services had piqued Wetherald's ambitions, and he solicited their account on behalf of the Pettingill Agency. When Wetherald asked if Pinkham wanted to advertise, Lydia's son responded positively, "If I ever find an honest agent who can write the kind of copy I want." It was not, therefore, just Hubbard's double-dealing that had driven Pinkham out of newspaper advertising but also this owner-manager's concerns about copy. In working with Hubbard, Pinkham had stayed within his mother's copy strategies, and he reentered the potentially lucrative but risky arena of extensive newspaper advertising only when he found professional assistance that addressed his needs for development and reliability, along with an attentiveness to his firm's needs that the traditional agent could not provide. Wetherald immediately operated very much like a company man, and eventually he did become a Pinkham employee. He first placed an advertisement for them in January 1890—an appropriate marker in the move to new agency practices—and provided extensive services for the Pinkhams over the course of almost four decades, reassuring and enriching the family in the process.[62]

As the advantages of specialized copywriting became more appreciated, freelance writers provided an option for an advertiser who wanted to turn to a specialist for assistance. Yet until after 1890, freelances rarely contributed to the development of advertising content and styles. Typically they wrote individual bits of copy for fixed fees, such as $25 for a poem or $10 for a "funny little dialogue." The work was sporadic, highly competitive, and clients expected their copy within a day or two.[63] These conditions discouraged the kind of long-term relationships between client and copywriter that might have fostered deeper understandings of the clients' products and marketing problems. Most freelances' work might just have well been prepared for any number of different advertisers as for any one of them. Even freelances who did make excellent reputations for themselves did their best work while focusing their attention on single products, either as employees or as single-client agents or freelances.

The careers of prominent copywriters Nathaniel C. Fowler Jr. and John E. Powers demonstrated the importance of specialization within the advertising process and the value of a strong client-centered relationship for successful and innovative copy. Fowler had written copy in several capacities before selling his Boston advertising agency in 1891 to specialize in writing copy. He wanted his own business and would not work within another agency, but he did not want to be distracted by the complications of space brokering; he had come to believe that one person could not do a competent job of both tasks. Having already built his reputation from writing successful advertisements for Columbia Bicycles beginning in 1883, Fowler had no difficulty in attracting new clients. Once he began to specialize, Fowler greatly influenced his field through several important and imaginative campaigns and through his prolific writing on advertising procedures and principles.[64] Powers, both as a young freelance and as a specializing employee for Wanamaker, took the time to research his patrons' customers to find out what they wanted. He studied his patrons' products and tried to figure out how to write copy that would match customers' desires with the products. After his years with Wanamaker, as a freelance working for many different campaigns, Powers gave people good reasons to buy Murphy Varnish or Carter's Little Liver Pills and other products, keeping him busy, affluent, and in the public eye for decades.[65] However, his failure in this stage of his career to tailor his work to specific clients lost at least one valuable account to a young innovator who did just that.

Claude C. Hopkins may well have been the first advertising professional to develop a deliberate, conscious notion of the marketing problem, that is, the relationships between product and market that need to be altered for improved sales. Most other innovators in advertising strategy and copywriting until then had worked intuitively, striking effective chords in their audiences more or less as P. T. Barnum had—by "instinct." Powers had made his contribution differently by deliberately developing a style that met higher intellectual and ethical standards than did most newspaper advertisements of the time; but then Powers, and soon others, applied that style unwaveringly to all sorts of advertising situations. Hopkins, on the other hand, came to believe that each product's marketing required a unique solution, and that that solution could only be discovered by studying the product, the people in its market, and how people reacted to the product and its competition. In other words, he gradually developed an inchoate sense of both the marketing problem, soon central to advertisers' strategies, and market research, the modern key to addressing marketing problems.

When Hopkins first entered advertising, he had not yet formed the sophisticated notions that he eventually espoused; still, in 1887 or 1888 he had enough of the idea to take the account for Bissell carpet sweepers from Powers, even though Hopkins was merely the Bissell bookkeeper at the time and

Powers was at his reputation's peak. According to Hopkins's telling, Powers had prepared a promotional brochure for Bissell that the ambitious young man read and offered to improve upon. Although Hopkins admired Powers's style, he convinced his manager that Powers "knew nothing about carpet sweepers. He had given no study to our trade situation. He knew none of our problems. He never gave one moment to studying a woman's possible wish for a carpet sweeper." Hopkins then prepared a pamphlet "based on knowledge of our problems" that persuaded the firm to cancel Powers's contract. When Powers sued for his fees, Bissell prevailed by arguing that the professional's pamphlet was incompetent by comparison with that prepared by Hopkins. From this beginning, Hopkins went on to develop his formula for "Reason Why" advertisements, always starting with the importance of examining each "trade situation" for its specific problems and working out unique solutions accordingly.[66]

Three men who eventually came to some measure of fame or fortune at copywriting worked full time in that capacity for others before 1890. Of the three, only John E. Powers reached his professional prime by the end of the 1880s; Claude Hopkins had just gotten his start by then, and both he and the third one of the trio, Artemas Ward, achieved their greatest reputations during the decades after 1890, setting precedents and standards for the field. Ward produced all of his early advertising material for Enoch Morgan's Sons, a company that had manufactured soaps in New York since 1809. The Morgan family decided in 1869 to advertise one of their products nationally and selected the scouring soap for which their family doctor had devised a Latin-sounding name, Sapolio. Throughout the 1870s the firm built a national market for Sapolio with advertisements that were lively and amusing, featuring cartoons and jingles from the start, and hiring professional artists and writers, including Bret Harte, to attract and please audiences. Spending grew apace: $15,000 for 1871, $30,000 for 1884, $70,000 for 1885, and $400,000 for 1896. The bulk of the 1885 media spending went out for bill posting and streetcar signs; the next largest category was novelties, stunts, and miscellaneous expenses; magazines and newspapers came in third. The posters included six-foot-tall chromolithographs, to be hung in the windows of wholesalers as samples of the smaller lithographs available to retailers and consumers. Trade cards were distributed by the many hundreds of thousands. In 1884, the firm decided to double its advertising budget and to move into the national marketplace more aggressively, so it hired Artemas Ward to guide and to write the new campaigns. Ward was a city-bred man and he believed that people traveling on streetcars provided an excellent market for this inexpensive cleansing product. He wrote copy that equated cleanliness with patriotism and happiness and that assiduously equated Sapolio with cleanliness for those who had to do their own or other people's cleaning. Reportedly, passengers enjoyed the jingles and read them aloud to each other. For instance:

A clean nation has ever been a strong nation
Fortify with Sapolio.

Another ran:

A Bright Home makes a Merry Heart
Joy travels with Sapolio.

And another:

Two servants in two neighboring houses dwelt
But differently their daily labor felt
Jaded and weary of her life was one
Always at work and yet 'twas never done
The *other* walked out nightly with her beau—
But then she cleaned with Sapolio.

Ward developed other lines and campaign themes over the years, playing on the Spanish-American War, the Western frontier, even devising a fantasy community, Spotless Town, where everyone's lives revolved around satisfying their needs for cleanliness.[67] His concentration on a single product served that product well and built Ward's reputation as a leading specialist and innovator in advertising. In the early years of the next century, Ward and the Morgans even had to reassess their strategies because it seemed that the messages for Sapolio often attracted more attention for themselves than the product, a complication that continues to arise with overly clever copy.

In sum, the best of the three options for acquiring specialized copywriting before 1890 entailed hiring a writer who learned about the employer's products and markets and become engaged in resolving that firm's specific marketing problems. However, most advertisers believed then, and still do, that they could not afford such a specialized employee, or they preferred the flexibility of moving between creative specialists. As a result, advertisers hesitant about creating their own advertising messages most frequently turned to freelance writers and advertising agents for assistance. Before the 1890s, however, neither of these types of professionals was set up or inclined to focus attention and effort exclusively on individual clients and their marketing problems. Neither group understood yet the importance of that focused attention; so the majority of the most-focused, most-innovative copywriters were owner-managers and company officers with an inclination for doing that kind of work themselves. Only after further and deeper changes in the structures and personnel and needs of national advertisers, and ad agencies' competition for their patronage, did advertising agencies take the lead in innovating style and content.

# 6

## Competition and Control
### Business Conditions and Marketing Practices

*The manufacturer once made everything in one shop, and sold to everybody near him. Now he only makes one or a few things, and must supply more customers, who are widely scattered. The consumer, who once looked to the comparatively local jack-at-all-trades producer to supply all his wants, must now use the products of numerous and remote manufacturers. Thus there is an ever-widening distance between the producer and the consumer. . . . Only the printer's ink can bridge the distance.*

—Emerson P. Harris, in the *Inland Printer*, 1890

Both contemporary and recent observers have agreed that the styles and content of American advertisements for consumer products began to change significantly in the 1890s. Explanations for the changes, then and since, generally credit specialists in advertisement writing and design who used their expertise to persuade advertisers—that is, businesspeople who advertise—to relinquish the creation of their public messages.[1] But what drove this process, and was it this simple? Concurrent developments in U.S. business structures and practices were the context for professionalization and specialization of advertising practices, and they can provide a more satisfying explanation. Although internal dynamics such as competition between specialists pressured them to expand their range of activities, the predominant forces for change were external to the field. After all, no matter what other functions advertisers choose to pass on to advertising specialists, they must always initiate and pay for the advertising process; they ultimately decide if and how their campaigns are to be conducted. Advertisers, including industrialists, had been creating their own copy and designs for decades before the 1890s. This chapter examines why many, especially the largest national advertisers, elected to relinquish this aspect of their business activity after 1890.

By the 1880s, many manufacturers began to concern themselves with a set of marketing problems related to controlling and maximizing the flow of their goods through distribution channels to the consumer. This set of issues arose in the 1870s and 1880s for those manufacturers who sought to profit from the greatly multiplied productivity and control over labor that new, continuous-process machinery made possible. Even firms manufacturing complex, hand-assembled items like bicycles, pianos, and furniture increased their productivity by relying on components produced on continuous-process machinery. In order to benefit from their investments in these expensive innovations, manufacturers had to develop large, national markets for the high volumes of goods the technologies could produce. (This dynamic did not involve batch-production firms, such as carpet, textile, and costume jewelry manufacturers, whose advertising rarely expanded into the national consumer markets during this period; most of their marketing continues to operate through salespeople and trade advertisements and activities. This chapter focuses instead on the firms involved with consumer products, marketed directly to consumers.) Without vastly increased sales, the new productivity would glut the marketplace, and capital-intensive factories would have to close. Although labor costs could be cut when a factory closed, the machines and plant entailed fixed expenses that had to be paid whether in use or not. Manufacturers often met these marketing problems by cutting costs, occasionally below the break-even point. Yet the demand for consumer goods was, and is, only partially cost driven, and manufacturers gradually came to use advertising to expand demand. The soap, tobacco, beer, grains, matches, canned-goods, and, of course, patent-medicine industries were among the earliest to generate high volumes of consumer goods with the new production technologies, and marketers within each of these industries experimented with various innovations in marketing and advertising in order to maximize inventory turnover.[2]

Nineteenth-century American marketing thrived on complex systems of mutual dependencies between countless numbers of firms and independent middlemen. Looking at these systems from a century later, it is easy to see a dramatic change in their dynamics in the 1890s and early 1900s. The numbers of manufacturing firms in many industries fell because of bankruptcy and merger, and many middlemen lost their independence by various means, including the replacement of many mutual dependencies with vertical and horizontal integration that consolidated—some say rationalized—managerial power. (Vertical integration entails the merging of production firms, backward to include suppliers, and forward to include distributors. Horizontal integration entails firms merging at the same level of production or distribution.) Yet profound changes in cultures and economies such as this rarely—maybe never—occur so suddenly as they appear later. The dynamics of one period generate the conditions of the next, changing conditions and giving new advantages to some of those who operate differently. In this fashion, the advertising practices that flourished in the earlier era contributed to the changes that, in turn, rewarded new advertising practices.

Distribution channels that flow between producers and their customers map all marketplaces. In the complex systems of mutual dependencies between independent entities that characterized U.S. business before the mid-1890s, salespeople, wholesalers, and retailers, plus advertising suppliers such as printers and publishers, filled the channels and took up the tasks of moving information, goods, and money in all directions. When some manufacturers adopted new, capital-intensive, high-speed production, transportation, and communication technologies, their interests relative to the existing business systems changed, and their efforts to gain greater control over suppliers and markets propelled the advertising changes that prevailed in the 1890s, although they began in the previous decade and had not run their course by the next. Their efforts to create a new business system—although they were generally piecemeal and not intended to build systems—led to mergers and to a whole range of experiments with new marketing techniques, including the use of trademarks and new advertising methods.

## The Merits of Trademarks and Trade Names

All during the nineteenth century, manufacturers developed their uses of trademarks for many of the same market control reasons that many of them eventually merged their firms. Prior to the 1870s, relatively few products were marked with identifying brands because most goods were generic and sold in bulk. Before then, only patent medicines and some alcohol and cosmetic products yielded sufficient profits to support the consumer-sized packaging required to carry identifying marks. Once the second phase of industrialization was well under way in the 1870s, it gradually became cost-effective to market countless industrially produced goods packaged in consumer-sized units.[3] Trademarks served to identify and thereby to differentiate between the varied goods of competing producers and distributors, and so marketers' appreciation of their potential usefulness grew. Trademarks also function as memory hooks for advertising appeals, acting as symbols with which promoters link their advertising messages to their products in the minds of consumers and middlemen. Advertising a trademark sufficiently well can help to replace the traditional push of sales forces and middlemen with the modern pull of specific demand from consumers. This change could lower manufacturers' distribution and sales costs by raising their control over the marketplace. A well-advertised trademark can help make demand relatively inelastic and minimize the impact of the business cycle by generating a constant level of specific demand. In addition, manufacturers sought to prevent retailers and wholesalers from substituting cheaper products for advertised, trademarked products; early on, some promoters recognized that only extensive advertising could assure that consumers would "accept no substitute."

In part because of a somewhat narrow sense of the trademarks' identification functions, a majority of nineteenth-century brand names simply named the goods' inventors or manufacturers, reflecting the owner-managers' close ties with their firms and products. For them, the trademark functioned as "evidence of manufacturing origin," rather than the "symbol of qualities" it later became, to borrow Neil Borden's distinction.[4] As the century wore on, trademarking practices became more flexible, incorporating illustrations and different words for drawing attention to advertising messages and products. Even so, many continued using their own names or portraits, as did Dr. John Woodbury, a dermatologist who in the 1870s created the facial soap that made his fame and fortune. After he accidentally cut the neck off his portrait, leaving only the face, while experimenting with it as a trademark, "it thereupon occurred to me as being just the illustration needed, since it was both original and peculiarly adapted for my facial soap. When carried out . . . the idea was so successful that I have used no other since."[5]

By the end of the century, trademarks and company names began to function quite independently of company founders.[6] In some cases a founders' name continued under new ownership, as when Henry L. Pierce bought the Walter Baker Chocolate Company in the 1880s. When owners had so many products that to brand them all with only the same surname was undesirable, or if they understood the potential power of the trademark as a focus for favorable associations, they began to name their various products after something other than themselves. Tobacco processing companies and soap manufacturers devised a plethora of brand names, keeping the owners' names as the umbrellas that covered their entire lines. Cyrus McCormick and his brothers gave the various models of their harvesters different names, keeping the family name for the company and the line.

Many others avoided symbolic names, however, until the 1880s, when they began to appreciate the marketing value of trademarks. The Procter & Gamble Company sold soap from 1837 until 1879 under the company name, adding only descriptive words, such as "white soap." Following a legendary production accident in 1879, a second generation of Procters and Gambles, cousins to each other, added a floating soap to the many kinds the firm already sold. Harley Procter believed that this floating soap merited special marketing, and a reading of one of the Psalms in church inspired him to name the soap Ivory. After three years and the adoption of innovative machinery, he convinced the family to advertise Ivory extensively and thereby established the brand as the "99 44/100 per cent pure" soap that floated.[7]

Patent-medicine sellers were among the first to appreciate the marketing value of a well-known trademark in promoting products that combined broad claims with narrow objective differentials—a marketing problem that calls for creating a sense of difference regardless of actual sameness. As advertising agent George P. Rowell reflected, "the value of a trademark that has been created by advertising nobody can tell." Indeed, he and others often described the success of a patent medicine in terms of how well established its trademark had become, favorably noting branded products that had achieved far greater success than other, identical products, judged by the extents to which their various trademarks had become established through advertising.[8] Rowell greatly admired Col. David Hostetter, one of the nation's most successful patent-medicine producers, who had advertised extensively since 1853. Rowell routinely measured success by its dollar value, and Hostetter had profited enough to leave one of the two largest "medical" fortunes, an estate of $18 million. Through renowned advertising expenditures, Hostetter created a worldwide recognition of, and reputation for, his mark, which included an illustration of St. George slaying the dragon. This traditional symbol of strength and triumph over evil represented a tonic with only 4 percent herbal content, 64 percent water, and 32 percent alcohol. With what amounted to an average proportion of alcohol, rather more water and less herbs than most, Hostetter earned Rowell's praise for advertising his otherwise nondescript product to success.[9]

A different set of conditions prevailed upon Rowell in 1891 when he decided on the name Ripans Tabules for his own proprietary medicine. He came upon the meaningless acronym for the product's ingredients after deciding against the traditional surname, following the logic that the "best protection for a trademark is the name of the inventor, but if the inventor ceases to be the owner that fact sometimes makes trouble for the actual proprietor." Moreover, Dr. Fred, Rowell's accomplice in this venture, who was then in medical school, "was not anxious to be made famous by having his name attached to a proprietary article with which his connection was likely to be brief. I, on my part, had no wish to become widely known except as an advertising agent." Rowell also found later that the mystery of the name's meaning served his advertising purposes well by piquing consumers' curiosity.[10]

That effective advertising created the value of any trademark also became clear to many manufacturers and distributors outside of the patent-medicine business. For example, W. T. Blackwell & Company came to dominate the tobacco market with its Bull Durham brand in the late 1870s through intensive national advertising that focused on the trademarked Bull. Julian S. Carr, one of three Blackwell partners, in 1877 took charge of an aggressive campaign that featured the Bull in a wide variety of drawings, with poses that ranged from serious to jovial, from frisky to distinguished, and all quite anatomically explicit, raising eyebrows everywhere, much to the firm's gratification and profit. Carr also hired four sets of painters in the 1880s to paint the Bull trademark on surfaces throughout the country and to keep the images looking fresh. In the last three months of 1883 alone, Carr spent $150,000 on extensive national campaigns in country newspapers and city dailies, offering $60,000 in premiums. In 1899, the "famous Durham Bull" appeared as a massive electric sign in New York City. Because of Bull Durham's impressive marketing successes, James Buchanan Duke convinced his partners in W. Duke, Sons, and Company to turn to cigarette manufacturing in 1881 rather than to confront the Bull head on.[11]

William L. Douglas's experience exemplified the process of building a trademark's preeminence. Douglas started his first small manufactory in Brockton, Massachusetts, in 1876, immediately turning to advertising to sell his modestly priced men's shoes, first through the mails, then through retail shoe stores, and finally through his own chain of stores. He asserted in 1891 that using his face as a trademark and publicizing it widely was "the means of my great success in advertising." His earlier, less personalized, trademarks were stolen each time they became well known, and he felt that his decision to use his likeness came from an exceptional insight:

> When I first began advertising I had no idea of a Trade Mark except such as were in general use, such as a shoe, which seemed to be at that time the only thing I could use; but after my advertisement had been before the public for a short time it struck me very forcibly that something must be originated to identify my line of goods so that the public might be able to distinguish between my goods and those of my competitors. . . . My mind ran over the broad field of Trade Marks in use, and P. T. Barnum came into my mind. The thought struck me very forcibly, as he had used his picture successfully and had been a prosperous advertiser.

Very likely, the many patent-medicine sellers who featured their portraits on their packages as well as their trademarks also influenced Douglas's decision. Contemporaries noted two remarkable accomplishments for the famous trademark, in addition to Douglas's wealth, as signs of its overwhelming effectiveness. The first occurred in 1881, when an envelope mailed from Daytona, Florida, reached Douglas in Brockton within two days, even though it carried no more identification on it than his trademarked portrait. Equally impressive, although likely due at least in part to factors other than Douglas's advertising prowess, was his becoming, in 1904, in George Rowell's words, the "Democratic Governor of Republican Massachusetts."[12]

Trademark legislation in the nineteenth century was flawed and inadequate, despite the value that manufacturers and merchants attributed to their names and symbols, so the numbers of marks registered underestimate the growth in trademark usage. The first federal trademark law passed in 1870, and 121 marks were registered that year. Before the law was declared unconstitutional in 1879, 7,668 more trademarks were registered, averaging 778.9 for each year of its existence. In 1881, a second act permitted registering marks used in commerce with foreign and Native American nations, but not until 1905 did Congress pass another trademark law that applied to interstate commerce. Nonetheless, in the intervening years, marks were registered apace to gain international standing, averaging 1,500 annually. With the new law, registrations for 1905 totaled 4,490; for 1906, 10,568; and the more than 28,000 by 1909 indicated a good measure of pent-up demand for trademark protection, despite mergers that had absorbed thousands of competing firms.[13] A 1906 article in AD Sense responded to this growth by addressing the legal and marketing uses of the trademark because they were "so universally used now."[14] Manufacturers had worked for such legislation individually and through their trade association, the National Association of Manufacturers (NAM), formed in 1895. In the association's journal, American Trade, eight articles appeared between October 1897 and June 1902 calling for increased judicial and legislative protections for trademarks. In Theodore C. Search's presidential address at the association's second annual meeting in 1897, he urged the members to work through their legislators for adequate trademark protection. Furthermore, a special session on patents and trademarks at the convention resolved that since NAM represented "the allied manufacturing interests of the United States," it appreciated "the great value of trademarks as an aid to commerce, and also the imperative necessity of national legislation, which will effectually protect trademarks and private brands against imitations and forgery"; NAM therefore encouraged members to petition Congress "to provide a criminal remedy for the infringement of such marks."[15] *Iron Age* published editorials and articles on the importance of trademark protection, including a reprinted series of three papers read at the Congress of Patents and Trade-Marks in Chicago in 1893. One paper declared that "the more the manufacturer advertises his trade-mark goods the more the imitator fattens and flourishes." This "robbery of [the manufacturer's] name and profits" also makes "the people . . . defenseless victims" because they "have learned to depend upon certain trade mark articles."[16]

Both legal and marketing strategies offered trademark protection. Advertising agents, such as Artemas Ward, promoted additional legal protections for trademarks and applauded actions taken to enforce established marks.[17] A professor at the University of New York who had studied the existing trademark law spoke at length during the first convention of the International Advertising Association in 1904. He argued for greater protection through new legislation intended to protect this "very valuable form of property." His audience agreed to "investigate trademark conditions and decide what measures, legislative or otherwise, can be adopted to remedy frauds and abuses."[18] Although the Act of 1905 left much to be desired, it remained the basic federal trademark law, with amendments, until passage of the Lanham Act in 1946. Between these two acts, manufacturers refined the 1905 legislation by repeated adjudications in the federal courts.[19] By their marketing uses of trademarks and their defenses of their trademarks in the courts, manufacturers changed the marks' legal and conceptual standing from merely indicating products' origins to serving as valuable marketing tools.[20]

In the absence of legal protections, and using only their rather unsophisticated sense of how to promote associations with their marks, most early advertisers had developed their brands simply through large volumes of advertising. An editorial in *Advertising Experience* was typical in declaring that there is "only one way to protect a trade mark—keep on advertising it." That was also "the way to make it valuable."[21] Some advertisers sought notoriety for their trademarks by emblazoning the countryside, as well as print, with their product names. Many brand-name advertisers spread their names throughout the landscape, led by Bull Durham Tobacco, Dr. Kilmer's Swamp Root Kidney Medication, Rising Sun Stove Polish, and that survivor of rural-scenery advertising into the late twentieth century, Mail Pouch Tobacco.

The nineteenth century's intense competition combined with the Crash of 1893 to reward businesses that experimented with ways to enhance their control over the marketplace. As a result, the importance of the trademark became more and more apparent to manufacturers as well as to the advertising professionals with whom they increasingly worked, and innovations in marketing strategies and techniques accelerated. For that reason, a *Printers' Ink* editorial of 1905 explained manufacturers' recent "intense, anxious interest in both advertising and the consumer" in terms of their realization "that this is a golden age in trade-marks." That was, the editorial contended, and Frank Presbrey agreed in his 1929 *History and Development of Advertising*, "a time when almost any maker of a worthy product can lay down the lines of a demand that will not only grow with years beyond anything that has ever been known before but will become in some degree a monopoly." Furthermore, everywhere "there are opportunities to take the lead in advertising—to replace dozens of mongrel, unknown, unacknowledged makes . . . with a standard trademarked brand, backed by the national advertising that in itself has come to be a guarantee of worth with the public."[22] By 1929, Presbrey could comfortably assert that advertising itself was the mark of worth, and implicitly of progress, in sharp contrast to the imposing factory images or heroic innovators that had marked goods as progressive in earlier eras.

## Demand and Trademarked Products

Aggressively advertising branded goods directly to consumers offered some manufacturers opportunities to control their markets and to avoid cost-cutting competition. Although faith in the marginal profitability of continuous-process machinery often induced individual manufacturers to compete by reducing prices whenever hard times threatened volume, this strategy risked not only profits but survival. According to Neil Borden, efforts to maintain price stability despite economic cycles and seasonal factors can succeed if an advertising program can create sufficient goodwill and, hence, brand loyalty. The goods that tend to be the most successful at maintaining prices are those that are "habitual," such as cigarettes, and those that have been able to establish a level of differential desirability independent of prices, or that may even play on high pricing, such as luxury goods. Although Borden argued that market and social conditions inevitably impinge on the most intense advertising campaigns, he concluded that the capacity of advertising to stabilize demand and prices can be significant.[23] However, before this notion became an operating principle for American businesses, protecting domestic markets with tariffs and opening international ones by whatever means necessary fostered some of the major political debates of the nineteenth century.[24]

# Competing for Market Share

Industries using continuous-process machinery to produce consumer goods led the evolution of American marketing from the mid-1880s into the new century as they tried to overcome the apparent disadvantage that products within a single industry tend to be very much alike. In advertising these physically undifferentiated products, firms attempted to create a distinctive reputation and a favorable sense of differentiation—that is, "goodwill"—in the minds of consumers. (In recent decades, this notion of a product's goodwill has been divided into a rather large set of product characteristics, such as appeal, personality, image, reputation, and product loyalty.) The $10,000 that Henry L. Pierce agreed to pay Walter Baker's widow annually for the right to the Baker name and trademark when he purchased the chocolate company in the 1880s shows the value he attributed to the goodwill accompanying a mature trademark.[25]

Royal Baking Powder was a favorite among advertising's advocates; they often cited its success as evidence of the differentiation of "a common commercial product that has nothing secret in its composition or in the manner of its compounding," according to a *Printers' Ink* article of 1895. Entitled "The Power of Advertising," this article referred to the Royal Baking Powder Company's recent contract with wholesale grocers "which the grocers find very distasteful" and complained that "there was not a living profit in handling the goods." Nonetheless, they could not refuse to carry this brand, even "under irksome conditions." Why were wholesalers and retailers so "powerless"? It was because a "large number of housewives will have no other kind," even though Royal had no real claim for a higher quality than any other brand. Royal's expenditure on advertising had yielded this success; hence, the "publicity obtained therefrom is an asset, a property as real as stocks or bonds, and its ownership should be maintained and guarded as strictly by our courts as that of any other personal possession." In short, "such a property may be created by judicious advertising." In 1905, another writer in *Printers' Ink* declared that at least "fifty percent of the advertising being done today is for the purpose of creating *property in trademarks*."[26] Royal Baking Powder, like Sapolio, Pears' Soap, and Ivory Soap consistently led the lists of products advertised and sold on a massive, national scale, exceeding all but the top patent medicines through the 1880s and 1890s. These four, all marketing products with little or no objective differential from their competition, pioneered in establishing regular, constant schedules with national magazines. They also numbered among the companies that developed and promoted slogans and catch-phrases. Royal's simple copy focused on its slogan, remaining relatively constant as the size of the placements grew. Usually the advertisements read only, in large clear type, "Royal Baking Powder—Absolutely Pure." A few additional lines of copy occasionally took up to 10 percent of the space to argue, "This powder never varies, a marvel of purity, strength and wholesomeness." In 1893, the founder was offered $13 million for the goodwill of the company—that is, its trademark—because of estimates that it would take more than seven years of annual advertising expenditures of $500,000 to displace Royal's standing in the market.[27] Royal's sole emphasis on purity and confidence was not unique, and it reminds us of consumers' concerns about products' safety before regulations began to offer protection. But since all products made such claims, Royal's advantage came from making the claim so much more often and more clearly than its competition.

### Tools for Increasing Demand

The goodwill that advertising can bring to a trademark can facilitate competition for market share, as the prowess of Royal Baking Powder marketing demonstrated. The constant iteration of the name, the slogan, and the claims for Royal's purity convinced a plurality of consumers to prefer it over other brands. However, none of the trade's encomia to Royal ever mentioned that its advertising had in any way added to the aggregate number of people using baking powder or to the total volume of their usage. Most contemporaries assumed the size of this market to be a given. Industrialists other than patent-medicine makers who turned to producing commodities with continuous-process technologies often expected guaranteed success because they assumed that the lower costs resulting from higher productivity and a less-skilled labor force assured a profitable share of a fixed market—in spite of the fact that competition on this basis within existing markets often led to ruinous price cutting. In response to these market conditions, some continuous-process manufacturers of consumer goods learned to follow the lead of patent-medicine purveyors and some inventors, who sold by creating or stretching markets. Such manufacturers consequently began to experiment with ways of generating wide demand for their products. Tobacco's Duke and others selling branded products to the general consumer came to believe that advertising to get consumers to ask for products—the pull strategy—together with mergers could help them control their markets, could stimulate the flow of goods through the distribution channels, and increase their control over those channels.

The evolution of modern cigarette selling demonstrated the potentials of using marketing strategies to maximize turnover in such capital-intensive, consumer-oriented industries. The earliest strategies in cigarette marketing, in the 1870s, aimed for the elite consumer because of the high costs and low pro-ductivity of hand rolling cigarettes. In order to increase productivity, John F. Allen and Lewis Ginter, owners of a major tobacco company in Richmond, Virginia, offered a $75,000 reward for the invention of a mechanical cigarette roller. James Albert Bonsack won the contest in 1880 with a continuous-pro-cess machine that could manufacture and package 70,000 cigarettes in a ten-hour day, compared with the 2,500 that, on average, a skilled worker could produce in a day. In a few years, the machine's productivity rose to 120,000 cigarettes per day, and Allen and Ginter were overwhelmed by what they had gotten for their prize money. They could not envision a way to mass-market such enormous quantities of cigarettes and in 1885 gave up on the Bonsack mechanized cigarette-producing technology. James Duke of Durham, whose company was making cigarettes in North Carolina, on the other hand, had al-ready started building a large production and marketing organization that in-corporated specialized management techniques as well as Bonsack's machin-ery. After Allen and Ginter had relinquished their rights to favorable royalty fees on the Bonsack machines, Duke negotiated for a guaranteed low royalty, making his cigarettes the market's cheapest. In order to sell the outpouring of inexpensive cigarettes, Duke developed marketing strategies that featured na-tional advertising campaigns so extravagant that they distressed both his part-ners and his competition.[28]

Duke's confidence that extensive advertising could sell unprecedented numbers of cigarettes followed from his experiences after deciding in 1881 not to compete against the dominant brand in loose tobacco, Bull Durham, and instead to pursue aggressive advertising in the cigarette market. Initially, un-certainty about future federal cigarette taxation had made both jobbers (the contemporary term for wholesalers) and retailers reluctant to distribute Duke's new, unknown brands. After two years of struggle and a brief plant closing, and when the tax issue was settled, Duke jumped back into the market with lower prices, higher promotional offers, and broader advertising than his com-petitors. Sales reached almost $600,000 in 1885, the year he acquired the rights to use the Bonsack machinery at reduced royalty rates. By 1890, he was spending about 18 percent of gross revenues on advertising, approximately $800,000 annually, to achieve sales of $4,500,000.[29]

Duke's advertising goals after 1885 were fourfold, all reactions against his earlier near failure: he sought to increase the numbers of cigarette smokers, to build brand loyalty, to increase his market share, and to eliminate the jobbers' control over the distribution channels. Forcing the other cigarette companies into fierce "tobacco wars" fought through expensive advertising campaigns, Duke drove the profits out of most of the older firms. By 1889, he succeeded in controlling the market's activities to such an extent that his rivals felt obliged to accept his terms in forming the "Tobacco Trust," the American Tobacco Company. Then, Duke and three of the top five companies agreed to merge, deciding that the wasteful rivalries had gone far enough. The fifth owner, Lewis Ginter, continued to reject the merger, however, until Duke threatened him with escalation. Acknowledging that he had neither assets nor credit to buy out Allen and Ginter, Duke declared, "I make $400,000 out of my business every year. I'll spend every cent of it on advertising my goods as long as it is necessary. But I'll bring you into line." Less than a year later, Ginter agreed to merge.[30] Shortly after the merger, American Tobacco virtually controlled all stages of the distribution channels. Consumer demand for its cigarettes rose high enough to keep the factories working and to ensure that every middleman between the trust's factories and the consumers had to carry the brands Duke advertised.[31] This reduced the roles of tobacco retailers and jobbers merely to supplying consumers' brand-specific demand.

The impetus that propels goods through distribution channels, from manufacturers to jobbers to retailers toward the final consumer, always results from expectations about what one level of distribution can sell profitably to the next level closer to the consumer. Traditional markets operate largely on a "push" dynamic, as salespeople exert most of the pressure that moves goods from one stage to the next and middlemen assume the risk of assessing what can be sold most profitably at the next stage. Prior to the development of new transportation and communication networks and the introduction of continuous-process industrial technologies, this dynamic served manufacturers well. After that juncture, however, increasing numbers of manufacturers, like Duke, trying to sell to the general consumer, began to reappraise their relationships with middlemen, deciding that they were too much at the mercy of these intermediaries. The middlemen's judgments and interests, they felt, intervened between them and consumers; for instance, until 1883, tobacco smokers did not have the choice to purchase Duke's cigarettes because jobbers and retailers were reluctant to stock new brands.

Duke and many other manufacturers adopted "pull" rather than, or in addition to, "push" marketing strategies. In a consumer-oriented marketing system, advertisements generate specific demand that pulls goods through the distribution channels because consumers ask their retailers for them. Retailers in turn order those goods from jobbers, who then acquire them from manufacturers. Louis E. Asher, a turn-of-the-century Sears executive, described the success of Richard Sears's copy by saying that it "pulled." Sears himself claimed that the copy in his advertisements "almost pulled the ink off the paper."[32] Moreover, retailers and jobbers will often anticipate consumer demand by stocking goods they know are heavily advertised. For example, in the 1870s, the Pinkhams decided to use newspaper advertisements because they found that this medium pulled. That is, unlike the pamphlets with which the family started their advertising, the newspaper copy generated enough consumer demand that wholesalers and retailers felt compelled to carry Lydia Pinkham's Vegetable Compound.[33] George Rowell, like many others, described a successful advertisement as one that "possessed pulling qualities."[34]

Advertisers and their advisers observed each others' various rates of success in experimenting with consumer advertising's pulling potential. They learned from each other to attempt to generate a constant demand through their promotions, seeking to diminish the effects of the recessionary periods of the business cycle. As early as 1870, George Rowell suggested that advertisers might be able to avoid the slow sales that most businesses experienced during dull times "by conspicuous display of special inducements to purchasers, to stimulate [business] into activity." At all times, the "advertiser who knows his business expends his money freely but judiciously." Furthermore, "when the timid advertiser withdraws" because of slow sales, the judicious advertiser "has the field to himself, and he diligently cultivates it." Such strategies, Rowell claimed, could thereby turn dull times to the advantage of the clever advertiser, for whom they would "only mean a little less activity, if anything."[35] This way, Sapolio sales figures overrode the seasonal cycle that had marked them for years when Artemas Ward took charge of the product's advertising campaigns; Ward claimed that, thereafter, "the sales in the slow months were so increased that all months came to look alike to Sapolio."[36]

## Advertising for Market Control over Middlemen

As manufacturers of consumer-directed products participated in the symbiotic expansions of transportation and communication networks, industrialization, and urbanization, many sought to expand beyond their local and regional markets, especially in hard times when decreased demand worked against increased productivity. As they did, other incentives for market control emerged. The distances between them and consumers grew both geographically and operationally as increasing numbers of middlemen intervened in the distribution channels to keep moving the flows of goods, information, and money between manufacturers and consumers. Nineteenth-century marketing systems, with their webs of jobbers, drummers, and retailers, continued to function well enough for most parties along the distribution channels, as long as manufacturers' products did not require specialized handling and expertise or were not effectively interchangeable. Despite the obvious differences in selling these two types of products, the manufacturers of each shared at least one common problem: their interests increasingly diverged from those of the jobbers and retailers, who had controlled marketing patterns since the first decades of the century. Furthermore, manufacturers no longer required the investment support of the traditional, large wholesaler; they were now able to fund their operations through other sources, including the accumulation of capital from their own profits.[37] In the cases of manufacturers trying to market to consumers either novel technologies (such as the new sewing machines and harvesting implements discussed above) or perishable goods (such as ice, dressed meats, and beer) firms often integrated forward to develop their own marketing networks. They needed to ensure that goods were handled properly and that customers received proper instructions for using the goods.

Despite the mutual dependencies that defined these relationships within the distribution channels, all parties sought their own interests, of course, and conflicts between them grew. Duke's experience with jobbers' and retailers' reticence in carrying his first cigarette brands inspired the American Tobacco Company's establishment of retail cigar outlets. In the 1890s, *Iron Age* reported distress from both retailers and manufacturers over the question of whether these outlets should sell goods directly to the public;[38] retailers were able to retard a product's sales without malice simply by neglecting to display samples left by a drummer.[39]

The traveling salespeople who took jobbers' and manufacturers' claims and order forms to retailers throughout the hinterlands had also begun to provoke the ire of those whose goods they represented. Local agents and commercial travelers had become major fixtures in the marketing channels once railroads had made both travel and delivery to outlying areas increasingly convenient and fast, replacing retailers' own travels to central distribution cities to stock their shelves. In the best of cases, the salesmen were honorable fellows whose work could be made more effective if a retailer's familiarity with a product through advertising "open[ed] the way for trade," as one book advised.[40] Because some drummers were less than honorable, however, a contemporary advertising guide suggested replacing them altogether with advertisements to consumers and retailers, which served instead as "The Best Kind of Drummer." An advertisement "has most of the merits and none of the vices of the 'travelling man,' besides many advantages that are entirely its own. . . . [It] doesn't get drunk. It doesn't play faro. It doesn't bring in any supplementary bill of 'expenses.' It requires no 'commission.' It never sets up in business for itself on the credit it has built up at your expense, or has artfully filched from you."[41] C. W. Post, for instance, believed that, in any case, drummers passing messages to consumers through retailers simply could not convey the attributes of innovative products such as his "scientific suspenders" or Postum, the cereal coffee, as effectively as could the advertisements he wrote himself.[42] Others observed that salesmen were "very expensive and inefficient" compared with printers' ink in distributing information about projects and that they never did reach the consumer directly to produce "knowledge value" that could pull products through retail.[43] In sum, advertisements' pull could replace altogether the drummers' push; this would move control over marketing processes higher up the channels, that is, to the manufacturers.

For branded consumer goods that were more or less interchangeable, whether patent medicines or threads or sad irons, manufacturers faced a different marketing problem. But again it was one that set them at odds with jobbers and retailers. They aimed at generating general demand with their advertisements that could pull their *types* of products through the distribution channels, but that was usually a by-product of their primary goals; namely, to generate specific demand that ensured that consumers asked for their brands only, as had Royal Baking Powder and Duke. Jobbers and retailers often exploited general demand and asserted their influence on the market by substitution. Substitution occurred in two forms, and both entailed replacing a heavily advertised product with a similar one at some point in the channel on the way to the consumer. Retailers perpetrated the most frequently occurring form when they took advantage of their customers' reliance on their advice in the days before self-service shopping. When retailers recommended substitutes, they did so because nationally advertised products often had fixed prices that were advertised, allowing retailers less markup than did other brands. In the second form of substitution, both wholesalers and retailers blatantly substituted products with similar names or labels for the heavily advertised products. The frequent warnings found in advertisements and on packages to "avoid counterfeits," to "beware of substitutes," and "none genuine without . . ." expressed manufacturers' concerns about substitution.

Successfully built, specific demand undermined the jobbers' and retailers' traditional influence and made it difficult for them to keep a product out of their inventories. Even before 1870, some patent-medicine purveyors had learned this strategy by experimentation. When the highly successful patent-medicine producer David Hostetter described his own practices, he compared his early marketing with his policy of set prices in the 1860s.

> In the early years of our business, we kept ourselves in the keenest of poverty in order to use our money in advertising. . . . At that time we had no standard price for our bitters, preferring rather to allow the seller to reap the profit, while we were sat-

*Specialization as Progress*

isfied to know that the article was bought, and that good remuneration did in nowise lessen the energy of the seller. As years passed by we more and more extensively commended our bitters through the newspaper channel and by means of almanacs, thereby creating an incessant demand, actually compelling druggists and others to keep the article at the risk of losing customers. Thus we progressed, until to-day Hostetter's Bitters can be obtained in almost any part of the globe.[44]

Hostetter's shift from a push to a pull strategy recognized and exploited the advantages of the specific demand that his advertisements had generated for his brand. With virtually no legal protection against substitution, other manufacturers, too, came to realize that the pull generated by frequent and extensive advertising offered the best available protection for their trademarks and their sales volume, preventing the interjection of similar, competing products that exploited the general demand for them.

Although the absolute numbers of wholesalers, distributors, and retailers continued to grow, by the 1910s both jobbers and retailers had lost most of their influence over the flow of goods, largely because of manufacturers' marketing strategies.[45] Once consumers regularly sought out specific brands, this dynamic pulled manufacturers' goods through the distribution channels with relative independence from the middlemen. The rise of self-service shopping in the 1920s and later nearly completed the decline of retailers' influence over most consumers' decisions about products. For instance, the patent-remedy Castoria did well through the 1880s and 1890s without salesmen altogether, relying on mothers to insist on the medication advertised extensively with the slogan "Children cry for it."[46]

Advertising agents responded to these issues rather slowly, other than to encourage more and more direct advertising. For this reason, an 1886 advertisement for N. W. Ayer & Son encouraged manufacturers to advertise directly to their consumers through newspapers. Ayer warned, "Dealers are <u>important</u>, but <u>sometimes</u> your competitor offers him better inducements, & away he goes. Talk to the man who USES your line of goods. Once get <u>him</u> and he'll STICK as long as you give him satisfaction."[47] In 1891, a two-part article in *Printers' Ink*, describing the role of advertising for manufacturers, lumped them together with wholesalers and did not argue for their independence from the power of jobbers, merely suggesting that brand-name advertisements should precede traveling salesmen into a district to cause the retail customer to ask for "particular goods."[48] Nonetheless, in a few more years, advertising agencies increasingly claimed an ability to enhance the manufacturers' control over their marketing channels. At an Ayer agency internal Business-Getting Conference in 1905, Harry Nelson McKinney, partner in the agency, declared that "the most dissatisfied man today is the manufacturer." The "manufacturer finds that he is helpless in the hands of the jobber . . . and our great business is to show the manufacturer that he ought to own his own trade by making the demand direct from the consumer. . . . We have got to think what makes advertising pay." McKinney urged the agency to seize this opportunity for "business-getting."[49] Yet even McKinney, one of the leading agency figures in the modernization of advertising practices after 1890, did not take up this new challenge until long after many manufacturers and their internal specialists had already recognized the role of advertising in themselves controlling marketing channels.

Truman A. DeWeese began one of the earliest books on advertising principles in 1908 by assessing the relationship between advertising, manufacturers, and middlemen. "Advertising is an evolution of modern industrial competition. . . . Through the magazines, newspapers, and other forms of publicity the producer now reaches hundreds of thousands of possible customers, whereas under the old system of distribution he reached only the jobber and wholesaler through traveling salesmen." DeWeese concluded that the up-to-date "manufacturer now creates a demand for the goods through advertising, thereby forcing the dealer to carry a good stock."[50] By 1912, George Frank Lord, another leading figure in the transitional period of the advertising profession, publicized his own agency by linking advertising and manufacturers' interests: "*If you are a manufacturer* I can show you how scientific advertising can keep your factory running at full capacity, increase the turn-over of your capital and your net annual earnings, put you instead of your jobbers in control of your product, and build up a future-sale asset of ever-increasing value."[51] By this time, many advertising professionals had become sensitized to the major marketing problems confronting the manufacturer and offered their advertising expertise as solutions.

Tying together the trademark with these issues of controlling the manufacturers' marketing channels, the J. Walter Thompson agency published a pamphlet in 1911 entitled *Things to Know About Trade-Marks*. The presentation introduced the trademark by explaining how we have come to "take Shakespeare on faith" as "the greatest man that ever put pen to paper." That "Shakespeare's name has become a sort of trade-mark of good literature" demonstrated the power of "*recognized distinction*" through reputation. After explaining how trademarks had become essential to the modern business world, the pamphlet pronounced that the "trade-mark is the connecting link between the manufacturer and the ultimate consumer. By the use of trade-marks, widely advertised, manufacturers are able to build up a trade that becomes, to a great degree, independent of jobber, wholesaler, and retailer. In the public mind a trade-mark grows, in time, to mean a certain standard of quality, workmanship and material." The introductory analysis concluded that a "trade-mark has no inherent, natural value. Whatever it is worth is the result of advertising in some form, plus the desirable qualities of the goods that it represents."[52]

Many observers applauded this "disappearance of some old business methods," that eliminated old, tangled marketing networks. "An Evolution in Trade" in the *New York Times* in 1889 considered the decline in the jobbers' "supremacy" from their former positions as "old-time merchant moguls" an indication of progress. As a result of these developments, "the step from the producer to the consumer had become comparatively cheap and direct. Now the competition was to sell goods and the buyer got all the benefit." Reasons for the improvements included the "immense increase in domestic manufactures" as well as "ready cash" available after the Civil War and inexpensive and rapid freight due to the expansion of transportation networks. In conclusion, "to all appearances the tendency is more and more toward this more agreeable and, what is far more important, toward the more economical system of transacting business."[53]

## Concentration and Marketing

The 1890s experienced a watershed in American business history. Investment in capital equipment, productivity, and competition had grown apace in the previous decades. Then in the 1890s and into the first years of the twentieth century, the concentration of industrial assets into fewer, larger firms dominated developments in national business organization and practices. Some producers achieved dominance in their industries by driving out or merging with competition or else erecting barriers to entry that minimized competition at the national level. Thousands of firms that had been owned and managed in the traditional entrepreneurial style merged during this period to form corporations owned by stockholders and managed by people who were neither owners nor their kin. In both circumstances, the growing sizes of the firms involved made it easier to control national markets, to raise capital, and to consolidate operations. The large numbers of small and batch manufacturers and retailers that have continued to operate and advertise in the United States have rarely influenced twentieth-century developments in national advertising; therefore, the remainder of this study will focus on the advertising of corporations that manufactured and marketed branded consumer goods on a large scale.

The concentration of industrial assets around the turn of the century marked a distinct change in the national profile of American business. During the 1880s, according to business historian Alfred D. Chandler's count, eight industrial trusts formed and six survived to operate within the national marketplace. Prior to this time, the only firms that approximated the modern national corporation were in transportation, communication, and finance. From this beginning, and after New Jersey's 1888 general incorporation law, by 1906 fully 328 mergers had occurred, with the period of greatest consolidation from 1895 to 1904, peaking in 1899. Between 1895 and 1904, more than 1,800 industrial firms disappeared into consolidations; 1,028 firms disappeared in 1899 alone. For example, by the time that the American Tobacco Company was broken up by Supreme Court order in 1911, it had absorbed more than 200 firms.[54]

The majority of the mergers prior to 1906 consolidated relatively equal competitors who hoped to gain control over their business conditions, including access to large-scale capital, and to maximize production and distribution efficiencies. (Many of the mergers fall outside this study because their constituent firms produced capital and industrial goods and did not sell through consumer advertising.) Although the depression that began in 1893 had devastating effects on the total volume of consumer product sales (prices dropped drastically, bottoming out in 1896 and 1897), it accelerated the national character of the marketplace as industrialists sought national exposure to counteract reductions in their local sales. Furthermore, the merger movement that followed the crash combined local producers into national corporations seeking national, even international, markets. Industrial overexpansion in the years prior to the Crash of 1893, particularly in the capital-intensive industries with high fixed costs, set the stage for competition that drove many businesses to try various methods of price-setting to avoid competition in prices after the crash. The legal and practical advantages of the merger as an alternative made it, along with extensive and innovative advertising techniques, the method of choice for controlling the marketplace. (The reasons for mergers also included the advantages of integration forward and backward to achieve economies of scale, control of transportation, and the control of suppliers as well as the control of market and distribution networks, including both wholesalers and retailers.) As economist Edward Sherwood Meade explained in 1909, "the *régime* of free competition was productive of manifold hardships to the manufacturer. Competition might·be considered the life of trade, but at the close of the last industrial depression it was regarded as the death of profits." It was, Meade concluded, "highly desirable from the manufacturer's view-point to stop, or at least to abate, this struggle, which benefited nobody save the consumers. . . . The producers were tired of working for the public." Meade also argued that mergers maintained product quality that might otherwise be sacrificed to intense competition, "improved" management's position relative to labor, and reduced their "vulnerability" to jobbers.[55]

In 1891, Emerson P. Harris asked in the *Inland Printer,* "Who will give us a science of philosophy of advertising, or the data from which to construct it?" He asked whether advertising was simply something "forced upon one by his neighbors," whether it actually created new customers or increased purchasing by present customers? Did it "really create value?"[56] An answer emerged out of the despair of the 1890s depression. Continuous-process industries composed of relatively equal firms marketing both consumer and capital products without significant differentiation experienced the most severe price competition. Marketers observed fewer price declines on packaged, trademarked, nationally advertised consumer goods than on products sold in bulk or on locally manufactured brands, regardless of whether or not a given industry had attempted to establish price-agreement pools.[57] This lesson combined with the mergers to afford maximum control over the marketplace. Both manufacturers and their communications professionals noticed. From here on, corporate manufacturers addressing consumers directly determined the character of national-brand advertising.

## Changes in Corporate Management

A *Printers' Ink* editorial declared 1905 as the year when manufacturers "suddenly . . . developed an intense, anxious interest in both advertising and the consumer."[58] This "anxious interest" actually developed over years, but it had recently accelerated, in part because the "solid phalanxes" of the "manufacturing world" to whom *Printers' Ink* referred were not the same people who had owned and managed most industries even a decade earlier. Moreover, they were not even the same *type* of people. The nineteenth-century individualistic entrepreneurs, the traditional captains of industry who had jealously guided every facet of their companies' activities, had largely lost their domination over large-scale U.S. business before 1900. To some degree this transition in personnel simply resulted from the passing of time. The first generations who had founded most industries were leaving the helm either because of age or because a later generation was working vigorously to drive them out, taking advantage of conditions alien to their elders. For instance, the upstart Duke, the cigarette manufacturer mentioned above, had early on forced his older competitors in the tobacco market to merge into a corporation that he could control. Similarly, the youthful owner of Quaker Oats, Henry Parsons Crowell, formed the American Cereal Company after the field's former leader had lost his factory and was outnumbered in his efforts to continue imposing his traditional owner-manager ways on the oats cereal market. Andrew Carnegie ceased his holdout against J. P. Morgan's creation, United States Steel, and sold his interests in Carnegie Steel to consummate his retirement. International Harvester was formed after Cyrus McCormick Sr. and his bitter rivals had died. The Shredded Wheat Company merged with the National Biscuit Company after Henry Drushel Perky and his immediate successor had died. What George P. Rowell concluded in 1905 about the advertising field held true throughout the new business world: "Conditions are changing, and only young men can be expected to keep up with the times."[59]

This generational factor does not, however, explain why the retiring owner-managers were not simply replaced by a new generation of owner-managers, as had generally happened up until the 1890s. Instead, the evolution of organizational size and the consequent changes in structure and operations account for the transformation in personnel that followed shifts from entrepreneurial capitalism through financial capitalism to managerial capitalism. Key to these shifts' impacts on advertising is the resultant distancing of ownership from managerial control.[60] Railroad magnate Senator Leland Stanford represented the traditional owner-managers' beliefs regarding their proper business responsibilities and prerogatives during a debate on the Interstate Commerce Act, arguing against the act because it would diminish the railroad owners' freedom to run their businesses. It amounted to an attack on ownership—because the essence of ownership, he asserted, was control.[61] Yet as a result of the mergers and the generational changes at the end of the century, owners had less and less of their own identity and sense of worth tied up in the operations and reputations of the companies that composed their assets. Owners were increasingly just stockholders. Even members of boards of directors who were major stockholders managed only indirectly, through layers of specialized managers.[62] New accounting practices reflected this transition, resulting from the need to inform owners and the public on the activities of corporate managers.[63] The names of the new conglomerates no longer identified their founders; Carnegie Steel and McCormick Harvester were gone, subsumed under United States Steel and International Harvester.[64]

The demands of forming and running these new corporations rewarded new styles of leadership. One of James Duke's advantages after entering the cigarette arena was that he, like Gustavus Swift and John D. Rockefeller in their respective fields, was "an innovator not thoroughly grounded in the previous competitive methods" of his industry, according to Glenn Porter. Duke's earliest business decisions, such as removing his firm from the competitive fray of the overpopulated loose-tobacco market, did not indicate any novel insight on his part. But thereafter his inexperience and flexibility allowed him to instigate advertising expenditures that betrayed his enthusiasm, appalled his partners, and almost cost his firm bankruptcy. Duke's first success resulted from what might have been an impulsive decision in 1883 to get a jump on his competition in an uncertain market, and his "vigorous, imaginative merchandising" quickly raised his company into the ranks of the top five cigarette companies.[65]

By 1885, Duke's marketing organizations and strategies had compelled the other cigarette companies to follow his innovations in order to survive. The four sets of owners other than Duke who, with him, formed the American Tobacco Company in 1890 represented the traditional owner-manager style of entrepreneurship, while Duke was the harbinger of the future with his style of financial/managerial capitalism. As each group presented and defended its interests during the merger negotiations, it became clear that the attitudes of the traditionalists and the junior participant diverged in ways that exacerbated their business differences. Consequently, the five sets of participants rarely talked for any length of time before tempers flared and the meetings broke up. In part, the differences expressed during the negotiations simply reflected the antagonisms that remained from years of bitter, almost ruinous, competition. As the junior party to the negotiations, and the innovator whose activities had challenged the traditional patterns of competition and brought the others unwillingly into the negotiations, Duke absorbed personal attacks in pursuit of his long-term business ambitions. Francis S. Kinney, one of the traditional owner-managers whose advertisements had always borne his surname, later reported that each of the older businessmen was reluctant to see his company absorbed into a combination. In order to compromise with the pride that each man felt for his own company, they declared a two-to-three-year "interregnum" during which the firms would operate as independent branches of American Tobacco, keeping their original names and structures.[66] The antagonisms that surfaced during the negotiations and the traditional entrepreneurs' attempts to preserve their firms' identities expressed the importance they felt for operating their own firms. Yet the press of the new business conditions required that they choose between financial and personal considerations.[67] In the end, financial factors won out.

These same conditions pushed the Deerings and McCormicks into International Harvester Company in 1903, along with three other firms, but only with great difficulty, again because of long-term rivalries and concerns about the loss of company and family identities. After three failed attempts over twelve years, a fourth negotiation succeeded with an awkward merger. Each of the companies kept separate brand names for six years, despite the expenses of duplicating catalogs and products. Even upon final consolidation, they preferred management by strangers to sharing it with each other; below the position of president, there was "nothing but employees."[68]

The move to corporate management also changed the nature of leadership, altering the criteria for success at the industrial helm. Both the sizes of the new corporations and their organizational structures surpassed any one person's ability to oversee and direct all of any firm's activities. The sorts of entrepreneurs who had the independence, self-assurance, and drive to start up new industries based on technological innovations were not then, nor are they now, the sorts of people who can usually manage a mature industry's bureaucracy successfully. Twentieth-century inventor entrepreneurs who had difficulty in making the transition from a high-risk, highly innovative business venture to a bureaucratic corporation include Henry Ford, Edwin Land of Polaroid, and Steve Jobs and Steve Wosniak of Apple. The traditional qualities of the "ideal entrepreneur" who combined "the traits of inventor, discoverer, conqueror, organizer, and merchant"[69] do not apply to established firms. The chief requirement for ordinary success in modern business has become the intellectual ability and emotional capacity for specialization within large, complex organizations that reward cooperation. To become an exceptional success, one now has to be able to manage such an organization, attending carefully to the management of specialized managers. Successful industries have had to combine technological and marketing innovations in order to prosper.[70] In the period before 1890, grand successes in consumer industries generally resulted from the propitious convergence of both types of abilities in a single ambitious person. In contrast, after 1890 the corporate structure facilitated, and successes within it increasingly required, teams of people bringing together their various experiences and types of expertise. Production specialists and marketing specialists took up very different assignments in the new, departmentalized bureaucracies.

Specialization and its legitimizing professionalization ranked among the most important ramifications of the turn-of-the-century growth of business organizations, paralleling contemporary developments in other growing fields such as medicine, law, academia, and science.[71] As businesses expanded, the advantages of increasing the division of labor among the growing legions of managers became apparent. For example, much of Duke's success with his oligopoly came from his ability for culling personnel from its composite firms and bringing like-minded experts together to manage the various operations of the American Tobacco Company. When he could not find the expertise he needed in the old companies, he "developed" specialists.[72] Many businesses ultimately explored and exploited so-called Scientific Management with its systematization of the division of labor to try to maximize efficiency and control

*Specialization as Progress*

at all levels of operation. For instance, the ideal corporate salesman no longer determined his company's distribution policies in an area; rather, he became an order-taker, in both senses of the word. Under the era's new principles of "scientific management," the new "scientific salesman . . . works for the house and the house works for him. . . . He believes that he should be a closer and not a missionary." This new breed of salesman should be, moreover, "thoroughly informed in full detail of the advertising plan" so that he can use it to the firm's advantage. He should not be encouraged to develop his own selling arguments, because despite the best of intentions, he could undermine the company's long-range marketing plans.[73]

Beyond the benefits of efficiency and mutual cooperation, social benefits also accrued to managers as they came to identify themselves as a distinct group between owners and laborers. As managerial specialists came to control the operations of their firms, they applied their class's main criterion for self-worth; namely, competence in one's profession, and, accordingly, they distributed tasks among other specialists. They assigned their firms' advertising and publicity operations to advertising and publicity professionals. Furthermore, as bureaucratic structures increasingly rewarded managers for conformity and efficiency rather than innovation, they turned to creativity specialists.

Advertising decisions, devolving either to in-house specialists or outside advertising professionals, were therefore only a portion of the managerial functions that cleaved from the top levels of management. Under the new business conditions, advertising practitioners and their advocates frequently cautioned the owners and managers of large firms against trying to do their own advertising preparation. As William H. Maher wrote in *Printers' Ink* in 1893, "the larger the firm the less time the owner can spend in advertising."[74] In 1895, Lord & Thomas, the leading advertising agency west of New York City at the time, promoted themselves, and the advertising trade in general, by advising owners and managers that "every employee should be better skilled in his particular branch of your business than you are. You expect it of him. Division of labor—every man to his specialty—that brings success. If you employ us to prepare and place your advertising you will find it more profitable than taking up your own time with the details."[75] Even companies like DuPont that remained family firms with family officers during and after the great merger movement grew too large not to set off advertising functions into a newly created department. After a century of close control over advertising by officers aided by advertising managers, "DuPont advertising became a separately conducted divisional activity" in either 1907 or 1908, then reorganized and expanded in 1911. In 1919 and 1920, Irenee DuPont still received inquiries about advertising addressed to him as president of the company. He had long since directed them to the advertising department, and in at least one case he responded to an inquiry with, "I am sorry to say that I have not followed our advertising particularly closely."[76]

Many corporation heads came to appreciate the value of specialization in advertising, including James Duke, who prided himself on his marketing prowess yet transferred the American Tobacco Company's advertising planning to N. W. Ayer & Son after 1900. He had come to recognize the advantages of a different sort of specialization than that which came with having been "raised in tobacco," and now he sought the services of selling expertise.[77] C. L. S. Tingley, president of the Pennsylvania Street Railway Association and vice president of the American Railways Company, advocated specialization with a letter to the *Electric Railway Journal* around 1910. He stated that "it is economy to employ competent persons to prepare that [advertising] message and place it before the public, and therefore [one] employs a skilled advertising man." When a nonspecialist writes an advertisement, "the message usually lacks the punch because the railroad man is a railroad man; he knows the facts and he presents his message to the public in a manner which the public doesn't understand, or he fails to emphasize a salient point, or he overburdens it with detail."[78]

Owners and top management retained the prerogative to approve the advertising campaigns devised by their specialists, but they chose to exercise decreasing influence as the years passed, only asserting their authority when specialists required correction. So in 1920 Irenee DuPont "seriously object[ed] to the expression 'The World's greatest chemical industry'" in a sample of advertisements that he had been sent by his advertising director. DuPont believed that this was "the kind of 'horn blowing' so uniformly practiced by those who are unfit, as to at once awaken a feeling of distrust." He sought to "make the whole much more dignified and impressive, not to claim too much."[79] Increasingly typical, however, was the man described by in-house publicist Arthur Warren as "the chief" of the American Steel and Wire Company, Pittsburgh, who "always" approved his advertising specialist's expenses and plans. Warren derided the company's "old-fashioned advertising" that predated his arrival and for which it was "getting no return." With his specialized skills as a journalist-turned-adman, Warren "undertook to make a change in industrial advertising, and make it effective."[80] This notion of effectiveness was, by 1904, becoming the new criterion for good advertising as the practitioners professionalized into a cohort of communication experts.

During the halcyon years of precorporate (or owner-managed) American industrialization, between the depressions of 1873 and 1893, it was reasonable for industrialists to act confidently on their beliefs that better, cheaper mousetraps, advertised extensively but intuitively, would suffice to ensure their success. The crisis of the 1890s depression challenged this faith and accelerated the decline of the owner-manager manufacturer in nationally marketed consumer goods; it rewarded experimentation with innovative ways to hold and to expand markets. The National Association of Manufacturers, organized two years into the depression, addressed the needs for aggressively pursuing both national and international markets.[81] Maintaining and increasing general demand for product lines as well as the specific demand for individual brands became the subjects of more widespread and deliberate national efforts. The importance of maintaining and expanding high-volume production and sales to support capital-intensive, continuous-process industries plus the specialization of management within industry motivated many managers to seek professional advertising assistance in what many correctly interpreted as different market conditions that called for new marketing practices.

# 7

# The Competition to Modernize
# Advertising Services

*The competition among business men to broaden out and find new fields for their products leads to advertising and is an encouraging feature. But the competition among advertising solicitors, among advertising agents, is exceedingly strong, and that competition is leading to a demand for far more service from the advertising agent than was the case ten years ago, or even five years ago.*

—W. W. Douglass, at an Ayer & Son "business-getting conference," 1905

## Advertisers' New Concerns Attract New Services

By the 1910s, U.S. manufacturers of trademarked consumer goods who sought specialized advertising assistance outside their firms generally turned to advertising agencies. Before the economic crises of the 1890s, however, even the largest advertisers only rarely patronized advertising agents for services other than distributing their messages. Instead, job printers, publishers, and freelance artists and copywriters provided most advertisers' creative resources on those occasions when they did turn outside their own firms.

At the start of the 1890s, it was not at all clear that *any* single profession would come to dominate advertising creation, advertising agents least of all, given their prevailing attitudes and practices; and as late as 1900, consumer-directed advertising could still have modernized in any of several directions. If we look back, some directions seem now to have had poor prospects, despite their adherents' efforts. Given public attitudes even then about mailed promotional material or items included in shopping bags at stores, it is hard now to see how job printers could have continued to compete effectively with periodicals in providing major advertisers with attractive media that would enter consumers' homes. Other directions seem to have had better prospects: publishers might have expanded their own creative services, as Cyrus K. Curtis did, and thereby dominated transactions with advertisers. All major advertisers might have fully developed their internal advertising departments, as did many, or they might have worked closely with a single agency, as Procter & Gamble did with Procter & Collins from the 1890s until 1912.[1] Together, publishers and advertisers might have destroyed the commission system upon which agents had come to depend. Yet by 1920, advertising agencies securely claimed authority in creating advertisements—after three decades of rivalry for advertisers' patronage, during which several groups responded in their own ways to the changing business conditions.

Manufacturers of trademarked consumer goods fueled the processes by which advertising agencies came to prepare advertisers' messages. Then, as now, advertisers initiated the advertising process, determined which messages would go public, where and how they would be distributed, and then paid the bills. High-volume manufacturers of branded consumer goods drove the field's modernization at the end of the century because they increasingly set store by their promotional programs, and in the context of industrial consolidation and specialization, they were willing and able to act on their marketing needs. As their marketing mix shifted away from personal selling because of growing distances and organization sizes, printed media—novelties, catalogs, and letters, as well as periodicals—became more important in reaching not only consumers but distributors of consumer goods and industrial purchasers. Firms' expenditures generally rose with their size, if not proportionally, at least relative to lower-volume producers, and as the costs and marketing consequences of conducting advertising programs rose, making decisions about them became more complex and risky. Manufacturers competed for audiences' attention and loyalty and expanded their markets by patronizing the most prestigious and— to use their phrase—"up-to-date" communications media they could afford. This patronage subsidized technological, stylistic, and distribution innovations when publishers and job printers competed for advertising accounts. Each round of this spiral resulted in trying new ideas and extending distribution that, in turn, set off further rounds of competition. As their costs and exposure rose, advertisers' concerns grew. They began to think about efficiency and effectiveness in content and style as well as in reach and frequency. Media producers and growing numbers of all types of advertising specialists responded to and encouraged manufacturers' concerns for placing and creating advertisements by altering their own practices and organizations in a variety of ways. When changes pleased advertisers, for whatever reason, the fortunate specialists prospered. Altogether, changes made by advertisers, printers and publishers, and advertising practitioners shaped their fields' separate but parallel and reciprocal modernizations.

Advertisers' efforts to reduce the likelihood of poor decisions in placing their messages added to the costs of their marketing when they tried strategies such as blanketing markets or placing with the most popular publications. This latter strategy contributed to a tendency toward concentration among the magazines and big-city newspapers that occurred alongside with the merger movement in manufacturing. Those publications with incremental edges in circulation attracted more advertising revenues, with which they could in turn improve themselves and attract more circulation, and so on. In similar circular fashion, the advertisers' costs in using the most advantageous publications rose, and marketing costs contributed to manufacturer consolidations. Operating within those corporations, advertising managers, rather than owner-managers, faced a long series of questions, some new, some old. The managers for, say, a household product might decide to place advertisements in the *Ladies' Home Journal* and a half-dozen other obvious, but expensive, choices. That decision made, though, others remained: how much to spend during any period of time; whether to pay extra for preferred placement or full pages; how frequently to place the messages; and what, if any, newspapers to use? Advertising budgets grew apace, but each opportunity for expansion again increased the advertisers' choices and expenses. Furthermore, as the complexity and costs of decisions increased, the demand to justify those decisions rose. Once managers rather than owners shaped budgets, their plans to expend amounts that seemed exorbitant by the common practice of the immediate past called for objectifiable rationales, validation by expertise, and positive results. Whims, instincts, and flamboyance served owner-managers well enough, but they ill-suited the new generations of corporate managers. (Owner-mangers can still follow their whims in ways not open to managers. Steve Jobs's dramatic "1984" Superbowl commercial for the Macintosh computer debut was a recent case in point.)

Other factors determine the results of an advertising program besides decisions about placement, and as appreciation of these factors grew, they, too, added to the advertising managers' concerns. As some publishers, job printers, and a growing cohort of advisers, copywriters, and artists had begun to argue, the content and appearance of an advertisement had a material impact on its selling effectiveness. Placing one's card frequently into appropriate periodicals, simply filling small amounts of space with heavy and clichéd copy, sending out lovely calendars, or printing trade cards with portraits of one's self or one's factory or one's product, or even with stories about product benefits, no longer sufficed. Even the most imaginative messages on lithographed show cards and trade cards came under criticism by self-appointed experts addressing advertisers from countless sources. While content and style did not yet receive the highest priority universally, even the raising of such questions complicated the criteria for decisions; hence, the need for more careful consideration by advertisers and their advertising managers. Furthermore, the increasing prestige and circulations of preeminent magazines made certain that advertisements placed therein would be seen by the spouses and peers of many interested parties. Comparisons with other advertisements, both those of competitors and ads in general, were inevitable and added to the pressure (on both the advertiser and the creator) to sponsor effective messages and images. Moreover, by the end of the 1890s, most major advertisers became too concerned with effectiveness and originality to be content with material not specifically created for their products by specialists whose new status as experts validated their output. All of these variables, plus the more obvious motivations to sell ever more, pressed for new and improved methods of devising advertisements and campaigns. Because of trends toward managerial specialization throughout large-scale businesses, such as hiring experts, including efficiency experts, "improvement" and progress entailed specialization on all fronts. Production specialists and marketing specialists took up very different assignments in and for these new, departmentalized bureaucracies. The question remained, however, which specialists would take over advertising?

In this period of flux, when the only certainties seemed to be marketing's increasing importance and costs, manufacturers explored a good many options for help with their creative processes. In a few instances, major advertisers even held public contests for advertising ideas, attracting hundreds of entries.[2] After 1890, as expenditures grew even faster than before, the petitioners seeking some measure of the advertisers' patronage multiplied. The variety of media and specialists competing to serve advertisers included printers, publishers, freelance or employed copywriters and artists, and advertising agencies. Neither precedent nor authority nor institutional structures made it clear to whom advertisers should turn. As one adviser to manufacturers explained in 1902, the "advertising medium that succeeds most nearly in gaining the confidence of the advertiser, and hence in participating in just the right degree in the elaboration of his plan, will not only secure the most business, but it will keep it year after year."[3] The same maxim held true for advertising specialists. Their competition moved advertising practices into new stages of activities, including self-analysis and reform.

Swindles, scams, and nuisances of various kinds darkened advertising's reputation throughout the nineteenth and early twentieth centuries. Public and trade debates on advertising practices included a case that focused on an ancient form that had come to be much abused; "scenery" advertising was hotly criticized as "defamation of the landscape." This case indicates something of advertising's profile in this period and illustrates how practitioners attacked nonperiodical media (from which they could glean no commissions) in the names of modernization, efficiency, and public spirit. In doing so, they attempted to distance their field from such practices that tainted the public's opinion, as did this "defamation of the landscape," because of the broad brushes with which critics of advertising painted.

Advertisers of many different products covered visible surfaces in both rural and urban areas with their messages. Rarely did these more than urge the use of products, sometimes stating, but often not, their proprietors' names, so it was not their contents that offended; still, they disturbed viewers of both rural and urban scenery. Between 1851 and 1900, "defamation of the landscape" was one of the most frequent topics related to advertising written about in the *New York Times*. One editorial half-seriously speculated that the late increases in insanity might be caused by the "abiding anger with which sensitive minds are filled by the enforced contemplation of . . . scenery . . . covered with monstrous legends vaunting the merits of multitudinous wares."[4] In their turn, and in their field's defense, advertising practitioners came to protest landscape advertising as inappropriate, given their modern understandings. An 1893 article in *Printers' Ink* declared that "rock painting and the desecrating of landscapes are practically obsolete, and are not countenanced by reputable contractors. All sign-advertising men of wide experience say that landscape spoiling hurts the reputation of the advertiser and injures the character of the article advertised," because it gave "unpleasant notoriety and not advertising." Additionally, writers for the trade press regularly joined the general protest with titles such as "Prevention of Cruelty to Landscapes."[5] As the only occupation entirely identified with advertising, the agents' reputations as a whole suffered more from criticisms of any advertisements than those of any other trade, including the publications carrying the advertisements or the printers who produced the noncommissionable advertisements. Clearly, in 1890 the advertising agents' path to credibility and authority was not a simple one, and there were plenty of other trades seeking the advertisers' growing expenditures and, therefore, their confidence.

# Rivals for Advertisers' Patronage

## *Job Printers*

Media producers—job printers and publishers—had provided most of the advice advertisers had received during the nineteenth century, and they had provided it, on request, without charge, as a necessary service to attract and hold customers. Job printers' interactions with advertisers especially included creative services. Because publishers sold audiences—that is, circulations—as their foremost commodities, their assistance to advertisers in creating advertisements was a secondary consideration, even though it affected their publications' appearances, their clients' satisfaction, and possibly the messages' performance. Job printers, on the other hand, had only their printed products and preparation services to sell; appearance, client satisfaction, and performance were everything. Industrialists' trade journals often critiqued catalogs in terms of their attractiveness, writing style, expensiveness, and "salesmanship," indicating to advertisers the importance of all of these variables and advising them to insist on top quality from their printers.

Manufacturers' trade journals advised them to seek guidance from their printers on all of their promotional materials to achieve effectiveness. They also warned their readers against printers who failed to provide them with anything more than "heavy coated paper and cheap ornamentation."[6] Accordingly, leaders among job printers increasingly sought advertisers' patronage by offering to improve their products as advertising instruments. For example, Livermore and Knight, a partnership originally formed in 1883 between a printer and an engraver, promised clients "every type of assistance needed in merchandising goods." Their slogan became "printing with service," and, according to a company history written in 1925, that service made their products effective advertisements.[7] Job printers had always exercised great influence on the contents of advertisements outside of periodicals, particularly because of the widespread use of stock images in lithographed show cards, trade cards, calendars, and so on. Using their experience and the feedback they received from sales of their own nonadvertising prints to the public, printers developed expertise on what sorts of images attracted attention and pleased viewers, even if they did not study the marketing effects of such images. By the mid-1890s, printers' own advertisements and articles in their trade press promoted their creative services to advertisers as a feature for competing with each other and with the periodical press for advertising accounts. For instance, an 1897 headline for the Imperial Engraving Company of Chicago announced that "Advertising Ideas by The Imperial are Impressive."[8]

Printers reminded each other, as Paul Nathan did in his 1900 book on the business aspects of printing, that the "intelligent job printer will never permit himself to forget that printing is allied to advertising, and that almost all of the printing that he does depends in some way upon its success as an advertisement or as an advertising medium." A full chapter addressed the importance of printers' becoming "students of advertising, that they may be able to advise and assist their patrons in the production of printing that will be profitable." In explicit contrast to the 1870s, when printers had not found it appropriate to assist their customers with their copy, Nathan warned that "times have changed." Instead, "the printer who can do nothing but print well is a good enough man for the production of reprint work, but the printer who writes and edits copy is the man to whom new work should be given." Nathan also advised printers who "felt a lack of ability to write and edit for their customers" to hire a writing specialist skilled in the new styles of preparing copy. After all, "if advertisements do not pay, they are sooner or later discontinued," and the printer who can "show a customer how to make his printing profitable" will prosper along with his customer. A Philadelphia printing firm advertised that they did "not feel that our responsibility ends with the preparation and production of printed matter—we rest content only when our client assures us that he is more than satisfied with the RETURNS from the printed matter sent out."[9]

Writing in *AD Sense: A Magazine for Business Builders* in 1906, Leroy Fairman argued even more strongly in favor of printers' responsibilities to their advertising clients. He declared that a person "has no business being a printer unless he is by nature, or training, or both, a competent advertising man, for the reason that most of the matter which the average printer puts into type is advertising of some sort or another." The successful printer "must understand just what the elements of salesmanship are and see that they are embodied in the copy." Fairman instructed printers who received a piece of copy from their customers to "sit down, and analyze it from the standpoint of the consumer or the dealer, or whoever it is to go to. If [a printer] is not competent to do this, he should enlist the assistance of an advertising man who is." He declared that the "true printer looks upon a piece of manuscript from the point of view of salesmanship." Fairman urged printers to develop their advertising expertise because "advertising agents and advertising men are handling millions of dollars worth of printing [business that] belongs to the printer."[10] Fairman's indignation at the advertisers' move away from the job printer recognized but did not forestall the trends well set by 1906.

In their efforts to solicit some of this business, printers advertised extensively to advertisers, both retail and manufacturing. They placed their own advertisements as indications of the quality of their work in both industrialists' trade journals as well as in their own trade's publications, the latter to attract potential clients actively seeking out a printer. Printers received frequent advice from their own journals on how to advertise, including warnings such as, "People expect your advertisements to be specimens of your work. . . . Advertising is a power, be careful with it. Treat it with as much respect as you do a dynamo."[11] In the two decades before World War I, many job printers advertised nationally to manufacturers in trade journals, such as the *Tobacco Leaf*, the *American Grocer*, the *Factory*, and *Iron Age*, offering creative services as well as printing. The Grand Rapids Engraving Company advertised in 1901 that they knew "how to make the strong, striking designs that attract attention," and that they could "do the work your local printer lacks facilities for." They could do "[a]ll the work—writing—illustrating—printing—addressing—mailing." Similarly, the A. B. Morse Co., "The Factory Print Shop," offered to produce circulars for manufacturers with "more of the order-landing, dollar-drawing power."[12]

A leading advocate of and adviser to the printing trade, the *Inland Printer: A Technical Journal Devoted to the Art of Printing*, contained not only information about printing technologies and supplies but also articles and editorials advising printers and their clients about advertising practices. The journal showed its readers, both printers and businesspeople who bought printing, frequent samples of advertisements among its examples of fine printing, expanding this function in the mid-1890s. "Notes on Publicity" was a feature column in 1894 through 1896, replaced in 1897 by "Printing and Publicity Problems." These columns advised printers on useful and effective advertising practices, evaluated advertisements, and offered news on the advertising field, such as meetings of practitioners. Other articles indicated the importance the editors attached to knowledge about advertising. Examples included "Sentences that Sell Goods," "The Question of Publicity," "Noticeable Progress in Advertising Methods," and "Advertising Experience." The *Inland Printer* praised a printer who in 1894 offered "to take over the whole task of designing, writing and compiling a catalogue or pamphlet, as well as the mechanical parts, entirely off a customer's hands, making a price to correspond. The customer will have nothing to do but read and be pleased until his work is delivered."[13]

In light of the new concerns for effective selling, advisers in many journals often warned printers not to place too high a priority on their printing skills if that in any way compromised the selling value of their compositions. One editorial pointed out that it is "a question if a too attractive poster really gives returns to the advertiser"; striving for beauty could reduce "that subtle influence called 'pull'." Printers had to be sure that their poster artists combined their "talents with enough commercialism" to make their products effective selling tools. Neither the individual printer nor the field would benefit if "the guile-less merchant [is] forced without his knowledge to become a patron of the arts at the expense of his advertising account." As one regular contributor expressed it, the "user of printers' ink wants to be advertised, and people don't care so much about good printing as they do about good sense."[14] In 1908, *Profitable Advertising* published an article entitled "The Progress of Design in Advertising" that explained recent improvements in advertising art, praising a new generation of printers "of a very different caliber from the old-time printer. . . . These men know the power and value of art, as applied in business, and they have lifted a few printing establishments to a plane undreamt of by the generation before this."[15] Over years of learning from feedback what style of printing "'takes' with the class addressed or in the country or locality where it is intended to seek trade," printers could help their clients target their messages.[16] Job printers who most successfully competed for advertising revenues combined sensitivity and skills in printing, art, and business. Even so, as the periodical media's share of advertisers' patronage grew, that of job printing continued to decrease, although the absolute volumes of both areas expanded. According to the chief clerk of the U.S. Census, W. S. Rossiter, printing and publishing, together, ranked seventh among American industries by 1905, compared with twenty-first in 1850.[17]

Turn-of-the-century job printing, despite new methods of reproducing images and additional creative services, declined in its importance to advertisers, relative to the periodical presses, in part because the latter themselves could increasingly include pictures. Printing technologies developed rapidly to reduce labor costs and increase speed substantially through this period, but overall this helped to shift the balance of attractiveness to periodicals. In the first decade of the new century, photolithography, photoengraving, halftones, and electrotypes accelerated the mechanical reproduction of images, quickly replacing slower and more expensive forms of chromolithography, for both publishers and job printers. The job printers' advertisements, such as posters, trade cards, and calendars, gradually lost their status as state-of-the-art visual communications media, although periodicals' artwork did not begin to compare in quality with their output for decades. Major advertisers continued to offer high quality prints, "elegant gravures . . . real works of art," as premiums to both retailers and consumers; but increasingly they did so through periodical advertisements.[18] And even though the volume of catalogs, booklets, and circulars continued to increase in selling both to consumers and to the trades because of the ease with which photoengraved images of merchandise could be printed, job printing still fell behind the dollar value of advertisements in pe-

*Specialization as Progress*

riodicals. By 1900, the periodical press dominated advertising media in both volume and the creative attention advertisers were willing to pay to it and for it.[19] The complexities and unreliability of getting ephemera into consumers' homes and workplaces became more serious obstacles at the same time that magazines and newspapers improved their successes at meeting this challenge. The medium of choice for achieving national reach by the early 1900s, magazines maintained that position until broadcasting (first radio, and later, television) challenged their hegemony.

In the meantime, popular reactions against "scenery" and public advertisements reinforced advertising agents' continuing campaign against noncommissionable advertisements to disincline national advertisers from using traditional, nonperiodical media. Attacks on printed, nonperiodical media varied widely, but they generally came from either publishers or people who specialized in periodical advertising, such as advertising agents and copywriters. In a similar vein, during the 1920s, some of the most vociferous attacks against advertising on radio broadcasts came from advertising agents and periodical publishers who perceived a threat to their revenues. In 1893, the manufacturers' and hardware dealers' trade journal *Iron Age* allied itself with periodicals in this debate and criticized storekeepers who "displayed promiscuously" too many "gaudy and senseless placards" to qualify for the "modern, progressive class" of merchant. Only those that were "really attractive [might] be displayed to advantage, providing they are not too many."[20]

Printers defended themselves against increasing numbers of attacks with varying degrees of success. In some cases they criticized the advertising specialists. An editorial in the *Printer and Bookmaker* in 1898 argued on behalf of streetcar advertising that it "is useless for newspapers to decry" this format because "it pays those who make use of it" and must "be treated as a rival that has come to stay."[21] This was still "the printer's age," as printers remained "the chronicler of all achievement and the salesman of the industrial products of the world."[22] But primacy within the field of printed consumer advertising was quickly moving to publishers and away from job printers. So much so, that when Frank Presbrey wrote his history of advertising in 1929, he recognized only two significant categories of nineteenth-century advertising lithography: the "artistic" posters of the French and the large billboard posters of American theater and circus.[23] Of course, job printers could still prosper (as they have to the present) in two niches of the advertising market. The first niche results when "small business men comparatively, that is, those who could not afford an advertising man, bring their work with the understanding that we are to take charge of the whole thing."[24] The second niche continued because advertisers still approached job printers for nonperiodical advertisements, but did so through their agents or advertising managers; so this "demand for the best that the reproductive arts can produce sends many advertisers to the lithographers." And, "the great public . . . actually expects and relishes its advertising novelties."[25]

## Periodical Publishers

Electrotype plates and halftones for illustrations and other advances in preparing and printing magazines and newspapers combined with rapidly growing circulations to add to the appeal of the periodical press as advertising media. Not only did illustrations become less expensive and more attractive, gradually including color in magazines, but typography, too, improved. Both newspapers and magazines improved their overall appearances with lighter, finer typefaces, increased numbers of illustrations that were themselves lighter because they could now include shades of grey, and, in the larger publications, the gradual acceptance of white areas in both editorial and advertising space. In the 1880s, many magazines made their pages more attractive as advertising media by starting to distribute advertisements throughout their pages, rather than isolating them at the back.[26]

Advertisers also found newspapers and magazines increasingly useful because of their remarkable growth in circulations, paralleled by more deliberate, although still primitive, market segmentation. Advertising revenues both fueled and rewarded the expansions in newspaper and magazine circulations, which continued unabated, as they had ever since the outbreak of the Civil War. Their distribution systems reached directly into peoples' homes and places of business, giving them a major advantage over all job-printed advertisements other than mail circulars (junk mail), which lack the benefit of being welcomed into homes on a regular basis.

Many newspapers began, in the 1890s, to alter their appearances and content in order to appeal to women, responding to the budding recognition of women's importance in consumer decisions that accompanied what Edward Kirkland has termed the "feminization" of the U.S. marketplace. Participating in this widespread trend, the newspapers competed with the flourishing new magazines that attracted national advertisers of food, household, and women's personal-care products.[27] Many newspapers also increased their circulations and thereby their claims to higher advertising rates by exploiting the popular appeals of yellow journalism. Yet others aimed for a "certain type" of reader rather than the amorphous large numbers that "yellowness" could bring; rather than resort to sensationalism, these papers sought "respectable readers"—and, of course, the advertisers who were trying to reach that "better class" of reader.

A *New York Times* editorial in 1897 cited a letter from "one of the largest advertisers in New York City," congratulating the paper on its "clean and dignified" coverage and hoping "to be able to increase our advertising with you in the early future." The editorial noted that some advertisers questioned whether readers of the "new journalism" had "the means to purchase goods" and concluded that "one reader who examines his paper with intelligent attention that overlooks nothing in its contents is worth more to the merchant whose advertisement appears in that paper than 300 boys who buy the other kind of paper merely to read about a prize fight."[28] Whether snobbishness or an understanding of marketing conditions and variables motivated this editorial, some large city newspapers targeted affluent markets to attract both national and major local advertisers, although most papers worked simply for large numbers.

With the merger movement consolidating regional and local markets, national, brand-name advertising comprised more and more of the total advertising revenues throughout the country.[29] To help daily newspapers around the country attract and negotiate with national advertisers and advertising agencies, the American Newspaper Publishers Association (ANPA) formed in 1887. One of its first projects circulated reports on advertising agents, helping member newspapers to distinguish the reliable ones from those less likely to pay for the space they commissioned. By 1899, the inadequacies of this reporting system convinced the trade association to publish a regular listing of recognized advertising agencies who had a professional right to commissions. These listings also blacklisted agents who were bad financial risks or whose practices hindered the trade, even though many individual newspapers continued to accept whatever advertising they were offered.[30]

The absence of regularized practices for placing newspaper advertisements provided a major source of inefficiencies and irritation, requiring constant negotiations that added substantially to all parties' expenses and efforts as well as to each one's inclination to doubt the integrity and worthiness of the other. Unreliable newspaper rate cards allegedly informed potential advertisers of publications' circulations and their rate schedules for buying space, but the rates and puffed circulations listed simply indicated the levels at which to open negotiations. Advertisers and advertising agents protested these deliberate inaccuracies for decades, the latter led in their indignation by George P. Rowell in his legendary crusade against the abuses. The absence of standardized rates of commission for advertising agencies who bought space for clients also caused uncertainties. The ANPA recommended a 15 percent rate in 1889, lowering this to 10 percent in 1894. Negotiation remained the determinant factor, however. Prominent publishers could insist on lower commissions, and desperate publishers accepted advertising orders from anyone, furthermore granting them high commissions, to the dismay of established, reputable advertising agents.[31] These problems generated inefficiencies and gave the short-term advantage to unscrupulous agents and publishers, punishing all for the unreliability of some. Worst of all, they detracted from the credibility of both groups in the eyes of the advertisers, injuring agents and newspapers alike to whatever extent they reduced advertisers' confidence in their services and in the entire process. Until more professional standards were established in the early twentieth century, personal reputation and negotiation remained the best means by which one businessperson could decide to trade with another. As a result, agents and newspapers known for their reliability and integrity drew clients to them, setting standards both by example and by the failures of less trustworthy competitors.

Although newspapers differed widely in their efforts to draw on various segments of their potential audiences, magazines came into this period of transformation with a tradition of addressing the "better classes." J. Walter Thompson had helped to convince national advertisers of the advantages of magazines precisely because of their differentials in appeal. Targeting, or market segmentation, remains the modern magazines' greatest claim on advertisers' patronage. Many of the magazines that aimed for the prosperous and literary classes had refused product advertising until the 1880s, when they had to defray the costs of competing with new magazines that used innovative printing technologies and paid writers and artists unprecedented fees. As magazines became prominent advertising media within the overall expansion of consumer advertising through the 1890s, their numbers actually declined significantly,[32] paralleling the bankruptcies and consolidations in business generally brought on by the decade's depression. Of the thousands of journals that jumped into the primordial frays after the Civil War, only a few succeeded in laying claim to large audiences—and, therefore, massive advertising revenues. By 1900, the leaders included the *Ladies' Home Journal, Munsey's,* the *Delineator, McCall's, Cosmopolitan, Harper's, Century, Scribner's, Woman's Home Companion, Colliers,* and *McClure's.* The advertising rates per inside page for these journals ranged from $250 to $800; in 1900, the *Ladies' Home Journal* successfully commanded $4,000 for its back cover, the most expensive position that year.[33] Those publications that established incremental advantages in their credibility as advertising media in the 1880s and 1890s generally continued to attract more readers and then more advertisers in a mutually reinforcing cycle, profiting from deliberate policies to build themselves as advertising media.

Cyrus K. Curtis's early establishment of the *Ladies' Home Journal* and, later, the *Saturday Evening Post* as the nation's commercial pacesetters followed from his appreciation of the lucrative potentials from operating a periodical primarily to attract advertising revenues, rather than as a source of subscription revenues. Even though legend has it that Louisa Knapp Curtis had to prod her husband into being more sensitive to his female audience's perspectives, his early acquiescence in her judgment and editorship evinced a predisposition to strategic experimentation in appealing to worthwhile markets. Other magazine publishers copied, more or less effectively, his spending of unprecedented amounts on popularly written and designed publications geared to the prosperous classes and their petitioners.[34] Curtis first relinquished editing the *Journal* to Mrs. Curtis, then, in 1889, to Edward W. Bok, so he could turn his efforts entirely to directing his own advertising and that of the advertisers in his pages. As late as 1906, he informed a young man from *Printers' Ink* that, "I can hire men to conduct the editorial affairs of my magazines and to look after the circulation satisfactorily, but the *promotion* of the business is a matter I feel it is my duty to attend to myself." He fully credited his successes at building a huge publishing empire to his abilities in advertising, for himself *and* for those who came to him to distribute their messages, a fitting belief for someone who published to benefit advertisers, not readers.[35]

After having built up the *Ladies' Home Journal* to unprecedented circulations, Curtis sought to reform the publishing/advertising matrix, all the better to enhance the advertising trade. Wielding his circulation, especially among the classes of women increasingly recognized as the purchasing agents for most affluent families, as his power base, he insisted on raising standards for advertising practices, or creating them where none existed. Although he confronted opposition from both advertisers and advertising agents, he and other reformers ultimately elevated both the public's and the advertisers' opinions of magazine advertising, encouraging the former to patronize the products that appeared in his journals and the latter to exploit that opportunity. Some of his reforms required also that advertising agents raise their own standards of performance. Through his lessons for advertisers, their agents, and other publishers, Curtis self-consciously served the advertisers of the coming age, the national, brand-name manufacturers, rather than the advertisers of the past age, encouraging the former and curbing the latter.

Early on, Curtis opposed patent medicines and their domination of national advertising's general image. He first discouraged them from advertising in the *Ladies' Home Journal*; then in 1892 he forbade them altogether. His editor, Bok, and other writers crusaded against the misrepresentations addressed later by the Pure Food and Drug Act of 1906.[36] By censoring the products that applied to advertise in his publications, Curtis legitimized those that appeared.

As a 1907 biography in *Printers' Ink* put it, Curtis's "columns [are] so clean that an advertisement in [them] is almost equivalent to a business rating for the advertiser"; hence, "the more rejected and the greater [the] restrictions, the more comes in." In 1906, an ad for the Curtis Publishing Company in the *American Grocer* reminded "Mr. Manufacturer" that, "not all the people in the country could or would buy your wares." After extolling the "economy of appeal" of the millions reached by Curtis's circulations, the message concluded with some justification, "Of one thing you may be sure—our advice is candid. With our advertising columns frequently crowded for space, we are under small temptation to lead you astray." Curtis institutionalized his standards in *The Curtis Advertising Code*, published in 1910 and bound in red leather with gilt-edged, rounded pages. With these twenty-one rules, Curtis sought "to conduct our advertising columns as to command the confidence of our readers and lead them to greater dependence upon the printed message." The rules excluded fraudulent ads, "extravagantly worded" ads, those that "knocked" other products, as well as advertisements for alcohol, medicines, mail-order lines, and businesses that violated Curtis's business or ethical standards.[37] Ernest Elmo Calkins, one of the most important advertising professionals in the early twentieth century, endorsed Curtis's achievements by dedicating *The Business of Advertising* to Curtis in 1915, as "the man who has done most to put the modern conduct of advertising on the right basis."[38]

Curtis taught national-brand advertisers lessons about both strategy and content. He and his staff encouraged them to take a longer view of their advertisements' effects—to build their reputations rather than attempt to achieve immediate sales through unseemly promotions.[39] By dissuading advertisers from withdrawing programs that did not achieve fast results, Curtis prompted advertisers to study feedback patterns and to attempt to find unique ways to present their wares for forming strong and productive associations in the readers' memories. To the same end, Curtis hired Charles Coolidge Parlin in 1910 to establish a department of "Commercial Research," that is, market research. Parlin's reports created unprecedented information with which Curtis representatives could act as consultants to potential and actual advertisers. Curtis also required that he or his staff approve of the styles and contents of advertisements before placing them in his pages. In particular, he always rejected displays filled with heavy type or that were too crowded, and advertisers often protested his rejections of their ready-made electrotypes. Some refused to conform, such as Sears, Roebuck, and Company, which was not allowed to advertise in the *Ladies' Home Journal* until Richard Sears no longer controlled the firm's advertising policies, since Sears persisted in leaving no white space around densely printed copy. By 1892, only two leading advertising agents had hired full-time copywriting specialists, George P. Rowell and F. Wayland Ayer; yet in that year Curtis hired an advertising copywriter, a typesetter, and an artist to create new designs and to improve existing designs for advertisers.[40]

Other publishers ambitious to gain advertisers' patronage also increased their efforts on behalf of copywriting and layout during this transition period. As the National Association of Manufacturers' *American Industries* explained to industrialists in 1902:

> It is because the publisher cannot afford to take a man's money on any misapprehension whatever that the most long-headed among them not only employ honest devices to obtain advertisements, but also exert themselves afterwards to the utmost to have the advertising pay. They are willing personally or through their various solicitors to study the real advertising problems of a business almost as hard as the advertiser himself must do. . . . [T]hey are only too glad to help him prepare his copy; they are glad to go to the trouble and expense of writing copy over and over again, and of changing it, and of having it displayed to the best advantage, and in short, by striving in every way to employ their own experience to advantage, to have the advertiser come as near as possible to making all the money by means of his advertising appropriation that he possibly can.[41]

Despite all this, no one publisher could satisfy national advertisers' full range of needs under the existing business conditions. The continuing disorder and disrepute of the business dealings between advertisers, advertising agents, and magazine and newspaper publishers, fueled by a deep sense of competition, worked against publishers routinely serving advertisers without intermediaries. Even Curtis's services and reforms on behalf of advertisers, singly and collectively, were clearly self-interested, and were recognized as such. Although some publishers shared Curtis's ambitions to win advertisers' confidence and thereby to establish their profession as the first to which advertisers turned, others sought their profits from advertisers more narrowly, selling only circulation claims, and often unreliable claims at that, feeding distrust. Manufacturers, and advertisers generally, pressured publishers and agents alike to provide accurate information: "The advertiser has a right to know just what he is getting for his money—who reads the paper, where they read it, what parts of it the various classes of its subscribers read," and so on.[42]

The individualism, constant negotiation, and lack of standardization that characterized nineteenth-century business practices in general had functioned reasonably well in advertising, if not smoothly, as long as the parties involved remained small and localized. As more and more advertising operations approached national scale between 1890 and 1910, however, the systems by which those advertisers interacted with publishers approached such magnitude that the traditional mechanisms added increasingly unacceptable costs and uncertainties to each transaction. Magazine publishers found themselves in an ironic position, attracting advertisers who sought their national reach, but as a group, raising the advertisers' concerns about reliability, as did the newspaper publishers, because of the scale and uncertainty of the transactions. Because advertisers' contacts with job printers still remain largely localized, or mediated by salespeople, for job printing these conditions have continued until the present without causing practical difficulties. (The formation of the American Lithographic Company, a trust, in 1892 had little impact on the creative responsiveness of printers to their proximate customers.) Advertising agents, likewise, have generally dealt with their clients on a face-to-face basis, so that advertisers could watch them more closely. The working relationships of these three groups—advertisers, printers and publishers, and advertising practitioners—remained essentially adversarial and filled with constant negotiation as the depression of the 1890s wore on. Their mutual dependence only served to exacerbate their certainties that each was at the mercy of the other and would be aggressively exploited without eternal vigilance. So each advertiser went into the fray seeking to negotiate favorable deals with publishers, demanding bargains and benefits, whether agencies handled their negotiations or not.

Even more than the disorder and mutual distrust that characterized transactions between advertisers and publishers, the cumulative costs that advertisers faced when putting together a campaign, publication by publication, worked against Curtis's ambitions to bypass agents, even when publishers gave commissions directly to advertisers. National advertisers generally wanted to maximize their reach through many publications and to do so efficiently. Working and negotiating with each publication, and having an original advertisement created for each, increased transaction costs significantly. The cumulative transaction costs of using more than a few magazines in this manner were prohibitive; for newspapers, such costs had long since given agents their livelihoods. Then, too, what if an advertiser liked one publishers' creations well enough to want to use it in other publications? So, despite the attractions of fitting advertisements to each publication and its audiences and retaining at least some portion of commissions that otherwise went to agents, such a noncentralized, highly redundant system could not compete with a more centralized, less complex alternative. By 1913, even the Curtis Publishing Company had ended its battle with advertising agency predominance. That year it published a book addressed to manufacturers on the subject of efficient advertising and recommended repeatedly that they turn to advertising agents "to be shown how to do it."[43]

## Publishers of Handbooks and Trade Journals

For the price of a book or a subscription, handbooks and journals gave advice to advertisers. During the 1890s and early 1900s, as advertising became an increasingly important component of firms' marketing mixes, published advice sources proliferated, some focusing on advertising alone, others part of more general publications. For instance, as the decades progressed, trade journals in most fields, from the *American Brewers' Review* to *Iron Age*, offered advice on all aspects of advertising with increasing frequency. In its third issue, *System*, a journal aimed at all business owners and managers—manufacturing and distributing alike—announced that each issue thereafter would feature the "promotion of trade [in no] fewer than two articles."[44] Still, most of the advice in manufacturers' journals was in the nature of encouragements to do more advertising and to do it better. The National Association of Manufacturers' journal, *American Industries* ("Of, By and For Manufacturers of the United States"), warned that advertising and selling were "the real problem of the business" of manufacturing. In the first issue, 1902, "The Advertising Man" began a series of guidance articles because "there is no business man of whatever kind, no advertiser of any of these classes, who does not constantly wish to do better and better advertising." Competition required it.[45] Catalogs, for instance, made up a major component of marketing for industrialists, whether they sought trade with consumers, retailers, wholesales, or other manufacturers, and *American Industries* published full-page columns regularly on catalog styles and content. These articles carried such titles as "Glimpses of Salesmanship in Catalogs" and "As Others See Them in their Catalogs" and reminded manufacturers that a firm's well-constructed catalog "indicates that similar care and judgment are bestowed on the articles which it manufactures."[46] Despite all this help from their own trades, advertisers continued to receive the most prolific and specific advice on how to improve their advertising from printers' journals and those in the advertising field, especially *Printers' Ink*, *Profitable Advertising*, and the *Inland Printer*, which wrote for both advertisers and specialists in advertising and printing. Other journals sometimes referred their readers to one of these.[47]

Gradually, through the 1890s and into the early 1900s, advice through the trade journals evolved from an emphasis related to buying advertising media—buying more, and selecting media wisely—to content. A series of columns in the *American Grocer* in 1900 by William Woodhouse Jr. summarized many of the stylistic criticisms current among advisers in print to the trades. Wood-house joined countless others with warnings to advertisers to avoid "silly and unnecessary" superlatives and multiple typefaces in a small "card" jammed with information. He admonished, "One point well taken is better than a dozen just hinted at." Similar criticisms had increased in the preceding decade along with a growing recognition of the importance of making "your advertising a silent salesman." Woodhouse responded to an example "of the good, non-paying, old-fashioned, price-listy order—things and prices, with scarcely any descriptions or facts," by reminding retailers that they would "discharge any salesman who, when a customer approached him turned himself into a walking price list and jabbered things and prices into the customer's ears."[48] Criticism and suggestions increasingly offered after 1890 included advice to focus on consumers' interests and concerns.

Handbooks, alongside journals, mostly helped small advertisers, especially retailers who patronized local newspapers and job printers and who could not afford billings enough to interest agencies. These handbooks ranged from brochures freely disseminated by journal publishers to brochures or bound books produced and sold by "experts." Sometimes handbooks, and occasionally journals, even disseminated template layouts and copy for advertisers to adapt. One handbook told jewelry store owners that they had, "in this book, placed at your disposal. . . absolutely everything that a high salaried advertising man in your own employ could give you—and you are free from his vagaries and independent of his help." The reader who was "intelligent, progressive, and hence open to conviction," would surely appreciate this volume as "one of the best possible investments."[49] Many of the advertising field's leading spokespersons published similar advice. The *Ad-School* promoted itself as "owned, published and pushed by practical Advertising Men who know what they are talking about."[50] George P. Rowell subtitled his *Printers' Ink* "The Little Schoolmaster in the Art of Advertising," and through it he circulated advice and suggestions aplenty. Like *Profitable Advertising,* the slogan of which was "We Show You How to Do It," *Printers' Ink* encouraged advertisers to "study all that you can lay your hands on of advertising literature." But at the same time readers were warned against depending on "book learning" and advertisements that were "clipped," "ready-made," or "stock cut." Charles Austin Bates sought to profit from all angles: he wrote manuals to guide self-advertisers, columns that insisted on professional copywriting, and copy for clients who could afford his individual attention. Despite all these various options for aid through print and printers, by the middle 1890s advertisers who could afford it were increasingly advised to turn to the "successful professional ad man."[51] Writing copy, designing layouts, and placing messages became increasingly specialized, and therefore the work of specialists, whether freelance or at advertising agencies. Advertising journals continued to offer advice to nonspecialists through the 1910s, but by that time they had begun to assume that all but the smallest of advertisers had specialized assistance, either in-house or from the outside.

## Freelance and In-House Specialists

During this transition period, freelance copywriters and artists offered their creative services, interjecting themselves into the advertising process. A rare few, most notably John E. Powers, had such reputations that they prospered at their copywriting for a variety of clients. Other copywriters often promoted themselves aggressively in both paid advertisements and in the columns they wrote for the trade and general presses. Charles Austin Bates and Nathaniel Fowler Jr. were among the most prominent of those freelances who boosted themselves and their profession loudly and immodestly. Bates claimed that "in nine out of ten cases, my work has been very much more productive of results than anything [clients] had previously used. That sounds egotistical, but it isn't. It's a fact." Bates believed that acknowledging his "egotism pure and simple" was the best strategy for building clients' confidence in his services. In promoting himself he repeatedly described his background, his experience, his facilities, his personnel, and his contacts, as well as his ambition to be the leading "specialist in advertising."[52]

Freelances without Powers's, Bates's, or Fowler's reputations could most easily acquire accounts that were relatively small and so not attractive to those publications, and the few agencies, willing to provide creative services in the 1880s and 1890s. They could also find work with advertisers unwilling or unable to put a creative specialist on salary or to work with one for an extended length of time. None of these types of clients offered good prospects for the long run; so, except for a relatively few, the vicissitudes of getting and keeping clients, negotiating terms, and consumating payment made steady employment either with advertisers, publishers, or agents more attractive to all concerned. Freelance copywriters and artists who took on space buying for their clients simply joined the ranks of competing advertising agents if they succeeded, as did Bates in the 1890s. Fowler, on the other hand, gave up space buying altogether in order to devote his energies entirely to copywriting; he could command the extra cost and inconvenience to the advertisers. Although some analysts suggested at that time that freelances and advertising agents complemented each others' work—that copywriters and artists "sold" through their ideas, and the agents conducted "business"[53]—freelance creative specialists simply could rarely compete with those whose labors appeared to be free, subsumed under the agencies' fees or commissions.

Besides their costs, distance from their clients disadvantaged freelance copywriters. As Claude C. Hopkins's success in the late 1880s in winning the Bissell advertising account from Powers demonstrated, an intimate understanding of a client's markets, products, and marketing problems made for a superior advertising program. By most accounts of the time, the best way to acquire such intimacy came from inside a firm, not by an occasional contact. As *American Industries* argued in its first issue, "Perhaps the most important qualification for the advertising manager of the live concern—for it is never too much to dignify him by that name—is that he should understand the spirit of the business; understand it as the head of the concern does; understand it as hardly anybody else in the organization does." Because "no two manufacturing, or jobbing, or retailing propositions, are exactly alike . . . they cannot be studied from the same point of view, . . . regardless of what anybody else is doing." Hence, "the advertising problem connected with a good business is worthy of the closest attention of the brightest mind in the concern." A few years later, in 1905, another writer indicated that advertising "must be one of the most important branches of the business and just as skilfully [sic] handled as any other, even if the head of the concern himself has to devote part of his time to it."

In the creation of appropriate advertisements for a firm, the importance of intimacy with the enterprise argued for hiring in-house advertising specialists. As managers replaced owner-managers in the increasingly bureaucratic firms that sponsored national campaigns, advertising responsibilities did fall onto a variety of shoulders, including employees. During this transitional period many firms chose to hire specialized advertising copywriters as well as managers, especially if they placed advertisements directly with periodicals and obtained discounts in lieu of commissions. By 1890, a few stars, such as both John E. Powers and Artemas Ward at times, received lordly incomes when under salary as in-house specialists. As the *American Grocer* explained then, a "man would have been considered insane five and twenty years ago who would have paid writers of advertisements salaries ranging, as they do now, from $10,000 to $25,000."[54] Yet many firms preferred minimizing their costs and imposed copywriting on someone already employed to do other tasks; this gave the benefits of intimacy but lost the benefits of specialization. Against all these options, having an agency that did all the work in order to compete for billings commissions appeared attractive, especially once agencies began to appreciate the importance of learning about their clients. This alternative minimized firms' overhead and maximized their flexibility, should they want a change of tack. When, after 1900, many publishers increasingly refused to give discounts to any but bona fide agents, in-house copywriters became even less attractive to most firms.

## Agencies Respond to the Changing Environment

As major advertisers of branded consumer goods shifted their expenditures to the published, commissioned media during the 1890s, they vastly expanded the niche filled by agents, as well as their rewards. Newspapers grew in size, number, and amount of illustration as the national scope and sheer volume of advertising expenditures grew. Fueled by past advertising revenues and the promise of more, magazines by mid-decade provided a whole new level of access to consumers' attention at home and at work. Agents stood to prosper if they could hold on to their decades-old claim on commissions for facilitating many of these placements. Even though they entered the decade with the advantage of their experience and contacts with publishers, their privileged twentieth-century position as advertising authorities was in no way assured. Agents still operated idiosyncratically at a time when the increasing complexities and magnitude of the communications and marketing networks were inclining advertisers to reward greater coordination and systematization, not only between parties, but within the professions serving them. The evolving business culture of the period, with the decline of owner-managers and the rise of corporations and their layers of specialists and managers, also favored formalized, standardized transactions. How and why advertising agents responded as they did to these changing circumstances, and their varying successes and failures in doing so, determined the nature of their profession in the twentieth century.

In order to take advantage of the opportunities presented by national advertisers' growing expenditures and win advertisers' patronage as a matter of authority and routine, agents had to convince advertisers that specialized, independent agencies optimized their clients' profits. This required both improving their collective reputations for honest dealings and developing services that satisfied high-volume advertisers. Advertising practitioners with an eye to the future encouraged these goals, both for individual businesses and, as importantly, for their profession. Such long-term thinking, rare before 1890, became commonplace by the 1910s. Reformers within the field believed that more efficient and effective services to the advertisers would increase the field's viability and public profile. Because the figures who prospered most visibly did follow these principles—such as Ayer, Rowell, and Thompson—their examples as much as their words led the field.

## The Commission System

Ironically, the commission system put agencies at risk even as it provided their greatest advantage. On the one hand, other sectors, including advertisers and publishers themselves, calculated how to hold or acquire the large sums that commissions transferred to agencies. On the other, the commission system had accustomed most large advertisers to paying for their advertising space through agents who first deducted their agreed-upon percentage then forwarded the balance to publishers. This provided an established mechanism by which advertising agents could provide clients with additional creative and planning services without charging extra for them, giving them a substantial edge over other contenders for advertisers' patronage. If agencies had had to set up a fee system for their services, the inefficiencies of micronegotiating for each service would likely have made their status as untenable as that of competing fields. (Many agencies moved toward a fee system in the 1970s, but that came after decades of standardized practices, quite unlike the earlier, highly volatile, distrustful environment for negotiating.)

The very advantages that the commission system gave advertising agents brought it under heavy criticism and challenge. Threats to it surfaced whenever advertisers considered buying their own space and claiming commissions from the publishers, instead of going through an independent agent. Although the knowledge and networks that reputable agents had built up offered important benefits, the lure of retaining the publishers' commissions—from 5 to 25 percent—tempted both advertisers and publishers to bypass agents. More large advertisers could have chosen to develop their own internal advertising departments to plan, create, and place advertisements; such practices could have centralized manufacturers' advertising efforts within their own firms, although for smaller firms this would have strained their resources, further exacerbating the concentration of industry. Under such conditions, agents would have held only smaller clients' patronage.

Most publishers held deeply seated objections to the very aspects of commissions that pleased the advertisers; namely, that the agents' compensation diminished the publishers' revenues, rather than increased the advertisers' expenditures. Cyrus Curtis believed that agents served advertisers rather than publishers; therefore, the agents' payments should not derive from publishers' commissions. Despite his influence, however, Curtis could not keep advertisers from agencies. He could only complain about the commission system, lower his commissions to 10 percent for a time, and insist that agencies' commissions not be shared with advertisers as a means of competition between agencies.[55] Like Curtis, publishers generally—along with anyone trying to regularize practices—objected to abuses by which agents rebated portions of their commissions to their clients in order to compete aggressively with other agents. Protests appeared in print, yet because this practice gave the advertiser an edge in negotiating with agents, advertisers did not generally object. Rebates exacerbated negotiations and added to transaction costs and irregularities, but the practice intensified during difficult times, when agencies competed most vigorously. Rebates were widely held in poor repute because they figured in much of the public discussion about abuses of railroad rates during this period. Rebates reminded both agents and publishers that the advertisers' interests drove the system, and would do so unless the two services sectors could coordinate and standardize practices.

Although advertisers used the commission system to their advantage, a deep conflict of interest lay within it and other forms of space brokering, such as Rowell's $100 system, whereby advertisers could get one-inch "cards" placed in one hundred newspapers for $100. Agents justified their compensations by assuring their clients that they placed advertisements efficiently and effectively. But they could, and some did, increase their incomes by placing more advertisements than optimal, by placing advertisements in publications that offered them favorable commissions or discounts, by placing advertisements only in papers in which the agents had purchased space at wholesale, by neglecting to pass on savings from publishers, and so on. Advertisers often suspected their agents of deceit, duplicity, or incompetence and switched when they thought another agent might serve them better, or they quit periodical advertising altogether, as did Charles Pinkham, for a time.[56]

Through all this controversy, advertising agents claimed that the commission system allowed fair value to all parties—publishers, advertisers, agents, and consumers alike—as long as each dealt honestly and forthrightly. Agencies willing and able to absorb the costs of additional services and receive their only compensations from the traditional publishers' commissions gave clients the sense that they were getting something for nothing. Such agents set the pace for the field and warded off the encroachments of others who offered their services to advertisers. Conversely, commissions also added materially to the attractiveness of the national advertisers as clients, because their extensive billings allowed their agents sufficient compensation to take on the additional functions. So despite the commission system's profound problems and often negative impacts on agent/advertiser/publisher relations, it survived, and the independent advertising agent survived with it, because agents collectively were able to convince advertisers and their managers that their services came honestly and competently, at no extra charge, with a fair profit to all parties.

## Serving Advertisers

Charles Pinkham's 1889 decision not to advertise in periodicals rather than trust an agent of the traditional school who had exploited the conflict-of-interest potential of the commission system reflected this sense that the agent/client relationship was fundamentally cutthroat and unstable. Pinkham returned to newspaper and magazine advertising only when a member of the new generation of advertising men offered not only straightforward dealings but increased services. The new Pinkham campaign began in January 1890, a harbinger of the coming transition.[57]

Agencies that grew the most under the new business conditions after 1890 absorbed more and more of the advertisers' tasks, eventually internalizing and centralizing all advertising activities except what must remain the advertisers' tasks: initiating a campaign, approving it, and paying for it. These agencies reduced the complexities and costs of the transactions involved in creating and placing advertisements, satisfying advertisers' objective concerns. Moreover, as advertisers began to expect greater effectiveness in their advertisements' messages, as well as efficiency in their placement, aggressive agencies satisfied those concerns, too, as the next chapter will show. Agencies' authority as creative experts grew simply by *creating;* their own efforts over time conferred expertise, and their self-promotions enhanced it. Agencies that specialized their internal operations paralleled their industrial clients' trends and helped to convince them of their credibility as modern businesses. As Boston manufacturer C. J. Bailey effused in 1893, "Where is the prosperous business concern of to-day that has not experts in every department? And the greatest of them all is he who writes, or manages, the advertising department. . . . To-day the writing of advertisements is a profession." According to Bailey, every successful business required professionals, either in-house or in agencies, to create and manage its advertisements.[58]

Effective, attractive services had to be client-centered; otherwise clients could just as well seek out harried freelances or inexpensive manuals. Charles Austin Bates insisted, therefore, that a copywriter could service an advertisers' unique marketing problems only by knowing "enough about the other man's business to be able to explain it clearly, forcibly, convincingly, to the reader who knows nothing about it." Moreover, "he must be able to do something for this man's business that the man cannot do for himself. He must understand the business, in some measure, as its proprietor understands it, and he must also understand it from the advertising standpoint."[59]

The major advertisers with large billings that agencies could most profitably serve accepted and rewarded this centralization of crucial functions in agencies most readily when they got assurances of square dealings with reputable, up-to-date firms. Advertisers wanted assurances that their bottom line, their total costs for advertising through agents, was their best possible deal for the most effective campaign. The systemic reforms that George P. Rowell and Frances Wayland Ayer had begun to promote in the 1870s did not make much headway as long as most clients prided themselves on their powers of negotiation. Owner-managers in the nineteenth-century tradition did not see the need of a true agent who made independent judgments on their behalf; nor did they trust agents to do so. Because principals determine what agents' functions they will reward, the Rowell-Ayer proposals for client-centered, nonnegotiating relationships saw limited application until advertisers changed their character and needs in the 1890s. Then advertising agents found it profitable to recognize the priority of advertisers' interests as the source of all the field's revenues.

### Changing Clients

As leading agents increasingly began to feel the need to improve their field's reputation and professionalism, they recognized that the public identified advertising in general with the advertised businesses. When asked about honest advertising in a 1903 interview, Fowler acknowledged that, "as advertising is a part of business, it will be neither better nor worse, neither more truthful nor less truthful, than is the business of its day. The truthfulness of advertising is on the same level as the business it represents, neither above nor below it."[60] Consequently the high profiles of patent-medicine and alcohol advertising fueled the public's ambivalence toward advertising; such advertised products sold widely and well, but highly vocal sectors of the nation objected loudly to those successes, especially during the Progressive era. At the same time that the temperance movement was providing arguments against advertising alcohol, the nostrums' exaggerated claims and often dubious ingredients made easy and appropriate targets for journalists, medical doctors, clergy, citizens' groups, and legislators. In 1894, the Harvard psychologist William James wrote a letter to the editor of the *Nation* that protested more eloquently than most against "the medical advertisement abomination." He declared that this "evil is increasing with formidable rapidity," and "the authors of these advertisements should be treated as public enemies and have no mercy shown."[61]

James's diatribe presaged the Progressive Era's assault on patent medicines and their advertisements, along with other abuses in the consumer marketplace. An essay appearing in two popular magazines of 1906 regretted that "escape from the ingenuity of the modern quack advertiser is impossible." The author attacked all advertisers, but especially the most "poisonous of all," which dispensed "falsehoods about pills, [and] distasteful notices about the human physiology" and took "an unfair advantage of human nature."[62] Although the Pure Food and Drug Act that finally worked its way through Congress in 1906 was largely stripped of its provisions against false advertisements by lobbyists' efforts, its very existence reflected widespread public reactions against the promotion of patent medicines, reinforced by the American Medical Association's determination to gain control over the pharmaceutical market.[63] As the most visible and most objectionable single category of advertiser (since alcohol advertisements rarely reached into bourgeois homes), the patent-medicine promoters drew negative attention to the entire practice of advertising, and the aspersions cast on them spread to the entire field.

This public outcry reinforced economic and structural incentives for agents to begin changing the mix of their most lucrative accounts in the 1890s, eliminating alcohol and patent-medicine purveyors and adding corporations marketing other consumer products or services nationally. N. W. Ayer & Son gradually censored its clients, starting in 1896 when Ayer and his partner Henry N. McKinney began rejecting liquor accounts and instructed their staff not to solicit or accept new brewery accounts. After 1899, the Ayer agency had no clients selling wines or spirits, and it ceased work on all liquor accounts in 1903. Ayer had great respect for Cyrus K. Curtis and, in his history of the firm, Ralph Hower speculates that Curtis's policies at the Ladies' Home Journal reinforced Ayer's own personal opposition to alcohol and support for temperance. In 1900 and 1901, the agency stopped working with two of its major patent-medicine accounts, drastically cutting its revenues and, as Ayer stated several years later, resulting in "a year's business without profit." Ayer and his partners had decided that because patent-medicine promotion "had finally reached the point at which it became necessary to make or fake miracles to secure commensurate results . . . we thought ourselves better off without it."[64] As with the open-contract system that was not fully in effect even twenty years after its announcement, Ayer did not rigidly follow his restrictive policy immediately. Nonetheless, as a result of these decisions, the agency's income from patent medicines dropped from 15.01 percent of total revenues to 3.44 percent from 1900 to 1901. The agency ceased soliciting or accepting new nostrum accounts after 1902, and after 1905 altogether ceased placing patent-medicine advertisements. This decision coincided with stepped-up campaigns against patent medicines in the *Ladies' Home Journal* and *Collier's Weekly* and comparable declarations against nostrum advertising by other agencies. Three years after the Pure Food and Drug Act of 1906, Ayer solicited "no business from manufacturers or dealers in alcoholic beverages, no patent-medicine advertising, no questionable financial or speculative propositions." As a promotional booklet asserted in 1909, N. W. Ayer & Son had "erected the most remarkable advertising structure that the world has ever seen—independent, watchful, alert, competent, honest, reliable."[65]

Although most other agencies did continue to accept some patent-medicine advertising, the number who did so among the leaders of the profession declined as the public expressions of distress at the alleged panaceas increased. J. Walter Thompson began insisting at least as early as 1887 that the medical journals that he handled were "not the vehicles for quack nostrums, but are THE mediums for very many proprietary articles which are prescribed by physicians in their practice." In 1895 and thereafter for at least a decade, Thompson also promoted his agency by indicating that the "customers I desire . . . [are] legitimate advertisers of the better class—only those in whom the publishers and readers can have confidence that they will fulfill every representation." In contrast, there were "quacks in advertising as in medicine. We do not want their business at any price."[66] Of course, as special agent for many magazines well into the 1890s, the Thompson agency continued to profit from innumerable transactions with patent-medicine vendors, even though a good many of them came through other agencies.

Beyond leaders' recognition of the ethical and publicity merits of moving away from controversial clients, major economic and structural incentives rewarded other changes in clientele. Typically, a plethora of small accounts filled agencies' portfolios before the middle 1890s—too many to provide with creative services without raising fees or losing profits. Here, again, the interaction between changes in the overall business environment drove and then reinforced changes in advertising practices. Creating ads for a single aggressive corporation could yield billings approaching those of all of the firms it had subsumed in mergers. As corporate advertisers sought creative assistance to help achieve greater effectiveness and efficiency in addressing their marketing problems, they sometimes even expended larger amounts on media buying than the sum of the parts. Agents' billings per consolidated company certainly increased, yielding directly proportional commissions and paying for additional client-centered services. This cycle clearly made the large national accounts of companies manufacturing consumer goods the most attractive clients. N. W. Ayer & Son, Lord & Thomas, and most others that prospered in the early twentieth century actively solicited such accounts. Smaller agencies that could not attract corporate accounts suffered losses in their billings when their former clients disappeared into mergers.

In the 1880s, even before giving up the revenues from their alcohol and patent-medicine accounts, Ayer and McKinney had begun to seek larger accounts. At first they hoped simply to increase their billings overall, but later they realized that reducing their total number of accounts would enable them to serve and attract large clients better. By 1900, N. W. Ayer & Son handled accounts for Hires' Root Beer, Montgomery Ward's mail-order company, Mellin's Baby Food, Burpee Seeds, the N. K. Fairbank Company, which produced many popular household products, eleven Standard Oil subsidiaries, and, most importantly, the National Biscuit Company.[67] The same year that Ayer closed its largest patent-medicine accounts, 1900, the agency also began a self-promotion campaign targeted at the large-scale manufacturing corporations coming to dominate national consumer markets, aiming to convince those manufacturers that their market dominance did not eliminate the need for advertising their goods. Booklets such as "Concerning Staples" argued that manufacturers attempting to sell their merchandise on a large scale required advertising to maintain demand. In the next few years, many such firms began working with the Ayer agency, including the American Tobacco Company, H. J. Heinz, the International Silver Company, the American Sugar Refining Company, the Cadillac Company, and Steinway & Sons. In 1905, the Ayer agency helped the New York Mutual Life Insurance Company through a crisis in its public reputation by "institutional," or image, advertising. In this case, and starting in 1908 with both the American Telephone and Telegraph Company and Western Union Telegraph Company, the agency began to develop advertising campaigns suited to clients who needed to promote something other than short-term sales.[68]

### Changing Personnel and Structures

The trend toward managerial specialization that progressed within manufacturing corporations contributed to these advertisers' interests in new standards for advertising practices. The parties engaged in negotiations between printers/publishers, advertisers, and/or advertising agents were decreasingly owner-managers, but managerial employees with very different skills and sources of authority. Reading the character of one's business rivals with acumen had been a matter of pride, and part of the nineteenth-century repertoire of entrepreneurial abilities when business was conducted on a scale that allowed personal contact and judgment. But the new corporate business environment required bureaucratic protocols and standards; employers relinquished ordinary negotiations to employees who might have to conduct them at some distance. In setting up such protocols and standards, advertising specialists inside the firms or in agencies lifted tasks off the shoulders of increasingly specialized managers who did not share the precorporate owner-managers' personal incentives for controlling their firms' advertising; nor did they have the expertise, confidence, or authority to justify increasing expenditures as rational and reasonable, and not just capricious.

In order to provide additional services, growing agencies during this transitional period found that internal specialization into departments was as necessary as divisions of labor were in other areas of business. The traditional nineteenth-century agency had functioned adequately with fewer than ten workers, with owner-managers soliciting as well as servicing accounts. Even in the remarkably large Ayer agency, which had 112 workers in 1890, partners directed every detail. Agents then typically boosted themselves by asserting that they attended to their clients' needs personally. For instance, through at least the last years of the nineteenth century, J. Walter Thompson's copy for his agency was largely written in the first-person singular. Typical statements included, "While magazines are my specialty, I deal in all of the large publications," and "I . . . give my personal attention to all business of this nature."[69] This contrasted with a 1909 book that referred to the agency and its personnel throughout, even in Thompson's signed "Introduction," by the first-person plural or as "The J. Walter Thompson Company." This publication also listed the various departments into which the agency had been divided by that time, underlining each of them for emphasis.[70] Similarly, F. Wayland Ayer stated in 1907, then with 238 on staff, that one of his agency's early improvements was to separate important functions: "This, then is one of our oldest 'standards' that *the man who meets advertisers and the man who meets publishers should work independently of each other*." The agency's publicity went so far as to scoff at other agencies' claims of "personal attention and personal service." This was in 1909, when its fortieth-anniversary promotion argued on behalf of the superiority of division of labor and large organizations. The older and "fallacious" proposition disregarded the important reality that "no man ever lived who is equally good at all kinds of work, and modern advertising embraces many lines of effort." The best people in any line, Ayer said, were even more likely than the ordinary to neglect areas outside of their expertise.[71] Agency self-promotions in this new phase instructed advertisers to find the best talent in large, well-coordinated organizations—firms like those the national advertisers themselves ran.

Not all agencies successfully transformed themselves from being owner-managed, relatively undifferentiated enterprises into highly structured, departmentalized organizations. George Rowell's agency declined at the end of the century because he had not restructured it according to an effective division of labor. Tellingly, he misconstrued his agency's decline by attributing it to his own shift of attention to *Printers' Ink* and the *Directory*. In true nineteenth-century fashion, he summoned up "a homely proverb" in explanation: "He who by the plough would thrive, / Himself must either hold or drive."[72] Both J. Walter Thompson and F. Wayland Ayer were younger men who built organizations better able to make the transition into the twentieth century. Nevertheless, Thompson resisted the assumption of creative services, and his staff's specialties were distributed disproportionately and could not meet the needs of the changing business environment. His agency was consequently in great difficulty when Thompson sold it to Stanley B. Resor and several other members of the firm in 1916. At that time, the agency's two hundred employees, most of them solicitors and clerks, served more than two hundred small accounts. As Resor coarsely recounted, "the copy department consisted of one very deaf former editor of the *Springfield Republican*, one deaf artist and a dumb [speech-impaired] artist."[73] Resor aggressively reconstructed the agency and its activities, and the J. Walter Thompson Company quickly regained its prominence. N. W. Ayer & Son survived its founder better than the others because Ayer had always sought to build an organization according to what best suited the advertisers; he also was willing to bring in strong partners to share responsibilities, notable among them, McKinney. As a result, his agency led in each of the responses that the advertising field made to the evolution of business during his lifetime, balking only at the final step of modernization, namely, joining with his competitors in a professional association. Ayer fit the stereotype of the nineteenth-century, inner-directed businessman, contrasting sharply with the socially pliant personality more typical of the modern advertising man. As an in-house historian for Ayer, Inc., stated, "Wayland Ayer could just have well been a banker as an advertising man."[74] His interests were in building a profitable, respectable business, and he had little attachment to any particular internal structure as long as it succeeded at that goal.

## Professional Associations

Initially, reformers within the ranks of the advertising practitioners wrote and argued as individuals about their field's activities and participants. In the course of defending and promoting their occupation, however, many professionals increasingly worked at institutionalizing it, developing standards, and forming a modern profession. Just as manufacturers had found it advantageous to concentrate their facilities and functions, advertising practitioners and members of other occupations began to see that some form of concentration could benefit them, too. Outside of production, however, there was little or nothing to gain in the way of economies of scale through horizontal or vertical integration at this stage, and so the models of merger, incorporation, or unionization were not appropriate for these occupational groups. Therefore, in seeking the benefits of cooperation and common standards, most occupational groups, including advertising practitioners, began to move toward professional associations.[75] Whether speaking as individuals or single agencies or in nascent professional organizations, advocates and reformers worked in three directions: urging publishers and fellow practitioners to raise their individual standards for conducting business; encouraging peers to improve the efficiency and effectiveness of their services; and justifying their positions within business activities and culture more broadly.

The mix of early associations in this field evinced just how unclear people who worked in advertising were about what constituted an advertising profession. The first associations generally included the advertising managers and special agents of publications, in-house managers employed by manufacturing and other advertisers, and independent advertising agents and their personnel. The most influential of this type of association, by far, was the Sphinx Club of New York, organized in 1896 to promote a "clearer understanding of the problems of advertising and a betterment of advertising" through discussions and the collegiality of its members from advertising institutions across the country.[76] In 1902, it established the National Society for the Investigation and Suppression of Fraudulent Advertising in order to protect the readers of newspapers and magazines and to improve the public's confidence in advertisements overall.[77] Articles in the *New York Times* applauded reformist actions by the Sphinx Club, as did others, including Charles Arthur Carlisle of Studebaker Brothers Manufacturing Company, writing in 1902 for the National Association of Manufacturers in *American Industries*. He praised its work "against fraudulent advertising," concluding that the agent who participates in such reform activities will also give "to his client his best talent in the expenditure of an advertising appropriation." In some cases, membership of "advertising clubs" ranged even farther afield. Some member clubs of the Associated Advertising Clubs of the World were "merely town-boosting clubs," formed to advertise their communities, according to Earnest Calkins. By the 1910s, however, the various associations increasingly included people "engaged in advertising work or in advertising a particular business."[78] As one of the most aggressively modernizing advertising publications expressed it in 1902, whatever the form, "the club idea in advertising" was a boon to "the development of advertising as a profession."[79]

In addition to calling for organized, internal enforcement of honesty in advertising practices, an editorial in *Profitable Advertising* in 1908 suggested that other efforts be made "To Regulate the Experts." This response to criticisms about advertising experts insisted that solutions would have to affect the field collectively. "It is perhaps the greatest brake on the wheels of genuine advertising that there are in the business so many men who are so poorly equipped to practise it, and so unable to do justice to those who spasmodically employ them." Although all professions had "incompetents," other fields had "standards for estimating the attainments of their professors, at least." The editors lamented that "in advertising there are no standards."[80] George French, a leader in systematizing advertising practices in the early twentieth century, declared that the "most imminent problem now before the advertising profession is this question of legitimizing and standardizing the work of the advertising man." He asserted that there had previously been "a sufficient excuse for the chaos that reigned in advertising, in that it was so young a business." That excuse had become obsolete by 1909, French insisted, and it was time that advertising be "put on a better and more luminous basis."[81]

Although many reformers in advertising sought the security and distinction of standards for preparation and admission to the profession, as in medicine and law, none of the many associations that advertising practitioners formed ever succeeded at that. Since the 1910s, they have developed mechanisms to recommend and to pressure members to conform to standards of ethics, but they have rarely been able enforce them. The Truth-in-Advertising movement of the 1910s attempted such self-regulation. It began when Samuel C. Dobbs observed that "something is wrong. . . . All advertising is under suspicion, good, bad, and indifferent." The movement he launched directed its collective efforts at the public's opinion explicitly in order to forestall regulation. As George French, a vocal participant in the movement, stated in 1915, advertising sought "to relieve itself of a certain odium that [had] accumulated against it as the conscious assistant to unworthy efforts to dupe or defraud the people." The movement's self-policing entailed setting up vigilance committees to purge false advertisements and thereby improve consumers' and state officials' confidence in what remained.[82] In a range of other settings, various loose coalitions of agencies and individuals worked toward goals analogous to those of other professional associations. Their accomplishments included regularizing and standardizing interactions with publishers and clients, cooperating to achieve political, business, and social goals, and encouraging innovation.[83]

The most influential of all advertising associations, both locally and nationally, began with the formation of the New York City Association of Advertising Agencies in 1911. From its inception, this organization performed one of the essential functions of an effective professional association, namely, the exclusion of nonspecialists. Soon other cities, notably Philadelphia, Chicago, and Boston, organized allied associations, and out of this network came the American Association of Advertising Agencies (AAAA) in 1917. Eventually, this organization became the hub for advertising professionals around the nation. The second largest continuing organization is the American Advertising Federation (AAF), formed by the merging in 1967 of the Advertising Federation of America and the Advertising Association of the West, both founded around 1905. The AAF's objectives likewise seek to promote the field and to do so by promoting high professional standards.

By 1917, most advertising professionals who continued to operate had successfully made the transitions in their functions discussed here as well as the alterations in their professional attitudes that are the final subjects of this study. This timing also coincided with several major changes in advertising's relationships with the body politic. These included the beginning of the U.S. government's innovative, and often troubling, promotional efforts to rally the nation to World War I, the passage of the Internal Revenue Act, which accorded advertising costs the status of a fully deductible business expense, and the continuing transition of American businesses into corporate structures.

## Agencies Triumph

The standards for an advertising agency's satisfactory service had evolved by 1920 from simply making reasonably trustworthy placements to providing full planning and creative functions. Ayer and his partner Henry McKinney realized during the 1890s that their own interests were served best by generating advertising plans based on clients' individual needs. As Daniel M. Lord, Chicago's leading agent, explained in 1903 to a group of businessmen involved in all aspects of advertising, "the conditions surrounding the business [had] changed" since his first years as an advertising man. The modern advertising agency "is not only a conduit through which business passes from advertiser to newspaper," Lord declared, "but is a developer of business, and through their agency, through their work, a manufacturer is enabled not only to increase his trade and his profit, but not infrequently adopt new methods and more satisfactory methods for developing his business." The benefits of the agency came "not only so far as saving money, but in more efficient work, in choice of media and more efficient copy." So every advertiser could benefit by working with a good agency, even at the cost of the publishers' commissions that would go to compensate the agent.[84]

In the past, Lord acknowledged, the parties involved in advertising had not been so able to trust each other. But "we have gone through the usual evolution of business—the dishonest advertising agent—the dishonest paper—the dishonest advertisers—and to-day the successes in each of these lines are the ones that are making the money—the ones that are looked up to—the ones that are respected." Just as Rowell and Ayer had led the field by prospering with their client-centered emphasis on honesty and service, Lord concluded that "as time goes on the honest advertising man is bound to be of more influence, fill a bigger space in the business world and be a factor to reckon with in all successful manufacturing business, or any line that is seeking general publicity. . . . In short, he stands as a leader in the development of business to the advertiser, to the publisher, and last—to his own profit."[85]

Although Lord overstated his case when he relegated profit to the bottom of his list of priorities, he understood that, by then, successful advertising agencies had to reposition themselves in order to attract the patronage of major national-brand advertisers. A factor in N. W. Ayer & Son's successful solicitation of the National Biscuit Company account in 1898 was a letter of recommendation from a Chicago publisher to the new corporation's chairman of the board, Adolphus Green, that praised the agency's experience and capacities as "the most skilled in handling advertising in all its aspects. And this I *know— they're honest*."[86] The Ayer agency's success with this account, generating the famous Uneeda campaign discussed in the next chapter, followed from the close attention paid by McKinney to Green's requests, the product, and market conditions. Such successes widely taught both practitioners and advertisers that honesty and client-centered service characterized a productive and mutually profitable agent/client relationship; their examples likely had more impact than any reformers' pronouncements.

The R. J. Reynolds Company account solicited by William M. Armistead for N. W. Ayer & Son became one of the agency's most lucrative accounts and demonstrated to advertisers and agents alike the merits of a fully coordinated working relationship. Armistead had joined Ayer in 1909, and two years later he decided to approach the tobacco company because he liked its Prince Albert brand. Although Reynolds was not on Armistead's soliciting list and did not sell outside of the South at that time, the agent "decided the company could be made a national institution by using 'Prince Albert' as a spearhead." When Armistead met with Reynolds, the tobacco man showed him twelve brands owned and promoted by the American Tobacco Company and expressed his regret that "we cannot meet this competition with one brand." The adman countered with the proposition that marketing twelve brands could be "only one-twelfth as strong as one brand" and then suggested a concentrated advertising program to promote Prince Albert. Armistead's proposal required that Reynolds stop his practice of working directly with printers, as when, in 1900, he introduced himself to a printer in New York City and negotiated a large contract for chromolithographed signs. After Reynolds agreed to the program, Ayer & Son developed a series of advertisements and submitted them to him. Although Reynolds had been accustomed to having a strong hand in his advertising copy until then, he responded that he "would not change a word for $500." Nor did he ever reject or change any other copy that was submitted to him thereafter. Shortly after the successes of this model campaign, Reynolds determined to put a cigarette on the market and in 1913 launched Camel cigarettes, following an elaborate and expensive marketing and advertising plan from N. W. Ayer & Son. Combining the remarkable successes of both the Prince Albert and the Camel campaigns, R. J. Reynolds moved from fourth to first place among tobacco companies.[87] These campaigns convinced many of the remaining skeptics to allow advertising specialists to provide a full range of marketing services.

Through the first decade of the new century, the printing trades and their advocates continued to defend publishers and job printers against the advertising specialists' growing presumption of priority and overall authority in the field. They often urged printers to win advertisers' patronage by providing creative services rather than leaving them to advertising agents. In 1907, the *Printing Art* declared that the "interests of the advertiser and printer are so closely interwoven that the printer must always be looking toward a higher efficiency in this product."[88] This statement notwithstanding, by the end of the old century, their position had clearly become defensive. In response to an article in George Rowell's *Printers' Ink* defaming the compositor, the *Inland Printer* found it necessary in 1899 to insist upon the importance of printers' most specialized functions; the printer was not "merely . . . a machine to execute the desires of the so-called advertising 'doctor,' 'expert' or 'schoolmaster.'" Printers, said the response in the *Inland Printer*, resisted such insinuations, which had found a "place in advertising journals and which are calculated to mislead advertisers" into minimizing the importance of the compositor and his expertise.[89] But by 1910, recognizing that the battles for large accounts were effectively over, the *Inland Printer* urged its readers to work with "advertising men." The best of all possible worlds by then seemed to be compositors' working with agencies, each acknowledging the other's expertise, the former "making artistry from crude material," the latter creating the message and insisting on "classy" typography that maximized impact. Moreover, the "advertising agencies are good people to work for. . . . [T]hey are much more amenable to reason, where the question is one of practicality, than is the average customer, who may think he knows something about type, but whose taste is atrocious and whose ego abnormal." The *Inland Printer* confirmed this approach by reprinting an article from *Harper's Weekly* concluding that the "advertising solicitor in the main is a good fellow. His object in life is definite, legitimate and altruistic. He wants to succeed, by making others succeed. He may be persistent, unquenchable, unduly enthusiastic and sometimes *too* pushing. But he means well."[90] This was a mixed review, certainly, but one resigned to the new order of things.

Even the Curtis Publishing Company had relinquished its claims on the advertisers' primary loyalties in advertising matters by 1913, quite satisfied to collect revenues from advertisers working through agencies that had taken on full creative responsibility:

> Some ten years ago certain agencies began to write copy and to prepare illustrations for their clients, because they found that by this means they could more readily induce men who dreaded the technical details, to advertise. To do this they began to find it necessary to inquire into the client's problems, and to find out what his lines of argument were. Then they began to suggest selling arguments. Next they saw ways of correlating other selling plans with the advertising. . . . Thus step by step grew the well-equipped agency of today . . . which is beginning to make the word "advertising agent" a misnomer. For "advertising" is today but one feature of the work of a real agency.

By this time, "the agent is the real advertising man."[91] According to some reports, 97 percent of all national advertising in 1917 was placed through agencies.[92] Although advertising agents had not yet gained the full confidence of advertisers or the public, in twenty years, advertisers' interests in centralized and specialized services had pushed the other contenders for "the real advertising man" into more narrowly specialized niches of their own. Out of the fluid conditions and practices of the turn of the century, a new system for creating advertisements had crystallized.

# Part Three

## CONSUMPTION AS PROGRESS

# 8

# Taking Advertisements
# toward Modernity

*Clear-headed men no longer rush into print merely to satisfy a vanity for having their name and business autobiographies emblazoned on paper. . . . [T]he up-to-the-scratch business man now-a-days wants value received for every dollar spent in print publicity. He wants returns—sales—practical prestige that makes for better, bigger trade.*

—The Hoeflich Printing House's *Profitable Talks on Printing* 3 (1915)

## Rising Expectations for Effectiveness

Advertisements became "modern" as specialists competed with each other to provide advertising services after 1890. As national, brand-name advertisers gradually gave up directing and writing their own messages after 1880, agents, printers, publishers, freelances, and advertisers' employees vied for authority and patronage in the new niche for professional assistance. In the unsettled business environment that followed the Crash of 1893, progressive and up-to-date specialists urged that efficiency and effectiveness—the watchwords of the era—become the criteria for advertising prowess and progress. As difficult as they are to ascertain, then as now, efficiency and effectiveness argued against advertisers' using costs as the sole criteria for advertising decisions, against manufacturers' using product price as their primary promotional message, against messages that pleased advertisers instead of engaging consumers, and against nonspecialists' creating messages, this last despite the great successes of owner-managers' promotions throughout the century.

In order to improve their claims to the advertisers' patronage, leading agencies began to restructure their operations so that their highest profile became that of communication experts operating as intermediaries between advertisers and consumers, even though, to this day, media buying still occupies a major portion of agency personnel. In the course of this restructuring over three decades, specialists participated in the development of the consumer-oriented approaches that have come to characterize twentieth-century advertisements. Then, as now, it remains to be pointed out, advertising agencies prosper best by serving their clients, who are their first audiences. Therefore, *consumer-oriented* did not, and does not, refer to *serving* consumers and their interests. Consumer-oriented messages are designed to appeal to and *influence* consumers by calculating what visual and verbal stimuli can evoke the desired responses. Neither does use of the term *consumer-orientation* mean that advertising specialists quickly, if ever, got past their own intuitions and biases simply because they sought to override their clients' intuitions and biases.[1]

Promoting oatmeal as a breakfast cereal provides a case in point of the evolution of advertising creation. After leading producers merged, they battled over advertising styles, debating price and production emphases against a plethora of attempts to appeal to consumers' emotions. The rolled-oats industry began in the United States in 1854, pioneered by Ferdinand Schumacher. It epitomized the type of processing firm that required high turnover to profit from expensive technologies that could put products—many newly available or newly available in large quantities—into distribution channels to be pushed by sales forces or pulled by consumer demand. By the 1870s, Schumacher had successfully pioneered oatmeal with stark newspaper copy, first locally and then nationally. His accomplishments at convincing many consumers that oats were an economical food that was fit for them as well as for their horses encouraged competitors to enter the market, and by the mid-1880s prices began to fall rapidly. His competitors attempted pools, which Schumacher either ignored or sabotaged. Then in 1888 they merged into the American Cereal Company; Schumacher agreed to join them only after negotiating extremely favorable concessions.[2]

Schumacher never accepted the desirability of cooperation within the new corporate structure, however, and he continued to micromanage his activities within the firm, even refusing to employ a stenographer or typist. He also continued to see himself at odds with his former competitors; actually, he *was* at odds with them—because he and they approached business differently. In marketing strategies, Schumacher held onto the production ethos by which volume processing and price reduction were not only tools in competition but the industrialists' major contribution to progress. Like Carnegie and Rockefeller, Schumacher genuinely believed that lowering prices for processed goods legitimated both business and personal fortune; Henry Ford never believed that any goal was more important than his lowering of automobile prices by high-volume production techniques. Schumacher's promotional strategies— namely, announcing price and nutritional benefit, distributing samples, and declaring his product's quality—had served well, and he saw no reason to change. In contrast to Schumacher's strategies (he had never made any effort to make his product more attractive to consumers except by price cutting) the corporation's directors sought to improve their product's superficial features, to experiment with packaging, and to advertise to develop brand loyalty so that they could maintain their price level. Schumacher staunchly resisted these elaborations, believing that consumers needed only to be convinced to buy oatmeal as a cheap, digestible, safely produced protein source. All else was a waste of resources and a distraction from the problem of generating primary demand for oatmeal.[3] Despite Schumacher's objections, the American Cereal Company experimented broadly with style and content in advertising during the 1890s, relieved from price competition because of the mergers and because this cheap source of nutrition was relatively depression-proof. Henry Parsons Crowell, one of the corporation's prime movers, in contrast to Schumacher had had no experience with milling or any form of production when, around 1881 at the age of twenty-six, he purchased the mill that produced Quaker Oats. With K. B. Newell, a director who worked as its advertising manager, Crowell applied many of the tactics long used to sell patent medicines, in- cluding alleged scientific endorsements, customer testimonials, premiums, and the printing of sales arguments and recipes on the packaging. Crowell also sup- ported story-line advertisements (narratives with plots) and puffing—that is, paid insertions that appeared in publications as stories or reports without de- claring themselves as advertisements. In all of these stories, consumers of Quaker Oats dramatically achieved their fondest desires because of the cereal. The firm conducted these practices—which must have seemed erratic, even dissembling, to Schumacher—on a massive scale, with extensive national placements through magazines and newspapers.[4]

The continued antagonism between Schumacher and his former competi- tors gave American Cereal Company's experimentation with advertising strategies special significance. Because Schumacher opposed applying brand- enhancing promotions or nonbusinesslike messages, the corporation's directors negotiated a two-brand program. While Crowell and Newell marketed Quaker Oats, Schumacher insisted that his name be continued on a separate "brand" of the same product, F. S., with an identical advertising budget. The adver- tisements for F. S. followed the owner-manager tradition that featured the pro- ducer's identity and prestige, and they all read alike: "The trademark F. S.

stands for Ferdinand Schumacher, who is probably better known than any other man in the country as a manufacturer of Pure Food Products. The brand F. S. on a package of flour or cereal is a guarantee to the purchaser that the quality is the *best* that can be had in the market." In what amounted to a market test, F. S. sales declined while Quaker Oats sold well. Schumacher continued to deny that any advantage accrued to advertisements that addressed consumers' lives and emotional interests instead of stating basic product merits and his own accomplishments. Moreover, he demanded that his brand be allowed to undersell Quaker Oats by rebates and discounts. Even with this, the F. S. brand suffered declining sales, meanwhile costing the company substantial profits; in the end, a proxy fight ensued, and by 1899 Schumacher had retired. Unlike C. W. Post and W. K. Kellogg, who lived on through their cereals' brand names, Schumacher's reputation died before he did.[5]

The American Cereal Company spoke to the public through the abstract figure of a jovial Quaker gentleman. In 1877, this symbol began its work for one of the original oatmeal firms as a small, serious man in dark clothing, but it evolved to a rotund, smiling, brightly drawn figure. The image appeared on packages to remind consumers of the countless times it appeared in advertisements, at fairs and expositions, or on special cross-country trains, always advising them on how to improve or preserve their health, or even their careers and romances. The cereal's advertising claims ranged from the sublime, "Children fed on Quaker Oats will develop strong, white teeth," to the ridiculous, "On four successive occasions [a woman filed for divorce because she] has asked her husband to bring home a package of Quaker Rolled Oats, and each time he has failed to do so." What the new messages held in common made them stepping stones to modern advertising: no officer of the trust represented the firm to the public, none signed the labels, and they included no mentions or images pertaining to production, other than references to what directly affected consumers, such as cleanliness. The Quaker figure, whether drawn or walking around in costume, did not own or operate the firm; it did not exist other than as a conduit for promotional messages intended to attract and resonate with popular humor and consumers' interests. It had no purpose other than selling oatmeal on behalf of a corporation that belonged to and represented no single person. In 1901, the Quaker Oats Company formed, identifying the corporation with its symbol, but not with its owners, or even their country.[6]

Besides the much publicized successes of Quaker Oats and others such as Columbia Bicycles and Duke's cigarettes, business owners and managers alike received many signals that strongly urged updating advertising methods. Electoral politics of the 1890s, culminating in the 1896 presidential election, offered businesspeople a convincing lesson in the power of advertising, supplemented generously and expensively by other forms of structured publicity.[7] Most trade journals featured articles and editorials on the subject, and advertisements by agents and printers and publishers did what they could to add to the sense of urgency. An *Iron Age* editorial explained in 1896 that "the bicycle has been more extensively, expensively and ingeniously advertised than any other article ever placed on the market. . . . This is the result of the sharp and incessant competition. Makers do not do this because they like to keep their earnings in circulation—it is an essential part of the business and constitutes a large item in the cost." *American Brewers' Review* editors quoted *Printers' Ink* in one of their continuing criticisms of brewers' advertisements: "Yet, despite the millions poured out by brewers in this country every year for advertising, beer still remains one of the products about which the public knows least. Who will tell the story of beer properly?"[8] With such admonitions everywhere, including the specter of ruin represented by competitors' advertisements, the businessperson concerned with promoting a firm's wares could hardly avoid worry lest "his competitor, beating him in what might be called the aggregate of selling methods, will beat him in the selling." New business conditions required giving "continual study" to advertising, according to the first issue of the National Association of Manufacturers' journal *American Industries* in 1902, and the advertiser "who has not been so progressive as his competitor, nor so apt in adapting his own general proposition to the conditions which surround him" was fated to "exclusion" from the market.[9]

How was a manufacturer to pursue a "progressive" advertising course? According to all advice, the first step entailed recognizing that effectiveness rather than low media costs had to be the advertiser's top priority. This comprised both effective media planning and advertisement content. As *American Industries* put it, "if periodicals 'pay,' it is clear that the right periodicals will pay better than the wrong ones, and that the right kind of 'copy' will pay better than the wrong kind."[10] Although frequency and reach, or exposure per dollar, were easily understood measures of bargaining skills and business acumen, buying space by seeking the lowest price for the maximum exposure could be a false economy. Not all circulations were equally valuable. A 1904 advertisement for N. W. Ayer & Son explained that in distributing an advertisers' expenditures, "the cost per line per paper is of infinitely less consequence to the advertiser than that the right thing shall be said in the right way, in the right paper, at the right time, and in the right place, and this combination of right things does not come by accident or without experience."[11]

Earnest Elmo Calkins wrote in 1915 about the transformation in advertisers' expectations for effectiveness that he had helped foster. "The manufacturer who uses this great force to sell his goods has begun to submit it to the same tests to which he submitted his shop costs, sales or shipping methods. Long ago he admitted that advertising is a necessity. Now he asks can it be made more exact. . . . The manufacturer who bought advertising as a commodity began to scrutinize more sharply what he was buying. Now if he is wise he is buying it as a service, or rather as a commodity made more valuable by a service."[12] That service was best obtained from advertising agents, according to the bulk of the literature aimed at manufacturers in their own presses and elsewhere after 1895. One writer predicted in 1898 that advertisers would come to turn to specialists even if agencies' costs were not wholly met by publishers' commissions. The advertising business "exists because men want help in their advertising," less for the "clerical service" of buying space and more for the "vital thing" of copy.[13] The second step to progressive advertising, accordingly, was to seek the services of a progressive advertising specialist.

During the 1880s, Harry Nelson McKinney had developed a strategy for soliciting accounts at N. W. Ayer & Son that was widely acknowledged as the most successful in the business. He investigated a prospective firm's products and markets, calculating how best to improve on its current marketing by more efficiently placing periodical advertisements. In the 1890s, McKinney began to seek out new, larger accounts, including financial institutions such as the major insurance companies and, especially, the foremost manufacturers of staple commodities. By 1891, the agency was prepared to assist with copy on a regular basis, and McKinney set an industry standard by acquiring the National Biscuit Company account in 1898 and helping to launch its Uneeda Cracker campaign.[14] By 1905, at the same agency meeting in which McKinney pointed to the manufacturers' dissatisfaction with their inability to control jobbers, he called on his colleagues to seize upon that dissatisfaction as an opportunity for "business-getting" by making the advertisers' messages pay. They had to think "down below the surface" to come up with effective copy.[15] By the turn of the century, an agency slogan, "make advertising pay the advertiser," applied to preparing advertisements as well as to placing them, and all leading advertising agencies had similarly begun to form new types of relationships with their advertising clients.

## Intermediaries Between Advertisers and Consumers

As advertising specialists gradually took on planning and creating their clients' messages, they became, in effect, a new sort of intermediary. Unlike jobbers, wholesalers, and retailers, who had often operated at odds with manufacturers, agencies explicitly, if not selflessly or without conflict, worked for, and at the behest of, the advertisers. In 1910, a *Harper's Weekly* article stated that even with small accounts the "advertiser becomes [the agents'] client. He [the ad agent] either writes his advertisements or supervises the writing of them. He organizes selling campaigns, takes a personal interest in the advertiser's business and becomes a sort of *aide-de-camp* or business counsellor to him."[16]

In addition to mediating between advertisers and publishers, specialists began to mediate, as they saw it, between advertisers and their markets. To compete with each other by promoting the levels of consumption that manufacturers sought, advertising specialists had to learn to persuade audiences on behalf of their clients. They eventually added new directions to commercial communications by learning to research markets and to seek out consumer reactions to products as well as to specific advertisements and overall campaigns. By doing so, they aimed at developing an awareness of the marketplace that advertisers, particularly the industrialists, had formerly neglected, but increasingly appreciated and rewarded when it sold goods. As a result, crude market analyses gradually began to replace advertisers' judgments about who the audiences were and what they wanted. Even so, it was specialists' intuitions and biases that began to replace advertisers' intuitions and biases. They succeeded if they could convince advertisers that those intuitions and biases sold.

For firms to accept the displacement of nonspecialist insiders by professional outsiders for producing their public messages, even when the latter were management-level employees instead of top management or owners, required the backdrop of deep changes in organizational structures and functions then restructuring high-profile American businesses. Although much of U.S. business still occurs in smaller firms, the national brand-name advertising that dominates the consumer marketplace largely comes out of managerially operated corporations. The growing distance of ownership from managerial controls resulting from mergers and generational changes meant that stockholders sought profits rather than their sense of worth or identity in the operations and reputations of the companies they owned. Middle managers more and more controlled businesses' daily activities. Even if founders of, or heirs to, firms that had merged wanted to maintain a hand in the new corporations' activities, they generally had to do so as upper-level, or even middle-level, managers. Consequently, no one person's identity was integrally connected with such firms in the way the founding owner-managers' had been. In some cases, the merger process pushed even the most prominent figures from firms' corporate identities, as when Edison's company became part of General Electric and Carnegie's became part of U.S. Steel.

The bureaucratization of the corporate structure accelerated the acceptance of the professional outsiders' roles. In contrast to the entrepreneurs' circumstances, the corporate environment rewarded receptiveness to other people's ideas and interpretations, fostering the "other-directedness" that David Riesman has posited. While Riesman dated the transition to a culture characterized by an "exceptional sensitivity to the actions and wishes of others" at mid-twentieth century, Louis Galambos has argued that "the other-directed man was already working for Standard Oil in the 1890s. By the early 1900s, his values were displacing individualistic concepts, at least in the middle class."[17] This transition in the context for corporate decision making manifested itself in both an increasing appreciation of the value of investigating and responding to audiences in order to persuade them and a willingness to pass the responsibility for this task to specialists.

Even in this new corporate environment, advertising specialists did not come by the authority to direct advertising campaigns automatically. To the persuasive impact of publicized marketing successes they added their frequent arguments for why and how this transition to outsiders could benefit advertisers. As one analyst wrote in the general press in 1903, "even when a man doing a large business is thoroughly competent to advertise it himself, as many of them are, he does not have the time to give to this one of the many departments into which modern business divides itself." He also contended that "the view now generally taken in the business world" altogether dismissed nonspecialists' capacity to do their own advertising. When such a business owner or manager protested, "I think I ought to know how to advertise my own business," the proper response was, "Yes, you ought to, but you are one man in a hundred if you do." Assessments of the new marketing conditions echoed endlessly in the trade press to tell decision makers that they needed to change their practices.

> The old methods were sufficient for their day, when there was little competition and the men who dared advertise largely made fortunes with small intellectual effort; but now advertising is a profession in itself, and men of enterprise are fain to employ skilled writers and equally skilled artists to tell the public about their business. . . . The business men are finding that it is one thing to know what you wish to say and quite another thing to know HOW to say it, and that, while they may know the former, it is usually better to hire special talent to do the latter.[18]

So, even if the officers of a firm had the time or the ability to communicate well to their consumers, they could certainly not have the perspective on their business to know what should be conveyed to a distant audience in order to maximize selling effectiveness.

**Plate 1.** Jacob Estey left no doubt about his contributions to progress in technology, production, and the social graces. His portrait and that of his manufactory each appear twice in this large, chromolithographed poster, circa 1890, for the Estey Organ Company.

**Plate 2.** A French opera of the 1890s told the story of a destitute young woman who ruined her reputation by posing for this painting in which a courtesan looks directly into our gaze, rather than glancing away decorously. Fortunately for her, a fine young man understood that her inner virtue remained unsullied and married her. Shortly thereafter, Lorillard Tobacco Company adapted this striking theatrical poster from the opera, without attribution or explanation, for its chromolithographed show card, saying nothing about their tobacco.

**Plate 3.** Music was an important component of the good, bourgeois life in the late nineteenth century; homesteaders, for instance, sometimes even moved their pianos and reed organs out into the open air for family photographs to show their level of social graces. This chromolithographed poster for the Sterling Piano Company, circa 1885, is adorned by Charles A. Sterling's portrait, factory, home interior, and, very likely, his grandchildren, in this promotion of not only his pianos but their (and his) place in the social progress of the era.

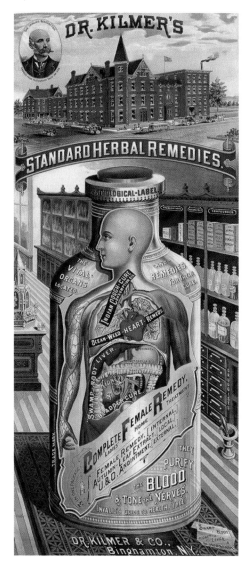

**Plate 4.** An anatomical image in a medicine bottle indicates which of Dr. Kilmer's Standard Herbal Remedies cured ailments of which organs. Dr. Kilmer, "The Invalid's Benefactor," displayed his portrait, his business and residential structures, and a retail outlet for his curatives. This chromolithographed hanger (a poster meant to hang from a metal strip at the top) presents the advertiser as a hero of progress in medicine, production, and distribution; circa 1885.

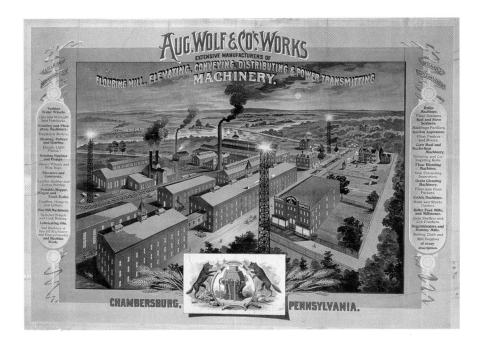

**Plate 5.** In a visually dramatic manner, this chromolithographed show card implied a close tie between production, product, and producer for the August Wolf Milling Company. Having to run the factory at night, using the latest of lighting technologies, demonstrated the demand for the products listed alongside the image of heroic production. The owner's residence (far right) and retail outlet add to the indicators of his personal success and dedication to his firm; circa 1890.

**Plate 6.** Elegant young ladies often enjoyed leisure and luxury—but here their pleasure is as much a product of the factory outside their fashionable window as is the champagne they share. The woman dressed in street clothing has come to visit what is likely the home of the Diamond Wine Company's owner, where modest amounts of fermented beverages were considered healthful and social. Chromolithographed poster, 1896.

**Plate 7.** The several layers of images in this chromolithographed poster for the New Home Sewing Machine tell a story that credits industrialization with making possible the new cultural and material standards for bourgeois women. Standards expanded to include sewing complex clothing for themselves and their children and cultivating artistic activities in the spare time that their new domestic technologies presumably afforded them; circa 1885. Courtesy of David and Bettie Briggs.

**Plate 8.** Helen Lansdowne created this magazine advertisement as part of a sensual campaign for John H. Woodbury's Soap, setting the pace for evocative national, brand-name advertising. This full-page ad combines a strikingly intimate romantic scene and headline with two older practices: heavy, black type on white packaging that still carried Woodbury's portrait as its trademark and an offer of the picture as a premium. *Ladies' Home Journal* 33, no. 9 (1916): 58.

The outside "experienced specialists" argued that they offered manufacturers the best sources of perspective feedback so that they might "Repeat the successes—not the failures," according to H. B. Humphrey, a Boston advertising agent, in 1901. Later Humphrey used the forum of NAM's *American Industries* to explain the importance of the "experienced advertising man [who] seeks out the vital points—he looks at the advertiser's business from the buyer's viewpoint—he is an outsider, and sees the features which interest him as a layman, and with his ability for handling words, can present these features to his readers in a way that is convincing, as though he was one of them and talking with them and not at them."[19] Herbert N. Casson, who wrote on advertising as a time-and-motion expert, addressed the necessity for increasing the distance between specialists and advertisers with the concept of the admen as "professional outsiders." He concluded that "business men live too close to their work. They never see how it looks from the outside." Casson reviewed a long series of innovations in science, technology, and business by newcomers to those fields. Advertising, along with other aspects of managing in modern business, should be left to the professional outsider who can "put corporations in touch with the public" and "create new standards of efficiency."[20] In the business culture of the times, appeals to specialization, efficiency, and effectiveness were hard to deny.

In making their claims to create more effective advertisements than advertisers could, specialists pointed in a specific direction of change, toward consumer-oriented, not advertiser-oriented content. To some, this conversion came as a personal revelation. William J. Raddatz became one of Cleveland's leading advertising professionals after leaving his position at the Morgan Lithography Company, a major printer of advertising show cards and other noncommissionable media. As a salesman for Morgan, he had prospered according to his ability to please the advertisers who were the job printer's customers. In 1911, he broadcast his new ambition as if it were a redemption: "I will today drop my identity as a seller of posters and burn incense at the alter of the buyer rather than that of the seller." In doing so, Raddatz rejected "the antiquated theory of poster advertising," which was "simply a process of crying one's name to the four corners of the earth with the wild hope of bringing your goods to the attention of someone without any regard for the impression you would create after you had this much coveted attention."[21] By joining the ranks of those who managed the "impression" they made once they had their audiences' attention, Raddatz recognized that he had to lessen his concern for selling advertisements to the advertisers. Competing for and serving clients now entailed providing them with successful advertising campaigns that gave priority to appealing to the consumer. Conversely, agents had to be less concerned with satisfying the advertisers' short-term, intuitive predilections. This dual realization became a rallying cry for advertising professionals, giving them direction for their professionalization.

Rather than perceiving any ambiguity or irony in their new ambition, or in the compromising position of the intermediary, the new profession of specialists adopted a self-righteous tone. They often spoke of themselves as the doctors or attorneys of business, and the new consumer-interest advertising became a medicine of sorts that advertisers should swallow for their own long-term interests.[22] The most bitter pill of all those they offered was the prohibition against advertisers' boosting themselves through their advertisements. As a freelance copywriter and adviser through the trade press, Nathaniel Fowler Jr. depended entirely on the patronage of advertisers, yet he frequently asserted that "it doesn't make a particle of difference whether the advertiser is pleased or not, so long as the advertisement does its business." Nor, he said, did it matter whether the advertisement pleased the advertiser's "wife and his doctor and his lawyer and his artistic friend." Fowler went so far as to suggest that advertisers "paste these lines on your desk: 'The advertisement is for the buyer's eye, not for the seller's.'"[23] Advertising professionals often expressed this principle to advertisers in colorful ways, such as admonishing them that, "it is not by his own taste, but by the taste of the fish, that the angler determines his choice of bait." Writing in *Language for Men of Affairs*, a series of business texts, James Melvin Lee explained the importance of researching audiences in sections entitled "Investigating the Basis of Appeal" and "Studying the Consumer's Taste." Lee emphasized his point with a parable about a wise manufacturer who had advertisements on his wall that had never gone to press. This possibly apocryphal businessman explained that "they are advertisements which I greatly admire personally, but which I know would never sell my products. By framing them and hanging them on my office walls, I can still enjoy them." According to Lee, even insisting upon approving the advertisements created by advertising professionals was not wise for the manufacturer.[24]

This lesson was easier for some advertisers than others. In some cases the transfer of creative initiative and authority was smooth, as when Arthur Warren became the in-house advertising specialist for a major manufacturing firm. He claimed that the officers of the corporation were sufficiently pleased with the effectiveness of his advertising that they never countered his plans or expenses.[25] In some cases, owners still managed their firms but felt burdened by advertising, doing it only to meet the competition, and they willingly passed the task on. The *Inland Printer* described this type of individual as having "spent a *whole hour* (!) in preparing 'copy'" and then sent it to all newspapers alike for years at a time, "relieved when the copy was mailed and the space filled."[26]

In other cases, however, advertisers resented and opposed the suggestions of the specialists they had hired or commissioned to prepare their advertisements. For instance, Stanley Resor at J. Walter Thompson Company recalled recommending that Gerhard Mennen change his logo and the design of the tin container for his major product, baby talcum powder. Mennen's trademark featured his own portrait, and the tin container was, as Resor described it, "decorated with the picture of a baby with the muscle of a John L. Sullivan and glowering with [a] Mussolini glare." Mennen had intended to show the happy effects of his talcum on a baby, and since he did not want to cast aside decades of product-association with that image, he adopted more "modern" symbols only "when the business had begun to suffer."[27] N. W. Ayer & Son personnel frequently responded to a client's comments about not liking copy with the "equally unanswerable argument that the copy is not intended to please him but rather to sell goods to a different class of people." At other times, a client's opposition resulted from "his instinctive distrust of unfamiliar ideas and methods." The outcomes of the ensuing clashes of wills varied, but the agency's records indicated, according to Ralph Hower, that "where the client has complied with [a] request for non-interference, both the advertising results and the relations between N. W. Ayer & Son and client have shown a noticeable improvement." Clients could be lost, however, over such disagreements, and some clients were rejected who refused to follow the agents' creative lead, such as when Ayer refused to handle Sears & Roebuck advertising because of Richard W. Sears's inflexibility. Livermore & Knight reported that, before 1900, "some trade was lost by their refusal to prepare advertising solely according to the taste of customers."[28] And in yet other cases, trade journals and other advisers warned advertisers against agents who offered their services to flatter "their unconscious egotism. Most business men are so completely possessed with the thought of their own goods that they are unable to put themselves in the position of the public who know nothing of them and care less."[29] In some cases, advertisers simply resented "a foolish outgo" of their "hard-earned money" on something that did not immediately produce results, as Claude Hopkins experienced with meat processors Swift & Company.[30]

The irony that advertisers were served best by advertisements that pleased them less than they appeared to please consumers resulted in a growing distance between advertisers, their agents, and their advertisements. However, it also testified to the apparent effectiveness of the advertising campaigns that professionals created during this transition period. For instance, when the Welch grape-juice business was twenty years old, William Armistead of N. W.

Ayer & Son discussed their advertisements with Dr. Welch and Edgar Welch, president and vice president of the firm. When Armistead and his colleagues suggested changes in their advertising, the Welches were "indignant." After much discussion, however, they agreed to a trial, and their business increased 40 percent during the first year of the new campaign.[31] Had the new styles of advertisements not appeared to market more effectively than those produced by the advertisers themselves, the arguments for specialized planning and copywriting could not have upset traditional practices so quickly. Such product successes could have been due to other factors, such as demographic changes, new communication technologies, competitors' failures, or fads. What matters here is that advertisers and their advisers attributed the successes to what they controlled, namely, the marketing.

## Rejecting the Past's Copy and Design

The changes in advertising styles and content after the early 1890s did not occur because of any inevitable modernization. Nor did advertisements change simply because the professionalizing field of advertising specialists "took over" creating advertisements and exercised their budding expertise. Instead, advertisers, printers, publishers, and advertising specialists changed their output as they engaged in highly competitive and sometimes acrimonious interactions, all within a context of new printing technologies and new trends in American culture that both affected and reacted to the changes in advertising. The printing developments made it possible to increase vastly the volume and quality of pictures available to the public everywhere, but especially in periodicals. Gradually, the old-style one- or two-inch "cards" were pushed to the backs of publications or onto designated "classified" advertising pages and by 1900 larger ads—quarter-page, half-page, and full-page—increasingly became frequent, if not standard, especially for major advertisers in magazines. Photolithography, photoengraving, and screened halftones, all means of mechanically preparing images for printing, replaced chromolithography, engravings, and woodcuts as the technologies of choice for nonperiodical advertising in the 1880s and 1890s, with offset printing after 1900. The ensuing decline of trade cards and other ephemera was only one of many blows to formerly dominant advertising media, although manufacturers and wholesalers did increase their use of illustrated catalogs and circulars in lieu of distributing samples; calendars and other ephemera—such as fast-food giveaways—have remained widespread in retail promotions and in nonconsumer advertising. Once advertising agents could distribute illustrated advertisements through periodicals, this strengthened their case for newspapers and magazines as advertising media. Photomechanical printing processes also reduced designers' dependence on printers and engravers for generating images, as anyone's illustrations (drawn or photographed) could be reproduced directly, without the intermediary of a printer's hand to redraw them. Photography's "constant feast for the eyes" itself gave advertising designers much greater freedom from both artists and printers.[32]

The cultural context for these transitions in advertising included the period's many reactions against nineteenth-century culture, including design and prose styles. The extravagances of decoration that had characterized Victorian design became fashion's new target. Fashion's arbiters no longer felt the preceding century's strong needs for a reaction against mechanization and urbanization, a means of legitimating industrial products, or a celebration of industrialization's abundance.[33] So powerfully had these three older impulses reinforced each other that the penchant to elaborate had rarely been restrained; decades of lighting devices, furniture, clothing, and even industrial equipment bore its influence. In this spirit, nineteenth-century advertisers and their printers and publishers had relished applying the new abundance of typefaces, borders, and dingbats. Flourishing these devices showcased printers' expansive styles, technical prowess, and ownership of the required technologies, all the while proclaiming advertisers' power to command such resources. Letterpress posters and handbills, as well as newspaper advertisements, often featured as many, or more, different typefaces as they had lines of type. Even an old letterpress printer had to admit, though, that lithographers had "led the typographic printer in the pursuit of the beautiful and truly artistic in printing."[34] Lithographers had gloried in their abilities to design a new typeface with which to brandish each advertiser's name, and with no need to follow a straight line at all. The taste for printed extravagance began to fade only after decades of enthusiasm had sated the leaders among printers and publishers. By the mid-1880s, the trade press had already begun to caution its readers—advertisers and printers alike—"against crowding every ornamented font in the office into one job." Advisers began to warn that using "gingerbread, filigree work turned out under the guise of artistic printing, while valuable as showing what patience and effort can accomplish, is practically worthless. . . [in part] because it is frequently out of character to the nature of the work for which it is used." Admonitions to avoid the seductions of ornamentation continued for decades, such as the *Printing Art*'s 1907 recommendation of "plain type": despite contentions that "this is an age of novelty," a "touch is usually all that is necessary, and the same is true of ornaments."[35]

Printing was not the only field to move away from its nineteenth-century fashions. By the end of the century many Americans, and particularly leaders of the mainstream culture, had begun to react against the complexity of Victorian visual styles as manifested in all forms, from architecture to home decoration to advertisements. Designs, visually isolated figures, and abstractions increasingly replaced pictures and detailed scenes. Writing styles experienced an analogous shift away from elaborate, "literary," or "flowery" constructions. Major magazine editors, for instance, began to demand a simple, speechlike style from authors that persuaded rather than expressed—a "forceful," commonsense prose that communicated straightforward ideas and sold the reader on editorial policy.[36] As the modernist impulse filtered into popular culture, advisers in both commercial art and copy picked up on its "progressive" movement away from tradition and guided advertisers accordingly. Just as modernist intellectuals defined their cause, in part, as a reaction against traditions, progressive advertising advisers defined their work as up-to-date according to how it moved away from traditional techniques and messages. They also used the modernist languages of expertise, efficiency, and Scientific Management, invented for industry, and applied them to convince industrialists to leave their public messages to the experts on writing with emotional appeal. These commercial rebels acted selectively, however, in rejecting the past. For instance, they eagerly sought to distill and preserve the essence of success from entertainers' and patent-medicine vendors' carnivalesque excesses and apply it to their own messages.

The practitioners' movements away from traditional advertisements in the name of effectiveness led them increasingly away from an emphasis on price advertising. They could hardly claim an important place for ad-writing skills if advertisements only publicized prices. Of course, competition based on characteristics other than price was not new; it was as old as consumer preferences themselves. The amenities retailers offer, for instance, can influence people's decisions on where to conduct their trade. Likewise, producers of similar goods can advertise incidental advantages in quality, service, or changes in style; both price and nonprice competition exist in different balances in all markets.[37] Patent-medicine purveyors and entertainers since ancient times had adopted lively narratives and other appeals in their advertisements; some manufacturers and merchants did likewise.

Then under the pressure of the 1890s' marketing conditions, all forms of competition intensified. Initially, price competition did characterize many firms' marketing strategies as they competed for shrinking markets, both industrial and consumer. However, those purveyors and manufacturers of consumer goods whose market positions allowed them to avoid desperate price cutting, such as Quaker Oats, increasingly developed consumer-oriented promotional strategies after 1893. For a while, manufacturers turned to the kinds of images printers had been selling for decades as stock images—pretty, humorous, or evocative pictures altogether irrelevant to the products being advertised. In periodicals and on trolley cars, doggerel and other light copy abounded, sometimes providing more fun for readers than it was persuasive, as, for instance, Artemas Ward's later stories of Sapolio's Spotless Town. A surge of such messages in both published and ephemeral media testified to the growing sense that it mattered less what an advertiser said or portrayed than that it be pleasing to consumers.

All early selling arguments had followed from advertisers' idiosyncratic and intuitive notions of what they wanted to communicate to consumers, or from what they thought consumers' interests ought to be, with varying degrees of appropriateness and accuracy. This nonprice competition did not yet qualify as consumer-oriented, particularly when the messages satisfied first advertisers' interests other than selling, such as social aggrandizement or claims about the advertisers' contributions to progress. Whether or not such messages appealed to consumers and sold products, consumers' interests did not inform them. As corporate directors and their advertising agents and internal specialists started to react against those traditional orientations in marketing, they instead put together deliberate programs to develop messages intended to play to consumer interests. Of course, what they actually played to were their own senses of consumer interests, since that was all they knew; but they did know to aim for personal, familial, social emotions. The experiment in internal competition between Quaker Oats and the F. S. brand vindicated this strategy by increasing both primary demand for oatmeal and secondary demand for Quaker Oats. Although consumers did not see completely new types of advertisements right away, neither did they see Quaker Oats advertised by factory scenes or statements or images that hinted at the founders' or owners' wealth and successes. What this pre–World War I transition to modern advertising entailed, therefore, more clearly than a general or immediate adoption of new techniques, was the elimination of advertisements that were not consumer oriented.

## Experiments in Modernizing Advertising Images

Printers and publishers continued to influence advertising styles as the only source for the production of images in mass quantities, regardless of who originated the designs. For instance, the first U.S. example of the art poster, the favorite medium of art nouveau and already the fashion in Europe, appeared when Harper and Brothers' editors asked Edward Penfield, head of their art department, to design a unique poster for the April 1893 issue of *Harper's*. They wanted something quite different from typical magazine posters, with their rows of type listing upcoming contents. Penfield produced a design, rather than a detailed picture, that he later credited for setting the pace for "simplicity and good composition" in American commercial design. This poster showed a man intently reading a magazine, oblivious to the rain falling about him; it showed no other detail, and the only copy read, "HARPER'S FOR APRIL." Penfield claimed that he had not yet seen contemporary French posters and that this was "only an experiment."[38] This experimental style became the rage for publishers' advertisements and covers, as well as illustrations.

Another contemporary commercial artist who helped set the design pace in the United States with his work, Will H. Bradley, was a printer as well as artist, controlling both design and production from his advertising agency and press.[39] With models such as these in publishing and printing, art nouveau fashions spread into advertising styles, particularly for those consumer industries, such as bicycles and cameras, that deliberately projected innovative profiles. For instance, the winner of Columbia Bicycles Company's second poster-design contest in 1896 was none other than the young Maxfield Parrish, who left his mark on decades of advertising and illustrating.[40] Although pure forms of this "art poster" style with its minimal copy and often unnatural shapes and color schemes never dominated American product advertising, the popularity of the style among publishers, printers, and artists exerted a powerful pull toward simple, high-impact messages as the new standard for commercial design, with or without direct relevance to the advertised goods. Art Deco and streamlining, representing speed and efficiency, carried this trend into later decades.[41]

These and other new design trends for attractive but usually irrelevant images surfaced between the realization that advertisements had to appeal to their audiences and the establishment of advertising specialists' authority in determining how. Everyone knew (as they still do) that the first object of an advertisement was to get its audience's attention, and that its second object was to interest its audience somehow. A message cannot sell before it has accomplished these two goals. Many advertisers, such as Thomas Barratt, had mastered these arts and continued to do so with questions ("Have you used Pears' Soap?"), testimonials (Lillie Langtry for Coca-Cola as well as for Pears' Soap), and other imaginative fare. Joel Benton, a frequent writer in the advertising trade press, commented in 1893 that because of the growing competition for audiences, "the advertiser, above all others, needs to 'invoke attention and fasten remembrance.'" As a result of this need, "a change has been rapidly coming, within a very few years, calculated to make the style almost more important than the thing said. This may reverse, possibly, the order of nature, but it does not allow any more than the proper stress upon the prime value of making an impression."[42]

In 1896, when Charles Austin Bates categorized the three ways of using pictures in advertisements—representing an article, illustrating the selling argument, and "merely because it is pretty and will attract a passing glance"—he did not strongly recommend one over the others, insisting mostly on artistic and typographic skill.[43] The printers' art and artists had the most credibility to date in achieving the "appearance" advertisers and their specialists sought. For good reasons, job printers—more so than periodical printers with their technological limitations—had already presaged many of the fashions that developed in advertising styles after 1890, when appealing to consumers became a deliberate advertising goal. They had long since collected feedback on consumer preferences from the sales of their noncommissioned or speculative prints.[44] The resulting sensitivity to their markets' tastes and interests made their consumer-directed images dramatically different from those producer-oriented images they printed at the behest of manufacturers. Derived instead, for the most part, from what advertising analysts came to call human-interest subjects (see chapter 3), these generic images were first created expressly by the job printers to sell according to popular tastes.

Because of printers' own marketing activities, consumer-oriented images existed in their stock prints long before questions about appealing to consumers arose in the advertising field more generally. As a result, advertisers and their advisers turned often to the printers' generic images for their initial forays into consumer-oriented images, and a new fashion came into vogue. After 1895, countless advertisements appeared in both periodicals and ephemeral media sporting images with only minimal references to the advertisers and their products. These pictures, often without a detailed background or with a studio background, featured only the advertisers' names or trademarks for identification, unless a model or drawn figure held or looked at the product. Often the only means of distinguishing such advertisements from stock advertisements was how the advertisers' names were printed; a letterpress overprint rather than having the name incorporated into the design indicated a stock ad that could very well appear for another advertiser, too. To avoid this, large advertisers frequently purchased "exclusives" from printers or electrotype makers, buying exclusive rights to use one or a set of images originally generated on speculation and sold through a printer's catalog or samples. For instance, W. Duke, Sons & Company, New York, purchased a series of trade cards with cowboy scenes as an exclusive from Koerner & Hayes, Buffalo, beginning in 1888. J. & P. Coats Thread Company purchased a series of trade cards entitled

"Grotesque Mice" in the 1899 catalog of Butler & Kelley, New York City.[45] These images borrowed from the same conceptual categories as the stock images produced by printers for decades. Instead of appearing only in ephemeral media, they now flowed into periodical media as technological improvements permitted, mediated by advertising practitioners.

Advertisers and their advisers very often explained this fashion in terms of progress in "good taste." It became a constant concern and resulted in an intermediate stage, preliminary to the fully-modern advertisements that emerged by World War I. In part this minimalist approach to layout manifested a reaction against the flash and hard sells of the patent-medicine and entertainment advertisements, then bringing disfavor upon the whole field. Yet notions of advertising as simply "putting one's name before the public" were not new and had resulted in vast quantities of advertisements in all media through the nineteenth century, when "experts" had critiqued them as simplistic. By the middle 1910s, when "good taste" glowed like a beacon to advertising practitioners trying to improve their field's professionalism and public esteem, the fashion for such advertisements presented them as elegant, not mindless. The trade press often encouraged printers to attend schools of decorative art in night school or similar educational venues as an important source of guidance not best learned in the shop.[46] The practice of purchasing fine art unrelated to the business or product being promoted had actually begun at least as early as 1886, with Thomas A. Barratt's purchase of a painting by Sir John Millais to use in advertising Pears' Soap.[47] This success led to other, less notable, attempts at applying fine art, such as the Robert Portner Brewing Company's reproduction, just after 1900, of a woman's portrait from an "original by Asti, valued at $2,000, and pronounced by connoisseurs his masterpiece." This statement on the back of the poster also announced that the "picture will make a handsome ornament to your home *and* can be secured without any printing."[48] The "fine art" strategy peaked around the turn of the century, flourishing from the mid-1890s to near 1910.

In the search for an iconography that would succeed in appealing to the "better" sorts of audiences of both genders, both printers' and advertising specialists' journals encouraged the use of women's pictures as a "surer attraction" than all else, particularly "a woman's winsome face" or the "human form divine—mostly female,"[49] and often only slightly covered, depending on the product and the audience. *Printers' Ink* explained in 1895 that the apparent irrelevance of women's faces and figures to tobacco hardly disqualified them from advertisements: they attracted men's attention.[50] Yet women's images were not confined to appeals to men during this period, or since, for that matter. A 1902 article on "Beauty in Advertising Illustration" in *Cosmopolitan* explained that advertisers had discovered that "a first-class magazine was valuable because it was the companion of the hour of rest." To reach such a fine readership in the heart of their homes, "every cranny and nook of art is being ransacked" to make the advertisements attractive. While some inventive artists succeeded in creating truly unique and memorable images, "the search for novelty . . . seems now to be focusing itself most often in the direction of beautiful faces. Such are eternally new and always to man or woman delightfully interesting." The era of "indelicate drapings" had passed because "good taste required that everything offensive should be eliminated, and that that advertisement was most effective which attracted all and offended none."[51]

As Robert C. Ogden, manager of Wanamaker's in New York City, explained to the Sphinx Club in 1898, the "advertiser has a mission in uniting in some degree the fine and useful arts." He advised advertising professionals to "[w]age warfare against the spirit that sneers at art applied to advertising as a degradation." Key to accomplishing this progress was to use "no illustration that is not artistic," because the costs of reproducing and distributing advertisements so greatly outweighed the costs of "original designs" to make slighting the latter a false economy.[52] In a more positive mode, the *Inland Printer* asserted that because commercial art had been able to "keep pace with modern progress," art had drawn "business up to a more elevated plane," to the benefit of both business and art.[53] The prestige that might come to advertisers as patrons of art motivated William Haskell Simpson of the Santa Fe Railway to take credit for having directed his firm to become "the first road in the land to take art seriously, as a valuable advertising adjunct. We have never skimped. We use the very best art that can be bought." (Simpson commissioned art of the Southwest, especially of, not usually by, Native Americans, to encourage tourism.)[54] As part of the movement to fine art, or at least fine commercial art, many artists followed the practice of signing their works, as initiated in the United States by Penfield with his *Harper's* posters, leaving traditional anonymity behind. Palmer Cox became famous for his elfin Brownies as they frolicked through countless advertisements; and Maude Humphrey (mother of Humphrey Bogart) painted innumerable charming scenes of children, winning fame in association with Ivory Soap as well as for her children's books. By the end of the first decade of the new century, Howard Chandler Christy, Will H. Bradley, J. C. Leyendecker, Maxfield Parrish, Harrison Fisher, and others had all begun to reap the rewards of celebrity. (Rarely did copywriters sign their work; Elbert Hubbard was an exception.) In these and other ways, the increasing importance of the advertisements' appeals paralleled the diminishing prominence of the advertisers, as heroic figures, in the messages. For the duration of this pursuit of art, advertisers who could not or chose not to commission a commercial artist for a custom rendition might sacrifice all relevance to their products on the altar of good taste, sending their names into the public market with an irrelevant but "artistic" stock image.

The *Inland Printer* led advertising art and fashions by example and advice. In the middle 1890s, its editors and contributors increasingly offered advice about advertising images in its own pages. In April 1894, for instance, the masthead took on an art nouveau look, and the lead article discussed Aubrey Beardsley's work; in that one issue, twelve articles and three editorials, plus one letter, two poems, and miscellaneous smaller items, all addressed advertising matters.[55] The journal asked Will H. Bradley to design a new cover about the same time. He convinced editors instead to change covers regularly, rather than staying with one for years, and his and others' contributions showed the impact of cosmopolitan styles.[56] In December 1899, for the last issue of the century, the journal reproduced seventy-two of its covers, explaining what technologies had made them possible. The first cover in the series, "one of the early covers" (1887), presents a striking contrast to all of the others, showing a dense glorification of industrial imagery and technological progress related to printing: three vignettes portray printers at work in idealized settings; telephone and telegraph lines flow through the title; a goddess figure composes type along one side of the cover, and a crowned male presides over the whole. The cover that appeared from July 1891 through September 1893 referred to printing as "The Art Preservative of Arts," but showed no press. Covers changed monthly after March 1894 until at least 1900, but only twice did presses appear: once as a heroic printer struggled to turn down the screw of an ancient press, and again, on the last cover of the series, as an abstracted antique and oversized press frames a dandy clearly not dressed for work. The intervening designs featured highly stylized schemes that included nature scenes and, most commonly, images of women by influential commercial artists such as Will H. Bradley and J. C. Leyendecker.[57]

The practice of using fashionable but largely irrelevant images for attracting audiences, evoking pleasant emotions and good taste, never went unchallenged, even in its heyday.[58] Criticisms of irrelevance that had begun in the 1890s mounted in the new century as analysts and advisers increasingly emphasized that selling was the ultimate, if not the first, function of advertisements. Advisers on design increasingly stressed that while "the better the art the better the ad," the "power and value of art, as applied in business" depended on bridging "the gap between art for its own sake . . . and art for the sake of publicity."[59] As George Frederick explained, "art is a commodity," and its value to advertisers depended on its capacity to evoke emotional responses that promoted selling.[60] In 1906, *Ad Sense* insisted that illustrations "should

*Consumption as Progress*

relate exclusively and specifically to the articles advertised." Any other images might be worthless or "positively detrimental." Moreover, the "question is not, Is the illustration attractive? but, Is it effective as well as attractive?—not, Will it make people smile? but, will it help to open the purse-strings of the particular class I am trying to reach?" Artists, by this thinking, had to be held in check because they are "prone to give the ornamental side of the work precedence and make the advertising idea secondary."[61] Advisers had come to realize that "merely attracting attention is the easiest part of advertising, and if this were all that is desired, then notoriety would answer the purpose."[62] As the *American Druggist* advised those advertisers who were still preparing their own messages in 1906, "the Pointless Cut should be the *bete noir* of every advertiser." Inappropriate, irrelevant illustrations could "ruin the effect" of advertisements, either by "having nothing whatever to do with the text" or because they induce the advertiser to write messages "to match the poor cuts."[63] By this time, standards for advertising images had come to consider their usefulness in selling as well as getting attention and pleasing audiences.

## The Decline of the Industrialists' Imagery

During the heyday of the irrelevant, pretty image, the motifs that nineteenth-century industrialists had favored declined in frequency. In part this followed from the same growing appreciation that had brought generic images to the fore; namely, that messages must first of all appeal to their audiences. The decline of industrialists' images also followed from the increasingly frequent and pointed arguments on behalf of messages that were "nearest to the mind of the reader" in order that they might "have some 'pull,' some influence to action."[64] The advertising and printing trade presses aggressively advocated this shift away from the older styles and motifs to advertisements aimed at consumers. The argument against industrial imagery centered on the ad practitioners' growing claims for their authority regarding the relative effectiveness of consumer-interest advertising and on women as consumers. Building positive cases for redirecting advertising messages and increasing advertising success did not suffice, however, because advertisers frequently enough opposed the shift, challenging the specialists' judgment. Moreover, specialists had to justify their work—in-house, freelance, or in agencies. If continuing as before were adequate, why change? Therefore advertising experts aggressively assaulted the older practices of emblazoning advertisers' names, their own or their children's portraits, or their factories' portraits across their printed emissaries to the public. Ralph Hower has recorded some of the difficulties that

N. W. Ayer & Son had in dealing with clients' lack of cooperation over these matters before World War I. Many of the greatest difficulties occurred when Ayer's clients insisted on having their names and pictures placed prominently in their advertisements. The agency's personnel then had to persuade the advertisers "tactfully" that "such sops to vanity hindered the work of advertising."[65] The *Inland Printer* also rued the advertisers' too frequent request to have their own portraits "crowded in." Another analyst expressed his relief in 1903 that "there is an abatement of the man with the bald head and chin whiskers or close-cropped pompadour, whose 'face is on every package.'" He was very glad that the time had passed when "we were bored to death by the advertiser who insisted that we admire the profile, three-quarters, and front view of his manly and heroic head. It was like looking through a rogue's gallery to glance over the advertising pages of a popular monthly."[66]

In 1900, Nathaniel C. Fowler Jr. published one of his several volumes that, among other things, coached advertisers and their advisers to direct their copy to consumers in appropriate, meaningful language and to attend to their audiences' interests. In the chapter entitled "Personal Publicity," Fowler argued against the traditional motifs of self-aggrandizement: "Advertise the goods for sale and not the folks who sell them." It was "vanity and conceit" to promote one's self by name or portrait, because "no man is as great as the business he has made." In step with the advertising literature of the day, Fowler's advice was starkly anathema to the traditionally intimate linkage between a business and its owner-manager. The fervor of his arguments in this matter indicated Fowler's sense of crusading for a still-unpopular cause among manufacturers.[67] He did not, in fact, think much of producers or production, relative to the importance of goodwill—a firm's positive public image—in building business success. After all, the "factory may burn to ashes. . . . The members of the firm may die. . . . But the good of advertising never changes." He continued the attack on the producers' values by declaring, "The buyer of a thing is not the maker of it; he is interested in the result, not in the steps to the result. He does not care how a thing was made. . . . The picture that appeals to him is the one that shows what he wants, doing what he wants it to do."[68] So not only must the advertiser keep himself out of his advertisements, but he must keep his production facilities out, too. To demonstrate his advice, Fowler collected more than one hundred of the "best advertisements" in a separate section. Not surprisingly, none of these "specimens of success, [included] for the reader's benefit," show factories or advertisers' portraits.[69] After 1890, other advertising professionals who publicized samples of what they considered good advertising, as did J. Walter Thompson from at least 1895 through the 1910s, never included advertisements that showed factories, and only rarely owners' portraits.

Trademarks made an analogous and significant shift toward greater human interest and away from founders' or owners' surnames and portraits during these same years. Advising manufacturers to think carefully about their trademarks in 1893, *Iron Age* declared that there is "vastly more in a trade-mark than merely business egoism." Through advertising and packaging, the producer should "keep the name before the trade until it became better known than his own. . . . A short name takes the fancy." Firms' and founders' names were "too long for mankind generally to bother with." Frank Presbrey included a chapter entitled "Enter the Human-Interest Trade-Mark" in his 1929 history of advertising. This movement in the 1890s he credited to those improvements in printing technology that had made "the half-tone reproduction of humans in action" possible;[70] his theory, however, does not explain why advertisers did not simply employ better reproductions of the same old trademarks and other symbols, such as their places of business. Two letters from the Anderson Preserving Company, sent out in 1898 and 1899, demonstrate how the factory could be replaced by symbols with more human interest without a change in the printing technology employed.[71] The reverse sides of both pieces of stationery, both printed by the same technology, were covered with various company trademarks and images of packages, a choice that shows the importance this firm accorded to trademarks. Sent out during the firm's transition into modern promotional styles, the letter written in 1898 displayed a traditional factory scene at its top; the letter sent the following May highlighted instead the figure of a jolly monk, one of the firm's new trademarks.[72] The change was conceptual, not technological.

Printers and those who advertised to them in the *Inland Printer*, such as manufacturers of printers' machinery and supplies, paralleled the trends in consumer advertising, even though, generally speaking, other manufacturers of industrial machinery continued to employ industrial images in their trade-journal advertisements through the twentieth century. The printing trade used industrial images in relatively equal numbers with nonindustrial images into the mid-1890s; then the latter increased in frequency. Printers and their suppliers reduced their uses of industrial imagery earlier than most other industrialists for many reasons. Because they produced images, their credibility as advisers and suppliers depended on their responsiveness to feedback from their customers—and their customers' feedback from their own audiences. Since this feedback indicated the popularity of nonindustrial images with consumers, such images were not as irrelevant to these producers as they were to other manufacturers and merchants who bought stock images for their advertisements. They represented, after all, evidence of the printers' products. In 1894, as the *Inland Printer* began to champion advertisements with "pull," printers' own advertisements with factories or machines declined. Instead of what Fowler called "still life engines" standing alone, these advertisers began the practice, only recently questioned, of picturing irrelevant figures alongside their machines. Most often they depicted women in various drapes, but also cupids, flowers, and other popular motifs.[73]

By 1910, factories, engines, and other industrial scenes were gone, as were most founders' portraits from all but a few consumer advertisements. The most notable exceptions included owner-managers like Henry Ford, and others, such as electricity power companies, who continued to promote their sense of the value of production to progress. C. W. Post, for instance, kept factories on his letterhead and in his food-product advertisements at least into the 1910s. The copy he wrote described his overcoming obstacles in his own life and pursuing a "long and exhaustive study of food and beverage." His accomplishments had improved the "healthful welfare of millions" and "repaid him a hundredfold." He personally wrote loving descriptions of his buildings and factories for publicity.[74] Trade journals have generally continued undeterred in industrial imagery. The technological sublime can be found in advertising, art, and industrial design through World War II, although the streamlined imagery resembled only slightly the actual, dirty, noisy, and complex means of production. On the rare occasion when factory images were advocated in the advertising trade press for consumer ads after 1900, it was clear that they were no longer "natural"; that is, their purposes needed to be explained and justified.[75]

In addition to the advertising professionals' rejection of these motifs in favor of imagery that was more consumer oriented, other factors contributed to the decline of industrial imagery, including the increasing popular association of factories with blight and hardships, rather than heroic innovation. The Progressive Era's frequent associations of factories with child labor, with other abuses of labor and ensuing unrest, and with increasing concerns about the impacts of pollution and lack of industrial hygiene on the general public contributed to the changing perceptions of industrialization.[76] General reactions against the complexity of Victorian visual styles also played a part in this shift. They combined with the twentieth century's intensifying saturation of stimulus to make it difficult to attract and hold audiences' attention long enough to view the traditional, complicated advertisements that showed factories and multiple vignettes; ad writers believed that a *story* could hold attention, but not an unnarrated picture. At the same time, factory architecture also became simpler, safer, and more efficient, eliminating much of the architectural detail that had made the early buildings visually interesting.[77] In addition, the evolution of corporate capitalism ensured the ultimate demise of producers' portraits and surnames from advertisements for lack of motivation on the part of the advertisers themselves. Yet these last two developments explain only why advertisers would allow the older motifs to fall into disuse, not why admen labored so diligently to expedite the transition. This shift was central to their growing sense of professional justification, as the next chapter will demonstrate.

## Modernizing Copy

Even while copywriting was the advertisers' domain, advertising practitioners began to offer their advice, increasing the volume and intensity of that literature during the decades after midcentury. Since they could only justify, and continue, their livelihoods if advertisers appeared to profit from sales attributable to advertising, they sought to "make advertising pay the advertiser," in Frances Wayland Ayer's phrase, by helping to sell the advertised article. Still, as long as practitioners defined their occupation in terms of the buying and selling of publication space, most of their help drew on that experience. So George Rowell offered precious little advice on copy in his early career, merely cautioning advertisers that, to find their fortunes, they should pay "attention to their manuscript compilations." In his 1870 book on advertising practice, advice on writing took up only 3 of 207 pages, vaguely recommending that a "notice of any kind, to be read, must be readable" and that "novelty attracts attention." He concluded that shrewdness was a major asset in coming up with effective copy, but he offered no recipe for it, only describing the praiseworthy inventiveness of successful advertisers. Years later, in the first volume of *Printers' Ink,* Rowell's advice continued to emphasize advertising volume and placement, but he did feature an article in the first year asking advertisers if their messages were "properly worded and displayed."[78] With increasing frequency as the years progressed, his journal warned advertisers to avoid "exaggerations and misrepresentations," to write "plainly, lucidly, simply," as they did when they talked to customers, and reminding them that they were "talking still through printers' ink." By 1891, the year Rowell hired a full-time copywriter for his own agency, *Printers' Ink* included a regular column by Artemas Ward, a high-profile copywriter.[79]

During the 1890s, freelance writers and other specialists began to advise advertisers on copy. Fowler began the chapter on writing advertisements in his 1893 tome on *Building Business* with the epigram, "'Tis not so much how much is said—'tis how it's said." His most frequent advice, however, reflected the changes since Rowell first wrote, recommending that advertisers turn to professional ad writers "to more often succeed than to fail." For those many advertisers writing their own messages, he recommended a variety of strategies, including regular revisions, not "radical changes," of style, and always they should remember to "[a]dvertise the goods for sale, not the men who sell them." Fowler insisted that advertisers not feature their name prominently. In any case, if "the advertisement has anything in it worth reading it will be read, and the advertiser's name discovered," however small its size. Importantly, because an "advertisement is a silent drummer" and people generally resist drumming, "it is absolutely necessary that the advertisement should be so written that the reader will absorb it before he has time to remember the conventional apathy he may suppose he possesses." So Fowler recommended large, uncrowded spaces with strongly stated headlines and a few, well-written words that emphasized a single point—for "a statement cannot be too broad and strong, if it be true." Above all, he said, "the advertisement should be written for the eye of the reader, not as a means of personal gratification to the advertiser." A few years later, Fowler reminded advertisers that the "good of advertising is in the good it does. If the advertisement brings results it must be a good advertisement. Not what we think is good, but what does good, is good, in advertising and in everything else."[80]

Since advertisers wanted copywriting that sold, the practices of face-to-face salesmanship provided the foundation for many of the ideas about improving advertising strategies. According to an oft-repeated story, John E. Kennedy gave Albert D. Lasker the key to understanding advertising in three words— and twenty years later, Lasker still credited Kennedy with the revelation that advertising was "salesmanship in print." In 1905, Kennedy was a copywriter of considerable repute, making the fabulous annual income of $28,000, writing for a patent-medicine company; Lasker was just beginning what would be a long, prominent career at Lord & Thomas in Chicago. Kennedy's insight reinforced John E. Powers's earlier lessons for the field and fostered the institutionalization of forthright and "reason why" advertising strategies; that is, honestly explaining benefits from audiences' perspectives, rather than piling on the conventional superlatives. Both of these principles functioned as slogans to the new field, serving to encode and communicate standards and goals, building new conventions. Kennedy's observation made especial sense to his contemporaries in light of the large role that the sales force played in business at all levels then.[81] It must be said, however—Kennedy's celebrity, notwithstanding—long before his widely publicized disclosure, other advisers had told advertisers to write copy as printed salesmanship. For instance, in 1891 *Printers' Ink* admonished advertisers who tried to use "graceful and dignified diction" at the expense of "plain and blunt" and "commonplace" language. "Write precisely as you would talk to a customer." Above all, "recollect that what you are doing is done to please the public—not yourself or your highly educated friends."[82] Charles Austin Bates likewise reminded his readers in 1899 that if they "deserve patronage there are reasons for it. Your ad should tell the reasons rather than the mere fact that you are deserving." Moreover, advertisers "should never say anything in an ad that [they] would not say personally to a customer." In other words, Bates recommended, "just recall what you said to the last half dozen customers you waited upon, and you will almost invariably recall good material for an ad."[83] Through the 1890s, *Printers' Ink* repeated this message again and again. That Kennedy learned something of this approach from Bates's early criticism of his work indicates the extent to which it had been in the air for a decade.[84]

## Intuition versus Science

In theory, good copy has always been defined as copy that sold the advertised product or service. Yet measuring selling efficacy has never been as easy as comparing copy with conventions and other fabricated criteria. And determining whether a product or service sold or not because of its advertisements has never been as easy as correlating promotional practices with sales figures and assuming causal links. Many promoters, from entertainers like P. T. Barnum, to patent-medicine vendors like Lydia Pinkham, industrialists like Cyrus McCormick, publishers like Cyrus Curtis, and advertising specialists like Nathaniel Fowler, certainly possessed an intuitive sense of how to market successfully, and they sold their wares. They often defied "common sense" or established procedures in some way because, in Lasker's words, "they inherently felt it within themselves." Yet many others' intuitions had failed them, and, moreover, intuition formed a poor foundation for a nascent profession in the new, increasingly corporate and bureaucratic business environment. Lasker and others recognized that the field needed to move beyond intuition to study content and strategies that could be communicated, systematized, and taught,[85] and by the end of the century, the move away from intuition, or at least its appearance, was already well under way.

Practitioners sought a veneer of system and objectivity for advertising activities, borrowing at first from the established profession of selling—though face-to-face selling certainly requires intuition, as do psychology and Scientific Management, to which they turned next. Advertising specialists still vary in their willingness to admit that creating advertisements remains, in the end, a matter of intuition aided by research and technique. If nothing else, qualification as experts in this transitional period required rejecting their most flamboyant predecessors' stained reputations and instead seeking ways to create and judge advertising messages for which they could claim objective, even scientific, standards. In 1894, *Profitable Advertising* warned, "Experimental advertising is dangerous." Only "men of genius," such as those noted for having generated large fortunes by their advertising skills, should attempt advertising for themselves. Everyone else should either consider not advertising at all or call upon "an expert." Advertising had become a science, and it required a knowledgeable practitioner "to make it a success," both in terms of buying space and "imparting a 'pulling' quality to the advertisements themselves."[86] Although science in the strict sense relies on experimentation, individual advertisers were advised not to contribute their own expenditures to the cause, instead to rely on the experience gained on others' accounts. Hence, John Lee Mahin's 1900 headline reassuringly, if misleadingly, declared that "Advertising is no longer an experiment."[87]

Advertising professionals' claims that they could accurately predict consumer responses belied Claude Hopkins's emphasis on the lessons from feedback that compared successes and failures. Earlier than most, Hopkins made "an everlasting argument . . . against dealing with people in the mass." He developed an approach to advertising in the 1890s that based appeals on what he believed was important to consumers and wrote to them as if he were writing to them individually, even when he told them to follow the crowd. For instance, Hopkins researched and explained product features that might well not have been unique but that had not been previously publicized. Even if a feature "embodies no great advantages" but might appeal to consumers, such as steam-cleaning beer bottles, he believed that whatever "pains" a firm took to excel should be told. As long as no competitor had done so first, Hopkins claimed that the "product will come to typify those excellences." His autobiography relates scores of experiences, personal as well as professional, from which he calculated lessons in advertising through feedback. He tried to assess audiences' interests with personal conversations. He claimed to stay close to "simple people" to keep his perspective fresh. "I learn what they buy and their reasons for buying. Those reasons would surprise many who gain their impressions from golf-club associates." Despite his often homespun storytelling, Hopkins also developed some of the earliest objective feedback mechanisms, doing so first by following his intuition rather than self-consciously attempting to mimic scientific methods. Early on, he attended to sales figures and other consumer responses to products and advertisements, systematically collecting information to test and compare the worth of his copy. Extending Kennedy's notion of advertising as salesmanship, he compared advertising messages, "one by one, on a salesman's basis, and [held] them responsible for cost and result."[88]

Together, the results of his intuitive experimentations formed a "system" to which he and others could attach the label of "scientific advertising," the title of a book he published in 1923. Freely admitting his frequent mistakes in the course of learning each lesson, Hopkins presented these techniques to the field as the means of avoiding intuition's weaknesses by accruing expertise.

Not all advocates of progressive advertising argued for its place as a science. Many emphasized instead the art of preparing an effective message. Earnest Elmo Calkins, looking back on early debates from 1915, advocated a balance of the "statistical, bookkeeping, exact mind" with creativity, which "presupposes, in addition to experience, a certain touch of temperamental adaptability." Such creativity requires "common sense, shrewdness and imagination" to plan and prepare advertisements. Psychological studies could inform and assist the creative processes, and explain after the fact what sold and what did not, but, Calkins declared, studying psychology cannot "make a good advertising man out of one who has not a certain feeling for the work, any more than a study of prosody and versification will make a poet." Therefore, no "working formula or set of rules" could replace intuition in reckoning with "the human element." Calkins saw in these searches for system "the same progress as shown by the older professions," going "through many throes and many theories in its attempt to find itself" as specialists' ambitions responded to manufacturers' demands with research and art.[89]

Another debate over the nature of advertising during these transitional years—whether or not advertising created desires—had major implications for the development of creative techniques. If, on the one hand, advertising "at its best is news," as early analysts, even Bates as late as 1896, had generally concluded, "it merely caters to an existing demand" that might "lie dormant."[90] If, on the other hand, advertising "creates trade," as Fowler claimed as early as 1893, this laid a heavier burden of expectations on the field. The marketing crisis that followed the Crash of 1893 fueled the stronger claim, and by the turn of the century, analysts assumed that successful advertisements attracted attention, tempted a reading, interested the reader, created desires, and turned desires "into resolves to have or see" the advertised goods.[91] The outcome of this debate—namely, that advertisements were to generate demand through their salesmanship—meshed with the larger picture of advertising's expanding roles in the marketing mix. In order to accomplish this expanded list of expectations for their services, practitioners increasingly felt the need to develop their techniques.

During this transitional period, then, advertising practitioners found themselves looking both backwards and forwards for guidance. Many sought direction from the newspaper training that had prepared them to write for public consumption. For instance, John Wanamaker hired Joseph Appel from his newspaper job in 1899 when Appel wrote to tell him that advertising should "be made news."[92] Another news reporter, Lasker, instead looked back paradoxically both to Powers's honesty and "reason why" techniques and to patent medicine, declaring repeatedly that it was from the latter that "we learned this art, and well we might, because there was no limitation on them as to what they could do." The entrepreneurs operating in that arena had virtually no restrictions imposed on their imaginations by either product or convention, and so, collectively, they tried everything. Both their competitors, other advertisers, and advertising practitioners took notice and learned. An article in the general press in 1903 corroborated that "the patent-medicine men were pioneers in the advertising business. If they did not originate the display advertisement, they were among the first to use it on a large scale, and it was their success that taught other business men how to increase their trade." Even in the midst of the public debates that led up to the Pure Food and Drug Act of 1906, the latter author could proclaim that the "world at large may not owe very much to the old patent-medicine advertisers, since it canceled the debt long ago by giving them comfortable fortunes; but modern advertising must acknowledge their tuition."[93] Successful advertising, it appeared, required avoiding the offenses perpetrated by the nostrum masters while learning from their techniques to open consumers' purses.

Having taken on the task of "creating trade," advertising practitioners began to explore how they might accomplish it. Looking at the lessons of the past, with an eye to their future, they experimented. According to Calkins, the "so-called advertising expert then is the man who studies the causes of great successes with the idea of applying them to other articles and other markets. It is for him to eliminate as far as possible the uncertainty, the waste, the non-essentials; to change advertising from an art to a science—or, at least, to a profession worthy of the ambition and energy of trained minds."[94] Fowler advised in 1893 that advertisers make their messages "lively" by mixing them "with Brains," particularly, "the choicest cells of genuine cranial gray matter."[95] The mix of brains, enthusiasm, and ambition led to a lively state of experimentation and growth. While it is certainly not the case, as Lasker claimed in 1925, that by 1915 all the "fundamental principles of advertising" had been discovered and disseminated,[96] the velocity and volume of experimentation in the years after 1900 exploded, yielding many of the "principles" as well as the arts still in use today. Firms' willingness to spend unprecedented sums and agencies' eagerness to distribute those sums lured growing numbers of ambitious individuals with business, journalism, and university backgrounds, sharing a range of motives from financial to the lure of excitement. They gave free rein to their imaginations; some of their offerings appeared to improve sales, and those in turn fanned the flames. The causes and dynamics of this experimentation and the activities, ideas, and advertisements resulting from these explorations into technique and strategy call for a full study to do them justice. The new approaches took advertising strategies and contents ever farther away from their roots.

## Seeking to Persuade

Charles Austin Bates summarized the problem of persuasion in 1903 when he declared that "the whole purpose of a printed advertisement is to carry a definite and convincing impression to the mind of the reader."[97] By that time, the options for achieving that "definite and convincing impression" included attempting various systems. Bates's older notion, a view also held by others, that advertisements simply communicated news to awaken existing wants no longer sufficed. George French, who wrote frequently on advertising's functions in the new century, in 1915 declared, "It is now one of the minor functions of advertising to announce or give notice. Its major function is to persuade." Moreover, advertising's "office now is to develop the need or the desire. It ignores the necessity, for the most part. At the best, the necessities of the people form but one of the less considered elements of advertising, as it is now understood and practiced." In other words, French explained, the advertiser tries "to create . . . a necessity in the lives of the people that has no economic or moral basis in fact. Whether the motive is to seek out real needs or to create fictitious needs, the motive for modern advertising runs along the attempt to persuade people."[98]

Herbert Casson advocated Scientific Management as a means of achieving persuasion, applying Frederick W. Taylor's notions of creating "a new habit of thought" in order "to make UNCONCERNED people take notice" and then "to persuade UNCONCERNED people to purchase."[99] Success entailed increasing the probabilities of appealing to consumers by increasing sensitivity to their interests and needs in ways quite alien to traditional advertisers, who operated on their intuitive senses of what messages to disseminate and who had succeeded whenever their intuitions by chance struck a chord.

The trade literature offered advertisers and specialists alike endless instructions for striking the chords of consumers' purchasing responses. At one end of the range of options fell relatively simple insights on improving advertising's access to people at their most vulnerable moments, such as observations that magazines' excellence as advertising media resulted because they are "peculiarly the companion of leisure hours, when the mind is free to accept new impressions."[100] Other oft-repeated basic suggestions warned not to offend readers, either with extravagant claims following the old patent-medicine and circus patterns, or with crude humor. The central theme of all this advice, via countless articles and books, called for consumer-interest messages, despite lingering resistance from some advertisers. Ubiquitous calls for uncluttered layouts linked them with positive human reactions, as in the claim that "ventilation in an advertisement suggests healthfulness and prosperity," as opposed to display that "looks as though its owner was afraid some little quarter of an inch of space would be paid for without being utilized, [which] puts the prospective customer in an unconscious attitude of dealing with a close-fisted merchant."[101] Writers should avoid jargon and stilted language, and instead use human interest and humanity. "Sympathetic copy" included "not so much . . . of the merits of the article as of what the company could do for the reader, if he would let them." Advertisements constructed by following this advice possessed "that human sympathy which the good salesman puts into his selling efforts."[102] By the turn of the century, the desirability of "humanity" became less an issue than how to apply it to "cold type."[103]

### Simplicity

The earliest criticisms of advertisements' contents discouraged the usual practice of simply placing a small "card" that merely identified a firm or product and tacked on a superlative or two. Once most advertisers had learned that lesson, critics addressed the ensuing enthusiasm with which advertisers filled their advertisements. More often than not, critics focused on advertisers' overfilling their spaces, trying to pack content into a given space; the common tendency, encouraged in *Iron Age* as late as 1896, entailed claiming "nothing which is not strictly true, but never fail[ing] to claim all the truth."[104] In contrast, most advisers by then argued against compound messages, whether in lists of claims or clusters of images, by pointing to the vanguard of layouts and copy that were successful in either notoriety or sales, and also appealing to new standards of "good taste." Early in the 1890s, the *Inland Printer's* editors complained that advertisers' habits could be "hackneyed and obsolete" in this respect.[105] In 1900, the same journal excused a printer's own advertisement as "too florid in style for those having a critical taste in printing" with the guess that "the printer is looking to please the ideas of his trade and not his own." As J. Walter Thompson emphasized in 1895, "*Always* keep in each and every Ad., no matter what the size may be, one leading Idea, Trademark or Design. There is nothing else so forcible and lasting as this. Tell your story over and over, with all its variations, in a series of ads., *but always* stick to the Idea and to the *Point*."[106] The advertising mainstream followed this advice for both copy and art.

Urging advertisers to favor simple and direct messages followed an easy logic, given the period's intensifying level of stimulus saturation, in rural areas as well as in cities and towns. If ever it had been possible to attract and hold audiences' attention long enough to view the traditional, complicated advertisements with factories and multiple vignettes, or to read long lists of goods or lists of superlatives describing offerings, it was so no longer. Decades of competition had generated voluminous printed media, both ephemeral and periodical, and, according to *Metropolitan Magazine,* this had made the "busy American loath to read. His eyes must be attracted, coaxed, cajoled." As a result, "to-day the advertising columns of high-class mediums are nearly as attractive from a literary and artistic point of view as the regular text and illustrations."[107] Ad specialists, as a rule, came to want simpler styles that did not interfere with their messages.[108] This said, how could ads win their audiences' attention and interest?

## *Planning*

With advertisers' growing demands for effectiveness and efficiency in both creating and placing advertisements, advertising professionals competed by developing services that featured basic planning and other previously neglected activities. As an expert on "scientific advertising" explained in 1911, "No great achievement, and certainly not the winning of an indifferent public, can be done without a Plan." Although "four-fifths of our selling is still of the slambang, hit-or-miss species," there were enough successfully planned advertising campaigns to inspire others.[109] The most obvious components of an advertising plan are decisions about the advertising message and placing that message. These are, however, the end products of decision making, with or without a deliberate plan. By the 1890s, advertising professionals were already aware of some considerations that contradicted intuitive notions of how they should plan and evaluate their advertising, such as that immediate sales might not be the best indicators of a campaign's worth. For instance, in 1892, William Maher evaluated the "staying power of an advertisement" and advised advertisers to consider the long-term impact of their messages as investments in goodwill. Likewise, improving public attitudes toward companies could be an intermediate step to long-term sales.[110]

As part of their intense competition for accounts and their clients' competition for markets, specialists experimented in techniques for market analysis, planning, and creation during the transition period after the mid-1890s, resulting in campaigns such as Procter & Gamble's outstandingly successful marketing of Crisco shortening, starting in 1911.[111] *American Industries* noted the rapid pace of change in 1904, praising advertisements that contained "appeals to the general public that would have seemed heretical a year or two ago."[112] Of the countless examples of marketing innovations under the new regime, a single case can illustrate the nature of the advertising professionals' new roles and exemplify the impact that an advertising innovator could have in service of a powerful corporate advertiser.

The National Biscuit Company campaign for Uneeda Biscuit was considered extraordinary when initiated, but its remarkable success made it a model for a level of market analysis and planning that, within two decades, became the norm for major national accounts. Three years after the National Biscuit Company (NBC), later Nabisco, took shape from mergers in 1898, the corporation established a policy that it would no longer compete by price. Instead it would compete by "constantly increasing capitalization" to maximize efficient buying, production, and distribution, and "above all things and before all things, to improving the quality of our goods and the condition in which they should reach the consumer." In order to achieve this, NBC's chairman of the board, Adolphus Green, organized the production of a standardized, high-quality, and packaged biscuit—the traditionally popular soda cracker. Green sought assistance with the advertising and marketing problems involved and soon awarded the account to N. W. Ayer & Son, represented by Henry McKinney. Thereafter, the two men worked closely together to develop a long-range plan to market this yet-unnamed product.[113]

McKinney and Green cooperated on planning and executing all of the activities for what would become the largest national advertising campaign for a single product to date. They began by devising a name, both making suggestions, and finally agreeing on McKinney's idea, Uneeda Biscuit. Placing the agency's full capabilities at Green's disposal set a precedent for the extent of a major agency's assistance to a client. Most importantly, both Green and McKinney agreed on the importance of setting the highest priority on planning. Copy, artwork, packaging, and advertising placement were generated and coordinated within both the agency and the corporation to meet the overall strategies. This unique planning produced a nationally distributed series of teaser advertisements, placed in newspapers and store displays and on billboards and streetcars. The first of these messages simply stated "Uneeda Biscuit," without explanation. Every few days, a new message, such as "Do You KNOW Uneeda Biscuit?" added to the mystery. (Questions were not new to copywriting at this time, as evinced by examples cited earlier, such as Genin's and Macy's discussed in chapter 1, and Barratt's for Pears' Soap in chapter 2. Nonetheless, the use of questions rose in frequency as consumer-oriented advertising grew.) Demand for the new product was almost immediate, once its introduction solved the mystery. Sales for this biscuit, with its guarantee of quality based on an elaborately designed, consumer-sized package, soon challenged the tradition of purchasing crackers out of barrels. Consumers, particularly urban consumers, readily bought these goods, innovatively packaged and sealed from moisture and vermin, even at roughly twice the cost per pound of those sold out of barrels. The Uneeda Biscuit marketing campaign worked so well that soon production fell behind demand. NBC then built new plants.[114]

To Adolphus Green, the Uneeda Biscuit campaign had much the character of a crusade; to N. W. Ayer & Son, it was less a crusade than a challenge. McKinney and Ayer understood the benefits of serving well the manufacturers of large volumes of branded, standardized, consumer goods. The tie between the two firms lasted until 1935, fulfilling another of Ayer and McKinney's post-1890 ambitions: they wanted long-term relationships with active and high-volume clients. The lessons of the Uneeda Biscuit campaign impressed many advertising professionals seeking direction. Planning for entire marketing campaigns rather than individual advertisements had begun to attract attention already, but this success quickly moved it into prominence. Although Ayer and McKinney had experimented with rudimentary market research for an occasional client as far back as 1880, they had never yet applied it at such depth. Even after this lesson, they still did not establish a separate planning department until ten years later, dispersing the planning function throughout the agency in the meantime.[115]

In the new century, the importance of planning and research reached general acceptance. The *Inland Printer* had already warned its readers in 1895 that although "everyone who has anything to do with it [advertising] feels assured he can excel," it was "wise to seek the advice of students of the science" in view of the varieties of research on markets that major publishers conducted on behalf of advertisers to eliminate guesswork in placing ads.[116] Daniel Starch, originator of a still-active readership feedback service, wrote in 1914 that "success and failure are not matters of good or bad luck. Complete analysis of a proposition and careful execution of the plans bring results with as reasonable certainty in an advertisement as cause and effect follow each other in any other controllable human affairs."[117] In 1915, Calkins addressed the importance of planning to effective advertising campaigns; he observed that "shrewd manufacturers keep advertising men at work two years before a single line of publicity is sent out" on a new product line. "Some time ago the advertising man extended his work from advertising pure and simple to a study of sales problems." This included spotting a "weak point in the manufacturing policy" by studying products, trademarks, distribution channels, and competitors. Because "the manufacturer has demanded better ground for his advertising plan," and because "the advertising man, ambitious to develop a surer method, has neglected no field of research . . . this present, more scientific method of basing advertising upon the real facts, whatever they are, wherever they may be found, has come into its own." These areas of study included "the laws of the human mind, the laws of supply and demand, the natural channels of trade, [and] the shopping habits of women."[118]

## Targeting Markets

An important aspect of sensitivity to markets is knowing who populates the markets for different products; therefore, market segmentation—that is, dividing the general population into advertising targets according to their interests and demographics—has become an essential tool for planning campaigns and preparing tailored messages. In principle, it could work more reliably than impulse, intuition, or the preparers' own tastes. This tool for enhancing effectiveness and efficiency infiltrated advertising practices only haltingly after J. Walter Thompson raised its profile in order to convince advertisers to buy space in the magazines he represented. As early as 1887, Thompson argued that a medium's "character" was more important to advertisers than the wider circulation they could get more cheaply from newspapers. Advertisers should, therefore, favor publications that have "entrance to the *better class* of homes, where the other is never admitted." Thompson continued: "The great bulk of business, aside from the necessaries of life, comes from the people of moderate or independent means associated with at least fair refinement and culture. The ignorant classes have no inclination to spend money for other than the necessaries of life; the poor have none to spend. Hence, judicious advertisers seek to reach people having both TASTE for their goods and the MEANS to gratify it."[119] Even so, as long as advertisers continued to care more for getting optimal circulation than for creating audience-sensitive messages, targeting remained a tool at most for placing advertisements strategically, rather than creating them with audiences in mind. Even after the mid-1890s, when copywriters slowly began to think about addressing specific classes or genders, they never used the term with its implied focus and precision.

Although most advertising agents brokered their space by contending that their offerings were superior to their competitors, few besides Thompson argued their cases with much more than the same types of superlatives other advertisers used in their copy before 1890. Most agents remained primarily concerned with selling large volumes of space and with competing through price per unit of circulation, rather than audience appropriateness. Just as most advertisers sought broad audiences rather than finely targeted ones, some delineations were so crude that they assumed there was only one class of people whom all advertisers cared to reach. Thus a soap manufacturer declared that he had confined his advertising "entirely to newspapers. The man who does not read a newspaper does not use soap!"[120] Although the general level of discourse on market refinements began to rise in the 1890s, for years the arguments merely claimed that particular publications or agents' lists of publications reached the "better classes."[121] An 1895 advertisement in *Printers' Ink* read simply that the "class of people you desire to reach are those to be found through advertising in *The Sun,* New York."[122] Country papers and their brokers or syndicates plied potential advertisers with a broad type of segmentation by which they might reach a desirable audience. They told mail-order advertisers, for instance, that country storekeepers could not keep large enough inventories to satisfy "people in country towns." Occasionally using the drawing card of fond memories, they encouraged advertisers also to aim for another market: the city gentleman who read his hometown paper from cover to cover "with boyish eagerness."[123] Aiming for both sides of the rural/urban coin may have stretched the reliability of such targeting, but it told advertisers that they ought to be thinking about it.

Keying advertisements offered a systematic and relatively inexpensive means of targeting, and trade publications of all sorts encouraged its use, beginning about 1900. Well before that, some advertisers, such as Colonel Pope of Columbia Bicycles, had come to the method on their own. Advertisers could evaluate the effects of varied content or varied publications by placing different advertisements containing different, keyed, contact information and usually slightly different addresses, and then tracking responses to the keyed addresses.[124] Gradually, targeting did become more refined for both placement and copywriting purposes, taking into account data from population surveys, primitive market surveys, and the accumulated experience of advertising professionals. The targeting of audiences had yet to yield the techniques of surveying and interviewing, much less setting up focus groups to explore people's thoughts or including representatives to help create messages. In 1911, Casson still criticized the field because "perhaps the most frequent cause of failure in selling is the vague this-is-for-nobody-in-particular aspect of the advertisement. There is no aim—no direct appeal." Casson believed that advertisers too rarely appealed directly to the two most obvious targets, women and farmers.[125]

By the early 1890s, however, the trade literature had begun to discuss women as a market, and therefore as an audience, oftentimes as an undifferentiated audience. In 1894, the *Inland Printer* featured an analysis of ten advertisements by "feminine eyes." In an unusually lengthy article that coincided with the journal's new "artistic" masthead, M. Georgia Ormond advised advertisers to appeal to women's "delicate sensibilities" with beauty, occasional inoffensive humor, and constant bargains.[126] Targeting the prosperous classes of women was an early and frequent refinement. An advertisement for the *Ladies' World* in 1894 offered to reach women because they "Can't vote, Can't sit on juries, Can't put down riots;—BUT—They can and do purchase over eight-tenths of all articles purchased for the household and used by the family." The illustration's elegantly dressed woman combined class discrimination with gender. The journal argued its case later for women as more lucrative targets than millionaires; they were "the best buyers—women of the well-to-do class who can and do buy your goods."[127]

For decades after recognizing women's purchasing power in the 1890s, most advertisers and their advisers labored mightily to figure how best to reach them without ever taking on women as copywriters. Despite having Kate E. Griswold as publisher and editor, *Profitable Advertising* rarely mentioned women in any role other than targeted consumers. An exception, written by "Miss Progress" in 1893, pointed to the logical advantages of women writing to women.[128] The men in most agencies continued to struggle to prepare messages appealing to women through the 1920s, although some women were hired, usually at relatively low salaries, to provide the "woman's viewpoint," usually in retail advertising.[129] On rare occasions, an article in the general press announced that "advertising needs women" to write, illustrate, and critique. Women could help advertisers avoid endless "blunders," and they could do this, readers were assured, "without altering or searing their best natures."[130] With no sense of the procedure's inadequacies, Calkins told of an agency's calculating how best to impress upon women the social errors inevitable from an improper choice of writing paper. "The answer comes from various sources: from the inner consciousness of the advertisement writer, from his friends, from the manufacturer of the paper, from his salesmen, from the dealers. The opinions of all these are considered."[131] But not, apparently, the opinions of women. Appel likewise prided himself on having learned at Wanamaker "to assume the attitude of the customer and give such information as the customer would ask for were she talking to the salesman over the counter."[132] Awareness of a market segment clearly did not necessarily entail seeking its input for well-tuned copywriting.

Helen Lansdowne was the great early exception. In 1908, when she joined a major agency handling nationally advertised branded products, she began to provide a genuine "women's view." Stanley Resor recruited her to help the J. Walter Thompson agency at the branch he had opened in Cincinnati; the agency still specialized in magazines for the home, and most of its 'large accounts wished to sell products to women. Lansdowne had written advertisements for several firms already: Procter and Collier (Procter & Gamble's agency), a nationally prominent streetcar advertising organization, and for retailers advertising in a Cincinnati newspaper. She had just received an offer of a position in the streetcar advertising firm's New York office when Resor made his offer. She accepted it and came to national acclaim immediately as the creative force to whom Procter & Gamble—in a rare excursion outside of Procter and Collier—turned for its Crisco campaign. She continued as one of the top figures in U.S. advertising for the next five decades, mostly selling women's products—even promoting government policy for women's war efforts in both world wars—and vigorously mentoring other women as she went. Lansdowne married Resor in 1917, and together they rebuilt the J. Walter Thompson agency into one of the world's largest.[133]

Just as some advisers increasingly advocated reaching for the "women's view" through selective publications, they also cautioned advertisers and their agents against using the same space-buying policies for the "classes" as for the "masses."[134] In 1918, the *Delineator* produced a report that combined gender awareness, economics, demographics, and class chauvinism that won favorable notice from advertising professionals. By assessing how much women, as compared with men, spent on household goods, and how much different classes of women spent relative to each other, the *Delineator* analysts concluded that the optimal targets of advertisements for household goods were families of "comfortable income," rather than either the small numbers of wealthy women or the many poor women. There were, after all, seven million "worth-while families" who "constitute the good wholesome fiber of our race," and who can manage to have whatever they truly want. Of these families, the women were the true targets because "to get her results the woman has to spend"; therefore, copywriters should "attend to the workings of the home" and thereby overcome men's notions that "your meals leap to the table of their own accord . . . and that the children's clothes grow on them in the night."[135] By this time, leading advertising specialists knew they ought to reach people according to their demographics and interests, and that they should shape their appeals accordingly. Although it took decades for practitioners to move out into the worlds of their audiences on a regular basis, they wrestled with ways to communicate with them and to move them, sometimes turning for help to various systems, theories, and even to academic experts in psychology. Although practitioners projected their own expectations onto their audiences, in one way or another enough of them struck enough chords that their impacts, as recorded in sales and notoriety, were enormous.

## Exploring Human Psychology

Manufacturers' discomfiture in addressing the "pertinently and impertinently personal" had often precluded attempts at manipulating human interest. Not yet pragmatically or professionally distanced from the potential for embarrassment, an author in *Printers' Ink* warned advertisers that not all attempts to "address each reader individually, appealing to some want or supposed want, or asking a direct personal question" were fit carriers of commercial messages. Writing in 1894, William Kohn was likely reacting to the popularity of the Pears' Soap campaign that encouraged everyone to ask of everyone else, "Good morning! Have you used Pears' Soap?"[136] Nonetheless, the great success of this and other provocative campaigns encouraged others to attempt to elicit personal emotions (for example, anxiety or guilt) and to indulge in ever more personal, human-interest strategies with the help of specialists. In 1903, George Frederick asserted that the advertising specialists' duty required him to exploit the personal in a matter-of-fact way. "In the great swirling world of buying and selling and boosting, it is the office of the ad man to turn the tide of human caprice and money toward his employer's coffers. . . . In study he must run the whole gamut of human nature's emotions, and if he doesn't like his task of taking humanity at a disadvantage and using his knowledge of its weaknesses as a level to pry gold from its arms, he has but to resign. A man may be greater than his tools, but he cannot change the tools or their use." After all, a man "may sacrifice half his business to sentiment, but he does not hire an ad man to sacrifice it for him. He hires him that he may have the more wherewith to sacrifice."[137] So the advice that had originally come to advertisers as suggestions to assist them in preparing their own materials, increasingly by the turn of the century came as urgings that advertisers allow the experts a free rein in evoking consumer responses.

The effectiveness of designs, copy, and targeting can only be measured by feedback; that is, how well did any specific message draw out the desired response, whether making sales or getting votes? To obtain feedback, in the late 1890s inchoate market analyses began to replace intuitive judgments about who the audiences were and what interested them. Most of that research prior to the middle 1910s entailed setting up feedback loops, such as the tracking systems mentioned above. Some research, however, occurred in artificial settings, such as university and business-school classrooms and the new field of psychology, as a small but growing number of academicians joined advertising practitioners in studying advertising. Applying experimental psychology's techniques provided sources of feedback from artificial settings without the costs of time, media, and risking product reputation. In addition to the artificial settings, "psychological" testing differed from other sorts of experimentation by its stringent attempts to isolate variables of such phenomena as attention, learning, and motivation, and by obtaining feedback on them while attempting to hold other variables constant. Some techniques tried surveys and other means of questioning subjects. Sometimes more laboratory-like techniques presented subjects with stimuli, ranging from simple pictures and single words to colors, and measured some aspect of response. As Calkins defined it, psychologists study "the processes of the normal human mind," and from those understandings they deduce "the kind and character of advertising which will appeal, influence and create action."[138]

*Printers' Ink* appears to have initiated the advertising trade's discussion on psychology in advertising in 1895. That year, in "Human Nature as a Factor in Advertising," Oscar Herzberg concluded that "the advertiser who studies 'the noblest study of mankind' is apt to get the best results. Probably when we are a little more enlightened, the ad writer, like the teacher, will study psychology," because both must "influence the human mind." The next year an article on psychology ended with the statement that, if a man intended to become "a good advertiser, he must become perforce no mean psychologist." And another year later, the "Hidden Forces in Advertising" asserted that it "seems almost ridiculous to insist at this late day that advertising is founded on human nature; yet the fact is often forgotten." Still, the same piece also argued that advertisers of true genius "are born, not made," even though, all abilities require "cultivation and direction" through study.[139] In addition to numerous articles in *Printers' Ink* and other publications that advocated the study of human nature in general, several specifically mentioned the academic study of psychology. For instance, in 1908, *Profitable Advertising* recommended that, to ensure its effectiveness, practitioners study psychology formally, rather than by "common-sense".[140]

Claude C. Hopkins and many others around the turn of the century began to write of using psychology as the scientific tool that could help in knowing "how to appeal to . . . desires." In the competitive commercial world, whoever "wins out and survives does so only because of superior science and strategy." Hopkins did much better than survive; he, like others who had survived less well, believed that they had "discovered some enduring principles."[141] Advertising advisers began to offer their particular lessons about human nature and their notions of how those lessons related to promotional successes or failure, to which some added lessons from academic studies. Scholars of various persuasions, including faculty in the burgeoning business schools, began to offer their work and insights to practitioners, attesting to the growing interest in and respectability of advertising. As a result, the available instructions about understanding consumers and their interests included increasingly sophisticated insights from analysts' newly developed survey techniques and psychological investigations. Psychological experimenters also began to explore systematically just how and why people respond to stimuli, and specifically, how and why advertising layouts and verbal appeals vary in their effectiveness.[142]

By far the most deliberate and extensive campaign on the benefits of applying psychologists' principles to advertising began when *Mahin's Magazine* took the issue up as a crusade of sorts. John Lee Mahin had earlier published *System,* in which he advocated feedback systems for every type of business. In 1902, he invited Walter Dill Scott, professor of psychology at Northwestern University, to write what became a year-long series of articles based on work Scott had begun for a presentation to the Agate Club, Chicago's primary advertising organization. Scott also later wrote for the general press, most importantly in the *Atlantic Monthly* in 1904, and in several books. By the time of his second book, 1908, Scott had achieved considerable renown for his work. He returned the favor in part by dedicating *The Psychology of Advertising* to "that increasing number of American business men who successfully apply Science where their predecessors were confined to Custom." Scott's advice included suggestions that ads "awaken in the reader as many different kinds of images as the object itself can excite." In other words, piano makers should try to evoke memories of music and tone; food sellers should add taste to their product descriptions.[143]

By the 1910s, any number of "theories" about how best to do advertising circulated. Most of them laid some claim to psychological insights—that "ponderous word," according to one analyst in 1909, that "opens wide the door of opportunity to the advertiser"—that "relates to the study of the mind of man, the instrument we must play upon when we advertise."[144] As in many other fields struggling toward standardization, each advocate of a theory labeled his as "scientific" or "realistic" and the others as "mere theories." Hopkins, for instance, had "little respect for most theories of advertising, because they have not been proved"; his own principles, however, he considered well proven and therefore scientific.[145] In raising the field's claims on effectiveness, the psychological and other research methods contributed to the sense that Hugo Munsterberg, a Harvard psychologist, termed in 1909 "a certain contact between empirical psychology and business." As he warned, and others recognized, "many hundreds of millions are probably wasted every year on advertisements that are unsuccessful because they do not appeal to the mind of the reader."[146] Yet so often those insights deemed psychological were simply logical, such as Appel's epiphany, framed in John E. Powers's words, that advertising's goals were to "get seen," "get read," and "get sales." This "psychology of advertising in a nutshell" "hitched" together his college psychology studies and his practice of journalism to good purpose.[147]

By the mid-1910s, study and thinking about the psychology of advertising had advanced sufficiently to make synoptic texts useful, such as the 333-page *Advertising and Its Mental Laws* by Henry Foster Adams, a professor of psychology at the University of Michigan. Adams placed psychology on a par with economics as a science necessary to understand and succeed in advertising because it explored the "facts of the mental life—attention, sensation, perception, memory, reasoning, feelings, emotions—and also . . . the facts of the behavior of the individual." Adams encouraged advertising professionals to apply psychology's understandings of these mental processes to induce "a certain definite kind of action on the part of the reader." For instance, since stimuli elicit both emotion and action, carefully determining the types of stimuli to employ could serve advertisers well. As a case in point, Adams reproduced a Woodbury Facial Soap advertisement showing a young couple caressing romantically. He explained the sensual, sexual impact of this picture, which evoked "a contact or an internal sense" to enhance a message that could only come to the audience through sight, one of the less-potent "distance senses."[148]

Adams's example came from Helen Lansdowne's still-famous campaign, begun in 1910, that had launched Woodbury's sensual slogan "A skin you love to touch" (plate 8). (Years later, the slogan transformed into "The skin you love to touch.") In using this example, Adams corroborated Calkins's argument that science could only explain after the fact what intuition had created because Lansdowne said that she always relied on her intuition and her woman's perspective, not "science." Nonetheless, she, like Calkins and most modern copywriters, highly valued information and research on markets and products, and her intuition came into operation after having analyzed the available information.[149]

### Balancing Art and Copy

Notions of the proper balance of artwork and copy have never held constant but have changed according to fashion, prevailing technologies, and priorities. In the lithographed media of the nineteenth century, pictures dominated, the better to make use of the strongest communication technologies available. Commercial artists flourished in all printed media as technologies developed, reaching their greatest successes in publications after 1890. Into the 1920s and later, a few, such as Maxfield Parrish, J. C. Leyendecker, Harrison Fisher, Howard Chandler Christy, and Norman Rockwell, carried their signature styles to both magazine covers and the advertisements inside with large displays and often minimal copy. As publications became the preferred media for reaching consumers, however, copywriting moved into its ascendancy. This, after all, had been the first creative option in formats that for decades had had few pictorial opportunities. When those opportunities expanded in the 1890s, copywriters already had priority over artists within agencies and advertising departments for setting messages' themes and points. As advertising specialists gained a measure of confidence in using the growing number of pictorial options in publications to support their new responsibilities for writing copy, they experimented with coordinating the two means of appeal. Still, most leading advertising analysts through the 1950s believed that effective copy paved the high road to success, valuing pictures only as signs to attract audiences onto the road. By the 1910s, the creative advisers most in direct contact with advertisers' decision makers were "literary men" of the type their predecessors had regarded with disdain. (Cyrus K. Curtis and F. W. Ayer had considered themselves businessmen, not "literary men.") The new agents held college degrees and incorporated references to literature that reflected their educations and class.[150]

Printers came to terms with their declining influence with advertisers as copywriters ascended. The *Inland Printer* increasingly acknowledged the primacy of copy, although reluctantly at first, as in 1893 when commenting on the "purer, stronger diction" coming into use: "A line can be catchy quite as much in its essence as in its outer form—in what it says, as in the loudness with which it says it."[151] By 1910, the *Inland Printer* demonstrated the new terms on which printing and copywriting professionals cooperated with a series of suggestions on layout followed by this advice:

> Take this hint! The ad. man wants simplicity. Rarely will he pass a florid effort. He especially dislikes fancy borders. They interfere with his direct-talk effort, for he depends much more on his words to induce sales than on the art preservative. This may seem a stunning blow to the pride of the "artist" at the case, but it is a lesson he will have to learn, if he comes into intimate contact with agency work. And I heartily endorse this preference. It is not within his province to present the beauties of typography—rather the message he has to convey.[152]

The verbal message—the "direct-talk effort"—was the copywriters' domain, and those who dominated the field of newspaper and magazine advertising between 1890 and the mid-1920s insisted on the primacy of their contributions. Visuals were just illustrations to most of them, despite the acclaim many commercial artists received and Lansdowne's successes at balancing copy and visuals. Their copy often filled advertisements with lengthy argument and product details that contradicted copywriters' admonitions about clutter. But text was not clutter to these specialists—it was "clean," no matter how long, if it consisted of short, direct sentences. These "literary men," and occasionally women, wrote for their literate peers, so much so that *Profitable Advertising* and other advisers warned copywriters against writing for their peers rather than for "the men and women who are expected to read them."[153] Nobody knew yet how much time people spent reading advertisements, but the writers knew what they felt comfortable doing and what they believed pulled. Their successes at this stage of the art reinforced their beliefs and their authority, whether or not theirs were the most effective possible in this new milieu.

Copywriters provided much of the literature about their profession, in both popular publications and in the trade journals, enhancing the impact of their convictions. The writers prominent in the 1910s generally saw little merit in accompanying their messages with anything but the most minimal amount of illustration. They had come to maturity before printing technologies permitted cheap and easy pictures in periodicals. They also shared an interest in moving their profession's reputation away from its colorful lithographic heritage, disproportionately associated after 1900 with the notorieties of patent-medicine and circus advertising, rather than with the many manufacturers and publishers who had earlier used lithographed images extensively. Reasoned argumentation and information served their multiple concerns, employed their talents, and, they believed, sold products best. As Lasker put it, "it was copy—copy alone—that makes advertising pay."[154]

## Persuading in Peace and War

Among the strongest advocates of copy between 1890 and 1920 were Charles A. Bates, John E. Powers, John E. Kennedy, Albert Lasker, and Claude C. Hopkins. Of these, Hopkins most successfully systematized the pursuit of effectiveness and scientific advertising, throughout this period and into the 1920s. His famously successful campaigns (some of which took place when he worked for Lasker at Lord & Thomas) took obscure products to national leadership, among them Bissell carpet cleaners, Pepsodent toothpaste, and Palmolive soap and shaving cream. As a case in point, Henry Crowell invited Hopkins to launch a campaign for Quaker Oats' puffed cereals in 1908. Hopkins followed his customary practice of studying product processing and character-

## The Good Things
## Some Folks Have

**At breakfast today,** perhaps a million children found Puffed Grains on the table.

Crisp, toasted grains, puffed to eight times normal size. Grains that taste like toasted nuts.

**At dinner today,** on many a table these grains were served in soup. And many another housewife used them as a nut-like garnish for ice cream.

**At supper tonight,** countless bowls of milk were served with these Puffed Grains in them.

Thin, airy wafers — bubble-like and brown — grains four times as porous as bread.

**This afternoon,** legions of girls used these grains in home candy making. Used them in place of nuts. And armies of boys enjoyed the grains dry, like peanuts, when at play.

Forty million dishes per month are now served in all these delightful ways.

> **Puffed Wheat, 10c** *Except in Extreme West*
> **Puffed Rice,   15c**

**Your boys and girls** would enjoy these grains better than any other cereal food.

They are thin and fragile—steam-exploded—filled with a myriad cells. And terrific heat has given them a delightful almond flavor.

**Every food granule** has been blasted to pieces by Prof. Anderson's process. Inside of each grain there have occurred at least a hundred million explosions.

So these are whole grains made wholly digestible, as no other process can make them.

They are ideal foods—scientific foods—the best-cooked cereal foods ever created.

It's a pity to go without them.

### The Quaker Oats Company
#### Sole Makers

*Fig. 8.1.* Leading copywriters trying to set new, up-to-date standards for advertising content after the mid-1890s self-consciously wrote "reason why" messages. In this advertisement for the Quaker Oats Company, Claude Hopkins explained why mothers and children would fare better with puffed cereals. By guiding consumers to wise purchasing decisions, advertising professionals claimed to contribute to progress, while reducing production to a matter of metaphors. *Ladies' World* 34, no. 9 (1913): 21.

istics to find features attractive to appropriate markets. He visited plants with Alexander P. Anderson, developer of the technologies for puffed grains. He learned how the grains exploded in massive, gun-like devices and coined the slogan "shot from guns." An example of Hopkins's puffed-cereals advertising filled half of a large (16″ × 11″) page of the *Ladies' World* for September 1913 (fig. 8.1). Two stylized children look down into a massive bowl of cereal and milk that floats above "The Good Things Some Folks Have." The copy explained the different ways that "perhaps a million," "legions," and "armies" of people enjoy "countless" meals and snacks in the course of a day, adding up to "forty million dishes per month [which] are now served in all these delightful ways." The cereals were digestibly "thin and fragile" because "every food granule has been blasted to pieces by Prof. Anderson's process. Inside of each grain there have occurred at least a hundred million explosions." Because these were "ideal foods—scientific foods," it was "a pity to go without them." While the children's picture draws the gaze into the bowl and the headline, it comprises a small portion of the overall display. Without question, people responded to Hopkins's reason-why campaign, because it moved the once-failing product from obscurity to Quaker Oats' most popular ready-to-eat cereal.[155]

Copywriters labeled as "reason-why" techniques their attempts to project an apparently logical argument. Such messages might include, in an effort to engage the audience, features of the product and their benefits to the consumer. Whether such arguments actually appeal to reason, motivate buying, or instead justify purchases made for other reasons are still topics of debate within the trade. Reason-why techniques never dominated the ads in print, but their advocates' arguments dominated the literature in the first quarter of the century. Reason-why methods served both advertisers and ad writers by encouraging consumers to trust new products in a nearly unregulated marketplace. Rather than offer only tired superlatives or founders' portraits, the lengthy copy ostensibly assured consumers about products' reliability and safety. Detailed copy also gave consumers a language and framework within which to think and talk about the products. Beyond selling products, this approach also allowed advertising specialists to define and assert their professionalism as measured by their distance from past practices. In this capacity, reason-why played an important transitional role as advertising practices moved from the producers' messages to consumer-oriented messages mediated by the new advertising communication specialists.

Reason-why's transitional role—assuring consumers and addressing their interests and at the same time satisfying advertisers by focusing on their products—made it attractive to its users in automobile advertising. It dominated that arena well into the 1920s, even though more evocative marketing techniques were already in use in promoting other nationally advertised products. Auto advertisers were still largely owner-managers, and they generally ignored or rejected the notion that the reasons why people might want to purchase an item were not necessarily its objective and practical features and benefits. Advice to do differently existed as early as 1903, when a *Judicious Advertising* editorial quoted publisher Frank Munsey as having exclaimed that automobiling "will renew the life and youth of the overworked man or woman." The editorial confirmed, "This is good sound talk—*truthful talk*—and it offers a suggestion for strong convincing advertising argument for automobiling and for any automobile that *goes*." In contrast to this "sound talk" about benefits, most automobile advertisements had "a certain sameness" that belied the promotional potential so often expressed by enthusiasts such as Munsey. Automobile manufacturers had failed to keep up with the progress in advertising and were still clinging "to the old-time idea that the proper sort of an ad shows a cut of the machine, with a few stock phrases" about features, and a list of agents. "Let the makers catch up the spirit of enthusiasm—[and] stand out for work of the highest quality from those who prepare their announcements. The results will well repay the pains."[156]

Such "arguments" as this—emotional reasons why—were seldom used in automobile promotions for another twenty years. Instead, the ads emphasized the reliability of the production firms or the mechanical features of the products themselves, and always the costs. Just as Claude Hopkins devised copy about cereals shot from guns and steam-cleaned beer bottles by abstracting facets of production, he advised strategies specifically to reassure buyers and to build confidence, such as writing profiles about head engineers and glossing facts, such as "actual figures how quantity production reduced costs," especially for middle-class cars like the Hudson and the Studebaker.[157] So while he did not advocate portraying a factory as a matter of the producers' pride in industrial progress, he did feature aspects of production that he thought would attract consumers because of their presumed effects on the products. At a time when the absence of regulations combined with the novelty of many products to induce some uncertainty in consumers, this attention to production and product was truly consumer-oriented, even if copywriters still assumed that they somehow knew what consumers wanted to learn. In the case of automobile advertising, it was not that Hopkins did not share Munsey's personal enthusiasm for automobiling; he was an avid buff himself. He simply did not think of promoting automobiles in that fashion. The reason-why approach, which focused on mechanical features and reliability and economic efficiency, was intended to encourage and reassure buyers while giving them a manageable lexicon with which to feel expert and conversant about the new intimidating technology. Copywriters thereby gave emotional needs a veneer of rationality that was important for selling a new, expensive, complex technology.

The one type of emotional appeal in the selling of automobiles recognized as a tactical exception to this rule, even before the mid-1920s, appealed to elitism—that of both the producers and the consumers of the most expensive makes. As another leading copywriter, Earnest Elmo Calkins, observed, "mechanical excellence would be approached ultimately by all cars," so the finest cars should be distinguished instead by their "finish, beauty and luxury."[158] This practice fit a "gentleman's car, built by gentlemen" who were more concerned with their reputations than their fortunes.[159] Even these messages, with their elegant but static images, expressed the prestige attending ownership, but not the excitement. Only after the country had assimilated automobility (and when most leading major automobile makers had incorporated) did auto ads begin to apply the marketing techniques explored earlier by advertisers in other markets.[160]

At the same time as reason-why copy reassured and informed consumers—and sometimes misled them, according to critics—some innovators moved toward more evocative strategies. Copywriters Lansdowne and Calkins and psychologists Scott and Adams, for instance, believed that an effective "fusion of sensations," as Adams termed it, combined copy and picture to form the most effective advertising messages. Adams cited a study indicating that although some people disliked ads with all copy and others disliked the opposite, both groups reacted positively to ads split evenly between illustration and text. In addressing what sorts of images worked best, Adams declared that advertising "is very largely a visual affair" that is best done by using the "distance sense" of sight to evoke "organic and contact sensations."[161] Lansdowne achieved this impact with her Woodbury soap advertisements, Adams believed, and certainly her campaign sold soap: sales multiplied ten times in eight years. Successfully creating demand by evoking emotional responses through picture and copy, Lansdowne's messages continued for decades and pointed the way to powerful and controversial practices that appeared ever more frequently after World War I. The campaign for "A skin you love to touch" offered, both verbally and visually, sensual messages that were novel in marketing to proper women, although not entirely novel to their reading material. These messages implied that these most proper of women should seek such experiences and that the right soap could transform them—first their complexions, then their lives. As daring as they were, Lansdowne's Woodbury advertisements also pointed to the past: they offered copies of their illustrations as premiums. More tellingly, the soap packages pictured in the displays still bore John H. Woodbury's full name and head-only portrait. Such remnants of the traditional practices that featured the advertiser and what the advertiser held dear lingered on during the transition to full specialist control. Kellogg's cornflake advertisements in the 1910s, for instance, embedded a traditional Victorian box in stark, modernist, sometimes evocative designs.

The advertising field's experiences with World War I, including the work of the propaganda organ, the Committee on Public Information (CPI), taught its practitioners much about the potential for persuading audiences. The war's opportunities for experiments in the name of patriotism came when the field and strategists were already on a fast track. Taking advantage of these opportunities, in the name of patriotism, led to narrative styles that did more than offer consumers benefits, such as lovely complexions and romantic liaisons, and more than reasons-why for preferring one product over another. Copywriters moved to narratives that used illustrations to dramatize in no uncertain terms why citizens/consumers should or should not act in some way. Wartime exigencies warranted such strong admonitions as "Nail Lies Like These! . . . Get the Facts from Washington!" and "That Liberty Shall Not Perish from the Earth Buy Liberty Bonds." Ominous and dark illustrations often accompanied this copy, threatening a bitter world if citizens did not pitch in. Some instructions told readers to "Write Him Cheerful Letters," as drawings or photographs compared the effects of hopeful and sad letters on soldiers and hence on the war effort. Countless solicitations on behalf of the Red Cross asked for money and volunteers from "those who love America, believe in humanity, and have faith in God." As commercial artist Charles Dana Gibson explained, "One cannot create enthusiasm for war on the basis of practical appeal." The public must be aroused by the horrors of war.[162]

Copywriters and commercial artists let their imaginations range freely to discover threats to soldiers and the war effort posed by individual citizens' carelessness or lack of diligence. They sold the war through posters, magazines and newspapers, and the Four-Minute Men's speeches; it was a time when there was nothing to offer but everything to fear. In doing so, they learned what propagandists and proselytizers have long known; namely, the power of the narrative to define virtue and evil, to plant fear and doubt, and to promise only the surcease of anxiety as a reward for obedience. Most of all, they wrote to ensure that citizens examined their actions and those of the people around them for true patriotism. It was not enough to believe in one's own patriotism; there were certain requisite behaviors, and only those could satisfy this eternal judging. A CPI ad made this explicit, picturing a fierce-looking Columbia who declared,

*Consumption as Progress*

I Am Public Opinion. All men fear me! [Public opinion] will judge you not by an allegiance expressed in mere words . . . not by your mad cheers. . . .

But, as wise as I am just, I will judge you by the material aid you give to the fighting men who are facing death that you may live and move and have your being in a world made safe. I warn you—don't talk patriotism over here unless your money is talking victory Over There. *I am Public Opinion! As I judge, all men stand or fall!*[163]

So, in case patriotism might not be enough to ensure action, copywriters called on citizens' fear for their reputations and self-esteem.

Wartime copywriters developed new narrative powers to define values, to warn of the consequences of specific actions or inaction, and to label heroes or villains. To accomplish their political purposes, the propagandists wrote to and about citizens and soldiers—"you loving wives and sweethearts" and "our boys"—and not about objects. Reason-why became reason-why-or-else! Writers did not recommend or suggest or compare or describe or make claims about the worthiness of actions; instead they insisted that citizens' worthiness could be measured by how loyally they joined the cause and followed its instructions. This directness, of course, fit the official definition of the crisis and its urgent purposes.

When translated into product advertising targeted at consumers after the war, such boldness presented readers with instructions in several forms. Some copywriters, such as William H. Rankin and William C. D'Arcy, recognized and expounded on the usefulness of wartime activities for postwar commercial advertising.[164] Warnings and offerings gained force from narratives of personal failures and successes that, as during the war, hinged not on the consumers' own judgment but on whether or not they satisfied specific standards. Now the standards became whether or not readers purchased and used specific products, be they personal or house-care products or etiquette books. The rapidly developing narrative techniques resulted in long texts written and illustrated to instill fears of betrayal in business, fears of social disgrace, fears of grooming inadequacy, fears of harming one's children, and so on. Once developed, in the 1920s, parables, social tableaux, and visual clichés, as historian Roland Marchand terms them, taught the merits of products indirectly, less by description of features than by enacting the consequences of neglect or benefits of use.[165] In the meantime, exhortations, admonitions, and, increasingly, melodramas evolved, reducing the announcement styles of advertisements, with their declarations and superlatives, to a minor role. Extensive copy continued well into radio days, diminishing only with the advent of television when the level of popular culture made too many demands on audiences to favor lengthy copy.

Of course, stories about product benefits were not new to advertising, but

**Fig. 8.2.** Nineteenth-century advertisers made large claims for their products, but rarely, except for patent-medicine and cosmetic firms, did they promise personal transformations. Instead, they showed that people who were already competent, attractive, and progressive had the good sense to purchase and use their products. Therefore, Mrs. Enterprise most certainly used Dobbins' Electric Soap, leaving her time to attend to her child, whereas Mrs. Fogy struggled with ordinary soap as her neglected child cried. Two-part chromolithographed trade card, circa 1880.

their appearances as picture stories through the lithographic media, particularly trade cards, had long since become passé. In any case, those older picture stories did not offer miracles of consumption because the people portrayed in them did not experience transformations. Instead, two sets of people demonstrated what products could do for consumers: one set appeared incompetent and unattractive; the other set was competent enough to select the better product and therefore prosper. Double trade cards for Dobbins' Electric Soap and Rising Sun Stove Polish demonstrate both character and ethnic differences between "wise" and enterprising people, on the one hand, and "foolish" fogies on the other (figs. 8.2 and 8.3). Using the right product could not transform one into the other, but it could offer comforting evidence of one's belonging to the right sort of people in the first place—not unlike sacramental evidence of one's belonging to those graced by predestination for spiritual salvation. In contrast, patent-medicine purveyors did use before-and-after formats throughout the nineteenth century; but even they offered only cures, not personality or lifestyle transformations. Still, by promoting what products

**Fig. 8.3.** Elijah Morse, founder and manager of the Rising Sun Stove Polish Company, served his hometown of Canton, Massachusetts, as its congressman. His chromolithographed, double trade card, circa 1885, defined that achievement as the height of success, made possible when a wise man brought to his wife the best stove polish—an important asset to the well-run kitchen in the days of the cast-iron stove. The ads did not, of course, point out that manufacturing the product surely helped a man's career more than purchasing it. Morse's other advertisements often portrayed his factory and homes as evidence of his success.

could do for the consumer—and what failure to use them implied about one's character—these early advertisements presaged the narratives of the 1920s.

James Webb Young prepared the first of the notorious postwar appeals to social fears in 1919 as a full-page advertisement for Odorono, a woman's deodorant (fig. 8.4). This pace-setting advertisement appeared in a typical format for the decade: small illustration, prominent headline, and more than one-half page of tight copy. Its copy had the form of reason-why, but it ap-

*There isn't a girl who isn't have the irresistible, appealing loveliness of perfect daintiness*

# Within the Curve of a Woman's Arm

*A frank discussion of a subject too often avoided*

A woman's arm! Poets have sung of its grace; artists have painted its beauty.

It should be the daintiest, sweetest thing in the world. And yet, unfortunately, it isn't, always.

There's an old offender in this quest for perfect daintiness — an offender of which we ourselves may be ever so unconscious, but which is just as truly present.

### Shall we discuss it frankly?

Many a woman who says, "No, I am never annoyed by perspiration," does not know the facts — does not realize how much sweeter and daintier she would be if she were *entirely* free from it.

Of course, we aren't to blame because nature has so made us that the perspiration glands under the arms are more active than anywhere else. Nor are we to blame because the perspiration which occurs under the arm does not evaporate as readily as from other parts of the body. The curve of the arm and the constant wearing of clothing has made normal evaporation there impossible.

### Would you be absolutely sure of your daintiness?

It is the chemicals of the body, not uncleanliness, that cause odor. And even though there is no active perspiration—no apparent moisture—there may be under the arms an odor unnoticed by ourselves, but distinctly noticeable to others. For it is a physiological fact that persons troubled with perspiration odor seldom can detect it themselves.

Fastidious women who want to be absolutely sure of their daintiness have found that they could not trust to their own consciousness; they have felt the need of a toilet water which would insure them against any of this kind of underarm unpleasantness, either moisture or odor.

To meet this need, a physician formulated Odorono—a perfectly harmless and delightful toilet water. With particular women Odorono has become a toilet necessity which they use regularly two or three times a week.

### So simple, so easy, so sure

No matter how much the perspiration glands may be excited by exertion, nervousness, or weather conditions, Odorono will keep your underarms always sweet and naturally dry. You then can dismiss all anxiety as to your freshness, your perfect daintiness.

The right time to use Odorono is at night before retiring. Pat it on the underarms with a bit of absorbent cotton, only two or three times a week. Then a little talcum dusted on and you can forget all about that worst of all embarrassments—perspiration odor or moisture. Daily baths do not lessen the effect of Odorono at all.

### Does excessive perspiration ruin your prettiest dresses?

Are you one of the many women who are troubled with excessive perspiration, which ruins all your prettiest blouses and dresses? To endure this condition is so unnecessary! Why, you need *never* spoil a dress with perspiration! For this severer trouble Odorono is just as effective as it is for the more subtle form of perspiration annoyance. Try it tonight and notice how exquisitely fresh and sweet you will feel.

If you are troubled in any unusual way or have had any difficulty in finding relief, let us help you solve your problem. We shall be so glad to do so. Address Ruth Miller, The Odorono Co., 713 Blair Avenue, Cincinnati, Ohio.

At all toilet counters in the United States and Canada, 60c and $1.00. Trial size, 30c. By mail postpaid if your dealer hasn't it.

*Dr. Lewis B. Allyn, head of the famous Westfield Laboratories, Westfield, Massachusetts, says:*

*"Experimental and practical tests show that Odorono is harmless, economical and effective when employed as directed, and will injure neither the skin nor the health."*

Address mail orders or requests as follows:

For Canada to The Arthur Sales Co., 29 Colborne St., Toronto, Ont. For France to The Odorono Co., 38 Avenue de L'Opera, Paris. For Switzerland to The Agence Americaine, 6 Rue Du Rhone, Geneve. For U. S. A. to The Odorono Co., 713 Blair Avenue, Cincinnati, Ohio.

**Fig. 8.4.** James Webb Young's innovatively intimate advertisement for the Odorono Company attracted wide attention. It offended many readers of the *Ladies' Home Journal* enough for them to cancel their subscriptions, but it also sold a lot of deodorant. The intention of most copywriters of this era was to use illustrations in magazine and newspaper advertisements only to draw readers to the ads' lengthy texts, which were filled with stories and warnings. Such formats contrasted profoundly with the earlier, freestanding advertisements that narrated by means of pictures, using minimal text and rarely offering personal transformations. *Ladies' Home Journal* 36, no. 5 (1919): 168.

pealed to powerful or-else emotions. As a young couple danced in a romantic setting, the caption under them read, "There isn't a girl who can't have the irresistible, appealing loveliness of perfect daintiness." Young, a protégé of Helen Lansdowne Resor's, had self-consciously tried to balance propriety and his task of eliciting interest in the product's benefits; therefore, the headline only hinted at the subject of the message: "Within the Curve of a Woman's Arm." Yet he did inject into the copy candor about body processes unheard of in the *Ladies' Home Journal* since patent medicines had been expelled. Young did not threaten consumers with ill health, as had the nostrum sellers, but there were potent goads to anxiety just the same. Just as the CPI had denied wartime citizens the option of judging their own patriotism, Young's lengthy text informed readers in different ways that they could not "be absolutely sure of [their] daintiness" without this product. "It is a physiological fact that persons troubled with perspiration odor seldom can detect it themselves." In August, another Odorono advertisement appeared to use the voice of "a well-known business man" in a "courageous article" to tell women that their chances for success in business as well as social spheres could be spoiled by a "real menace" to which they were probably "utterly unconscious." Only proper applications of Odorono could end their offensiveness and salvage their romantic and business lives. In dismay over these breaches of decorum in the *Ladies' Home Journal*, more than two hundred people canceled their subscriptions. Sales of Odorono, however, increased 112 percent in the next year, and Young learned the merits of (to quote his "Curve of a Woman's Arm" ad) "a frank discussion of a subject too often avoided."[166]

As advertising practitioners and their advocates observed the internal progress of their field after 1890, they interpreted and touted their marketing successes as evidence of their own progress. By the turn of the century, they began to claim that their progress deserved credit for the progress of society as a whole. By 1920 they were sure of it.

# 9

# Modernity and Success

## Legitimating the Advertising Profession–I

*Nowhere has there been given a more notable response to the spirit of modern improvement than in the advertising pages of the current newspapers and magazines. Advertising itself is not a new thing, but its primitiveness of style was, until very recent times, a markedly persistent trait of it.*

—"Progress in Advertising," *Harper's Weekly*, reprinted in *Printers' Ink* (1897)

Long before advertising agents made broad claims about the impact of their activities on the ambient culture, they did participate in the progress discourse that pervaded nineteenth-century American culture. They observed with great satisfaction their own progress and that of others, although taking credit for none but their own and those they served. By the turn of the century, however, the advocates and practitioners of advertising expanded the range of their stake in progress to a third theme, namely, their profession's roles in national economic and cultural progress. Whereas the first two themes appeared consistently and in all forums, the third developed only gradually at the end of the 1890s, after which it flourished. So, before the 1890s, advertising's partisans could juxtapose articles on the general progress of the times next to articles on the growth of advertising and form no connection between the trends. For instance, in the late 1870s, N. W. Ayer & Son published an *Advertiser's Guide* that carried a regular column containing "Notes of Progress." These columns routinely recorded developments external to marketing, such as those in science, technology, and industry. Articles in the same issues remarked on how advertising was expanding and how "curious" its practices had been in earlier centuries, but made no reference to the types of events covered in

"Notes of Progress."[1] Progress was something to be noted and celebrated, but advertising practitioners still considered that only contributions to their own progress and that of their clients fell within their purview.

Proponents of the new and professionalizing occupation always wrote voluminously, both to justify its activities and to improve them. Trade journals, led first by *Printers' Ink* and later by *Profitable Advertising, Judicious Advertising,* and others, promoted the field to advertisers and debated its issues with fellow practitioners. Those who set the field's pace wrote with increasing frequency and intensity to sell their profession, targeting potential clients as a rule—George Rowell called *Printers' Ink* "a journal for advertisers"—but also the general public. As the Curtis Publishing Company argued in 1913 on behalf of the advertising agent, "because their calling is so young and the abuses have been so much more apparent than the merits, they still have to apologize for their calling."[2] And so they wrote to show how advertisements and their own activities and achievements had progressed, how they had served clients and publishers, and, eventually, how they served both industrial and social progress. Each theme appeared according to the challenges they experienced and to the stages their own development had reached. As people whose jobs entailed selling through the medium of print, they learned early on to sell themselves; in fact, as we have seen, even before they wrote advertisements for clients, they wrote ads for themselves. By the turn of the century, in their own defense and with considerable enthusiasm, they participated in the dramatic changes of the nation's ethos to that of a consumer culture, for which they believed that they provided the most essential services.

## The Advertising Profession Promotes Its Modernity

At every point, advertising practitioners observed that their field had developed substantially since its inception, and for that matter—because progress was, after all, the watchword of the century in every avenue of self-promotion and self-justification—since any given time, however recent. Even in 1849, Volney B. Palmer promoted his services in terms of their improvement by virtue of honesty and system over competitors' usual practices that fit more the trade of "our grandfathers."[3] As the pace of change accelerated, this sense of advancement intensified, and it provided a constant source of self-congratulation to practitioners. Early analysts of advertising repeatedly referred to the field as being in its infancy—already valuable, but in need of improvement. For instance, an editorial in the first issue of *Profitable Advertising* noted that the "crude, very crude" infancy of advertising already showed "a great improvement" that augured well for the future. Likewise, the J. Walter Thompson Company looked back on the field's history from 1910 and declared, "When we began business—away back in 1864—advertising was a rather puny infant, and there was some doubt as to whether it would pull through at all. And now look what a world-straddling Colossus it is. Advertising has turned out very well indeed." The agency took some pride in that development, "for we fed it with a milk bottle, figuratively speaking, in the early days, and have done what we could to shape its character for nearly half a century."[4]

### Distancing Advertising from Its Past

The advertising press as well as the general press often featured reflections on "old-time" advertisements. Until the 1890s, these always focused on the quaint and curious nature of the vintage messages. For instance, in 1874, Englishman Henry Sampson published the first full text written exclusively on the history of advertising. He sought, first, to correct the notion that advertising was "modern" in origin, and second, to show that outdated advertisements were "full of interest," even "highly suggestive of amusement." Sampson's treatment of advertising's changes was largely anecdotal; he noted advertising's growing importance to the economy only to justify collecting anecdotes about an "important branch of our present system of commerce."[5] Innumerable pieces in *Printers' Ink* and other U.S. journals for the trade also looked back on "old-fashioned" advertisements as quaint relics of the field's past. Articles or fillers with some kind of historical perspective appeared at least a dozen times each year in each of the various trade publications from 1888, when *Printers' Ink* began publication as the first successful trade journal for advertising in the United States.[6] In most cases before the mid-1890s, the articles simply itemized curiosities for amusement, retaining Sampson's anecdotal, quizzical manner.[7]

Starting in the 1890s, as advertising specialists began to create advertising copy, a distinct shift occurred in how observers compared the "modern" with the "old-time." The purely anecdotal article still appeared, of course;[8] however, observers slowly began to compare favorably the modern against the old-fashioned, usually to congratulate the growing corps of copywriters and artists who increasingly influenced advertising's output. For instance, an article reprinted in *Printers' Ink* from the *McKeesport Times* in 1890 noted that "advertisements are no longer the regulation musty affairs they used to be. They are among the most artistic and attractive features of the popular newspaper."[9]

Self-congratulatory comparisons often also self-promoted, as in 1895 when J. Walter Thompson, in "Antique versus Modern," an article in his annual promotional book, instructed advertisers in "the marvellous improvement of the present day": his article demonstrated some "modern" principles, contrasting "ancient cuts" with illustrations by "my artists."[10] Occasionally instructions made comparisons to inspire, rather than to sell. "In order to arrive at a correct and proper understanding of the ethical and scientific side of advertising, it is necessary to compare the old with the new, the obsolete with the 'up-to-date' style, the 'old fogy' way with the *fin de siecle* methods now practiced," according to one article in 1894. Despite advertising's recent progress toward becoming a science, it had not yet developed "straight out-and-out 'specialists' as that term is understood in the medical profession," and that important task required the comparison of failures and successes.[11]

Joel Benton noted in 1893 that the growing competition for audiences' attention had brought about an enhanced appreciation for style among advertisers and their writers.[12] A week after Benton's essay, a lead article in *Printers' Ink* declared that an "advertisement which an advertiser would have felt justified in spending a large sum of money in placing in newspapers some years ago would, in many cases, be rejected to-day as not being up to the mark." The editors also favorably noted the increased use of illustrations, especially "appropriate illustrations" done by the "good artists at the command of advertisers." Carroll D. Wright, U.S. commissioner of labor, commented in 1895 that the "science and skill displayed in advertising in modern times were not thought of in colonial days."[13] An editorial in the *New York Times* declared in 1900, "the progress is immense."[14] Walter Dill Scott, who studied the psychology of advertising at Northwestern University, declared a few years later in *Atlantic Monthly* that the "change has been so great that the leading advertisers say that in comparison with to-day there was in existence fifteen years ago no advertising worthy of the name."[15] Advertising professionals sought to put "manufacturers [and others] into a frame of mind where advertising will be still further removed from the old conception of it as circus posting and patent medicine promotion," according to Stanley Resor of the J. Walter Thompson Company in 1916.[16]

Advertising advocates also eagerly touted the effects of creative innovations. A representative of Lord & Thomas, the leading Chicago agency, wrote in 1894 that because of improvements in writing styles "ads [in periodicals] are now read with as much zest as is the reading matter." The following year, a *Printers' Ink* editorial declared that an "advertisement can be made so seductive and readable that I must continue to read it whether I want the thing it advertises or don't want it. In fact, the live advertiser is now a sharp competitor of the reading-material purveyor in the race for entertainment."[17] The pleasures that the new advertisements afforded their audiences, of course, mattered mostly because of their presumed effects on the advertisers' businesses.

The *Inland Printer* praised the way the new advertising methods "coaxed along" success by amusing readers. "Those who are responsible for the great advances made in advertising methods" have created "a distinct art, and a pleasing and profitable one at that. They . . . let the sunshine into business methods, and by their efforts the soil of publicity has been fructified beyond belief."[18]

But this appropriation of credit for the progress in advertising styles did more than simply justify the advertising agents' work; it also excluded other professions and noncommissionable, nonperiodical media from the field's claims for its growing authority. For instance, in 1905, H. B. Humphrey, president of a Boston agency, wrote "The Reason Why the Agency Is" for *American Industries*, the National Association of Manufacturers' journal. In the middle of his extended argument on behalf of agents and their practices, Humphrey asserted that the "agency has developed most of the general advertising." He ignored nonperiodical advertisements and their contributions to the field's development, as well as agencies' decades of not writing copy, declaring that in "the writing, designing and general construction of advertisements the agency has perhaps been of greatest service." Without explicitly saying so, Humphrey implied that it was through agents' efforts that the field had moved beyond "old, stereotyped forms (which were nothing more than business cards and formal announcements)." By neglecting to mention formats that had for decades provided countless colorful "forms" of advertising, with often engaging pictorial narratives (such as show cards, posters, trade cards, catalogs, and premiums), Humphrey, along with most other colleagues who wrote on advertising's place in business development, could claim that there was only one line of advertising history; namely, the one evolving in the periodical media under his trade's care. It followed from this narrow perspective that their progressiveness alone had moved the field from the old "cards" to the "present-day" appeals that were "direct, forceful, [and] personal."[19] *Printers' Ink* eagerly pointed out that its own role in the "interchange of ideas" between specialists had accelerated the pace of change.[20]

Ultimately, the comparisons with the past became scornful. The worst criticism one could make of an advertisement in the new century was that it did not make "any improvement upon the advertising of our grandfathers."[21] This scorn applied when referring to media as well as to styles and content. For instance, the critics against landscape advertising assured the public that such offensive practices were "doomed to follow in the wake of handbills and town criers," cursed by obsolescence as well as by public disfavor. On occasion, professionalization activists also repudiated the "Barnum Principle" of advertising. They claimed that although it was picturesque and often influential, it was

*Consumption as Progress*

also "inartistic, reactionary, and unsuccessful in the long run, and immoral."[22] Nonetheless, even the most aggressive of the field's advocates cautioned against originality for its own sake. Fowler warned that "progression's marching road is never straight"; moreover, "many a conventional advertisement, moldy with age, has assisted in bringing more business than many an advertisement teeming with originality." So while "progressiveness demands the new," success would best be found in a balance of "originality and conventionality."[23]

## Advertising Practitioners Tout Their Own Successes

The praises for advertisements' progress easily spread to include the people preparing them. In a lively few pages on history in *Building Business: An Illustrated Manual for Aggressive Business Men*, Nathaniel C. Fowler Jr. declared that so recently had progress been made that the "youngest business man can remember when [newspaper and magazine advertisements] were clumsily put together, interesting to nobody, and seldom read, even by the advertisers themselves. During the last ten years, and particularly during the last five years, the quality of advertising has passed through a fiery revolution."[24] How did Fowler explain this "fiery revolution"? Not given to understatement, he described the "brilliant minds of the country [who] are now giving attention to the preparation of advertising." Because advertising had become both an art and a science, the "man with the power to write a telling advertisement may have as fine a quality of brain excellence as he who can build literature, and create romance. . . . He will by and by find his monument in the same field with the memorials of the men who discovered the composition of electricity, or were able to regulate the sunshine."[25] Attracting ambitious, talented people signaled both progress past and progress to come.

Ten years later, in 1903, Daniel M. Lord, Chicago's leading agent, explained to New York City's Sphinx Club upon his retirement, not only had "the conditions surrounding the business changed" in recent years, but the advertising profession's responses to those changes had finally earned it a prominent position. "I can remember," Lord declared, "when the advertising agent was looked upon as something to be endured because he could not be cured, and I tell you, gentlemen, no time in the history of business has the advertising man stood so high in the estimation of the business world as he stands today."[26] The potential for prosperous careers appeared in many arguments for the profession's legitimacy after 1900, such as in the first words of John Lee Mahin's 1914 treatise on advertising: "This is the age of advertising. Within the memory of older men the ambitious youth was urged to enter the church or the army, to study law or the sciences. Now business is generally recognized as a world-dominating science. It is becoming more and more intricate and complex, and constantly calls for a higher grade of intelligence."[27] As a leading Chicago advertising analyst, trade-journal publisher, and promoter of psychological research in advertising, Mahin represented those who believed that advertising was the profession of the future.

As the field grew, the size of agencies grew, as did individual practitioner's incomes. The latter provided a major promotion point for both recruiting and professional legitimation. Claude C. Hopkins, writing in 1896 to "The Young Man in Advertising," demonstrated the successes of advertising professionals by comparing their incomes with those of other people in business. "There is nothing higher in business for a young man to attain to" because revenues were growing rapidly. In recruiting young professionals, Hopkins likened his burgeoning profession to a new gold-mining camp, "an unknown and promising field in business" to which young men were flocking to seek their fortunes.[28] In the 1906 memoirs of his long and important career in advertising, George P. Rowell also celebrated a multitude of fortunes made through advertising as evidence of the field's growth and success. Rowell admired most his chief competitor, Francis Wayland Ayer, who had created "the greatest institution of the sort that has thus far come into being in any part of the world." Hardworking and of exemplary character, Ayer had become the richest man in the business while pioneering his profession. It must be said that Rowell acknowledged Ayer's success out of more than graciousness; he used it to prove the viability of their shared profession, just as he used descriptions of his own and others' successes. He felt confident, therefore, in assuring young advertising men, "You are in business to earn a living. The line of business in which you are engaged is respectable."[29]

According to Fowler in 1900, a residual factor that still inhibited the growth of advertising and the specialists' incomes resulted from manufacturers who still did not adequately "understand even the rudiments of advertising." They paid "merely nominal clerk's wages" to the people "in charge of the expenditure of a princely fortune in advertising," meanwhile paying "enormous salaries" to other managers, not appreciating that "men of no experience, who are unable to command decent salaries," could not do justice to this "vital department."[30] Fowler and other advocates of the field had more convincing to do.

A rather ironic note sounded now and again in the various ways that advertising agents sought to evince their growth and successes. Despite the advisers' best efforts to purge advertisements of other advertisers' edifices, they frequently displayed or described their own buildings in their self-promotions.

That this was commonplace in the years before the mid-1890s is to be expected, but interestingly, the practice continued into the 1910s. For instance, in the same annual volumes that, from the late 1890s through at least 1909, J. Walter Thompson published for clients, showing collections of "first-class advertising" containing no edifices, the agency featured its own buildings. "A fine view" of the main office appeared in the frontispiece of most issues, along with an introductory article on "The Thompson Offices" that described and showed views of and from their other buildings. In 1909, the agency's *Blue Book* featured its six buildings around the country on the frontispiece.[31] Similarly, in 1905 both the J. Walter Thompson Company and Charles Austin Bates published booklets focusing attention on their places of business, *Where Good Advertising Is the Constant Product* (Thompson's) and *Good Advertising and Where It Is Made*, (Bates's).[32] Despite the professional copywriters' lack of sympathy for manufacturers who portrayed their facilities to boast of their successes and to demonstrate their capacity, they used those same arguments to show their own facilities. *Where Good Advertising Is the Constant Product* began: "An inside view of any great industry is always interesting." Four years later, the agency pointed out "the advantages of size"; clients could benefit by "a business dynamo" that was "ready for service of any magnitude." Carrying the metaphor forward, the Thompson agency referred to itself as "a producer of advertising electricity" that operated with efficiency and personal attention to clients because of "subdivision of labor."[33] Calkins, who admired Cyrus Curtis so much that he dedicated his 1915 volume to him, reprinted an ad that pictured the publisher's building with the headline "Visible Evidence of the Power of Advertising." Calkins described this as a "strong, dignified advertisement."[34] In fairness, advertising agents could not easily illustrate their services. Also, such selling points may well have interested clients and potential clients as businesspeople—who were assumed to operate more rationally than consumers—to warrant copywriters' violating their own rules; the factory has continued to flourish in trade-to-trade advertising. But in their attempts to eliminate industrial imagery from consumer advertisements, the pontificating copywriters seem not to have considered the possibility that such selling points about manufacturers' factories might also have interested consumers.

### Promoting Specialized Services

Specialized experience, skills, and various claims to system provided both the means to success for advertising professionals and their most basic source of legitimation. Early advertising practitioners had always argued for specialization's merits as their own best claim on advertisers' patronage. As noted earlier, George P. Rowell wrote in his memoirs, "These are the days of specialization even more than in the past. Advertisers are not looking for people who can do everything, they are more interested in those who can do some one thing well that nobody else can do at all." Similarly, an 1893 editorial in *Profitable Advertising* typically emphasized the importance and advantages of replacing nonspecializing "egoists" and their "superficial Knowledge" with "experts" in all phases of business.[35]

Medicine and law were the professions most frequently cited as standards for advertising professionalization. Nathaniel Fowler, for instance, claimed that his colleagues should be ranked with lawyers, not businesspeople. Their "art is of the essence of professional business rather than of business profession." It was "the expert's business to do that for business which business proper cannot do for itself." Charles Austin Bates identified himself as "a specialist in advertising" and defined the specialist as one "who devotes all of his brains and energy and time and energy to the study of one thing." Hence, a "specialist in advertising is a man who practices advertising as a doctor practices medicine, or a lawyer practices law." As J. Walter Thompson wrote "To Advertisers and Business Men," the "merchant who is his own lawyer or his own doctor does not fare much better than the merchant who does his own advertising."[36] As this professionalization discourse gained strength, some advertising practitioners of the 1890s and early 1900s referred to themselves as doctors of business, attorneys-at-advertising, or even publicity physicians.

Because placing advertisements in newspapers and magazines was the advertising professionals' earliest specialized service, it provided their first claim to professional stature. In 1874, Rowell wrote that only the best, most professional agency, which just happened to be his, could serve clients optimally. He had the most complete information about publishers and could get clients the lowest possible rates from publishers because of his agency's experience and high volume of business.[37]

Advantages accrued to both publisher and advertiser from competent advertising agents' knowledge and experience in placing advertisements. As full-time professionals, they saved advertisers time, avoided inconvenience and expense, and at the same time they assured publishers of more revenue with fewer risks. All parties could enhance their profits through the good offices of the agent. As early as 1876, N. W. Ayer & Son expressed concern for the entire practice of advertising because too many advertisers wasted their expenditures being unaware of newspapers' rates and circulations. "Every dollar squandered in this way is a direct injury to the advertising business." Only a genuine agent's experience and honesty could correct this problem, and many of the advertisements for specific agencies reiterated this theme.[38] In his history of the N. W. Ayer & Son agency, Ralph Hower demonstrates that professionals could in fact save even their most experienced clients substantial amounts in expenditure by both their expertise and their publishers' discounts for volume buying.[39] As Fowler summarized the argument, "Advertising agents make mistakes, and lose money for their customers, but they lose a great deal less money than will the customers themselves, if they attempt to handle that which they have no business to handle, and for which the advertising agent was specially created." If this were not true, the "larger part of all national advertising would not be in the hands of respectable and responsible advertising agents."[40]

Copywriting and planning joined the placing of advertisements in the advertising practitioners' claims to professional justification during the 1890s. The same pressures that induced ambitious practitioners to expand their services then also compelled them to promote their services to advertisers, in part to compete with each other and other service providers such as publishers and in part to legitimate their occupation. Perhaps because of the novelty of these creative functions, but also because their effectiveness was hard to demonstrate, specialists took to proselytizing their benefits to advertisers with even greater fervor than they had their placement skills. Using advertisements for their individual agencies' services, plus articles and books written for the trade and general presses, they informed the world just how difficult good copywriting was. Obtaining desirable results, therefore, required professional services. As George Rowell wrote in his memoirs, "There is an unsuspected difficulty in preparing advertising matter that will not seem tame and valueless beside the more glowing announcements."[41]

The year 1891 was a watershed in the matter of traditional versus professional copywriting. Reflecting the prevailing ambivalence, fully half of the hints in "Hints on Preparing Advertisements," a lead article by John S. Grey, suggested hiring a professional copywriter. Grey began, "Half a dozen years ago, if a man announced himself as an advertisement writer, he would have been regarded with contempt"; "we find things greatly changed, though, in '91." By then, wrote Grey, "people . . . [recognized] that men on whose work depends the successful or unsuccessful expenditure of hundreds of thousands of dollars per year are at least of as much importance in the world as self-satisfied scribblers on the newspapers." All this notwithstanding, Grey's concluding sentence reminded readers that "a regular weekly perusal of *Printers' Ink*" should satisfy the needs for advice of the "average country merchant."

George Rowell's ironic position as both an advertising agent and the publisher of *Printers' Ink* embodied this transitional ambivalence. In 1891, when he hired a full-time copywriter and an illustrator for his agency, he began to advertise its preparation services for those advertisers who wanted "good advertisements." A few months after Grey's article, Rowell announced his expanded services. Instead of competing on rates, "we make it our first business to see that [the advertiser] has a good advertisement; next that it shall go into the papers that are best for his purpose, and have a position where it is likely to be seen . . . and we charge the advertiser for the work that we do."[42] The advertising men's basis for professional legitimacy had clearly expanded since Rowell's early days, and he now offered advertisers two paths: they could seek assistance through *Printers' Ink* or through his agency. Artemas Ward, himself a prominent copywriter, wrote a regular column of copywriting advice for *Printers' Ink*. In 1891 he warned advertisers that it was "hard to be original" and cited Rowell's recent advertisement for *Printers' Ink* that offered subscribers the same quality of expertise for $2 a year for which John Wanamaker paid John Powers $10,000. Advertisers might therefore avail themselves of the advice in *Printers' Ink* and save themselves the costs of hiring talent and expertise.[43] In 1891, there was no single, clear path to take for self-promotion, for either advertisers or agents.

By 1893, in contrast, advertising professionals regularly advised that all but the smallest firms "always employ an advertising expert to write and an agent to place" advertisements, as William H. Maher explained. As businesses got larger, their owners could spend less time in advertising and were not likely to develop the "popular way of writing" as successfully as professionals. Others reinforced the notion that keeping up with the times and the trends was "a difficult progression, a restless seeking after new ideas, a constant activity in original thoughts and methods." Successful plans and purposeful advertisements required ambition and dedication.[44] As the 1890s advanced, calls increased for enhanced originality and individuality. As the number of advertisements grew, along with the efforts put into the messages, creativity became ever more important to attract attention, to distinguish between messages, and to make effective impressions through the use of human interest, sympathetic copy, and psychology. All of this called for professional skills and diligence.[45] H. B. Humphrey of Boston titled a 1900 advertisement "Unbelievers" to refute those businesspeople who "condemn advertising, saying that they have 'tested' it and failed to get results"; they had merely "made an experiment, having acted independently instead of employing the services of those experienced and skilled in the work." He advised advertisers to "repeat the successes, not the failures" and to use competent, successful professionals.[46]

*Profitable Advertising* constantly admonished advertisers to "Avoid Egotism. Consult the Expert." Even though advertising was still in an "experimental" stage, the "scientific advertising agent" had begun to make the effects of his work more predictable and therefore safer and more profitable for advertisers.

No longer could business owners expect to advertise their own products. "The careers of such successful men as Barnum, Hood, Ayer, and a number of other large advertisers who began in a small way, have entered too largely into the beginners' dreams of the future." These were men of "genius," whereas the "average experimental advertiser is not."[47] Nonetheless, Herbert Casson, an efficiency expert, explained in 1911 that advertising was still "so young and immature an art that many men believe they can write their own advertisements. So they can. So could men make their own boots . . . before factories . . . were invented." Since then, however, Casson wrote, "professional ways of doing these things . . . have proved to be so much better that the every-man-for-himself method has been abandoned." Only the professional copywriter could serve the interests of the advertiser and produce the most efficient and effective advertisements.[48]

Charles Austin Bates expressed his excitement at finding greater possibilities for worthwhile copywriting the more he did of it. At the same time, he declared his reluctance to work for clients who thought of advertising as "an exasperating but necessary evil"; his work succeeded where others' had not, and he expected clients to appreciate that "fact." He also pointed out that people turn to lawyers or doctors because of their preparation and knowledge. He had been a "student of advertising for ten years. . . . All of my business life has been spent in the way best adapted to fit me for my present business." With no pretense at modesty, Bates explained at length how his professionalism could save his clients' time and money. As discussed in chapter 7, he projected his "egotism pure and simple" as the best strategy for building clients' confidence in his services.[49]

As the importance of creative work grew through the 1890s, advertising practitioners and their advocates began to minimize the importance of placing advertisements in justifying their compensation and professional status. A typical article of the late 1890s asserted that the advertising business existed "because men want help in their advertising" less for the "clerical service" of buying space and more for the "vital thing" of copy. The "agent of the future will sell brains, not merchandise. . . . He will be a counselor, an advertising adviser, just as other men are now medical advisers and legal advisers."[50] Accordingly, Bates began a column in 1900 by indicating that the "mere placing of advertisements in a given list of papers is out of my line," for the "work of placing and checking advertisements is a clerical operation, requiring no particular ability." He did, however, also claim to obtain space at rates as low as anyone could, but at the same time charged more than mere space sellers because he gave more and better services: "The plans, and the copy, and the publications chosen are infinitely more important than the cost of the space." He compared buying his services with buying those of an architect, lawyer, "or any other professional man."[51]

The egotistical tone of the advertising professionals drew criticism, especially since these newly self-proclaimed specialists critiqued the egotism of advertisers so vigorously; they responded with even more self-promotion. An article in *Printers' Ink* defended against the "fad to sneer at the advertisement writers individually and as a class" with the assessment that most of the critics came "from insignificant sources." More important, however, the effectiveness of the professionals' work was demonstrated by the "fact that almost all successful advertisers employ advertisement writers, either in their own establishments, or occasionally, as they may need outside assistance." This proved "rather conclusively" that "the profession is not a useless one." The charge of egotism, moreover, could be applied to all advertisements by their nature. Why should people be in business if they did not believe in the superiority of their goods or services? "If it were not for egotism in the world, there would be no progress in any line."[52]

This proselytizing for specialized professional status based on the preparation of advertisements continued well into the twentieth century. After 1900, specific advice on copywriting in the trade journals was increasingly directed to practitioners, rather than advertisers, whereas advice to advertisers instead told them how to work with specialists and how to judge the advertisements prepared for them. Early in the century, Seth Brown wrote that buying advertising "includes buying space and brains." It required as much care and expertise as legal work and therefore as much competent professionalism. Yet business persons who would hire the most high-priced lawyer they could afford without questioning the rates still considered it astute business practice to bargain with and challenge the advertising professional. But Brown warned: "Buy space by the inch, where you can buy it cheapest. Advertising can't be bought by the pound. You can't buy brains as you do hay."[53]

### Searching for Standards through Science, Education, and Organization

System, efficiency, and science entered the practitioners' discourse early on to assure advertisers and the public that advertising costs and commissions did not waste advertisers' and consumers' resources. Many individuals, as well as journals and trade associations, consistently pledged their intentions to avoid inefficiencies due to poor judgment, lack of information, or conflicts of interest. As early as 1849, Volney B. Palmer addressed these concerns, promoting his method of "Systematic Advertising" for the achievement of the most effective trade on behalf of advertisers.[54] Through that century, one sort of system or another surfaced constantly in the literature and practice of space-brokering agents. As specialists began to take on creative services, they continued to search for and promote their own feedback devices.

By the turn of the century, *science* had become, even more than now, a word with which to conjure respectability and authority. Advertising's advocates used and debated the concept of science loosely, often using the term interchangeably with *system* or *technique* when referring to the search for guidelines by which to raise their effectiveness and efficiency. Some sought to exploit the positive connotations of science among progressive people. For others, *science* represented a distraction or even a danger that diminished the value of their intuition and experience.[55] For the most part, in the context of rapid and profound changes in business as well as in social and cultural settings, "laws" that might help to govern behavior as well as provide understandings attracted mainstream thinkers in all fields. In 1904, N. W. Ayer & Son expressed the sense in which most practitioners conceived of advertising as a science—a sense that offered them a guide to pragmatic behavior, a discourse of self-promotion, and a source of professional prestige. "Advertising today is a science requiring as deep thought, as great knowledge, as wide experience, as painstaking and conscientious work as any other science or business known to mankind. Its success depends, not upon thoughtless surface work, but upon a careful study of prevailing conditions and of a knowledge of the business as well as of human nature."[56] This usage simply borrowed the term to represent the diligence and learning from experience required for competent advertising.

In order to participate fully in progress, advertising practitioners and other progressive businesspeople believed that they had to take on modern business practices and attitudes. In the early 1890s, it was quite possible for a respected leader in the field like Fowler to call upon the powers of science without initiating a debate on the relative merits of science and intuition, or art. In fact, he called both sides of the coin in fast succession, as others often did, praising advertising's becoming a science at the same time as it reached "the platform of art."[57] After the turn of the century, however, a debate developed with considerable intensity because the question—advertising as art or as science—took on policy implications regarding educational and organizational goals for the profession. Many of the practitioners who had begun work before 1890 resisted innovations in education and organization along the lines taken by law and medicine; they held that such a direction entailed positioning their trade as a science to be studied in the abstract, rather than as a business art or skill best learned by experience in the field. Other leading specialists who addressed the matter head on, such as Earnest Elmo Calkins, Claude C. Hopkins, and

Truman A. DeWeese, argued on the one hand for a variety of balances between intuition and personal experience and, on the other, for the "rational" collection and evaluation of information and experimentation.

Quite a number of activists strongly advocated allying advertising practice with a formal sense of science. Psychologist Henry Foster Adams believed "it is possible to measure the development of any industry by the number of scientific laws which are applied by it." As always in such arguments, the "real gain" came from "a gain in efficiency" because applying laws to business "eliminates waste of material and of time."[58] George French, a prolific advocate of science as a key to advertising's progress, declared in 1909 that advertising specialists "must be able to justify the faith that is in them by other evidence than that of their works." Instead, "they must know how to apply advertising so that they may not waste seed and effort trying to get results from stony and thorny ground." This could occur "only through seeking out the scientific bases of advertising, and by a thorough study of them."[59] French argued frequently that "no branch of modern business practise can gain more actual benefit from the teachings and methods of pure science than can advertising." He anticipated that "when the day comes that sees advertisers [i.e., agents] admit that their business is a science, and sees them turn to science for guidance, the business of advertising will advance in efficiency to a point it now touches only in isolated cases." Although French was not satisfied with any psychological research yet conducted, he proposed applying scientific methods and knowledge to advertising "not only [as] the most fertile source of profit, but the most direct and certain fount of power" to attract attention and persuade audiences on behalf of advertisers. He pointed out that major critics of scientific advertising actually advocated many of the same goals of systemizing the field, but refused to call that science.[60]

In 1904, an academician wrote a series of articles that typified the enthusiasts' sweeping proposals for application of the various sciences and their concepts to advertising. "A science of advertisement will exist," Conway MacMillan believed, "when there is an orderly and accessible body of information setting forth 1. The structure, 2. The function, 3. The adaptation, 4. The geographical distribution, 5. The classification, and 6. The economic uses of advertisement." MacMillan laid out the subdivisions of this science, borrowing freely from both the physical and social sciences: anatomy addressed the advertisement's structure, physiology the function, ecology the adaptation of advertisement to the environment, and so on. This new science would employ the scientific method, establishing standardized units of measurement and "basal components" that consisted of "commodities, services and personalities." He boldly predicted that the literature of this new science would soon equal that of medicine, because "just as a world of living organisms has sprung from the womb of Nature so is a world of advertisement developing through human genius."[61]

Consistently, the central issue was raising productivity and profits for advertisers and specialists alike through more efficient and effective advertising. All points of the debate focused on this goal. Consequently, while the word *science* filtered into the trade literature as a source of innovation and validity with varying degrees of appropriateness and success, it was Scientific Management, or whatever various people thought that was, that had the greatest impact on the reality of advertising practices. A near obsession for efficiency affected U.S. businesses near the turn of the century (as it has since) and it spread into much of the popular culture in the first two decades of the twentieth century. Many leaders of the advertising field studied diligently to systematize and standardize their practices and to enhance both their effectiveness and their legitimacy thereby. Francis Wayland Ayer had already brought in an "efficiency engineer" in 1899 to analyze his agency and recommend ways to improve its productivity.[62]

Accordingly, even the astounding successes of the field since the mid-1890s were not enough if they inadequately served the advertising clients' needs for high productivity. Calkins in fact blamed some of advertising's problems in the new century on its having developed "too fast." "This headlong rush," he wrote, "has produced success rather than efficiency." The manufacturer was beginning to remedy the situation, Calkins reported, by insisting that advertising "be made more exact."[63] In like vein, Herbert Casson, an efficiency expert who worked as an advertising consultant, applied in depth the insights of Scientific Management to advertising. In 1911, he published what he believed to be "the first attempt . . . to apply the principles of Scientific Management to the problems of Sales and Advertising." The large amounts of money spent on advertising pointed to the "tremendous importance of efficiency" in advertising to avoid wasting those expenditures. Advertising specialists who learned the principles of system, strategy, and efficiency could use them to follow the inventors of new technologies in creating "better ways of doing the same old things."[64] Because advertisers valued effectiveness and efficiency, advertising specialists promised them.

It is not at all certain how deeply or widely these precepts about advertising practices actually changed agency operations directly. Certainly, ideas filtered down through leaders and spokespersons, but applications were less easy to devise and carry out. Lord & Thomas and John Lee Mahin, both major agencies in Chicago, applied what they could, and others, too, struggled with the transition. Stanley Resor, who strongly advocated modernization in the name of science and efficiency, in 1916 took over the J. Walter Thompson Company when conflicts between his generation and Thompson made retirement attractive to the founder and his remaining cohort. Resor defined science in the sense of system as "organized common sense." Immediately upon taking control of the agency, he reorganized it according to a division of labor deriving from Scientific Management principles: the goal was to have every employee able "to carry on his part of the work to the very fullest degree of perfection."[65] Resor often referred to the agency as a factory operating with people as the machinery. Shortly after he took over the declining agency, he announced to personnel that "the organization, as an organization, has been at fault up to date in not having clearly defined just exactly what the machinery of the organization is." To achieve the efficiency of a manufacturing plant, he intended to systematize "our machinery and our factory processes." The next year, he generalized his metaphor, applying it to advertising and selling as a whole. "More and more is the machinery of distribution acting *as* a machine. It is to the interest of the maker of every good commodity that this be the case."[66] For Resor and many others with the new views, progress required acting according to progressive principles.

Still, the traditionalists and progressives debated. Experience in the field had provided the best—the only—means in the nineteenth century for training and selecting advertising specialists. Even commercial artists had no institutional training opportunities per se until the turn of the century. By that time, however, debates raged in the trade press and at trade meetings about how best to provide recruits who could carry the business forward. These debates were intimately linked with the concurrent debates over whether advertising practices could be systematized sufficiently to approach scientific status, because as Lasker, Kennedy, Calkins, and other practitioners recognized about this time, education required system, and a criterion for a true system was its teachability. Moreover, just as specialized skills in law and medicine required a qualifying formal education, those who most sought to develop the advertising field toward those pinnacles of professionalism sought also to found formalized educational programs through a variety of institutions, including universities and business schools.[67]

Traditionalists, by contrast, believed that all formal education, beyond the basics of literacy and numeracy, was irrelevant, even harmful, in the "real" and very particularistic world of business. Neither they, nor even those reformers promoting formalized education, as it turned out, hired graduates solely on the basis of their scholarship. Indeed part of the debates focused on just what a business education, and specifically an advertising education, entailed. Colleges, universities, and business schools started up courses beginning in the first decade of the century, expanding these in the coming years. That some of the courses grew out of journalism programs and others out of business programs reflected profoundly different views of what practicing advertising was all about, not to mention what it meant to educate someone for it; this dichotomy still holds at the end of the century. Some programs, especially within the leagues of correspondence schools and night schools, took advantage of the ambitions of students more hopeful than realistic about the likelihood of their finding careers with their unstandardized learning from books. The growing numbers of courses and students evinced the field's increasing favor among the ambitious, but they also fueled the arguments of the traditionalists when graduates were unemployable. Although some cheered the schools' "mission of sending into this mass of conservatism a leaven of young and energetic brain matter that will stir it all into activity," others warned that this would cost the field its common sense.[68]

Central to the debates about science and education were questions of standards and who should set them. Many explained the problem after 1900 as a lack of standards in the field. *Profitable Advertising* and most advocates, but not all, argued that professional organizations offered the best solution for this problem, just as they had for law and medicine.[69] Leaders of the early generations of practitioners, like F. Wayland Ayer, believed that reforms should, and could, be enacted only by individuals, on moral and practical grounds. Despite others' great efforts to organize advertising specialists, no permanent or reasonably effective association could address the many questions of standards and prestige until the formation, in 1917, and subsequent solidification of the American Association of Advertising Agencies. However, neither that organization nor any other could resolve the divisive issues related to standards in education.

A series of questions held constant through the debates on the merits and directions of professionalization. These included how best to raise specialists' credibility to their clients, how to raise their public esteem, and how to raise their self-esteem. These concerns led quite logically to questions about how best to raise standards and performance, in terms of both ethics and results. These latter issues tied into education and association because they entailed recruiting, training, and screening new practitioners. Because there were more answers to these questions than leaders and organizers could reconcile, no resolutions were institutionalized during this transition period, between 1890 and 1917. In the meantime, specialized service stood out as the dominant and recurring theme in advertising agents' self-advocacy. It provided a strong focal point of agreement around which practitioners could finally organize, but only after it had begun to acquire legitimacy in the larger business and public cultures. As H. B. Humphrey explained to manufacturers, "the well-equipped agency is an assembly of specialists," and since "study and practice along a special line bring better results than diversified effort; so the need for the agency will always exist."[70]

### Success by Serving the Successes of Others

Volney B. Palmer set the basis on which advertising practitioners defended and justified their work. This owed less to Palmer's prescience than to his recognition that his success completely depended on serving others' needs. In 1850, Palmer stated that his "extensive connections in business, his experience and practical knowledge, his long-established agency for the best newspapers in every part of the United States, and his systematic manner of advertising to the greatest possible benefit of the advertisers, whether on a large or small scale, have rendered his offices . . . highly beneficial to the public and not unprofitable to himself."[71] The material evidence that he had served well—namely, his multiple offices and his own profit—fit the era's criteria. Just as nineteenth-century industrialists used the evidences of their successes as evidence for the quality of their products, advertising practitioners routinely used their own successes as agents for others to demonstrate the value of their services.

Initially, advertising agents had balanced dual loyalties as intermediaries between publishers and advertisers. In serving two types of businesses throughout their first half century, advertising specialists often argued for the importance and merits of their services to both. Yet conflicts of interest accompanied this dual agency. If agents maximized revenues to publishers and thereby their own revenues through commissions, they did so at the expense of the advertisers. On the other hand, if advertisers were dissatisfied with their costs relative to their gains, both agents and publishers lost revenues in the long run. Francis Wayland Ayer and George P. Rowell were the first to publish the professional and personal risks of mixed loyalties to publishers and advertisers. Their conversions led the field and, by the 1890s, most advertising specialists gave advertisers their primary loyalties, the rest gradually identifying themselves as newspaper or magazine agents. Even so, in whichever of the two directions advertising practitioners faced, service to each formed the bases for justifying their occupation.

### Serving Publishers' Successes

The close, if not always congenial, relationships between advertising agents and the commissionable media—newspapers, journals, and magazines—were

*Consumption as Progress*

often discussed in the advertising trade press. Many of the first generations of agents felt a strong affinity for the press, as did George P. Rowell, who often expressed a more comfortable bond with publishers than with advertisers, although he knew that he must primarily serve the latter. Advertising agents and their trade publications often praised the roles of the press in raising the character of the nation, matching or bettering the fervor of others who declared, as did Carroll Wright, that the "development of the printing and auxiliary industries is a true index to the progress of civilization and the advance in all arts and manufacturers."[72] Rowell, like many other advertising agents, gave the periodical press a good deal of credit for that broad progress. Without the press "we should immediately fall back to a level with those who lived in the ages of ignorance and despotism. 'Tis only through this agency that we are better than they and enjoy liberties and privileges of which they never dreamed." Moreover, "business would come to a stand-still, markets be unsteady; stocks unobtainable at any fixed value, and everything else uncertain and fluctuating." Therefore, "no man, be he ever so shrewd and intelligent, can hope to succeed in any avocation without thoroughly and energetically advertising his business through the newspaper." One writer in *Printers' Ink* defended the general press from criticism during the tumultuous mid-1890s by rejecting the notion that it needed defense. "It has thoroughly vindicated itself as a force that is at once both a security and an inspiration for all the interests of material prosperity and moral welfare and progress."[73]

In part, these tributes to the press in the advertising literature may have flowed from a deliberate concern to appease publishers, on whose favor and commissions the agencies depended. On the other hand, the motivation could have derived from the advertising practitioners' desire to take some measure of vicarious credit for the contributions to progress with which they accredited the press. To warrant this connection, the practitioners often articulated their beliefs that they shared important interests with publishers. Through their frequent contentions that publishers should grant bona fide agents exclusive rights to commissions, the advertising professionals reminded publishers of the mutuality of their interests. "The advertiser who starts out under the guidance of a competent agency is likely to spend his money more judiciously, and as a consequence, to invest more money in the newspapers eventually than he who trusts to his untrained judgment."[74] The advertising agent's professional standards also inclined him to expect publishers' appreciativeness for his services. Rowell wrote that the unreasonable occurrences sometimes complained of by publishers were never "invented" by the advertising agent, who "likes to have the conditions simple, so that the work will go smoothly, and the bill may be paid in full."[75]

Conversely, just as Rowell once gave credit to revenues from patent medicines for saving the life of the New York *Herald* in its early days, advertising agents frequently credited advertising for publishers' profits. Printing a speech given to the Sphinx Club of New York, *Printers' Ink* declared that advertising "is the breath of life to the trade journal" because its high publication costs required the income additional to subscriptions. The *Inland Printer* often reminded its readers, once in a rhyme that belied the seriousness of the assertion, that "Success depends alone upon the advertising man"—by whom they meant the papers' employee who compiled and solicited advertising. "He works more men and hours than the other all combined; / To him belongs the victor's crown—this brave catch-as-catch-can, / Keen, money-getting, business-booming advertising man." Editors and all others "were mere assistants."[76] Although this verse put things both lightly and extremely, the point was clear. J. Walter Thompson, the agent who had once controlled most national magazine advertising, wrote in 1908 that the American magazine was "a national institution." Its "progressive" and "magnificent monument to American enterprise, American genius, and American skill," however, "would be impossible without the advertising section."[77] In the thick of World War I, *Printers' Ink* assured its readers that Congress "could hardly declare general advertising non-essential without making the same interdiction of local and retail publicity," because eliminating all these would destroy the press and "hurl the country back at one swoop into the dark ages," making both democracy and the war effort impossible.[78]

Accordingly, when advertising practitioners formed associations, with or without publishers, these invariably lobbied publishers to recognize their common goals of maximizing advertising revenues by maximizing advertisers' long-term confidence. An organizer of the American Advertising Agents' Association in 1900 explained that the group did not "expect to revolutionize the advertising agency business, but merely desired by means of this organization to help each other and the publishers with whom we are so closely allied."[79] Cooperation between agencies and publishers appeared to many practitioners essential to improving the business overall. With or without that cooperation, advertising agents wanted recognition for their contributions to the publishers' profits and accomplishments.

### Serving Advertisers' Successes

Advertising agents had never doubted the efficacy of advertisements as selling devices. Their confidence that good commercial messages, placed well and placed frequently, could elicit the desired responses at reasonable cost formed the core of their self-advocacy as individuals and as a trade. Typically, practitioners solicited accounts by promoting both advertising's efficacy generally as well as their own services. Early on, George Rowell asserted that the "importance of advertising is undisputed and universally admitted. The extent to which it is carried proves beyond doubt its usefulness, and advantages. The man who advertises once is sure to do so again. . . . It opens the most direct road to success and offers equal inducements to all parties."[80] In his memoirs almost four decades later, Rowell celebrated a multitude of fortunes made through advertising, including patent-medicine sellers, publishers, merchants, and manufacturers, as he had in the intervening decades.

Assuming advertisements' "business-building" powers, practitioners claimed to contribute to the success of any business that used their services. They credited advertising even for successes not mediated by an agent. The first issue of *Printers' Ink* in 1888 expressed this confidence on a grand scale. One article credited the first English advertisement for a commercial product with initiating the popularity of tea in England. A second article compared the rebuilding of London and Chicago after their great fires: because the London fire occurred in 1666, the city's businessmen could not benefit from the "prodigious" advertising opportunities available to their counterparts in Chicago in 1871; hence, London rebuilt more slowly—or so the story went.[81] "A good advertisement is the doctor of business. When a business is good you will need it to keep healthy, and when it is poor, you must have it to invigorate it," explained Rowell in 1891.[82] Anecdotes and analyses in the trade literature constantly expressed pride, along with an element of pragmatic self-promotion, in the many fortunes they could in any measure attribute to their efforts. S. M. Pettengill, for instance, demonstrated Volney B. Palmer's contributions to the business world by citing some of the many merchants who had increased their profits because his mentor had convinced them to advertise. Rowell, in turn, praised Pettengill for having placed advertisements for even more successful advertisers, including patent-medicine mogul Dr. J. H. Schenck and Robert Bonner, publisher of the New York *Ledger*.[83] Many patent-medicine successes were so spectacular that the general press celebrated them until Progressive reformers discredited such products and practices. The *New York Times* highlighted some of these under the headline "In Printer's Ink the Secret: Vast Fortunes made by the Patent-Medicine Kings"; as discussed earlier, the article concluded that "a pot of printer's ink is better than the greatest gold mine."[84]

Charles Austin Bates, like his peers before 1900, rated advertisements and the entire occupation primarily by success in selling and making profits. "Americans are the best and most successful advertisers in the world. They spend more money for advertising than any other nation, and they make more money out of it."[85] For Bates, this burgeoning enterprise required no other justification. An 1896 advertisement for Rowell's agency reinforced this promise of advertising's immediate benefits by showing a goddess of justice weighing the small cost of an advertisement against bags of money, spilling over in their abundance, on "the results" side of a scale. The first line of type read: "Successful advertising means getting back more money that is paid out."[86] Every practitioner held out this same lure in some form, as when the pioneer copywriter John E. Powers reminded his fellows that clients "are in business for a profit; we mustn't lose sight of that."[87]

The bicycle industry afforded analysts an attractive illustration of advertising's powerful impact in helping to build a new and quite respectable industry. Advertising had served bicycle manufacturers first in pioneering the safety bicycle—"educating the public to the beauties and pleasures of cycling"— and then in competition between makers. Colonel Albert A. Pope introduced the safety bicycle with extensive advertising, generating a fad in the 1890s and making his fortune. In this he was assisted by "the best artists, the best writers," including Nathaniel Fowler, and the most expensive advertising media in and outside of periodicals. Pope and others credited his advertising with "the great popularity bicycling has to-day—in the tremendous growth the bicycling business has witnessed." By 1897, his firm produced six hundred bicycles daily and spent more than $500,000 annually to advertise them.[88]

The same iconography of success—the factories and machines—that induced manufacturers and advertising agents alike to portray their facilities in their advertisements inspired an 1892 editorial in *Profitable Advertising* the "Monuments of Success in Advertising that Stand in Every City." The journal proclaimed that these "great marts of retail trade, the vast structures, and mills, and factories" were "irrefutable demonstration of the money, the success, the prosperity that are open to those who advertise." On the other hand, "small buildings, small stores, offices up four flights-of-stairs, in a dingy room, in charge of a half-starved clerk; in rapidly diminishing business . . . can be found the irrefutable demonstration that there is no avenue to success in these days except that of advertising." Such successes resulted from the national distribution of products "which except for advertising, would never have attained more than a limited local sale."[89]

Often encouragements and cautions against failing to advertise, or advertising carelessly, unsystematically, or unprofessionally, marched side by side. Thus "men that know how to advertise never fail to receive abundant returns," whereas "80 per cent of the business firms in this country that fail are those that never advertise." Failures included "old-timers, slow-goers, men of the back-number genus," who rejected advertising as "wholly valueless to

·themselves" and who "rely on their past record, their long standing, and anti-quated signboards. But in this bustling, hustling, rustling age of sharp competition and quick bargains, it won't do to rely too much on prestige or pedigree."[90] If failing to keep pace by advertising doomed a business, it was also true that "wild and illegitimate methods which promise quick riches . . . ultimately lead to failure and oblivion." Steadily practicing sound advertising, in contrast, would bring the ambitious "safely and surely to Success."[91] In this light, advertising appeared a solid, essential business activity.

In all such claims for their importance to clients' successes, as in the praises for professional specialization cited earlier, advertising practitioners argued for their individual and collective worth. They rarely explored other factors, such as demographic changes, new communication technologies, competitors' failures, or whims, which might have explained advertisers' successes. If their clients succeeded, *they* had succeeded. If their clients' successes had merit, so did theirs. A refinement of this genre of claim increasingly supplemented it, focusing on service as an end it itself worthy of professional pursuit; profits alone satisfied less as justification, although they defined success. As Calkins asserted in 1915, by professionalizing, by "studying the underlying problems of advertising," the specialist had "qualified as a responsible adviser to his clients. The advertiser, feeling this new force in advertising, gets a new confidence, is more wary in the selection of his advertising agent, and at the same time more trusting when he has selected him." This new dynamic "must ultimately result in removing much of the uncertainty that exists both in the state of mind of the advertiser and in the actual results obtained."[92] The J. Walter Thompson agency promoted its agents' services after 1900 by saying that they would be "almost as much your representative as if he were actually in your employ. He will become for the time being an additional and valuable part of your business machinery, while remaining a part of ours and participating in its constant impetus." The Thompson Method brought "inevitable success."[93]

Touting advertising service as the key to professional legitimacy at the turn of the century fit into wider changes in business practices and mainstream attitudes. In the nineteenth century, the success and esteem of business owners and managers most often derived from their acumen in developing and using innovative technologies or financial tools to produce goods or to build communication and transportation networks; at least, the popular ethos ascribed to that generalization. To keep public favor, great successes also required philanthropy, or stewardship, as Carnegie called the wealthy classes' control over material assets. In the early decades of the twentieth century, however, service to the community joined the acceptable justifications for success. This change occurred in part because managers of productive wealth seldom owned it after

1900, because Progressive era reformers vigorously critiqued the notion of stewardship, and because managers became an important new class in need of legitimation. The Chicago businessmen who founded the Rotary Club in 1905 captured the mix of social and material ambitions in this new ethos by inventing a "service club" that also addressed businessmen's social and business needs. In the 1920s, they adopted the slogan "He Profits Most Who Serves Best."[94] The increasing complexities of doing business (just as of living in cities) also called for new and expanded services to facilitate operations. Working in this context, advertising practitioners had recognized all along that service was their only commodity, and therefore they prefigured the overall shift from production and stewardship to service as publicized justifications for business activities and success. They were, in function as well as title, agents, and after the general shift in attitudes, they could place some pride in serving. Accordingly, in 1913, the Associated Advertising Clubs of America made public service their declared goal as part of their quest for professional stature.[95] As one agent described his firm, "The difference is service—The Power Service for Advertisers is enthusiastic, personal service that vitalizes and animates every separate and distinct form of effort and welds them all into a perfect business-bringing chain."[96] In 1910, the *Inland Printer* reprinted an article from *Harper's Weekly* stating that the advertising solicitor "wants to succeed, by making others succeed."[97] More than that, this was the only way to succeed.

By the 1917 formation of the Association of American Advertising Agencies, service to clients had become the expressed focal point of professional purpose. Even so, and even among those pursuing professional cooperation, practitioners widely disagreed on what service should entail. But they generally did agree that setting standards for service was a high professional priority. In 1918, therefore, the association adopted a definition of service prepared at the J. Walter Thompson agency shortly after its reorganization under Stanley Resor. According to this statement, those "on whom we must depend for our business," both media and advertisers, "have a right to demand" such a standardized service.[98]

Advertising specialists initially defined their profession's progress and successes pragmatically, according to individual financial accomplishments, including their own. When the field's champions began to describe their contributions to the business community explicitly and deliberately as service to clients, they also began to develop another category of legitimation: they began to reinterpret the range of advertising's impact far beyond individual business successes. It would now encompass the nation's economy, national industry, and prosperity. This was progress writ large.

# 10

# The Appropriation of Progress
## Legitimating the Advertising Profession–II

*You of the advertising world are the pioneers in the development of business, you are in the vanguard of progress, discovering new fields of endeavor and wider possibilities of development. . . . Industry, commerce and business are the life of a nation and make the nation prosperous and powerful. You make commerce and business prosperous and powerful; and have become an integral and important part of our business world and, indeed, of our social economy. . . .*

*Service and sacrifice—these are the watchwords now.*

—Senator Hiram W. Johnson, speaking to
the Associated Advertising Clubs of the World, St. Louis, 1917

Thirty years before the entry of the United States into World War I, the advertising field had no major trade journal, no organization, and certainly no profile that could incline a senator and former governor of California to praise it publicly. Yet by 1917, Senator Johnson was not alone when he linked advertising not only with business prowess and progress, as of old, but also with *national* prowess and progress; he even linked the advertising practitioners' work to the "service and sacrifice" of the nation in wartime. Governor Frederick E. Gardner of Missouri, welcoming participants to the same 1917 convention of the Associated Advertising Clubs of the World, explained that they could do national service and ensure military victory if they kept business going in a "steady, unbroken" manner. "By so doing you will not only write advertisements—you will write history."[1]

During the thirty years after 1890, advertising practitioners, individually and in groups, responded to the many challenges discussed earlier in this study by changing profoundly how they conducted their business. Not all practitioners actually adjusted their practices, and not all who did change followed the direction the field took collectively, but the overall movement was resounding. Under these and other, nonbusiness, pressures, advertising agents and their advocates also altered how they thought about their trade. Their precarious, rapid, and uneven professionalism after 1890 motivated intensive self-assessment in search of self-esteem and public esteem. In this, advertising specialists joined the nation's bourgeoisie as they organized and professionalized, trying to make sense of their places in the rapidly changing cultural context.[2] In large measure, however, their pursuit of legitimacy was also quite specific and pragmatic, required by their dependence on other businesses for their livelihood; they had to convince both publishers and advertisers of the merits of their services. As discussed in chapters 8 and 9, all advertising specialists had to prove that they achieved more than "a foolish outgo" of someone else's "hard-earned money," as Gustavus F. Swift accused Claude Hopkins. As *Printers' Ink* explained in 1895, the advertising practitioner "has less chance to veil his egotism than has any other business man," having "nothing to advertise but himself and the superior brand of brains which he owns."[3] Also, compounding their other legitimating tasks, as nonproducers in a culture that still valued production as the foremost, if not only, means of gauging professional merit, they had to make a case for their very existence within the business world and within the wider culture. If clients and publishers made money from advertising, that could have sufficed to keep advertising agents in business, but that function alone would hardly have justified such glowing claims as Johnson and Gardner made to the Associated Advertising Clubs. F. Wayland Ayer's distress in 1874 when his father's old friend considered him "nothing but a drummer" showed that some trades servicing business carried little enough prestige.

Besides criticisms focused on advertising's costs and apparent unproductiveness, other public concerns about patent-medicine promotions and various dubious practices, such as scenery advertising, inspired both internal reforms, as discussed in chapter 7, and prolific self-promotion. Several Progressive Era public-policy debates also addressed advertising expenditures and impacts. The Trademark Act of 1905 and the Pure Food and Drug Act of 1906 occasioned such opportunities for self-justification, as did the Internal Revenue Act of 1917. The latter debate raised questions that included not only the business and social consequences of advertising but also its impacts on forests and air and water pollution because of the high volume of paper it consumed. The outcome—very likely influenced by lobbying as well as debates—was a major victory for advertisers and their agents: advertising was awarded the subsidized tax status of a fully deductible business expense.[4] The Truth-in-Advertising movement of the 1910s likewise directed its efforts at public opinion explicitly to forestall regulation.[5] As George French, a vocal participant in the movement, stated in 1915, advertising sought "to relieve itself of a certain odium that [had] accumulated against it as the conscious assistant to unworthy efforts to dupe or defraud the people."[6] During World War I, specialists volunteered on a massive scale for projects like the Committee on Public Information, the Red Cross, and army recruiting. These efforts came out of personal and collective ambitions to demonstrate the practice's potency in a patriotic and highly visible forum. "Advertising's hour of opportunity" had struck, according to activist William D'Arcy in 1918.[7] Leading proponents had by then joined the increasing numbers of businesspeople, including the founders and early clients of public relations, who recognized the importance of citizens and consumers as a public audience for their legitimating discourse.

## Advertising Keeps Pace with Progress

The traditional praise for advertising's roles in individual successes had not, by 1890, led anyone to generalize about its roles in business as a whole, much less in national progress. As late as 1893, but before the crash, even Nathaniel Fowler Jr. simply juxtaposed the concurrent growth in the size of advertising with the national economy: "Advertising has kept pace with the times; it has run ahead of the times; and it proposes to keep ahead of the times." Neither explicitly nor implicitly did he claim that the growth of his field influenced the economy. Other writers also commented on how advertising had been able to "keep pace with modern progress," but they did so without claiming any credit for that progress. Indeed, even after the turn of the century, *Judicious Advertising* joined many others still giving "thanks to progress [that] the world in general has come to regard the art of publicity in a vastly different light." Similarly, articles in the *New York Times* employed advertising volume as an indicator of national prosperity: "No other kind of property reflects the financial condition so quickly and so accurately."[8]

The trade press in the 1890s mixed countless accolades about advertising's growth with hundreds of testaments to its power to bring individual successes, but, with rare exceptions, did not generalize from these achievements to advertising's impact on the general conditions of business. Many topics offered opportunities to conceptualize a broader impact beyond individual businesses' successes, yet authors maintained the narrow interpretation of advertising's contribution to success and profits in countless other articles and essays in the trade press during the 1890s.[9] For example, in 1891 A. I. Teele began "The Mission of Advertising" by stating, "Advertising is becoming one of the great commercial factors of the business community of the world." An impressive array of financial statistics about advertising's expansion supported his assessment of its potential as "one of the most powerful allies that the business man can call to his aid." Like the authors cited in the preceding chapters, Teele intended to inspire individual decision makers with the potential benefits to them of well-run advertising programs, because "the bright, quick advertiser takes trade from his slower neighbors." Teele believed that the future promised "a better grade of advertising matter" from "the professional expert,"[10] but he saw no broader impact from that other than stiffer competition.

Similarly, in 1896 an exceptionally long article in *Printers' Ink* led off in a fashion that hinted at a broad justification of the advertising field in terms of national benefit: "Within the last quarter of a century a new phase of commerce has developed itself, a new power for business advancement has arisen, and new methods and ideas have come in vogue for the conduct of trade." The present must therefore "be hereafter chronicled as the advertising age. . . . From a simple side issue the obtaining of business publicity has become a most important factor in commercial success." Despite this opening, however, the perspective of the title, "Profitable Stories," prevailed, and the body of the article itemized the stories of twenty-two companies whose successes could be attributed to substantial advertising.[11] It never mentioned the national growth of industrialization as a whole or theorized any role for advertising beyond the progress based on individual successes.

Another golden opportunity to place advertising into the larger context of national progress through innovation and industry occurred in 1896 when *Printers' Ink* carried an article on "Advertising for Inventors." The advertising practices of a company that brokered patents filled more than two pages, but the style and content followed exactly the usual weekly article that discussed some company or another and its successes due to strong advertising. The special nature of the business or any special significance that might derive from advertising's assistance to inventors in the age of invention received no notice.[12]

Charles Austin Bates was not one to be lax in puffing his field, and his first use of the language of progress in print appeared in 1895. In the same article in which he described the spread of the "gospel of advertising," Bates claimed that "each year's progress [in advertising] has been more rapid than the preceding year." Advertising "is becoming more and more certain. Business men learn more about it every day. They have more confidence in it. . . . As advertisers become more enlightened, weak and dishonest agencies find it harder and harder to eke out an existence."[13] Bates thereby made another strike on behalf of professional pride and standards, this time borrowing from the discourse of progress, but not yet crediting advertising for progress outside of its immediate operations.

With the end of the century approaching, "The Future of the Advertising Agent" was an appropriate title for an 1898 lead article in *Printers' Ink*. This subject also presented a good opportunity for broad statements about the role of the advertising profession within the business community and the national economy. The bulk of the article, however, focused on controversies about newspaper rates and forms of compensation; the broadest generalization simply reaffirmed the typical pragmatic orientation: "What creates advertising is the desire of man for money. He thinks he can get it through advertising. This desire is stimulated by the success of those who do advertise."[14]

The effusion about individual successes and advertising's progress in the 1890s made even more remarkable the absence in the advertising press of any transcending commentary about the field's causal relationships to the grander trends of industrialization and material progress that the popular and trade presses featured. Inspiring phrases that might have introduced broad claims for advertising's impact on business and progress were confined to individual cases. When interviewed for *Printers' Ink*, Robert Bonner, publisher of the New York *Ledger* and a legendary advertiser, declared, "The life of business is advertising." His frame of reference, however, was the individual businesses whose examples he cited as evidence. The interviewer also endorsed the traditional measures of legitimacy by concluding, "As Mr. Bonner's wealth has been estimated at five millions, his views are something more than theories."[15]

Francis Wayland Ayer, a leader of the old guard, wrote in 1895 on the attainments of advertising. He showed weak advertisements from earlier times and pulled together impressive statistics on the growth of many aspects of the field over the century. He interpreted all this "history of advertising" as "a record of the adaptation of business methods to modern business conditions"; in other words, as a reaction to the marketplace. He concluded:

> Enterprise is ever seeking expression. Advertising has always been the expression of enterprise. The few meager, colorless announcements of 1795, written with a dull and heavy pen, fittingly expressed the enterprise of that day. At the close of a century of marvelous progress the enterprise of to-day finds expression in advertising of every conceivable form, in every available place, in the preparation and illustration of which have been combined the best obtainable skill of hand and brain.

Ayer's vision of the future saw advertising serving business and consumers by telling "the story of the better things which the opening century will unfold to

the better-seeking millions of America."[16] Even its role as an information conduit was culturally passive—Ayer took no credit on behalf of advertising for
"the better things" or the "better-seeking millions." Whether Ayer saw no
need or no grounds for it, he claimed no credit for advertising beyond the services into which it had grown. Growth was proof enough of his profession's
worth.

## Advertising Sets the Pace of Progress

Nonetheless, interspersed throughout the newsiness and tales of growth
and individual success, achieved or promised, a new argument for legitimation
slowly developed. Its early manifestations evinced an inchoate awareness that
advertising might have broader economic and cultural impacts than those usually propounded. Volney B. Palmer's 1849 vision of a future system of trade
"entirely different from that of our grandfathers" credited "Systematic Advertising" in part for that future.[17] This first agent expressed a rare sense of his
field's impact, as it turned out. Much later, during the transitional decade of
the 1890s, advocates began to explore the relationships between advertising
and success, success and progress, and advertising and progress in diverse ways,
almost as if there were a suspicion in the air that there was some grand connection that remained elusive. Unlike the ubiquitous statements about advertising's aiding a business's successes, the following exceptions to the common
pattern are unique expressions. An 1892 essay on "The Next Great Profession" presented advertising as a second-order cause of progress. The first cause,
"the most potent force in life," was ambition, "the vital principle of progress."
Advertising served progress as "the handmaid of ambition." Because the age
was "a commercial one," advertising functioned as "the voice of ambition calling in the wilderness of human industry. It is the interpreter who makes
known the wants of individual ambition to the world."[18] Despite this glorified
connection between advertising and progress, the idealized scheme did not yet
strike a responsive chord with others as the key to advertising's legitimacy. The
intervening factor of ambition, with all its controversial qualities, had still to
be expunged from the connection's public profile and replaced with service.

In the meantime, other writers explored the possibilities that advertising
had broader impacts than on individual businesses. In 1893, a Boston manufacturer contributing to Fowler's *Building Business* loosely hinted at a wider perspective in juxtaposing advertising and general progress. He expressed his
wonderment at the "long strides that have been taken in inventions, manufacturing, printing, electrotyping, and the wholesale and retail business of the

country. . . . It is true that we are living in a progressive age, and that nothing succeeds like success." Bailey concluded that "judicious advertising" offered the only means by which a successful business could be built, but he did not connect it causally with the larger progress. The next year, a eulogy for "The First Subscriber to *Printers' Ink*" pointed to a budding awareness of advertising's importance outside of business. It told of a man not involved in the trade in any way, but who subscribed solely to satisfy "his interest and curiosity" about "the rising power and importance of the art and practice of advertising."[19] Such Victorian clichés were common among the period's bourgeois classes and were the earliest views in the trade press that placed advertising in a broad, progressive perspective. Significantly, neither of the two statements originated within the trade, but trade advocates did recognize and publish both as evidence of the legitimacy of their field. Perhaps observers of this young profession were in a better position than participants to speculate on its place in the larger context of development in the business world.[20]

The devastation of the Crash of 1893 and its ensuing depression had a profound impact on the advertising practitioners' rhetoric. The trade press and the general press fluctuated between stories of distress and conjectures on relief from hard times. As might be expected, advertising's advocates encouraged businesses to work their individual ways out of depressed markets through aggressive advertising. Inspiring narratives typically demonstrated how "even in the face of financial depression and when personal solicitations had totally failed, bold newspaper advertising changed failure to success" for one firm or another. In 1896, George Rowell advertised his agency by showing two competitors reaching for advertising's hammer to strike the "iron of opportunity" while it was hot. "Business is going to boom. Everything points to plethoric prosperity. Money-making opportunities were never so good."[21] To no small degree, the severity of the depression itself compelled practitioners to develop more effective techniques and stronger arguments about advertising's potential for generating demand. The depression also contributed to industrial concentration, and advertising's supporters learned to promote their occupation as a means of maintaining and increasing consumption levels, rather than solely as a means of competition. More immediately, the depression created desperate conditions for advertising specialists, whose apprehensive, and often struggling clients and employers frequently cut advertising along with other "nonfixed" expenditures. The advertising press began immediately to push the case that advertising "creates trade"—a case that only a few, such as Fowler, had earlier claimed.[22]

Agents' own advertisements expressed their growing confidence about increasing trade for individual clients. The Boston advertising agency and publisher of *Profitable Advertising*, C. F. David, took out an advertisement a few months after the panic began, posing a question for business owners: "Can't afford to advertise because business is dull?" Using the image of a circle to convey the idea of circular thinking, the ad stated in the circle's top hemisphere, "It is dull because you don't advertise"; the bottom hemisphere held the converse,"You don't advertise because it is dull." Attempting to convince reluctant advertisers of the fallacy of such thinking, the message concluded, "We think this way: If your business is dull, *advertise* that you may *do well*. If you are doing well, *advertise*, that you may *do better*. *Let us show you how to do it*."[23] "The Outlook for 1894," an editorial at the end of 1893, encouraged businesses to use advertising with an attractive if not very sound argument: "There is as much or more money in the country than there was before the so-called period of depression. The only trouble is that it does not circulate freely. *Shrewd advertising will draw it out*."[24] The depression intensified the other pressures already motivating advertising professionals to promote the merits and legitimacy of their rapidly expanding services.

The pace at which advertising's advocates credited it with broad, progressive influences slowly gathered momentum through this decade. An 1893 essay merely reinforced the usual, limited arguments for advertising's benefits to businesses and newspapers until its concluding recommendations. Using the pen name "A Believer," the author called for all publishers to hire advertising experts and to allow them to have their "own private office, and be at the disposal of all customers of the paper." The writer recognized a third audience beyond businesspeople and publishers to whom advertising professionals should direct their legitimating arguments. Each paper "should have an article once in a while written by the [advertising] expert, which would tend to advance the idea of both advertiser and purchaser." Advertising's advocates needed to make "the great mass of the people thoroughly understand that the daily advertisements are of the utmost importance to them."[25] By the turn of the century, other "believers" did begin to address this third audience directly to promote the linkages between advertising and progress.

The phenomenon of interested outsiders instructing the advertising community on their place within the century's progress occurred again in a short article reprinted in 1895 by *Printers' Ink* from *Age of Steel*. "The Science of Advertising" included several of the usual assessments about the advertising trade but added progressive concepts that previous writings had lacked. It began by affirming that "advertising has become an essential part of modern business" and then described the variety of options available for publicizing businesses, which represented "a large investment of money and unshaken faith of businessmen." Like most contemporary analyses, the article indicated that "the evolution of advertising has kept pace with other things." However, unlike assessments that advertising was doing well to "keep pace" with business, this piece pointedly included advertising with several of the high-impact advances of the century, such as increased travel, literacy, and diffusion of art into the public arena. It concluded that "the businessman who would make his advertising pay, must keep pace with its progressive methods."[26] In other words, the field was making a kind of progress with which others must keep pace.

As advertising agents promoted themselves and their profession during this transitional period, they, too, began to broaden the conceptual range of their services' benefits. In 1894, Francis Wayland Ayer wrote, "Every one can see that Newspaper Advertising has grown with the country, but not every one realizes that it is largely by Newspaper Advertising that the country has grown." Ayer made "this distinction" to convince businesses to advertise in order to build their trade and to give "purchasers everywhere . . . a sign of enterprise, that raises a man in his own community . . . and that your bright competitor is going to adopt." Although Ayer's incentives and messages were traditional, his "distinction" hinted at a broader range for advertising's influence, and hence, its claims for legitimacy.[27]

The J. Walter Thompson Company's primary house organ in 1897 began its regular "Business Chat" by addressing a broadly legitimating paragraph to "Intelligent Business Men." With a rather reversed logic, the agency claimed that advertising "forms today so important a part of the prosperity of the individual, of the corporation, even of the nation, that here at the end of this progressive nineteenth century it has, by the subtle magic of brains, art and printer's ink, been developed into a veritable science." Two years later, the agency's new publication to advertisers, *The Thompson Red Book*, featured several pages on its new building and facilities and neglected to comment on advertising's expanding influence beyond business. Even so, the agency reinforced its own and the field's importance to modern business by insisting that the "merchant who does not believe in advertising does not believe in banks, insurance or other modern institutions. He is a relic of the lost ages." By contrast, progressive businesses knew that "vigorous advertisements lead the willing customers and drag the unwilling." For them, this agency kept on hand "modern tools and equipment in the shape of ideas and experience that will prove of value even to the veteran advertiser. Keep up with the procession."[28]

Although advertising professionals and commentators had occasionally begun to use the prevailing discourse about evolution and progress by the mid-1890s, until 1899 they made no explicit statement that advertising fostered progress in any general sense. Even an 1897 article entitled "Progress in Advertising" that *Printers' Ink* reprinted from *Harper's Weekly* praised the internal evolution of advertising's techniques without giving that evolution any credit for developments external to it, such as industrial growth. A tiny, free-standing filler item in *Profitable Advertising* the next year did catch the spirit of industrial progress and tied it to advertising through metaphor. "Good advertising," it asserted, "often marks the difference between profitless inaction and profitable activity; it is the fuel under the boiler that quickens industrial currents, the blow-pipe upon the flames of commerce, the extra steam that 'makes the wheels go round.'"[29] Even though it started with the usual goad to individuals, this little lyric contained the closest approximation to the progress discourse that would fully develop first in 1899 and then come to dominate the trade literature for decades after 1900. The trade literature before 1900 mingled the concepts of individual success, professional progress, and national economic or cultural progress with progress in the field of advertising, but the connections were not yet tightly or explicitly drawn.[30] At the end of the century, however, novel reflections powerfully applied the contemporary idealization of progress to the problem of legitimizing the advertising profession. The ensuing literature overflowed with such claims about advertising's progressive role and powers. The contrast between the nineteenth century's near absence of such claims and the following decades' abundance of them highlights the change in attitudes: the earlier advertising advocates had not simply assumed the connection between advertising and progress and not bothered to mention it.

The title and content of *Self Culture Magazine* reflected many of the Victorian era's strategies for both individual and collective progress. It provided, therefore, an appropriate publication for a lengthy article by Oscar Herzberg, managing editor of *Printers' Ink,* entitled, "The Century's Achievements in Business." Reprinted as a lead article in the advertising journal in October 1899, it announced, "More radical changes have been made in the conduct of business during the century now drawing to a close than in all the eras preceding." After a short history of American merchandizing since colonial times, Herzberg glorified advertising as "indeed, one of the great developments of the century. It has revolutionized business and made it possible to accomplish in a few years what otherwise would have taken generations to compass."[31]

At last, we find in Herzberg's analysis an explicit articulation of a progressive role for advertising in the business and industrial revolutions of the nineteenth century and, importantly, in material progress. He addressed at some length the benefits that accrued to industrial innovators, who could by then introduce their products to "the entire public almost literally at a bound." Herzberg expounded on the growth of trade that advertising made possible, benefiting both seller and buyer by developing markets for the "hundreds of improvements and articles by which life can be made more pleasant." Furthermore, "no force has conduced more [than advertising] to knit the world closely together, nor made our mutual interdependence more apparent." He welcomed the "increasing magnitude of commercial transactions requiring a large outlay of capital," seeing more benefits than costs in the resulting "tendency to centralization [that] has produced our great department stores, our great mills and factories, and other commercial enterprises." Herzberg finished with an emphatic proclamation of the cultural legitimacy of the business professions in general. They had outlived "the stigma which in former ages attached to commercial pursuits," and commerce "call[ed] into service the highest abilities of the best of our young men."[32]

## Advertising, Markets, and Progress

Just how much impact Herzberg's analysis had in furthering the association of advertising with general prosperity and progress is impossible to know. It did focus on and pull together the threads of the pertinent ideas for two broad and well-connected audiences: *Self Culture Magazine* offered self-improvement and information on timely subjects;[33] *Printers' Ink* was the most widely read advertising journal among practitioners and advertisers alike. One of Herzberg's ideas was the broadly accepted tenet among bourgeois Americans that progress was an important, transcendent criterion for judging the worth of individuals, groups, and their activities. A second was the predominant, although not universal, belief that industry's contributions to progress were paramount. The third idea had heretofore received comparatively little public attention; namely, that advertising could, and must, generate market demand for industry. Herzberg's linking these three strands together drew on the legitimating authority of both progress and industry to give the advertising field a new and powerful claim for its place in business and the nation. Someone had to be first to say this, and Herzberg's position at *Printers' Ink* made him a likely candidate. Whether or not Herzberg's spark lit the fuse, an explosion of interest in the linkage followed.

Through the 1890s, the trade's press had increasingly promoted advertising's potential for expanding the markets for specific goods, whether patent medicines or less dubious industrial goods. Looking back on that decade, that no one explicitly made a connection between this potential—industry's requirement for markets—and the widely touted material progress credited to innovations in industry indicates how narrowly advertising's advocates saw its influence then. Perhaps specialists had focused too intently on claims to win over clients, such as that advertising made it possible for individual businesses to enjoy successes. Perhaps also the trade carried so little prestige before its rapid-fire evolution of the 1890s that it took the whole decade to build to where someone could imagine staking this claim for it. Mounting public pressures on the advertising profession in the 1890s and later exacerbated the need for broader legitimation than individual business successes could provide. Yet what gave the argument its form and force derived from the debates about economic policies and events that dominated American politics through the 1890s.

## Markets and the Political Arena

Market-related issues lay behind major debates in late-nineteenth-century American politics. In particular, the national elections of 1888, 1892, and 1896, as well as many local contests, revolved in large measure around the relative benefits and costs of protective tariffs and whether voters saw themselves as beneficiaries or victims of public policies that attempted to govern the marketplace.[34] Although there were many subtle and obscure aspects of the arguments involved, the general public was well aware that the debates centered about the needs of both agriculture and industry to market goods and whether or not domestic markets should be protected from foreign competition. The era's evocative political economy issues about monetary policy fostered vigorous partisanship as well. Whether the country should have a gold or a bimetallic standard and whether it should sanction paper currency were in part argued according to peoples' beliefs about the money supply's impact on purchasing power, their own and that of their markets. The *Iron Age*, for instance, asserted after the 1896 "sound money" election that "consumption, which has been proceeding at a starvation rate, will return to a normal condition."[35] The drive for international markets and resources reinforced cultural paternalism in foreign policy debates, especially those involving expansion. In particular, the Spanish-American War had started and ended (1898), but the questions about governing the acquired territories and what goals should determine those decisions continued to receive attention in the press and in political debates for years. Indeed, Herzberg referred to the recent war as having "done much to draw attention to the commercial possibilities so long allowed to lie dormant," namely, "trade in tropical regions."[36]

In 1895, with the nation still deep in the throes of depression, Ohio Governor William McKinley received an enthusiastic response from the National Convention of Manufacturers in Cincinnati when he addressed the politics of markets. "It is a mighty problem to keep the wheels of industry in motion. They can not be kept in motion without markets. (Applause) They will not

*Consumption as Progress*

long produce beyond consumption." In a section of McKinley's speech entitled "Lessons of Progress," he declared, to more applause, "We want our markets for our manufacturers and agricultural products. . . . We want a reciprocity which will give us foreign markets for our surplus products." If a solution to this problem could be found, it would "improve our industrial situation and start this great country once more upon its march of triumph for the welfare of our own people and for the good of mankind everywhere."[37]

Although McKinley's rhetoric reflected the skill and ambitions of a rising political star (he became U.S. president in 1897), it did not exceed the typical bounds of contemporary discourse in recognizing the preeminence of industry and agriculture and the importance of marketing their goods. The next year, Thomas Dolan opened the first annual convention of the newly organized National Association of Manufacturers (NAM) by conveying the same themes in his presidential address. "Among the wealth-creators of the United States," he declared, "the manufacturers rank next after the farmers; and with the prosperity of both classes of producers the welfare of the nation is bound up in a positive manner." Dolan reviewed the benefits of industry to labor and to "the people" generally, and he found them "magnificent." Only by protecting the home markets, however, could the nation ensure "that industrial independence which is the condition of highest prosperity." The audience applauded when it heard, "Our own market is the best in the world." Dolan emphasized, moreover, that it "is the only market of which we may have absolute control; and the most ordinary considerations of business prudence should induce us to hold fast." Another speaker expounded on "The Home Market," calling for tariff protection of prosperity's "foundation stone . . . the home market of the American people, supplied by her own producer." This "sound business sense" remedy for "unequalled prosperity" also met with "prolonged applause" from the manufacturers.[38]

The challenges of marketing industrial goods dominate NAM's extant nineteenth-century records (the association was organized two years into the depression); however, advertising in order to expand the demand within existing markets seems not to have been considered. Protecting domestic markets through tariff policies and expanding international markets through negotiation with other producing nations and through international spheres of influence filled the discussions. For instance, at the association's first convention, four of seven agenda items related to foreign-trade matters, and a fifth called for "recognition of the Nicaragua Canal, and the control of the same by the United States Government." (The other two items addressed "cementing" the organization and "the advocacy of carefully considered legislation, to encourage manufacturing industries of all classes throughout the country.")[39]

What this preponderance within both agenda items and speech topics reveals is a static perspective on markets. In other words, markets were generally considered in demographic and geographic terms. Populations defined markets, and how much demand any given population represented was relatively fixed by its constituents' access to goods and abilities to purchase them. Accordingly, NAM and the various industrial trade journals incessantly urged political solutions to the problems of markets, only decrying "too much legislation" on other issues, such as regulation, when it suited them.[40]

By 1899, the political economy of markets had filled political debates and both general and trade presses for years. Despite this background, no one fully connected the well-publicized marketing successes of the patent medicines, Royal Baking Power, bicycles, and many other heavily advertised brand-name products to the rhetoric of these grand, political issues of national prosperity and progress. The perception of the scope of advertising's impact remained localized; that is, pertinent to advertisers' particular successes, the advertising media, and practitioners. Advertisers and advertising practitioners touted the successes, although no one before Herzberg presented them as representative of a generic solution to the larger problems of finding industrial markets on a broad scale. The spectacularly successful innovations by the National Biscuit Company and N. W. Ayer & Son in marketing Uneeda Cracker had recently taken off by the time Herzberg wrote, however. They may have contributed to his pulling together the three threads of industry, progress, and, finally, advertising's potential to generate demand within domestic markets. Whatever its sources, shortly after Herzberg made the connection, extrapolating from individual marketing successes to national prosperity and progress became a constant theme among advertising's champions. The "pot of printer's ink" that the *New York Times* had appraised as "better than the greatest gold mine" for patent-medicine vendors[41] could serve the national quest as well.

After the turn of the century, public events continued to fuel the general awareness of industry's needs for markets and the implications for national prosperity. Domestically, the merger movement peaked between 1898 and 1905, raising questions about monopolies among many citizens in their roles as consumers, businesspeople, laborers, or farmers. Among other things, the Panic of 1907 taught that such a "bankers' panic" might not devastate the economy for long if markets for industrial goods remained strong. International concerns kept the public's eye on industry's needs for markets. In addition to the continuing debates about the Spanish acquisitions, related international events included establishing the Open Door policy for China in 1900, beginning the construction of the Panama Canal in mid-decade, and sending the Great White Fleet around the globe in 1907 and 1908. Trade barriers were also a prominent issue in precipitating World War I in 1914. As these events dominated the United States' perspective on the world, growing numbers of successful marketing programs continued to fuel the advertising advocates' linkage between national progress and their marketing efforts.

## Advertising Agents and the Trusts

Advertising practitioners initially distrusted the concentration of industry, fearing that mergers would destroy traditional forms of competition, leaving monopolies with no incentive to advertise. They also worried that the firms remaining outside of trusts would not advertise to consumers enough to support the advertising trade. Whether discussions praised or attacked the trusts, the consensus in the business press by 1900 concluded that the "trend of modern business . . . is toward concentration of capital and perfection of organization. . . . No such movement can take place of course, without arousing active opposition from those who suffer from it, or who are overcome by it."[42] Both advertising practitioners and publishers feared that the advertising expenditures that provided their livelihoods would number among the "unnecessary expenses." Trusts, therefore, made up part of the business context imposing challenges and changes on the advertising field at the turn of the century.

An 1898 article by L. J. Vance in *Printers' Ink* opened by conceding that "the drift of things commercial is toward large aggregations of capital," then expressing his fears that "monopoly is the foe of advertising." If people had to buy from a monopoly, it "does not usually need to advertise." He compared the prolific advertising policies of the hundreds of competing bicycle companies with the minimal advertising in the oil market. Within the latter, the companies other than Standard Oil shared one-tenth of its business between them and advertised twice as much as the near monopoly. Trade presses (outside of the advertising field) lost major portions of their revenues when the industries that had previously advertised in them merged. Vance and many other analysts at this point held out only one hope for advertising; namely, that combinations might compete against each other, as had the cigarette corporations.[43]

Although hundreds of firms had disappeared into mergers by the end of the century, Jonathan Cutler began to see a ray of hope for the advertising field. Featured in a late 1899 issue of *Printers' Ink,* he reproved advertising practitioners and publishers who had shown "their lack of faith in advertising as a necessary element in business building." He believed, to the contrary, that while "trusts may temporarily decrease the amount expended for advertising . . . if there is any real value in advertising it is certain that in the long run the amount annually expended for it will grow with the years." Cutler comforted his readers by dismissing the fears that resulted because "just now trusts are like mysterious monsters." Even so, "time will prove them as amenable to the laws of trade and of competition as is the smallest of corner groceries." Cutler based his own faith on two examples of trusts engaged in major advertising programs—the newly formed National Biscuit Company and the pioneer American Tobacco Company. He advised small firms to compete with the conglomerates for local markets. Publishers and other advertising practitioners also needed to study the "local field" so that they might direct and encourage local advertisers to take on the trusts.[44] This fine advice still missed corporations' desires for market control and expansion, which pushed advertising expenditures ever higher after 1900.

The first two issues of *Printers' Ink* for the new century offered understanding and comfort. Emerson P. Harris explained that despite the contentions of "some economists, most trust promoters and all Socialists," competition was not the "prime cause of advertising." Instead, Harris interpreted advertising as "a necessary device in the modern system of distributing goods, a system by which selling can be done with far less expense than in any other way." Because of the nature and operation of modern industry, "what the automatic machine is to manufacturing goods, that the advertisement is to selling them, and as the machine thrives best where production is most highly organized and carried on on the larger scale, so advertising will be most extensively employed where distribution is most highly developed." As a result, trusts "will have no more incentive for abandoning the modern selling machine than throwing out the most improved machinery." Harris also noted the development of "special brands" and the essential role of advertisements by which the producer can "reach the consumer direct" to develop those brands.[45]

Harris acknowledged that the absence of competition might induce the trust "temporarily [to] withdraw all its advertisements under the misapprehension that its customers must come to it." But he insisted that corporations would have to advertise because "no trust is so independent that it need not seek its customers to the extent of informing them about its product." Moreover, advertising provides the "motive power by which modern selling in any branch is kept up with the procession" of production. Harris concluded by hinting at competition's potential to reemerge should a trust fail to advertise adequately to maintain its hegemony.[46] In doing so, he suggested a function of advertising that would not become the topic of mature analysis for another decade, namely, the role of advertising as a barrier to entry. Business operations had long been aware of this aspect of advertising, but they lacked the term and the focused deliberation on the subject that would develop by the 1910s. As early as 1893, the Royal Baking Powder Company had estimated that it would take $15 million of advertising expenditure for another brand to displace its dominance in the market. Two decades lapsed between recognition of the power of an established brand to stave off new competition (as the Royal Baking Powder Company in fact did) and the formalization of the notion that advertising could act as a barrier to entry.[47]

A reprinted essay from the *Chicago Tribune* in *Printers' Ink* refuted a *Yale Review* article that had anticipated the demise of advertising as a result of the industrial combinations and, to add insult to injury, considered that result beneficial. In disputing both aspects of this assessment, the *Tribune* piece argued, in part, that only trade advertising and not consumer advertising had been thus far reduced by the trusts. More importantly and more contentiously, it contended that advertising would always remain necessary to stimulate demand for "things not absolutely necessary" but that are the beneficial results of "industrial progress."[48]

For the next several years, *Printers' Ink* and other publications continued to assure their readers that industrial concentration would not destroy consumer advertising, although trade journals would likely continue to suffer. In 1902, for instance, the opening editorial of *Judicious Advertising*'s first issue offered a round of advice and encouragement to advertising specialists that included putting oligopolies on notice that "having the field to yourself doesn't signify that you shouldn't advertise. The Standard Oil company is not staying awake nights worrying about competition, but it takes printers' ink in liberal doses just the same."[49] Other reassurances came in the form of case studies of particular industries that continued to advertise despite dominating their markets. In 1907, one such study analyzed DuPont's "Powder trust," which spent several hundred thousand dollars each year in advertising. "Why is this expenditure made to advertise a virtual monopoly?" The answer, in short, explained the company's needs to maintain demand, to try to increase demand, and to keep up the public's confidence in the safety of DuPont products when properly used.[50] Edward Sherwood Meade, whose loyalties lay more with the trusts than with advertising agents, asserted in 1909 that if "the trust wishes to push its goods, it must advertise. Advertising is not a waste . . . but a productive expense [that] . . . brings the merits of the goods to the buyer's attention, and awakens the desire to purchase." Meade pointed out the successes of the National Biscuit Company and other corporations due to aggressive and innovative advertising.[51] Such heartening reports as this in the new century raised the field's confidence in its prospects in the face of the transformations of the business environment upon which it depended.

Consumers, in their roles as citizens, often protested vigorously against what they called the trusts' price-fixing and operating in constraint of free trade during the 1900s and 1910s. Nonetheless, as a whole, they continued to buy the most heavily advertised products of the conglomerates, even while their representatives and courts voiced their challenges.[52] Advertising practitioners' confidence grew out of such marketing successes, which at the same time waylaid their original fears about the trusts. Increasingly advocates attributed greater and greater portions of businesses' successes to advertising's ever more skillful persuasiveness.

## Opening Markets by Persuasion

Persuasion was the tool that advertising's advocates increasingly offered manufacturers of consumer goods in their crisis of markets. In the intensely competitive environment of the 1890s, practitioners had expanded and specialized their services. As they exercised and promoted their selling prowess, their confidence grew, individually and collectively, and they took credit for marketing successes, whatever the cause.[53] At the same time, the ubiquitous discourse on various industries' needs for markets, trusts or no trusts, fueled their sense of importance.

In 1893, Nathaniel Fowler Jr. argued for persuasion's importance in marketing, trying to disabuse advertisers of the notions that they should only advertise most when business was good and that they should advertise merchandise that was already selling well: "When business is brisk proportionate advertising should always accompany it," he wrote, "to direct trade more than to create it, to drive hesitating trade into those corners of the store which are seldom visited by general buyers." But when the times and business are dull, "a severe attack of business parsimony" is unwise; instead, the "progressive business man should lead, not follow, his customers." Especially in "dull and quiet times necessities are of more interest to people than luxuries, but half the people do not know all they really need until someone tells them, and the best friend on earth cannot give them this desired information more convincingly than can the well worded advertisement." By doing so, advertising "creates trade."[54] Conversely, ceasing a campaign could destroy a product's market, for patent medicines and bicycles alike. Almost twenty years later, as one of countless carriers of the same message in the meantime, Herbert N. Casson defined the "true ad" as "the one that brings in the new buyer—the indifferent buyer—the buyer who did not clearly know what he wanted until he saw the advertisement."[55] Iron Age reminded its readers that the "world did not know it wanted bicycles" until they were made "irresistible."[56] Arch Wilkinson Shaw, lecturer on business policy at Harvard University, explained that by "educating the public to perceive a particular need it has lying latent," instead of focusing on price, advertising actually reduced "destructive competition" and widened "the market for all makes of the article it describes."[57]

An 1896 "Treatise on Advertising" declared that in order to create trade, the "bright, ingenious and new" advertisements were "written and arranged with a view to influencing the popular mind, and no other form of current literature represents a better understanding of human nature."[58] Similarly, George French wrote in 1915 that because advertising's "major function is to persuade" it was "compelled to seek for a way into the minds of the people." In the modern, more "strenuous time," advertisers could not offer their goods and then "await the necessity or pleasure of the people." Therefore, advertising had now "to develop the need or the desire." The advertiser now "bends his energies to the task of persuading people to purchase his goods. He does not inquire whether there is a real need for his goods, and usually he does not concern himself about their utility in economic life." Effective advertising was therefore "a method of influencing people to subordinate their own judgment to the suggestions of the advertisers."[59] The many successful campaigns of recent years had "created new demands" and thereby made luxuries into necessities, according to the J. Walter Thompson agency in 1909; a "necessity is a luxury in universal demand."[60] All such cases encouraged advertising's advocates to take credit for providing the nation's businesses with adequate markets by expanding demand.

## Developer of Business

By the early years of the twentieth century, advertising's advocates had built their confidence and claims sufficiently to assert frequently and strongly the business community's dependence on its services. Advertising's importance to individual businesses remained a major component of the trade literature, but this growing rhetoric also professed the broader belief that business as a whole, and therefore the nation, depended on advertising for its vitality and prosperity. *Profitable Advertising* expressed this belief through allegory— the "good ship, *Nineteen Hundred*" portrayed on the cover of the first issue of the new century. The opening editorial explained that the ship's figurehead represented the goddess-figure "Prosperity and Plenty," and that the "Imp of Advertising, who is really responsible for all prosperity," rode "astride the bow with the reins in its hands."[61] In 1903, Daniel Lord, of Lord & Thomas, addressed the Sphinx Club in New York City on the same point but in a more straightforward manner, calling modern advertising and the agent who conducted it "a developer of business." Not only did advertising increase trade and profits directly, but its leading agents had come to perform innovative planning and program management for their clients. Together, these services improved the conduct of business, often helping manufacturers to develop new products and new markets.[62]

Unlike other professions that dealt with "some of the attributes of business," George French claimed in 1909 that "advertising *is* that business, makes it, creates it. While the other professions assist in the transaction of business, not one of them is essential to its life. . . . Without advertising business ceases, or would cease if ever the experiment were to be tried." Truman DeWeese, advertising manager of the Shredded Wheat Company, told the Sphinx Club that same year that advertising created new desires, one at a time. What was important was that each "new desire, multiplied in potency and pulling power thousands of times and thru all the changing moods of human fancy, is the thing that pulls business and piles up industrial wealth to colossal heights." Such persuasion "is the thing that builds factories, cities, and railroads, and all the instrumentalities that contribute to human happiness and human progress. It makes the luxuries of to-day the necessities of to-morrow." So, while advertising promoted one product at a time, its cumulative effect built the nation's business as a whole. *Profitable Advertising* insisted that "there is no profession, not excepting the so-called 'learned professions,' that is more vitally concerned in the progress and uplift of the world of business than is advertising."[63]

### Challenges of Distribution

The strongest case for advertising's importance, and therefore its legitimacy as a profession as its output and profile rose, derived from the growing concern that, by the turn of the century, industry's capacity to produce had surpassed the capacity of the existing markets to consume. Without new techniques for marketing—still called distribution at that time—industry could not continue growing, and worse, would face repeated slowdowns in order to sell off the inevitable surpluses. In countless ways, advertising's champions joined others who have explained this inherent difficulty within the modern industrial system. Stanley Resor's personal interests in studying history gave him a longer perspective than most of his fellows, and he interpreted the relative importance of production and distribution in terms of a shifting balance over time. Resor explained that in the early stages of industrialization, "production and distribution balanced each other, but productive forces increased faster than consumption and the need for selling then came into being." Salespeople and jobbers could not "keep pace with production," however, and in order to "keep the wheels turning in all these factories, some method of large scale selling had to be devised to keep pace with large scale production." Advertising, Resor concluded, had evolved to maintain the necessary balance between production and consumption.[64]

A manual for manufacturers sponsored by Curtis Publishing Company in 1913 also took a historical approach, ending its summary of U.S. business history with the assessment that manufacturing had become by 1900 "a fine art." On the other hand, "distribution and selling, little understood, offered new scope to genius in competition. No longer was it a problem solely of manufacture, with an eager public waiting to consume." That advertising "was seized upon is a tribute to the wisdom of American manufacturers. An economic need had arisen which had to be met if progress were to continue." Advertising, the manual contended, "would fully justify its existence if it did only these two things—increase the demand in present markets, and develop new markets; in other words, serve as an educational force in merchandizing." It did more than this, however, also acting as a form of "business insurance," assuring manufacturers of future markets as well.[65]

John Lee Mahin also credited advertising for industrial prosperity, asserting that convincing and evocative appeals could make a product "satisfactory and valuable to the buyer."[66] Writers and editors in *Mahin's Magazine* addressed this matter frequently. One conceived of a cyclic relationship between production and prosperity driven by consumption, arguing that the "factories are the chief wealthmakers of the nation" and that the "consumer is also the worker." Therefore, if workers could be persuaded to purchase what they produced, the "flitting five-dollar bill is chased around the circle" back to the manufacturer. An editorial insisted that if manufacturers only concerned themselves with the excellence of their production and their products, they would fail. They must use advertising's "Opportunity to gain an unobstructed, respectful, and even a welcome hearing" in order to generate demand for their products.[67]

So distribution—that is, marketing—had become the challenge of twentieth-century capitalism, according to the post-1900 advertising literature. The technological accomplishments of the previous century, and those assumed to come, had moved to the background for advertising practitioners because the achievements within most people's lifetimes had made invention and production appear relatively routine. With so much already accomplished, this particular group of businesspeople took for granted further developments in the technology of production. The ongoing imperative of markets to industrial prosperity, on the other hand, had been powerfully and urgently demonstrated in everyone's immediate experience. As DeWeese and many other proponents of advertising explained it, advertising was the only way to optimize marketing operations and to generate the profit that they knew "accrues from large volume and quick turn-over."[68] The problem that remained in 1900 and thereafter, they believed, was the "distribution of intelligence," which "but for the ad must be done by more expensive and less efficient means."[69]

The J. Walter Thompson Company had learned from the panics of 1893 and 1907 that "a manufacturing plant without business is not an asset, but a liability," and advertising was the best means of generating business for industry.[70] Still, not every manufacturer had "the courage of the plain logic of the situation," according to a 1909 editorial in which *Profitable Advertising* admonished those who continued to "stake fortunes upon brick or cement buildings, upon machinery, upon workmen; but they have not the courage to stake fractions of fortunes upon that business-maker which is able to guarantee them the fortunes they wish for." They needed to realize that the "buildings, the machinery, the workmen, and all of the elements of production, cannot guarantee the man a market for his proposed product. Advertising can. Of what avail are the factories, the machinery, the workmen, if there is not a market?" Countering the traditional criticism that advertising was unpredictable (reflecting John Wanamaker's admission that half his advertising was wasted, but since he did not know which half, he intended to continue apace), *Profitable Advertising* contrasted the "subordinate elements, uncertain elements, the gambling elements" with advertising—"the one element that may be absolutely depended upon." Not that advertising had been perfected yet. The journal called upon the "advertising interests" to support its study to develop a science of advertising for everyone's "knowledge and profit."[71]

DeWeese had occasion to promote advertising in the *Forum* as the best opportunity in 1902 for "The Young Man With Nothing But Brains." Distribution presented the most challenging and open career for such men during that "era of expansion which the politicians are talking about." The goals of industrial concentration were "to cheapen the cost of production and distribution," and the choice was to be part of the machinery of one or the other. Clearly, the ambitious young man would not want to be part of the former, since most of those problems had already been reduced to routine. Rather, the real challenges lay in the "great distributing machinery brought into existence by the era of combines" to lower the costs of distribution. Advertising was essential, DeWeese alleged, because it "converts the product of industry into coin. Without it the wheels of the factory would stop, and there would be industrial stagnation." Participating in the "battle of ideas" to "furnish the ideas for this new and vast twentieth-century system of publicity" was the modern alchemy, open to the "genius of publicity."[72]

## Defending Advertising's Costs

Advertising practitioners had acquired the habit of promoting their occupation during the nineteenth century as part of their dual attempts to legitimate their work and to gain patrons for it. In the next century, as the costs mounted, questions arose regarding these costs. Did advertisers, individually and collectively, receive adequate returns on these investments in marketing? Was advertising nothing more than an artificial cost dutifully but unnecessarily paid by manufacturers because their competitors paid it? There was also another question: Did the costs ultimately rest on the consumer? The rapidly increasing pervasiveness and impact of advertisements gave weight to these and like questions. The Progressive Era's scrutiny and criticisms of advertising content and practices intensified the pressure for answers. For instance, a statistician's analysis received coverage in the mainstream press when he concluded in 1900 that a "considerable portion" of advertising expenditures entailed "economic waste," particularly that which simply drew "trade to one seller at the expense of others."[73] As a result, advocates directed some of their legitimating arguments, especially that advertising was the new engine of progress, beyond their traditional business audiences to the public. They began to recognize the influence wielded by this third audience within the corporate commonwealth and to address its concerns.

The new century's need for answers to the question of whether advertising paid allowed advertising's advocates to reiterate their traditional arguments. The J. Walter Thompson Company repeated the standard explanation in 1909: the great and ever increasing volume of advertising was itself evidence for its effectiveness. Advertisers "do this year after year. Somebody pays for it, and finds it profitable, or it wouldn't be continued." The agency also rephrased the other traditional rationale for advertising's costs: aggressive advertisers had found the "asset of public confidence worth many millions of dollars" toward their individual successes, as substantiated by the "first-class ratings" in both Dun's and Bradstreet's listings held by all the leading advertisers.[74] Even so, the matter of waste climbed high on the agenda of professional organizations trying to raise their trade's standards, and thereby its prestige. The American Association of Advertising Agencies' 1918 "Report on Agency Service" highlighted the goal of serving the public by making "advertising better, and thus to eliminate waste and reduce costs." Likewise, the 1917 convention of the Associated Advertising Clubs of the World set lowering costs and reducing waste as top agenda items, placing them after only war-related issues.[75]

The question of who paid for the advertising costs brought out another set of answers based on the newly discovered relationship between industry, progress, and industry's needs for the market demand that advertising promised to supply. Daniel Starch, a professor at the University of Wisconsin and founder of the pioneer public-opinion research and marketing feedback organization, the Starch Reports, addressed this basis for legitimacy. He was especially concerned that advertising "has been charged with being responsible to a considerable extent for the increased cost of living. It would seem improbable, however, that advertising has contributed any appreciable amount to the prices for the necessities of life. For we must remember that advertising is on the whole an economical method of selling," and as such, it often "increased the number of sales and thus decreased the cost of manufacturing as well as of selling." In Starch's later textbook, he detailed data and reports from a 1914 *Printers' Ink* survey that documented claims that through the use of advertising, leading manufacturers had been able to reduce prices by increasing their rates of production, or they had improved on quality without raising prices.[76]

Many other advertising practitioners, users, and promoters developed aspects of this argument. Resor contrasted the power to generate business activity that came from the pull, or demand, that advertising could elicit from "a hundred millions of people" with the push of "the few hundreds or thousands of dealers" upon whom the traditional distribution channels had relied. Adrian Joyce of the Sherwin-Williams Paint Company itemized ways that advertising made distribution more efficient and increased sales, also making production more efficient. He summarized what had come by 1915 to be a standard argument in defense of advertising costs: in "taking care of the work of furnishing the supply to fill the demand, and in solving the problem of getting the goods from the factory to the consumer," advertising "reduces the cost of production, reduces the cost of selling, and reduces the price to the ultimate consumer, while at the same time standardizing the quality and the real value of the product." The frequency with which the trade press repeated these arguments attested to its sense of their importance in legitimating the advertising profession, grounding it in the industrial foundation for modern prosperity.[77]

The standardization of products that Joyce referred to was often presented as in itself a major benefit that consumers received from manufacturers' advertising. Not only could industrialists who advertised directly to consumers produce more and cheaper goods, but advertising required that those goods be held to a constant and high standard. As Calkins put it, "Advertising implies a contract between the maker and the public always to deliver the same goods under that same name." The value of a trademark to an advertising manufacturer flowed directly from the confidence that consumers had in its consistency and safety. Mahin and others cited many instances in which manufacturers worked to improve their products through better materials and production processes, and he argued that they did so out of a "feeling of responsibility." Because consumers were loyal to producers who accepted and acted on this responsibility, they developed a mutually beneficial relationship.[78] However accurate, these and like claims represented the field's growing confidence in the face of continued questions about its legitimacy.

So successfully had advertising's proponents built their field's authority in some circles by 1920 that they could find themselves protesting against advertisers' unreasonable expectations. A Lord & Thomas spokesman, for instance, worried that "many are seeking to do in advertising that which can't be done." He cautioned: "Advertising is not a panacea" for all business ills, as some believed. To those who expected too much of it, those "who are today indulging in an orgy of unwise and uneconomic advertising, we issue these words of warning—for the good of the cause." By that time, advertising was, according to this practitioner, "too great a power thus to be brought into disrepute" by unrealistic expectations.[79]

Arguments that tied together progress in industry and advertising while addressing the public's questions on its costs also appeared outside the trade press. In 1909 and 1910, *Collier's* published two series of articles on the merits of advertising as they affected the general population. After having been a leader among the muckraking magazines, *Collier's* took on a dual task: assuring readers that they could trust the advertisers in its pages and admonishing those duped by misleading advertisements that they read elsewhere. Very likely, both series had the further purpose of mollifying advertisers concerned as a result of earlier muckraking editorial policies. The shorter series consisted of four, feature-length articles at one-month intervals under the rubric "The New World of Trade," praising advertising's rapid expansion and its usefulness to businesses and consumers as a means of communication, while cautioning about the dangers that still lurked "for the gullible."[80] *Collier's* labeled its longer series "Advertising Bulletin" and usually placed these short, weekly pieces prominently under the table of contents. Besides assurances that advertisements placed in *Collier's* were reliable, the essays presumed to educate readers on advertising procedures and costs. Advertising, of course, supported the "best publications" in which the advertisements were "embellishments." Because advertising informed consumers about "the latest and best of everything in every nook and corner of the country," it benefited them as well as the advertisers and the publications that carried quality messages. In rather simplified form, a few of these popular pieces addressed the costs of advertising, always concluding that, ultimately, advertising reduced prices and raised the variety and quality of goods available. One of the *Collier's* articles ended: "*Advertising costs, but it pays, and the readers reap the benefits.*"[81]

*Leslie's Illustrated Weekly Newspaper* also supported its advertisers and its revenues by explaining advertising's effects on costs. In 1915, *Leslie's* published an article entitled "Who Pays the Advertising Bills?" later reprinting it as a hard-covered booklet with a preface by its advertising manager for distribution to major advertisers and whoever else might request a copy. The overall message explained that advertising was "paid for by the increased business" that it generated; advertisers recognized it as a "factor of economy in modern sales and distribution—a positive and potent influence in reducing the cost of living." Unfortunately, too many consumers "*misunderstood* [advertising] as a tax which is added to the price of the article advertised." *Leslie's* aggressive stance in favor of advertising made only token acknowledgement of past abuses in promoting quack medicines; after all, such purveyors exploited the public no more than did "fake reformers." Indeed, "trade-marks and national advertising are the two greatest public servants in business today. Their whole tendency is to raise qualities and standardize them, while reducing prices and stabilizing them." Production, on the other hand, was "easy enough," so distribution now determined which of the "fittest" businesses would survive.[82]

## Advertising as a Promoter of Cultural Progress

By virtue of advertising's role in the development of business, particularly industrial production, it substantially contributed to the material progress of the nation, according to its apologists. Advertising also contributed, they said, to the national progress and raised the level of what was commonly referred to as "civilization"—unintended benefits about which both advertisers and advertising practitioners could congratulate themselves. In this, advertising specialists joined the legions of others eager to participate in and take credit for civilization's progress—magazine editors, missionaries, explorers, reformers, educators, and so on. Advertising's support and subsidization of the press had long been celebrated and remained a major component of the field's claims to legitimacy. Twentieth-century observances of this benefit simply continued taking credit for a better and cheaper press to educate the population, as did *Collier's* "Advertising Bulletin" series.[83]

Subsidizing the press did not exhaust advertising's contributions to civilization, as advocates proclaimed them after 1899. In a 1903 interview, pioneer copywriter Fowler explained that the "social benefits" of advertising extended beyond the "popular education" made available by the contents of the popular presses. Advertisements themselves directly introduced the population to "right methods of living." Foremost on Fowler's list of these object lessons was the "liberal advertising of sanitary arrangements, health-foods, and other progressive commodities." Although there had been deleterious effects from advertising of "dangerous compounds, unhealthy foods, patent medicines, and the like," the "right kind of advertising, the advertising of the right kind of goods, is one of the great factors of civilization."[84]

Not surprisingly, Mark Twain observed earlier than most the implications of advertising's messages in the aggregate, and he remarked on their alleged capacity to improve civilization through hygiene, to be specific. Twain published *A Connecticut Yankee in King Arthur's Court* in 1889, when advertising for Pears' Soap covered the country and its slogans, including "Good morning, have you used Pears' Soap?" provided ripe targets for his satire. He applied his infamous blend of sarcasm and moralism to this phenomenon by devising an advertising campaign for "civilizing and uplifting" Camelot. His plan had two parts: first reducing the stature of the pompous "knight-errantry" by turning them into sandwich men selling soap; second, introducing, thereby, "a rudimentary cleanliness among the nobility," from whom "it would work down to the people."[85]

In contrast, when twentieth-century advertising practitioners and their advocates set about attributing "civilizing and uplifting" to advertising, they were quite in earnest about it. Since the mainstream culture placed a priority on material progress, and the ethos of the time precluded a strong governmental presence, business figures generally spoke as if they shouldered the responsibility for national betterment. Advertising specialists sought to place themselves at the level of other business leaders in this context by taking credit for cultural progress. Their access to both public venues and persuasion, "a way into the minds of the people," provided the inspiration as well as the means for this quest for leadership. They had developed access and persuasion first for trade, and now they were available for "higher purposes," since advertising had been "chosen as the medium of the new era."[86]

Of advertising's educational impact, Calkins wrote that it "modifies the course of a people's daily thoughts, gives them new words, new phrases, new ideas, new fashions, new prejudices and new customs." In doing so, "it obliterates old sets of words and phrases, fashions and customs" with greater effect than "any other one force, the school, the church and the press excepted." Its accomplishments included "the prevalence of good roads, rubber tires, open plumbing, sanitary underwear, water filters, hygienic waters, vacuum cleaners, automobiles, kitchen cabinets, pure foods . . . which the public has been taught by advertising to use, to believe in, and to demand."[87] Similarly, an editorial in *Profitable Advertising* asserted that a "large proportion of the welfare of our nation is in the keeping of advertisers" because of its effect on children and "upon that great class of people who are profoundly influenced by that which they read." The "educative, the character-forming, the sociological effect of advertising" seemed a positively "fruitful and suggestive subject."[88] Advertising's educational potential, according to DeWeese, comprised "news" enhanced by "psychological power." Combining these two attributes, advertising benefited people by making them require new and improved acquisitions to be content, such as, by 1908, the safety razor and breakfast cereal, which had clearly improved consumers' lives. Advertising "enlarges and expands the horizon of man's daily life and experience by bringing to his attention new commodities designed for his comfort and convenience, without which he would have been perfectly happy in his ignorance; but, having learned of their existence, he cannot find it in his heart to be happy or contented until he possesses them." Advertising thereby served the public.[89]

Arguments on behalf of advertising as popular education frequently emphasized that it taught people how to make their lives more pleasant and comfortable. J. Walter Thompson wrote for *Appleton's Magazine* that "advertisements educate the people to a knowledge of the comforts, conveniences, and luxuries of life and create the desire to share in their enjoyment." French refuted critics of advertising with evidence that "a large part of all the advertising that is done is for the purpose of giving consumers some valuable information" for their "comfort and happiness." DeWeese, in this vein, asserted that Kodak's advertising had "touched the button of joy in 100,000 homes, letting in the sunlight that preserves the faces of loved ones on the films of memory," just as advertising had brought the benefits of other progressive technologies to consumers, from watches to hams.[90]

*Collier's* "Advertising Bulletin" series brightly informed its readers about how the "University of Advertising" sought to teach them "the news of the world." The consumers' curriculum included "The Effect of Advertising," which encouraged them "instinctively [to] have faith in the goods that are known . . . through distinctive, honest advertising." Advertising, *Collier's* asserted, had had "ten times as much to do with the real progress of the human race as all the structural steel ever produced—or that will be produced." Otherwise magazines and newspapers could not exist, and "half of what most of us know about hygiene, sanitation, and physical culture we have learned either from the advertising pages or the things advertised." Indeed, "almost everything you can think of that has helped to make our homes pleasanter, our minds brighter, and our lives full of variety, has come to us because advertising provided a way through which we could be reached—all of us at the same time." Advertising was much more important than the invention or production of the technologies that it brought to people; without it, *Collier's* declared, "the world would be, industrially, decades behind where it is now."[91]

Yet all of these benefits from advertising did not come without imposing pressures on consumers, its supporters reminded readers, approvingly. Housewives, for instance, were compelled to respond to advertisements to care for their families' growing needs in modern times. In meeting their responsibilities, Curtis Publishing Company told advertisers, women competed with "other men's wives." Women's homes were their factories, and the popular magazines were their "own trade journals" from which they learned the necessary skills, materials, and tools of their trade.[92] To help women perform up to standards in the consumers' new environment, *Good Housekeeping Magazine* offered them "A Course in Scientific Shopping." These "talks" on shopping for food and clothing told women that goods advertised in reputable magazines were safer, more fashionable, and of better quality. The first article explained how advertising improved the quality and prices of goods. Only because the "American public is a receptive one" could the system work so well. This public "is a live, active growing, yearning mass [that] . . . wants to be told facts; it wants to be given suggestions" about being better, more efficient consumers. Somehow, women were to express their individuality at the same time that they selected the correct goods *"because they are advertised."*[93] For all of its joys, the life of the perfect consumer has never been easy or free from anxiety or conflicts.

As the end of the first decade of the twentieth century approached, advertising's apologists asserted a new sense of their field's broadening impact. Along with all his exhortations to his colleagues to increase their professionalism, French expressed his belief that advertising was already "the one art which interests every person, the one profession which enforces its tenets upon all who live, the one business which means profit or loss to every individual who earns or spends money. Whether we will or not, whether we know it or not, we are all dependent upon advertising."[94] Such a culture might well be called a consumer culture, and advertising's advocates had already begun to foresee such a vindication for their field as the reward for their efforts. As part of the transition in this perception of American culture and their roles in it, the J. Walter Thompson Company declared in 1909 that "America is the advertiser's Promised Land, turned into a reality." Advertisers and their marketing specialists had been able to build a nation of commercial successes because the American people were the most progressive in the world—the most receptive to advertising's "revolutionary" "form of progress." Thus, because "Americans are producers and spenders" who appreciate "improvements and inventions," advertising had only to present innovation's case in order for progress to unfold through consumption.[95]

No longer was advertising just a tool for others' successes, according to its growing literature. Nor was it just a commercial phenomenon. In 1915, Herbert W. Hess, a professor at the Wharton School of Finance and Commerce at the University of Pennsylvania, dedicated his book "to those who dream, hope, think and work for a constantly improving world thru productive advertising." For centuries, advertising had responded to the "particular needs and desires of the various epochs which mark the progress of the world." Now, however, it had become "a highly specialized element in the creative processes of life" and had altered the historical balance between its activities and its cultural environment. "To-day, far from being a passive or an unconscious factor in human existence, and far from complacently following the vacillating course of the public's footsteps, advertising has become a positive and productive force—a guiding factor in the shaping of the constantly changing public standards of life. It works with art and science in the evolution of human need and desire."[96] So far had the need to defend advertising passed from its advocates' concerns that their writings appeared to be more apologia for an already powerful force than efforts to establish its legitimacy. By 1909, Waldo Warren even celebrated the alleged "great moral by-product of advertising" that extended beyond "commercial significance." Besides "elevated" taste and the "spirit of enterprise" that ads inculcated, their guarantees led people "not only to be honest externally, but actually to become honest at heart."[97]

Notwithstanding this confident discourse, the pressures to justify advertising and its practices continued into the 1920s on multiple fronts, including national attempts to prevent then remove the tax subsidies that were implicit in establishing it as a fully deductible expense from income taxes (1917) and later to tax advertising (1920, 1926). French worried in 1915, for instance, about a residual distrust of the medium that meant that advertisers and their agents "have got to teach the people to trust them." Once advertising professionals perfect their trade through organization, study, and standards for honesty, they could bring the public "to the knowledge of what advertising can do for them." Their communications "may benefit the mass, or in some way minister to the mass," by bringing a "personal message from one who knows to many who are supposed to wish to know."[98] Even in the 1920s, the heyday of advertising's popular image, critics attacked its cultural, social, ecological, and economic impacts. For instance, Ralph Borsodi critiqued as *post hoc, ergo propter hoc* the "bad logic" by which advocates claimed to prove that improvements that followed the rise of national advertising were caused by it.[99]

# Advertising's Wartime Service

The entrance of the United States into World War I in April 1917 offered both challenges and opportunities. Debates over wartime taxation threatened the practice of advertising,[100] but the emergency also gave advertising's practitioners and advocates the opportunity to tie their new rhetoric of service to the fervor of wartime patriotism: they would serve the nation and thereby save it. Whether or not the nation, or any significant portion of it, accepted this enhanced self-portrayal, its champions evinced a conviction approaching arrogance—certainly a far cry from the limited claims, diffidence, and concerns that had marked the challenges and transitions of the 1890s. Even so, the initial reactions in *Printers' Ink* to the declaration of war presented a cautious interpretation of what good citizenship entailed in advertising. At the end of that first month, for instance, editors admonished readers to "Avoid Using Patriotism as Sales Argument." Patriotism was "a sentiment so lofty that it is almost sacred, and any attempt to attach a dollars-and-cents significance to it is nothing short of desecration." Doing so was "neither good taste nor sound business."[101] However, by May, how advertising professionals might best display their citizenship began to take on a more positive, but still tempered, tone. An editorial suggested that, just as machinery replaced manpower in industry to increase productivity, "creative selling" through advertising could free up sales personnel for military service and speed up "distribution all around."[102]

Two months into mobilization, the annual convention of the Associated Advertising Clubs of the World (AACW) provided the occasion for boosters to throw off all reserve in their claims on behalf of advertising's positive impacts. To serve business now meant to serve the nation's capacity to wage war. President Woodrow Wilson had sent a message congratulating the AACW on its intentions "to assist in mobilizing the best thought and promoting greater activity in all lines of business in these times of stress and exigency." The business arena was essential, but it was not advertising practitioners' only arena: Wilson also asked that the convention "be employed to steady business and clear the air of doubts and misgivings in order to make the greatest unity of purpose in winning the great war for democracy and civilization." Convention speeches reflected leaders' ambitions for advertising to make its mark—to serve and thereby to grow in power and prestige.[103] Twenty years of an expanding presence and professionalization, of serving business by creating its modern, public profile, had prepared advertising's advocates to forge, in the heat of wartime fervor, a new, three-way link between the national interest, advertising's persuasive capabilities, and practitioners' confidence that they could, given the forum and the cause, expand those capabilities.

Senator Hiram W. Johnson opened the convention with the glowing phrases featured at the start of this chapter, but he also admonished that "great profits must not be made out of this war." Honest and militant advertising could facilitate both "service and sacrifice" to ensure "tranquility and security, and permanent prosperity." The AACW president, Herbert S. Houston, asserted that just as the press had "brought democracy to the world . . . advertising is bringing and will always bring democracy to business." It was "a sure and unfettered force that works for freedom." But to make grand claims required grand achievements and public confidence, so "the service [advertising] renders" required responding to businesses' challenge "as to the character and cost of its service" by reducing costs and assuring "Truth." Only by doing so could the field "serve business and universal democracy." Louis W. Hill, chair of the board of the Great Northern Railway, warned against the "commercial crapehanger" who was reluctant to promote business and therefore was "quite as definitely a non-patriot as the man who refuses to fight." Instead, advertisers and advertising agents had "a big opportunity today to demonstrate to the world what enlightened publicity can do to further a great cause—the cause of freedom and democracy." That way, "even war [can become] an engine of national growth, and of a new and greater national development."[104] In all this, the older advocacy's strains of promoting business and developing the economy were mixed with the new goals of saving the nation and bettering civilization.

The boldness of advertising's self-aggrandizing rhetoric leapt forward when some of its top practitioners moved into war-related activities. The British helped to inspire this mobilization of opinion makers: they had already learned by 1917 that "advertising plays a very important part, indeed, when war becomes . . . not merely the clash of armed forces, one against the other, but a conflict between whole peoples." As J. Murray Allison informed the AACW convention, advertising in Britain had helped to recruit soldiers, had "persuaded" women to labor in factories, and had "taught" the citizenry "to work harder and produce more, to give up their useless luxuries"; it also taught them "the sin of waste and the glory of sacrifice." Allison argued that when aggressive advertising did not accompany loan drives or other efforts, untutored patriotism alone did not suffice, and projects failed. The "days were too big for the old methods." America now had a similar "advertising opportunity." "We, the pupils, feel proud to have blazed this trail for you."[105] The United States had not, in fact, lost any time in setting up a centralized public-opinion agency. On April 14, less than two weeks after the declaration of war, President Wilson, by executive order, established the Committee on Public Information (CPI) to promote the nation's militancy.[106]

AACW leaders figured prominently in the CPI, including the association's 1917 and 1918 presidents, Houston, and D'Arcy. At the organization's next annual meeting, after an intense year of discussion about advertising's service and merits in both wartime and the coming peace, D'Arcy presented a manifesto on advertising's potency and legitimacy. The CPI and other institutions had filled the year with aggressive experimentation, with evocative appeals in the name of patriotism, as outlined in chapter 8, exceeding anything previously used in product advertising. The public had responded energetically, and as always, copywriters and artists claimed triumph, assuming that their messages alone had persuaded. In that context, D'Arcy spoke to the convention. Besides repeating calls, by now routine, for maintaining commercial activity in wartime and preparing for peace, D'Arcy told his listeners that they were "as truly in the nation's service as that other representative body in the crisis that confronts democracy"—namely, Congress.[107]

The year's successes in selling wartime passion had fueled D'Arcy's ardor and taken it well past the stature claimed for advertising even one year earlier. "Probably no great world force has grown so much as advertising in the past few years," its "vital power" touching all practical needs and reaching "beyond to community needs and the very purposes of a nation." He shot right past the traditional claims that advertising existed as business's tool by proclaiming that it "is the forethought and not the afterthought of business." The past year's accomplishments had brought advertising to "the portals of brighter vision and greater service," including leading "the reorganization of the commercial world." In order to do so, the field "must mold a new consciousness in business public opinion." In peacetime, "individually and collectively we must organize and prepare for bigger understanding and use of advertising's power."[108] As it turned out, D'Arcy correctly surmised that neither advertising nor its relationships to public opinion would be the same again.

# Conclusion
## Patrons, Agents, and the New Business of Progress

*You trace your ancestry back to the very beginning of the universe; your charter is contained in the first spoken words in the book of Genesis: "Let there be light," it was commanded.*

*Yours is the profession of enlightenment. A promoter of commerce? Yes. An instrument of distribution? Assuredly. But you think too meanly of advertising if you confine it to these terms. It is an agency of civilization.*

—Joseph French Johnson, quoted in *Poster 11*, 1920

At the time he spoke these glowing phrases to the Associated Advertising Clubs' annual convention, Joseph French Johnson was dean of the New York University School of Commerce and president of the Alexander Hamilton Institute.[1] Respected within both the academic and business communities, he urged stronger ties between them for their mutual benefit. Nonetheless, the plausibility of Johnson's assertion that his audience "had some special justification" for their "faith and pride" in their profession did not rest on his personal credentials. He had not invented these accolades, nor was it likely that his speech, "Advertising as an Economic Force," introduced them to his audience. To the contrary, by 1920, the notion that advertising professionals were the agents of progress was becoming a commonplace among the field's advocates, if not the general public.

Historian Roland Marchand analyzes the messages that advertising agents created as the self-appointed "apostles of modernity" during the two decades after Johnson's 1920 speech. The "ad creators of that era," he concludes, "proudly proclaimed themselves missionaries of modernity" because they believed that they guided and improved the nation's desires and consumption.[2] That sense of certainty had a long history, including twenty years of aggressively building and promoting themselves as the solution to manufacturers' concerns about inadequate consumer demand. (The option of distributing income and resources enough to ensure *effective* demand rather than just desire occurred to few until well into the next crash, the Great Depression, when buying power—not desire—fell disastrously below the capacity to produce.) So Johnson could confidently equate progress with consumption in 1920 when he declared that "the quality of a people's civilization depends entirely upon the quality of their wants" and that people whose wants do not increase are "making no progress." Advertising contributes to progress, according to this view, because it "gives birth to new wants and so creates an economic demand for more goods, thus tending to increase the demand for . . . labor"; large-scale production and low prices also depend on advertising. Hence, Johnson admonished his audience to "keep the faith . . . [and proclaim] the good gospel of advertising not merely as an economic force, but as the prophet of progress, and the moulder of public opinion, which is the strength of democracy and the hope of our civilization."[3] In contrast, anyone vaunting such claims for advertising's impact on civilization in 1890 would have been considered a visionary, and indeed, no one is known to have committed such ideas to public record. Even as Johnson spoke, of course, critics found advertising's impact as pervasive as did Johnson but not so positively progressive.

Back in the 1890s, many Americans had explored new definitions of progress in the context of the decade's rapid changes and threats to economic order and security. In the course of trying to redefine their worldviews, some found pessimism more realistic than optimism; others sought confidence in technological enthusiasms. Progressive reformers sought to ensure improvement by activism that addressed the ills rooted in economic and demographic changes. Among business owners and managers trying to figure out this environment and work it to their advantage, some felt optimistic, some pessimistic, generally according to the trajectories their individual circumstances took.[4] For leaders in the advertising field, the 1890s and early 1900s were a period of astounding growth that linked them with the firms coming to dominate the national marketplace. Their products—the advertisements they created—filled and supported the nation's most popular media as they built and spread their clients' public profiles. These were heady days, as the burgeoning profession spent vast quantities of other people's money while reaping ever larger incomes for its practitioners. Given all this, their optimism grew.

As advertising expanded its range and marketing successes after the turn of the century, criticisms of it also deepened. No longer did proper citizens simply reject advertising agents as mere drummers or as dangerous nostrum promoters. Instead, the very successes that gave the profession its rising profile prompted attacks on it as being either symptomatic of, or a cause of, national ills.[5] World War I both exacerbated advertising practitioners' unsettled conditions—giving rise, for example, to debates on whether advertising should be taxed—and provided opportunities for aggrandizement. Since their circumstances, both positive and negative, did not make for a "harmonious, self-enclosed, perfectly functioning 'system'" wherein "the reality of everyday life" could be "taken for granted," to use Peter L. Berger and Thomas Luckman's phrases, these specialists felt strong impulses to verify, or legitimate, themselves and their activities.[6] In this context, practitioners asserted that they provided essential services and guidance along a new and improved road of progress. Their rhetoric, as well as internal reform efforts such as the formation of trade associations, reveal the vigor with which they threw themselves into this competition for business and cultural authority. For instance, an internal exchange within N. W. Ayer & Son the year after Johnson's speech confirmed their self-promoting mission but belied statements to date about their success. A recommendation moved up the agency's ranks for a concerted campaign to influence "the bankers of this country" because they did "not advance funds for the carrying on of advertising campaigns." "If the bankers knew more about the value of advertising and what it will accomplish under proper direction," this "should not only help business generally, and consequently our clients, but should also not be lacking in reward for ourselves."[7] Legitimacy had a clear financial payoff.

By the 1910s, after exploring and experimenting with persuasion on behalf of their clients and arguing for advertising's impact as an educational as well as promotional conduit, some advertising practitioners began to think about advertising messages as an arena for promoting themselves. This coincided not only with the important public debates on advertising's standing in the polity, discussed earlier, but also with the growing recognition by many in business of the importance of public opinion and the resulting patronage by businesspeople of public relations.[8] The Truth-in-Advertising movement was very much a public-relations campaign. At the same time, moreover, some advertising practitioners realized that they might very well apply their own expertise to their public-opinion needs and "advertise advertising." A few, such as George French, even insisted that the field's needs had created "an opportunity for another kind of advertising expert—the man who can advertise advertising."[9] As a result, during the 1910s, as advertising's profile as a factor in popular culture expanded, so did its advocates' claims for its achievements and potentials. A

*Vital Need of the Times*, for instance, anticipated the end of World War I, when advertising would "take its place as a vital public force." It would offer "countless suggestions for better living" and would also "interpret business to the public." In doing so, advertising would "have a tremendous value in creating a greater destiny for the United States." In part, its author claimed, this was necessary because the importance of distribution would supersede that of production after the war, and unless advertising performed the "great National service" of "enhancing the public appreciation of business enterprise," "industrial chaos [would] inevitably follow." The importance of advertising's responsibility was such that "if there is any future for civilization, there is just that same future for advertising."[10] Of course, all this rhetoric belied that the advertising field is not inherently progressive. Practitioners have generally criticized the use of advanced communication technologies from which they had devised no means of profiting, most especially chromolithography and the radio.

In 1919, N. W. Ayer & Son launched two extensive campaigns in the popular press to raise confidence in advertisements generally and in the agency specifically. First, to promote the agency to businesses, a series of house advertisements argued for the importance of advertising to modern business, the superior character of the business leaders who understood its potency, and the Ayer agency's unique capacity to provide the best services. Ayer's house advertisements no longer merely offered the agency's services to improve clients' profits; now they offered greatly expanded services only to those "commercial institutions" with "worthy products," and whose leaders fit the advertisements' characterization of the progressive businessman. Each monthly advertisement focused on one such quality and attributed it both to the class of client Ayer wished to serve and to the agency itself. The featured qualities included "the creative genius of industrial pioneers," and the "courage of faith in their products, in their methods of production, and in the markets of the country to consume, which has made our industrial leaders fear nothing but stagnation." Such courage made for progress, as several of the messages pointed out, and one message focused entirely on the world's postwar desire for progress and the capacity of industry and advertising, together, to provide it. Only by "service to mankind" could business and advertising be "true to the spirit of Progress"; as a consequence, advertising professionals had to keep their "finger on the pulse of humanity and diagnose desire while it is in the very process of development." So the Ayer agency advertisement, entitled "Progress," paid tribute to technological achievements with an abstract melange of scenes that included skyscrapers, massive machinery, airplanes, and an enormous dirigible, but insisted that, for industrial and social progress to continue, advertising had to "diagnose desire" on behalf of business.[11] Advertising had become a privilege to be withheld from unworthy aspirants; without it, neither individual business success nor general progress were possible.

In the second campaign, to promote the profession to the public, the Ayer agency distributed a second series of ads to newspapers and magazines, to be placed anonymously for the purpose of educating consumers "to the value of reading advertising." Unlike the agency's nineteenth-century promotions, all these messages emphasized confidence in the field's importance to society as a whole as well as to individual clients. The consumer-directed advertisements in this anonymous, 1919 "Advertising Advertising" series challenged their audience to be progressive. The agency wrote to publishers to explain the campaign as the first "systematic advertising campaign conducted in a broad way . . . to increase the value of advertising." If publishers contributed the space, this campaign promised to "increase interest in advertising on the part of the consuming public" and also encourage businesses to advertise. Ayer predicted the "greatest advertising era" ever, and both advertising professionals and publishers would benefit if the consuming public could be influenced to "regard advertising as commercial news."[12] More than a thousand newspapers and forty-eight magazines participated in the campaign, and the Ayer agency later took credit for increasing their subsequent advertising receipts.[13]

The tone of Ayer's anonymous consumer advertisements was friendly, bright, and assured. In contrast to the confidential tone of the letters to publishers, these ads gave no hint that advertising still required any legitimation; to the contrary, advertising appeared as the source of legitimation. It contributed to the nation and the general state of things by supporting the press and helping to distribute manufactured goods. The ads also aimed directly at the readers' day-to-day experiences as consumers. The first began with a headline that advised readers: "You'll spend the money—Get the most out of it." Consumers could get "the latest ideas and improvements" by reading advertisements and be able to "live better and dress better at less cost." On the one hand, the advice came ostensibly as a service to consumers to help them save money, make wiser purchases, and take advantage of the bounty offered by the merchants and manufacturers "who work for you." On the other hand, the agency interwove this advice with injunctions to read and heed the advertisements in order to keep up with "the daily record of progress":

Don't Miss the Advertisements
Read them as an investment.
Read them because they save you money.
Read them because they introduce you to the newest styles—the latest comforts
   for the home—the best of the world's inventions.

Read them as a matter of education.
Read them to keep abreast of progress.
Read them—*regularly!*

At the end of the first year's series, Ayer informed readers, "the reason the world is so much more comfortable and convenient a place nowadays, is because advertising has made it possible for merchants and manufacturers to tell you what they have to offer, without waiting for the news to spread by word of mouth."[14] Consumers ignored this advice at their peril because advertisements were their best means of keeping up with the times. Readers' well-being, and that of their families, depended on well-informed consumption.

In both the trade advertisements and in the popular series, N. W. Ayer & Son attributed modern progress to efficient distribution, that is, marketing. This consumption-oriented worldview imposed new responsibilities on both businesses and consumers to participate in the world's progress as defined by advertising professionals, if, that is, they wished to be up to date. Whether or not citizens and consumers accepted these standards is another story.

## The Ironies of Service by Persuasion

Advertising agents prospered only as clients valued their services to generate consumer demand. As a consequence, practitioners increasingly described their activities and contributions in terms of service, sometimes even minimizing the roughness of the competition in which they and their clients engaged. Claude C. Hopkins, for instance, criticized the old ways of "selfishness" that had been "bred in the idea that business is a fight, that sales must be forced, that competition must be undersold."[15] Advertising agents increasingly couched their self-promotion and legitimation rhetoric in the language of beneficent assistance, as did the large department-store retailers who had concluded that service offerings could best differentiate between competitors, and the businesspersons' service clubs that flourished during this period as another indication of their turn to public service as a means of legitimation as well as camaraderie.[16] The Associated Advertising Clubs of the World, for instance, placed "We Serve" on its banner above "Truth."[17] This said, ironies abounded in ad specialists' claims of serving both clients and consumers. In both cases, the advertising practitioners' notions of service reflected their own interests: promoting the stature of consumption in the advancement of progress and asserting their control over advertisers and consumers both—through service to each.

As advertising specialists served their clients after 1890 by extending their sovereignty over advertising practices, they often met with resistance. Clients' reluctance to relinquish control over their firms' advertisements made the specialists feel that their rightful authority in marketing matters was continually challenged, and their literature took an aggressive stance against their own patrons. Because of the irony that advertisers were often served best by advertisements attractive to consumers instead of themselves, the advertising professionals' growing influence and assertiveness testified to the perceived effectiveness of the marketing campaigns they created and waged. Earnest Elmo Calkins, for instance, acknowledged that some few manufacturers might "achieve greatness" by exercising their own talents for advertising; he surmised that it was more likely, however, that successful manufacturers "have had success thrust upon them by some competent, experienced advertising man, who may be the advertising manager, but who is far more likely to be a man in an advertising agency who has both natural bent and much experience to guide him."[18] Specialists also expressed their disdain for the production process in the language with which they justified eliminating industrial imagery from advertisements and with which they insisted on their superiority in operating advertising programs. John Lee Mahin even attributed improvements in production to manufacturers' realizing "that the advertising has committed [them] to maintaining a certain standard with the public. . . . Better merchandise is the result."[19]

Whether advertisers made their own decisions regarding their advertising or worked with specialists, they were admonished early on by Nathaniel Fowler Jr. that before seeking to lay the blame elsewhere they should "investigate the fault" in themselves for advertising that failed to draw.[20] Years later, George French, like many other analysts, still complained about advertising's clients. French wrote:

> About half the labor of expert advertising creators is wasted in trying to convince their clients that they really know their business, and in arguing them out of their wrong positions. The labor is all wasted, and it impairs the good agent's power to be obliged to struggle with his customer in order that he may be allowed to serve his customer as well as he can. This condition does not prevail in any other profession. It should not prevail in advertising. A man who wishes to advertise should study the science of advertising, or resign himself into the hands of someone whom he has reason to believe does know his business, and is honest.[21]

In an article entitled "Service" and directed to his co-workers at N. W. Ayer & Son, William Armistead explained that the "business [of advertising] carries with it a tremendous responsibility." Agents who took on this responsibility would not "accept the judgment of a client" if they knew it to be "unsound."[22] As the J. Walter Thompson Company expressed the proper, new order of things, modern advertising services could be most helpful "to the Manufacturer who *knows how to co-operate loyally and whole-heartedly with his Advertising Agency*."[23] So far had professional confidence grown that *Printers' Ink* warned advertising managers against "the habit of looking upon themselves as superior to any suggestions from their confreres in the manufacturing line of their businesses."[24] Without the transition to bureaucratic, often corporate, business operations wherein specialized managers rather than owner-managers made advertising decisions, such arrogance in the name of service would certainly have obstructed agents' work with client firms.

When advertising specialists looked in the other direction, to the consumers of brand-name products, their ambivalent position motivated a second set of ironies. The most obvious—and this is one still hotly debated by advertising professionals and others—was whether consumer-interest advertising served consumers' interests or manipulated and exploited them in the service of agents' and advertisers' interests. Also, while agents prided themselves on their abilities to perceive consumer interests and needs, they observed their targets through their own experiences—biased and distanced by class and gender; moreover, they were writing, in effect, for another audience altogether—their peers. Still another irony developed as the advertising professional's position relative to consumers became somewhat analogous to that of the king's minister who bears great respect for royal powers but little respect for the person wielding them and who employs wile and artifice to operate as the power behind the throne. By the 1920s and 1930s, this position had fostered agents' disdain and elitism.[25]

This last irony operated whenever experts gave advice on how to persuade consumers upon whose decisions their clients' fortunes, and their own, rode. Through the 1890s, for instance, Nathaniel Fowler Jr. told advertising experts repeatedly that they were subject to the will of the consumer; but once he made that clear he explained how best to influence those very consumers.[26] Likewise, in 1897, Oscar Herzberg advised attending to the tastes of readers in an article first printed in *Profitable Advertising* and then reprinted in *Printers' Ink*. He began by reminding advertisers and their writers that advertising is "greatly effected by our national traits and idiosyncrasies"; therefore, even though the advertiser "may laugh in his sleeve at the narrow-mindedness or the childishness of his public . . . if he is wise, he will make his profit out of its foibles."[27] Even as Herbert Casson explained the importance of his methods of persuasion, he also warned: "High above all corporations, and even above all laws, stands the great REASONABLE force of Public Opinion. In the last analysis, the People are the Boss."[28]

Through the 1910s, "Mr. Ultimate Consumer" and "Mrs. Consumer" were increasingly accorded the prestige of the "connoisseur." According to "Wants Created by Advertising" in *Modern Business Talks*, a widely used series published by the Alexander Hamilton Institute, consumers were "important personage[s] before whom every advertiser willingly prostrates himself, and whose every wish is law" because they do "the choosing." At the same time, the consumers' choices were educated "through the advertising of the day—that great free correspondence school in merchandising" that taught consumers "values."[29] Another advertising manual informed advertisers that the "consumers dictate" based "solely on their familiarity with the merits of a particular article, made known to them by the advertising of the manufacturer and proved worthy by experience."[30] Perhaps the most remarkable expression of this irony came from John B. Watson, the pioneering behavioral psychologist hired by Stanley Resor at J. Walter Thompson Company in 1921. Watson began his career in advertising feeling "a distinct need" to understand the audiences for his advertisements. To accomplish this he studied first to learn "about the great advertising god, the consumer," and then how to manipulate that very deity, although with more impact on the rhetoric of the field than on its output, as it turned out.[31]

Even during the heyday of reason-why advertising, which assumed that people make purchasing decisions on a rational basis, few advocates credited consumers with possessing the capabilities to benefit fully from industrial productivity on their own; consumers needed instruction from and about advertisements to maximize their benefits from that productivity. Emily Fogg-Meade, a professor of economics at the University of Pennsylvania, defined advertising as "a mode of education by which the knowledge of consumable goods is increased." She declared that "progress in consumption" depended on consumers' being educated in the "varied and harmonious use of goods." Unfortunately, in 1901, "the majority are little guided by intelligence. Their powers of discrimination and adaptation are imperfectly developed." Women, moreover, who made most decisions regarding consumer goods, particularly needed such education since they "have had little to lift their minds above the low level of domestic tranquility. Their lives are narrow and monotonous, and their capacities are deadened by hard work or the routine exactions of society." Without such education, people remained the slaves of "simple and undiversified habits."[32] Granting that women were educable offered hope for lifting their lives through consumption, as guided by advertising.

Education constituted a major component of Progressive Era reforms, and advertising specialists and advocates asserted that advertisements educated consumers on coping with modernity; this included, in part, making the best uses of modernity's abundance. Fogg-Meade, for instance, believed that advertising benefited a culture until "all the consumers are educated or a better means of training them [is] substituted," because it was "a force working toward social improvement." Psychologist Henry Foster Adams asserted in 1916 that "the standards of cleanliness, of sanitation, of health, have been advanced generations before their time by the educational campaigns which have been carried on by the national advertisers."[33] Since neither of these analysts practiced advertising themselves, their assessments evinced that the field was having some success in establishing its new profile.

Magazines eager to attract advertising revenues took on the tasks of instructing readers on the advantages of attending to the advertisements in their pages: they explained products and their uses to the uninitiated. Because upscale magazines for the home had taken the lead in eliminating patent-medicine advertisements, they could now present themselves as apt media for modern, honest messages. In this context, *Good Housekeeping Magazine* in 1909 provided its readers with "A Course in Scientific Shopping" to explain how credible advertising could further their abilities to "get the most value for the money expended." The first of this series assured readers that because advertising "has had to live down the odium of a past created by the quacks and charlatans who were its early devotees," both advertisers and "reputable and far-sighted publishers" had worked to "fill [advertisements] instead with real information about the desirable things for health, comfort and pleasure." Moreover, consumers could believe that "the manufacturer could not afford to jeopardize his large business by putting into cold type, subject to deliberate analysis and refutation by the public and his competitors, statements about his products that are not true."[34] *Collier's* 1909 and 1910 series of about fifty articles, discussed in chapter 10, likewise directed readers' attention to the advertisements in its pages; they were lessons in the "University of Advertising." This "store of practical knowledge" and "news of the world" as told through trustworthy advertisements allegedly brought more practical "benefit" to consumers than to the advertisers themselves.[35] In their relationship with consumers, publishers were caught in the same ambivalences as the advertising agents.

Approaches to advertising messages that did not consider rational appeals to be adequate selling techniques also gained credence in the years before World War I. At the same time that Fogg-Meade insisted that advertising was educational and should have rational content, she also advised advertisers to "excite desire by appealing to imagination and emotion." She believed that "the successful advertisement is obtrusive" and is read "involuntarily, and unconsciously it makes an impression . . . as it creeps into the reader's inner consciousness."[36] Professor Walter Dill Scott and others joined the search in the first two decades of the century for the most effective means of influencing consumers, searching for the means to elicit responses through triggering either instincts or voluntary choices that would lead to purchases. Amid the ambivalence and even confusion about the rationality or irrationality of consumers that pervaded the literature, advertising professionals were quite insistent that, one way or another, they offered consumers their best lessons in getting on in the modern world.

As copywriters and others explored ways of appealing to consumers' rational and irrational minds, what satisfied those advocates who needed to justify their professional activities was keeping the wheels of industry rolling and raising the nation's level of civilization; at least, these rationales filled the literature whenever the question of legitimation surfaced. Activities during World War I overcame whatever reticence remained in the field's vanguard about promotional techniques. In the name of patriotism, advertising creators learned to appeal to and exacerbate audiences' concerns, raising the specter of personal and national disaster to make irrational fears appear to be rational needs. Even so, George Creel, the journalist at the head of the Committee on Public Information, insisted that the CPI's functions were rational and educational. Famed commercial artist Charles Dana Gibson, on the other hand, directed the artwork—and much of the spirit of the CPI's messages—in keeping with his fervent belief that wartime persuasions required intensely emotional and imaginative appeals. Facts and practical concerns would not suffice; death and destruction had to be made salient to generate the levels of zeal and commitment necessary for the nation to mobilize effectively.[37] In 1915, George French had presaged the uses of advertising for noncommercial—that is, propaganda—purposes by cautioning that its powers could lend themselves to influencing public attitudes, even undesirably. Yet, overall, French not only approved of this potential—used properly—but wrote frequently to guide others in using advertising as a "new alliance between business and the gentler and more consequential phases of life."[38] Wartime propaganda was hardly "gentler" than commercial advertising, but it certainly was "more consequential." Its perpetrators wrote as if they knew the consumer/citizens' best interests even more than when they promoted products. With a mandate that made selling products pale by comparison, the CPI's writers and artists pushed the vanguard of persuasion to engage audiences' emotions through mass communications as never before.

After copywriters learned the lessons of the wartime propaganda, exacerbating consumers' existing anxieties and generating new ones became the order of the decades to follow. The demands to participate in mobilization had left no room for individual deliberations—one was either a good citizen and followed instructions or not. Likewise, the postwar advertisements for Odorono (deodorant) and Listerine (mouthwash) left no room for individual discrimination: if even your best friend wouldn't tell you, and you could not discern your own failings, you had no choice but to consume the product in question. Follow instructions, or be suspect; consume, or confront guilt and inadequacy. It was for your own good; and it served the writers well.

## Consumption and Progress

Struggles between material and spiritual urges have engendered much soul-searching throughout American history. The impacts of unprecedented abundance and material gratification through industrialization have raised even more questions and have intensified these deliberations for a century and a half.[39] By 1900, writers on behalf of the advertising profession added their voices to the discussion, taking an unequivocal position that equated a civilization's progress to progress in its material accumulation. In this view, advertising served the greater good by both enhancing and directing wants. As a member of the Curtis Publishing Company's Advertising Department explained in 1914, "if we believe in a constantly advancing civilization—if we believe that people ought to keep on trying to live a little better and have a little more comfort and a little more ambition, then we must believe that whatever shows people the way and rouses their ambition to possess—and to *produce* in order to possess—is a public service. Advertising does that."[40] The advertising practitioners' self-appointed task, therefore, was to increase consumption, and they went about it fervently, invoking Progressive Era rhetoric about raising the commonwealth through education.

Proclaiming the link between advertising and cultural progress at a time when the production ethos still dominated mainstream values, at least those to which most people would admit, required repeated references to production as the fount of legitimation. As the strength of the production ethos changed from the early years of the advertising agency, so did the references to them. In 1849, when the first American advertising agent, Volney B. Palmer, touted his Systematic Advertising, the production ethos strongly prevailed. Accordingly, furthering progress entailed increasing productivity, and Palmer offered his improvements in advertising practices as a means of reducing the numbers of people "engaged in traffic," that is, marketing. This would liberate "a great proportion of the agents and servitors of Commerce, to be engaged thenceforth in

Productive Labor."[41] By the turn of the century, however, the productive capacities of industry and agriculture seemed to have overwhelmed the population's capacity to consume, barring a rarely suggested (in the mainstream and business presses) redistribution of resources that could raise the effective demand of those less affluent than the bourgeoisie.[42] Especially after the Crash of 1893, high productivity levels had appeared to justify the advertising agents' devaluation of industry and production. "It is easy enough to produce," some declared, "but marketing is a vastly different matter."[43]

Even after 1910, however, advertising agents often drew on the legitimacy that still accrued to industry by adopting its language, as well as its edifice motifs. For instance, "The Machinery of Advertising" was the title for a chapter on advertising techniques in a book the Curtis Publishing Company published in 1913 for manufacturers who advertised to consumers. Stanley Resor used this same expression a few years later to describe the J. Walter Thompson Company's assets and facilities; he aimed to distinguish the firm from "an insurance solicitor or a book agent." Resor, one of the dominant figures in the field after 1916, also described his agency at various times as a "factory of special work" that operated with efficiency, system, and a rational division of labor. Similarly, a J. Walter Thompson Company internal document eagerly presented *building* advertisements as a metaphor that had been suggested by a manufacturer touring agency facilities.[44] Similarly, many attributed successful advertising to "hard work" that went beyond creative "genius," as did Earnest Elmo Calkins, who harkened back to master inventor Thomas A. Edison's aphorism on "perspiration" as the true source of creativity. Calkins insisted that "a certain delight in his work" marked the good advertising professional, just as it did anyone who performed well in any business.[45] (The term *hard work* is still used to legitimate highly visible, nonproduction vocations in late-twentieth-century culture; for example, acting, modeling, and sports.) In the same vein, advocates of the ascendancy of consumption frequently argued for consumption's legitimacy as a form of labor. A 1902 article in *Mahin's Magazine,* the "Hum of the Factory," declared that the "consumer is also the worker" by keeping money in circulation "for the comfort of the nation's toilers."[46] Others, like the J. Walter Thompson agency, bragged that "Americans are producers and spenders" and that that is what made the nation prosper. Unlike European peasants and workers who were "picturesque, and that is all" because they were not buyers, all Americans made the effort to be alert to every opportunity to learn about and purchase innovative goods. This kept money in circulation and created lively markets.[47]

Despite their borrowing of rhetoric from industry, advertising writers were so removed from the producers' set of values after 1910 that they began to reverse the traditional path of legitimation and boast that advertising "instills a *pride of manufacture*" in the employees and owners of an industrial firm.[48] Likewise, in the thick of the fashion for assaults on industrial imagery, copywriters had to take care to avoid "falling into the mannerisms and thought of the inventor" or maker of a product. Instead, they were advised to "approach the machine" from the perspective of the consumer's "environment," to understand "his position, his joys, his ambition."[49] Similarly, Calkins advised advertising automobiles with style, not mechanics, at a time when that industry's advertisements still reflected the interests of automobile firms' owner-managers.[50]

Marketing and advertising specialists rarely attributed consumer demand to products' features or consumers' capabilities to recognize them. Moreover, their distance from the challenges that remained in production grew with their distance from the client firms' operations and technological achievements. Advertising professionals' interests instead lay in selling products and in promoting their nascent profession's profile. Their militancy in taking charge of this arena for cultural politics eliminated heroic innovators, dramatic factory scenes, and other conventions of the owner/entrepreneurial advertising styles from most consumer advertisements. Their chauvinism also fueled their increasingly proconsumption rhetoric. The manufacturing of soap, by this view, deserved less credit for a clean, civilized populace than did the marketing of soap, which raised standards and expectations for cleanliness; this spin contrasted, for example, with the B. T. Babbitt's Best Soap signs and trade cards that featured factories as providing the impetus for world cleanliness (see chapter 3). Progress required consumption, and consumption required advertising.[51] This self-promoting confused marketing's *necessary* function for a *sufficient* function.

According to this interpretation of the relationship between consumption, production, and progress, there was no cultural contradiction within capitalism like the one Daniel Bell raised in his deliberations over material abundance decades later. Advertising's advocates, unlike Bell, did not regret that the "cultural, if not moral, justification of capitalism has become hedonism, the idea of pleasure as a way of life." What for Bell was the "double bind of modernity"—that capitalism required its denizens to defer gratification in order to work and invest but then to consume with minimal restraint—provided the positive driving force of progress for them. Material progress offered a new ethic from which all the other virtues, including daintiness, good taste, health, and even faith, could derive. Rather than deplore that "men constantly redefine needs so that former wants become necessities,"[52] advertising's boosters rejoiced that this was possible.[53]

# Promoting Consumption: Producers and Their Agents

Long before turning over their public messages to advertising specialists, many manufacturers had undermined the public profile of the production ethos through their own messages to promote consumption. Using the lush colors and design capabilities of chromolithography, many among them had sent into the popular culture millions of images of fantasy and abundance: giant-sized pies, overflowing jars of fruit preserves, luxurious vegetation, voluptuous and exotic women, plump, euphoric children . . . to list only a few of the most frequent motifs. Printers, it must be remembered, like furniture makers and other nineteenth-century producers of decorative artifacts, developed and used their technologies to compete in a market that equated elaboration with good taste, abundance with progress. Their stock images—those for sale directly to consumers as well as those available in bulk to advertisers—depicted plenty in countless ways. Advertisers purchased and commissioned both stock and unique images to take credit for the industrial cornucopia, itself a frequent motif in their messages. Of course, even when fantasy and abundance flourished in the producers' advertisements, founders or owner-managers always dominated such scenes with their names, and often their portraits. They loudly insisted that theirs was the credit for inventing and producing the abundance they made available, sometimes including their factories or warehouses as well as harbingers of the consumer culture. Even when they showed no factory, they often linked abundance with their production. One Thurber & Co.'s trade card promoted its products with a scene of toddlers amid large jars of preserves and jellies, the copy on the reverse identifying progress with moving production from the home to the factory, where it could be done "more tidily, skilfully, and economically." Only wise, economical consumption remained for homemakers who wished such plenty for their families.

Although the producers' images of abundance may have worn away at the work ethos they otherwise espoused and often practiced, those images also reflected a belief that while the volume of human needs may change, their types would not. This stands in distinction to the twentieth-century marketers' belief in the infinite mutability of needs; such a notion had been growing since at least the mid-eighteenth century but remained at the margins through the nineteenth.[54] So the producers' images featured abundance as an end in itself—an attraction that needed no additional explanation or lure. Although some images of abundance certainly violated bourgeois proprieties, even these did not offer to transform consumers' lives but rather to seduce their attentions and imaginations, as with erotic images of voluptuous, luxuriant, and exotic women.[55] Numerous though such images were, they made up but a small portion of the total of advertisements from this period. Moreover, manufacturers' picture stories that argued for their products' benefits to real people rarely, if ever, promised fanciful abundance—unrealistically improved conditions, often, but not fantasy. More importantly, these promises of improvement almost never offered personal transformations, with the notable exceptions, of course, of those made on behalf of patent medicines and cosmetics, always a step beyond the rest. Instead the producers' narratives compared two clearly different sets of people: those with the good sense to purchase their products and those without it. The advertisements for Union Sewing Machine, Dobbins' Electric Soap (fig. 8.2), and Rising Sun Stove Polish (fig. 8.3) typified the messages that the better sort of people, already capable and attractive, demonstrated their superiority—and improved it—with their choices of goods. Other techniques bypassed comparisons but advertised as a word to the already wise, like the Hoosier Manufacturing Company, which offered its kitchen cabinet to the "Busy, Competent Women" whose active and varied lives justified relief from "drudgery."[56]

Advertising agents completed the process of selling consumption when they removed all traces of the producers' roles in creating the abundance, focusing instead on consumers' alleged benefits from it. At the same time, they also reacted against Victorian visual and verbal extravagance. The resulting images and copy were leaner and more argumentative, as suited modernist fashions all around.[57] Reasons why—and, later, the dangers of why not—made for intense messages that sold abundance less joyfully and more artfully than had the first generations of promoters. By the 1920s, high-profile advertisements abandoned older assumptions about people's immutable character and promised the transforming magic of consumption, as suited the new notions of pliant personality.[58]

In many ways and for many years before 1910, producers had allied themselves with marketers of various kinds in order to sell their wares. In doing so, manufacturers, along with other advertisers, had supported both advertising media and agents since the middle of the nineteenth century. In the first half-century of the alliance between advertising agents and manufacturers, the manufacturers clearly dominated the relationship. As patrons with many options, including media outside of the agents' purview, owner-mangers maintained control over their promotional messages. At the end of that century, however, with the move toward incorporation and all that that entailed for the manufacturers of national, brand-name consumer products, advertising agents successfully gained a level of influence over promotional images that bordered on control, even though owners and managers, now different people, still held the purse and the final, decision-making authority. Although producers still paid for their messages, and therefore the agents' incomes, most allowed themselves and their motifs to be purged from the messages in order to increase consumption. There is no question that at every step of this process, however, the advertisers who advanced it did so by choice. Some others resisted, like Ferdinand Schumacher, Henry Ford, and the competitors whom James Buchanan Duke drove into the American Tobacco Company. These traditionalists' sales and profits suffered, as it turned out, if they persisted after their industries passed into their corporate phase. Producers who wished to compete nationally with brand-name consumer goods increasingly placed their public images into the hands of those who trumpeted consumption.

Success at selling goods and, most important, success at capturing brand-name advertisers' patronage allowed advertising specialists to escalate their profession's claims and reverse their earlier sense of dependency. They prospered, collectively and individually, only as long as their patrons believed that they marketed effectively, but their increasingly aggressive advocacy of consumption—as guided by their lights—belied their deputy status. Placing their joint activities in the larger frame of raising consumption to preserve production allowed them to invert their sense of the client/agent power dynamic and thereby fueled the intensity of the antiproduction rhetoric. As a result, the advocates of the advertising profession did not just take on the mantle of progress, they aggressively appropriated it from industry. A. P. Johnson, advertising manager of the Chicago *Record-Herald,* expressed this appropriation in 1913 by observing: "It is the contention of others that modern invention, improved facilities of transportation, the telegraph and telephone have helped to raise advertising to its present importance in the business world." Then Johnson emphatically reversed the causal logic: "Advertising is not the result of progress. It has made progress. Advertising is not the result of modern invention, because it has been the channel through which all improvement, betterment and achievement have been fostered and popularized." As if this insight had been widely accepted, he asserted that advertising "occupies today a position equal in importance to that of any factor in modern civilization."[59] By the 1920s, advertising content routinely embodied the consequent view that consumer decisions, guided by advertising professionals, drove progress on the personal, societal, and economic levels.

Producers have provided the goods for the consumer culture, although they did not do so alone. Producers, with merchants, also directed the early phases of introducing and promoting goods into the marketplace. When industrialists first began advertising to consumers, they created their messages to compete for cultural authority as well as for market success, seeking to promote both themselves and their products as bearers of progress. Conditions for marketing brand-name consumer goods changed, however, by the end of the nineteenth century, at the same time that owners of those industries increasingly gave up day-by-day control over their firms. In their competition for market success, owners turned over the creation of their firms' advertising messages—and public profiles—to advertising specialists, who were engaged in their own competitions for business and cultural authority. The specialists' advertisements promoted consumers and consumption, not producers and production, while employing ever more powerful means of communicating to audiences. Successes at selling their clients' goods gave advertising specialists authority in business and also allowed them to lay claim to cultural authority by reaching for the mantle of progress as the stewards of consumer demand. Yet, advertising practitioners were, and remain, deputies who serve at the pleasure of their patrons. Their clients have sponsored advertising's role in the consumer culture at the expense of the production ethos, trading off cultural authority for financial success. In making these tradeoffs, American business transformed what it meant to advertise progress.

# Appendix:
# Distribution of Advertising Revenue,
# 1870–1890

A lack of sufficient evidence makes it difficult to determine who advertised in the nineteenth century and how much. The variety of media through which businesses advertised and the absence of records for them preclude accuracy, except, at most, for specific cities in limited time periods. Before 1880, only the roughest of estimates is possible. According to assessments from the 1870s, most advertisers were small enterprises with small advertising budgets, aside from the relatively few exceptions, primarily patent-medicine sellers and the growing but still limited ranks of nationally advertising manufacturers. According to the best possible calculations, retailers ranked with medicine sellers and entertainers as the major categories of advertisers around 1870, although they advertised only regionally. By the end of the nineteenth century, the major department stores were, individually, among the largest advertisers in the country.[1]

As part of his 1874 listing of patrons of advertising agencies, ranked by volume of ad placements in periodicals, George P. Rowell placed first "the patent medicine men." Then he itemized the following groups: those seeking agents, "which includes dealers in subscription books, sewing machines, patent rights, and the thousand and one articles which may be sold by hawkers or pedlers [sic]"; the only other substantial advertisers he listed were those offering investment possibilities, including bonds, lands, and businesses. Rowell estimated that only ten individual advertisers expended about $100,000 annually in the newspapers; "perhaps fifty or more" expended about $20,000; hundreds spent between $1,000 and $10,000; and ten thousand "send advertisements beyond their immediate neighborhood, rang[ing] from one dollar upward, according as hope, caprice, their desire to experiment, or their means of paying may dictate."[2] In Rowell's 1870 book *The Men Who Advertise*, publishers in a variety of fields accounted for twenty-two of the forty-eight successful examples cited. Most of these did not fit into any of Rowell's 1874 categories because they were generally newspaper publishers who advertised locally to boost their circulations and therefore functioned without the aid of advertising agents. Sixteen manufacturers, including four piano or organ artisans, made up the next largest group of *Men Who Advertise*; ten patent-medicine manufacturers and/or promoters made their field third; then seven merchants, one entertainer—P. T. Barnum—and five others of miscellaneous occupations completed the count.[3] (Few of the people Rowell wrote of followed a single profession rigorously: many patent-medicine purveyors, publishers, and manufacturers also operated stores or other businesses at some time, in addition to what I have surmised to be their primary activities.) None of these figures include spending on nonperiodical media through job printers, data that are wholly unavailable for this period on a national basis.

In his history of the N. W. Ayer & Son agency, Ralph Hower calculated the percentages of advertising volume placed by Ayer during various years according to categories of commodity groups. He found that Ayer's early clientele comprised dozens of small accounts, many of them so small that he could not trace the nature of their businesses. Hower's calculations for 1877 and 1878 roughly corroborate Rowell's assessments, taking into account that their categories and sources differed. Over these two years, 20.7 percent of Ayer's billings—that is, dollar volume spent by clients for advertising through the agency—came from "patent medicines and treatments." The second largest group, "books, tracts, etc." amounted to 10.7 percent, with "jewelry and silverware" next at 9.45 percent, followed by "dry goods and clothing" (7.45%), "greeting cards and chromos" (7.25%), then "seeds and nursery stock" (6.8%). Together, these various categories of manufactured goods, leaving aside the patent medicines and seeds and nursery stock, add up to 34.85 percent. The several remaining categories of manufactured goods yield another 21.1 percent of Ayer's billings for 1877 and 1878, totalling 55.95 percent manufactured goods, much more than the patent medicines taken alone. That leaves just under 25 percent for Ayer's many other clients, including "railroads and transportation" (0.75%) and "insurance and financial" (0.55%). Hower's tally does not discriminate between retailers and producers of manufactured goods. In both cases, however, the goods being advertised were, indeed, manufactured, and therefore indicate the level of advertising activity based on promoting those types of goods. Even most medicinals were industrially produced and used industrially produced packaging. Hower, because he could not trace the identities or products of all of Ayer's early clients, therefore calculated these early percentages using only the total amounts actually identified as his base. The figures cited here average the figures Hower gave for 1877 and 1878, the only years before 1900 for which he published calculations.[4] The overall impression from Rowell and Hower confirms the long-standing observation that patent-medicine sellers did indeed make up the primary single category of advertisers placing advertisements through agencies before 1890. Nonetheless, the manufactured goods promoted through the newspapers during this period, "the thousand and one articles" to which Rowell referred, add up to a substantial proportion of the whole.

# Abbreviations for Archival Sources

BLC

Bella Landauer Collection
New-York Historical Society
170 Central Park West
New York, N.Y. 10024

HM&L

Hagley Museum and Library
P.O. Box 3630
Wilmington, Del. 19807

JWTCA

J. Walter Thompson Company Archives
Manuscript Department
William R. Perkins Library
Duke University
Durham, N.C. 27706

MHC

Michigan Historical Collections
Bentley Historical Library
University of Michigan
Ann Arbor, Mich. 48109-2113

NWA

N. W. Ayer Archives
Ayer Corporate Communications
Worldwide Plaza
825 Eighth Avenue
New York, N.Y. 10019

*(Now housed at the Archives Center, National Museum
of American History, Smithsonian Institution,
Washington, D.C. 20560)*

WCBA                      Warshaw Collection of Business Americana
Archives Center
National Museum of American History
Smithsonian Institution
Washington, D.C. 20560

WRHS                      Western Reserve Historical Society
10825 East Boulevard
Cleveland, Ohio 44106

# Notes

## Introduction

1. Fred Danzig, editor, "Advertising and Progress," *Advertising Age* 39, no. 48 (1988): 1.
2. Susan Ingalls Lewis corrects the stereotypical notions about women's business inactivity in "Female Entrepreneurs in Albany, 1840–1885," *Business and Economic History* 21, 2d ser. (1992): 65–73.

## Chapter 1. Marketing Problems and Advertising Methods as America Industrialized

1. See the essay on sources for a brief review of histories of advertising.
2. Henry Sampson, *A History of Advertising from the Earliest Times* (London: Chatto and Windus, 1874; repub. Detroit: Gale Research, 1974), pp. 34–36, 44–48; Richardson Wright, *Hawkers and Walkers in Early America* (Philadelphia: J. B. Lippincott, 1927), pp. 22, 28, 30–41, 88–96, 178, 180; Robert Collison, *The Story of Street Literature: Forerunner of the Popular Press* (Santa Barbara, Calif.: ACB Clio, 1973), pp. 78–88; and Leslie Shepard, *The History of Street Literature* (Detroit: Singing Tree Press, 1973), pp. 81–106.
3. Like more recent authors on marketing, Melvin Thomas Copeland of the Harvard Business School included advertising as only one chapter of eight in his 1920 textbook *Marketing Problems* (New York: A. W. Shaw, 1920).
4. E. P. Harris, "Random Thoughts on Trade and Advertising," *Inland Printer* 8 (December 1890): 202–3.

5.    Gregory G. Brunk, "Coins Stamped With Advertising: A Forgotten Chapter in Nineteenth-Century Advertising History," *Journal of American Culture* 14, no. 1 (1991): 63–80.

6.    George Francis Dow, "Trade Cards," *Old-Time New England* 26 (April 1936): 114–35.

7.    Glenn Porter and Harold C. Livesay, *Merchants and Manufacturers: Studies in the Changing Structure of Nineteenth-Century Marketing* (Chicago: Ivan R. Dee, 1989; first published 1971), p. 2, n. 2; Neil McKendrick, John Brewer, and J. H. Plumb, *The Birth of a Consumer Society: The Commercialization of Eighteenth-Century England* (Bloomington: Indiana University Press, 1982); Richard L. Bushman, *The Refinement of America: Persons, Houses, Cities* (New York: Knopf, 1992).

8.    David M. Potter, *People of Plenty: Economic Abundance and the American Character* (Chicago: University of Chicago Press, 1954), esp. pp. 166–75. Johnson is quoted in Sampson, *History of Advertising*, p. 200.

9.    Alfred D. Chandler, *The Visible Hand: The Managerial Revolution in American Business* (Cambridge: Belknap, Harvard University Press, 1977), pp. 17–19; Porter and Livesay, *Merchants and Manufacturers*, pp. 5–6; Stuart M. Blumin, *The Emergence of the Middle Class: Social Experience in the American City, 1760–1900* (Cambridge: Cambridge University Press, 1989); and Charles Sellers, *The Market Revolution: Jacksonian America, 1815–1846* (New York: Oxford University Press, 1991).

10.   James Harvey Young, *The Toadstool Millionaires: A Social History of Patent Medicines in America before Federal Regulation* (Princeton: Princeton University Press, 1961), pp. 3–15.

11.   Potter, *People of Plenty*, p. 168; Young, *Toadstool Millionaires*, pp. 165–66.

12.   Young, *Toadstool Millionaires*, pp. 40–41, and passim.

13.   Sampson, *History of Advertising*, chs. 3 and 4; Young, *Toadstool Millionaires*, p. 42.

14.   Paul Starr, *The Social Transformation of American Medicine* (New York: Basic Books, 1982), pp. 127–34; Young, *Toadstool Millionaires*, esp. pp. 52–57, 137–59.

15.   *Massachusetts Spy*, Worcester, 10 October 1821. This and other advertisements will be reproduced as accurately as possible as to grammar, spelling, and typographic emphases of the originals.

16.   *New York Tribune* 25, 26 May 1865, pp. 3, 5.

17.   Daniel Pope, *The Making of Modern Advertising* (New York: Basic Books, 1983), pp. 45–46; Gerald J. Baldasty, *The Commercialization of News in the Nineteenth Century* (Madison: University of Wisconsin Press, 1992), p. 109.

18.   Stephen Fox, *The Mirror Makers: A History of American Advertising and Its Creators* (New York: William Morrow, 1984), pp. 14–16; Young, *Toadstool Millionaires*, p. vii and throughout.

19.   Chandler, *Visible Hand*, pp. 25–26, 207–23; Bill Reid Moeckel, *The Development of the Wholesaler in the United States, 1860–1900* (New York: Garland Press, 1986); Porter and Livesay, *Merchants and Manufacturers*, pp. 8–11; Timothy B.

Spears, *100 Years on the Road: The Traveling Salesman in American Culture* (New Haven: Yale University Press, 1995).

20. James M. Mayo, *The American Grocery Store: The Business Evolution of an Architectural Space* (Westport, Conn.: Greenwood Press, 1993).

21. *New York Tribune* 25, 26 May 1865, pp. 2, 3, 5, 8.

22. Susan Porter Benson, *Counter Cultures: Saleswomen, Managers, and Customers in American Department Stores, 1890–1940* (Urbana: University of Illinois Press, 1986), pp. 12–13; Chandler, *Visible Hand*, pp. 224–26; Robert Hendrickson, *The Grand Emporiums: The Illustrated History of America's Great Department Stores* (New York: Stein and Day, 1979), pp. 26–29.

23. See appendix regarding calculation of expenditures during this period.

24. By significant contrast, even though some food stores were parts of chains as early as the 1890s, the stores themselves remained relatively small neighborhood businesses until home refrigeration and the spread of automobiles made possible the supermarkets of the 1930s. Home refrigeration reduced the necessity for daily food shopping, and automobiles made it possible to carry home sufficient quantities for several days at a time. Richard S. Tedlow, *New and Improved: The Story of Mass Marketing in America* (New York: Basic Books, 1990), pp. 191–92, 226–45.

25. Chandler, *Visible Hand*, p. 27; Robert W. Twyman, *History of Marshall Field & Co., 1852–1906* (New York: Arno Press, 1976), pp. 97, 184.

26. Benson, *Counter Cultures*, p. 13; Chandler, *Visible Hand*, p. 227; Twyman, *Marshall Field & Co.*, pp. 4, 25–26, 127, 179.

27. *New York Tribune* 25, 26 May 1865, p. 5.

28. Chandler, *Visible Hand*, pp. 218, 225; Hendrickson, *Grand Emporiums*, pp. 35–38; Ralph M. Hower, *History of Macy's of New York, 1858–1919: Chapters in the Evolution of the Department Store* (Cambridge: Harvard University Press, 1946), pp. 90, 94; Norris, *Advertising*, p. 16; James Playsted Wood, *The Story of Advertising* (New York: Ronald Press, 1958), pp. 186–87.

29. Twyman, *Marshall Field & Co.*, pp. 6, 17, 18, 43, 108–9, 173–75.

30. George P. Rowell, *The Men Who Advertise: An Account of Successful Advertisers* (New York: Nelson Chesman, 1870), pp. 47–48; Chandler, *Visible Hand*, pp. 226, 228; Wood, *Story of Advertising*, pp. 184–86.

31. Hower, *Macy's*, pp. 54–65.

32. Chandler, *Visible Hand*, pp. 230–31; Boris Emmet and John E. Jeuck, *Catalogues and Counters: A History of Sears, Roebuck and Company* (Chicago: University of Chicago Press, 1950), pp. 19–22; Tedlow, *New and Improved*, pp. 259, 272–73.

33. Twyman, *Marshall Field & Co.*, p. 147.

34. Emmet and Jeuck, *Catalogues and Counters*, p. 20.

35. Rowell, *Men Who Advertise*, p. 48.

36. Frederick Dwight, "The Significance of Advertising," *Yale Review*, o.s. 18 (August 1909): 199.

37. Neil H. Borden, *The Economic Effects of Advertising* (Chicago: Richard D. Irwin, 1944), esp. pp. 27, 681–708, 870, 881.

38. McKendrick et al., *Consumer Society*, pp. 2, 9, 31–32, 53, 65–67, 69, 77, 97, 100, 131–32, 139.

39. Bushman, *Refining America*.

40. Chandler, *Visible Hand*, pp. 308–9; Moeckel, *Development of the Wholesaler*, pp. 5, 112–24; Porter and Livesay, *Merchants and Manufacturers*, pp. 2–12, 152, 154–58, 215–19.

41. Chandler, *Visible Hand*, p. 307; Rowell, *Men Who Advertise*, p. 10; Wood, *Story of Advertising*, p. 189.

42. Lawrence B. Romaine, *A Guide to American Trade Catalogs, 1744–1900* (New York: R. R. Bowker, 1960), p. 315.

43. *New York Tribune* 25, 26 May 1865, p. 2.

44. Rowell, *Men Who Advertise*, p. 133.

45. Ibid.

46. *New York Tribune* 25, 26 May 1865, p, 5.

47. The story of the long competition between Singer and Howe and, more particularly, Singer's success, is a long and often told one. For an analysis of the early Singer business and the transition to the manufacture of complex machines, David A. Hounshell, *From the American System to Mass Production, 1800–1932: The Development of Manufacturing Technology in the United States* (Baltimore: Johns Hopkins University Press, 1984), pp. 82–99, 105–7, 135–38.

48. WCBA, Sewing Machine Collection, box 3, folders 1–3.

49. Chandler, *Visible Hand*, pp. 302–4, 402–5; Hounshell, *American System*, pp. 84–85, 89; Porter and Livesay, *Merchants and Manufacturers*, pp. 194–95.

50. Hounshell, *American System*, pp. 5–6, 99, 136–37.

51. Chandler, *Visible Hand*, pp. 305–7, 406; Hounshell, *American System*, pp. 5–9, 154–62; William T. Hutchinson, *Cyrus Hall McCormick: Seed-Time, 1809–1856* (New York: Century, 1930), pp. 327–51; Cyrus McCormick, *The Century of the Reaper* (Boston: Houghton Mifflin, 1931), pp. 20, 43–44.

52. Hutchinson, *McCormick: Seed-Time*, pp. 327–51; William T. Hutchinson, *Cyrus Hall McCormick: Harvest, 1856–1884* (New York: Appleton-Century, 1935), pp. 76, 97, 490–92, 713; McCormick, *Century of the Reaper*, pp. 43–47, 99.

## Chapter 2. Owner-Manager Control of Advertising

1. For instance, in 1896 Henry King called advertising columns "a history of society." "A Treatise on Advertising," *Printers' Ink* 17, no. 9 (1896): 17–19; reprinted from *Once A Month*. See the essay on sources for recent examples.

2. Glenn Porter and Harold C. Livesay, *Merchants and Manufacturers: Studies in the Changing Structure of Nineteenth-Century Marketing* (Chicago: Ivan R. Dee, 1989; first published 1971), p. 127.

3. See the essay on sources regarding the importance of small businesses, then and now.

4. "The Men Who Succeed," editorial *Manufacturers' Gazette* 16 (5 April 1890).

5. Seymour Eaton, *One Hundred Lessons in Business* (Boston: Seymour Eaton, 1887), title page and Lesson One, n.p.

6. T. C. McLuhan, *Dream Tracks: The Railroad and the American Indian, 1890–1930* (New York: Harry N. Abrams, 1985). Editorial, *Printers' Ink* 12, no. 2 (1895): 4–5; "The Reason Why the Agency Is," H. B. Humphrey, *American Industries* 4, no. 9 (1905): 9; Nathaniel C. Fowler, "Advertising," in Howard P. Dunham, *Business of Insurance* 3 (New York: Ronald Press, 1912), esp. pp. 242–46.

7. Andrew Carnegie, *The Empire of Business* (New York: Doubleday, Page, 1902).

8. William Chazanof, *Welch's Grape Juice: From Cooperative to Corporation* (Syracuse: Syracuse University Press, 1977); Welch's 1922 statement is quoted in George Burton Hotchkiss and Richard B. Franken, *The Leadership of Advertised Brands: A Study of 100 Representative Commodities Showing the Names and Brands That are Most Familiar to the Public* (New York: Doubleday, Page, 1923), pp. 67–68.

9. "Notes of a Speech Made by Mr. Stanley Resor to New Members of the Company, May 4, 1931," p. 5, JWTCA; Hotchkiss and Franken, *Leadership*, pp. 100–102.

10. Otto Leisy, memo (Cleveland, 1910), WRHS Library, MSS 4143, container 1, folder 2.

11. Quoted in James Oliver Robertson, *American Myth, American Reality* (New York: Hill and Wang, 1980), pp. 174–75.

12. Peter C. Wensberg, *Land's Polaroid: A Company and the Man Who Invented It* (Boston: Houghton Mifflin, 1987), p. 5.

13. For example, "A Talk with a Successful Advertiser," *Profitable Advertising* 1, no. 8 (1892): 338; "Advertising Did It," ibid. 2, no. 3 (1892): 70–72; "Advertising 'The Columbia,'" ibid. 7, no. 8 (1897): 275–78; C. A. Bates, "Some of America's Advertisers," *Printers' Ink* 12, no. 1 (1895): 27–35; "Profitable Stories," ibid. 14, no. 6 (1896): 17–25, reprinted from the *San Francisco Call*.

14. George P. Rowell, *The Men Who Advertise: An Account of Successful Advertisers* (New York: Nelson Chesman, 1870), pp. 49–52; the Estey statement is from a catalog, circa 1875, quoted in Penrose Scull, *From Peddlers to Merchant Princes: A History of Selling in America* (Chicago: Follett Publishing, 1967), p. 55.

15. Maurice Rickards, *The Rise and Fall of the Poster* (New York: McGraw Hill, 1971), p. 21.

16. Richard W. Flint, "Printing, Advertising and Showmanship in 19th-Century America," *AB Bookman's Weekly* (May 4, 1987): 1949–61.

17. *Printers' Ink* 4, no. 16 (1891): 548.

18. Both quotations in James Playsted Wood, *Story of Advertising* (New York: Ronald Press, 1958), pp. 148, 157.

19. Neil Harris, *Humbug: The Art of P. T. Barnum* (Chicago: University of Chicago

Press, 1973), esp. pp. 51–54, 194, 247–48; John W. Merten, "Stone by Stone Along a Hundred Years with the House of Strobridge," *Bulletin of the Historical and Philosophical Society of Ohio* 8, no. 1 (1950): 15–18, 22; Manuel Rosenberg, "Billing 'The Greatest Show on Earth': Interview with Nelson Strobridge, President, The Strobridge Lithographing Company, Who Produced the Barnum & Bailey Circus Posters for More than Fifty Years," *Artist & Advertiser* (February 1931): 4–7, 25; Wood, *Story of Advertising*, pp. 148–57.

20. Harris, *Humbug*, pp. 3–5, 63–67, 73–75. James Harvey Young, *The Toadstool Millionaires: A Social History of Patent Medicines in America before Federal Regulation* (Princeton: Princeton University Press, 1961), esp. pp. 52–57, 137–59; Paul Starr, *The Social Transformation of American Medicine* (New York: Basic Books, 1982), pp. 127–34.

21. Quotations in Harris, *Humbug*, pp. 22, 53–54.

22. Henrietta M. Larson, *Jay Cooke, Private Banker* (Cambridge: Harvard University Press, 1936), pp. 18–20, 72–73, 106–7.

23. Larson, *Jay Cooke*, pp. 126–31, 168–73; James M. McPherson, *Battle Cry of Freedom: The Civil War Era* (New York: Oxford University Press, 1988), pp. 442–43; Ellis Paxson Oberholtzer, *Jay Cooke: Financier of the Civil War*, 2 vols. (Philadelphia: George W. Jacobs, 1907), l: 388–91, 577–78.

24. "How to Succeed in Business," *Advertiser's Gazette* 1 (May 1867): 1, WCBA, Advertising Collection, box 5.

25. For an example of such an industry, see Judith McGaw, *Most Wonderful Machine: Mechanization and Social Change in Berkshire Paper Making, 1801–1885* (Princeton: Princeton University Press, 1987), pp. 246–50, 256.

26. George P. Rowell, *The Men Who Advertise: An Account of Successful Advertisers* (New York: Nelson Chesman, 1870), pp. 31–32.

27. Young, *Toadstool Millionaires*, pp. 137–38

28. Newspaper clipping, publication unnamed, New York City (21 September 1875), scrapbook, Andrew Campbell Collection, HM&L, accession 1314, box 44; Young, *Toadstool Millionaires*, pp. 138–39.

29. Charles M. Cobb, Catalog for auction held 5–6 April 1991, Nashua, New Hampshire.

30. George Presbrey Rowell, *Forty Years an Advertising Agent, 1865–1905* (New York: Printers' Ink Publishing, 1906), pp. 14, 400–401, 450; "The House of Ayer and Its Modern Development," editorial, *Advertising Success* 2, no. 5 (1900): 11–15.

31. "In Printer's Ink the Secret," *New York Times*, 14 October 1894, p. 21.

32. A small sample of the many critiques of scenery advertising includes "Objectionable Methods," *New York Times*, 28 May 1877, p. 4, col. 6; "Ads on Rocks," *New York Times*, 22 May 1896, p. 11, col. 3; "Prevention of Cruelty to Landscapes," *Printers' Ink* 8, no. 10 (1898): 51; Young, "The Great Outdoors," *Toadstool Millionaires*, ch. 8, pp. 111–24. Gerald J. Baldasty, *The Commercialization of*

*News in the Nineteenth Century* (Madison: University of Wisconsin Press, 1992), pp. 109–10, on conflicts of interest between newspapers and their patrons.

33. The American Medical Association was one of the leaders in the fight against patent medicines; its reports on the contents and effects of these products can be found in *Nostrums and Quackery: Articles on the Nostrum Evil and Quackery Reprinted, with Additions and Modifications, from the Journal of the American Medical Association*, 2d edn. (Chicago: American Medical Association Press, 1912).

34. Boris Emmet and John E. Jeuck, *Catalogues and Counters: A History of Sears, Roebuck and Company* (Chicago: University of Chicago Press, 1950), pp. 26–30, 36–40, 42–45, 59–63; Richard S. Tedlow, *New and Improved: The Story of Mass Marketing in America* (New York: Basic Books, 1990), pp. 259, 263–65, 272–73.

35. Quoted in Tedlow, *New and Improved*, p. 272.

36. David A. Hounshell, *From the American System to Mass Production, 1800–1932: The Development of Manufacturing Technology in the United States* (Baltimore: Johns Hopkins University Press, 1984), pp. 160, 168–69, 173; William T. Hutchinson, *Cyrus Hall McCormick: Seed-Time, 1809–1856* (New York: Century, 1930), pp. 327–51; William T. Hutchinson, *Cyrus Hall McCormick: Harvest, 1856–1884* (New York: Appleton-Century, 1935), pp. 76, 76n, 97, 364–65, 490–91, 520–21, 627–37, 713; Cyrus McCormick, *Century of the Reaper* (Boston: Houghton Mifflin, 1931), pp. 33, 43–47, 231.

37. Hutchinson, *McCormick: Harvest, 1856–1884*, pp. 637, 712–13, 735. Hutchinson quotes McCormick Jr. from *Farmers' Advance* (April–May 1886).

38. George P. Rowell, "Who Are the Patrons of Advertising Agencies?" *Advertiser's Gazette* 8 (March 1874): 4. See appendix for more detail.

39. Stephen Fox, *The Mirror Makers: A History of American Advertising and Its Creators* (New York: William Morrow, 1984), pp. 32–34; Salme Harju Steinberg, *Reformer in the Marketplace: Edward W. Bok and the Ladies' Home Journal* (Baton Rouge: Louisiana State University Press, 1979), pp. 1–10; Wood, *Story of Advertising*, pp. 210–16.

40. Fox, *Mirror Makers*, pp. 32–34; Ralph M. Hower, *The History of an Advertising Agency: N. W. Ayer & Son at Work, 1869–1939* (Cambridge: Harvard University Press, 1939), pp. 111, 418–19; Wood, *Story of Advertising*, pp. 211–12.

41. Frank Presbrey, *The History and Development of Advertising* (Garden City, N.Y.: Doubleday, Doran, 1929), pp. 98, 100, 386, 394, 395–96; Wood, *Story of Advertising*, pp. 221–28.

42. Presbrey, *History and Development of Advertising*, p. 395; Wood, *Story of Advertising*, p. 225.

43. Quoted in Porter and Livesay, *Merchants and Manufacturers*, p. 223.

44. Matthew A. Shannon, *One Hundred Years of Premium Promotions, 1851–1951* (New York: Premium Advertising Association, 1951), pp. 2–3; Felix Shay, *Elbert Hubbard of East Aurora* (New York: William H. Wise, 1926), pp. 27–28; Wood, *Story of Advertising*, pp. 234–35.

45. Elbert Hubbard, *Advertising and Advertisements* (East Aurora, N. Y.: Roycrofters, 1929), pp. 7–19 and passim; Shay, *Elbert Hubbard*, 29–30.

## Chapter 3. Printers, Advertisers, and Their Products

1. Charles Francis, *Printing For Profit* (New York: Bobbs-Merrill and Charles Francis Press, 1917), pp. 7–8, 10. For other printers' assessments of their contributions to civilization, see William H. Bushnell, "The Status of the Printer," *Inland Printer* 3 (July 1886): 607–9; editorial, "The Printer of the Future," ibid., 45 (July 1910): 538; S. H. Horgan, "The Future of Photoengraving," ibid., 45 (July 1910): 587–88.

2. Editorial, "Have We Reached the End?" *Inland Printer* 3 (September 1886): 748–49.

3. Hazel Dicken-Garcia, *Journalistic Standards in Nineteenth-Century America* (Madison: University of Wisconsin Press, 1989), pp. 36–39, 88–89.

4. Ibid., pp. 86–88, 89–92, 202.

5. Ibid., pp. 65, 89–90, 229–30.

6. Stephen Hess and Milton Kaplan, *The Ungentlemanly Art: A History of American Political Cartoons* (New York: Macmillan, 1968), pp. 62–65; Charles Press, *The Political Cartoon* (East Brunswick, N.J.: Associated University Presses, 1981), pp. 36–48, 208, 212–18.

7. William Murrell, *A History of American Graphic Humor,* 2 vols. (New York: Whitney Museum of American Art, 1933), 1: 171.

8. Ibid., 1: 155, 183, 229; ibid., 2: 2, 33, 36, 70; Richard Samuel West, *Satire on Stone: The Political Cartoons of Joseph Keppler* (Urbana: University of Illinois Press, 1988), pp. 5, 9, 108–11, 215, 257, 258, 313.

9. Albert Bigelow Paine, *Th. Nast: His Period and His Pictures* (Princeton, N.J.: Pyne Press, 1974; first published 1904), pp. 3, 84, 94, 96, 109, 111, 112, 527, 531.

10. Hess and Kaplan, *Ungentlemanly Art*, pp. 43, 122, 136; Murrell, *American Graphic Humor*, 2: 31, 103. Also, F. Penn, "Newspaper Illustrators—Charles Nelan," *Inland Printer* 13 (July 1894): 344–46; Sheridan Ford, "Illustrated Daily Journalism," ibid.: 346–47; "Brownies" by Palmer Cox in ad for Buffalo Printing Ink Works, ibid.: 385.

11. This phrase comes from the 1933 President's Research Committee on Recent Social Trends, quoted in Daniel J. Czitrom, *Media and the American Mind from Morse to McLuhan* (Chapel Hill: University of North Carolina Press, 1982), p. 126. See the essay on sources for histories and analyses of lithography and its cultural roles.

12. Diana Korzenik, *Drawn to Art: A Nineteenth-Century American Dream* (Hanover, N.H.: University Press of New England, 1985), pp. 1–2, 83, 137–40, 153–60, 202–3, 226–27, 242, and passim. George Ward Nichols, *Art Education Applied to Industry* (New York: Harper & Brothers, 1877), pp. 9, 21; editorial, "The Engraver's and Printer's Art in America," *Inland Printer* 8 (March 1891):

509. Katharine Morrison McClinton, *The Chromolithographs of Louis Prang* (New York: Clarkson N. Potter, 1973), pp. 119–36; Peter C. Marzio, "The Democratic Art of Chromolithography in America: An Overview," in *Art & Commerce: American Prints of the Nineteenth Century*, Museum of Fine Arts, Boston (Charlottesville: University Press of Virginia, 1975), pp. 89–90, 98.

13. Korzenik, *Drawn to Art*, pp. 215, 225; Clarence P. Hornung and Fridolf Johnson, *200 Years of American Graphic Art* (New York: Braziller, 1976), pp. 76–77; West, *Satire on Stone*, pp. 1–3, 393–95; John W. Merten, "Stone by Stone Along a Hundred Years with the House of Strobridge," *Bulletin of the Historical and Philosophical Society of Ohio* 8, no. 1 (1950): 1–48, quotations p. 28.

14. Quotations from Peter C. Marzio, *The Democratic Art: Chromolithography 1840–1900, Pictures for a 19th-Century America* (Boston: David R. Godine, 1979), pp. 1, 47, 211; Saul E. Zalesch, "What the Four Million Bought: Cheap Oil Paintings of the 1880s," *American Quarterly* 48, no. 1 (1996): 77–109.

15. Sally Pierce and Catharina Slautterback, *Boston Lithography, 1825–1880* (Boston: Boston Athenaeum, 1991), pp. 13–14; Larry Freeman, *Louis Prang: Color Lithographer, Giant of a Man* (Watkins Glen, N.Y.: Century House, 1971), pp. 82–86; Korzenik, *Drawn to Art*, pp. 161–63; Marzio, *Democratic Art*, pp. 105–6; McClinton, *Chromolithographs of Louis Prang*, pp. 21–22.

16. James Parton to L. Prang & Co. (29 December 1866), in *Prang's Chromo: A Journal of Popular Art* 1, no. 1 (1868): 1, reproduced in McClinton, *Chromolithographs of Louis Prang*, p. 12.

17. Contemporary quotations from Marzio, "Democratic Art," pp. 98–99. Russell Lynes, *The TasteMakers* (New York: Harper & Brothers, 1949), pp. 66–70, 79–80.

18. Nichols, *Art Education*, p. 44.

19. L. Wells, "Commercial Art," *Inland Printer* 15 (May 1895): 181.

20. Jacob A. Riis, *How the Other Half Lives: Studies Among the Tenements of New York* (New York: Dover, 1971, first published 1890), pp. 16, 96, 123, 198, 217.

21. James Parton to L. Prang & Co. (29 December 1866), in *Prang's Chromo: A Journal of Popular Art* 1, no. 1 (1868): 1, reproduced in McClinton, *Chromolithographs of Louis Prang*, p. 12.

22. For example, "Bookless Homes," reprinted from *United States Paper-Maker* in *Inland Printer* 3 (August 1886): 701; editorial, "Progressive Journalism," ibid. 8 (January 1891): 314; A. W. Engarde, "Artistic Advertising," ibid. 11 (August 1893): 388; C. F. Thwing, "The New Century Influences," reprinted from *Leslie's Weekly*, ibid. 25 (May 1900): 250. Dicken-Garcia, *Journalistic Standards*, pp. 29–62, 278.

23. S. N. Dickinson advertisement, 1845; *Saturday Evening Post* advertisement, 1849; courtesy Jack Golden. Hatch calendar information courtesy Don J. Lurito.

24. McClinton, *Chromolithographs of Louis Prang*, pp. 120–26.

25. Advertisement for Chicago Pneumatic Tools, *Inland Printer* 26 (January 1901): 677.

26. Francis, *Printing for Profit*, pp. 7–8, 10; T. D. Parker to editors, "On the Internal Economy of Printing Offices," *Inland Printer* 4 (August 1887): 758–59; advertisement for C. B. Cottrell & Sons, ibid. 8 (June 1891): 823. Also, Alton B. Carty, "The Progressive Printer," ibid. 8 (April 1891): 593–94; Henry Lewis Johnson, "How Engravers and Printers Advertise," ibid. 13 (August 1894): 433–34; Charles H. Cochrane, "One Hundred Years of Progress in Printing," ibid. 26 (January 1901): 604–8; editorial, "The Progress of Printing," *Inland Printer* 3 (February 1886): 269–70; Gustav Boehm, "The Liberty of the Press," pt. 2, ibid. 3 (September 1886): 729–30; editorial, "The Engraver's and Printer's Art in America," ibid. 8 (March 1891): 509; William Bushnell, "'Dull Times,'" ibid. 8 (September 1891): 1042–43; "An Old-Time Printer," "We Want More Labor-Saving Devices and Material," ibid., p. 1043.

27. Francis, *Printing for Profit*, p. 219; Pierce and Slautterback, *Boston Lithography*, pp. 15–16.

28. "Concerning Printing-Inks," *Inland Printer* 3 (October 1885): 1–5; "The Type-foundries of the United States, No. III—The Central Typefoundry, St. Louis," ibid., 8 (April 1891): 638. Also, Roderic C. Penfield, *"The Ladies' Home Journal,"* in *Inland Printer* 11 (April 1893): 49–50.

29. Robert Jay, *The Trade Card in Nineteenth-Century America* (Columbia, University of Missouri Press, 1987), pp. 36, 38; Marzio, *Democratic Art*, pp. 99, 149, 198.

30. Catalog of Thomas Sinclair & Son (Philadelphia, 1885), Catalog Collection, HM&L. The firm was listed as Thomas Sinclair and Co. in Philadelphia at least as early as 1854. Marzio, *Democratic Art*, p. 15.

31. McClinton, *Chromolithographs of Louis Prang*, pp. 5–21, 27, 29, and passim.

32. "High Art on Card-Board," *New York Times*, 3 December 1882, p. 4. Jay, *Trade Card*, pp. 36–39; Marzio, *Democratic Art*, esp. pp. 6, 176, 191–96; McClinton, *Chromolithographs of Louis Prang*, pp. 37, 104; David Tatham, "John Henry Bufford: American Lithographer," *Proceedings of the American Antiquarian Society* 86 (April 1976): 52–53, 66–67.

33. Elizabeth Harris, *The Boy and His Press*, catalog for exhibition of same name, National Museum of American History (Washington, D.C.: Smithsonian Institution, 1992).

34. A. H. M., "Division of Responsibility," *Inland Printer* 7 (April 1890): 588. The journal's standing in the profession had the sanction of major trade organizations; for example, ibid. 7 (October 1889): 21.

35. Francis, *Printing For Profit*, p. 164.

36. Ibid.

37. "A Printer," "Advertising for Printers," *Inland Printer* 24 (March 1900): 878–79. Also, H. A. Blodget, "The Printing Office Salesman," *Inland Printer* 11 (July 1893): 303–4; Paul Nathan, *How to Make Money in the Printing Business* (New York: Lotus Press, 1900), pp. 71–78. An unfortunate consequence of this practice from the historians' perspective is the dearth of historical records about specific negotiations.

38. "Some Printing Offices of Cleveland, Ohio," *Inland Printer* 15 (June 1895): 294.

39. Gustavus Boehm, "The Nervus Rerum of Mercantile Success: A Chapter on Advertising," *Inland Printer* 3 (May 1886): 455–57.

40. Nathan, *Printing Business*, pp. 36, 39.

41. A Printer, "Advertising for Printers," *Inland Printer* 24 (January 1900): 603–4.

42. Nathan, *Printing Business*, p. 36. Also, editorial, "A Plea for the Printer and for the Man Who Pays," *Inland Printer* 25 (April 1900): 41–42; Francis, *Printing for Profit*, p. 9; Luna Lambert Levinson, "Images That Sell: Color Advertising and Boston Printmakers, 1850–1900," in *Aspects of American Print Making, 1800–1950*, ed. James F. O'Gorman (Syracuse: Syracuse University Press, 1988), pp. 9–11; Marzio, *Democratic Art*, p. 5.

43. A Printer, "Advertising for Printers," *Inland Printer* 24 (March 1900): 878–79; "An Organized Campaign for Publicity," editorial, *Inland Printer* 35 (September 1905): 844–86; editorial, "Street Car Advertising," *Printer and Bookmaker* 25, no. 5 (1898): 280–81.

44. O. F. Byxbee, "Newspaper Advertising *vs.* Schemes," *Inland Printer* 20 (October 1897): 161–62; editorial, "Unproductive Advertising," ibid., p. 169; editorial, "A Short-sighted Policy," ibid. 3 (October 1885): 23.

45. This dynamic played out again when large general-circulation magazines suffered revenue losses because broadcasting captured much of the general market advertising, first with radio in the 1920s and then television in the 1960s. Cable and satellite television currently challenge the networks' and local stations' revenues for the same reasons.

46. Gerald J. Baldasty, *The Commercialization of News in the Nineteenth Century* (Madison: University of Wisconsin Press, 1992), esp. pp. 59–60; Dicken-Garcia, *Journalistic Standards*, pp. 29–62; Jeffrey Rutenbeck, "Toward a History of the Ideologies of Partisanship and Independence in American Journalism," *Journal of Communication Inquiry* 15, no. 2 (1991): 126–39.

47. Quoted in James Playsted Wood, *The Story of Advertising* (New York: Ronald Press, 1958), p. 213. Also, Salme Harju Steinberg, *Reformer in the Marketplace: Edward W. Bok and the Ladies' Home Journal* (Baton Rouge: Louisiana State University Press, 1979).

48. Horace Greeley, *The Great Industries of the United States* (Hartford: J. B. Burr, Hyde, 1873), pp. 67–68.

49. "To Have and To Hold," *Inland Printer* 26 (December 1900): 432. Reprinted from *Newspaper Maker*.

50. Baldasty, *The Commercialization of News*, pp. 16–23, 59; Dicken-Garcia, *Journalistic Standards*, pp. 39–40, 43, 56–58, 61–62, 281.

51. Sarah Stage, *Female Complaints: Lydia Pinkham and the Business of Women's Medicine* (New York: Norton, 1979), p. 92.

52. Edwin Emery, *The Press and America: An Interpretative History of Journalism* (Englewood Cliffs, N.J.: Prentice-Hall, 1962), pp. 172–73, 209–18, 257–59, 311; Hornung and Johnson, *American Graphic Art*, pp. 47–51.

53. Emery, *Press*, pp. 403–5, 407; Frank Presbrey, *The History and Development of Advertising* (Garden City, N.Y.: Doubleday, Doran, 1929), pp. 236–40.

54. Ralph M. Hower, *The History of an Advertising Agency: N. W. Ayer & Son at Work, 1869–1939* (Cambridge: Harvard University Press, 1939), p. 20; and Daniel Pope, *The Making of Modern Advertising* (New York: Basic Books, 1983), p. 117.

55. *Commercial and Financial Chronicle* 6 (January-June 1868): passim; Presbrey, *History and Development of Advertising*, p. 389; obituary for James Pyle, *American Grocer* 63, no. 4 (1900): 10.

56. West, *Satire on Stone*, pp. 108–11.

57. Emery, *Press*, pp. 403–5, 407. Hornung and Johnson, *American Graphic Art*, p. 75; Presbrey, *History and Development of Advertising*, pp. 236–40.

58. Francis Procter, "Discounts to Advertising Agents—To Whom Should They Be Given, and How Much," *Inland Printer* 7 (October 1889): 21; W. H. H., "A Word About Outside Advertisers," *Inland Printer* 7 (December 1889): 250; E[merson]. P. Harris, "The Basis of Advertising Rates," *Inland Printer* 7 (April 1890): 588; idem, "Needed Reform in Advertising Rates," *Inland Printer* 11 (May 1893): 127–29.

59. Frank Luther Mott, *A History of American Magazines*, vol. 3, 1865–1885 (Cambridge: Belknap, Harvard University Press, 1957), pp. 9–12; Wood, *Story of Advertising*, pp. 193–98; James Playsted Wood, *Magazines in the United States: Their Social and Economic Influence* (New York: Ronald Press, 1949), pp. 84–89.

60. Mott, *American Magazines, 1865–1885*, p. 5.

61. Ibid., pp. 37–39; Boris Emmet and John E. Jeuck, *Catalogues and Counters: A History of Sears, Roebuck and Company* (Chicago: University of Chicago Press, 1950), p. 19.

62. Wayne E. Fuller, *The American Mail: Enlarger of the Common Life* (Chicago: University of Chicago Press, 1972), pp. 123, 125, 127, 132–33; Emery, *Press*, p. 345.

63. Ellen Gruber Garvey, *The Adman in the Parlor: Magazines and the Gendering of Consumer Culture, 1880s to 1910s* (New York, Oxford: Oxford University Press, 1996), ch. 1, pp. 16–50; Pat Gilmour, ed., *Lasting Impressions: Lithography as Art* (London: Alexandria Press, 1988), p. 28; Hornung and Johnson, *American Graphic Art*, passim; Jay, *Trade Card*, p. 3; Marzio, *Democratic Art*, pp. 191–92.

64. *Puck* and *Frank Leslie's Illustrated Newspaper* were exceptions to this rule as both of these popular journals featured lithographed illustrations by the 1870s.

65. Tommy Dodd, letter to editors, *New York Times*, 6 May 1875, p. 6, col. 7; Samuel Hall, New York, advertisement, *Inland Printer* 7 (January 1890): 313. Also untitled, uncredited article in *New York Times*, 19 March 1879, p. 4, col. 6.

66. Jay, *Trade Card*, pp. 29–32; Nina de Angeli Walls, *Trade Catalogs in the Hagley Museum and Library* (Wilmington, Del.: Hagley Museum and Library, 1987).

67. Quoted in Marzio, *Democratic Art*, p. 99.

68. I. L. Cragin & Co., "Confidential to Retailers," *Merchants' Review* 3 (29 April 1881): 625.

69. William T. Hutchinson, *Cyrus Hall McCormick: Harvest, 1856–1884* (New York: Appleton-Century, 1935), pp. 712–13.

70. Catalog of Thomas Sinclair & Son (Philadelphia, 1885), Catalog Collection, HM&L.

71. WCBA, Sewing Machine Collection, box 2, folders 7–19.

72. I. L. Cragin & Co., "Confidential to Retailers," *Merchants' Review* 3 (29 April 1881): 625.

73. The Jno. B. Jeffery Printing Co., Chicago, to the secretary of the Northern Indiana and Southern Michigan Agricultural Society, South Bend, Indiana, April 30, 188[?]. WCBA, Printers and Printing Collection, box 4.

74. Catalog of Thomas Sinclair & Son (Philadelphia, 1885), Catalog Collection, HM&L.

75. This figure represents the best judgment of current authorities. Interview with Dave Cheadle, of the Trade Card Collectors' Association, Denver, Colo., 22 January 1996.

76. Merten, "Stone by Stone."

77. For example, the promotions in *Catalogue of Signs for Advertising,* Robert Hartmann (New York, 1901), p. 1, WCBA, Advertising Collection, box 7.

78. T. P. Archibald of the University Press, Cambridge, Mass., to R. M. Colt, General Passenger Agent, Fonda, Johnstown & Gloversville Railway, Gloversville, New York, 29 December 1908. WCBA, Printers and Printing Collection, box 4.

79. William Jillson, treasurer, Duck Co., Willimantic, Connecticut, to James Hamersley, Printer, 17 July 1863. WCBA, Printers and Printing Collection, box 4.

80. G. J. Cooke, president, Metropolitan Printing Co., New York City, to R. M. Colt, General Passenger Agent, Fonda, Johnstown & Gloversville Railway, Gloversville, New York, 4 April 1909. WCBA, Printers and Printing Collection, box 6.

81. Arthur M. Allen of the A. M. Allen Press, Troy, New York, to R. M. Colt, General Passenger Agent, Fonda, Johnstown & Gloversville Railway, Gloversville, New York, 7 July 1910. WCBA, Printers and Printing Collection, box 6.

82. Henry F. Gilq, secretary, D. Lutz & Son Brewing Co., Allegheny, Pennsylvania, to Theodore Leonhardt & Son, Philadelphia, 21 November 1898. HM&L, Leonhardt Lithographer Collection, accession 1020, 1021.

83. Alfred Edgell of the Edgell Co., Philadelphia, to R. M. Colt, General Passenger Agent, Fonda, Johnstown & Gloversville Railway, Gloversville, New York, 7 July 1910. WCBA, Printers and Printing Collection, box 12.

84. Theo. L. DeVinne, "Typography in Advertisements," *Inland Printer* 8 (April 1891): 657; S. K. Parker, "'Taste' in Jobwork," ibid. 8 (August 1891): 959; Arthur K. Taylor, "The Reason for the Remarkable Number of Millionaire Printers," ibid. 17 (September 1896): 523–624. Also, "Give Your Customers a Press Proof," ibid. 3 (February 1886): 273, reprinted from *Pacific Printer;* editorial, "A Plea for the Printer and for the Man Who Pays," ibid. 25 (April 1900): 41–42.

85. "Division of Responsibility," *Inland Printer* 7 (April 1890): 588.

86. Sinclair H. Hitchings, "Fine Art Lithography in Boston: Craftsmanship in Color, 1840–1900," in *Art & Commerce*, pp. 117–19; Marzio, *Democratic Art*, pp. 170–71.

87. The two signs by Prang are described in Levinson, "Images That Sell," pp. 95, 98. The two Donaldson Brothers' signs are in the WCBA, Advertising Collection, oversize portfolio drawers.

88. *Railroad Advocate* (8 November 1856) quoted in John H. White Jr., "Locomotives on Stone," *Smithsonian Journal of History* 1 (1966): 49–50.

89. The Delaware & Lackawanna Co. chose not to distribute *The Lackawanna Valley* as a chromolithograph, but they did use two versions of the *Delaware Water Gap* as promotional prints. Nicolai Cikovsky Jr., "George Inness's *The Lackawanna Valley:* `Type of the Modern,'" in Susan Danly and Leo Marx, eds., *The Railroad in American Art: Representations of Technological Change* (Cambridge: MIT Press, 1988), pp. 71–91.

90. T. C. McLuhan, *Dream Tracks: The Railroad and the American Indian, 1890–1930* (New York: Harry N. Abrams, 1985).

91. Charles W. McCurdy, "American Law and the Marketing Structure of the Large Corporation, 1875–1890," *Journal of Economic History* 38 (September 1978): 631–49.

92. Hutchinson, *McCormick: Harvest, 1856–1884,* pp. 491, 712–13.

93. Linus Pierpont Brockett, *The Commercial Traveler's Guide Book* (New York: H. Dayton, 1871), cited in Levinson, "Images That Sell," p. 84.

94. Bill Reid Moeckel, *The Development of the Wholesaler in the United States, 1860–1900* (New York: Garland Press, 1986), pp. 117–29; Glenn Porter and Harold C. Livesay, *Merchants and Manufacturers: Studies in the Changing Structure of Nineteenth-Century Marketing* (Chicago: Ivan R. Dee, 1989; first published 1971), pp. 141–46, 192, 194–95, 208; Timothy B. Spears, "'All Things to All Men': The Commercial Traveler and the Rise of Modern Salesmanship," *American Quarterly* 45, no. 4 (1993): 524–57; Spears, *100 Years on the Road: The Traveling Salesman in American Culture* (New Haven: Yale University Press, 1995); and Olivier Zunz, *Making America Corporate, 1870–1920* (Chicago: University of Chicago Press, 1990), pp. 176–77, 184–85.

95. Driscol, Church & Hall, wholesaler's warehouse photograph taken in Boston, Providence area, circa 1885. Glass negative collection of Frame Central, Boston.

96. Marshall Bros, circular, circa 1885, BLC.

97. Humphreys' Medicine Co., advertisement, *American Druggist* 19 (January 1890): 12.

98. Sidney A. Sherman, "Advertising in the United States," *Publication of the American Statistical Association* n.s. 7, no. 52 (1900): 119–62.

99. O. Kling, "Money Thrown Away," reprinted from the *Denver Road* in *Printers' Ink* 4, no. 13 (1891): 446.

100. Enoch Morgan's Sons spent a total of $72,000 on advertising in 1885, including $8,300 for sign painting and $19,400 for "stunts and miscellaneous." Presbrey, *History and Development of Advertising*, p. 394.

101. Marzio, *Democratic Art*, p. 3.

102. Stage, *Female Complaints*, p. 110.

103. A search through the Western Reserve Historical Society's collections, including the Kovel Collection, Cleveland, in 1990, yielded this itemization.

104. "Among the Dealers," *Tobacco Leaf* 36 (8 March 1899): 4.

105. "The Man Behind the Counter," *Tobacco Leaf* 36 (30 August 1899): 6. After 1890, the plethora of giveaways, including trade cards and posters, lost their prominence as advertising media, although the variety remained for decades. W. F. Hofert, ed., *Advertising Specialty Manufacturers' Directory*, 1st edn. (Chicago: Schulman Bros., 1917), and *Blue Book of Advertising Products* (Oak Park, Ill.: W. F. Hofert, 1927). By 1930 they were reduced to "junk" mail and two relatively minor categories in terms of total expenditures, point-of-purchase advertising and "novelties," or specialty advertising, now generally used for retail, business-to-business, and franchise promotions

106. "Quaint Devices in Trade," *New York Times*, 18 June 1882, p. 9; "High Art on Card-Board," *New York Times*, 3 December 1882, p. 4.

107. Marzio, *Democratic Art*, pp. 127–28; Mott, *American Magazines, 1865–1885*, pp. 7–8.

108. "Ethel" belongs to the Kovel Copllection of the Western Reserve Historical Society in Cleveland.

109. Thurber, Whyland, & Co., advertisement, *American Grocer* 43, no. 23 (1890): 57.

110. "Advertising Souvenirs," editorial, *Business* 12, no. 1 (1892): 17. Garvey, *Adman in the Parlor*, ch. 1, pp. 16–50.

111. Cream of Wheat, "The Object of Advertising Is to Bring People Into Your Store," *American Grocer* 63, no. 1 (1900): insert at pp. 8, 9.

112. Edward Chase Kirkland, *Dream and Thought in the Business Community, 1860–1900* (Ithaca, N.Y.: Cornell University Press, 1956), pp. 2–3. Also, Irvin G. Wyllie, "Social Darwinism and the Businessman," *Proceedings of the American Philosophical Society* 103 (October 1959): 629–35.

113. Warren B. Catlin, *The Progress of Economics: A History of Economic Thought* (New York: Bookman, 1962), p. 327. H. G. Wells, *The Work, Wealth and Happiness of Mankind* (London: Heinemann, 1932), p. 253; JoAnne Yates, *Control Through Communication: The Rise of System in American Management* (Baltimore: Johns Hopkins University Press, 1989).

114. H. A. Blodgett, "The Printing Office Salesman," *Inland Printer* 11 (July 1893): 303–4.

115. Irvin T. Geistweit, "John B. Stetson," *Trade Magazine*, 2 (May, 1894), pp. 239–45; Charles Austin Bates, "Some of America's Advertisers," reprinted from *Peterson's Magazine* in *Printers' Ink* 12, no. 1 (1895): 27–35; "Profitable Stories," reprinted from the *San Francisco Call* in *Printers' Ink* 14, no. 6 (1896): 17–25. In

*The Rise of Silas Lapham*, William Dean Howells refers obliquely to Dr. Kilmer several times as "the kidney-cure man" who generated ubiquitous advertisements. William Dean Howells, *The Rise of Silas Lapham* (New York: Signet Classics, 1980; serialized first in *Century*; first published in book form, 1885).

116. Gail F. Stern, "Ethnic Images in Advertising" exhibition, Balch Institute for Ethnic Studies (Philadelphia, 1984); Fath Davis Ruffins, "Type, Archetype, or Stereotype: Ethnic Images in Advertising," conference paper presented at "Selling the Goods: Origins of American Advertising, 1840–1940," Strong Museum, Rochester, New York, 10 November 1990.

117. A similar pattern existed in the editorial content of newspapers; even papers that did target minorities and ethnic groups only rarely reported on their activities beyond their immediate communities. Dicken-Garcia, *Journalistic Standards*, p. 70.

118. Jan Garnert, "Seize the Day: Ethnological Perspectives on Light and Darkness," *Ethnologia Scandinavica* 24 (1994): 38–59, esp. pp. 52–57; idem, *Anden i lampen: Etnologiska perspektiv på ljus och möker* (Stockholm: Carlsson, 1993), pp. 155, 264n.; Anne Hollander, *Seeing Through Clothes* (New York: Viking, 1978), pp. 85, 88, 157–58, 169, 185, 213; Marina Warner, *Monuments and Maidens: The Allegory of the Female Form* (New York: Atheneum, 1985), pp. 277, 315, 320–25.

119. This information on Sterling's residence courtesy of Dorothy A. Larson, director, Derby (Conn.) Historical Society. Telephone conversation (25 August 1994).

120. *Young America: Stories and Pictures for Young People* (Boston: Aldine, 1888).

121. For this and other factory scenes in consumer-targeted advertisements of this period, Pamela Walker Lurito (Laird), "Advertising's Smoky Past: Themes of Progress in Nineteenth-Century Advertisements" in Robert Weible and Francis R. Walsh, eds., *The Popular Perception of Industrial History* (Lanham, Md.: American Association of State and Local History, 1989), pp. 175–212.

122. For a measure of the mixed responses to industrialization and urbanization, see the essay on sources.

123. Michael Adas, *Machines as the Measure of Men: Science, Technology, and Ideologies of Western Dominance* (Ithaca: Cornell University Press, 1989); Carolyn Marvin, *When Old Technologies Were New: Thinking About Electric Communication in the Late Nineteenth Century* (New York: Oxford University Press, 1988), pp. 35–39.

124. David Riesman, with Reuel Denney and Nathan Glazer, *The Lonely Crowd* (New Haven: Yale University Press, 1961), pp. 15, 21, 115, 116.

125. For theoretical approaches to interpretation across cultures, see the essay on sources.

126. "Ayers Hair Vigor for the Toilet," for J. C. Ayer, Lowell, Mass., paper show card, circa 1890; seal of Kentucky Whiskey, for B. S. Flersheim Merc. Co., Kansas City, Mo., large metal sign, circa 1905.

# Chapter 4. Advertising Progress as a Measure of Worth

1.   William Deering & Co., *One of the Triumphs of the 19th Century* (Chicago, 1893).

2.   Joseph Addison, *Tatler* no. 224 (12–14 September 1710).

3.   Peyton Paxson, "Charles William Post: The Mass Marketing of Health and Welfare" (Ph.D. diss., Boston University, 1993), pp. 206–7.

4.   Jackson Lears uses the phrase "Victorian compromise" in a similar manner, "respectability, rooted in tense ambivalence," regarding aesthetics of fashion. My use is quite compatible, although it carries a broader application of the notion regarding the moral ambiguity of material prosperity. "Beyond Veblen: Rethinking Consumer Culture in America," in Simon J. Bronner, *Consuming Visions: Accumulation and Display of Goods in America, 1880–1920* (New York: Norton, 1989), p. 85. For analyses of historical U.S. ambivalences regarding luxury, see the essay on sources.

5.   For an introduction to the rapidly growing literature on nineteenth-century U.S. bourgeois culture, see the essay on sources.

6.   Alan Dawley, *Class and Community: The Industrial Revolution in Lynn* (Cambridge: Harvard University Press, 1976), p. 35.

7.   T. L. Haines, *Worth and Wealth: Or the Art of Getting, Saving, and Using Money* (New York: Standard Publishing, 1884), pp. 48–49, 53; William Dean Howells, *The Rise of Silas Lapham* (New York: Signet Classics, 1980; serialized first in *Century*; first published in book form, 1885).

8.   Seymour Eaton, Lesson One, "Sound Business Advice," in *One Hundred Lessons in Business* (Boston: Seymour Eaton, 1887), n.p. Also, Henry B. Hyde, "Hard Work and Success," *Inland Printer* 25 (September 1900): 814; reprinted from *Monetary Times*.

9.   Cited in Richard M. Huber, *The American Idea of Success* (New York: McGraw-Hill, 1971), pp. 39–41. For James A. Garfield's instructions to business students in 1869, Eaton, Lesson One, "Sound Business Advice," in *One Hundred Lessons*, title page.

10.   F. W. Thomas, "To the Young Man in the Printing Business," *Inland Printer* 8 (July 1891): 866–67.

11.   William M. Thayer, *Onward to Fame and Fortune, Or, Climbing Life's Ladder* (New York: Christian Herald, 1893), p. 3. Also, *Iron Age* and *Inland Printer*, passim, for cases.

12.   Huber, *American Idea of Success*, p. 367.

13.   Jerome Paine Bates, *The Imperial Highway to Fortune, Happiness, and Heaven* (Chicago: George W. Borland, 1881), p. 25.

14.   Edward Chase Kirkland, *Dream and Thought in the Business Community, 1860–1900* (Ithaca, N.Y.: Cornell University Press, 1956), pp. 145–54; John G. Cawelti, *Apostles of the Self-Made Man* (Chicago: University of Chicago Press, 1965), pp. 75–76, 87–92.

15. Bates, *Imperial Highway*, p. 25.

16. This biblical exhortation (Proverbs 22: 29) appeared widely; examples include Eaton, *One Hundred Lessons in Business,* n.p.; Thayer, *Onward to Fame and Fortune,* front cover; and Thomas H. Jones, "The Hardwareman's Influence in the Development of the Country," speech before the Ohio Hardware Association, published in *Iron Age* 57 (30 January 1896): 499–500.

17. David Riesman, Reuel Denney, and Nathan Glazer, *The Lonely Crowd* (New Haven: Yale University Press, 1961), p. 146. See the essay on sources for literature on nineteenth-century business culture.

18. Carnegie is quoted in Alfred L. Thimm, *Business Ideologies in the Reform-Progressive Era, 1880–1914* (University, Ala.: University of Alabama Press, 1976), p. 205; William T. Hutchinson, *Cyrus Hall McCormick: Harvest, 1856–1884* (New York: Appleton-Century, 1935), pp. 494; Cyrus McCormick, *The Century of the Reaper* (Boston: Houghton Mifflin, 1931), p. 80.

19. Hutchinson, *McCormick: Harvest, 1856–1884,* p. 735.

20. Andrew Carnegie, *Triumphant Democracy, or Fifty Years' March of the Republic* (New York: Scribner's Sons, 1886), passim; Huber, *The American Idea of Success,* p. 95; Kirkland, *Dream and Thought,* pp. 158–60; Charles Sellers, *The Market Revolution: Jacksonian America, 1815–1846* (New York: Oxford University Press, 1991), p. 27; and Irvin G. Wyllie, *The Self-Made Man in America: The Myth of Rags to Riches* (New Brunswick: Rutgers University Press, 1954), pp. 76–77.

21. Bates, *Imperial Highway,* p. 99.

22. Kirkland, *Dream and Thought,* pp. 154–58.

23. "The Greatest Wealth Producers," editorial, *Iron Age* 51 (8 June 1893): 1289.

24. Carnegie, *Triumphant Democracy,* pp. 109, 116–17, 231–33, 265, and passim.

25. Michael Adas, *Machines as the Measure of Men: Science, Technology, and Ideologies of Western Dominance* (Ithaca, N.Y.: Cornell University Press, 1989), pp. 3–7, 134, and passim; Thomas P. Hughes, *American Genesis: A Century of Invention and Technological Enthusiasm, 1870–1970* (New York: Viking, 1989), p. 1 and passim.

26. Donald Davis, *Conspicuous Production: Automobiles and Elites in Detroit, 1899–1933* (Philadelphia: Temple University Press, 1988), pp. 3–8, 11, 88, and passim.

27. Davis, *Conspicuous Production,* pp. 83a, 83c, 83g, 88, and passim.

28. Pamela Walker Laird, "'The Car Without a Single Weakness': Early Automobile Advertising," *Technology and Culture* 37 (1996): 796–812.

29. Landes concludes this section with the remark that the "labouring poor" were "undoubtedly of another mind." David S. Landes, *The Unbound Prometheus: Technological Change and Industrial Revolution in Western Europe from 1750 to the Present* (Cambridge: Cambridge University Press, 1969), pp. 122–23.

30. J. H. Plumb, "The Acceptance of Modernity," in Neil McKendrick, John Brewer, and J. H. Plumb, *The Birth of a Consumer Society: The Commercialization*

*of Eighteenth-Century England* (Bloomington: Indiana University Press, 1982), pp. 316–17, 332–33.

31. Leo Marx, *The Machine in the Garden: Technology and the Pastoral Ideal in America* (Oxford: Oxford University Press, 1964), p. 197. See the essay on sources for literature on progress and attitudes toward technological changes.

32. Lewis O. Saum, *The Popular Mood of America, 1860–1890* (Lincoln: University of Nebraska Press, 1990), pp. 9, 203–16; Saum, *The Popular Mood of Pre–Civil War America* (Westport, Conn.: Greenwood Press, 1980), pp. 184–89.

33. Charles A. Beard, "Introduction" to J. B. Bury, *The Idea of Progress* (London, 1920), p. xxxi; Merritt Roe Smith, "Technological Determinism in American Culture," in Merritt Roe Smith and Leo Marx, *Does Technology Drive History? The Dilemma of Technological Determinism* (Cambridge: MIT Press, 1994), pp. 26–33.

34. Beard, "Introduction," to Bury, *The Idea of Progress*, pp. xxxi–xxxii, xl; Peter J. Bowler, *The Invention of Progress: The Victorians and the Past* (London: Blackwell, 1989), pp. 29, 151, 194–93; Smith, "Technological Determinism," pp. 2–8, 26–33; Marx, "The Idea of 'Technology' and Post-Modern Determinism," in Smith and Marx, *Does Technology Drive History?* pp. 240, 249–51.

35. As skeptical as many moderns are of technological progress in the real world, the popularity of *Star Trek* and its spin-offs belie total pessimism.

36. James H. Hoyt, "Our National Progress," speech at Hardware Dinner, Cleveland, Ohio, *Iron Age* 57 (27 February 1896): 551–62.

37. This monument now stands outside the National Portrait Gallery in Washington, D.C.

38. *Trade Magazine: Helpful Hints to Merchants and Business Men* 2 (May 1894): front cover. Representations of gender differ significantly in these portrayals. For a discussion, Pamela Walker Laird, "Progress in Separate Spheres: Selling Nineteenth-Century Technologies," *Knowledge and Society* 10 (1996): 19–49.

39. John F. Kasson, *Civilizing the Machine: Technology and Republican Values in America, 1776–1900* (New York: Penguin, 1976), esp. pp. 40, 166, 171–80; Leo Marx, *The Machine in the Garden: Technology and the Pastoral Ideal in America* (Oxford: Oxford University Press, 1964), p. 195; Marx, "The Railroad-in-the-Landscape: An Iconological Reading of an Icon in American Art," in Susan Danly and Leo Marx, eds., *The Railroad in American Art: Representations of Technological Change* (Cambridge: MIT Press, 1988), pp. 183–208; Smith, "Technological Determinism," pp. 9–25; Marianne Doezema, "The Clean Machine: Technology in American Magazine Illustration," *Journal of American Culture* 11 (winter 1988): 73–92.

40. Edward Bellamy, *Looking Backward, 2000–1887* (New York: New American Library, 1960, first published 1888); Henry George, *Poverty and Progress* (New York: Robert Schalkenback Foundation, 1937, first published in 1879); Horace Greeley et al., *The Great Industries of the United States: An Historical Survey of the Origin, Growth, and Perfection of the Chief Industrial Arts of the Country* (Hart-

ford: J. B. Burr and Hyde, 1872), p. 46; T. E. Willson, *The National Hand-Book of American Progress: a Ready Reference Manual of Facts and Figures from the Discovery of America to the Present Time* (New York: E. B. Trat, 1884).

41. Kirkland, *Dream and Thought*, pp. 163–67.

42. Tom Lutz, *American Nervousness, 1903: An Anecdotal History* (Ithaca, N.Y.: Cornell University Press, 1991), esp. pp. 3–7. Dr. George M. Beard offered a contemporary analysis of these problems in "Causes of American Nervousness," reprinted in *Popular Culture and Industrialism, 1865–1900*, ed. Henry Nash Smith (New York: New York University Press, 1967; first published 1881), pp. 57–70.

43. Earl J. Hess, *Liberty, Virtue, and Progress: Northerners and Their War For the Union* (New York: New York University Press, 1988), pp. 120–21. Also, Karen Halttunen, *Confidence Men and Painted Women: A Study of Middle-Class Culture in America, 1830–1870* (New Haven: Yale University Press, 1982), and John F. Kasson, *Rudeness and Civility: Manners in Nineteenth-Century Urban America* (New York: Hill & Wang, 1990).

44. S. C. Ferguson and E. A. Allen, *The Golden Gems of Life, or, Gathered Jewels for the Home Circle* (Cincinnati: Central Publishing, 1883), pp. 118–19.

45. James Russell Lowell, "The Present Crisis," *The Poetical Works of James Russell Lowell* (Boston: Houghton, Mifflin, the Cambridge edition, 1978).

46. Lewis Mumford, *Technics and Civilization* (New York: Harbinger Books, Harcourt, Brace, & World, 1963; first published 1934), p. 185. Also, Bowler, *Invention of Progress*, esp. pp. 1–3, 9, 13, 192–93, 200.

47. William O. Stoddard, *Men of Business* (New York: Scribner's Sons, Men of Achievement series, 1893), pp. 31–32.

48. Erastus Wiman, "How Fortunes Are Made," *American Grocer* 43, no. 3 (1890): 12, reprinted from the *New York Tribune*, 4 January 1890.

49. Kirkland, *Dream and Thought*, pp. 7–9.

50. Joshua Ronen, "The Entrepreneur and Society," in Paul J. Albanese, ed., *Psychological Foundations of Economic Behavior* (New York: Praeger, 1988), pp. 143–48.

51. For example, editorial "Too Much of a Good Thing," *Inland Printer* 4 (August 1887): 730–31; and Ricardo (Richard Ennis), "Leisure Gleanings of A Printer," ibid. (July 1887): 646–47; "Production and Demand," anon., *Iron Age* 58 (3 December 1896): 1109. The essay on sources provides some of the key studies in this regard.

52. Louis Galambos, *The Public Image of Big Business in America, 1880–1940: A Quantitative Study in Social Change* (Baltimore: Johns Hopkins University Press, 1975), p. 14.

53. Richard A. McDermott, "The Claim to Power: The Foundations of Authority in American Industry, Lowell, 1820–1850" (Ph.D. diss. Brandeis University, 1985), pp. 17–22, 61–62; Tamara Plakins Thornton, *Cultivating Gentlemen: The Meaning of Country Life among the Boston Elite, 1785–1860* (New Haven: Yale

University Press, 1989), pp. 1–12, 143–45, 192–212. Also, Robert F. Dalzell Jr., *Enterprising Elite: The Boston Associates and the World They Made* (New York: W. W. Norton, 1987), esp. pp. 157–8, 223, 229–31.

54. Francis X. Sutton et al., *The American Business Creed* (Cambridge: Harvard University Press, 1956), p. 11.

55. Wells, Richardson & Co.'s Lactated Food, trade card, circa 1880.

56. Steele & Price, *The Hand and Cornucopia* (Chicago, 1878), p. 11.

57. Cawelti, *Apostles of the Self-Made Man*, p. 196. Also, Huber, *American Idea of Success*, pp. 367–68, 396, 452–53.

58. Henry Adams, *The Education of Henry Adams* (Boston: Houghton Mifflin, 1946; first published 1906), p. 466.

59. John Reps, *Views and Viewmakers of Urban America: Lithographs of Towns and Cities in the United States and Canada, Notes on the Artists and Publishers, and a Union Catalog of Their Work, 1825–1925* (Columbia: University of Missouri Press, 1984), esp. pp. 53–55. Quote from J. D. Van Slyck, *Manufacturers*, two volumes, Representatives of New England (Boston: Van Slyck, 1879), p. v.

60. Helena E. Wright, "The Image Makers: The Role of the Graphic Arts in Industrialization," *IA: The Journal of the Society for Industrial Archeology* 12, no. 2 (1986): 5–18; and "Selling an Image: Views of Lowell, 1825–1876," in Robert Weible and Francis R. Walsh, eds., *The Popular Perception of Industrial History* (Lanham, Md.: American Association of State and Local History, 1989), pp. 141–64, esp. pp. 141, 144, 154, 156, 160. McDermott, "The Claim to Power," pp. 14, 16, 17, 21–22; *Lowell Views: A Collection of Nineteenth-Century Prints, Paintings, and Drawings* (Lowell, Mass.: Lowell Historical Society, 1985).

61. Robert Bell, Alexandria Chemical Co., to Leonhardt Lithographer Co. (January 28, 1898, February 9, 1898, and February 15, 1898), Leonhardt Lithographer Collection, accession 1022, Soda House MSS, Hagley Museum and Library, Wilmington, Delaware. Abbreviations and underlining are in originals.

62. The insight belongs to Joseph J. Corn; letter (30 October 1992). Julie Wosk, *Breaking Frame: Technology and the Visual Arts in the Nineteenth Century* (New Brunswick: Rutgers University Press, 1992), pp. 15, 68–69.

63. The Knickerbocker Press (New York, 1896) advertising booklet, n.p., WCBA, Printers and Printing Collection, box 2, folder 1.

64. Alfred D. Chandler, *The Visible Hand: The Managerial Revolution in American Business* (Cambridge, Mass.: Belknap Press, 1977), pp. 250, 292–93. The Family Match tin, circa 1888, is in the collection of the WRHS, Tobacco Shop.

65. G. G. Green, *Green's Diary Almanac, 1880* (Woodbury, New Jersey), pp. 11, 29. This story originally appeared in the 1878 almanac.

66. The quotation from the 1889 almanac is on page 17. The 1885–1886 and 1880 almanacs are the author's. All other G. G. Green materials are in WCBA, box 12, folders 19–25.

67. This book was distributed to dealers and retailers for customers' perusal. G. G. Green, *Home of August Flower and German Syrup* (Woodbury, N.J., 1889), WCBA, Patent Medicine Collection, box 12, folder 25.

68.  Marx, "The Railroad-in-the-Landscape," pp. 190–93.

69.  J. Valerie Fifer, *American Progress: The Growth of the Transport, Tourist, and Information Industries in the Nineteenth-Century West* (Chester, Conn: Globe Pequot Press, 1988), frontispiece and pp. 191–205, 208; p. 421, n. 13.

70.  For additional examples, Pamela Walker Lurito (Laird), "Advertising's Smoky Past: Themes of Progress in Nineteenth-Century Advertisements," in Robert Weible and Francis R. Walsh, eds., *The Popular Perception of Industrial History* (Lanham, Md.: American Association of State and Local History, 1989), pp. 175–211.

71.  *Dr. King's Guide to Health* (Chicago: H. E. Bucklen, 1903), pp. 2, 8.

72.  Marx, "Closely Watched Trains," p. 28. "The Flight of the Fast Mail" painting can be found at the Henry Ford Museum, accession no. 76.44.1.

73.  Pamela Walker Lurito (Laird), "The Message Was Electric: Electricity as a Motif in Advertising," *IEEE Spectrum* 21 (September 1984): 84–95.

74.  Carolyn Marvin, *When Old Technologies Were New: Thinking About Electric Communication in the Late Nineteenth Century* (New York: Oxford University Press, 1988), esp. pp. 3, 5–6, 128–32, 164–79; David E. Nye, *Electrifying America: Social Meanings of a New Technology* (Cambridge: MIT Press, 1990), esp. pp. 1–6, 35–36, 51–54, 142, 147, 174, 368–79.

75.  For analyses of ancient goddess figures as symbols of truth and progress, Jan Garnert, *Anden i lampan: Etnologiska perspektiv på ljus och mörker* (Stockholm: Carlsson, 1993), pp. 154–56; idem, "Seize the Day: Ethnological Perspectives on Light and Darkness," *Ethnologia Scandinavica* 24 (1994): 38–59, esp. pp. 51–58; Marina Warner, *Monuments and Maidens: The Allegory of the Female Form* (New York: Atheneum, 1985), pp. 277, 315, 320–25.

76.  Dennis Stillings and Nancy Roth coined this term in "When Electroquackery Thrived," *IEEE Spectrum* 15 (November 1978): 56–61.

77.  George A. Scott, *90 Years of Pleasure! A Treatise on Electricity and Electro Magnetism* (London: Pall Mall Electric Association, 1887), n.p., WCBA, Patent Medicine Collection.

78.  Dr. Thomas's Electric Bitters, flyer, circa 1890.

79.  Other examples from this period include Electric Fruit Jar, Electric Shoe Dressing, Electric Cleanser, Kil-lol Electric Bug Killer (a liquid that came in a bottle), Bogle's Electric Hair Dye, and even Electric Light Oil and Electric Light Candles (which were made of wax).

80.  *Die zweite industrielle Revolution: Frankfurt und das Elektrizität, 1880–1914* (Frankfurt: Historisches Museum Frankfurt, 1981). Courtesy Dr. Bayla Singer.

81.  H. J. Heinz Co. streetcar advertisement, circa 1900, Edison Institute, Dearborn, Mich., ID no. 69.152.3; and Heinz trade card, circa 1895.

82.  Henry Perky is quoted in William Cahn, *Out of the Cracker Barrel: The Nabisco Story from Animal Crackers to Zuzus* (New York: Simon & Schuster, 1969), pp. 208–16. "Short Trips to Great Industries, Shredded Wheat: A Visit to Oread In-

stitute, of School of Domestic Science, Worcester, Mass.," *American Grocer* 63, no. 19 (1900): 8–9.

83. Green's August Flower Boshee' German Syrup chromolithograph show card, circa 1885. WCBA, Patent Medicine Poster Collection.

84. Kirkland, *Dream and Thought*, p. 34; esp. the chapter "The Big House," pp. 29–49. Riesman, *Lonely Crowd*, pp. 120–23.

85. "Rising Sun in Canton," *Canton Journal* (July 8, 1904): 9.

86. "The Story of a Successful Advertiser," *Profitable Advertising* 7 (January 15, 1898): 296–99.

87. Author's interviews with Edward H. Bolster in Canton, Mass., July 24, 1985, board member, Canton Historical Society. Obituary, *Canton Journal* (10 June 1898).

88. Thorstein Veblen, *The Theory of the Leisure Class: An Economic Study of Institutions* (New York: Vanguard, 1926; first published 1899), pp. 74, 77, 81–83.

89. Laird, "Progress in Separate Spheres," pp. 19–49.

90. Veblen, *Theory of the Leisure Class*, pp. 81–82.

91. Ibid., p. 83.

92. Quoted in Russell Lynes, *The Tastemakers* (New York: Harper & Brothers, 1949), pp. 77–80. Wendy Gamber, "'Reduced to Science': Gender, Technology, and Power in the American Dressmaking Trade, 1860–1910," *Technology and Culture* 36 (1995): 455–82.

93. WCBA, Pattern Industry Collection, box 1, folders 1, 2; box 3, folders 27, 32.

94. Ruth Schwartz Cowan, *More Work for Mother: The Ironies of Household Technology from the Open Hearth to the Microwave Oven* (New York: Basic Books, 1983).

95. Paul B. Hensley, "Time, Work, and Social Context in New England," *New England Quarterly* 65 (December 1992): 531–59; Mark M. Smith, "Old South Time in Comparative Perspective," *American Historical Review* 101 (December 1996): 1432–69.

96. Time and its proper uses were major themes in this period's culture, as manifested in advertisements and other expressions of peoples' concerns. See the essay on sources for major analyses.

97. WCBA, Agricultural Machinery Collection, box 8.

98. Esp. Glenna Matthews, *"Just a Housewife": The Rise and Fall of Domesticity in America* (New York: Oxford University Press, 1987), pp. 145–50; and Susan Strasser, *Never Done: A History of American Housework* (New York: Pantheon, 1982), ch. 11, pp. 202–23.

99. David S. Landes, *Revolution in Time: Clocks and the Making of the Modern World* (Cambridge: Belknap, Harvard University Press, 1983), p. 2.

100. Lears, "Beyond Veblen," pp. 85, 91–93, and Jackson Lears, *Fables of Abundance: A Cultural History of Advertising in America* (New York: Basic Books, 1994).

101. Colton Packing Co. advertisement in *American Grocer* 43, no. 2 (1890): 4.

# Chapter 5. Early Advertising Specialists

1. For histories of the advertising agency, see the essay on sources.
2. Daniel Pope, *The Making of Modern Advertising* (New York: Basic Books, 1983), p. 130; *The Trow Business Directory of New York City* 65 (New York: Trow Directory, 1892). Manhattan comprised New York City until 1898.
3. Claude C. Hopkins, *My Life in Advertising* (New York: Harper and Brothers, 1927), pp. 15–16; Ralph M. Hower, *The History of an Advertising Agency: N. W. Ayer & Son at Work, 1869–1939* (Cambridge: Harvard University Press, 1939), pp. 31–32; James Playsted Wood, *The Story of Advertising* (New York: Ronald Press, 1958), pp. 137, 140–11.
4. George Presbrey Rowell, *Forty Years an Advertising Agent, 1865–1905* (New York: Printers' Ink Publishing, 1906), pp. 33, 324, 325, 381; Rowell, "Miscellany," *Advertiser's Gazette: A Magazine of Information for Advertisers* 1 (New York: December 1867): 2.
5. George P. Rowell, *The Men Who Advertise: An Account of Successful Advertisers* (New York: Nelson Chesman, 1870), p. 199. Also, *Advertisers Gazette* 1, no. 7 (New York, 1867): 1. WCBA, Advertising Collection, box 5.
6. *Printers' Ink* 4, no. 5 (1891): 180; Rowell, *Forty Years*, p. 436.
7. Hower, *Advertising Agency*, pp. 98–99. Stephen Fox, *The Mirror Makers: A History of American Advertising and Its Creators* (New York: William Morrow, 1984), pp. 152–55; Wood, *Story of Advertising*, pp. 405–9.
8. Advertisement placed in *Bill Poster* (November 1900), no page number indicated on loose sheet, NWA.
9. Quoted in Daniel Pope, *The Making of Modern Advertising* (New York: Basic Books, 1983), pp. 114–15.
10. George P. Rowell, "What is an Advertising Agent?" and "Who Are the Patrons of Advertising Agencies?" *Advertiser's Gazette* 8 (March 1874): 3–4.
11. Hower, *Advertising Agency*, pp. 221–23, 249–50; Rowell, *Forty Years*, p. 324–26.
12. Volney B. Palmer, *Business-Men's Almanac* (New York, 1850), n.p., WCBA, Advertising Collection, box 3.
13. Hower, *Advertising Agency*, p. 118; letterheads of H. P. Hubbard's The International Newspaper Agency (New Haven, 1885) and T. C. Evans Advertising Agent (Boston, 1886). Both letterheads are in WCBA, Advertising Collection, box 2.
14. "How to Succeed in Business," *Advertiser's Gazette* 1 (May 1867): 1, WCBA, Advertising Collection, box 5; "Improved Business Methods," *Printers' Ink* 1, no. 20 (1889): 515; editorial copy, ibid.: 529.
15. Rowell, *Forty Years*, p. 332.
16. Fox, *Mirror Makers*, pp. 20–21; Rowell, *Forty Years*, p. 473.
17. Artemas Ward, "Some Final Words about Substitutes," *Art in Advertising: An Illustrated Monthly for Business Men* 4 (October 1891): 41–42.

18. Advertisement for N. W. Ayer & Son in *Farm Implement News* n.s. 7, no. 2 (1886): 1, NWA.

19. Fox, *Mirror Makers*, pp. 20–21; Rowell, *Advertiser's Gazette* 1 (June 1867): 1, WCBA, Advertising Collection, box 5; ibid., 8 (March 1874): 6; Rowell, *Forty Years*, pp. 161–63, 358–59, 365.

20. Rowell, *Forty Years*, pp. 358–59, 365; "Do Your Advertisements Pay?" *Printers' Ink* 1, no. 9 (1888).

21. Pope, *Modern Advertising*, p. 120; Rowell, *Forty Years*, pp. 463–64.

22. Louis Galambos and Joseph Pratt, *The Rise of the Corporate Commonwealth: U.S. Business and Public Policy in the Twentieth Century* (New York: Basic Books, 1988), pp. 25, 29.

23. Alfred D. Chandler, *The Visible Hand: The Managerial Revolution in American Business* (Cambridge: Belknap, Harvard University Press, 1977), esp. pp. 36–38.

24. Rowell, *Forty Years*, pp. 237–49.

25. Hower, *Advertising Agency*, pp. 69–70.

26. Ibid., esp. pp. 62–87; Pope, *Modern Advertising*, 117, 130–32.

27. Hower, *Advertising Agency*, pp. 69–72, 604–5, 635; Rowell, *Forty Years*, pp. 237–49; Albert Davis Lasker, *The Lasker Story: As He Told It* (Chicago: Advertising Publications, 1963), pp. 10, 12.

28. Rowell, *Forty Years*, p. 443.

29. Hower, *Advertising Agency*, pp. 67–69.

30. Rowell, *Forty Years*, p. 442.

31. *The Book of the Golden Celebration* (Philadelphia: N. W. Ayer & Son, 1919), p. 6, NWA.

32. Lasker, *Lasker Story*, p. 16.

33. Hower, *Advertising Agency*, pp. 88–90.

34. Ibid., pp. 72–75, 77, 405–11.

35. Hower has taken this quotation from an unidentified Philadelphia newspaper, dated 12 May 1887, that described an Ayer staff banquet. *Advertising Agency*, p. 109.

36. Ibid., reprinted on p. 110.

37. N. W. Ayer & Son, *Directory* (Philadelphia, 1888), p. 7, WCBA, Advertising Collection, box 2; *Manual for Advertisers* (Philadelphia, 1888), n.p., WCBA, Advertising Collection, box 1.

38. Frank Presbrey, *The History and Development of Advertising* (Garden City, N.Y.: Doubleday, Doran, 1929), pp. 271–72; Rowell, *Forty Years*, p. 145; "Some Basic Roots of the J. Walter Thompson Company," unsigned MS for an internal history (New York, 1958), p. 3, JWTCA.

39. Stanley Resor, "Some of the contributions which the J. Walter Thompson Company Has Made to Advertising Thought and Practise over the Last Sixty Years," MS (25 April 1931), p. 2, JWTCA; house advertisement for J. Walter Thompson, 1889, JWTCA.

40. Quoted in Fox, *Mirror Makers*, pp. 30–31.

41. Hower, *Advertising Agency*, pp. 98–99; Presbrey, *History and Development of Advertising*, pp. 348, 460–61; Resor, "Contributions," p. 2; "Some Basic Roots of J. Walter Thompson Company," unsigned MS for an internal history (New York, 1958), p. 35, JWTCA; J. Walter Thompson to Mr. B. M. Morris (10 August 1895), form letter in the collection of Jack Golden.

42. "Some Basic Roots," p. 3; house advertisement for J. Walter Thompson Company, 1889, JWTCA.

43. "J. Walter Thompson, Man at the Helm: The First Champion of Magazine Advertising," *Profitable Advertising* 8, no. 1 (Boston, 1898): 18–19.

44. Rowell, *Forty Years*, p. 441. Also, Presbrey, *History and Development of Advertising*, p. 271.

45. Charles E. Raymond, "An Advertising Man's Story," pp. 9–10, 25, JWTCA.

46. Rowell, *Advertiser's Gazette* 8 (March 1874): 5; the second statement is quoted from Rowell's 1872 *Advertiser's Gazette*, in Pope, *Modern Advertising*, pp. 133–34; Rowell, *Forty Years*, pp. 328–29.

47. S. M. Pettengill & Co., *Catalogue of 1,200 Cooperative Newspapers with Their Rates of Advertising* (1876), n.p., WCBA, Advertising Collection, box 3.

48. I. N. Soper, "Preface," *Advertisers' Manual* (New York, 1874), p. 3, WCBA, Advertising Collection, box 9.

49. Fox, *Mirror Makers*, pp. 13–14; Hower, *Advertising Agency*, pp. 94–97; Charles Raymond, "An Advertising Man's Story," MS (1923), pp. 9–10, JWTCA.

50. Stanley Resor, untitled speech (4 May 1931), p. 9. JWTCA. *Direct Acting—High Pressure* (New York City: J. Walter Thompson, 1889), p. xiii, JWTCA.

51. Pope, *Modern Advertising*, pp. 123–24, 194–95; Rowell, *Forty Years*, pp. 370–80.

52. Joseph H. Appel, *Growing Up With Advertising* (New York: Business Bourse Publishers, 1940), pp. 72–73; Hower, *Advertising Agency*, pp. 94–95; Pope, *Modern Advertising*, pp. 134–35; Presbrey, *History and Development of Advertising*, pp. 303–9, 316, 423, 469; Wood, *Story of Advertising*, pp. 231–33.

53. Pope, *Modern Advertising*, pp. 134–35, 187–88; Presbrey, *History and Development of Advertising*, pp. 303–9; Wood, *Story of Advertising*, pp. 231–33.

54. "Catching the Public Eye," *New York Times*, 27 September 1885, p. 4.

55. Hower, *Advertising Agency*, pp. 94–97.

56. Ibid.; advertisement for N. W. Ayer in 39th edition of *Ayer & Son's Standard Lists* (October 1889), n.p., NWA.

57. "Advertising Agents' Commissions," *Profitable Advertising* 1, no. 1 (Boston, 1891): 5–6.

58. "To Advertisers and Businessmen," *J. Walter Thompson's Illustrated Catalogue of Magazines Compiled for the Use of Advertisers* (Philadelphia, 1887), p. 7; *Direct Acting Pressure*, booklet (Philadelphia, 1889), p. xiii.

59. Raymond, "An Advertising Man's Story," pp. 8–9, JWTCA. Rowell, *Forty Years*, p. 453.

60. Sarah Stage, *Female Complaints: Lydia Pinkham and the Business of Women's Medicine* (New York: Norton, 1979), pp. 30–37, 39–44, 90, 95, 101, 107–8; James

Harvey Young, *The Toadstool Millionaires: A Social History of Patent Medicines in America before Federal Regulation* (Princeton: Princeton University Press, 1961), pp. 104, 247–48.

61. Raymond, "An Advertising Man's Story," pp. 8–9, JWTCA; Stage, *Female Complaints*, pp. 108–10.

62. Quoted in Stage, *Female Complaints*, pp. 111–12.

63. "Catching the Public Eye," *New York Times*, 27 November 1885, p. 4.

64. Fox, *Mirror Makers*, p. 36; Presbrey, *History and Development of Advertising*, pp. 310–13; Wood, *Story of Advertising*, p. 276.

65. Presbrey, *History and Development of Advertising*, pp. 423, 469; Wood, *Story of Advertising*, p. 233.

66. Fox, *Mirror Makers*, pp. 52–53; Claude C. Hopkins, *My Life in Advertising* (New York: Harper & Brothers, 1917), pp. 38, 40–41; Wood, *Story of Advertising*, pp. 287–89.

67. Fox, *Mirror Makers*, p. 23; Presbrey, *History and Development of Advertising*, pp. 394–95; Rowell, *Forty Years*, p. 413. The jingles are quoted in Wood, *Story of Advertising*, pp. 247–49.

## Chapter 6. Competition and Control

1. For histories of advertising agencies and professionals, see the essay on sources.

2. See the essay on sources on business history.

3. Richard B. Franken, *Packages that Sell* (New York: Harper & Brothers, 1928); Thomas Hine, *The Total Package: The Evolution and Secret Meanings of Boxes, Bottles, Cans, and Tubes* (Boston: Little, Brown, 1995).

4. Neil H. Borden, *The Economic Effects of Advertising* (Chicago: Richard D. Irwin, 1942), p. 30.

5. Russell Howland, "Dr. Woodbury, Dermatologist," *Profitable Advertising* 7, no. 1 (1897): 47.

6. A column directed to "Entrepreneurs" in 1995 indicates the continuing strength of the impulse for founders to name small businesses after themselves despite countervailing advice that this "makes the business look small and un-professional." Courtney Price, "Take Time to Find Right Name for Your Business," *Rocky Mountain News* (Denver), 1 February 1995: 38A.

7. Alfred D. Chandler, *The Visible Hand: The Managerial Revolution in American Business* (Cambridge: Harvard University Press, 1977), pp. 250, 296; David Powers Cleary, *Great American Brands: The Successful Formulas that Made Them Famous* (New York: Fairchild Publications, 1981), pp. 172–76; Editors of *Advertising Age*, *Procter & Gamble: The House that Ivory Built* (Lincolnwood, Ill.: NTC Business Books, 1988); Frank Presbrey, *The History and Development of Advertising* (Garden City, N.Y.: Doubleday, Doran, 1929), p. 396.

8. George Presbrey Rowell, *Forty Years an Advertising Agent, 1865–1905* (New

York: Printers' Ink Publishing, 1906), pp. 82, 400, 402–5; James Harvey Young, *The Toadstool Millionaires: A Social History of Patent Medicines in America before Federal Regulation* (Princeton: Princeton University Press, 1961), pp. 104, 166–67.

9.  Rowell, *Forty Years*, p. 390; George P. Rowell, *The Men Who Advertise: An Account of Successful Advertisers* (New York: Nelson Chesman, 1870), pp. 183–84; Young, *Toadstool Millionaires*, pp. 126–28.

10. Rowell, *Forty Years*, pp. 375–76.

11. David I. Carlton, "The Revolution From Above: The National Market and the Beginnings of Industrialization in North Carolina," *Journal of American History* 77 (September 1990): 445–75, esp. pp. 464–65; Glenn Porter and Harold C. Livesay, *Merchants and Manufacturers: Studies in the Changing Structure of Nineteenth-Century Marketing* (Chicago: Ivan R. Dee, 1989; first published 1971), p. 201; Nannie May Tilley, *The Bright-Tobacco Industry, 1860–1929* (Chapel Hill: University of North Carolina Press, 1948), pp. 549–50; "Among the Dealers," *Tobacco Leaf* 36, no. 11 (1899): 4.

12. The quotation is from "Some Famous Advertisements and How They Originated," *Art in Advertising: An Illustrated Monthly for Business Men* 4 (October 1891): 32–33. "Some of America's Advertisers," Charles Austin Bates, *Printers' Ink* 12, no. 1 (1895): 32; Stephen Fox, *The Mirror Makers: A History of American Advertising and Its Creators* (New York: William Morrow, 1984), pp. 24–25; Rowell, *Forty Years*, pp. 124, 255. Also, editorial, "The Value of a Trade Name," *Iron Age* 51 (26 January 1893): 183.

13. Registrations for 1881–1904 total 36,017. Calculations are based on *The Statistical History of the United States From Colonial Times to the Present*, with an introduction by Ben J. Wattenberg (New York: Basic Books, 1976), pp. 956, 959.

14. Ferdinand Goss, "Trade marks and Unfair Competition," *AD Sense* 21, no. 1 (1906): 17–20.

15. Theodore C. Search, annual presidential address to the National Association of Manufacturers, *Convention Reports, 1895–1898* (23 August 1897), pp. 8–23; ibid, pp. 65–70; National Association of Manufacturers Archives at HM&L.

16. J. M. Battle, "The Present Condition of the Trade-Mark Law in the United States," *Iron Age* 52 (26 October 1893): 760. Also, "Trade-Marks From the Manufacturer's Point of View," ibid., pp. 760–61; and Elijah A. Morse, "Trade-Marks," ibid., pp. 761–62.

17. For instance, *Printers' Ink* 4, no. 14 (1891): 471; 15, no. 7 (1896): 57; and 60, no. 1 (1907): 25; *Ad Sense* 14, no. 6 (1903): 461–62.

18. J. L. Steuart, "The Value of Trademarks," speech delivered at the First Convention of the International Advertising Association, St. Louis, October, 1904. Reported and quoted in "What Happened in St. Louis," *Printers' Ink* 49, no. 3 (1904): 6, 8.

19. Beverly W. Pattishall, "Two Hundred Years of American Trademark Law," *Trademark Reporter* 68 (March–April 1978): 121–47.

20. Frank Schecter, "The Rational Basis of Trade-Mark Protection," *Harvard Law Review* 40 (1927): 813.

21. *Advertising Experience* 4, no. 2 (1896): 15.

22. Quoted in Presbrey, *History and Development of Advertising*, pp. 444–45.

23. Borden also pointed out that competitive advertising can raise or lower selective demand for particular brands, affecting relative prices in one industry. Borden, *Economic Effects*, pp. 512–17, 850–53.

24. Joanne Reitano, *The Tariff Question in the Gilded Age: The Great Debate of 1888* (University Park: Pennsylvania State University Press, 1994).

25. Daniel Pope, *The Making of Modern Advertising* (New York: Basic Books, 1983), p. 69.

26. Greg Boorman, "The Power of Advertising," *Printers' Ink* 13, no. 9 (1895): 8. The second citation was quoted in Pope, *Modern Advertising*, p. 69.

27. Presbrey, *History and Development of Advertising*, pp. 338–39, 362, 365, 392–93, 396. Pope, *Modern Advertising*, pp. 199, 202.

28. Chandler, *Visible Hand*, pp. 249–50, 290–92; Porter and Livesay, *Merchants and Manufacturers*, pp. 202–3; Jane Webb Smith, *Smoke Signals: Cigarettes, Advertising, and the American Way of Life* (Richmond: Valentine Museum, 1990), pp. 15, 17; Tilley, *Bright-Tobacco Industry*, pp. 557–59, 570–72, 575.

29. Pope, *Modern Advertising*, pp. 52–54; Porter and Livesay, *Merchants and Manufacturers*, pp. 202–3; Tilley, *Bright-Tobacco Industry*, pp. 557–58.

30. Carlton, "Revolution From Above," p. 465; John Wilber Jenkins, *James B. Duke: Master Builder* (New York: George H. Doran, 1927), pp. 85–88, 117–19; Pope, *Modern Advertising*, pp. 52–54; Porter and Livesay, *Merchants and Manufacturers*, pp. 212–13; Tilley, *Bright-Tobacco Industry*, pp. 557–58, 575.

31. Jenkins, *James B. Duke*, pp. 85–88, 117–19; Tilley, *Bright-Tobacco Industry*, pp. 557–58, 575.

32. Richard S. Tedlow, *New and Improved: The Story of Mass Marketing in America* (New York: Basic Books, 1990), p. 272.

33. Sarah Stage, *Female Complaints: Lydia Pinkham and the Business of Women's Medicine* (New York: Norton, 1979), p. 37.

34. Rowell, *Forty Years*, p. 392.

35. Rowell, *Men Who Advertise*, pp. 97, 200.

36. Quoted in Fox, *Mirror Makers*, pp. 23–24; Rowell, *Forty Years*, p. 413.

37. Porter and Livesay, *Merchants and Manufacturers*, pp. 127, 212–25.

38. For examples, "What Retailers Say in Regard to Sales to Their Customers by Manufacturers and Jobbers," editorial, *Iron Age* 51 (20 April 1893): 927–28; "Selling to Consumers," anon., ibid., 52 (5 October 1893): 628; and "Should Manufacturers Sell to Consumers? A Merchant's View of the Situation," anon., ibid., 58 (8 October 1896): 700.

39. A.F.G., "Two Cases," *Iron Age* 51 (2 March 1893): 526–27.

40. William H. Maher, *On the Road to Riches: Practical Hints for Clerks and Young Business Men* (Toledo: William H. Maher, 1889; first edn. 1878), p. 175.

41. Jno. H. Bentley, *Advertisers' Handy Guide* (Chicago, 1880), p. 16.

42. Peyton Paxson, "Charles William Post: The Mass Marketing of Health and Welfare" (Ph.D. diss., Boston University, 1993), p. 190.

43. E[merson]. P. Harris, "Wanted: Data for the Science of Advertising," *Inland Printer* 8 (July 1891): 867.

44. Quoted in Rowell, *Men Who Advertise*, p. 184.

45. Bill Reid Moeckel in *The Development of the Wholesaler in the United States, 1860–1900* (New York: Garland Press, 1986), esp. pp. 112–25; Porter and Livesay, *Merchants and Manufacturers*, pp. 3, 10, 11, 166–79, 212–13, 215–19; Chandler, *Visible Hand*, pp. 298, 308; Jenkins, *James B. Duke*, pp. 85–88, 117–19; Marquette, *Brands, Trademarks, and Good Will*, pp. 62–63; Quentin J. Schultze, "Manufacturers' Views of National Consumer Advertising, 1910–1915," *Journalism Quarterly* 60 (spring 1983): 10–15, 34; Tilley, *Bright-Tobacco Industry*, pp. 557–58, 575.

46. Presbrey, *History and Development of Advertising*, p. 391

47. N. W. Ayer & Son, advertisement, *Farm Implement News* n.s. 7, no. 2 (1886): 1, NWA.

48. Allston Ladd, "Advertising by Manufacturers and Wholesalers," *Printers' Ink* 4, no. 22: 407–8, and no. 13: 444–45 (1891).

49. Harry Nelson McKinney, transcript of informal address at Business-Getting Conference, N. W. Ayer agency, New York (5 January 1905), NWA.

50. Truman A. DeWeese, *The Principle of Practical Publicity, Being a Treatise on "The Art of Advertising"* (Philadelphia: George W. Jacobs, 1908; first published 1906), p. 1.

51. George Frank Lord, *Let Me Help You Make Money Through Advertising* (Chicago: Lord Advertising Agency and George Frank Lord, 1912), n.p., WCBA, Advertising Collection, box 2.

52. *Things to Know About Trade-Marks: A Manual of Trade-Mark Information* (New York: J. Walter Thompson, 1911), pp. 7, 10, 11, JWTCA.

53. "An Evolution in Trade," *New York Times*, 7 April 1889, p. 10, cols. 3–4.

54. Chandler, *Visible Hand*, pp. 292, 320, 330, 331–32, 337; Naomi R. Lamoreaux, *The Great Merger Movement in American Business, 1895–1904* (Cambridge: Cambridge University Press, 1985), pp. 1–2; Ralph L. Nelson, *Merger Movements in American Industry, 1895–1956* (Princeton: Princeton University Press, 1959), pp. 5, 6, 34.

55. Edward Sherwood Meade, *Trust Finance: A Study of the Genesis, Organization, and Management of Industrial Organizations* (New York: Appleton, 1909), pp. 23–24, 65–66, 69–74, 76–85.

56. Harris, "Wanted: Data for the Science of Advertising," p. 867.

57. Lamoreaux, *Great Merger Movement*, pp. 18, 45.

58. Reprinted in Presbrey, *History and Development of Advertising*, pp. 444–45.

59. Rowell, *Forty Years*, p. 470.

60. See the essay on sources for analyses of the changes in business management and organization during this period.

61. Joseph Dorfman, *The Economic Mind in American Civilization, 1865–1918* (New York: Viking, 1959), p. 121.

62. Chandler, *Visible Hand,* p. 491; Melvin T. Copeland and Andrew R. Towl, *The Board of Directors and Business Management* (Boston: Graduate School of Business Administration, Harvard University, 1947), pp. 5, 7, 8, 15; Meade, *Trust Finance,* p. 86.

63. David F. Hawkins, "The Development of Modern Financial Reporting Practices among American Manufacturing Corporations," *Business History Review* 37 (autumn 1963): 166–99.

64. In his index to *Visible Hand,* Chandler lists nine corporations of this time period whose titles began with *United States,* eight with *United,* nine with *International,* three with *Continental,* and thirty-four with *American* (pp. 587–607).

65. Patrick G. Porter, "Origins of the American Tobacco Company," *Business History Review* 43 (spring 1969): 59–76, esp. 64–65.

66. Ibid., pp. 67–73.

67. Meade, *Trust Finance,* p. 87.

68. John A. Garraty, *Right-Hand Man: The Life of George W. Perkins* (New York: Harper & Bros., 1957), pp. 127–46. On the "harvester wars," see also Cyrus McCormick, *The Century of the Reaper* (Boston: Houghton Mifflin, 1931), pp. 99–120.

69. Werner Sombart, "Capitalism," in *Encyclopedia of the Social Sciences,* Edwin A. Seligman, ed., vol. 3 (New York: Macmillan, 1937), p. 201.

70. Borden, *Economic Effects,* pp. 27 and 881; also, pp. 681–708 and 870.

71. On specialization and professionalization during this period, see the essay on sources.

72. Jenkins, *James B. Duke,* pp. 111, 160–63.

73. Charles W. Hoyt, *Scientific Sales Management* (New Haven: George B. Woolson, 1913), pp. 3–5, 66, HM&L.

74. William H. Maher, "Who Shall Write the Advertisement?" *Printers' Ink* 8, no. 2 (1893): 83–85.

75. Advertisement, Lord & Thomas, Chicago, *Printers' Ink* 13, no. 7 (1895): 71.

76. Edwin R. Manchester to W. A. Hart, cover memo for "History of DuPont Advertising Leadership" (June 15, 1948), Manchester/DuPont MSS, HM&L; Manchester, "140 Years of DuPont Advertising" (1948), Manchester/DuPont MSS, HM&L; Irenee DuPont to *New York Commercial,* 28 June 1919, DuPont MSS, accession 1662, box 3, no. 49, HM&L; Irenee DuPont to Grayson M-P. Murphy, 22 September 1919, DuPont MSS, accession 1662, box 3, no. 49, HM&L.

77. Ralph M. Hower, *The History of an Advertising Agency: N. W. Ayer & Son at Work, 1869–1939* (Cambridge: Harvard University Press, 1939), p. 117; Jenkins, *James B. Duke,* pp. 162–63.

78. Cited in F. B. Wright Jr. to W. H. Collins, 29 December 1914, WCBA, Advertising Collection, box 7, "Miscellaneous Correspondence." Wright was a New York advertising counsel who specialized in public utilities.

79. Irenee DuPont to C. F. Brown, 26 November 1920, DuPont MSS, accession 1662, box 3, no. 49, HM&L.

80. Arthur Warren, "Secrets of Business 'Booming' Revealed," *New York Times*, 28 February 1904, p. 13.

81. For example, "The Battle for Markets," an editorial in the first volume of *American Trade*, declared that "Publicity is the need of the hour." *American Trade* 1, no. 12 (1898): 88, National Association of Manufacturers Archives, HM&L.

## Chapter 7. The Competition to Modernize Advertising Services

1. Editors of *Advertising Age, Procter & Gamble: The House that Ivory Built* (Lincolnwood, Ill.: NTC Business Books, 1988), pp. 16, 165.

2. For instance, Burpee Seed Co.'s contest was reported in *Printers' Ink*, 4, no. 7 (1891): 252; *Comfort Magazine*'s contest in *Printers' Ink* 4, no. 14 (1891): 491; the Columbia Bicycle Co. held a contest in 1896 that attracted about one thousand entries. David W. Kiehl, "American Art Posters of the 1890s," in idem., ed., *American Art Posters of the 1890s* (New York: Metropolitan Museum of Art, distrib. Harry N. Abrams, 1987), p. 20.

3. "Character in Business and in Publicity," in "By The Advertising Man" column in *American Industries* 1, no. 3 (1902): 4.

4. Editorials, "Ads on Rocks," *New York Times*, 22 May 1896 and 23 May 1896, and editorial, "Public Advertising—Corrections of Abuses," *New York Times*, 1 September 1898, p. 6. James Playsted Wood, *The Story of Advertising* (New York: Ronald Press, 1958), pp. 182–83. An interesting discussion of landscape advertising, and other comments on advertising practices, can be found in the first chapter of William Dean Howells, *The Rise of Silas Lapham* (New York: Signet Classics, 1980; serialized first in *Century*; first published in book form in 1885).

5. S. G. Harvey, "Some Facts about Sign Advertising," *Printers' Ink* 8, no. 10 (1893): 343–44; "Prevention of Cruelty to Landscapes," ibid. 25, no. 8 (1898): 51. Also, editorial, ibid. 11, no. 2 (1894): 64; Richardson Evans, "Advertising as a Trespass on the Public," *Living Age* 208 (13 July 1895): 131–40, reprinted from *19th Century*; Seymour Eaton, *Sermons on Advertising* (New York: J. Walter Thompson, 1907), n.p.

6. "Certain Important Advertising Pointers by the Silent Partner," *American Industries* 4, no. 4 (1905): 3.

7. Livermore & Knight, Advertisers, *Fifty Years of the Pioneer Spirit* (Providence, R.I.: Livermore and Knight, 1925), n.p., HM&L.

8. Imperial Engraving Co., Chicago, *Inland Printer*: 20 (November 1897): 277.

Also, Peter Marzio, *The Democratic Art: Chromolithography 1840–1890; Pictures for a Nineteenth-Century America* (Boston: David Godine, 1979), esp. pp. 6, 176, 191–96.

9. Paul Nathan, *How to Make Money in the Printing Business* (New York: Lotus Press, 1900), pp. 9, 36–37, 39–41; Hoeflich Printing House, Philadelphia, *Profitable Talks on Printing* 3, no. 1 (1915): 2–3, WCBA, Printers and Printing Collection, box 12. Also, "Why the Printer is Becoming a Factor in Advertising; Advertising is Printed Salesmanship," editors, *Printing Art: A Monthly Magazine of the Art of Printing and of the Allied Arts* 9 (July 1907): 304; "Hints for Customers," editors, *Inland Printer* 35 (May 1905): 214–15.

10. Leroy Fairman, "What is a Printer?" *AD Sense: A Magazine for Business Builders* 21, no. 2 (1906): 96–98.

11. F. F. Helmer, "Advertising for Printers," *Inland Printer* 25 (May 1900): 248–50.

12. Advertisement for Grand Rapids Engraving Co., *System* 1, no. 3 (1901): n.p.; advertisement for A. B. Morse Co., *Factory* 1 (February 1901): 174.

13. "Sentences that Sell Goods," *Inland Printer* 15 (April 1895): 56; "The Question of Publicity," ibid. 15 (June 1895): 278; "Noticeable Progress in Advertising Methods," ibid. 15 (July 1895): 381; F. W. Thomas, "Advertising Experience," ibid. 17 (September 1896): 624–25; Walter L. Gallup, "Range of Advertising Ideas," ibid. 13 (July 1894): 354–55.

14. "The Art Poster as an Advertisement," ibid. 20 (October 1897): 41–42; Musgrove [sic], "Printing and Publicity Problems," ibid. 20 (November 1897): 348. Also, William D. McJunkin, "How Type Tells in Advertising," ibid. 35 (July 1905): 512–14.

15. "The Progress of Design in Advertising," *Profitable Advertising* 17, no. 12 (1908): 1238–40.

16. "Hints for Customers," editors, *Inland Printer* 35 (May 1905): 214–15.

17. W. S. Rossiter, "The Growth of the Printing Habit," *Printing Art* 9 (August 1907): 361–68.

18. For instance, "The Object of Advertising Is to Bring People into Your Store," ad for Cream of Wheat, *American Grocer* 63 (3 January 1900): insert between pp. 8 and 9.

19. Rossiter, "Printing Habit"; Sidney A. Sherman, "Advertising in the United States," *Publication of the American Statistical Association* 7 (December 1900): 119–62.

20. M. W. Carleton, "How to Keep the Store Neat and Clean," *Iron Age* 51 (6 April 1893): 812–13.

21. Editorial, "Street-Car Advertising," *Printer and Bookmaker* 25 (January 1898): 280–81.

22. Rossiter, "Printing Habit," p. 368.

23. Maurice Rickards, *The Rise and Fall of the Poster* (New York: McGraw Hill, 1971), p. 21; Frank Presbrey, *The History and Development of Advertising* (Garden City, N.Y.: Doubleday, Doran, 1929), pp. 496, 502.

24. Helmer, "Advertising for Printers," *Inland Printer* 25 (May 1900): 248–50.

25. "Gains of Lithography for Advertising," editors, *Profitable Advertising* 18, no. 3 (1908): 265–66; C. F. B. "Posters," *Printers' Ink* 12, no. 10 (1895): 17–18. Also, "Trend Toward Lithography," editors, *Profitable Advertising* 18, no. 3 (1908): 215.

26. For examples of the many contemporary reports on these changes, H. Chirpe, "Photolithography," *Inland Printer* 15 (June 1895): 298–99; James H. Plummer, "Newspaper Advertising vs. Solicitation," *Printers' Ink* 11, no. 21 (1894): 907–8, 910; "Photo-Mechanical Printing," ibid. 11, no. 21 (1894): 910; "Photography in Advertising," ibid. 14, no. 9 (1896): 3–4. See the essay on sources for printing technologies histories.

27. Edwin Emery, *The Press and America: An Interpretative History of Journalism*, 2d edn. (Englewood Cliffs, N.J.: Prentice-Hall, 1962), pp. 345, 398–402, 423–26; Edward C. Kirkland, *Industry Comes of Age: Business, Labor, and Public Policy, 1860–1897* (New York: Holt, Rinehart & Winston, 1961), p. 273; William Leach, *Land of Desire: Merchants, Power, and the Rise of a New American Culture* (New York: Pantheon, 1993), pp. 91–92; Presbrey, *History and Development of Advertising*, pp. 355, 437.

28. "Advertisers Will Withdraw Patronage," *New York Times*, 10 March 1897, p. 6. Also, "Yellowness," ibid., 31 July 1898, p. 16.

29. Daniel Pope, *Making of Modern Advertising* (New York: Basic Books, 1983), p. 30.

30. Emery, *Press*, pp. 396–402.

31. Pope, *Modern Advertising*, pp. 127–38, 154–63; Emery, *Press*, pp. 398–400, 402; Ralph M. Hower, *The History of an Advertising Agency: N. W. Ayer & Son at Work, 1869–1939* (Cambridge: Harvard University Press, 1939), pp. 433–34.

32. Frank Luther Mott, *A History of American Magazines*, vol. 4, *1885–1905* (Cambridge: Harvard University Press, 1957), pp. 11, 20–24. For other analyses of the relationships between advertising and magazine history, see the essay on sources.

33. Presbrey, *History and Development of Advertising*, pp. 436–37.

34. Edward W. Bok, *A Man From Maine* (New York: Scribner's Sons, 1923), pp. 91–93; Stephen Fox, *The Mirror Makers: A History of American Advertising and Its Creators* (New York: William Morrow, 1984), pp. 32–34; Hower, *Advertising Agency*, pp. 111, 418–19; Salme Harju Steinberg, *Reformer in the Marketplace: Edward W. Bok and the Ladies' Home Journal* (Baton Rouge: Louisiana State University Press, 1979), pp. 1–10; James Playsted Wood, *The Curtis Magazines* (New York: Ronald Press, 1971), pp. 8–14, 23; Wood, *Story of Advertising*, pp. 210–16.

35. Wood, *Curtis Magazines*, pp. 10, 63–64, 66–67, 72.

36. Hower, *Advertising Agency*, pp. 111, 449; Presbrey, *History and Development of Advertising*, pp. 531–33, 534; Steinberg, *Reformer in the Marketplace*, pp. 20, 98–106; Wood, *Story of Advertising*, pp. 327, 336–40; Wood, *Curtis Magazines*,

p. 29; James Harvey Young, *Pure Food: Securing the Federal Food and Drugs Act of 1906* (Princeton: Princeton University Press, 1990), p. 197.

37. "Who's Who—and Wherefore: Cyrus Curtis," *Printers' Ink* 58, no. 1 (1907): 32–34; *American Grocer* 63, no. 11 (1906); Wood, *Curtis Magazines*, pp. 63–66.

38. Earnest Elmo Calkins, *The Business of Advertising* (New York: Appleton, 1915), frontispiece, p. v.

39. Steinberg, *Reformer in the Marketplace*, p. 32.

40. Presbrey, *History and Development of Advertising*, p. 474; Steinberg, *Reformer in the Marketplace*, pp. 27–28; Wood, *Curtis Magazines*, pp. 73–79.

41. The Advertising Man, "Character in Business and in Publicity," *American Industries* 1, no. 3 (1902): 4.

42. Ibid.

43. Richard J. Walsh, *Selling Forces* (Philadelphia: Curtis Publishing, 1913), p. 67.

44. "Forthcoming Articles," *System* (March 1901): cover.

45. The Advertising Man, "The Real Problem of the Business; Advertising and Selling," *American Industries* 1, no. 1 (1902): 5.

46. "Glimpses of Salesmanship in Catalogs," *American Industries* 1, no. 5 (1902): 10, and "As Others See Them in Their Catalogs," ibid., no. 2 (1902): 8.

47. For examples, Nathan, *How to Make Money in the Printing Business*, p. 37; "Representative Trade Journals in the Printing, Book Making, Advertising, Stationery, Paper Making and Allied Trades," *Inland Printer* 17 (August 1896): 558; F. F. Helmer, "Advertising for Printers," ibid. 26 (December 1900): 486–91.

48. William Woodhouse Jr., "Retailers' Advertising," *American Grocer* 63, no. 1 (1900): 13; and Woodhouse, "A Letter and a Pointer," *American Grocer* 63, no. 13 (1900): 10–11.

49. *The Jeweler's Advertiser: A Systematized Compendium of High Class, Specialized Advertisements for the Retail Jewelry Trade* (Chicago: Jeweler's Advertising, 1908), pp. iii–v.

50. "The Ad-School," *System* 1, no. 8 (1900): n.p.

51. W. L. Agnew, "The New Advertiser," *Printers' Ink* 20, no. 8 (1897): 3–4; also, Artemas Ward, "Stray Shots," ibid. 4, no. 10 (1891): 345–46. Other publications of this period included *Brains for the Retailer and Advertiser, Fame, Poster,* and *Judicious Advertising: A Monthly Publication Devoted to General Publicity.*

52. Charles Austin Bates, "My Own Business Again," *Printers' Ink* 11, no. 8 (1894): 21; Bates advertisement "The Art and Literature of Business," ibid. 12, no. 10 (1895): 28–31.

53. "Ad 'Experts' Talk," *Printers' Ink* 13, no. 6 (1895): 3–6; and 13, no. 7 (1895): 3, 10.

54. The Advertising Man, "The Real Problem of the Business; Advertising and Selling"; The Silent Partner, "Certain Important Advertising Pointers," *American Industries* 4, no. 4 (1905): 3; "Reduced Net Profits," editors, *American Grocer* 43, no. 26 (1890).

55. *Inland Printer* published a good example of the arguments for regularizing com-

mission practices in the form of a speech to the National Editorial Association. Francis Procter, "Discounts to Advertising Agents—To Whom Should They Be Given, and How Much," 7 (October 1889): 48. For an example of a tight argument against advertising commissions, William J. Reilly, *Effects of the Advertising Agency Commission System* (New York: William J. Reilly, 1931). See Pope's *Modern Advertising* for a lengthy discussion of the commission issues.

56. The Advertising Man, "Character in Business and in Publicity"; Hower, *Advertising Agency*, pp. 62–67.

57. Sarah Stage, *Female Complaints: Lydia Pinkham and the Business of Women's Medicine* (New York: Norton, 1979), p. 110.

58. Quoted in Nathaniel C. Fowler Jr., *Building Business: An Illustrated Manual for Aggressive Business Men* (Boston: The Trade Co., 1893), p. 500.

59. Charles Austin Bates, *Good Advertising* (New York: Holmes Publishing, 1896), p. 49.

60. "A Conversation with Nathaniel C. Fowler, Jr.: Advertising, Past, Present, and Future," *Arena: The World's Leading Review* 29 (June 1903): 638–43.

61. William James, "The Medical Advertisement Abomination," letter to the editor, *Nation* 58 (1 February 1894): 84–85.

62. "Hypnotic Advertisements," n.a., *Living Age* 251 (3 November 1906): 317–18; reprinted from *Saturday Review*.

63. Louis Filler, "The Poison Trust," ch. 12, *Crusaders for American Liberalism* (Yellow Springs, Ohio: Antioch Press, 1961, first published 1939), pp. 142–56; Paul Starr, *The Social Transformation of American Medicine* (New York: Basic Books, 1982); *Nostrums and Quackery: Articles on the Nostrum Evil and Quackery Reprinted, with additions and Modifications, from The Journal of the American Medical Association* (Chicago: American Medical Association Press, 1912), pp. 7–9, 11.

64. Hower, *Advertising Agency*, pp. 111–14, 211; Francis Wayland Ayer, "Talk," at N. W. Ayer & Son Business-Getting Conference (9 September 1908), NWA.

65. Hower, *Advertising Agency*, pp. 112–14, 639; George Presbrey Rowell, *Forty Years of Advertising: 1869–1909* (Philadelphia: N. W. Ayer & Son, 1909), p. 48.

66. *J. Walter Thompson's List of Prominent Medical Journals* (New York: J. Walter Thompson, 1887), p. 1, JWTCA; *J. Walter Thompson Advertising* (New York: J. Walter Thompson, 1895), p. 9, JWTCA; *J. Walter Thompson Advertising* (New York: J. Walter Thompson, 1897), p. 7, JWTCA; *J. Walter Thompson's List of Prominent Medical Journals*, p. 2.

67. Hower, *Advertising Agency*, pp. 114–15, 211–15.

68. Ibid., pp. 116–17.

69. *J. Walter Thompson's Illustrated Catalogue of Magazines* (New York: J. Walter Thompson, 1891), p. 97, JWTCA.

70. *The Thompson Blue Book on Advertising* (New York: J. Walter Thompson, 1909), pp. 5, 15, JWTCA.

71. F. Wayland Ayer, speech at Business-Getting Conference (5 April 1907), NWA; Rowell, *Forty Years*, pp. 31–34. The agency had 163 on staff in 1900, 298 in

1910, and 496 in 1920. Hower, *Advertising Agency*, pp. 93–94, 119–23, 126–31, 221–24, 539.

72. Rowell, *Forty Years*, p. 468.

73. "Notes of a Speech Made by Mr. Stanley Resor to New Members of the Company, May 4, 1931," p. 9, JWTCA; Pope, *Modern Advertising*, p. 142.

74. Author's interview with F. Bradley Lynch, retired director of corporate communications, Ayer, Inc., June 18, 1990. Hower, *Advertising Agency*, pp. 145, 148.

75. See essay on sources for trends in professional association.

76. Quoted in Presbrey, *History and Development of Advertising*, p. 542.

77. "Movement against Fraudulent Advertising," *New York Times*, 9 October 1902; "National Society for the Investigation and Suppression of Fraudulent Advertising Formed by the Sphinx Club," *New York Times*, 23 November 1902; Charles Arthur Carlisle, "Merit as an Asset in Publicity," *American Industries* 1, no. 9 (1902): 3.

78. Calkins, *Business of Advertising*, pp. 344–46.

79. "The Club Idea in Advertising," *Mahin's Magazine* 1, no. 3 (1902): 24–29.

80. "To Regulate the Experts," editors, *Profitable Advertising* 18, no. 5 (1908): 417–18.

81. George French, *The Art and Science of Advertising* (Boston: Sherman, French, 1909), pp. 284–85.

82. H. J. Kenner, *The Fight for Truth in Advertising: A Story of What Business Has Done and Is Doing to Establish and Maintain Accuracy and Fair Play in Advertising and Selling for the Public's Protection* (New York: Round Table Press, 1936), pp. 16–17; George French, "Truth in Advertising," appendix to *Advertising: The Social and Economic Problem* (New York: Ronald Press, 1915), pp. 21, 242–58; Pope, *Modern Advertising*, pp. 202–6, 213–26; Quentin J. Schultze, "Advertising, Science, and Professionalism, 1885–1917" (Ph.D. diss., University of Illinois, 1978), pp. 174–86.

83. Examples of the discussion in "Movement against Fraudulent Advertising," *New York Times*, 9 October 1902; "National Society for the Investigation and Suppression of Fraudulent Advertising Formed by the Sphinx Club," *New York Times*, 23 November 1902. George French, *The Art and Science of Advertising* (Boston: Sherman, French, 1909), pp. 284–85, 291; "The Club Idea in Advertising," *Mahin's Magazine* 1, no. 3 (1902): 24–29.

84. D[aniel]. M. Lord, "The True Function of the Advertising Agent," *Judicious Advertising* 1, no. 5 (1903): 18–21.

85. Ibid.

86. Victor F. Lawson to Adolphus Green, quoted in William Cahn, *Out of the Cracker Barrel: The Nabisco Story from Animal Crackers to Zuzus* (New York: Simon & Schuster, 1969), pp. 68–69.

87. William M. Armistead, "Recollections," typescript memo (1954), n.p., NWA; Hower, *Advertising Agency*, pp. 151, 328. Theodore Regensteiner, *My First Seventy-Five Years* (Chicago: Regensteiner, 1943), pp. 112–13. The calculation of

Reynolds's position takes into account the break up of the American Tobacco Co.'s trust because that had occured in 1911.

88. "Why the Printer is Becoming a Factor in Advertising; Advertising is Printed Salesmanship," editors, *Printing Art* 9 (July 1907): 304.

89. A Printer, "'Expert' Ad. Writers and the Compositor," *Inland Printer* 24 (October 1899): 77.

90. Louis F. Fuchs, "Concerning Agency Composition," *Inland Printer* 45 (April 1910): 61–63; Alphonsus P. Haire, "The Theatrics of Advertising," *Harper's Weekly*, reprinted in *Inland Printer* 45 (April 1910): 63.

91. Walsh, *Selling Forces*, pp. 67–70, 84. Note that the time frame given here is rather shorter than the actual period of changes.

92. Schultze, "Advertising, Science, and Professionalism," p. 76.

## Chapter 8. Taking Advertisements toward Modernity

1. Roland Marchand, *Advertising the American Dream: Making Way for Modernity, 1920–1940* (Berkeley: University of California Press, 1985).

2. Alfred D. Chandler, *The Visible Hand: The Managerial Revolution in American Business* (Cambridge: Belknap, Harvard University Press, 1977), pp. 293–94; Arthur F. Marquette, *Brands, Trademarks, and Good Will: The Story of The Quaker Oat Company* (New York: McGraw-Hill, 1967), pp. 13–20; 40–44; Harrison John Thornton, *The History of the Quaker Oats Company* (Chicago: University of Chicago Press, 1933), pp. 25–28, 87–88.

3. Chandler, *Visible Hand*, p. 294; Naomi R. Lamoreaux, *The Great Merger Movement in American Business, 1895–1904* (Cambridge: Cambridge University Press, 1985), p. 36; Marquette, *Brands, Trademarks, and Good Will*, pp. 24, 40–44, 59–61; Thornton, *Quaker Oats Company*, pp. 88–91.

4. Marquette, *Brands, Trademarks, and Good Will*, pp. 50–54; Thornton, *Quaker Oats Company*, pp. 30–32, 88–110.

5. Marquette, *Brands, Trademarks, and Good Will*, pp. 54–61.

6. Thornton, *Quaker Oats Company*, pp. 32–33, 67–70, 90–110.

7. R. Hal Williams, *Years of Decision: American Politics in the 1890s* (New York: Knopf, 1978), pp. 67, 100–103, 115–17, 119–23.

8. "Who Will Tell the Story of Beer to the Public?" editors, *American Brewers' Review* 21 (1907): 458.

9. "Cost of a Bicycle," editors, *Iron Age* 57 (11 June 1896): 1369–1370; The Advertising Man, "The Real Problem of the Business; Advertising and Selling," *American Industries* 1, no. 1 (1902): 5.

10. The Silent Partner, "Certain Important Advertising Pointers," *American Industries* 4, no. 4 (1905): 3.

11. "Our Opinion of Advertising," advertisement for N. W. Ayer & Son, placement unknown (5 June 1904), NWA.

12. Earnest Elmo Calkins, *The Business of Advertising* (New York: Appleton, 1915), pp. 183–84, 199.

13. Newcomb Cleveland, "The Future of the Advertising Agent," *Printers' Ink* 25, no. 9 (1898): 3–6. Also, H. B. Humphrey, "The Reason Why the Agency Is," *American Industries* 4, no. 9 (1905): 9.

14. William Cahn, *Out of the Cracker Barrel: The Nabisco Story from Animal Crackers to Zuzus.* (New York: Simon & Schuster, 1969), pp. 68–69; Ralph M. Hower, *The History of an Advertising Agency: N. W. Ayer & Son at Work, 1869–1939* (Cambridge: Harvard University Press, 1939), pp. 88–90, 114–15, 117, 224–26, 639.

15. Harry Nelson McKinney, transcript of informal address at Business-Getting Conference, N. W. Ayer agency, New York (5 January 1905), NWA.

16. Alphonsus P. Haire, "The Theatrics of Advertising," *Harper's Weekly*, reprinted in *Inland Printer* 45 (April 1910): 63.

17. Louis Galambos, *The Public Image of Big Business in America, 1880–1940: A Quantitative Study in Social Change* (Baltimore: Johns Hopkins University Press), pp. 14–15; David Riesman, with Reuel Denney and Nathan Glazer, *The Lonely Crowd* (New Haven: Yale University Press, 1961), pp. 22, 139; Olivier Zunz, *Making America Corporate, 1870–1920* (Chicago: University of Chicago Press, 1990).

18. Henry C. Sheafer, "A Study in Advertising," *Arena: The World's Leading Review*, New York, 29 (April 1903): 383–90.

19. H. B. Humphrey, "The Reason Why the Agency Is," *American Industries* 4, no. 9 (1905): 9; H. B. Humphrey Co. advertisement, *System* 1, no. 4 (1901): n.p. Also, The Silent Partner, "Certain Important Advertising Pointers."

20. Herbert N. Casson, *Ads and Sales: A Study of Advertising and Selling from the Standpoint of the New Principles of Scientific Management* (Chicago: A. C. McClurg, 1911), pp. 160–67.

21. William J. Raddatz, untitled article, *Signs of the Times* 14, no. 57 (1911): 8, MS 3480, container 1, folder 1, WRHS.

22. For instance, "Avoid Egotism. Consult the Expert," editors, *Profitable Advertising* 4, no. 1 (1894): 69–70; A Printer, "'Expert' Ad. Writers and the Compositor," *Inland Printer* 24 (October 1899): 77; Nathaniel C. Fowler Jr., "The Advertising Counselor," *Profitable Advertising* 17, no. 8 (1908): 821–22.

23. Nathaniel C. Fowler Jr., "Fact vs. Theory: A Discussion of the Sense and Nonsense of Advertising," *Advertising Experience: The American Advertiser's Illustrated Magazine* 4, no. 2 (1896): 5; Fowler, *Fowler's Publicity: An Encyclopedia of Advertising and Printing, and All that Pertains to the Public-seeking Side of Business* (Boston: Publicity Publishing, 1900), p. 739. Also, Theodore Hamilton, "Yellow Advertising," *Printers' Ink* 22, no. 6 (1898): 14; Casson, *Ads and Sales*, p. 71.

24. James Melvin Lee, *Language for Men of Affairs*, vol. 2, *Business Writing* (New York: Ronald Press, 1920), pp. 375, 380–81. Also, O. C. Harn, "An Aid in the Securing of Results," *Profitable Advertising*, 18, no. 2 (1908): 142–43.

25. Arthur Warren, "Secrets of Business 'Booming' Revealed," *New York Times*, 28 February 1904, p. 13.

26. Walter L. Gallup, "Neglected Opportunities in Advertising," *Inland Printer* 13 (July 1894): 315–16.

27. "Notes of a Speech Made by Mr. Stanley Resor to New Members of the Company, May 4, 1931," p. 5, JWTCA; George Burton Hotchkiss and Richard B. Franken, *The Leadership of Advertised Brands: A Study of 100 Representative Commodities Showing the Names and Brands That Are Most Familiar to the Public* (New York: Doubleday, Page, 1923), pp. 100–102.

28. Hower, *Advertising Agency*, pp. 372–74, 382; Livermore & Knight, Advertisers, *Fifty Years of the Pioneer Spirit* (Providence, R.I.: Livermore & Knight, 1925), n.p., HM&L.

29. Editors, *American Brewers' Review* 21 (1907): 460.

30. Claude C. Hopkins, *My Life in Advertising* (New York: Harper & Brothers, 1927), pp. 53–57.

31. Armistead, "Recollections."

32. S. C. Stevens, "Photography in Ads.," *Printers' Ink* 24, no. 2 (1898): 8, reprinted from *Metropolitan Magazine*. Also, "Photography in Advertising," n.a., *Printers' Ink* 14, no. 9 (1896): 3–4, reprinted from *American Journal of Photography*.

33. John F. Kasson, *Civilizing the Machine: Technology and Republican Values in America, 1776–1900* (New York: Penguin, 1976); Julie Wosk, *Breaking Frame: Technology and the Visual Arts in the Nineteenth Century* (New Brunswick: Rutgers University Press, 1992).

34. Charles Francis, *Printing for Profit* (New York: Bobbs-Merrill, 1917), p. 54.

35. "Specimens Received," editors, *Inland Printer* 4 (December 1886): 223–24; "Give Us Good Plain Work," editors, *Inland Printer* 3 (April 1886): 402; Frederick F. Turner, "Effectiveness in Job Printing," *Printing Art* 9 (June 1907): 241–42. Also, R. C. Harding, "Concerning Fashion and Taste," for a recognition of how much "fashion affects individual taste" in printing styles. *Inland Printer* 15 (July 1895): 377.

36. John Higham, "The Reorientation of American Culture in the 1890's," in *The Origins of Modern Consciousness*, John Weiss, ed. (Detroit: Wayne State University Press, 1965), pp. 25–48; Cecelia Tichi, *Shifting Gears: Technology, Literature, Culture in Modernist America* (Chapel Hill: University of North Carolina Press, 1987); Ann Uhry Abrams, "From Simplicity to Sensation: Art in American Advertising, 1901–1929," *Journal of Popular Culture* 10 (winter 1976): 621–28; Christopher P. Wilson, "The Rhetoric of Consumption: Mass-Market Magazines and the Decline of the Gentle Reader, 1880–1920," in *The Culture of Consumption: Critical Essays in American History, 1880–1980*, T. J. Jackson Lears and Richard Wightman Fox, eds. (New York: Pantheon, 1983), pp. 39–64, esp. pp. 48–50.

37. Arthur Robert Burns, *The Decline of Competition: A Study of the Evolution of American Industry* (New York: McGraw-Hill, 1936), p. 375. Neil H. Borden,

The Economic Effects of Advertising (Chicago: Richard D. Irwin, 1944), pp. 158, 424–26, 602–6, 860.

38. David W. Kiehl, "American Art Posters of the 1890s," in idem., ed., *American Art Posters of the 1890s* (New York: Metropolitan Museum of Art, distributed by Harry N. Abrams, 1897), pp. 11–15.

39. Nancy Finlay, "American Posters and Publishing in the 1890s," in Kiehl, *Art Posters*, p. 46.

40. Each of the first two contests attracted at least one thousand posters. "Advertising Did It," n.a., *Profitable Advertising* 2, no. 3 (1892): 70–72; "Advertising 'The Columbia,'" ibid. 7, no. 8 (1897): 275–77; Kiehl, "American Art Posters," p. 20.

41. "The Artistic Pictorial Poster: High Art in Advertising," editors, *Profitable Advertising* 4, no. 10 (1895): 291–97; "The Decline of the Fancy Poster," editors, *Printer and Bookmaker* 25 (January 1898): 279–80.

42. Joel Benton, *Printers' Ink* 8, no. 2 (1893): 18–19.

43. [Charles Austin Bates], "Pictures in Advertising," *Advertising Experiences* 4, no. 2 (1896): 11; Bates, *Good Advertising: A Practical Book* (New York: Holmes Publishing, 1896), pp. 577–90.

44. A Printer, "'Expert' Ad. Writers and the Compositor."

45. Interview with Dave Cheadle, Trade Card Collectors' Association, Denver, 22 January 1996.

46. For instance, George Ward Nichols, *Art Education Applied to Industry* (New York: Harper & Brothers, 1877), pp. 9, 21; editorial, "The Engraver's and Printer's Art in America," *Inland Printer* 8 (March 1891): 509; and "Analysis of Decorative Printing," editors, *Inland Printer* 20 (October 1897): 43; also, "The Commercial Artists' Association of Chicago," editors, *Inland Printer* 24 (March 1900): 865. In addition to organizing artists, this latter group set up evening art classes.

47. Frank Presbrey, *The History and Development of Advertising* (Garden City, N.Y.: Doubleday, Doran, 1929), pp. 98, 100.

48. This undated poster and two others dated 1900 and 1903 for the Robert Portner Brewing Co., Alexandria, Va., are in WCBA.

49. F. Penn, "Some Notes on Publicity," *Inland Printer* 16 (February 1896): 539; "Notes on Publicity," editors, *Inland Printer* 17 (April 1896): 88.

50. Editorial, *Printers' Ink* 12, no. 2 (1895): 4–5.

51. John Brisben Walker, "Beauty in Advertising Illustration," *Cosmopolitan* 33 (September 1902): 491–500.

52. "The Sphinx Club Dinner," *New York Times*, 14 April 1898, p. 7.

53. W. L. Wells, "Commercial Art," *Inland Printer* 15 (May 1895): 181.

54. T. C. McLuhan, *Dream Tracks: The Railroad and the American Indian* (New York: Harry N. Abrams, 1985), pp. 18–28.

55. "Aubrey Beardsley," *Inland Printer* 13 (April 1894): 27.

56. Finlay, "American Posters and Publishing in the 1890s," in Kiehl, *Art Posters*, pp. 48–49.

57.  "The Inland Printer's Covers," editors, *Inland Printer* 24 (December 1899): 389–96.

58.  "Opinions on Display in Advertisements," editors, *Inland Printer* 11 (July 1893): 310–11. Also, "The Artistic Pictorial Poster: High Art in Advertising," editors, *Profitable Advertising* 4, no. 10 (1895): 290–97; "Poster Show at Paris Exposition," editors, *Inland Printer* 24 (March 1900): 845; "The Professional Beauty," n.a., *Printers' Ink* 12, no. 8 (1895): 13; C. F. B., "Posters," ibid. 12, no. 10 (1895): 17–18; "Columbia Bicycle Posters," C. F. B., ibid. 15, no. 6 (1896): 25; "The New Advertiser," editors, ibid. 20, no. 8 (1897): 3–4.

59.  "The Progress of Design in Advertising," editors, *Profitable Advertising* 17, no. 12 (1908): 1238–40.

60.  J. George Frederick, "First Principles of Advertising," *Judicious Advertising* 1, no. 8 (1903): 23.

61.  "Advertising Illustrations," editors, *Ad Sense* 20 (May 1906): 452–55. Also, "The Art Poster as an Advertisement," *Inland Printer* 20 (October 1897): 41–42; William D. McJunkin, "How Type Tells in Advertising," *Inland Printer* 35 (July 1905): 512–14; Louis F. Fuchs, "Concerning Agency Composition," ibid. 45 (April 1910): 61–63.

62.  George Sherman, "Advertising," *Inland Printer* 35 (August 1905): 733–35.

63.  Frank Farrington, "Business Building," *American Druggist* 49 (23 July 1906): 49–50; ibid. 49 (27 August 1906): 106–7.

64.  Henry Lewis Johnson, "How Engravers and Printers Advertise," *Inland Printer* 13 (August 1894): 433–35.

65.  Hower, *Advertising Agency*, pp. 378–82.

66.  "A Plea for the Printer and for the Man Who Pays," editors, *Inland Printer* 25 (April 1900): 41–42; Penrhyn Stanlaws, "The Lack of Art in Publicity," *Profitable Advertising* 10, no. 12 (1901): 885–90.

67.  Nathaniel C. Fowler Jr., *Fowler's Publicity: An Encyclopedia of Advertising and Printing* (Boston: Publicity Publishing, 1900), pp. 517–19.

68.  Fowler, *Fowler's Publicity*, pp. 520–21, 654.

69.  Ibid., pp. 273–300.

70.  Presbrey, *History and Development of Advertising*, pp. 382–87.

71.  The Anderson Preserving Co. had roots deep in the nineteenth century, having shared a common ancestor with the Campbell Soup Co.

72.  John T. Cox, secretary, and V. S. Anderson, treasurer, Anderson Preserving Co., to Theo. Leonhardt & Son (2 December 1898 and 4 May 1899), HM&L, Leonhardt Lithographer Collection, accessions 1020 and 1021.

73.  For instance, "A Plea for the Printer and for the Man Who Pays," editors, *Inland Printer* 25 (April 1900): 41–42; F. F. Helmer, "Advertising for Printers," ibid. 25 (May 1900): 248–50. For example advertisements, see those for the Card Electric Motor and Dynamo Co., *Inland Printer* 17 (September 1896): 613; and Sanders Engraving Co., ibid. 26 (October 1900): 31. Fowler, *Fowler's Publicity*, p. 654.

74.  Advertisements and other items in Post Family Collection, box 1, folders 3, 4,

and 5, MHC. Charles W. Post, "The Door UnBolted: Come In," Post Family Collection, box 1, folder 4, MHC.

75. A. Rowden King, "The Factory and Its Relation to the Advertising Department," *Printers' Ink* 72, no. 10 (1910): 30, 32–35.

76. For early efforts against air pollution, Christine Meisner Rosen, "Businessmen Against Pollution in Late Nineteenth-Century Chicago," *Business History Review* 69 (1995): 351–97.

77. Lindy Biggs, *The Rational Factory: Architecture, Technology, and Work in America's Age of Mass Production* (Baltimore: Johns Hopkins University Press, 1996); Pamela Walker Lurito [Laird], "Advertising's Smoky Past: Themes of Progress in Nineteenth-Century Advertisements," in Robert Weible and Francis R. Walsh, eds., *The Popular Perception of Industrial History* (Lanham, Md.: American Association of State and Local History, 1989), pp. 175–212; John R. Stilgoe, "Moulding the Industrial Zone Aesthetic: 1880–1929," *American Studies* 15 (April 1982): 5–24.

78. George Presbrey Rowell, *The Men Who Advertise: An Account of Successful Advertisers* (New York: Nelson Chesman, 1870), pp. 146–48, 181; "Do Your Advertisements Pay?" *Printers' Ink* 1, no. 9 (1888).

79. "Improved Business Methods" *Printers' Ink* 1, no. 20 (1889): 506, originally published in *Table Talk*; John S. Grey, "Hints on Preparing Advertisements," *Printers' Ink* 4, no. 9 (1891): 311–12; Artemas Ward, "Stray Shots," ibid. 4, no. 9 (1891): 312.

80. Nathaniel C. Fowler Jr., *Building Business: An Illustrated Manual for Aggressive Business Men* (Boston: The Trade Co., 1893), pp. 243–62; idem, "Fact vs. Theory: A Discussion of the Sense and Nonsense of Advertising," *Advertising Experience* 4, no. 2 (1896): 5.

81. Albert Davis Lasker, *The Lasker Story As He Told It* (Chicago: Advertising Publications, 1963), pp. 20–21, 34–35. Most analysts integrated this concept into their work, such as Casson, *Ads and Sales*, ch. 2, pp. 13–21; and S. Roland Hall, *The Advertising Handbook* (New York: McGraw-Hill, 1921), pp. 12–14; Hopkins, *My Life in Advertising*, pp. 121–22.

82. John S. Grey, "Hints on Preparing Advertisements," *Printers' Ink* 4, no. 9 (1891): 311–12.

83. Charles Austin Bates, *The Dry Goods Book* (New York: Charles Austin Bates Syndicate, 1899), pp. 9–11.

84. Stephen Fox, *The Mirror Makers: A History of American Advertising and Its Creators* (New York: William Morrow, 1984), pp. 49–50. For instance, John S. Grey, "Hints on Preparing Advertisements," *Printers' Ink* 4, no. 9 (1891): 311–12; Calkins, *Business of Advertising*, p. 334.

85. Lasker, *Lasker Story*, p. 21.

86. "Avoid Egotism. Consult the Expert," *Profitable Advertising* 4, no. 1 (1894): 69–70. Also, "Sentences that Sell Goods," editors, *Inland Printer* 15 (April 1895): 56.

87. Mahin Advertising Co. advertisement, *System* 1, no. 1 (1900): n.p.

88. Claude Hopkins, *My Life in Advertising*, passim, esp. pp. 73, 79–82, 116, 146, 150–56, 173, 175–76, 204.

89. Calkins, *Business of Advertising*, pp. 89, 198–99, 202–3, 207, 266–67.

90. Bates, *Good Advertising*, p. 1. Also, Joseph H. Appel, *Growing Up With Advertising* (New York: Business Bourse Publishing, 1940), p. 24.

91. Fowler, *Building Business*, pp. 19–22; G. H. E. Hawkins, "An Addressed Delivered Before the Adcraft Club of Detroit," *Brains for the Retailer and Advertiser* 30, no. 13 (1907): 5–7; Charles Lee Prator, "The Mission of the Ad," ibid. 30, no. 13 (1907): 7.

92. Appel headed Wanamaker's advertising department from 1901 or 1902 until 1936. Appel, *Growing Up With Advertising*, pp. xx, 24, 34.

93. Lasker, *Lasker Story*, pp. 21, 43; Henry C. Sheafer, "A Study in Advertising," *Arena* (April 1903): 383–90. Also, Hopkins, *My Life in Advertising*, pp. 73–74.

94. Calkins, *Business of Advertising*, p. 8.

95. Fowler, *Building Business*, pp. 19–22.

96. Lasker, *Lasker Story*, p. 47.

97. "Charles Austin Bates' Observations," *Judicious Advertising* 1, no. 12 (1903): 22.

98. George French, *Advertising: The Social and Economic Problem* (New York: Ronald Press, 1915), pp. 24–27.

99. Casson, *Ads and Sales*, pp. 70–72.

100. John Brisben Walker, "Beauty in Advertising Illustration," *Cosmopolitan* 33 (September 1902): 491.

101. Philo C. Darrow, "The Philosophy of Advertising," *Profitable Advertising* 9, no. 11 (1900): 767–70.

102. O. C. Harn, "An Aid in the Securing of Results," *Profitable Advertising* 18, no. 2 (1908): 142–43.

103. Humphrey, "The Reason Why the Agency Is."

104. Untitled column filler, *Iron Age* 58 (16 July 1896): 145.

105. "Our Designs," *Inland Printer* 8 (June 1891): 835. Also, A Printer, "Advertising for Printers," *Inland Printer* 24 (January 1900): 603–4.

106. "Antique versus Modern," *J. Walter Thompson: Advertising* (New York: J. Walter Thompson, 1895), p. 16, JWTCA. Also, Fowler, *Building Business*, p. 258; John S. Grey, "Hints on Preparing Advertisements," *Printers' Ink* 4, no. 9 (1891): 311–12; W. A. Engarde, "Artistic Advertising," *Inland Printer* 11 (August 1893): 387–88; F. Penn, "Some Notes on Publicity," *Inland Printer* 16 (February 1896): 539; Cha[rle]s Paddock, "The Selling Element in an Ad," *Printers' Ink* 20, no. 3 (1897): 17.

107. S. C. Stevens, "Photography in Ads.," *Printers' Ink* 24, no. 2 (1898): 8, reprinted from *Metropolitan Magazine*.

108. Louis F. Fuchs, "Concerning Agency Composition," *Inland Printer* 45 (April 1910): 61–63.

109. Herbert N. Casson, *Ads and Sales: A Study of Advertising and Selling from the*

*Standpoint of the New Principles of Scientific Management* (Chicago: A. C. Mc-Clurg, 1911), p. 22.

110. O. C. Harn, "An Aid in the Securing of Results," *Profitable Advertising* 18 (July 1908): 142–43; William H. Maher, "The Aftermath of Advertising," *Printers' Ink* 7, no. 24 (1892): 787–89.

111. Both the primary and secondary literatures are replete with tales of these marketing accomplishments. See the essay on sources for recent scholarship in marketing history.

112. "Suggestions by the Advertising Man," n.a., *American Industries* 3, no. 5 (1904): 12.

113. Cahn, *Out of the Cracker Barrel*, pp. 65–70. The National Biscuit Co.'s 1901 policy statement is quoted in Chandler, *Visible Hand*, p. 335.

114. Cahn, *Out of the Cracker Barrel*, pp. 70–73, 83, 90–93; Hower, *Advertising Agency*, pp. 115–16.

115. Cahn, *Out of the Cracker Barrel*, pp. 93, 126–27, 132, 225; Hower, *Advertising Agency*, pp. 89–91, 93.

116. "Sentences that Sell Goods," editors, *Inland Printer* 15 (April 1895): 56.

117. Daniel Starch, *Advertising: Its Principles, Practice, and Technique* (Chicago: Scott, Foresman, 1914), p. 16.

118. Calkins, *Business of Advertising*, pp. 183–201.

119. *J. Walter Thompson's Illustrated Catalogue of Magazines Compiled for the Use of Advertisers* (New York: 1887), pp. 8–14, JWTCA. Also, Fowler, *Building Business*, pp. 104–5.

120. This statement was attributed to Frank Siddell, "The Philadelphia soap man." *Printers' Ink* 11, no. 1 (1894): 11, column filler.

121. Richard Ohmann, *Selling Culture: Magazines, Markets, and Class at the Turn of the Century* (London: Verso, 1996), pp. 112–14.

122. Advertisements for the *Sun*, *Printers' Ink* 13, no. 9 (1895): 8.

123. Advertisement for Boyce's Big Weeklies, *Printers' Ink* 15, no. 9 (1896): 16; advertisement for Atlantic Coast Lists, *Printers' Ink* 15, no. 5 (1896): 2. Also, John Chester, "Country Newspapers," *Printers' Ink* 14, no. 6 (1896): 25.

124. Bates, *Good Advertising*, p. 16. For examples of later recommendations, "Keying Advertisements," *American Druggist* 36, no. 4 (1900): 105, reprinted from *Printers' Ink*; John Lee Mahin, "Interesting All Kinds of People," *System* 1, no. 1 (1900): n.p; A. H. Zenner, "Ascertaining the Results of Advertising," *System* 1, no. 4 (1901): n.p.; The Silent Partner, "Certain Important Advertising Pointers," *American Industries* 4, no. 4 (1905): 3; Hopkins, *My Life in Advertising*, p. 154.

125. Casson, *Ads and Sales*, p. 88. Also, Starch, *Advertising*, pp. 91–95.

126. M. Georgia Ormond, "Comparisons in Advertising," *Inland Printer* 13 (April 1894): 30–33.

127. Advertisements for the *Ladies' World* in *Printers' Ink* 11, no. 4 (1894): 147; ibid. 11, no. 6 (1894): 213.

128. Miss Progress, "Woman in the Business World," *Profitable Advertising* 3, no. 1 (1893): 27–28.

129. Marchand, *Advertising the American Dream*, esp. pp. 32–35.

130. "Where Advertisers Blunder," *Overland Monthly* 36 (July 1900): 84–85.

131. Calkins, *Business of Advertising*, p. 210.

132. Appel, *Growing Up With Advertising*, p. 28.

133. Edd Applegate, ed., *The Ad Men and Women: A Biographical Dictionary of Advertising* (Westport, Conn.: Greenwood Press, 1994), pp. 262–71; Fox, *Mirror Makers*, pp. 81, 86–88. Helen Woodward was also a prominent copywriter, but she worked later and for less duration than Lansdowne.

134. For example, Richard A. Pick, "Advertising Inconsistencies," *Printers' Ink* 60, no. 1 (1907): 8.

135. *Mrs. John Doe* (New York: Butterick Publishing, 1918), pp. 5–13, 23.

136. William Kohn, "Pertinently and Impertinently Personal," *Printers' Ink* 11, no. 4 (1894): 158–59.

137. J. George Frederick, "First Principles of Advertising," *Judicious Advertising* 1, no. 8 (1903): 23.

138. Calkins, *Business of Advertising*, p. 202.

139. Oscar Herzberg, "Human Nature as a Factor in Advertising," *Printers' Ink* 13, no. 14 (1895): 3–4; Joel Benton, "Psychology of Advertising," *Printers' Ink* 14, no. 2 (1896): 14; O[scar] Herzberg, "Hidden Forces in Advertising," *Printers' Ink* 20, no. 5 (1897): 10, first published in *Fame*.

140. David Gibson, "The Common Sense of Psychology," *Profitable Advertising* 17, no. 9 (1908): 955.

141. Hopkins, *My Life in Advertising*, pp. 187–88.

142. Jean M. Converse, *Survey Research in the United States: Roots and Emergence 1890–1960* (Berkeley: University of California Press, 1987), pp. 88–91; Merle Curti, "The Changing Concept of 'Human Nature' in the Literature of American Advertising," *Business History Review* 41 (winter 1967): 335–57; David P. Kuna, "The Concept of Suggestion in the Early History of Advertising Psychology," *Journal of the History of the Behavioral Sciences* 12 (1976): 347–53; Quentin J. Schultze, "Advertising, Science, and Professionalism, 1885–1917" (Ph.D. diss., University of Illinois, 1978), esp. ch. 3.

143. Schultze, "Advertising, Science, and Professionalism," pp. 93–94; Walter Dill Scott, series, "Twelve Papers on Psychological Topics," *Mahin's Magazine* 1, nos. 1–12 (1902–1903); Scott, "The Psychology of Advertising," *Atlantic Monthly* 93 (January 1904): 29–34; Scott, *The Theory of Advertising: A Simple Exposition of the Principles of Psychology in their Relation to Successful Advertising* (Boston: Small, Maynard, 1904); Scott, *The Psychology of Advertising* (Boston: Small, Maynard, 1908).

144. George French, *The Art and Science of Advertising* (Boston: Sherman, French, 1909), pp. 28–29.

145. Hopkins, *My Life in Advertising*, p. 173.

146. Hugo Munsterberg, "Psychology and the Market," *McClure's Magazine* 34, no. 1 (1909): 87–93.

147. Appel, *Growing Up With Advertising*, p. 105. Chapter 5 is titled "Psychology in the Practice of Advertising." Also, Stanley Resor, "The Machinery of Our Business," in News Bulletin (typescript) no. 17 (New York: J. Walter Thompson, 26 September 1916), p. 6, JWTCA.

148. Henry Foster Adams, *Advertising and Its Mental Laws* (New York: Macmillan, 1916), pp. 18–20, 277, 296, 298–99, 311–14.

149. Applegate, *Ad Men and Women*, pp. 262–71; Fox, *Mirror Makers*, pp. 81, 86–88.

150. Sally Wyner, "A Literary Product: The Relationship of American Literature and Advertising Copy" (Ph.D. diss., Harvard University, 1995). Also, Marchand, *Advertising the American Dream*, esp. ch. 2.

151. W. A. Engarde, "Artistic Advertising," *Inland Printer* 11 (August 1893): 387–88.

152. Louis F. Fuchs, "Concerning Agency Composition," *Inland Printer* 45 (April 1910): 61–63.

153. "The Appeal of the Advertisement," 18 (April 1909): 1076–77. See Marchand, *Advertising the American Dream*, for some of the consequences of succumbing to this temptation.

154. Lasker, *Lasker Story*, pp. 44–49.

155. Thornton, *Quaker Oats Company*, pp. 243–48; Hopkins, *My Life in Advertising*, pp. 143–46. *Ladies' World* 34, no. 9 (1913): 21.

156. "The Automobile Industry and Its Advertising Possibilities," *Judicious Advertising* 1, no. 7 (1903): 15–17.

157. Hopkins, *My Life in Advertising*, pp. 109–21; Donald Finlay Davis, *Conspicuous Production: Automobiles and Elites in Detroit, 1899–1933* (Philadelphia: Temple University Press, 1988), p. 91.

158. Calkins, *Business of Advertising*, pp. 205–7.

159. Davis, *Conspicuous Production*, pp. 59–60.

160. Pamela Walker Laird, "'The Car Without a Single Weakness': Early Automobile Advertising," *Technology and Culture* 37 (October 1996): 796–812.

161. Adams, *Advertising and Its Mental Laws*, pp. 196–97, 204, 276.

162. Stephen Vaughn, *Holding Fast the Inner Lines: Democracy, Nationalism, and The Committee on Public Information* (Chapel Hill: University of North Carolina Press, 1980), p. 150. Vaughn reproduces a series of examples on pp. 159–88.

163. Ibid., p. 169.

164. Ibid., pp. 192, 319 n.89.

165. Marchand, *Advertising the American Dream*, summary pp. 10–24.

166. Advertisement for Odorono, *Ladies' Home Journal* 36, no. 5 (1919): 168. Fox, *Mirror Makers*, pp. 87–88; Applegate, *Ad Men and Women*, p. 355; Julian Lewis Watkins, *The 100 Greatest Advertisements: Who Wrote Them and What They Did* (New York: Dover, 1959), pp. 30–31. *Ladies' Home Journal* 36, no. 8 (1919): 113.

# Chapter 9. Modernity and Success

1. N. W. Ayer & Son, "Notes of Progress," *The Advertiser's Guide: A Magazine Devoted to the Interests of Advertisers and Newspaper Publishers* 1, nos. 1–4 (1976–1977); ibid. 2, nos. 1–2 (1877); "Curious Facts About Advertising," ibid. 2, no. 1 (1877): 2–3; "The Growth of Advertising," ibid. 2, no. 2 (1877): 18–19, NWA.

2. Richard J. Walsh, *Selling Forces* (Philadelphia: Curtis Publishing, 1913), p. 84.

3. Volney B. Palmer, *Business-Men's Almanac for the Year 1849* (New York), n.p., WCBA, Advertising Collection, box 3.

4. "The Advertising of the Future," *Profitable Advertising* 1, no. 1 (1891): 7; J. Walter Thompson Co., postscript to P. V. Bunn, *Friendly Talks to Managers* (New York: J. Walter Thompson, 1910), pp. 46–49, JWTCA.

5. Henry Sampson, *A History of Advertising from the Earliest Times* (London: Chatto & Windus, 1874), pp. 1–2, 556–57.

6. See the essay on sources for the research basis of this conclusion.

7. Examples include *Printers' Ink* 1, no. 1 (1888): 17; "Advertising of a Country Store 70 Years Ago," *New York Times*, 8 April 1978, p. 2; "The Seller to the Buyer: History and Curiosities of Advertising," ibid., 26 January 1879, p. 5.

8. "The Dawn of Advertising," *Printers' Ink* 13, no. 25 (1895): 57–58; "First New York Advertising," ibid. 15, no. 6 (1896): 49–51, reprinted from *New York Evening Post*; "Some Old Time Advertisements," *AD Sense* 14 (June 1903): 457; "A Study in Antiquities," *Judicious Advertising* 1, no. 8 (1903): 37–38.

9. "Newspapers Before the War," *Printers' Ink* 2, no. 30 (1890): 730, reprinted from the *McKeesport Times* (Pa.).

10. J. Walter Thompson, "Antique versus Modern," *J. Walter Thompson Advertising* (New York, 1895), pp. 13–17.

11. R. G. Ray, "The Ethics of Advertising," *Printers' Ink* 11, no. 21 (1894): 904–7.

12. Joel Benton, "Style in Advertising," *Printers' Ink* 8, no. 2 (1893): 18–19.

13. Carroll D. Wright, *The Industrial Evolution of the United States* (Meadville, Pa.: Chautauqua-Century Press, 1895), p. 68. Also, Henry King, "A Treatise on Advertising," *Printers' Ink* 17, no. 9 (1896): 17–19; Charles Austin Bates, *Printers' Ink* 13, no. 26 (1895): 68–69; Frances Bellamy, "The Literature of Business," *Reader Magazine* 16 (August 1904): 244–51; Frederick Dwight, "The Significance of Advertising," *Yale Review* 18 (August 1909), o.s.: 197–205.

14. "Changes in Advertising Matters," *Printers' Ink* 8, no. 3 (1893): 115–16; "About Advertisements," *New York Times*, 2 August 1900, p. 6. Also, W. L. Agnew, "The New Advertiser," *Printers' Ink* 20, no. 8 (1897): 3–4; "Progress in Advertising," ibid.: 42, reprinted from *Harper's Weekly*; Francis Wayland Ayer, "Fiftieth Anniversary Speech" (4 April 1919), n.p., NWA.

15. Walter Dill Scott, "The Psychology of Advertising," *Atlantic Monthly* 93 (January 1904): 29–34.

16. Stanley Resor, "New York Notes," News Bulletin no. 17, typescript (New York: J. Walter Thompson, 29 September 1916), p. 3, JWTCA.

17. "The Value of Display," *Printers' Ink* 10, no. 20 (1894): 602; "Advertisements That 'Have Influenced Me'," ibid. 13, no. 19 (6 November 1895): 4–5.

18. "Noticeable Progress in Advertising Methods," *Inland Printer* (July 1895): 381. Also, "A Glance at the Past," *Profitable Advertising* 8, no. 1 (1915): 11–14.

19. H. B. Humphrey, "The Reason Why the Agency Is," *American Industries* 4, no. 9 (1905): 9–10.

20. Henry Romaine, "The Interchange of Ideas," *Printers' Ink* 14, no. 7 (1896): 59.

21. Frank Farrington, "Business Building," *American Druggist* 49 (15 October 1906).

22. Editorial, *Printers' Ink* 11, no. 2 (1894): 64. Herbert L. Willett, "The Barnum Principle in Advertising," *Mahin's Magazine* 1, no. 5 (1902): 19–23. Also, S. G. Harvey, "Some Facts about Sign Advertising," *Printers' Ink* 8, no. 10 (1893): 343–44; "Prevention of Cruelty to Landscapes," ibid. 25, no. 8 (1898): 51; "Side-Show Phases of Advertising," ibid. 26, no. 1 (1899): 14; Walter R. Hine, "The Advertising of Foods: Why the Manufacturer Who Advertises Should Be Encouraged," *Good Housekeeping Magazine* 48 (March 1909): 383–86.

23. Nathaniel C. Fowler Jr., *Fowler's Publicity: An Encyclopedia of Advertising and Printing, and All that Pertains to the Public-seeking Side of Business* (Boston: Publicity Publishing, 1900), pp. 532–33.

24. Nathaniel C. Fowler Jr., *Building Business: An Illustrated Manual for Aggressive Business Men* (Boston: The Trade Co., 1893), pp. 13–14.

25. Fowler, *Building Business*, pp. 13–14.

26. D[aniel]. M. Lord, "The True Function of the Advertising Agent," *Judicious Advertising* 1, no. 5 (1903): 18–21.

27. John Lee Mahin, *Advertising: Selling the Consumer* (New York: Doubleday, Page, 1914, for Associated Advertising Clubs of the World), p. 3.

28. Claude C. Hopkins, "The Young Man in Advertising," *Printers' Ink* 16, no. 7 (1896): 6. Also, Truman A. DeWeese, "The Young Man With Nothing But Brains," *Forum* 32 (February 1902): 695–99.

29. George Presbrey Rowell, *Forty Years an Advertising Agent, 1865–1905* (New York: Printers' Ink Publishing, 1906), pp. 204–5, 325, 441–54.

30. Fowler, *Fowler's Publicity*, pp. 691–93.

31. J. Walter Thompson agency, *The Thompson Red Book on Advertising* (New York, 1899), frontispiece and pp. 3–6; and *The Thompson Blue Book on Advertising* (New York, 1904–1905 and 1909).

32. J. Walter Thompson Co., *Where Good Advertising is the Constant Product* (New York: 1905); Charles Austin Bates, *Good Advertising and Where It Is Made* (New York, 1905), JWTCA.

33. J. Walter Thompson Co., *Where Good Advertising is the Constant Product*, n.p.; idem, *Thompson Blue*, p. 9.

34. Earnest Elmo Calkins, *The Business of Advertising* (New York: Appleton, 1915), p. 251. Also, Walsh, *Selling Forces*, pp. 274–81; "The Curtis Publishing Company," *Profitable Advertising* 18, no. 5 (1908): 466–77.

35. Rowell, *Forty Years*, p. 441; "Concentration, the Secret of Success," editorial,

Profitable Advertising 3, no. 6 (1893): 170–72. Also, George H. Powell, *System of Advertising Instruction* (New York, 1903), p. 7, WCBA, Advertising Collection, box 7.

36. Nathaniel C. Fowler Jr., "Mr. Fowler Stands Up," *Profitable Advertising* 1, no. 4 (1891): 138; Charles Austin Bates advertisement "The Art and Literature of Business," *Printers' Ink* 12, no. 10 (1895): 28–31; *J. Walter Thompson's Illustrated Catalogue of Magazines, Compiled for the Use of Advertisers* (New York, J. Walter Thompson, 1887), pp. 4–7. Also, R. G. Ray, "The Ethics of Advertising," *Printers' Ink* 11, no. 21 (1894): 904–7; Fowler, "The Advertising Counselor," *Profitable Advertising* 17, no. 8 (1908): 821–22.

37. *Advertiser's Gazette*, p. 5. Also, Rowell, *Men Who Advertise*, pp. 3–4; N. W. Ayer & Son, "Wise Advertising," *1888 Directory* (Philadelphia, N. W. Ayer & Son, 1888), p. 7, WCBA, Advertising Collection, box 2.

38. *J. Walter Thompson's Illustrated Catalogue of Magazines, Compiled for the Use of Advertisers* (New York, J. Walter Thompson, 1887), pp. 4–7; N. W. Ayer & Son, "Our Aims," *Advertiser's Guide: A Magazine Devoted to the Interests of Advertisers and Newspaper Publishers* 1, no. 1 (June 1876): 1, NWA; Pierce W. Hart, "Advertising as a Practical Science," *Printers' Ink* 4, no. 12 (1891): 407–8; George P. Rowell Advertising Co. advertisement "The Search Light of Business," *Printers' Ink* 11, no. 18 (1894): 720.

39. Ralph M. Hower, *The History of an Advertising Agency: N. W. Ayer & Son at Work, 1869–1939* (Cambridge: Harvard University Press, 1939), pp. 283–84.

40. Fowler, *Building Business*, p. 221. Also, J. Walter Thompson, "A Live Businessman," *The Religious Press* (New York: J. Walter Thompson, 1887), n.p., JWTCA; "A Prominent Advertiser's Wise Decision," editorial, *Profitable Advertising* 3, no. 3 (1893): 70–71; C. W. Scofield, General Advertising Agent, to Riehle Brothers, 2 April 1879, WCBA, Advertising Collection, box 3; *J. Walter Thompson's Illustrated Catalogue of Magazines, Compiled for the Use of Advertisers* (New York, J. Walter Thompson, 1891), p. 97.

41. Rowell, *Forty Years*, p. 376.

42. John S. Grey, "Hints on Preparing Advertisements," *Printers' Ink* 4, no. 9 (1891): 311–12; George P. Rowell & Co. advertisement "To Advertisers," *Printers' Ink* 4, no. 23 (1891): 756.

43. Artemas Ward, "Stray Shots," *Printers' Ink* 4, no. 10 (1891): 345–46.

44. William H. Maher, "Who Shall Write the Advertisement?" *Printers' Ink* 8, no. 2 (1893): 83–85; Henry Romaine, "Ambition in Advertising," *Printers' Ink* 15, no. 4 (1896): 70. Also, "Ad 'Experts' Talk," *Printers' Ink* 13, no. 6 (1895): 3–6; *Printers' Ink* 13, no. 7 (1895): 3–10.

45. For example, Joseph Eldridge Esray, "Publicity's Progress Impeded by Tradition," *Profitable Advertising* 8, no. 11 (1899): 593–94; J. A. Richards, "Individuality in Advertising," ibid.: 660.

46. H. B. Humphrey advertisement "Unbelievers," *Advertising Success* 2, no. 5 (1900): 6, WCBA, Advertising Collection, box 5. Also, D. M. Lord, "The True

Function of the Advertising Agent," *Judicious Advertising* 1, no. 5 (1903): 20; J. Walter Thompson Co., *Advertising* (New York: J. Walter Thompson, 1897), pp. 17, 19–21, JWTCA; J. Walter Thompson Co., "A Business Chat," *The Thompson Red Book on Advertising: A Register of Representative Organs and How to Use Them* (New York: J. Walter Thompson, 1899), p. 1, JWTCA.

47. "Avoid Egotism. Consult the Expert," editorial, *Profitable Advertising* 4, no. 1 (1894): 69–70. Also, "Sentences that Sell Goods," *Inland Printer* 15 (April 1895): 56.

48. Herbert N. Casson, *Ads and Sales: A Study of Advertising and Selling from the Standpoint of the New Principles of Scientific Management* (Chicago: A. C. McClurg, 1911), pp. 71–73.

49. Charles Austin Bates, *Printers' Ink* 11, no. 8 (1894): 21; Bates advertisement "Art and Literature," *Printers' Ink* 12, no. 10 (1895): 28–31.

50. Newcomb Cleveland, "The Future of the Advertising Agent," *Printers' Ink* 25, no. 9 (1898): 3–6.

51. Charles Austin Bates, "A Distinctly Egotistical Talk to General Advertisers," *Profitable Advertising* 9, no. 12 (1990): 868–69.

52. "Criticising the Critic," *Printers' Ink* 12, no. 10 (1895): 37–38.

53. Seth Brown, "Buying Space and Buying Advertising," *Printers' Ink* 31, no. 3 (1900): 3–5. Also, editorials in *AD-ART: A Magazine of Ideas and Suggestions, in Text and Illustrations, for All Who Write Advertisements* 5, no. 1 (20 December 1902): 1–2; *AD-ART* 5, no. 5 (17 January 1903): 2, WCBA, Advertising Collection, box 5.

54. Volney B. Palmer, *Business-Men's Almanac for the Year 1849* (New York, 1849), n.p., WCBA, Advertising Collection, box 3.

55. For a detailed discussion of this issue and its implications for advertising education and organization, see Schultze, "Advertising, Science, and Professionalism," esp. pp. 93–125.

56. N. W. Ayer & Son advertisement, "Our Opinion of Advertising" (5 June 1904), NWA.

57. Fowler, *Building Business*, p. 14.

58. Henry Foster Adams, *Advertising and Its Mental Laws* (New York: Macmillan, 1916), p. 19.

59. George French, *The Art and Science of Advertising* (Boston: Sherman, French, 1909), p. 30.

60. French, "The Practise of Advertising: As to Science and Theory," *Profitable Advertising* 17, no. 9 (1908): 916–19. Also, French, "First Lessons in the Art of Advertising: The Second Lesson, Dealing with Science and Art, and Their Importance as Fundamentals of Advertising," *Profitable Advertising* 18, no. 8 (1909): 778–81; French, *Advertising: The Social and Economic Problem*, pp. 44–58; "Scientific Selling," *The Ayer Idea In Advertising* (N. W. Ayer & Son, Philadelphia, 1912), pp. 29–32; Daniel Starch, *Advertising: Its Principles, Practice, and Technique* (Chicago: Scott, Foresman, 1914), p. 16.

61. Conway MacMillan, "Adology, Part II, Science of Advertisement," *White's Class Advertising* 2, no. 11 (November 1904): 21–25, WCBA, Advertising Collection, box 6.

62. Hower, *Advertising Agency*, pp. 122–23.

63. Earnest Elmo Calkins, *The Business of Advertising* (New York: Appleton, 1915), p. 183.

64. Casson, *Ads and Sales*, pp. vi, 60, 145. Also, Charles Frederick Higham, *Scientific Distribution* (London: Nisbet, 1916).

65. Resor believed he had derived this definition from Thomas Huxley. "The Agency and the Representative," speech, 3 November 1919, p. 4, JWTCA.

66. Stanley Resor, untitled speech (September 1916), p. 1, JWTCA; idem, "What Magazine Advertising Is Accomplishing," speech, 4 June 1917, p. 13, JWTCA. Also, idem, "News Bulletin," J. Walter Thompson Co., no. 20 (1916), pp. 3, 6, JWTCA; Walsh, *Selling Forces*, p. 56. Peggy J. Kreshel, "The 'Culture' of J. Walter Thompson, 1915–1925," *Public Relations Review* 16, no. 3 (1990): 80–93.

67. Schultze, "Advertising, Science, and Professionalism," esp. pp. 132–57; Schultze, "'An Honorable Place': The Quest for Professional Advertising Education, 1900–1917," *Business History Review* 56 (spring 1982): 16–32.

68. Henry C. Sheafer, "A Study in Advertising," *Arena* 29 (April 1903): 383–90.

69. For instance, "To Regulate the Experts," editorial, *Profitable Advertising* 18 (1908): 417–18.

70. Humphrey, "The Reason Why the Agency Is," pp. 9–10. Also, W. Hull Western, "Manufacturer and Machinery Dealer and His Advertising," *American Industries* 4, no. 19 (1906): 11.

71. Volney B. Palmer, *Business-Men's Almanac for the Year 1850* (New York, 1850), n.p., WCBA, Advertising Collection, box 3.

72. Wright, *The Industrial Evolution of the United States*, p. 185.

73. George P. Rowell, *The Men Who Advertise: An Account of Successful Advertisers* (New York: Nelson Chesman, 1870), pp. 198–99; Henry King, "The American Press," *Printers' Ink* 14, no. 7 (1896): 3–6. Also, "Newspapers Before the War," *Printers' Ink* 2, no. 30 (1890): 730, reprinted from the *McKeesport Times* (Pa.); "The Evolution of the Newspaper," *Printers' Ink* 27, no. 12 (1899): 10–12.

74. "The Present Unsatisfactory Condition of the Advertising Agencies," *Printers' Ink* 21, no. 9 (1897): 37.

75. Rowell, *Forty Years*, pp. 321–22.

76. Rowell, "Miscellany," *Advertiser's Gazette: A Magazine of Information for Advertisers* 1 (New York: December 1867): 2; Charles T. Root, "Trade Journalism in Its Relation to Advertising," *Printers' Ink* 26, no. 3 (1899): 38–45; Nixon Waterman, "The Ad. Man," *Inland Printer* 13 (July 1894): 335, reprinted from *Chicago Evening Journal*.

77. J. Walter Thompson, "Reaching the Millions," *Appleton's Magazine* 37 (May 1908): 610–14.

78. "What's the Advertising Outlook for 1918?" editorial, *Printers' Ink* 101, no. 12 (1917): 3–4, 6, 104, 106–8; quotation from p. 108.

79. "The Present Unsatisfactory Condition of the Advertising Agencies," *Printers' Ink* 21, no. 9 (1897): 37; "Advertising Agencies Organize," *Advertising Experience* (March 1900), in J. Walter Thompson Press Clippings, 1890–1903, JWTCA. Also, W. L. Beadnell, "Their Interests Are Mutual," *Printers' Ink* 4, no. 14 (1891): 487, reprinted from *American Advertiser Reporter*; Charles T. Root, "Trade Journalism in its Relation to Advertising," paper read before Sphinx Club of New York, reprinted in *Printers' Ink* 26, no. 1 (1899): 38–45. The American Advertising Agents' Association formed in 1900 was not a direct predecessor of the American Association of Advertising Agencies formed in 1917.

80. George P. Rowell, "How to Succeed in Business," *Advertisers' Gazette: A Monthly Journal Devoted to the Interests of Advertisers and Newspaper Publishers* 1, no. 7 (May 1867): 1, WCBA, Advertising Collection, box 5.

81. *Printers' Ink* 1, no. 1 (1888): 17.

82. George P. Rowell & Co. advertisement, "Doctor of business," *Printers' Ink* 4, no. 16 (1891): 563.

83. S. M. Pettengell, "V. B Palmer's Sales Approach," *Printers' Ink* 3, no. 26 (1890): 686; Rowell, *Forty Years*, pp. 25, 71–74, 124.

84. "In Printer's Ink the Secret: Vast Fortunes made by the Patent-Medicine Kings," *New York Times*, 14 October 1894, p. 21; "Men Who Have Advertised Themselves to Fame and Fortune," *Printers' Ink* 11, no. 17 (1894): 659–60. Also, "The House of Ayer and Its Modern Development," *Advertising Success* 2, no. 5 (1900): 11–15. This refers to J. C. Ayer Co., a leading patent-medicine company.

85. Charles Austin Bates, *Good Advertising* (New York: Holmes Publishing, 1896), p. 9.

86. George P. Rowell Co., *Printers' Ink* 14, no. 2 (1896): 80.

87. John E. Powers, "New Ways to Keep Shop," *Judicious Advertising* 1, no. 9 (July 1903): 33–34.

88. G. H. Powell, "Bicycle Advertising," *Profitable Advertising* 1, no. 2 (1891): 85–86; "Advertising Did It," *Profitable Advertising* 2, no. 3 (1891): 70–72; "Advertising 'The Columbia,'" *Profitable Advertising* 7, no. 8 (1898): 275–78.

89. "Monuments of Success in Advertising that Stand in Every City," *Profitable Advertising* 2, no. 10 (1892): 294–95.

90. "Honest Advertising," *Printers' Ink* 13, no. 26 (1895): 68, reprinted from *American Investment*; R. H. Sylvester, "The Value of an Advertisement," *Art in Advertising* 4, no. 2 (1891): 40.

91. "Parable of the Traveler and His Good Fairy," *Judicious Advertising* 1, no. 7 (May 1903): 26–27.

92. Calkins, *The Business of Advertising*, pp. 98–99.

93. J. Walter Thompson Co., *The Thompson Blue Book on Advertising* (New York, 1904–1905), pp. 7–9.

94. David Shelley Nicholl, *The Golden Wheel: The Story of Rotary, 1905 to the Present* (Plymouth, U.K.: Macdonald & Evans, 1984), pp. 6, 77; *Rotary? The University Group Looks at the Rotary Club of Chicago* (Chicago: University of Chicago Press, 1934), pp. 2–3, 5; Bruce A. Kimball, *The "True Professional Ideal" in America* (Cambridge, Mass.: Blackwell, 1992), pp. 199, 293, 300; Thomas J. Peters and Robert H. Waterman Jr., *In Search of Excellence: Lessons from America's Best-Run Companies* (New York: Harper & Row, 1982), pp. 157–82.

95. Schultze, "Advertising, Science, and Professionalism," pp. 60, 62, 64, 72.

96. William S. Power Co., "The Power Service for Advertisers," *Industry: A Magazine of Commerce and Finance*, n.s. 2, no. 6 (June 1907): 397.

97. Alphonsus P. Haire, "The Theatrics of Advertising," *Harper's Weekly*, reprinted in *Inland Printer* 45 (April 1910): 63.

98. National Committee on Agency Service, "Report on Agency Service" (1918), p. 11, JWTCA.

## Chapter 10. The Appropriation of Progress

1. "War Time Service the Note of St. Louis Convention," *Printers' Ink* 99, no. 10 (1917): 3–4.

2. This interpretation draws, in part, on Peter L. Berger and Thomas Luckman, *The Social Construction of Reality: A Treatise in the Sociology of Knowledge* (Garden City, N.Y.: Doubleday, 1966), esp. pp. 23, 67, 97–99. For major sources on professional and business culture trends of this era as well as theoretical resources, see the essay on sources.

3. Claude C. Hopkins, *My Life in Advertising* (New York: Harper & Bros., 1927), p. 56; "Criticising the Critic," the editors, *Printers' Ink* 12, no. 10 (1895): 37–38.

4. John G. Burke, "Wood Pulp, Water Pollution, and Advertising," *Technology and Culture* 20 (1979): 175–95.

5. George French, "Truth in Advertising," appendix to *Advertising: The Social and Economic Problem* (New York: Ronald Press, 1915), pp. 242–58; H. J. Kenner, *The Fight for Truth in Advertising: A Story of What Business Has Done and Is Doing to Establish and Maintain Accuracy and Fair Play in Advertising and Selling for the Public's Protection* (New York: Round Table Press, 1936); Daniel Pope, *The Making of Modern Advertising* (New York: Basic Books, 1983), pp. 202–6, 213–26; Quentin J. Schultze, "Advertising, Science, and Professionalism, 1885–1917" (Ph.D. diss., University of Illinois, 1978), pp. 174–86.

6. French, *Advertising: The Social and Economic Problem*, p. 21.

7. William C. D'Arcy, "The Achievements of Advertising in a Year," *Printers' Ink* 104, no. 2 (1918): 17–18. Stephen Vaughn, *Holding Fast the Inner Lines: De-*

mocracy, *Nationalism, and The Committee on Public Information* (Chapel Hill: University of North Carolina Press, 1980), pp. 142–43, 192.

8. Fowler, *Building Business*, p. 14; W. L. Wells, "Commercial Art," *Inland Printer* 15 (May 1895): 181; editorial, *Judicious Advertising* 1, no. 8 (June 1903): 12; "Indexes of Prosperity: The Return of Good Times Shown in the Newspapers— Circulation Up, More Advertising," *New York Times*, 22 February 1895, p. 8; "A Measure of Prosperity," *New York Times*, 9 January 1900, p. 6. Also, Henry King, "A Treatise on Advertising," *Printers' Ink* 17, no. 9 (1896): 17–19.

9. See the essay on sources for the basis of this assessment.

10. A. I. Teele, "The Mission of Advertising," *Profitable Advertising* 1, no. 2 (1891): 37–38. Also, "Cocoanuts and Cocoanuts, Advertising Talk in a New Dress," *The Thompson Red Book*, p. 9.

11. "Profitable Stories," *Printers' Ink* 14, no. 6 (1896): 17–25, reprinted from the *San Francisco Call*.

12. Octavus Cohen, "Advertising for Inventors," *Printers' Ink* 14, no. 7 (1896): 56–58.

13. Charles Austin Bates, *Printers' Ink* 13, no. 26 (1895): 68–69.

14. Newcomb Cleveland, "The Future of the Advertising Agent," *Printers' Ink* 25, no. 9 (1898): 3–6.

15. "Interview of Robert Bonner," *Printers' Ink* 8, no. 18 (1893): 547–49.

16. F. W[ayland] Ayer, "Advertising in America," in Chauncey M. Depew, ed., *One Hundred Years of American Commerce*, vol. 1 (New York: Greenwood Press, 1968; first published 1895), pp. 76–83. Depew's work is a two-volume collection of analyses on the state of American business with essays written by a person prominent in each area.

17. Volney B. Palmer, *Business-Men's Almanac for the Year 1849* (New York, 1849), n.p.

18. T. C. Quinn, "The Next Great Profession," *Profitable Advertising* 2, no. 2 (1892): 37.

19. Nathaniel C. Fowler, *Building Business* (Boston: The Trade Co., 1893), p. 500; "The First Subscriber to *Printers' Ink*," *Printers' Ink* 11, no. 4 (1894): 137.

20. *Printers' Ink* 15, no. 3 (1896): 5; John Brisben Walker, "Beauty in Advertising Illustrations," *Cosmopolitan* 33 (September 1902): 491.

21. James H. Plummer, "Newspaper Advertising vs. Solicitation" *Printers' Ink* 11, no. 21 (1894): 907–8; George P. Rowell Advertising Co. advertisement "The Iron Is Hot," *Printers' Ink* 15, no. 5 (1896): 112.

22. Fowler, *Building Business*, pp. 19–22.

23. C. F. David advertisement, "Can't Afford to Advertise?" *Profitable Advertising* 3, no. 1 (1893): 26.

24. "The Outlook for 1894," editorial, *Profitable Advertising* 3, no. 7 (1893): 200–201.

25. "Education in Advertising," *Profitable Advertising* 3, no. 1 (1893): 5.

26. "The Science of Advertising," *Printers' Ink* 13, no. 7 (1895): 24, reprinted from

*Age of Steel.* Also, "Modern Advertising," *Printers' Ink* 13, no. 19 (1895): 23, reprinted from the *Whiting Sun* (Kans.).

27.    Francis Wayland Ayer, "Dictated by F. W. A.," *Manual for Advertisers* (Philadelphia: N. W. Ayer & Son, 1894), NWA.

28.    J. Walter Thompson Co., "A Business Chat," *Advertising* (1897), p. 5, JWTCA; "Cocoanuts and Cocoanuts, Advertising Talk in a New Dress," *The Thompson Red Book on Advertising* (1899), p. 9, JWTCA. Also, "Evolution in Trade Methods" *Printers' Ink* 15, no. 7 (1896): 57, reprinted from *Paper and Ink.*

29.    "Progress in Advertising," *Printers' Ink* 20, no. 8 (1897): 42, reprinted from *Harper's Weekly*; *Profitable Advertising* 8, no. 1 (1898): 19

30.    For instance, Henry King, "A Treatise on Advertising," *Printers' Ink* 17, no. 9 (1896): 17–19.

31.    Oscar Herzberg, "The Century's Achievements in Business," *Printers' Ink* 29, no. 2 (1899): 3–5, reprinted from *Self Culture Magazine*.

32.    Herzberg, "The Century's Achievements in Business," pp. 3–5.

33.    *Self Culture Magazine* became *Modern Culture* in 1900. Frank Luther Mott, *A History of American Magazines*, vol. 4, *1885–1905* (Cambridge: Belknap, Harvard University Press, 1957), p. 54–55.

34.    Joanne Reitano, *The Tariff Question in the Gilded Age: The Great Debate of 1888* (University Park: Pennsylvania State University Press, 1994).

35.    "The Victory for Sound Money," editorial, *Iron Age* 58 (5 November 1896): 869.

36.    Herzberg, "The Century's Achievements in Business," p. 4.

37.    William McKinley, "Opening Speech," to the National Convention of Manufacturers, 1895, National Association of Manufacturers *Convention Reports, 1895–1898*, n.p., National Association of Manufacturers Archives, HM&L.

38.    Thomas Dolan, "Opening Speech," *Program* of the First annual convention of the National Association of Manufacturers, 1896, National Association of Manufacturers (NAM) *Convention Reports, 1895–1898*, n.p.; Thomas McDougall, "The Home Market," ibid., NAM Archives, HM&L. Later, "The Battle for Markets," an editorial in the first volume of NAM's *American Trade*, declared that "Publicity is the need of the hour." *American Trade* 1, no. 12 (1898): 88, NAM Archives, HM&L.

39.    National Association of Manufacturers *Convention Reports, 1895–1898*, n.p.

40.    McDougall, "The Home Market." Also, "The National Association of Manufacturers," editorial, *Iron Age* 57 (30 January 1896): 309; "Reciprocity Treaties: Summary of the Views of Many Firms," ibid. (26 March 1896): 756–58; "Reciprocity Treaties: Additional Evidence from Manufacturers," ibid. (2 April 1896): 805–6; "Banquet Issue: Annual Banquet of the Crockery Board of Trade," *Crockery and Glass Journal* 51 (15 February 1900): 33–46.

41.    "In Printer's Ink the Secret: Vast Fortunes made by the Patent-Medicine Kings," *New York Times*, 14 October 1894, p. 21; "Men Who Have Advertised Themselves to Fame and Fortune," *Printers' Ink* 11, no. 17 (1894): 659–60.

42. *Thirtieth Annual Report of the [Massachusetts] Bureau of Statistics of Labor*, p. 60, cited in Edward C. Kirkland, *Industry Comes of Age: Business, Labor, and Public Policy, 1860–1897* (New York: Holt, Rinehart & Winston, 1961), p. 277. Also, "Trusts and Prices," editors, *American Grocer* 43, no. 3 (15 January 1890): 7; "Ideal Combinations," editors, *Iron Age* 58 (15 October 1896): 731; "Production and Demand," anon., *Iron Age* 58 (3 December 1896): 1109.

43. L. J. Vance, "Trade Combinations and Advertising," *Printers' Ink* 12 (1898): 63; also, "Advertising *vs* Trusts," *Printers' Ink* 26, no. 8 (1899): 16.

44. Jno. Cutler, "On Trusts and Advertising," *Printers' Ink* 29, no. 6 (1899): 3–4.

45. Emerson P. Harris, "Trusts and Advertising," *Printers' Ink* 30, n. 1 (1900): 17.

46. Ibid.

47. Pope, *Making of Modern Advertising*, 68–70; Neil H. Borden, *The Economic Effects of Advertising* (Chicago: Richard D. Irwin, 1944), pp. 859, 873–74.

48. "Advertising and Economics," *Printers' Ink* 30, no. 2 (1900): 8, reprinted from the *Chicago Tribune*.

49. Editorial, *Judicious Advertising: A Monthly Publication Devoted to General Publicity* 1, no. 1 (1902): 15.

50. "How the Powder Trust Advertises—And Why," *Printers' Ink* 60, no. 2 (1907): 3–4, 6.

51. Edward Sherwood Meade, *Trust Finance: A Study of the Genesis, Organization, and Management of Industrial Organizations* (New York: Appleton, 1909), pp. 75–76. Also, "Views by the Advertising Man; Trust Advertising, 'Commissions,'" anon., *American Industries* 3, no. 3 (1904): 7.

52. George Burton Hotchkiss and Richard B. Franken, *The Leadership of Advertised Brands: A Study of 100 Representative Commodities Showing the Names and Brands That Are Most Familiar to the Public* (New York: Doubleday, Page, 1923); Pope, *Making of Modern Advertising*, pp. 95–97; Susan Strasser, *Satisfaction Guaranteed: The Making of the American Mass Market* (New York: Pantheon, 1989), pp. 272–75, 278–82.

53. Borden, *Economic Effects*, pp. 27, 162, 163, 166–67, 436, 438, 512, 517, 848–51, 879, 881.

54. Nathaniel C. Fowler Jr., *Building Business: An Illustrated Manual for Aggressive Business Men* (Boston: The Trade Co., 1893), pp. 19–22.

55. Herbert N. Casson, *Ads and Sales* (Chicago: A. C. McClurg, 1911), p. 72. Also, Humphrey, "The Reason Why the Agency Is."

56. Franklin L. Sheppard, "Market Prices and Competition: Their Origin and Suggestions for Remedying their Evils," *Iron Age* 57 (14 May 1896): 1187; "Cost of a Bicycle," *Iron Age* 57 (11 June 1896): 1369–70.

57. Arch Wilkinson Shaw, *An Approach to Business Problems* (Cambridge: Harvard University Press, 1916), pp. 202–3, 214–16.

58. Henry King, "A Treatise on Advertising," *Printers' Ink*, 17, no. 9 (1896):17–19. Also, Charles Austin Bates, *Printers' Ink* 13, no. 26 (1895): 68–69; Frances Bellamy, "The Literature of Business," *Reader Magazine* 16 (August 1904): 244–51;

Frederick Dwight, "The Significance of Advertising," *Yale Review*, o.s. 18 (August 1909): 197–205.

59. George French, *Advertising: The Social and Economic Problem* (New York: Ronald Press, 1915), pp. 24–27, 38.

60. "Advertising Luxuries," *The J. Walter Thompson Book* (New York: J. Walter Thompson, 1909), pp. 48–49; also, *Advertising as a Selling Force* (New York: J. Walter Thompson, 1909).

61. Cover illustration and description in "From 'P.A.'s' Point of View," *Profitable Advertising* 9, no. 8 (1900): cover and p. 555.

62. D[aniel]. M. Lord, "The True Function of the Advertising Agent," *Judicious Advertising* 1, no. 5 (March 1903): 18–21.

63. French, *Art and Science of Advertising*, p. 39; Truman A. DeWeese, "Advertising as a Business-Building Force," *Profitable Advertising* 18, no. 12 (1909): 1190–93; "From 'P.A.'s' Point of View," *Profitable Advertising* 18, no. 1 (1908): 21–23.

64. Resor, "The Agency and the Representative," typescript of speech before the Representatives Club, 3 November 1919, p. 1, JWTCA. Also, "Production and Demand," anon., *Iron Age* 58 (3 December 1896): 1109; Francis Bellamy, "The Literature of Business," *Reader Magazine* 4 (August 1904): 244–51, esp. p. 246. Daniel Bell regretted the necessity for this linkage from his less sanguine view of advertising's cultural impact. *The Cultural Contradictions of Capitalism* (New York: Basic Books, 1978).

65. Richard J. Walsh, *Selling Forces* (Philadelphia: Curtis Publishing, 1913), pp. 23–24, 152–53.

66. John Lee Mahin, *Advertising: Selling the Consumer* (New York, 1914), pp. 5, 17, 19, 20.

67. George B. Waldron, "The Hum of the Factory," *Mahin's Magazine* 1, no. 4 (July 1902): 22–24; editorial, ibid. 1, no. 6 (September 1902): 15.

68. Truman A. DeWeese, *Keeping a Dollar at Work: Fifty Talks on Newspaper Advertising Written for the N. Y. Evening Post* (New York Evening Post, 1915), p. 8. Also, "Decennial Anniversary of the New York Council of the American Association of Advertising Agencies" (13 April 1921), p. 51, reprinted in Richard Turnbull, "Genesis of the American Association of Advertising Agencies," typescript prepared for the American Association of Advertising Agencies (January 1969).

69. Emerson P. Harris, "Trusts and Advertising," *Printers' Ink* 30, no. 1 (1900): 17.

70. J. Walter Thompson Co., *The J. Walter Thompson Book* (New York: J. Walter Thompson, 1909), p. 18, JWTCA.

71. "From 'P.A.'s' Point of View," *Profitable Advertising* 18, no. 12 (1909): 1180–81. Also, Shaw, *An Approach to Business Problems*, p. 128.

72. Truman A. DeWeese, "The Young Man With Nothing But Brains," *Forum* 32 (February 1902): 695–99.

73. Sidney A. Sherman, "Advertising in the United States," *Publication of the American Statistical Association* 7 (December 1900): 119–62, quotations on p. 156.

Sherman did agree, however, that advertising was necessary to maintain demand for manufactured goods and thereby did contribute to progress, pp. 158–59.

74. J. Walter Thompson Co., *The J. Walter Thompson Book*, p. 19, JWTCA. Also, Truman A. DeWeese, *Book on Advertising*, The Business Man's Library, vol. 7 (Chicago: System, 1907), pp. 6–10.

75. Resor, "Report on Agency Service," p. 8; "War Time Service," p. 4, JWTCA.

76. Starch, *Advertising: Its Principles, Practice, and Technique*, pp. 15–16; Starch, *Principles of Advertising* (Chicago: A. W. Shaw, 1923), pp. 79–88.

77. Resor, "What Magazine Advertising Is Accomplishing," speech, 4 June 1917, p. 13, JWTCA. Adrian D. Joyce, "Advertising as an Economizer of Selling Expense," *Judicious Advertising* (1915): 114–16, NWA. Also, "Advertising and Economics," *Printers' Ink* 30, no. 2 (1900): 8, reprinted from the *Chicago Tribune;* Truman A. DeWeese, *The Principles of Practical Publicity*, 2d edn. (Philadelphia: George W. Jacobs, 1908), pp. 2–3; Paul Terry Cherington, *Advertising as a Business Force: A Compilation of Experience Records* (New York: Doubleday, Page, 1913), pp. 458–60; French, *Advertising: The Social and Economic Problem*, pp. 59–69; Resor, "Two Means of Saving Labor and Reducing Cost," editorial prepared for *Public Ledger* (6 May 1918), p. 4, JWTCA.

78. Calkins, *The Business of Advertising*, pp. 11, 97; Mahin, *Advertising: Selling the Consumer*, pp. 24–25. Also, Shaw, *An Approach to Business Problems*, pp. 203–9.

79. Anonymous source quoted in James Melvin Lee, *Language for Men of Affairs* (New York: Ronald Press, 1920), vol. 2, *Business Writing*, pp. 444–45.

80. Samuel Hopkins Adams, "The Art of Advertising," part 1 of "The New World of Trade," *Collier's* 43 (22 May 1909): 13–15; "Fair Trade and Foul," part 2, ibid. (19 June 1909): 19, 20, 16; "Traps and Pitfalls," part 3, ibid. (24 July 1909); "The Publisher and the Public," part 4, ibid. (21 August 1909).

81. "Advertising Bulletin No. 4: The Cost of Advertising," *Collier's* 43 (22 May 1909): 5. Also, "Advertising Bulletin No. 15: Advertising Decreases the Cost of Advertising," 43 (7 August 1909): 5.

82. Maurice Switzer, *Who Pays the Advertising Bills?* (New York: *Leslie's Illustrated Weekly Newspaper*, 1915), WCBA, Advertising Collection, box 9. Also, George B. Waldron, "What America Spends in Advertising," *Chautauquan* (Springfield, Ohio) 38 (October 1903): 155–59.

83. In particular, "Advertising Bulletin No. 5: Advertiser and Publisher," *Collier's* 43 (29 May 1909): 5. Also, J. Walter Thompson, "Reaching the Millions."

84. "A Conversation with Nathaniel C. Fowler, Jr.: Advertising, Past, Present, and Future," *Arena: The World's Leading Review* 29 (June 1903): 638–43. Also, Charles Arthur Carlisle, "Advertising Men's Dinner," *New York Times*, 24 September 1904, p. 2.

85. Mark Twain, *A Connecticut Yankee in King Arthur's Court* (New York: Tom Doherty Associates, 1991; first published 1889), pp. 93–95.

86. French, *Advertising*, p. 38. Also, "From 'P.A.'s' Point of View," *Profitable Advertising* 18, no. 1 (1908): 21–23.

87. Calkins, *Business of Advertising*, p. 9.

88. "From 'P.A.'s' Point of View," *Profitable Advertising* 18, no. 1 (1908): 23–24.

89. DeWeese, *The Principles of Practical Publicity*, pp. 8–10.

90. J. Walter Thompson, "Reaching the Millions," *Appleton's Magazine* 37 (May 1908): 610–14; French, *Advertising: The Social and Economic Problem*, p. 69; Truman A. DeWeese, "Advertising as a Business-Building Force," *Profitable Advertising* 18, no. 2 (1909): 1190–93.

91. "Advertising Bulletin No. 7: The University of Advertising," *Collier's* 43 (24 July 1909): 5; "Advertising Bulletin No. 20: Making Life Pleasant," ibid. (11 September 1909): 5; "Advertising Bulletin No. 18: How Advertising Helps the World Move," ibid. (28 August 1909): 4. Also, Waldo P. Warren, "By-Products of Advertising," ibid., 42 (6 February 1909): 34.

92. Walsh, *Selling Forces*, p. 231.

93. "The Advertising of Foods: Why the Manufacturer Who Advertises Should Be Encouraged," *Good Housekeeping Magazine* 48 (March 1909): 383–86; "The Commerce of Clothes," ibid. (April 1909): 524–26.

94. French, *Art and Science of Advertising*, p. 17.

95. J. Walter Thompson Co., *The J. Walter Thompson Book*, pp. 5–9, JWTCA.

96. Herbert W. Hess, *Productive Advertising* (Philadelphia: J. B. Lippincott, 1915), pp. ii, 1.

97. Waldo Warren, "By-Product of Advertising," *Collier's: The National Weekly* 42 (6 February 1909): 34.

98. French, *The Art and Science of Advertising*, pp. 31, 287, 291.

99. Burke, "Wood Pulp, Water Pollution, and Advertising"; Ralph Borsodi, *National Advertising vs. Prosperity: A Study of the Economic Consequences of National Advertising* (New York: Arcadia Press, 1923), quote from pp. 16–17.

100. Burke, "Wood Pulp, Water Pollution, and Advertising"; Charles Gilbert, *American Financing of World War I* (Westport, Conn.: Greenwood Publishing, 1970), p. 63. An example of the debates regarding wartime taxation of publishers and advertising can be found in "Tax on Intelligence," editors, *New York Times*, 25 May 1917, p. 10: 2, 7.

101. "Avoid Using Patriotism as Sales Argument," editors, *Printers' Ink* 99, no. 4 (1917): 118.

102. "Advertising and the Man Famine," *Printers' Ink* 99, no. 7 (1917): 114–15.

103. "War Time Service the Note of St. Louis Convention," *Printers' Ink* 99, no. 10 (1917): 3–4.

104. "War Time Service the Note of St. Louis Convention," *Printers' Ink* 99, no. 10 (1917): 3–4; Herbert S. Houston, "Advertising as the Instrument of Democracy; The Shortcomings Have Been Steadily Corrected," *Printers' Ink* 99, no. 10 (1917): 8, 10; Louis W. Hill, "Advertising's Part in National Prosperity," *Printers' Ink* 99, no. 10 (1917): 12, 17–18. Also, Vaughn, *Holding Fast*, esp. pp. 141–43; Daniel Pope, "The Advertising Industry and World War I," *Public Historian* 2, no. 3 (1980): 4–25.

105. J. Murray Allison, "Advertising as the Quick Rescuer in England's Crisis," *Printers' Ink* 99, no. 10 (1917): 51–52, 55–56.

106. The Committee on Public Information, headed by journalist George Creel, also participated in censorship and nonadvertising propaganda activities. Stewart Halsey Ross, *Propaganda for War: How the United States Was Conditioned to Fight the Great War of 1914–1918* (Jefferson, N.C.: McFarland, 1996), esp. pp. 218–37. Also, Vaughn, *Holding Fast*.

107. William C. D'Arcy, "The Achievements of Advertising in a Year," *Printers' Ink* 104, no. 2 (1918): 17–18.

108. Ibid.

# Conclusion

1. Joseph French Johnson, "Advertising as an Economic Force," *Poster* 11 (August 1920): 23–25, 59, 61.

2. Roland Marchand, *Advertising the American Dream: Making Way for Modernity, 1920–1940* (Berkeley: University of California Press, 1985), esp. pp. xxi, 1–24, 233–34. Marchand's analysis shows how this attitude played out in advertisements of the 1920s and 1930s.

3. Johnson, "Advertising as an Economic Force," pp. 24, 59.

4. See the essay on sources for a summary of studies of business peoples' operations and attitudes during this era.

5. For instance, "Magazine Advertising," editorial, *Current Literature* 34, no. 1 (January 1903): 9; Frederick Dwight, "The Significance of Advertising," *Yale Review* 18 (August 1909): 197–205. "Hypnotic Advertisements," n.a., *Living Age* 251 (13 November 1906): 317–18, reprinted from *Saturday Review*.

6. Peter L. Berger and Thomas Luckman, *The Social Construction of Reality: A Treatise in the Sociology of Knowledge* (Garden City, New York: Doubleday, 1966), esp. pp. 23, 67, 97–99.

7. Amos Stote, memo to [William M.] Armistead and [George H.] Thornley (16 February 21); H. E[ugene] Wheeler to Armistead (17 February 1921); Armistead to F[rancis] W[ayland] A[yer] (18 February 1921), NWA. Also, F. Wayland Ayer, "A Half Century of Advertising," *The Next Step* 1, no. 5 (1921): 3–5, 13–17, 21.

8. Arthur Twining Hadley, president of Yale University, wrote an important example of the many contemporary tracts on the growing appreciation for the power of public opinion in *Standards of Public Morality* (New York: Macmillan, 1914), esp. pp. 9–14. Ron Pearson, "Perspectives on Public Relations History," *Public Relations Review* 16, no. 3 (1990): 27–38; Alan R. Raucher, "Public Relations in Business: A Business of Public Relations," *Public Relations Review* 16, no. 3 (1990): 19–26; Richard S. Tedlow, *Keeping the Corporate Image: Public Relations and Business, 1900–1950* (Greenwich, Conn.: JAI Press, 1979), pp. 15–19.

9. George French, *The Art and Science of Advertising* (Boston: Sherman, French, 1909), pp. 289–90.

10. Felix Orman, *A Vital Need of the Times* (New York: Felix Orman, 1918), pp. vii–xi, 45, 74, 116. Also, E. S. Hole and John Hart, *Advertising and Progress* (London: Review of Reviews, 1914).

11. N. W. Ayer & Son, *House Advertisements*, bound collection of advertisements placed during 1919 (Philadelphia: N. W. Ayer & Son, 1920), n.p., NWA.

12. N. W. Ayer & Son, form letter to newspaper publishers, 25 September 1919, NWA; N. W. Ayer & Son, form letter to newspaper and magazine publishers, 2 January 1919, NWA.

13. Paul F. Stacy, "Advertising Advertising," undated page from *The Next Step* (c. 1921), NWA.

14. N. W. Ayer & Son series of advertisements "Advertising Advertising" (1919), NWA. Earlier examples abound of publications themselves encouraging their readers to have confidence in their advertisers' products. For instance, *Country Life in America* 11 (March 1907): 603; ibid. 11 (April 1907): 634.

15. Claude C. Hopkins, *My Life in Advertising* (New York: Harper & Brothers, 1927), pp. 69–70, 72, 77.

16. Jeffrey A. Charles, *Service Clubs in American Society: Rotary, Kiwanis, and Lions* (Champaign: University of Illinois Press, 1993).

17. William C. D'Arcy, "The Achievements of Advertising in a Year," *Printers' Ink* 104, no. 2 (1918): 17–18.

18. Earnest Elmo Calkins, *The Business of Advertising* (New York: Appleton, 1915), p. 66.

19. John Lee Mahin, *Advertising: Selling the Consumer* (New York: Doubleday, Page for Associated Advertising Clubs, 1914), p. 183.

20. Nathaniel C. Fowler Jr., *Building Business: An Illustrated Manual for Aggressive Business Men* (Boston: The Trade Co., 1893), p. 248.

21. French, *Art and Science of Advertising*, p. 243. Also, pp. 33, 281–84, 287.

22. W[illiam] M. Armistead, "Service," *The Next Step* 1, no. 1 (1920): 3–4, 7.

23. J. Walter Thompson Co., foreword to *Modern Advertising Agency Service* (Toronto: J. Walter Thompson, n.d., circa 1914), n.p., JWTCA.

24. A. Rowden King, "The Factory and Its Relation to the Advertising Department," *Printers' Ink* 72, no. 10 (1910): 30, 32–35.

25. Marchand, *Advertising the American Dream*; passim; Daniel Pope, *The Making of Modern Advertising* (New York: Basic Books, 1983), pp. 249–50; Jackson Lears, *Fables of Abundance: A Cultural History of Advertising in America* (New York: Basic Books, 1994), esp. pp. 118–20, 184, 204–7.

26. Nathaniel C. Fowler Jr., "Fact vs. Theory: A Discussion of the Sense and Nonsense of Advertising," *Advertising Experience: The American Advertiser's Illustrated Magazine* 4, no. 2 (December 1896): 5. Also, Fowler, *Building Business*, passim.

27. Oscar Herzberg, "Some American Traits that Effect Advertising," *Printers' Ink* 20, no. 6 (1897): 8.

28. Herbert N. Casson, *Ads and Sales: A Study of Advertising and Selling from the Standpoint of the New Principles of Scientific Management* (Chicago: A. C. McClurg, 1911), pp. vi, 60, 145. Also, Charles Frederick Higham, *Scientific Distribution* (London: Nisbet, 1916).

29. "Wants Created by Advertising," Talk 15, *Modern Business Talks* (New York: Alexander Hamilton Institute, 1915), pp. 3–4, HM&L.

30. Richard J. Walsh, *Selling Forces* (Philadelphia: Curtis Publishing, 1913), p. 138. Also, James Playsted Wood, *The Curtis Magazines* (New York: Ronald Press, 1971), p. 76.

31. "Psychologists in Marketing: John Broadus Watson—1878–1958," *The Marketing and Social Research Newsletter of the Psychological Corporation* (4 December 1959): 3–4, JWTCA; Stephen Fox, *The Mirror Makers: A History of American Advertising and its Creators* (New York: William Morrow, 1984), pp. 85–86.

32. Emily Fogg-Meade, "The Place of Advertising in Modern Business," *Journal of Political Economy* 9 (March 1901): 218–42.

33. Fogg-Meade, "Place of Advertising," pp. 235, 236; Henry Foster Adams, *Advertising and Its Mental Laws* (New York: Macmillan, 1916), p. 27.

34. Walter R. Hine, "The Advertising of Foods: Why the Manufacturer Who Advertises Should Be Encouraged," *Good Housekeeping Magazine* 48 (March 1909): 383–86.

35. E. C. Patterson, "Why You Get Your Money's Worth When You Buy Advertised Goods," *Collier's* 43, no. 14 (26 June 1909): 5; "The University of Advertising," ibid., no. 18 (24 July 1909): 5.

36. Fogg-Meade, "The Place of Advertising in Modern Business," p. 231.

37. Stephen Vaughn, *Holding Fast the Inner Lines: Democracy, Nationalism, and The Committee on Public Information* (Chapel Hill: University of North Carolina Press, 1980), pp. 149–50, 191.

38. George French, *Advertising: The Social and Economic Problem* (New York: Ronald Press, 1915), pp. 24–27, 38.

39. For expositions of the issues, including several that place advertising at the center of the debates, see the essay on sources.

40. *Obiter Dicta* (Philadelphia: Curtis Publishing), no. 8 (1914): 4, WCBA, Advertising Collection, box 9. Also, Charles Frederick Higham, *Scientific Distribution* (London: Nisbet, 1916), esp. pp. 1–4, 51. Later examples include Neil H. Borden, *The Economic Effects of Advertising* (Chicago: Richard D. Irwin, 1944), pp. 27, 681–708, 870, 881; Maxwell Sackheim, *My First Sixty Years in Advertising* (Englewood Cliffs, New Jersey: Prentice-Hall, 1970), p. 215; *In Behalf of Advertising: A Series of Essays Published in National Periodicals from 1919–1928* (Philadelphia: N. W. Ayer & Son, 1929); and William D. Patterson, ed., *America: Miracle at Work* (New York: Prentice-Hall, 1953).

41. Volney B. Palmer, *Business-Men's Almanac for the Year 1849* (New York: Volney B. Palmer, 1849), n.p., WCBA, Advertising Collection, box 3.

42. Many visionaries, including the popular Edward Bellamy and Henry George, proposed redistribution systems to increase effective demand, but these ideas had little impact on policy before the Great Depression of the 1930s, when the failure of consumers' effective demand, not desire, shut down industry and gave credence to Keynesian analysis.

43. Maurice Switzer, *Who Pays the Advertising Bills* (New York: reprinted from *Leslie's Illustrated Weekly Newspaper,* 1915), pamphlet, n.p., WCBA, Advertising Collection, box 9.

44. Walsh, *Selling Forces,* pp. 55–65; Stanley Resor, "New York Notes: The Machinery of Our Business" News Bulletin (typescript) no. 20 (New York: J. Walter Thompson, 17 October 1916), pp. 3–6; Resor, "The Agency and the Representative," p. 4. Committee on Standardization, J. Walter Thompson Co. internal document (1919), p. 1, JWTCA; Resor, "Speech in Class," J. Walter Thompson Co. internal document (September 1916), pp. 1–3, JWTCA.

45. Earnest Elmo Calkins, *The Business of Advertising* (New York: Appleton, 1915), pp. 335–37. Also, Richard J. Walsh, *Selling Forces* (Philadelphia: Curtis Publishing, 1913), pp. 23–24; Truman A. DeWeese, "The Young Man with Nothing But Brains," *Forum* 32 (February 1902): 695–99.

46. George B. Waldron, "The Hum of the Factory," *Mahin's Magazine* 1, no. 4 (July 1902): 22–24.

47. "The American Public," *The J.W.T. Book* (New York: J. Walter Thompson, 1909), pp. 6–7.

48. Walsh, *Selling Forces,* pp. 152–53.

49. Johnson, *Library of Advertising,* pp. 56–58.

50. Calkins, *The Business of Advertising,* p. 205. Pamela Walker Laird, "'A Certain Sameness': Early Auto Advertisements," *Technology and Culture* 37 (October 1996): 796–812.

51. The priority of production to progress had not, of course, lost its advocates. For instance, National Association of Manufacturers statements quoted in Marian V. Sears, "The American Businessman at the Turn of the Century," *Business History Review* 30 (1956): 382–443, esp. p. 401; Charles H. Harding, "Tariff, Exports; Home Market Expansion," *American Industries* 1, no. 17 (1903): 7; Carroll D. Wright, "Modern Industry a Social Force," *American Industries* 1, no. 20 (1903): 1–2. And, of course, Henry Ford proclaimed the superiority of production throughout his lifetime.

52. Daniel Bell, *The Cultural Contradictions of Capitalism* (New York: Basic Books, 1978), pp. 21–22, 66, 69–70, 254.

53. The rejoicing continues. Fred Danzig, editorial essay, "Advertising and Progress," in *Advertising Age* 39, no. 48 (9 November 1988): 1.

54. Christopher J. Berry, *The Idea of Luxury: A Conceptual and Historical Investigation* (New York: Cambridge University Press, 1994); Neil McKendrick, John

Brewer, and J. H. Plumb, *The Birth of a Consumer Society: The Commercialization of Eighteenth-Century England* (Bloomington: Indiana University Press, 1982); Wolfgang Schivelbusch, *Tastes of Paradise: A Social History of Spices, Stimulants, and Intoxicants* (New York: Pantheon, 1992).

55. See Lears, *Fables of Abundance*, esp. pp. 102–13, 148–53.

56. *Good Housekeeping Magazine* (November 1913): 215.

57. Cecelia Tichi, *Shifting Gears: Technology, Literature, Culture in Modernist America* (Chapel Hill: University of North Carolina Press, 1987).

58. Warren I. Susman, "'Personality' and the Making of Twentieth-Century Culture," in *Culture as History: The Transformation of American Society in the Twentieth Century* (New York: Pantheon, 1984), pp. 271–85.

59. A. P. Johnson, *Library of Advertising* (Chicago: Chicago University of Commerce, 1913), pp. 5–6.

# Appendix

1. Daniel Pope, *The Making of Modern Advertising* (New York: Basic Books, 1983), pp. 21–33, 135.

2. George P. Rowell, "Who Are the Patrons of Advertising Agencies?" *Advertiser's Gazette* 8 (March 1874): 4.

3. George Presbrey Rowell, *The Men Who Advertise: An Account of Successful Advertisers* (New York: Nelson Chesman, 1870), p. 5.

4. Ralph M. Hower, *The History of an Advertising Agency: N. W. Ayer & Son at Work, 1869–1939* (Cambridge: Harvard University Press, 1939), pp. 114, 635–38.

# Essay on Sources

## Primary Sources

So often, historians' tasks entail exploring one body of evidence (in my case, American advertisements between 1870 and 1920) and then explaining it by reconstructing pertinent contexts (in this case, mainstream U.S. business conditions and cultures of that period) from other evidence. An understanding of these varied forms of evidence helps to locate them.

The primary advertising media between 1820 and 1920 were printed, and they entered the public arena in two very different ways, although both processes started with the advertisers, the businesspeople who advertised. Publishers produced the newspapers and magazines that distributed and now preserve one category of advertisements. Researchers find these readily in libraries across the country, bound or on microforms, always well ordered and dated. Besides their accessibility, these materials lend themselves to sampling strategies and are, therefore, the advertising examples most often used in research. Job, or contract, printers produced the other broad category of historical advertisements, now called ephemera, which include posters, trade cards, catalogs, calendars, and other brightly colored, free-standing forms, along with flyers and direct mail. The most publicly salient advertisements of their day, they have become the most elusive, residing in museums, archives, and private collections. Impossible to catalog by every variable that can interest a researcher, and often difficult to store and date and sample, these resources remain underused treasures.

The collections of historical advertisements in all printed formats and business materials in the Warshaw Collection of Business Americana and the

Center for Advertising History in the Archives Center of the National Museum of American History, Smithsonian Institution, Washington, D. C., offer unexcelled resources. The Hagley Museum and Library, Wilmington, Delaware, also holds superlative collections, plus vast manuscript and published materials in business history. The Bella Landauer Collection in the New-York Historical Society also holds many hundreds of thousands of vintage advertisements. Historical museums and archives everywhere often have small collections—that is, a thousand or two—of trade cards to give researchers some sense of their one-time abundance.

The reasons why businesspeople created, paid for, and disseminated their messages in these various media lay in their perceptions of their business and cultural needs. Trade journals, together with mainstream popular publications, can give a sense of that background. *American Industries* (New York), *Iron Age* (New York), and *System* (Chicago) served wide ranges of business fields and so are invaluable references. In addition, every form of manufacturing, retailing, and other business activity had its specialized trade journals—all worth exploring for each trade's concerns and practices. Frank Luther Mott's five-volume encyclopedia provides invaluable references and descriptions of journals in every field to help guide a research project. I primarily used *A History of American Magazines*, vol. 3, *1865–1885*, and vol. 4, *1885–1905* (Cambridge: the Belknap Press of Harvard University Press, 1957).

Especially influential popular guidance manuals of the period include Seymour Eaton, *One Hundred Lessons in Business* (Boston: Seymour Eaton, 1887); T. L. Haines, *Worth and Wealth: Or the Art of Getting, Saving, and Using Money* (New York: Standard Publishing, 1884); William H. Maher, *On the Road to Riches: Practical Hints for Clerks and Young Business Men* (Toledo: William H. Maher, 1889, 1st edn. 1878); and William M. Thayer, *Onward to Fame and Fortune, Or, Climbing Life's Ladder* (New York: Christian Herald, 1893). The high degree of consistency between such materials and, more important, between them and biographical and other cultural and business sources helped to reassure me that they reflected mainstream values regarding masculine virtues in and out of business.

Between advertisers and advertisements intervened two important groups of professionals. The printers' influence diminished as the advertising practitioners' (agents, copywriters, artists) rose in the years between 1870–1920. *The Inland Printer: A Technical Journal Devoted to the Art of Printing* (Chicago) preserves both printers' concerns and their advice regarding advertising. *Printers' Ink* (New York City) dominated the advertising trade press from its start in 1888 through the period of this study. Its volumes contain advice to and concerns of both advertising practitioners and advertisers, circulating widely to both groups. Other later journals that became increasingly important included *Profitable Advertising* (Boston), *Judicious Advertising: A Monthly Publication Devoted to General Publicity* (Chicago), and *Advertising and Selling* (New York City).

Influential trade books, largely directed to advertisers through the late 1890s when the literature for practitioners expanded rapidly, included Charles Austin Bates, *Good Advertising* (New York: Holmes Publishing, 1896); Nathaniel C. Fowler, Jr., *Building Business: An Illustrated Manual for Aggressive Business Men* (Boston: The Trade Co., 1893) and *Fowler's Publicity: An Encyclopedia of Advertising and Printing, and All that Pertains to the Public-seeking Side of Business* (Boston: Publicity Publishing, 1900); and George Presbrey Rowell, *The Men Who Advertise: An Account of Successful Advertisers* (New York: Nelson Chesman, 1870).

In the later period, the trade literature split in two: that still directed as advice to advertisers and that newly directed to ambitious or aspiring advertising practitioners. Influential books in this newer category include Henry Foster Adams, *Advertising and Its Mental Laws* (New York: Macmillan, 1916); Earnest Elmo Calkins, *The Business of Advertising* (New York: D. Appleton, 1915); Herbert N. Casson, *Ads and Sales: A Study of Advertising and Selling from the Standpoint of the New Principles of Scientific Management* (Chicago: A. C. McClurg, 1911); Truman A. DeWeese, *Book on Advertising*, The Business Man's Library, vol. 7 (Chicago: System Company, 1907); George French, *The Art and Science of Advertising* (Boston: Sherman, French, 1909); James Melvin Lee, *Language for Men of Affairs*, vol. 2, *Business Writing* (New York: Ronald Press, 1920); John Lee Mahin, *Advertising: Selling the Consumer* (New York: Doubleday, Page, 1914); and Daniel Starch, *Advertising: Its Principles, Practice, and Technique* (Chicago: Scott, Foresman, 1914).

Prominent advertising agents and agencies wrote invaluable retrospectives, especially N. W. Ayer & Son, *Forty Years of Advertising: 1869–1909* (Philadelphia: N. W. Ayer & Son, 1909); Claude C. Hopkins, *My Life in Advertising* (New York: Harper and Brothers, 1927); Albert Lasker, *The Lasker Story As He Told It* (Chicago: Advertising Publications, 1963), and George P. Rowell, *Forty Years an Advertising Agent, 1865–1905* (New York: Printers' Ink Publishing, 1906).

For building the picture of how advertisers, printers, and advertising practitioners interacted and made their decisions, I found archival resources essential. The richness of both the Archives Center at the National Museum of American History and the Hagley Museum and Library cannot be overstated in this area. For two of the most prominent early agencies, I relied on the J. Walter Thompson Company Archives in the William R. Perkins Library,

Duke University, Durham, North Carolina, and the N. W. Ayer Collection, now at the Archives Center of the National Museum of American History. The Library of Congress, the Denver Public Library, and Baker Library of the Harvard Business School house suberb collections of trade journals and books.

The conclusions and generalizations I have made in this book draw on a thorough reading of all the pertinent materials, in all formats, held in the above archives and libraries for the period before 1920. I thoroughly surveyed *Printers' Ink*, working through it on a page-by-page basis from its first issue in 1888 through 1900, intermittently from 1901 through 1906, thoroughly again for 1907, and intermittently thereafter. I carefully examined *Profitable Advertising* for its first ten years, 1891 to 1900, as well as for 1908 and intermittently in between. *Judicious Advertising* was more difficult to locate in full runs; hence, my survey of it is not exhaustive for any set of years. I also read the *Inland Printer* thoroughly for 1885 to 1900, 1905, and 1910, and *Iron Age* for several years in the 1890s. More modest surveys of other journals and materials supplemented these resources and assured that they represented the relevant attitudes and practices.

## Secondary Sources

### *Advertising*

Histories of advertising vary widely in their usefulness as sources of information and interpretation. (This essay, like the book, regretfully neglects resources on advertising history outside of the United States.) Two histories stand out from the field. Daniel Pope's *The Making of Modern Advertising* (New York: Basic Books, 1983) is by far the most useful analytical narrative of the business history of advertising through the 1920s. In *Advertising the American Dream: Making Way for Modernity, 1920–1940* (Berkeley: University of California Press, 1985), Roland Marchand provides a model interpretation of the field and its output for that period. He elegantly shows how agents in the 1920s and 1930s played out their social ambitions and prejudices through the advertisements they created.

Three other histories of the field provide much useful information on the history of agents and various advertisers and their campaigns, although they explain these histories from agents' perspectives alone: Stephen Fox, *The Mirror Makers: A History of American Advertising and Its Creators* (New York: William Morrow, 1984); Frank Presbrey, *The History and Development of Advertising* (Garden City, N.Y.: Doubleday, Doran, 1929); and James Playsted Wood, *The Story of Advertising* (New York: Ronald Press, 1958). Ralph M.

Hower's *The History of an Advertising Agency: N. W. Ayer & Son at Work, 1869–1939* (Cambridge: Harvard University Press, 1939) gives a detailed narrative of one of the most influential of the early agencies. Quentin J. Schultze examined the early attempts to professionalize advertising and infuse it with scientific methodology and rhetoric, although he credits disproportionately Chicago advertising activists for these trends. "Advertising, Science, and Professionalism, 1885–1917" (Ph.D. diss., University of Illinois, 1978). Richard W. Pollay has provided an annotated bibliography of published advertising resources in English before 1979 in *Information Sources in Advertising History* (Westport, Conn.: Greenwood Press, 1979).

For earlier essays on the relationship between advertisements and culture and evaluations of vintage advertisements' historiographical value, see John M. Staudenmaier and Pamela W. Laird, "Advertising History: A Survey of Recent Literature," *Technology and Culture* 30 (October 1989): 1031–16; and Pamela W. Laird, "The Challenge of Exhibiting Historical Advertisements," *American Quarterly* 43 (September 1991): 464–85.

### Marketing

Advertising is often the most publicly obvious arm of marketing. Neil H. Borden assessed advertising's importance as part of the whole with a historical perspective in his important study *The Economic Effects of Advertising* (Chicago: Richard D. Irwin, 1944). Susan Strasser's *Satisfaction Guaranteed: The Making of the American Mass Market* (New York: Pantheon, 1989) links the business decisions of many advertisers with their marketing processes and concerns. She offers example upon example of experiments that helped to define and build American advertising prowess. Richard Tedlow details four important case studies of marketing innovation in *New and Improved: The Story of Mass Marketing in America* (New York: Basic Books, 1990). Regina Lee Blaszczyk demonstrates how firms producing for the consumer market began to understand that the marketing process should include consideration of consumer interests in product design and production, as well as in advertising, in *Imagining Consumers: The Business of Product Design and Innovation* (Baltimore: Johns Hopkins University Press, forthcoming).

On retailing history, Susan Porter Benson, *Counter Cultures: Saleswomen, Managers, and Customers in American Department Stores, 1890–1940* (Urbana: University of Illinois Press, 1986), and William Leach, *Land of Desire: Merchants, Power, and the Rise of a New American Culture* (New York: Pantheon, 1993), provide overviews and context for the many histories available on specific retailers or regions.

The complex changes in product distribution within the marketplace require the special attention provided by Bill Reid Moeckel, *The Development of the Wholesaler in the United States, 1860–1900* (New York: Garland Press, 1986); Glenn Porter and Harold C. Livesay, *Merchants and Manufacturers: Studies in the Changing Structure of Nineteenth-Century Marketing* (Chicago: Ivan R. Dee, 1989; first published 1971); and Timothy B. Spears, *100 Years on the Road: The Traveling Salesman in American Culture* (New Haven: Yale University Press, 1995).

## Business Context

The business environment for marketing changed profoundly during the period of this study. Important background resources for manufacturing firms managed by their owners and others that did not mass-produce goods include Mansel G. Blackford, *A History of Small Business in America* (New York: Twayne, 1991); Stuart W. Bruchy, ed., *Small Business in American Life* (New York: Columbia University Press, 1980); and Philip Scranton's studies, *Proprietary Capitalism: The Textile Manufacture at Philadelphia, 1800–1885* (Cambridge: Cambridge University Press, 1983), and *Figured Tapestry: Production, Markets, and Power in Philadelphia Textiles, 1885–1941* (Cambridge: Cambridge University Press, 1989).

Firms moving toward mass production, national distribution of branded consumer goods, and corporate structures developed the highest profiles in the marketing revolutions of this period. Alfred D. Chandler, *The Visible Hand: The Managerial Revolution in American Business* (Cambridge: the Belknap Press of the Harvard University Press, 1977), is essential reading for these, as is Edward C[hase] Kirkland, *Industry Comes of Age: Business, Labor, and Public Policy, 1860–1897* (New York: Holt, Rinehart, and Winston, 1961); Louis Galambos and Joseph Pratt, *The Rise of the Corporate Commonwealth: U.S. Business and Public Policy in the Twentieth Century* (New York: Basic Books, 1988); and David Hounshell, *From the American System to Mass Production, 1800–1930: The Development of Manufacturing Technology in the United States* (Baltimore: Johns Hopkins University Press, 1989). Naomi R. Lamoreaux, in *The Great Merger Movement in American Business, 1895–1904* (Cambridge: Cambridge University Press, 1985), analyzes the formation of corporations in this critical period.

Trademarks are an elusive topic in the scholarly literature. I found these sources most helpful: Frank Schecter, "The Rational Basis of Trade-Mark Protection," *Harvard Law Review* 40 (1927): 813; Daniel McClure, "Trademarks and Unfair Competition: A Critical History of Legal Thought," *The Trademark*

Reporter 69 (1979): 305–56; Mira Wilkins, "The Neglected Intangible Asset: The Influence of the Trade Mark on the Rise of the Modern Corporation," *Business History* 34 (January 1992): 66–95; and Wilkins, "When and Why Brand Names in Food and Drink?" in Geoffrey Jones and Nicholas Morgan, eds., *Adding Value: Brands and Marketing in Food and Drink* (London: Routledge, 1994).

## Business Culture

Bringing ideological order to their volatile environment required that nineteenth-century businesspeople explain its dynamics to themselves while justifying their actions within it. Progress and success by participating in progress stood out as legitimating beliefs in the dominant American culture of this period. Yet most of the voluminous literature on progress as an idea examines what philosophers have thought about it. A different literature pertains to the nineteenth-century advertisers who touted their contributions to progress and defined them in terms of their participation in technological advances and the social ramifications of those advances. Two collections of essays are particularly helpful in tying together these components of the American mentality: Merritt Roe Smith and Leo Marx, eds., *Does Technology Drive History? The Dilemma of Technological Determinism* (Cambridge: MIT Press, 1994); and Steven L. Goldman, ed., *Science, Technology, and Social Progress* (Bethlehem: Lehigh University Press, 1989). John M. Staudenmaier's "Perils of Progress Talk: Some Historical Considerations" in the latter volume helps us now to gain enough perspective on attitudes toward progress to be able to analyze their manifestations in others. David E. Nye explicates the attitudes that have made up the *American Technological Sublime* (Cambridge: MIT Press, 1994). Tom Lutz examines some of the personal costs of progress as defined in the mainstream culture a century ago in *American Nervousness, 1903: An Anecdotal History* (Ithaca: Cornell University Press, 1991).

Key explorations of the relationships between cultural values and the new machines include John F. Kasson, *Civilizing the Machine: Technology and Republican Values in America, 1776–1900* (New York: Penguin, 1976); Leo Marx, *The Machine in the Garden: Technology and the Pastoral Ideal in America* (Oxford: Oxford University Press, 1964); David Nye, *Electrifying America: Social Meanings of a New Technology, 1880–1940* (Cambridge: MIT Press, 1990); Herbert L. Sussman, *Victorians and Machines: The Literary Response to Technology* (Cambridge: Harvard University Press, 1968); and Julie Wosk, *Breaking Frame: Technology and the Visual Arts in the Nineteenth Century* (New Brunswick: Rutgers University Press, 1992). The value that mainstream Americans placed on time intensified over the course of that century. Mark M. Smith's quite recent article, "Old South Time in Comparative Perspective," *American Historical Review* 101 (1996): 1432–69, contains a lengthy and useful review of the literature on the history of time and an insightful new interpretation of how central "clock consciousness" has been to notions of Western modernity.

Competing for business success gave the successful a claim on moral and cultural leadership, so they felt. Of the abundant reviews and analyses of nineteenth-century success literature, I found the following to be the most useful: John G. Cawelti, *Apostles of the Self-Made Man* (Chicago: University of Chicago Press, 1965); Richard M. Huber, *The American Idea of Success* (New York: McGraw-Hill, 1971); Irvin G. Wyllie "Social Darwinism and the Businessman," *Proceedings of the American Philosophical Society* 103 (October 1959): 629–35; and Irvin G. Wyllie, *The Self-Made Man in America: The Myth of Rags to Riches* (New Brunswick: Rutgers University Press, 1954).

Two short but useful studies of attitudes during this era are John Higham, "The Reorientation of American Culture in the 1890s," in John Weiss, ed., *The Origins of Modern Consciousness* (Detroit: Wayne State University Press, 1965), and Marian V. Sears, "The American Businessman at the Turn of the Century," *Business History Review* 30 (1956): 382–443. For a discussion of how businesspersons can become leaders when their activities develop attractive social symbolism, see Sigmund Diamond, *The Reputation of the American Businessman* (Cambridge: Harvard University Press, 1955). Edward Chase Kirkland provides a valuable overview of businesspeoples' operations and attitudes in *Dream and Thought in the Business Community, 1860–1900* (Ithaca, New York: Cornell University Press, 1956).

Some of the most important insights about nineteenth-century business culture come from sociologists and historians who have studied movements away from it. *The Lonely Crowd*, by David Riesman, Reuel Denney, and Nathan Glazer (New Haven: Yale University Press, 1961) remains a classic in this genre. William H. Whyte Jr. analyzed the strains between the prevailing rhetoric of individualism that denied, well into the mid-twentieth century, the overwhelmingly bureaucratic nature of large U.S. organizations and their requirements for cooperative action in *The Organization Man* (New York: Simon and Schuster, 1956).

The following studies detail how the managerial style and skills appropriate to bureaucratic organization developed: Alfred L. Thimm, *Business Ideologies in the Reform-Progressive Era, 1880–1914* (University: University of Alabama Press, 1976); JoAnne Yates, *Control through Communication: The Rise of System in American Management* (Baltimore: Johns Hopkins University Press, 1989); and Olivier Zunz, *Making America Corporate, 1870–1920* (Chicago: University of Chicago Press, 1990). Thimm and others, especially Louis Galambos, "Technology, Political Economy, and Professionalization: Central Themes of the Organizational Synthesis," *Business History Review* 57 (winter 1983): 471–93; Harold Perkin, *The Rise of Professional Society: England since 1880* (London: Routledge, 1989); and Robert H. Wiebe, *The Search for Order, 1877–1920* (New York: Hill and Wang, 1967), address the rise of specialization, professionalism, and professional associations by which businesspeople tried to control and understand their fields' expanding activities, competition, and their political and social environments.

## Printing and Publishing

This study required examining printing and publishing in terms of their business practices, technological capabilities, and their cultural and business relationships. Paul Nathan's *How to Make Money in the Printing Business* (New York: Lotus Press, 1900) offers a splendid—primary—look at all these factors. For lithography, no single resource addresses all of these aspects as well as do Peter C. Marzio, *The Democratic Art: Chromolithography 1840–1900, Pictures for a 19th-Century America* (Boston: David R. Godine, 1979); and John Reps, *Views and Viewmakers of Urban America: Lithographs of Towns and Cities in the United States and Canada, Notes on the Artists and Publishers, and a Union Catalog of Their Work, 1825–1925* (Columbia: University of Missouri Press, 1984). Helena E. Wright emphasizes the symbiotic relationship between industry and the graphic arts in "The Image Makers: The Role of the Graphic Arts in Industrialization," *IA: The Journal of the Society for Industrial Archeology* 12, no. 2 (1986): 5–18. Diana Korzenik, *Drawn to Art: A Nineteenth-Century American Dream* (Hanover, N.H.: University Press of New England, 1985), explicates some of the cultural and economic significances of printing during this era. Resources abound on specific printers or groups of printers who worked in particular towns. Katharine Morrison McClinton's *The Chromolithographs of Louis Prang* (New York: Clarkson N. Potter, 1973) is a fine example of this genre, focusing on a key individual in nineteenth-century commercial printing.

The businesses and cultural roles of publishing magazines and newspapers differed greatly from those of job printers. Edwin Emery wrote the standard history in *The Press and America: An Interpretative History of Journalism*, 2nd edn. (Englewood Cliffs, N.J.: Prentice-Hall, 1962). Gerald J. Baldasty, *The Commercialization of News in the Nineteenth Century* (Madison: University of Wisconsin Press, 1992) offers a more recent interpretation that focuses on the relationships between news content and business practices. Cyrus K. Curtis was a focal person in this history, and James Playsted Wood, in *The Curtis*

*Magazines* (New York: Ronald Press, 1971) provides a useful starting point for that figure and his activities. Frank Luther Mott's magazine-by-magazine descriptions mentioned earlier provide essential references for popular journals and trade journals. Ellen Gruber Garvey's *The Adman in the Parlor: Magazines and the Gendering of Consumer Culture, 1880s to 1910s* (New York: Oxford University Press, 1996) provides a valuable analysis of the successes of magazines in bringing advertisements into the home. Richard Ohmann's *Selling Culture: Magazines, Markets, and Class at the Turn of the Century* (London: Verso, 1996) interprets the dynamics between publishing and advertising and their ambient culture.

## The Consumer Culture

The classic critique of the consumer culture remains Thorstein Veblen's *The Theory of the Leisure Class: An Economic Study of Institutions* (New York: Vanguard, 1926, first published in 1899). Each decade since Veblen wrote has produced volumes analyzing the consumer culture, and the recent scholarly literature on the consumer culture grows at a remarkable rate. The burgeoning literature includes many of the volumes cited elsewhere in this essay, such as Bushman, Garvey, Leach, Marchand, and Ohmann. Conversely, the seminal collection of essays edited by T. J. Jackson Lears and Richard Wightman Fox, *The Culture of Consumption: Critical Essays in American History, 1880–1980* (New York: Pantheon, 1983), addresses many of the above topics.

One category within this field explores the meanings and impacts of advertisements on popular culture and behavior. Major sources in this area include Stuart Ewen, *Captains of Consciousness: Advertising and the Social Roots of the Consumer Culture* (New York: McGraw-Hill, 1976); Jackson Lears, *Fables of Abundance: A Cultural History of Advertising in America* (New York: Basic Books, 1994); William Leiss, Stephen Kline, and Sut Jhally, *Social Communication in Advertising: Persons, Products, and Images of Well-Being* (Toronto: Methuen, 1986); and Michael Schudson, *Advertising, The Uneasy Persuasion: Its Dubious Impact on American Society* (New York: Basic Books, 1984). Each of these has great merit but also some limitations because of the common tendency to examine advertising messages without reference to both their cultural and business contexts. Too often, analysts take sample messages to be representative of a larger field of advertising messages or other cultural media, or presume to assess messages' impacts on audiences, or even on the larger society beyond their audiences, without adequate contextualization. Even for today, with vastly more information at hand from feedback and motivation research, any such conclusions should be suspect. However intriguing and worth reading, insights regarding the meanings and impacts of past forms of popular culture limit their credibility to the depth of their evidence about how subjects experienced those forms.

Another literature seeks out the dynamics and manifestations of the consumer culture. Essential readings in this area include Neil McKendrick, John Brewer, and J. H. Plumb, *The Birth of a Consumer Society: The Commercialization of Eighteenth-Century England* (Bloomington: University of Indiana Press, 1982); Christopher J. Berry, *The Idea of Luxury: A Conceptual and Historical Investigation* (New York: Cambridge University Press, 1994); Richard L. Bushman, *The Refinement of America: Persons, Houses, Cities* (New York: Alfred A. Knopf, 1992), Simon J. Bronner, ed., *Consuming Visions: Accumulation and Display of Goods in America, 1880–1920* (New York: W. W. Norton, 1989); Daniel Horowitz, *The Morality of Spending: Attitudes Toward the Consumer Society in America, 1875–1950* (Baltimore: Johns Hopkins University Press, 1985); T. J. Jackson Lears, *No Place of Grace: Antimodernism and the Transformation of American Culture, 1880–1920* (New York: Pantheon, 1981); Grant McCracken, *Culture and Consumption: New Approaches to the Symbolic Character of Consumer Goods and Activities* (Bloomington: Indiana University Press, 1988); David M. Potter, *People of Plenty: Economic Abundance and the American Character* (Chicago: University of Chicago Press, 1954); Wolfgang Schivelbusch, *Tastes of Paradise: A Social History of Spices, Stimulants, and Intoxicants* (New York: Pantheon, 1992); Warren I. Susman, "'Personality' and the Making of Twentieth-Century Culture," in *Culture as History: The Transformation of American Society in the Twentieth Century* (New York: Pantheon, 1984), 271–85; and Nicholas Xenos, *Scarcity and Modernity* (London: Routledge, 1989).

## Patent Medicines and Circuses

Patent-medicine purveyors and entertainers shared many advertising practices and cultural roles in nineteenth-century America. The most useful studies on patent medicines and their makers are Sarah Stage, *Female Complaints: Lydia Pinkham and the Business of Women's Medicine* (New York: W. W. Norton, 1979); Paul Starr, *The Social Transformation of American Medicine* (New York: Basic Books, 1982); and James Harvey Young, *The Toadstool Millionaires: A Social History of Patent Medicines in America before Federal Regulation* (Princeton: Princeton University Press, 1961). Nothing gives a better understanding of how and why that century's most notorious entertainment promoter flourished than Neil Harris's *Humbug: The Art of P. T. Barnum* (Chicago: University of Chicago Press, 1973).

## World War I

The United States' mobilization for World War I had a huge impact on advertising techniques. The rapid evolution of advertising practices in nationalist propaganda as well as in product advertising during and immediately after World War I calls for a full-length study. In the meantime, two works provide excellent context and some of the specifics of these developments: Stephen Vaughn, *Holding Fast the Inner Lines: Democracy, Nationalism, and The Committee on Public Information* (Chapel Hill: University of North Carolina Press, 1980); and Daniel Pope, "The Advertising Industry and World War I," *The Public Historian* 2, no. 3 (1980): 4–25. An early study, James R. Mock and Cedric Larson, *Words That Won the War: The Story of the Committee on Public Information, 1917–1919* (New York: Russell & Russell, 1968; originally published 1939), is also useful.

## Gender

Although this study directs its attention to advertising messages that were, with rare exceptions, produced by men with little regular input from women, women were very much frequent subjects and intended audiences for many of those messages. Interpreting women's images in those advertisements, as with any other images, requires recognizing who created them and in what contexts. My recent article "Progress in Separate Spheres: Selling Nineteenth-Century Technologies," *Knowledge and Society* 10 (1996): 19–49, explicates gender in messages that advertised new technologies and carries an extensive bibliography on women and U.S. culture, 1870–1920.

### Interpreting Messages

What does it mean to interpret someone else's messages? Do we aim to explain what messages meant to their creators, to their audiences and ambient society, or what they mean to us, the interpreters? Failure to specify a level of explanation usually presumes the first two of these "aims," but results in the third. For anything but the third, limitations on evidence determine the limitations of interpretation. In helping me to define and clarify my perspective, I found the following theoretical approaches the most useful: Peter L. Berger and Thomas Luckman, *The Social Construction of Reality: A Treatise in the Sociology of Knowledge* (Garden City, N.Y.: Doubleday, 1966); James W. Carey, some of whose work has been republished in *Communication as Culture: Essays on Media and Society* (Winchester, Mass.: Unwin Hyman, 1989); Robert Darnton, *The Great Cat Massacre and Other Episodes in French Cultural History* (New York: Vintage, 1985), especially the introduction and concluding chapter; Mary Douglas, *Implicit Meanings: Essays in Anthropology* (London: Routledge & Kegan Paul, 1975); and Mary Douglas and Baron Isherwood, *The World of Goods* (New York: Basic Books, 1979). Essential treatments of the political functions of cultural symbols can be found in T. J. Jackson Lears, "The Concept of Cultural Hegemony: Problems and Possibilities" *American Historical Review* 90 (June, 1985): 567–93; and C. Wright Mills, *The Sociological Imagination* (New York: Oxford University Press, 1959).

# Index

advertising agencies, and media: competition with printers and publishers, 225–6, 245–6; and nonperiodical media, 86–88; and publishers, 165–70, 312, 322–4, 366–7; reforms, 165–7, 214, 235–8, 240–3, 316–21, 327–8. *See also* commissions; media, advertising; publishers

advertising agencies, and services: client-centered, 165–8, 234–5, 243–6; creative services, 171–5, 243–6, 254, 312–6; early, 155–63; as intermediaries, 156–8, 254–60; specialization of, 155, 164–71, 231, 239–40. *See also* advertising practitioners; copywriters

advertising practitioners: attitudes toward consumers, 370–3, 375–6; expansion of services, 254–60, 269–70, 281–7, 311–5, 368–70; promote their field, 161, 163, 229, 243–6, 293, 304–16, 321–2, 330–7, 354–61, 365–8, 374–6, 379; specialization within, 39–40, 51, 155, 164–71, 206–8, 213, 229–31, 311–6, 369–70; success of profession, 304–11, 322, 329, 363–6; tensions with clients, 257–60, 369–70, 376, 378–9; views on advertising's history, 1, 169, 305–9, 331–3, 337. *See also* commercial art; copywriters; layout and design; political cartoons; *and specific practitioners*

advice literature, 40–1, 103–5, 454–5. *See also* success

agricultural equipment, 36–7, 99–101, 99f, 204–6. *See also* McCormick, Cyrus

alcohol advertising, 81, 141–2, 224, 235–8, 252–3, plate 6

almanacs, 48–9, 87–8, 128

ambition, 104, 334, 350. *See also* success; Victorian culture, American

American Advertising Federation, 243

American Association of Advertising Agencies (AAAA), 242–3, 321, 324, 328, 351

American Cereal Company. *See* Quaker Oats Company

*American Industries*, 88, 189, 225, 227, 230, 253, 257, 282, 308, 454. *See also* National Association of Manufacturers; trade journals

American Tobacco Company, 194–5, 202, 205, 238, 244, 344, 379. *See also* Duke, James Buchanan

announcements, advertisements as, 7, 13, 16–7, 20f, 21, 59, 279

Appel, Joseph H., 278, 286, 291

Armistead, William M., 244–5, 259–60, 369–70. *See also* N. W. Ayer & Son

art in advertising, 263–4, 266–9. *See also* layout and design

artists. *See* commercial art; layout and design; political cartoons; *and specific artists*

Associated Advertising Clubs, 241, 328–30, 351, 359–60, 368

associations, professional, 240–3, 321, 461. *See also* professionalization; *and specific associations*

August Wolf Milling Company, 123–4, 126, 130, 136, plate 5

automobile advertising, 107–8, 295–7, 376

Ayer, Francis Wayland, 53, 157, 160, 164, 236, 239–40, 292, 319, 330; on advertising field, 312, 333–4; on history, 1, 333, 337; personal traits, 166–7, 310; and reform, 235, 243–4, 321–2; on service, 166–8, 243–5. *See also* N. W. Ayer & Son

Ayer, James C., 48–9, 70–1

Ayer, N. W., & Son. *See* N. W. Ayer & Son

B. T. Babbitt's Best Soap, 54, 97, 130, 376

commissions, 47, 157–8, 160, 211, 220–1, 225–6, 232–4, 237, 323–4. *See also* advertising agencies, and media: and publishers; advertising agencies, and media: and reforms; conflicts of interest; publishers: policies on advertising

Committee on Public Information, 298–9, 331, 361, 373. *See also* World War I

competition, 8, 13, 116–7, 210–3, 225–6, 262–3, 281, 335, 343–6, 368, 377–80. *See also* business culture; cultural authority, competition for; demand; marketing channels

conflicts of interest, 157, 160, 233, 322–4, 368–73

conspicuous consumption, 137–45

conspicuous production, 107–8

consumer concerns, 351–4, 367. *See also* public concerns

consumer culture, 354–8, 367–8, 370–6, 378–80, 462–3; early, 17, 32–3, 137

consumer-oriented messages, 250–2, 284–91, 377–80; in copy, 46, 273–4, 280, 292–3, 294f, 295–8, 302f, 367–8, plate 8; defined, 250; early, 25–6, 127–8; in images, 69, 150–1, 150f, 269–72, 302f, plate 8 (*see also* printers: impact on advertisements; stock images); reasons for, 254–60, 262–3, 269, 272–3, 279–80, 370–1; strategies, 284–91, 372–4

consumer products, national brand-name, 7–8, 31–2, 184, 210–3, 221, 231, 235–8, 243–5, 281–4, 338–9, 354–8. *See also* trademarks

consumption as progress, 5, 7, 294f, 367–8, 370–2, 374–6

Cooke, Jay, 46–7, 73

copywriters, 274–5, 292–3, 294f, 295–9, 301, 302f, 303, plate 8; freelance, 176, 178–81, 229–31. *See also* advertising practitioners; Hopkins, Claude C.; Powers, John E.; *and other specific copywriters*

copywriting, advice on, 216–7, 224–5, 227–31, 273–5, 279–81, 313–5; ascendancy, 292–3; nonprofessional, 97–100, 176, 181–2; retail, 24–31

copywriting specialization, 207–8, 217–8, 224–5, 228, 239–40, 243–5, 273–8; early, 53–6, 171–82; reasons for, 210–3, 216, 231–2, 234–5, 243–5, 254–60, 274–5

corporate-management, 203–9, 238–9, 327–8, 378–9; and advertising decisions, 212–3, 237–8, 255–7, 275, 278; specialization within, 206–8, 238–40

corporations: and advertising, 41, 202–8, 342–6; and mergers, 184–5, 201–2, 417n64

Corticelli Best Twist, 92f, 93

Cox, Palmer, 62, 267. *See also* political cartoons

Crash of 1893, 202, 249, 335, 375. *See also* corporations: and mergers

creativity, 213, 313–6

Creel, George, 373. *See also* Committee on Public Information

Crofutt, George, 129

Crowell, Henry Parsons, 203–4, 251–2, 293. *See also* Quaker Oats Company

cultural authority, competition for, 101–17, 140–1, 377–80

Currier & Ives, 69, 110

Curtis, Cyrus K., 52–3, 211, 222–6, 232–3, 292, 311, 461–2; on reform, 223–6. *See also* Ladies' Home Journal; publishers

Curtis, Louisa Knapp, 52–3, 223. *See also* Ladies' Home Journal

Curtis Publishing Company, 246, 349, 357, 374–5. *See also* Ladies' Home Journal

Potter, David, 18, 25, 463

Powers, John E., 29, 314; on advertisers, 173–4, 326; advice of, 174; as copy-writing specialist, 176, 178–80, 229–30, 274, 291

Prang, Louis, 63–4, 66, 68–9, 77, 81. *See also* chromolithography

premiums, 54, 56, plate 8

Presbrey, Frank, 191, 219, 271, 456

price advertising, 27–30, 262–3, 346–7

printed media: effectiveness of, 49, 82–91; reach of, 15–6, 62–3, 73–7, 83–5, 90–1. *See also specific media and technologies*

printers, 70, 81, 461; competition be-tween, 71–2, 76–81, 86, 217–20, 245; impact on advertisements, 70–1, 76–81, 271–2, 292, 454–6 (*see also* stock images); as producers, 65*f*, 66, 67*f*, 68, 70, 106, 377; and technolo-gies, 64, 66, 68, 76–8, 86, 377. *See also* job printing; publishers; *and specific technologies*

printers, and advertisers, 70–2, 77–81, 86, 91, 122–3, 211–2, 215–9, 245, 292; mutual dependency of, 57, 70–6, 156, 226

*Printers' Ink*, 71, 162–3, 228, 245, 289, 305, 313–4, 324, 370, 454, 456; on advertising field, 306–8, 316, 332–3, 335, 337–9, 343, 359; on copy, 273, 370. *See also* trade journals

printing: and culture, 57–68, 65*f*, 461; and education, 63–64, 66; growth, 87; and progress, 57–8, 64, 65*f*, 66; tech-nologies, 70–7, 211–2, 218–20, 260–1, 271. *See also* chromolithogra-phy; Prang, Louis

Procter & Gamble, 80, 85–6, 90, 186–7, 211, 282, 287. *See also* soap advertising

production: as metaphor, 294*f*, 344, 357, 375–6; as progress, 3, 5–6, 101, 450n51, plates 1, 6, & 7

production ethos, 66, 67*f*, 68, 101–2, 105–8, 120–8, 124*f*, 125*f*, 126*f*, 137, 140–2, 143*f*, 330, 338–9, 374–80, 450n51; attacks on, 369, 375, 377–80. *See also* industrial imagery

professionalization, 206–8, 223–6, 240–3, 245–6, 277–8, 295, 460–1; of advertising field, 305–6, 311–22, 330–1. *See also* advertising agencies, and media: reforms

*Profitable Advertising*, 8, 218, 228, 286, 289, 305–6, 314–5, 321, 326, 336, 338, 347–8, 350, 355–6, 370, 455–6

progress, 14, 33, 331; advertising field's claims to promote, 331–9; demands of, 140–8; and industrialization, 31–2, 108–10, 112*f*, 113–6 (*see also* indus-trial imagery; production ethos); as legitimation, 102, 108–17, 304–5, 329–30, 338–40, 354–8, 361, 363–8; and materialism, 3, 31–2; popular ideas of, 2–3, 14, 108–10, 111*f*, 113–7, 304–5, 317, 339, 344–5, 364. *See also* consumption as progress; production: as progress

Progressive Era, 23, 235–8, 272, 328, 330–1, 342, 345–6, 351, 371, 374

propaganda. *See* Committee on Public Information

proprietary products, 18. *See also* patent medicine advertising

psychology, 288–91, 297, 372–3

public concerns: about advertising, 23, 77, 214, 240–3, 330–1, 358; about costs, 351–4; about products, 49–50, 295–7, 367–8, 393n33. *See also* Pro-gressive Era

public relations, 102, 365. *See also* Truth-in-Advertising

publishers: as advertisers, 52–3, 73, 75; policies on advertising, 74–5, 162–3, 221–6, 232–4, 323–4; and progress, 323, 354; reforms by, 223–6. *See also*

Singer Manufacturing Machine Company, 35–6
soap advertising, 53–6, 90, 97, 147, 148f, 192, 285, 297–8, 300–3, 300f, 301f, 355–6, 374, plate 8. *See also specific brands*
Social Darwinism, 116–7, 460. *See also* success: and personal merit
specialization, 155, 171, 311–2, 460–1. *See also* advertising agencies, and services; advertising practitioners; copywriters; copywriting specialization; corporate-management
Sphinx Club, 241, 267, 309, 324, 347–8
Starch, Daniel, 283, 352, 455
Steinway & Sons, 34–5, 238
Sterling, Charles A., 96, 141, plate 3
Stewart, Alexander T., 27–8. *See also* retail
stock images, 20f, 68–70, 148f, 149–51, 150f, 262–3, 265–9, 377. *See also* nonindustrial images; printers: impact on advertisements
street criers, 13–5
Strobridge and Company, 80. *See also* chromolithography
substitution, 162–3, 186, 196–200. *See also* marketing channels; trademarks
success, 14, 300f, 301f, 454, 460; as legitimation, 309–16, 322–8; period literature on, 40–1, 103–5, 454–5; and personal merit, 40–1, 102–17, 120–8, 137–40, 327–8; progress and, 120–8, 309. *See also* ambition; Victorian culture, American
Swift, Gustavus, 204, 330
symbols of progress. *See* abundance; industrial imagery; technological sublime
*System*, 227, 454. *See also* trade journals
systematic advertising. *See* advertising: systematic

target marketing. *See* market segmentation
tariffs, 340–3
Taylor, Frederick Winslow, 279. *See also* Scientific Management
technological sublime, 65f, 67f, 106–7, 111f, 112f, 129–30, 131f, 132–3, 134f, 135–7, 143f, 272, 459, plate 5; defined, 129
technologies: attitudes toward, 122, 295–7, 364, 366, 459; complex, 33–7, 184, 295–7. *See also* printing: technologies; technological sublime
Tedlow, Richard, 50, 457
testimonials, 20–2, 37, 59, 99. *See also* patent medicine advertising
Thomas Sinclair & Son, 69, 78–9. *See also* job printing
Thompson, J. Walter, 222, 237, 240, 320; on copywriting, 172–3, 280–1; and magazine advertising, 168–71, 284, 324; on reform, 161. *See also* J. Walter Thompson Company
Thurber, Whyland & Co., 90, 118
time, 145–8, 300f, 301f, 460
tobacco marketing, 186, 188, 190, 193–5, 197, 202–5, 244–5, plate 2
trade cards, 61f, 77–9, 92f, 99f, 148f, 300f, 301f. *See also* nonperiodical media
trade journals, 88, 97, 217, 227–9, 269, 272, 331–2, 357, 454–5; in advertising field, 161, 227–9, 305, 335, 338, 345; in printing field, 215–9, 227. *See also specific journals*
trademarks, 18–9, 21, 173, 177, 180, 352–3, 417n64; consumer-oriented, 252, 259, 270–1; and demand, 191–6; faces as, 186, 188–9, 259, 269–71, 298, 377, plate 8; functions, 185–91; laws, 189–90, 330; personal names as, 65f, 95f, 99f, 107, 119f, 121, 124f, 125f, 126f, 131f, 143f, 148f, 150f, 173,

The Library of Congress has cataloged the hardcover edition of this book as follows:


Laird, Pamela Walker, 1947–
   Advertising progress : American business and the rise of consumer marketing /
Pamela Walker Laird.
      p.   cm. — (Studies in industry and society)
   Includes bibliographical references and index.
   ISBN 0-8018-5841-0 (alk. paper)
    1. Advertising—United States—History.   2. Advertising—Social aspects—
United States—History.   I. Title.   II. Series.
HF5813.U6L34  1998
659.1´0973—dc21                                                         97-52039


ISBN 0-8018-6645-6 (pbk.)